ISBN 978-1-5282-1261-8
PIBN 10909186

1 MONTH OF
FREE
READING

at

www.ForgottenBooks.com

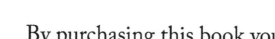

By purchasing this book you are eligible for one month membership to ForgottenBooks.com, giving you unlimited access to our entire collection of over 1,000,000 titles via our web site and mobile apps.

To claim your free month visit: www.forgottenbooks.com/free909186

English
Français
Deutsche
Italiano
Español
Português

www.forgottenbooks.com

Mythology Photography **Fiction**
Fishing Christianity **Art** Cooking
Essays Buddhism Freemasonry
Medicine **Biology** Music **Ancient
Egypt** Evolution Carpentry Physics
Dance Geology **Mathematics** Fitness
Shakespeare **Folklore** Yoga Marketing
Confidence Immortality Biographies
Poetry **Psychology** Witchcraft
Electronics Chemistry History **Law**
Accounting **Philosophy** Anthropology
Alchemy Drama Quantum Mechanics
Atheism Sexual Health **Ancient History**
Entrepreneurship Languages Sport
Paleontology Needlework Islam
Metaphysics Investment Archaeology
Parenting Statistics Criminology
Motivational

ECCLESIASTICAL HERALDRY

BY

JOHN WOODWARD. LL.D.

(RECTOR OF ST. MARY'S CHURCH, MONTROSE)

W. & A. K. JOHNSTON

EDINBURGH AND LONDON

1894

LIST OF SUBSCRIBERS.

Aberdeen Public Library (*per* Robert Walker, Esq., Librarian, *c/o* Messrs D. Wyllie & Son, Booksellers, Aberdeen).

Aberdeen University Library (*per* Messrs D. Wyllie & Son, Booksellers, Aberdeen).

Sir Charles Adam, Bart., Blairadam.

Charles Dexter Allen, Esq., Ex Libris Society, Hartford, Conn., U.S.A.

Mr E. G. Allen, Bookseller, 29 Henrietta Street, Covent Garden London (3 Copies).

Atkinson Free Library, Southport.

Miss Atlay, The Palace, Hereford.

Mr James Bain, 1 Haymarket, London, W. (2 Copies).

Messrs W. H. Bartlett & Co., Booksellers, 9 Salisbury Square, London, E.C.

Messrs Bell & Bradfute, Booksellers, 12 Bank Street, Edinburgh.

Thomas Bell, Esq., Hazelwood, West Ferry (*per* Mr G. Petrie, Bookseller, Dundee).

Frank Benison, Esq., 64 Regent Street, Leamington.

Joseph Bewley, Esq., Dublin (*per* Messrs Hodges, Figgis & Co., Booksellers).

Messrs Bickers & Son, Booksellers, 1 Leicester Square, London (5 Copies).

Mr B. H. Blackwell, Bookseller, 50 Broad Street, Oxford.

Mr F. Blackwell, Bookseller, Market Place, Reading.

Sir Arthur Blomfield & Sons, 6 Montague Place, Montague Square, London, W.

Rev. Archibald Harry Fletcher Boughey, Fellow of Trinity College, Cambridge.

Messrs T. Brear & Co. (Lim.), Booksellers, Bradford.

James Bromley, Esq., The Homestead, Lathom, Ormskirk.

Wm. Broughton, Esq.

J. Arthur Brown, Esq., Glasgow (*per* Mr Hugh Hopkins, Book- seller).

Mr William Brown, Bookseller, 26 Princes Street, Edinburgh (12 Copies).

I. Brunel, Esq., D.C.L., 15 Devonshire Terrace, Hyde Park, London.

William Buchan, Esq., Town-Clerk, Peebles.

Messrs J. & E. Bumpus (Lim.); Booksellers, 350 Oxford Street, London, W.

John William Burns, Esq., of Kilmahew, Cardross, Dumbarton-shire (per Messrs John Smith & Son, Booksellers, Glasgow).

The Most Noble The Marquis of Bute, Mount Stuart, Rothesay.

Rev. Thomas W. Carson, M.A., Clarisford, Cowper Road, Dublin.

Mr Thomas Carver, Bookseller, 6 High Street, Hereford.

Mr C. D. Cazenowe, 26 Henrietta Street, Covent Garden, London, W.C.

Charterhouse Library, Godalming.

Mr Chrystal, Bookseller, Market Street, Manchester (2 Copies).

Messrs Clarke & Hodgson, Booksellers, Leicester (2 Copies).

Mr W. F. Clay, Bookseller, 18 Teviot Place, Edinburgh (12 Copies).

Mr E. Clulow, Bookseller, Derby.

Mr E. W. Coates, Bookseller, Huddersfield.

G. E. Cokayne, Esq., M.A., Norroy King of Arms, Exeter House, Roehampton.

Patrick Cooper, Esq., Advocate, Aberdeen (per Messrs Lewis Smith & Son).

James Copland, Esq., Historical Department, General Register House, Edinburgh.

Mr Cornish, Bookseller, St. Ann's Square, Manchester (3 Copies).

Messrs Cornish Bros., Booksellers, Birmingham.

Leo Culleton, Esq., 25 Cranbourne Street, London, W.C.

James Davis, Esq., Grand Pump Room Library, Bath (2 Copies).

Messrs Deighton, Bell & Co., Booksellers, Cambridge (10 Copies).

Messrs A. & F. Denny, 304 Strand, London, W.C.

Thomas Dickson, Esq., LL.D., General Register House, Edinburgh.

Messrs Douglas & Foulis, Booksellers, 9 Castle Street, Edinburgh.

Mr W. Downing, Chaucer's Head Library, Birmingham.

Rev. Robinson Duckworth, D.D., Canon of Westminster, Little Cloisters, Westminster, S.W.

Archibald H. Dunbar, Esq., Younger of Northfield.

Rev. W. D. V. Duncombe, Custos of the College of Vicars Choral, The Cloisters, Hereford.

Messrs Ede & Son, 93 and 94 Chancery Lane, London.

Edinburgh Public Library (per Hew Morrison, Esq., Librarian, c/o Messrs Macniven and Wallace, Booksellers, Edinburgh).

John Edwards, Esq., 4 Gt. Western Terrace, Glasgow (per Messrs J. Smith & Sons, Booksellers, Glasgow).

Mr Hy. S. Eland, Bookseller, Exeter.

Rev. Hy. Ellershaw, M.A., Hatfield Hall, Durham (*per* Messrs Andrews & Co., Durham).

Mr A. Elliot, Bookseller, 17 Princes Street, Edinburgh (6 Copies).

Reginald S. Faber, Esq., 10 Primrose Hill Road, London, N.W.

The Rev. John Ferguson, B.D., The Manse, Aberdalgie (*per* Mr John Christie, Bookseller, Perth).

Rt. Hon. Viscount Fitz-Harris (*per* Mr B. H. Blackwell, Bookseller, Oxford).

Hy. O. Fleuss, Esq., 23 Bonham Road, Brixton Hill, London, S.W.

Rev. Herbert H. Flower, Pittodrie House, Castle Esplanade, Edinburgh (2 Copies).

J. C. M. Ogilvie-Forbes, Esq., Boyndlie House, Fraserburgh.

George Forsyth, Esq., Holy Rood, Armley.

Rev. J. T. Fowler, M.A., F.S.A., Bp., Hatfield's Hall, Durham.

H. B. Earle Fox, Esq., 9 Scarsdale Studios, Stratford Road, London, W.

Rev. Thomas Shipdem Frampton, F.S.A., St. Mary's Platt, Sevenoaks.

A. D. Weld French, Esq., 33 Fairfield Street, Boston, New England, U.S.A.

Messrs William George's Sons, Booksellers, Top Corner, Park Street, Bristol (4 Copies).

Messrs F. & E. Gibbons, Booksellers, Liverpool.

Glasgow University Library (*per* James MacLehose & Sons, Booksellers, Glasgow).

Messrs R. Grant & Son, Booksellers, 107 Princes Street, Edinburgh.

George Gray, Esq., Glasgow (*per* Mr Hugh Hopkins, Bookseller, Glasgow).

Everard Green, Esq. (Rouge Dragon), F.S.A., K.S.S., College of Arms, Queen Victoria Street, London, E.C.

Hartwell D. Grissell, Esq., M.A., Chamberlain to His Holiness Pope Leo XIII., Brasenose College, Oxford.

Robert Guy, Esq., Glasgow (*per* Mr Hugh Hopkins, Bookseller, Glasgow).

John Hall, Esq., The Grange, Hale, Altrincham (*per* Mr W. F. Clay, Bookseller, Edinburgh).

Rev. Robert J. Shaw-Hamilton, D.D., The Rectory, Tynan, Co. Armagh.

Messrs Harrison & Sons, Booksellers, 59 Pall Mall, London, S.W. (2 Copies).

Messrs Hatchards, Booksellers, 187 Piccadilly, London, W. (4 Copies).

Very Rev. William Hatt, Dean of Brechin, Muchalls, Stonehaven.

C. E. H. Chadwyck Healey, Esq., Q.C., 119 Harley Street, London, W.

Captain Clayhills Henderson, R.N., of Invergowrie (*per* Mr G. Petrie, Bookseller, Dundee).

Mr John Heywood, Bookseller, Manchester.

Harry W. Hitchcock, Esq., 20 Ashley Gardens, Victoria Street London, S.W.

Mr Hitchman, Bookseller, Cherry Street, Birmingham.

Messrs Hodges, Figgis & Co. (Lim.), Booksellers, 104 Grafton Street, Dublin (5 Copies).

Hugh Hopkins, Esq., Glasgow (*per* Mr Hugh Hopkins, 17 West Regent Street, Glasgow).

Isaac Hordern, Esq., Edgerton House, Edgerton, Huddersfield (*per* Mr Coates, Bookseller, Huddersfield).

Rev. Canon Hinds Howell, Drayton Rectory, Norwich.

Hull Subscription Library (*c/o* Alfred Milner, Librarian).

Rev. J. W. Hunter, S. Mary's Parsonage, Birnam, N.B.

Mr R. W. Hunter, Bookseller, 19 George IV. Bridge, Edinburgh.

Mr R. Jackson, Bookseller, Leeds.

R. D. Jackson, Esq. (*per* Messrs Bickers & Son, London).

Thomas E. Jacobson, Esq., Surgeon, Sleaford, Lincolnshire.

Robert Jeffrey, Esq., Glasgow (*per* Mr Hugh Hopkins, Bookseller, Glasgow).

The Right Rev. Hugh Willoughby Jermyn, D.D., Bishop of Brechin, Primus of Scotland, Forbes Court, Broughty Ferry.

Mr G. P. Johnston, Bookseller, 33 George Street, Edinburgh (8 Copies).

P. Landon, Esq., Putney (*per* Mr B. H. Blackwell, Bookseller, Oxford).

Edward B. Lees, Esq., Thurland Castle, Kirkby-Lonsdale.

Joseph M. Lochhead, Esq., The Laurels, Paisley (*per* Mr Alexander Gardner, Bookseller, Paisley).

Mr C. Lowe, Bookseller, New Street, Birmingham.

Mr George Lowson, M.A., B.Sc., High School, Stirling.

Messrs Lupton, Booksellers, Burnley (6 Copies).

P. Duguid M'Combie, Esq., of Easter Skene (*per* Messrs D. Wyllie & Son, Booksellers).

Miss MacDougall, Woodburn, Canaan Lane, Edinburgh.

Mrs H. MacGregor, Bookseller, 86 High Street, Dundee.

Alexander M'Kenzie, Esq., St. Catherine's, Paisley (*per* Mr Alexander Gardner, Bookseller, Paisley).

Messrs James MacLehose & Sons, Booksellers, 61 St. Vincent Street, Glasgow (2 Copies).

Messrs Macniven & Wallace, Booksellers, 138 Princes Street. Edinburgh (5 Copies).

Messrs M. J. Mansell & Co., Booksellers, 98. Darlington Street, Wolverhampton.

George W. Marshall, Esq., LL.D., Rouge Croix, College of Arms, London.

Mr E. Menken, Bookseller, 3 and 5 Bury Street, New Oxford Street, London, W.C. (4 Copies).

Messrs J. Menzies & Co., Booksellers, 12 Hanover Street, Edinburgh.

Midland Educational Trading Co. (Lim.), Corporation Street, Birmingham (2 Copies).

Mr T. Miles, Bookseller, Bond Street, Leeds (3 Copies).

J. W. Mitchell, Esq., Lyon Clerk, Colinton Mains, Colinton.

Mitchell Library, Glasgow (c/o Messrs W. & R. Holmes, Booksellers).

Alexander Moring, Esq., 52 High Holborn, London, W.C. (2 Copies).

Mr Frank Murray, Bookseller, Derby.

Wm. Neish, Esq., The Laws, Ringennie, Dundee.

Newcastle-upon-Tyne Public Libraries.

Rev. W. J. Oldfield, M.A., St. Paul's Missionary College, Burgh, R.S.O. Lincs.

Rt. Hon. Lord Oxmantown (per B. H. Blackwell, Bookseller, Oxford).

Messrs Parker & Co., Booksellers, 27 Broad Street, Oxford.

James Balfour Paul, Esq., Lyon-King-of-Arms, Edinburgh.

G. Petrie, Esq., Bookseller, 52 Nethergate, Dundee.

Mr W. N. Pitcher, Bookseller, 49 Cross Street, Manchester.

Mr William Potter, Bookseller, 30 Exchange Street East, Liverpool (3 Copies).

Mr Bernard Quaritch, Bookseller, 15 Piccadilly, London, W. (2 Copies).

A. Charles F. Radcliffe, Esq., Stackhouse, Settle, Yorkshire.

J. Brooking-Rowe, Esq., Castle Barbican, Plympton, South Devon.

Mr J. Sampson, Bookseller, York (2 Copies).

Samuel Sanders, Esq., Chalfont Grove, Gerrards Cross, Bucks.

Messrs Slatter & Rose, Booksellers, High Street, Oxford.

David Smith, Esq., 20 Carden Place, Aberdeen (per Messrs D. Wyllie & Son, Bookseller).

Mr W. J. Smith, Bookseller, North Street, Brighton (2 Copies).

Society for Promoting Christian Knowledge, John Dalton Street, Manchester.

Messrs N. Pitcher & Co., late Hy. Sotheran & Co., Booksellers, Cross Street, Manchester (3 Copies).

New Spalding Club, Aberdeen (*per* P. J. Anderson, Esq., Secretary.)

Messrs John & Thomas Spencer, Booksellers, 20 Market Place, Leicester.

Captain Stansfeld, Dunninald, Montrose (*c/o* Mr Mathew Welsh, Bookseller, Montrose).

Rev. W. Stephen, Dumbarton.

Mill Stephenson, Esq., 14 Ritherdon Road, Upper Tooting, London, S.W.

Mr B. F. Stevens, Bookseller, 4 Trafalgar Square, London (2 Copies).

Mr T. G. Stevenson, Bookseller, 22 Frederick Street, Edinburgh (3 Copies).

Rt. Hon. Earl of Strathmore, Glamis Castle, Glamis.

Mr Albert Sutton, Bookseller, 8 Deansgate, Manchester (2 Copies).

Rev. Arthur Symonds, M.A., St. Thomas' Rectory, Stockport, Cheshire.

Mr James Thin, Bookseller, 55 South Bridge, Edinburgh (6 Copies).

Mr W. J. Thompson, Bookseller, Ashford, Kent (2 Copies).

Mr William Tomlin, Bookseller, Cambridge (2 Copies).

John A. Traill, Esq., LL.B., W.S., 30 Drummond Place, Edinburgh.

Rev. Dr. Tupholme, St. Stephen's Vicarage, Ealing, London, W.

George S. Veitch, Esq., Friarshall, Paisley (*per* Mr Alexander Gardner, Bookseller, Paisley).

W. W. Waddell, Esq., Crail.

Henry Wagner, Esq., F.S.A., 13 Half Moon Street, Piccadilly, London, W.

Robert Crawford Walker, Esq., F.S.A., Scot., Dundee.

Messrs Walker & Laycock, Booksellers, Leeds.

Mr H. W. Wallis, Bookseller, Cambridge.

Mr Wardleworth, Bookseller, Brown Street, Manchester.

William H. Weldon, Esq., Windsor Herald, College of Arms, London, E.C.

Lieut.-Col. Gould Hunter-Weston, F.S.A., of Hunterston, West Kilbride, Co. Ayr.

Rev. Principal Whitefoord, M.A., Theological College, Salisbury.

Mr T. Widdison, Bookseller, Fargate, Sheffield.

ERRATA.

Page 54, line 32, "fig. 2" should be "fig. 1."

  ,,   76,   ,,   3, "fig. 32" should be "fig. 2."

  ,, 142,   ,, 29, "fig. 1" should be "fig. 2."

  ,, 144,   ,, 15, "Plate XXXVI." should be "Plate XIII."

  ,, 159,   ,,   9, "Gregory X." should be "Gregory IX."

  ,, 212,   ,, 27, "fig. 4" should be "fig. 6."

  ,, 215,   ,, 17, "fig. 3" should be "fig. 5."

  ,, 242,   ,,   4, "fig. 10" should be "fig. 9."

  ,, 248,   ,,   6, "Plate XI." should be "Plate XXX."

  ,, 280,   ,, 32, "preconised" should be "precognised."

INTRODUCTION.

ALTHOUGH the present volume is published independently, and a large portion of its contents has been in MS. for a considerable time, it may yet be considered as in some sort a continuation of, or supplement to, "A Treatise on Heraldry, British and Foreign," published in 1892. The reader will not therefore expect to find in it information which is already fully supplied in the larger work, and the present book is in no sense an introduction to Heraldry in general. On the contrary as it deals only with a limited but very interesting branch of Armorial Science it presupposes the possession of a certain knowledge of Heraldry on the part of its readers ; and though it is hoped that others who are as yet without that special knowledge may find in the pages of the work many matters of interest, it is obvious that a full appreciation of its information can only be made by those who have a fair acquaintance with the general subject. Manuals of, and Introductions to, Heraldry have been sufficiently abundant. For the most part compilations from their predecessors, and showing very little original investigation or research, the *crambe repetita* has been dished up *ad nauseam ;* but more advanced treatises, or books like the present, dealing more fully with particular branches of the subject than is possible in a general work, have been very few and far between. So far as I know no work of this kind exists at home or abroad. The object of this treatise is to deal with the science of Heraldry from an Ecclesiastical point of view: to give information as to the Armorial Insignia of Episcopal Sees, Abbeys, Religious Foundations, and Communities at home and abroad ; to indicate the various manners in which Ecclesiastics of different grades have borne their arms, and combined their personal with their official insignia ; and fully to describe those ornaments and external additions to the shield by which Ecclesiastical ranks and offices have been, and are, distinguished.

Accordingly the work consists of Two Parts. The *First* deals with the general use of Armorial Insignia by the Ecclesiastics of the Western Church from the earliest times to the present. This portion contains much curious and out of the way information on subjects which have never yet been fully treated by an English writer. Its information and illustrations have been gathered not only from collections of coins, medals, and seals, and from many scarce works, unknown to the general reader, which are only accessible in Public Libraries of the first class, but are also largely derived from the extensive notes made by me in a lengthened experience of over thirty years' travel in Italy, Germany, France, Spain, etc.

In the course of that time I have always had in mind a work on the present lines, and consequently have amassed, in an area which extends from the Peninsula to Poland and from Sicily to Sweden, the information which I have now the pleasure to make accessible. It is confidently hoped that the artist, and the collector of books, plate, seals, china, bookplates, etc., as well as the antiquary and student of Heraldry, will find here much that is useful and interesting.

The *Second Part* contains an enlargement and correction of the "Notice of the Arms of the Episcopates of Great Britain and Ireland, with Heraldic Notes," written by me in illustration of a series of illuminated coats of arms, published by A. Warren in 1868. This book (of which Her Majesty the Queen was pleased to accept the dedication) has been long out of print, and repeated requests have been made to me that its letterpress should be reprinted. This is now done, with much additional historical information, with some corrections, and a new series of plates.

This portion of the work also includes the arms of the numerous colonial Sees, and those of the chief Abbeys and Religious Houses, the Deaneries, and other ancient Ecclesiastical Foundations in England.

The Continental portion of this section contains the blazon of the arms of the Popes from 1144 to the present time; an account of the great Religious Principalities of the Holy Roman Empire; and much historical and heraldic information with regard to the principal Sees, Religious Houses and Chapters in Germany, Italy, France, Poland, and the Low Countries; as well as the arms and devices of the most important religious Orders and communities; and of the British and some foreign Universities.

The number of coats of arms blazoned in the work exceeds a thousand.

In the Appendices will be found much curious matter in the essays "On the use of Supporters by Ecclesiastics," and "On the Continental Chapters, with their *Preuves de Noblesse;*" and I venture here to direct the special attention of my readers to them, because considerations of space have required that they should be printed in smaller type than the rest of the work, and they are thus in some danger of escaping notice. As much of the subject matter of the book should be of interest to others besides those who belong to my own branch of the Catholic Church, I have been careful in the statement of facts to avoid any expression which might jar upon the sensibilities of those who differ from me on some theological matters ; I trust that the confidence in my fairness, which induced Ecclesiastics (and others) of high position in another communion to take an interest in the progress of the work, has been fully justified.

While I have been careful by the use of abundant references in the pages of the book to give the sources of my information with regard to matters which had not come under my personal observation, I think it right also to express here, in general terms, an acknowledgement of my obligations' to the published works on general heraldry of the great German armorial writers, SPENER and SIEBMACHER. The outlines of some of the illustrations have been taken from TRIERS, *Einleitung zu der Wapen-Kunst;* and from MAGNENEY, *Recueil des Armes.*

In some portions of the work I have been frequently indebted to POTTHAST'S invaluable *Wegweiser durch die Geschichtswerke des Europäischen Mittelalters*, and to JANAUSCHEK'S book *Originum Cisterciensium.*

My thanks are due to PERCEVAL LANDON, Esquire, of Hertford College, Oxford, for placing at my service the interesting and valuable notes on the *Heraldry of the Oxford Colleges* which he is now printing in the *Archæologia Oxoniensis.*

The excellent Index, which adds so greatly to the value of a book of this description, and which has been a work of more than usual difficulty, has been compiled by GEORGE HARVEY JOHNSTON, Esquire, who rendered the like service in the previous volumes.

In a work which deals so largely with names of persons and places, as well as with technicalities, errors (and not merely orthographical ones) will sometimes escape that which has appeared to be the closest and most careful vigilance. While I can hardly hope that my experience in this respect will be entirely different from that of my predecessors, or render this preliminary apology altogether unnecessary, I may yet say that I have done what I could to make it so. And in this connection I desire to express my thanks to my friend the Rev. J. MYERS DANSON, D.D., of Aberdeen, who has obligingly revised most of the proof sheets, and has thus been of very considerable assistance to me and to my readers.

"Feci quod potui; melius alter faciat opus."

JOHN WOODWARD.

MONTROSE, 1st Jan. 1894.

SYNOPSIS.

PART I.

CHAPTER I.

Military Origin of Armorial Bearings—Their adoption for Secular Purposes—Seals, authentic and forged—Personal Effigies on Ecclesiastical Seals — Seals of Benedictine and Cistercian Abbots—Personal Arms introduced—The various kinds of Seals—Ancient gems—Arms of Sees and Abbeys, how composed—The Crosier, or Pastoral Staff—Ecclesiastical Foundations of the Kings of France—Arms of Italian Sees—Arms assumed—*Preuves de Noblesse*—Brisures, Marks of Cadency, or of Illegitimacy, in Ecclesiastical Arms — The Mitre as a Heraldic Charge—Series of Seals of the Benedictine Abbots of Mölk —Arms on Ecclesiastical Vestments, etc.   pp. 3—31

CHAPTER II.

External Heraldic Ornaments, Spiritual and Temporal — The Coronet, its use on the Continent—The Temporal Sword—Helmets and Crests used by Ecclesiastics — Military Fiefs held by Ecclesiastics—The Church Militant—The Ecclesiastical Hat, etc. .   .   .   .   pp. 32—38

CHAPTER III.

ECCLESIASTICS BELOW ABBATIAL RANK.

Arms in a Cartouche—The *Biretta*, and the Ecclesiastical Hat—The Chanter's Baton—Protonotaries—Canons and *Chanoinesses*—Noble Chapters—Their Insignia—The use of the Amess, or

CHAPTER IV.

ABBOTS AND ABBESSES.

CHAPTER V.

BISHOPS.

CHAPTER VI.

ARCHBISHOPS, LEGATES, PRIMATES, PATRIARCHS.

APPENDIX D.

APPENDIX E.

APPENDIX F.

LIST OF PLATES.

PART I.

𝔈𝔠𝔠𝔩𝔢𝔰𝔦𝔞𝔰𝔱𝔦𝔠𝔞𝔩 ℌ𝔢𝔯𝔞𝔩𝔡𝔯𝔶.

CHAPTER I.

Military Origin of Armorial Bearings—Their adoption for Secular
Purposes—Seals, authentic and forged—Personal Effigies on
Ecclesiastical Seals — Seals of Benedictine and Cistercian
Abbots—Personal Arms introduced—The various kinds of
Seals—Ancient gems—Arms of Sees and Abbeys, how composed—The Crosier, or Pastoral Staff—Ecclesiastical Foundations of the Kings of France—Arms of Italian Sees—Arms
assumed—*Preuves de Noblesse*—Brisures, Marks of Cadency,
or of Illegitimacy, in Ecclesiastical Arms — The Mitre as a
Heraldic Charge—Series of Seals of the Benedictine Abbots
of Mölk—Arms on Ecclesiastical Vestments, etc.

IT is no part of the design of this treatise to deal in
detail with the Origin of Armorial Bearings, or to set
out the general principles which regulate their use.

It is sufficient to say here that arms as at present used
are distinctly of military origin, and arose from the
necessity of there being some means by which individuals,
though sheathed in armour which concealed the visage,
might be readily distinguished by their followers, in
warfare, or in those military exercises which were its
preparation and rehearsal. *Arma sunt distinguendi
causâ.* The devices adopted for this purpose, at first of
a simple character, emblazoned upon the shield, and
then spreading to the banner, the surcoat, and the
caparisons of the horses, were of such evident utility for

the purpose above indicated, that their use soon became general in civilised Europe ; and we may probably find in the gatherings of the princes and nobles of all nationalities for the Crusades the motive for the adoption of a more definite system to regulate the use of armorial bearings than had prevailed in earlier times, before they had become fixed and hereditary.

But armorial bearings were not only of value from a military point of view, they became of hardly less importance in civil life. The custom of authenticating legal documents by seals bearing the personal devices of the contracting parties, led the way to the adoption of heraldic insignia even by those to whom they were not necessary for military purposes. Shields of arms thus came to be adopted for Ecclesiastical dignitaries, for Bishoprics, Abbeys, and Religious Communities ; not merely because it often happened that, under the feudal system, they had to furnish for the military necessities of the state their quota of armed men whom it was needful to distinguish from others by the military insignia of banner or shield ; but because the adoption of a definite device was found both by Religious and Civil dignitaries and communities a very convenient way for indicating their status upon the seals attesting the authenticity of the charters and other documents to which they were appended.

Not only this, but the use of seals became compulsory by law. The *Statutum de apportis religiosorum* (35. Edward I., 1307) enacts that every religious House should have a common-seal, which should be in the custody not of the abbot only, as had been the case before, but of four others, "de dignioribus et discretioribus," of the convent ; and that every grant to which this seal was not affixed should be null and void.

This was not, as some have thought, because so few people in those times could write ; on the contrary, the majority of ecclesiastics and members of religious houses were at least equal to a formal signature ; but rather because, while signatures could be forged without great difficulty, the engraving of a seal demanded both time and special ability of a kind not generally found. Not that frauds were altogether precluded. Sometimes the matrices of metal were stolen to provide the means of authenticating forged documents. In 1318, for example, some clerics excommunicated by the Archdeacon of Poissy, treacherously attacked and mortally wounded the *sigillifer* of that ecclesiastic, robbed him of the "*scel aux causes*" (*v.* p. 9) of his master, and used it in the fabrication of letters of absolution. (Quoted by LECOY DE LA MARCHE from the *Registre du Parlement*, cited in the *Collection des Sceaux* of DOUET D'ARCQ.)

At other times, the same writer tells us, authentic seals were removed from the documents to which they belonged, and attached to others of more importance. A cleric of the Diocese of Narbonne was in 1282 cited into the Bishop's court at Carcassonne for a fraud of this kind. Here the authentic seal had been, by means of a heated blade of thin steel, removed from its document, and ingeniously attached to another.

Actual forgeries sometimes took place, as when in the eleventh century a goldsmith of Limoges counterfeited the seal of Pope URBAN II. for HUMBAUD, Bishop of that See (at the instigation of his archdeacon HÉLIE DE GIMEL), in order apparently to authenticate certain forged letters of the Pope. URBAN himself detected the fraud on his visit to Limoges. He instantly deposed the Bishop, and declared the very name of the Archdeacon to be infamous. The fate of the forger is left to our imagination—perhaps he had wisely decamped ! But to return ;—seals early became armorial. Moreover, the applicability of heraldic insignia to decorative purposes was soon perceived.

Whether carved in stone or wood for the adornment of the church, or glowing in their proper colours in the stained glass, or woven into the hangings, or embroidered on the vestments, or even enamelled on the sacred vessels to preserve the memory of a pious donor, the use of armorial insignia soon assumed very considerable importance from an Ecclesiastical point of view. It is in this aspect then that we purpose now to regard them, and it is the object of this book to give somewhat fuller information than exists in the treatises which deal with the general subject of Heraldry, with regard to the armorial insignia adopted by Religious Foundations, in Britain and on the continent of Europe ;—to describe the various external ornaments by which the various grades and offices in the ecclesiastical hierarchy have been distinguished both at home and abroad, and to indicate the various manners in which these official insignia were combined with the personal arms of the user.

.The examination of a good collection of mediæval seals will show us that at first the seals of Ecclesiastics were usually engraved with their personal effigy, within a band containing an inscription indicative of the name and rank of the person represented. These seals were usually, but not invariably, *vesica* shaped, or *en ogive.* LIÉBERT, Bishop of Cambray in 1057 ; and the Chapter of Notre Dame of Noyon, in 1174, used seals in the shape of a pear. (DEMAY, *Le Costume au Moyen Age d'après les Sceaux*, p. 23, fig. 14. Paris, 1880.) As early as the commencement of the eleventh century the Bishops of France had adopted great seals bearing their effigies. ARNOULD DE LISIEUX in 1130 (being then only Archdeacon of Seez) reproaches the prelates for this mark of ostentation, as he esteemed it. On the early seals only the bust of the bishop, or his figure at half-length, at first appeared (as was also the case on the early seals of the kings of France), and this custom continued in some dioceses up to the close of the century. In 1253 a seal of the *officialité*, or episcopal court, of Paris still bears a mitred bust, apparently the image of the diocesan. (Plate VIII., fig. 11.) Nevertheless the custom of representing the bishop at full length, standing or seated, had been adopted concurrently with the former usage, at least as early as the twelfth century. (LECOY DE LA MARCHE, *Les Sceaux*, pp. 254, 255.) Many early ecclesiastical seals, especially the counter-seals of Abbeys, and the personal seals of the Abbots, bear only a representation of the arm of the abbot issuing from the flank (usually the dexter flank) of the seal and holding a pastoral staff paleways. A good example, that of an Abbot of Melrose, is engraved in LAING, *Catalogue of Scottish Seals*, ii., No. 1164. The seal of oval shape bears the arm of the abbot, vested in the sleeve of his habit, and holding his crosier, or pastoral staff, in pale. The back ground is diapered with a reticulated pattern, and the legend is " MANUS ABBATIS DE MELROS." With this we may compare the small round *secretum* of the Capitular Seal of Melrose in 1292, which has a similar device with the addition of an estoile at the sinister side of the staff. The legend is "CONTRA SIGILL. DE MELROS." (LAING, *Scottish Seals*, i., 1077.) It is somewhat curious that this bearing is found, generally but not exclusively, on the seals of abbots and monasteries belonging, like Melrose, to the Cistercian Order. Thus the seal of the Abbots of Byland in 1186 (*British Museum Catalogue of Seals*, No. 2822); of Buildwas, twelfth century (*B. Mus.*, No. 2753); of Sibton in 1193 (*B. Mus.*, No. 4020); of Tintern, twelfth and thirteenth century (*B. Mus.*, No. 4194); of Vale Royal, twelfth century (*B. Mus.*, No. 4233); and of many other Cistercian foundations, are charged with the hand and pastoral staff. The seal of the Abbot of Holywood has the same bearings, but the crosier is backed by a tree. (LAING, *Scottish Seals*, i., 1043.) · The seals of the Benedictine Abbot of Eynsham, in the twelfth century; of RICHARD, Abbot of the Austin Canons at Grimsby in 1203; and of WILLIAM DE LEWKNOR, Precentor of Chichester, *circa* 1216 (*B. Mus. Cat.*, Nos. 3144, 3232, and 1484), all have the hand and crosier ; and it also appears, rather curiously, on the seal *ad causas* of the Chapter of Perugia, *sede vacante.* (GLAFEY, *Specimen decadem Sigillorum*, p. 25, Lipsiae, 4to 1849.) . The Benedictine Abbey of SAINT SEYNE had, in the eighteenth century, as its arms : *d'Azur à un dextrochère de carnation, habillé d'une manche large d'argent et tenant une crosse d'or posée en pal* (*Armorial Général de France.* Bourgogne, i., p. 152, No. 46). It may be noticed the same device appears on the tombstone of Abbot SUTTON, at Dorchester; and in several other instances (BOUTELL, *Christian Monuments*, pp. 53-55).

In course of time, as the convenience of Heraldic devices became generally recognised, a shield bearing the personal arms of the ecclesiastic was introduced, and it filled up conveniently the angle beneath the foot of the effigy in the base of the *vesica.* Mr W. H. ST. JOHN HOPE, Assistant Secretary of the Society of Antiquaries, says that "the earliest seal on which a shield occurs is that of WILLIAM DE LUDA, Bishop of Ely in 1290, who has the three crowns of the See of Ely beneath his feet. DAVID MARTYN (St. Davids, 1296) also has a shield under his feet, but it is charged with his own arms. (*Proceedings of Society of Antiquaries*, Feb. 3, 1887.) The BASSET arms, however, appear on the seal of FULK BASSET, Bishop of London, 1244-1259 (*B. Mus. Cat.*, No. 1909).

I may here borrow from Mr W. H. ST. JOHN HOPE'S paper on the "Seals of English Bishops" the following useful information : " Episcopal Seals are divisible into :—

(1) Seals of dignity, with (2) their counter-seals ; with which must be included (3) private seals, or *secreta ;* (4)

Seals *ad causas;* (5) Seals made for special purposes, such as the palatinate seals of the Bishop of Durham. And he appends the following note by C. S. PERCEVAL, Esq. LL.D., Treasurer of the Society, of Antiquaries, as to the uses of these various seals :—

"While the Seal of Dignity, as we have called it, or Great Seal, was used for charters, and other instruments affecting the property or rights of the See; or to authenticate copies (*vidimus* or *inspeximus*) of important documents such as Papal Bulls ; the *secretum*, or *sigillum privatum*, was for deeds concerning the private estate of the Bishop himself, the signet for sealing his private correspondence, both being occasionally used as counter-seals to the Great Seal. The seal *ad causas* was appended to copies of Acts of Court, letters of Orders, probates (where no special official seal was in use), marriage licences, testimonials, and similar instruments of a minor and transitory interest." (*Proceedings of the Society of Antiquaries*, 2nd S., xi., 271, *et seq.*). The counter-seal of RICHARD, Bishop of Winchester in 1174 (not in *B. Mus. Collection*) bears the words "*Sum custos et testis sigilli.*"

It is worthy of notice that as the earliest seals used in Christian times had been antique gems, usually set as finger rings, the use of these long continued as *secreta*, or counter-seals. It is no uncommon thing to find a pagan or a Gnostic gem used as a *secretum* by a Christian prelate. The *secretum* of GUILLAUME DE CHAMPAGNE, Archbishop of Sens in the twelfth century, is a gem bearing a remarkably beautiful bust of Venus. (LECOY DE LA MARCHE, *Sceaux*, fig. 8, p. 25.) This author remarks that these gems were sometimes Christianised by the addition of a legend. Thus the counter-seal of NICOLAS, Abbot of ST. ETIENNE at Caen, bore a *winged Victory* which was converted into an angel by the legend—" Ecce mitto angelum meum."

Warriors become ST. GEORGES by the addition of a lance and a dragon. The unmistakably pagan head of CARACALLA becomes that of the Prince of the Apostles by the simple addition of the words ο Πέτρος! The Monks of Durham turned the head of Jupiter into that of ST. OSWALD by a like process; "Caput Sancti Cswaldi." (*Vetusta Monumenta*, i., pl. xlix.) Mr PORTER gives an even more remarkable instance. The Monks of Selby converted the head of the Emperor HONORIUS into that of the BLESSED SAVIOUR, by the addition of the legend "Caput Nostrum Christus est!"

These gems are sometimes set upon the face of early seals. (This is so on the seal of BONIFACE of Savoy, Archbishop of Canterbury in 1266, where four antique gems are set, two on either side of the Archbishop's standing effigy. This is engraved in Mr HOPE'S paper; see also *Archæologia Cantiana*, vi., 215 ; and Mr PORTER'S excellent paper on the "Seals of the Archbishops of York," in *Proceedings of the Society of Antiquaries*, 2nd S., xiii., pp: 45, *et seq.*)

As seal engravers progressed in artistic skill more elaborate compositions were employed. The ecclesiastic was represented standing, or seated, under an architectural canopy which was often adorned with figures of patronal saints, and in addition to the shield of his personal arms others were introduced bearing the Royal Arms, or those of the Abbey, or See, over which he presided. WALTER REYNOLDS, Bishop of Worcester, 1308, is said to have been the first to place on either side of his effigy shields bearing the arms of England. Sir HENRY ELLIS considered that the use of the Royal Arms on ecclesiastical seals might refer to some high secular office held by the ecclesiastic, but as the custom is not confined to such cases, it is evident that this supposition is unfounded. Later, when the effigy of the bishop was moved into a subordinate position in the base of the shield, the shields of arms accompanied him thither.

The arms of Bishoprics, Abbeys, etc., were often a composition containing the effigies, or the conventional symbols, of the saints to whose honour they were dedicated. Thus the Cathedral Church of SALISBURY is dedicated to the Blessed Virgin, and so the shield of arms assumed for the See, bears: *Azure, the effigy of the Blessed Virgin holding in her arms the Holy Child or.* (Plate XXV., fig. 1.) The Arms of the See of LONDON are: *Gules, two swords in saltire proper the hilts in base or.* (Plate XX., fig. 4.) The sword is the emblem of the Apostle ST. PAUL to whom the Cathedral is dedicated. The ancient dedication of the Cathedral of Exeter was to SS. PETER and PAUL, and the symbols of both these Apostles are therefore combined in the arms of the See: *Gules, a sword in pale argent, the hilt in base or, surmounted by two keys endorsed in saltire of the last.* (Plate XXII., fig. 2.) The arms of the City and See of LISBON contain a boat on the prow and stern of which are perched two ravens. " Tem por armas . . . huma Nao com dous corvos discorrendo de poupa a proa." (*Nobiliarchia Portugueza,* p. 352, 1754.) These bearings commemorate the legend that the body of ST. VINCENT, exposed in an open boat, was guarded by ravens as it drifted on the sea to Lisbon from the Cape which now bears his name. The Church of COMPOSTELLA in Spain has for its arms the tomb of Santiago, the Apostle ST. JAMES, whose body is said to have been buried there, having floated from Joppa to Padron, twelve miles below Santiago, to be discovered eight centuries later.

The Abbey of S. ETIENNE at Dijon bore: *Gules, a palm branch in pale or, between three flint-stones argent.* Here the martyr's palm is combined with the instruments of the martyrdom of the saint whose relics were preserved in the abbey. The arms of the

Cathedral of S. ETIENNE at Auxerre are : *Azure, three stones or.*

The arms of Abbeys, and other religious foundations, were often a composition from the Armorial bearings of their founders. Thus the arms of the monastery of S. AGGAS, or AGATHA, founded by Lord SCROPE of BOLTON, were those of that nobleman (*Azure, a bend or*), with the addition of *a pastoral staff of the last in bend sinister.* (Plate I., fig. 8.)

The arms of the CHARTER-HOUSE were ; *Or, three chevrons sable,* the arms of its founder DE MANNY. The Abbey of RIEVAULX bore the arms of DE ROOS : *Gules, three water bougets, argent, over all a pastoral staff in pale or.*

It may be well to mention here that the pastoral staff, a staff with a head curved in imitation of a shepherd's crook, and originally of very simple formation (*see* Plate VIII.) is with equal propriety, and in full accordance with ancient English use, termed a crosier, or crozier.

In this book both terms will be used. The modern use by which the term *crosier* is applied to designate the cross borne, not by, but, before a Papal Legate or an Archbishop in his province, is an entirely mistaken and misleading one. (This cross will be spoken of in a future chapter.) The French term *crosse* denotes, not the archi-episcopal cross, but the ordinary crook-headed pastoral staff; and the word *crosier* has not, as is sometimes erroneously asserted, any connection with the French word *croix* or the English *cross*. Its real connection is with the word *crook*. In the contemporary narrative of the coronation of RICHARD III. (printed in *Excerpta Historica,* pp. 379 *et seq.*) we find the following passage :—" And then comyng the Crosse wt. a ryall procession, fyrst Prests wt. grey Amyses and then Abotts and Bushopes wt. meters on ther hedds & crosers in there hands; and the Bushope of Rochester bare the Cross before the Cardinall." Here in one sentence we have the processional cross borne before the Clergy; the Bishops who bore their own crosiers (as they ought to do still unless infirm in mind or body) and the archiepiscopal cross borne before the Cardinal-Archbishop.

The Rev. J. T. FOWLER, M.A., F.S.A., of Durham, who is a careful philologer and ecclesiologist, has shown that the terms "pastoral staff" and "crosier" are both rightly applicable to a bishop's crook, and that the term "crosier" does not, as is often imagined, properly belong to an archbishop's cross. "Crosier," he says, "in the form croce, crosse, croche, cruche, crocere, etc., may be shown by quotations to have been the proper English name of a bishop's staff from very early times. Pastoral staff is the English translation of the usual Latin term *Baculus Pastoralis*, used in the Pontificals, etc. And it may be rightly used, no doubt, by any who prefer four syllables to two, and a new term to an old one. The use of it in England appears to date from about the time when an archbishop's cross began to be called a crosier. The earliest example of this wrong application which I have hitherto found is in HOOK'S *Church Dictionary* (1842), where a crozier is said to be an archbishop's cross."

Mr FOWLER has printed in *Archæologia*, vol. lii., a most curious and interesting series of quotations and references in early writers, from 1330 downwards, which abundantly prove his case. He shows that the usual old English word for a bishop's (or abbot's) crook was croce, croche, or crosse. That when it was borne by another person for the bishop such person was called his crocer, croyser, or crosier; as was also the archbishop's or pope's cross-bearer. Next, that the bishop's staff was called in the fifteenth and later centuries a "croyser staff, crosiers staff, crosier's staff, or crosier staff, as if people connected it more closely with the clerk who commonly carried it than with the bishop himself."

Then the second member of the term, viz., "staff," was gradually dropped, and what had at first been called a croce, and then a crosier staff, was called simply a crosier, which use has continued to the present time. The application of the term crosier to the cross borne *before* an archbishop or legate is a modern error. An archbishop does not bear his cross himself, and when he pontificates he holds his crosier, or crooked pastoral staff, though it is quite true that on mediæval seals and stained glass he is often represented holding his cross.

"The blunder, once started, all at once sprang into astonishing vitality, as I find it adopted by even such writers as WEBB, HAINES, BOUTELL, LEE, BLUNT (in 1866, but corrected in 1884), SHIPLEY, MARRIOTT, MACKENZIE WALCOTT, Mrs JAMESON, FAIRHOLT, and others, also in several standard dictionaries, though not in that of SKEAT, who knows that crosier is not derived from cross, and that the word has always been used of a bishop's crook. The false derivation, plausible enough to those who have not gone into the matter, has no doubt had much to do with the propagation of the error. Is it too late to amend it? An archbishop's cross has been called a cross from 1460 to the present time, and the minister who carried it before the archbishop, while the prelate himself held his 'croce' or 'crosier,' was called the 'crossier' or 'croyser.' It is interesting to note that Roman Catholic writers of the old school, unaffected by the Anglican ecclesiological revival, such, for example, as Bishop JOHN MILNER, always used the terms in the old English way. But Dr ROCK and the younger PUGIN, while rightly calling the archi-episcopal cross a 'cross,' are shy of calling a bishop's staff a 'crosier,' and use the term 'pastoral staff.' Dr HUSENBETH in 1859 says of the latter, 'some have lately affected to call it the pastoral staff,' but expresses his decided preference for crosier, as hallowed by long usage. In 1866 he is 'aware that in

1. Abp. de Turey. 2. Jean de Flandre. 3. Harcourt.

4. Card. Altieri. 5. Card. Rappaciolo. 6. Card. Lugo.

7. Card. Barbarini. 8. S. Aggas. 9. Card. Geori.

10. Abp. Sterckx. 11. Calder Abbey. 12. See of Embrun.

strictness the term crosier belongs to a cross, but that by long usage it is applied to a Bishop's crook.' He is aware, that is, he has been led astray by Anglican ecclesiologists."

HUGO DE S. VICTOR admonishes us that in this staff three things are to be noted ;—the crook, the rod, the point, whose signification is thus given :—

> Attraho peccantes, justos rogo, pungo vagantes ;
> Officio triplici servio pontifici.

Or, as set out in the following distich :—

> Attrahe per curvum, medio rege, punge per imum ;
> Curva trahit quos virga regit, pars ultima pungit.

(*Vide* SPENER, *Opus Heraldicum*, pars. gen., cap. vii., p. 333.)

To return :—a singular example of monastic arms formed from the bearings of the founder is afforded by the coat of CALDER ABBEY, which is composed of the bearings of the three families which contributed to its aggrandisement : *Argent, three escucheons :* 1. *Or, a fess between two chevrons gules,* for FITZWALTER. 2. *Gules, three lucies hauriant argent,* for LUCY. 3. *Sable, a fret argent,* for FLEMYNG. (Plate I., fig. 11.) The Monastery of KIRKHAM bore the arms of ROOS, as given above for RIEVAULX, but substituted a bourdon, prior's staff, or crutch, for the crozier. A modern instance of the same usage is to be seen in the arms assumed for the modern foundation of the Abbey of MOUNT ST. BERNARD in Leicestershire. They are : *Or, a crosier in pale, with a sudarium sable ; on a chief Azure, three lions rampant or ;* the latter being the arms of the founder, DE LISLE.

Many other English examples will be found by the student in the list of the arms of Abbeys and Religious Houses in Great Britain, in Part II., of this book. The arms of the Abbey of ST. ETIENNE of Caen are a composition from the arms of ENGLAND

and those of the Duchy of NORMANDY; they form an interesting example of the curious heraldic arrangement known as dimidiation. The dexter half of the shield of the arms of ENGLAND (*Gules*, three *lions passant gardant in pale or*) is conjoined with the sinister half of the arms of the Duchy (*Gules*, two *lions passant gardant in pale or*), thus three of the lions' fore-quarters appear, but only two of the hind-quarters. (Plate II., fig. 1.)

In France, the Sees and Abbeys of Royal foundation often have as the "field" of their arms, the old Royal bearings of the Kings of FRANCE : *Azure, semé of fleurs-de-lis or*. Thus, the Cathedral of NOTRE DAME at Paris bears the above coat, known briefly as FRANCE-ANCIENT, and *Over all the effigy of the Blessed Virgin, supporting in her arms the Holy Child proper*. (SEGOING, *Armorial Universel*, planche 181. Paris 1679). The Canons of "LA SAINTE CHAPELLE DU ROI" at Dijon bore: FRANCE-ANCIENT, *Over all a palm branch in pale or ;* the emblem of the proto-martyr ST. STEPHEN (*vide supra*, and see also HOZIER, *Armorial Général de France*, Généralité de Bourgogne, i., No. 88). The Collegiate Church of ST. ANDOCHE in the town of Saulieu used : FRANCE-ANCIENT, *Over all a crosier and sword in saltire argent*. (The arms of the Sees of REIMS, LANGRES, LAON, and NOYON, similarly composed, will be found later on, at Plate X.) The Cathedral Church of ST. VINCENT at Macon bears : FRANCE-ANCIENT (*Azure, fleury or*) *thereon the figure of St. Vincent, vested in a white alb, and a dalmatic gules semé de fleurs-de-lis or, holding in his dexter hand a palm branch, and in the sinister the open Evangelistarium, proper*. The Cathedral Church of ST. VINCENT at Châlons bears : FRANCE-ANCIENT, *over all a sceptre gules with a flory head* (HOZIER, *Armorial Général de France*, Généralité de Bourgogne, tome ii., 225). The Benedictine Abbey of MOUSTIER ST. JEAN bore simply : FRANCE-

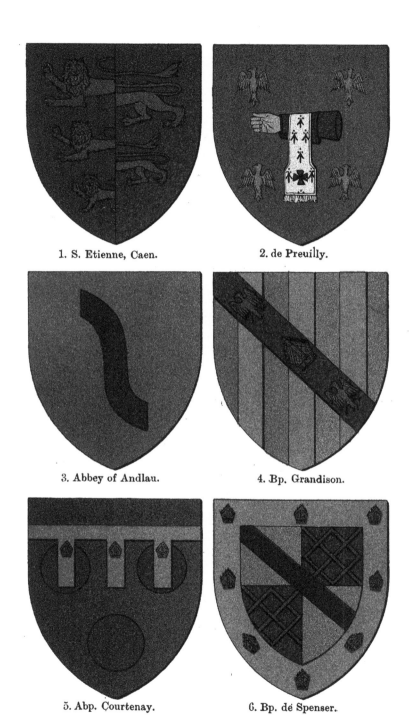

1. S. Etienne, Caen.

2. de Preuilly.

3. Abbey of Andlau.

4. Bp. Grandison.

5. Abp. Courtenay.

6. Bp. de Spenser.

ANCIENT. By the Chapter of LIMOGES the *semé* of FRANCE-ANCIENT is reduced to *five fleurs-de-lis or*, 3 and 2; which coat still appears in the old stained glass of the north aisle of the Cathedral of LIMOGES. There are examples in which appear the later arms of FRANCE (as borne since CHARLES V. reduced the *fleurs-de-lis* to three in honour of the Ever Blessed Trinity): *Azure, a passion nail between three fleurs-de-lis or*, are the arms of the famous Abbey of ST. DENIS near Paris; the burying place of the Kings of France. The Abbaye de ST. GERMAIN DES PRÉS similarly used: *Azure, on an escucheon argent between three fleurs-de-lis or, as many torteaux.*

The ancient arms of the Ducs D'ORLÉANS: FRANCE-ANCIENT, *a label argent in chief*, are the field of the arms borne by the CHARTREUSE D'ORLÉANS, *charged with a figure of Lazarus rising from the tomb argent* (HOZIER, *Arm. Gén. de France*, Généralité d'Orléans).

Many, perhaps most, of the French Sees have no official arms as distinct from those borne by the Cathedral Chapters; whereas in Germany, and in England (so far at least as concerns the Cathedrals of the "Old Foundation," *i.e.*, those which were in existence as such before the Reformation), the arms of the Deaneries or Cathedral Chapter are different from, though often formed upon, those of the See (*see* the arms of these Sees and Deaneries in Part II. of this work). The arms of the Chapter of POITIERS appear to be *Azure, a long cross botonny argent;* upon this the Bishop places an escucheon, *Barry of eight argent and gules.* Both coats occur with some frequency in the stained glass of the aisles of the Cathedral of Poitiers.

The official arms of the early Bishops of ALBI also, were identical with those which are still used by the Cathedral Chapter, viz.: *Gules, a cross pommetty or, adorned with pendant chains and precious stones.* It is said that this coat originated in the dedication of the ancient cathedral to the Holy Cross. But BERNARD DE CASTANET (1275-1308), who laid the foundation-stone of the present grand cathedral, dedicated to SAINTE CÉCILE, bore : *Gules, a tower argent, surmounted by a double cross ;* and, after the secularisation of the Chapter, he and his successors took this personal coat as the arms of the See.

In Italy many, perhaps most, of the Sees have arms, but they are not (so far as my pretty wide experience goes) frequently in use. While the arms of the Pope, and the personal arms of the Bishop or Archbishop are placed upon the façade, or are suspended within the church, the arms of the See are seldom or never seen. The curious inquirer may puzzle out at least some of them in the *Italia Sacra* of UGHELLI, and kindred works, but unless he has a special interest in the matter he is little likely to learn of their existence. I give just one or two here. TUSCULUM bears : *Gules, two keys in saltire tied by a cord in base or.* ANAGNI bears : *Gules, in chief an eagle displayed and in base a lion passant or.* The arms of SABINA are : *Gules, three sets of interlaced annulets between two bendlets or ;* of AQUILANI, *Argent, an eagle displayed sable, crowned or* (UGHELLI, *Italia Sacra,* t. i.).

In Germany, as formerly in England and Scotland, it was the custom for high Ecclesiastics to use indifferently their official arms, or their personal arms if they possessed any. It was then an easy step when seals became more elaborate, to represent both the official and the personal arms on the same seal, though upon different shields. In Italy when any official arms were used they were often made to occupy the *chief* or upper part of a shield divided *per fess ;* the personal arms of the Prelate being placed in the lower part, or base, of the shield.

In England it has been long the custom for Archbishops, Bishops, and Abbots to impale their personal with their official arms, just as a wife impaled the arms of her husband with her own ; the ecclesiastic being considered *maritus ecclesiæ*, and the official arms have assigned to them the dexter side, that being accounted the more honourable portion, of the shield. In later times Archdeacons and Chancellors impaled the arms of the See with their personal arms upon their official seals.

As will be shown more fully hereafter the arms of the Irish Sees date only from post-Reformation times. In Scotland, also, Bishops for the most part used only their personal arms, with of course the mitre and other external insignia pertaining to their ecclesiastical rank. This is still usually the case in the majority of the Sees of France, Belgium, and Southern Europe. In a few cases the personal arms of an illustrious Prelate were adopted by later Bishops as the bearings of the See :— of this we have examples in Part II. in the arms of MAINZ, HEREFORD, and WORCESTER.

In France the six great ecclesiastical Peers sometimes impaled, and other times quartered, the official arms of their Sees with their personal ones (*vide infra*, Plates IX. and X.). In Germany these arms were more frequently quartered, the official coat of the See or Abbey being generally placed in the first and last quarters, especially when the Bishop held but one Sec, and possessed no temporal lordships. But, when, as was in modern times frequently the case, several Sees with their dependent lordships were united under the rule of one Prelate, it was the custom to quarter all these official arms in the shield, and to place the personal arms of the Prelate in an escucheon *en surtout*.

These customs will be fully exemplified as we proceed. Of course many Prelates had by birth no right to bear arms at all. Many of those who have filled the highest places in the hierarchy have risen from the very humblest origin, by their personal merit, just as NICOLAS BREAK-SPEARE, the Anglo-Saxon thrall, attained to the Pontifical throne as ADRIAN IV. As it was then, so is it still. The late CELESTINE, Cardinal GANGLBAUER, Archbishop of VIENNA, was a Benedictine monk, of peasant birth; and on the occasion of his funeral, in 1889, the Emperor FRANCIS JOSEPH walked by the side of the Cardinal's peasant brothers and nephews. Mgr. KOPP, Prince-Bishop of BRESLAU, was the son of a cotton weaver at DUDERSTAAT. Mgr. DINDER, Archbishop of POSEN and GNESEN, was the son of a cobbler at ROSSEL. Mgr. KREMENTZ, Archbishop of COLOGNE, was the son of a COBLENTZ butcher, and his brother kept on the old butcher's shop. Cardinal SIMOR, late Archbishop of GRAN, and Prince-Primate of HUNGARY, was the son of a petty shoemaker at STUHLWEISSENBERG. Not long ago an infidel Belgian paper thought fit to sneer at Mgr. LAMBRECHT, Bishop of GHENT, as "only a peasant's son," and the instances noted above were, with others, contained in an article in reply published by a Catholic paper which gloried, and rightly gloried, in the facts stated. But although it has always been one of the boasts of the Catholic Church that persons of the lowest condition in life might aspire to the highest ecclesiastical dignities, there were yet some exceptions. For admission into many Chapters; and into the semi-military, semi-religious, Orders of Knighthood, such as the ORDER OF ST. JOHN OF JERUSALEM, or the TEUTONIC ORDER, it was essential that the candidate should be of noble birth; not necessarily titled, or of a Peerage family according to the improperly restricted use of the term *noble* which in modern times obtains among English-speaking people only, but *noble* as descended from ancestors who were *nobiles ;* that is, who were entitled to use armorial bearings which distinguished them from the *ignobiles*, or unknown. "Nobiles," said Lord - Chief-Justice COKE, "sunt qui arma antecessorum suorum proferre possunt" (quoted in Sir JAMES LAWRENCE'S *Nobility of the British Gentry*, p. 17, London, 1840). On the Continent many Sees and Abbacies could only be held by persons who were able to prove this nobility of descent for several generations. Thus, no person could formerly be consecrated Archbishop of CÖLN, or TRIER, or Bishop of BASEL, until he had publicly exposed for examination on the front of his future Cathedral the emblazonment of his thirty-two quarterings; that is a shield combining the arms borne by all his ancestors, both male and female, for five generations. The thirty-two quarters of JOHN HUGH ORSBECK, Archbishop and Prince-Elector of TRIER (1676-1711) are given for example in MENÊTRIER'S treatise on *Les Preuves de Noblesse*, p. 97.

Similar requirements, but varying in the number of generations, were made in Germany in most cases in which the Bishop or Abbot became invested in right of his ecclesiastical position with the temporal lordships which formed the endowment of the See or Abbey which he ruled.

The nobles who sat in the Diets of Germany were much too haughty to permit that Bishops and Abbots should sit and vote with them in their assemblies on a footing of equality, still less preside over them, and regulate their action, unless these Prelates were themselves of noble blood. Such requirements as those I have referred to above, originated therefore, not as is sometimes ignorantly asserted, in the pride of the clergy, but in the haughtiness of the lay nobles. It must, however, be confessed that the clergy were often infected by the spirit of the age, and were, unhappily, only too often not unwilling to "better the example" of their lay brethren. Pope NICHOLAS IV. excommunicated the whole Chapter of TRIER for refusing to admit to a prebend a person of ignoble extraction who had been nominated by him to that dignity. So early as 1227, Pope GREGORY IX. was called in to decide a dispute between the Bishop of PORTO who was his Legate in GERMANY, and the Chapter of STRASSBURG, who had refused to admit to a prebend the nominee of the Legate, on the ground that the person proposed was deficient in the requisite degrees of nobility. The papal decision went against the Chapter. (The decree is given in Baron VON LOWHEN'S *Analysis of Nobility*, pp. 170, 171. London 1754.)

In our own country men of all ranks have always been eligible for the highest ecclesiastical positions, and on attaining them have often, down to the present day, assumed armorial bearings for use upon their seals, etc., though frequently the connection of the Prelate with the family whose arms were adopted was, to say the least, extremely difficult of proof. Occasionally permission to use their arms was sought by the Prelate from the head and other members of the family to which he desired to attach himself.

In France, and probably in other countries, it is usual for a Bishop to invent for himself a coat of arms, if he is not entitled by birth to bear one. "Anciennement les prélats non nobles étaient anoblis personellement par leur charge, et pouvaient se choisir des armes. Cet usage s'est conservé, et actuellement tous les prélats, en prenant possession de leurs siéges adoptent un écusson, et une devise quand ils n'en ont pas de naissance." (*La Noblesse en France*, par BARTHÉLEMY, p. 321, Paris 1858.) Thus the present Bishop of LIMOGES bears : *Argent, on a cross sable the monogram of the labarum X P or.* Usually the arms thus assumed have a distinctly religious savour. WALTER REYNOLDS, Bishop of WORCESTER, and afterwards Archbishop of CANTERBURY, assumed : *Azure, on a cross or, between the symbols of the four Evangelists, five lions rampant gules armed and langued azure* (*Catalogue of Seals in British Museum*, No. 1217). Other examples will be found later in Chapter IV.

But though these assumptions were very general, there were exceptions even among high Ecclesiastics. Cardinal FRANÇOIS TOLET of the ORDER OF JESUS, "Prédicateur du Palais Apostolique" under seven successive Popes, never used any arms but the sacred name of JESUS in cypher, *Within an orle of five estoiles, all of gold in an azure field.* SARMIENTO DE MENDOZA, Bishop of JAEN, laid aside his illustrious paternal coat to take a simple Calvary cross, surrounded by a bordure charged with the words, "*Arma militiæ nostræ.*" On the other hand, GEORGE DA COSTA, Archbishop of LISBON and BRAGA, on his elevation to the Cardinalate assumed : *Azure, a wheel of St. Catharine or*, in memory of the Infanta CATHARINA (daughter of EDWARD, and sister of AFFONSO V., Kings of PORTUGAL), to whose favour he owed the commencement of his great fortune. This coat he impaled with his paternal arms : *Gules, six rib bones, in pairs, fessways in pale argent.*

The use of brisures, or marks of cadency, seems never to have been general in the case of Ecclesiastics. Even the illegitimate sons of Royal and Noble Houses often used the full paternal arms without any of the ordinary distinguishing marks of bastardy. It seemed as if admission into Holy Orders entirely obliterated any stain which might have been supposed to attach to their birth. "Si illegitimus sacris fuerit initiatus, non est opus transversam dictam lineam paternis insigniis addere, cum propter sacri ordinis dignitatem legitimus censeatur, imo ante susceptum ordinem numero sit legitimandus, quare quoq : nuptiis exinde inidoneus ac inter steriles numeratur." (SPENER, *Opus Heraldicum*,

p. gen., p. 359.) Thus ALEXANDER STUART, Archbishop of ST. ANDREWS (1509-1513), natural son of
JAMES IV., bore on his seal the full Royal Arms *sans
brisure* supported by the Royal unicorns, and having
the archi-episcopal cross behind the escucheon.

Another Archbishop of ST. ANDREWS, JOHN HAMIL-
TON (1549-1571), natural son of JAMES, Earl of ARRAN,
bore the quartered arms of HAMILTON and ARRAN,
without any brisure. His cross is placed, according to
custom, in pale behind the shield (*Scotichronicon*, ii.,
p. 284). Similarly JAMES, a natural son of JAMES, Lord
HAMILTON (elected to GLASGOW in 1547, and translated
to ARGYLL in 1558) bore on his seal in 1556 the quartered
arms of HAMILTON and ARRAN, *sans brisure*. (LAING,
Scottish Seals, ii., 1101.) JAMES, Earl of MORAY, Prior
of ST. ANDREWS, and Regent of SCOTLAND, natural son
of JAMES V., bears on his seal the full Royal Arms, with
a pastoral staff behind the shield (*ibid.*, ii., p. 156). The
seal of GEORGE DOUGLAS (natural son of ARCHIBALD,
Earl of ANGUS) consecrated Bishop of MORAY, 157¾,
bears his paternal shield, mitred, but without any brisure
(*ibid.*, ii., No. 1044.) So also, ANDREW, Bishop of
ARGYLL, (1613-1636) natural son of THOMAS, Lord
BOYD, bears on his seal in 1629 the full paternal arms
(*ibid.*, ii., No. 1102).

On the other hand PIERRE CHARLOT, Bishop of NOYON,
natural son of King PHILIP AUGUSTUS, bore the Royal
Arms of FRANCE-ANCIENT (*Azure, semé de fleurs-de-lis
d'or*), *debruised by a bend sinister argent.* JEAN, Bishop
of LIÈGE, Chancellor of FLANDERS, natural son of GUI,
Count of FLANDERS, bore on his seal in 1280 the arms
of that County (*Or, a lion rampant sable*) *debruised by a
crozier in bend argent* (Plate I., fig. 2, and see VRÉE, *Généalogie des Comtes de Flandre*, Plate 74). DAVID, Bâtard
de BOURGOGNE, son of PHILIP, Duke of BURGUNDY,
was made Bishop of TEROÜENNE, in 1451, and of

UTRECHT in 1455. He used the paternal arms *sans brisure*, with the coronet of a French Prince. His book-stamp is in GUIGARD, *Armorial du Bibliophile*, tome i., p. 29. Similarly, LOUIS DE NOGARET, Bishop of MIRÈPOIX (d. 1679), and his sister, LOUISE, Abbess of ST. GLOSME DE METZ (d. 1647), illegitimate children of JEAN LOUIS DE NOGARET, Duc D'EPERNON, bore on their book-stamps the full arms of NOGARET, without any mark of bastardy. (GUIGARD, *Armorial du Bibliophile*, ii., 149, 150.) LOUIS DE BASSOMPIERRE, Bishop of SAINTES, (d. 1676), son of Maréchal de BASSOMPIERRE, used no brisure to denote his illegitimacy. REYNAUD, *bâtard de Bourbon*, Archbishop of NARBONNE in 1472, bore: *Argent, a bend of* FRANCE-ANCIENT *thereon a fillet gules*, supported by two angels (the usual Royal Supporters of France) holding palms. (PÈRE ANSELME, i., p. 310.) The angels which support the Royal Arms of France have however azure dalmatics charged with the three golden fleurs-de-lis, and not the alb only. HENRI DE BOURBON, Bishop of METZ (son of HENRI IV. by HENRIETTE DE BALZAC D'ENTRAGUES, bore: FRANCE *a baton péri en barre d'argent*, with the fleur-de-lis coronet of a French Prince. (GUIGARD, *Armorial du Bibliophile*, i., 31.) The arms of CHARLES, Bâtard D'ORLÉANS, Bishop of LAON, and Pair de FRANCE, are given under CAMBRAY. THOMAS STUART, Archdeacon of ST. ANDREWS, 1443, natural son of King ROBERT II., bore the Royal Arms (*Or, a lion rampant within a double tressure flory counter-flory gules*) *debruised by a bend counter-componé argent and azure*. The shield is supported by two dragons sejant, as well as by an angel which stands behind it (LAING, ii., No. 931). I recently noticed a fine boss in the Musée des Antiquités, in the cloister of the Augustins at TOULOUSE which bears the arms: Quarterly, I. and IV.; quarterly, 1 and 4. *Or, three pallets gules* (County of FOIX); 2 and 3. *Or, two cows gules, clarinés azure* (the

County of BÉARN); II. and III. (. . . .) *on a chief*
(. . .) *three lozenges* (. . .). The whole shield
is debruised by a very narrow fillet in bend, which crosses
the I. and IV. grand - quarters. The shield has the
adjuncts of a crozier in pale behind its centre, on the
dexter side of the head of the staff is a mitre ; it appears
doubtful if there was ever anything on the other side
of the head for the sake of symmetry, but if there was
it has now disappeared.

The book-stamp of GABRIEL DE BEAUVEAU DE
RIVARENNES, Bishop of NANTES (1636-1667) shows
that he bore the arms of BEAUVEAU (*Argent, four lions
rampant two and two gules crowned, and armed, or*),
debruised by a baton péri en bande. (GUIGARD, *Armorial
du Bibliophile*, tome i., p. 81.)

Among a clergy bound to celibacy the ordinary marks
of cadency were not imperatively needful ; the external
ornaments which indicated their ecclesiastical dignity
sufficiently distinguished their arms from those borne by
other members of their families. In England since the
Reformation marks of cadency have been used and
omitted indifferently, but the arms of many Bishops
have been differenced by the introduction of small mitres
as charges within the shield. This is, indeed, no modern
custom. JOHN DE GRANDISON, Bishop of EXETER
(1327-1369) bore : *Paly of six argent and azure, on a bend
gules a mitre between two eagles displayed or ;* instead of
the three eagles which appeared on his paternal coat
(Plate II., fig. 4.) WILLIAM COURTENAY, Archbishop of CANTERBURY (1381-1396) bore : *Or, three
torteaux, a label throughout azure, on each of its points a
mitre* (sometimes three mitres) *argent* (Plate II.,
fig. 5).

In one of the windows on the south side of the choir in
YORK-MINSTER are represented the arms of Cardinal
BEAUFORT : the Royal Arms (France and England,

quarterly) *within a bordure componé azure and ermine, each of the azure compons being charged with a mitre argent.* (See *The Heraldry of York-Minster*, by Dean PUREY-CUST, plate x., p. 389, 4to, 1890.) I have not met with any instance of this use of the mitre in other examples of the Cardinal's arms.

Mitres also appear as differencing charges in the arms of Bishops BEKINGTON (BATH and WELLS), ALCOCK (ELY), BURGHILL and HALES (LICHFIELD), DE L'ISLE (DURHAM), PEPLOE (CHESTER), LUMLEY (LINCOLN),. GREY and LYHERT (NORWICH), and CARPENTER (WORCESTER). They also form the charge of the bordures which were used as differences in the arms of Bishops MARSHALL and STAFFORD. (EXETER), HEI-WORTH (LICHFIELD), BLUNDEVILLE and DESPENSER (NORWICH). The *azure bordure* of the DESPENSER arms (*Quarterly, argent, and gules fretty or, over all a bend sable*) *is charged with eight, but sometimes with fifteen, golden mitres* by Bishop DESPENSER. (Plate II., fig. 6.)

The arms of JOHN INNES, Bishop of MORAY, 1407-1410, still remain sculptured in the Cathedral at ELGIN. The coat (*Argent, three estoiles azure*) is differenced by the insertion of the head of a crozier between the estoiles.

The series of seals of the great Benedictine Abbey of MÖLK, or MELK, on the Danube in Lower Austria, which are engraved in HÜBER'S *Austria Illustrata*, afford good illustrations of the practices which prevailed from the thirteenth to the eighteenth century with regard to the disposition of arms upon the seals of Ecclesiastics. The seals of Abbots WALTER (1232), GERUNG (1277), FRIEDRICH (1292), and ULRIC (1312), bear simply their own seated effigies. That of Abbot OTTAKAR (1327) is the earliest which shows a shield of arms ; it is placed in the lower angle of the vesica, beneath the figure of the Abbot, and bears the arms of the Abbey : *Azure, a key with double wards, or rather two keys united in one*

. *handle or bow, argent.* The dedication of the Abbey is to
SS. PETER and PAUL. Probably the coat originally contained two keys with their wards interlaced (*see* examples
under the *Sees of England* in Part II.). The arms do not
appear on the seal of Abbot HEINRICH (1330), but are
engraved on the *secretum* of Abbot LUDWIG (1358). Personal arms are first added on the seal of Abbot GOTTS-
CHALK (1385). This bears the effigy of ST. BENEDICT ;
the arms of the Abbey appear on a shield on the right
hand, while one charged with the attire of a stag is placed
on the left. Abbot LUDWIG II. (1392) and LEONARD
(1432) use the double key as a device, beneath the feet
of the effigy, but not enclosed in a shield. Abbots
JOHN (1414), NICOLAS (1420), CHRISTIAN (1447), and
JOHN II. (1458), use the shield with the Abbey arms.
By Abbots WOLFGANG (1485), and JOHN SCHÖNBERG
(1551) the effigy of ST. BENEDICT is placed between
shields containing their personal arms on the dexter,
and those of the Abbey on the sinister. Abbots
MICHAEL GRIEN (1563) and URBAN (1568) yield the
place of honour, on the dexter side, to the Abbey arms.
Abbot KASPAR HOFFMAN (1590) quarters the arms of
the Abbey in the first and fourth with those of his
family in the second and third, and surmounts the shield
with a mitre. The five succeeding Abbots, whose seals
close the series, REINER LANDAU (1630), VALENTINE
EMBALNER (1639), EDMOND LÜGER (1677), GREGORY
MÜLLER (1680), and BERTHOLD DIETMAIR (1701), all
place the arms of the Abbey in an escucheon upon the
quartered shield of their personal arms, and surmount
the whole with a mitre enfiling a pastoral staff.

In modern times the Abbots of MELK bear in the 1st
and 4th quarters, *Or, an eagle displayed and dimidiated
sable armed gules issuing from the palar line;* in the 2nd
and 3rd are the personal arms ; and over all an escucheon of the arms of the Abbey, *Azure, the double key.*

Besides their constant use on seals, and monumental memorials, either of glass or of stone, armorial bearings are frequently found embroidered on ancient ecclesiastical vestments, and abroad this custom has never died out. Shields of arms thus appear embroidered upon the ends of the *vittæ*, or *fanons*, of the mitres ; on the orphreys of the cope and chasuble ; on the lower parts of the dalmatic and tunicle ; and on the stole, where they appear on each side at the level of the breast. The stole worn by the Pope is of red silk, thus embroidered on each breast with his personal arms with their usual accompaniments, the tiara and keys.

The arms of the donor are often embroidered on the vestments and altar fittings presented to churches. Even the corporals in CORPUS CHRISTI COLLEGE, CAMBRIDGE, were embroidered with armorial bearings (see *Report of the Historical MSS. Commission*, vol. i., p. 72). A chasuble given by ST. LOUIS of France to THOMAS DE BIVILLE, is of silk, embroidered with gold thread, and is composed entirely of lozenge-shaped compartments containing heraldic charges—the *fleur-de-lis* of FRANCE, the *castle* of CASTILE, the *lion* of LEON, and the *eagle displayed* of SAVOY - MAURIENNE (see *De Caumont Abécédaire d'Archæologie Religieuse*, where it is engraved at pp. 448-450).

In the celebrated case of SCROPE *versus* GROSVENOR (*temp.* RICHARD II.), the poet CHAUCER gave evidence of the use of the arms of SCROPE upon vestments, among other things.

On the seal of ANTHONY BEK, Bishop of DURHAM (1283-1310) his effigy is represented wearing a chasuble, on the breast of which appears the large *cross moline* of his arms (*Gules, a cross fer-de-moline ermine*). The Church of Durham inherited from him seven vestments, "cum una cruce de armis ejusdem quæ dicuntur ferrum molendini." Similarly the effigy of LOUIS DE BEAU-

MONT, Bishop of DURHAM (1318), as represented on his seal, wears a chasuble embroidered with his arms: *Azure, fleury and a lion rampant argent* (*Catalogue of Seals in the British Museum*, Nos. 2452 and 2459).

The orphreys of the celebrated Lyon House Cope, now at South Kensington, are heraldic, and contain the arms of ENGLAND, FERRERS, NEWBURGH, CASTILE and LEON, CLIFFORD, DESPENSER, GENEVILLE, GRANDISON, PERCY, MORTIMER, BASSINGBORNE, etc.

A curious reference to armorial bearings was made on the tomb of the Cardinal de PALUD, who was buried in the Abbey of TOURNUS. His arms were: *Gules, a cross ermine.* Accordingly on his tomb the Cardinal is vested as a priest; the stole, maniple, and the cross of the chasuble, are all of ermine; we may fairly conjecture that the colour of the vestment was red (MENESTRIER, *L'Art du Blason justifié*, pp. 81, 82).

On the celebrated PERCY shrine at BEVERLEY one of the sepulchral effigies represents a priest of that family, probably about the fourteenth century. On it the chasuble, alb, and maniple are ornamented with a series of twenty different shields of arms. (*See* Mr LONGSTAFFE'S "Old Heraldry of the Percies," in *Archæologia Æliana*, 1860; pp. 157, 192, etc.)

COLE mentions an altar cloth at ST. EDWARD'S Church at CAMBRIDGE, which had on it a coat of arms: *Or, a chevron nebulé argent and azure, between three choughs proper* (probably for the family of CROMER). We may refer also to the Inventory of the Goods of the Guild of the Blessed Virgin in BOSTON, taken in 1334. "Item, an altar cloth of tawny damaske wᵗ Egles standyng on bookes, wᵗ this l're, 🦅 crowned, of the gift of mʳ JOHN ROBYNSON esquyer, wᵗ the armes of the said mʳ ROBYNSON in the myddes of the altar cloth, wᵗ a frontell of the same therto belonginge havynge the seide armes at every end of the seide frontell." Other gifts of altar furnishing were made by the same person, and were all embroidered with the arms of the donor. (See *English Church Furniture at the Period of the Reformation*, edited by EDW. PEACOCK, F.S.A., *Herald and Genealogist*, iv., 169.) In Italy and Spain I have seen many sets of vestments, both for the officiants and for the altar, on each piece of which the arms of the pious donor are represented. At Wadstena in Sweden a set bears the arms of the great family of STURE (*Or, three nenuphar leaves in bend sable*).

CHAPTER II.

External Heraldic Ornaments, Spiritual and Temporal — The Coronet, its use on the Continent—The Temporal Sword—Helmets and Crests used by Ecclesiastics—Military Fiefs held by Ecclesiastics—The Church Militant—The Ecclesiastical Hat, etc.

WE have now to consider the several ornaments, external to the shield of arms, which have been in use to distinguish the different grades and offices of ecclesiastics.

They are of two kinds : those which indicate spiritual authority, and those which denote temporal rank or jurisdiction. Of the former class are :—the Papal Tiara, and the Keys ; the Pallium ; the Mitre ; the Patriarchal, Archi-episcopal, and Legatine Crosses ; the Crozier, or Pastoral Staff ; the Bourdon ; and the Ecclesiastical Hat. To the latter class belong the Coronet ; the Princely and Electoral Hats ; the Mantlings ; the Helmet and Crest ; the Temporal Sword ; and the Crosses and Badges of Knighthood ; or of Chapteral Rank.

The ensigns of spiritual authority which compose the first class fall naturally for consideration under the respective ecclesiastical ranks which they serve to distinguish ; and it will only be needful to offer in this place a few remarks upon the use by ecclesiastics of those external insignia which are by custom joined to the shield of arms as indications of secular rank or temporal jurisdiction.

Of these the most common is the coronet. This, though only used by ecclesiastics in our own country in the very rare cases in which they happen to be peers of the realm by descent, is in frequent use by foreign ecclesiastics for various reasons. We may remark here, that on the continent the use of coronets as heraldic ornaments is much more general than in these realms, where they are used only by princes and princesses of the Royal House; by peers and peeresses; and (according to modern usage but in violation of strict heraldic propriety) by the eldest sons (and their wives) of peers of the three highest grades. But upon the continent all the children of counts and barons use their father's coronet, and usually one of his titles also ; while in Italy even the remote cadets of great families often use their coronets ; add to their names such words as "dei Conti de . . . ," and have by general courtesy the title of the head of the family.

The following extract will suffice to indicate the modern usage in France. "L'ordonnance du 25 août 1817 établit la hiérarchie des pairs, réglant que les fils ainés prendraient le titre immédiatement inférieur à celui du père, et les fils puînés les autres titres pareillement inférieurs entre eux." (*La Noblesse de France*, p. 75.) Thus the eldest son of the Duc DES CARS, has the title of Marquis DES CARS, but his uncles, the brothers of the Duc, had respectively the titles of Comte, and Vicomte DES CARS. Similarly the eldest son of the Duc DE LEVIS is Marquis DE LEVIS ; his uncles bearing the title of Count, and Vicomte DE LEVIS. (Though the regulation applied only to *pairs de France*, the custom was soon adopted by other nobles who had not that dignity. There is not, however, uniformity of practice.)

Again, on the continent members of ancient noble and knightly families very generally use a coronet to indicate their descent, even though they may not have the right to use the specific title of baron, count, etc.; this is seldom understood by us, where a title is, wrongly, thought essential to nobility. As this is so in civil life,

D

it is consequently general for members of noble families to retain the coronet as an external ornament of their arms after they have been admitted into the ecclesiastical state.

Again, abroad coronets are used by ecclesiastics whether they are of noble families or not, when, as is frequently the case in Germany and elsewhere, temporal lordships are attached as endowments to ecclesiastical dignities held by them.

Again, in Germany and France, the dignity of Count, or Countess, was by Imperial or Royal grant, used by members of many noble-chapters in right of their canonries. And lastly the dignity of "Comte-Romaine" is still occasionally conferred by the Pope on ecclesiastics of eminence.

Examples of the use of coronets, both as indicative of noble descent, and as denoting the possession of temporal rank and jurisdiction acquired along with the ecclesiastical dignity, will be given in abundance as we proceed. Temporal jurisdiction, the *jus gladii*, is very frequently indicated by a naked sword, placed in saltire with the pastoral staff of the ecclesiastical dignity, behind the coroneted shield. (*See* Plates V., XV., XVI.) Sometimes the crosier and sword, instead of being in saltire behind the shield, are placed paleways on either side of it. (*See* Plate XIII., fig. 4.)

Not unfrequently one finds a person whose knowledge of Foreign Armory is probably derived from a French elementary book on Heraldry, and who will dogmatically insist that ecclesiastics have no right at all to use helmets and crests, though he seldom is consistent enough to suggest their return to the use of the "Popish" ecclesiastical hat. To such it is sufficient to say that a wider knowledge of Foreign Heraldry would have had the inevitable effect of modifying his statement as to "right," though he might retain, if he desired, his views as to propriety. But, after all, it is custom that determines the matter. In many countries the helmet and crest are not used by ecclesiastics in general, but our own country and Germany form exceptions to the rule. The great German herald SPENER, who discusses the propriety of the use of the helm by ecclesiastics, approves, but says that in any case, with or against propriety, practice has settled the matter so far as Germany is concerned. In Germany the use of helmets and crests by ecclesiastics has always been general as a result of that frequent union of temporal rank with spiritual dignity to which I have already made allusion. Abbots, abbesses, bishops, and archbishops were very frequently also secular princes, counts, or barons, holding the lands of their Sees or Abbeys immediately from the Crown; and bound consequently to furnish their feudal contingent of troops to their Royal or Imperial Superior, so that the use of military insignia to denote this fact was retained by clerics. (On the military fiefs held by ecclesiastics in Germany and on their forms of investiture, see the curious treatise of SCHILTER, *de Feudo Nobili*, 1696. Extracts therefrom are given in BURGERMEISTER, *Bibliotheca Equestris*, ii., 990 - 1015, Ulm, 1720. *See* also PRAUN, *von des Adels Heerschilden, etc.*)

Again, the temporal power and possessions belonging to the Spiritual Princes :—the Elector-Archbishops of MAINZ, CÖLN, and TRIER ; and to the numerous Prince-Bishops, and Abbots of the Empire,—were so great that these dignities were eagerly sought, and continually filled by churchmen who were already by inheritance in possession of military fiefs; while the custom of placing above the escucheon a crested helm for each fief which conferred on its possessor the right to a vote in the Circles of the Empire, naturally contributed to the retention of these military insignia by ecclesiastics. It must also be remembered that in Germany the crested helm is not looked upon, as among us, as a subordinate accessory to shields of arms, but is considered as being of at least equal importance with them.

In our own country helmets and crests are generally used by ecclesiastics below Episcopal rank, but the custom, which has not the same excuse as in Germany, has often, and not unreasonably, been denounced as a violation of strict heraldic propriety. Helmets and crests were intended for use in war and martial exercises, and there is consequently some incongruity in their employment either by ecclesiastics, or by ladies.

Instances may indeed be found in which the heralds of the gospel of peace have been led to take a very active part in offensive warfare, from the times of the Crusading Prelates, to our own day when, in the American War of Secession, Bishop LEONIDAS POLK led to battle the forces of the Confederate States. Even before the Crusades military ecclesiastics were found in the armies of the Frankish kings. GREGORY OF TOURS (lib. iv., cap. xliii., says) — "Fuerunt in hoc prælio Salonius et Sagittarius, fratres atque episcopi, qui non cruce cœlesti muniti, sed galea aut lorica sæculari armati, multos manibus propriis, quod pejus est, interfecisse referuntur." CHARLEMAGNE, in conjunction with the Church, endeavoured to reform these abuses (see *les Capitulaires*, lib. vi. et vii.). An old French Historian, GUIL. DE BRETON, mentions PHILIP DE DREUX, Bishop of BEAUVAIS, who at the battle of BOUVINES, in 1244, unhorsed, and beat out the brains of several of the enemy with a mace, so as not to break the letter of the law which forbade the use of the sword by ecclesiastics (*v. i.*, p. 95). JEAN DE MONTAIGU, Archbishop of SENS, was slain in battle in 1416. Another well-known story is that of the Pope who sent to demand the release of one of these martial prelates—styling him his beloved son. The King is said to have returned the coat of mail worn by the Bishop, with the text—"Know now, whether this be-thy son's coat or no!" (Gen. xxxvii., 32). (*See* VON LOWHEN'S *Analysis of Nobility*, p. 164.) So in Italy GUIDO TARLATTI, Bishop of AREZZO, was so eminent a warrior that his tomb erected in 1330 is richly sculptured with sixteen bas-reliefs of his battles and sieges. At the battle of BOUVINES. the Abbot of S. MÉDARD at SOISSONS himself led to battle a hundred and fifty of his vassals. In England, HENRY LE DESPENSER, the warlike Bishop of NORWICH (1370-1406), used on his *secretum* the shield of his personal arms, timbred with a mitre from which rises the crest, a dragon's head between a pair of wings. In the *Armorial de Gelre*, the arms and crest are given, but a helmet is interposed between the shield and the mitre. (*See* Plate V., figs. 1 and 3.) The seal of Bishop RICHARD COURTENAY, also of NORWICH (1413-15), bears a *couché* shield timbred with a crested helm. (*Catalogue of Seals in the British Museum*, No. 2050.) The use by the Bishops of DURHAM of crested and plumed helmets on their palatinate seals will be referred to hereafter.

Although an ecclesiastic may if he choose use helmet and crest, yet it is not necessary that he should do so. On the continent many ecclesiastics have contented themselves with bearing the arms of their family in a simple oval escucheon or cartouche. In most countries the use of the helmet and crest has been supplanted by the adoption for all grades of ecclesiastics of a flat, broad-brimmed, low-crowned hat, varying for each rank in its colour, and in the number of the *houppes*, or tassels, with which the ends of its cords or strings are adorned. The use of the ecclesiastical hat does not seem ever to have been general in this country to any great extent, or in Germany. Accordingly, when it is met with in this country on a book-cover, an engraving, or some work of art, it is (in accordance with the prevalent ignorance of foreign heraldic matters) nearly always taken to be indicative of the rank of cardinal, and is not unfrequently so described with an amount of positiveness corresponding to that of the assertor's ignorance.

CHAPTER III.

ECCLESIASTICS BELOW ABBATIAL RANK.—Arms in a Cartouche—*The Biretta*, and the Ecclesiastical Hat—Chanters' Batons — Protonotaries — Canons and *Chanoinesses*—Noble Chapters—Their Insignia—The use of the Amess, or Aumusse, at Home and Abroad—Mitred Canons and Dignitaries—Lay Honorary Canons—Priors and Prioresses—The *Bourdon*—The Pastoral Staff—Mitred Priors—Provosts and Deans — Official Arms of Cathedral Dignitaries — Clerical Members, and Officers of Military Orders of Knighthood, and Chaplains of the Order of St. John—Canons of St. George's Chapel, Windsor, etc.

IT has been noted above that many ecclesiastics abroad are content to use their family arms in a *cartouche*, or oval shield, without any external ornaments to indicate their ecclesiastical status. Thus LOUIS CLOQUET, "*chanoine diacre*" of the Church of REIMS at the commencement of the eighteenth century used for his book-stamp an oval cartouche, encircled by a branch of olive, and another of palm, and bearing the *armes parlantes : Azure, a chevron between three bells, in chief a crescent* (? for difference) *all argent.* (*Armorial du Bibliophile,* i., 161.) The library of JEAN DES CORDES, Canon of LIMOGES, who died in 1643, was acquired by Cardinal MAZARIN, and the books bear the arms of the Canon (*Azure, two lions rampant addorsed or*) in an oval escucheon without any mark of ecclesiastical dignity. NICOLAS DOINET, Canon of REIMS in 1722, bore: *Gules, on a fess or, three canettes sable,* in an oval escucheon encircled by palm branches. (GUIGARD, tome i., 184-185.)

The book-stamp used by JEAN DE SAINTE ANDRÉ,

Canon of NOTRE DAME at Paris, at the close of the sixteenth century, bears his arms (*Azure, a castle triple-towered argent, masoned sable, in chief three estoiles of five points or*) on an escucheon surmounted by a full-faced helmet with grilles, above which is placed a *biretta,* or four-cornered ecclesiastical cap. (Plate III., fig. 2.) There are several other examples of the use of the biretta, but I know no other where it is used thus to surmount a helmet. One where it surmounts a coronet is given later on at p. 48. PIERRE LE JEUNE, Canon, bore: *Gules, a chevron between in chief a sun in splendour, and in base a rose issuing from a heart, all or,* the shield timbred with a biretta. (GUIGARD, *Armorial du Bibliophile,* ii., 51.) FRANÇOIS ROBERT SECOUSSE, Doctor in Theology, Curé of ST. EUSTACHE in Paris, about 1750, used the *biretta* alone above the escucheon of his arms (*Azure, a chevron between two pierced mullets, and a garb; in chief a crescent, all or.* (The crescent was here not a mark of cadency but a regular charge—his brother, DENIS FRANÇOIS, who died in 1754, used the same arms.) MELCHIOR B. M. COCHET DU MAGNY (d. 1791), Canon of the Royal Chapel (la Sainte Chapelle) at DIJON, used the biretta alone, above the shield of his arms (*Argent, a cock gules.* (GUIGARD, i., 161.)

Much more general was the use of the ecclesiastical hat. The common priest's hat is flat, broad-brimmed, of a black colour, and had originally on either side a cord, or string, terminating in a single tassel. In later times, when ecclesiastics generally seem to have claimed and used something more than they were legally entitled to, the single tassel was replaced by a double one. This hat was represented above the shield, or oval *cartouche* containing the arms.

Members of a Regular Order often impaled its armorial bearings, or its device, with their personal arms, giving the place of honour on the dexter side of the shield to the bearings so assumed. Thus, the book-

1. Henri Baradeau, Canon of Paris.   2. Jean de St. André, Canon of Paris.

3. Boissel, Canon-Count of Lyon.

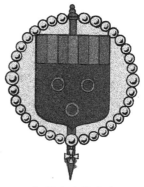

4. Colbert (Abbé).   5. Boisot (Prior).

plate of Frère JACQUES'RENAUD, of the Order of Friars-Preachers, at LYONS, bear the arms of the DOMINICAN ORDER (*v. post*, p. 143) impaling his personal coat : *Or, a fess gules between an eagle rising in chief and a horse courant in base proper.*

Protonotaries and Chanters were frequently, perhaps ordinarily, chosen from among the Canons. The Chanters, or Precentors, denoted their office by placing behind the shield of arms the baton with which they led the choral music, and which they are often represented as holding on early seals. The seal of HENRI, Chantre de TROYES in 1227, shows his standing effigy, holding in one hand a baton the head of which is a *fleur-de-lis,* and in the other a song book. (DEMAY, *Le Costume du Moyen Age après les Sceaux*, p. 293.) On the seal of GUILLAUME, Chanter of EVREUX in 1236, his effigy is similarly represented, but the baton is not floriated. On that of GAUTIER, Chanter of LE MANS, the figure holds a baton only. The counter-seal of the last bears a *cross potent fitché* (DEMAY, *Les Sceaux de la Normandie*, Nos. 2416, 2418).

MENESTRIER records (*l'Usage des Armoiries*, tome i., pp. 249-250) an example existing in his time in the Cathedral of NOTRE DAME at Paris, where on the tapestry representing the chief events in the traditional life of the Blessed Virgin there were also to be seen the arms of the probable donor, MICHEL LE MASLE DES ROCHES, Chanter, and Canon of NOTRE DAME at Paris, viz. : *Argent, a chevron between three rocks sable.* A baton surmounted by a fleur-de-lis is placed behind the escucheon. (*See* Plate IV., fig. 2.)

In the Chapel of the Chateau de VINCENNES is the tomb of RENÉ DE LAULNAY, Canon and Chanter, on which the baton is similarly placed in pale behind the shield.

On the book-stamp of the Abbé DORSANNE (Doctor in Theology, Canon, Chanter, and *Grande Vicaire* of

NOTRE DAME at Paris in 1715) his arms: *Argent, a chevron gules, on a chief azure three mascles or* (Correct GUIGARD'S *Blason*, i., 186) are in an oval escucheon, surmounted by a coronet. The chanter's staff is in pale behind the shield, and its head appears between a small mitre, and the head of a pastoral staff, head outwards. On a cope at BEAUVAIS the arms of a chanter are embroidered; in this case two batons are placed in saltire behind the escucheon. (MENÊTRIER, *les Ornemens des Armoiries*, p. 144.)

Protonotaries used the black flat hat, but this was differenced from that of the ordinary priest by the silken cordons on either side which were made to end in a series of three tassels, one above two.

In the choir of the Church of S. JACQUES at Antwerp I have noticed the monument of JACOB CHANNON, Protonotary, who died in 1714. His shield of arms (. . .) *a fess wavy* (. . .) *between three goat's heads erased* (. . .), *those in chief respecting each other, that in base affronté*) is surmounted by such a hat as that just described. So are the arms of the Protonotary DE BERNAGE: *Barry of six or and gules, on each piece of the last five saltires couped argent* (Plate IV., fig. 1, and see *l'Armorial Universel*, planche 73, Paris, 1679); and those of the Protonotary PIANELLI: *Per fess gules and sable, a fess raguly or* (MENÊTRIER, *Méthode du Blason*, p. 208, Lyons, 1718).

CHARLES DE GRASSALIO in 1545 says that the protonotaries' hats were turned up with green :—"Protonotarius Tymbrum addit ex pileo nigro, duplicata viridi colore." I have never myself remarked an example of this use, but the black hat had sometimes violet tassels appended to it. At REGENSBURG there is an example of the year 1462, above the shield of Doctor THOMAS PIRCKHAIMER, Protonotary, and Apostolic Referendary. At ROME it appears that the seven Apostolic

PLATE IV.

PROTONOTARY ᴀɴᴅ CHANTER.

1. De Bernage, Protonotary

Protonotaries use a red cord and tassels (*see* MONTAULT, *L'Année Liturgique à Rome*, p. 300). The number of *houppes*, or tassels, is now usually three, but there was formerly considerable variety in the matter. I observed in the Cathedral at VERONA the tomb of the Protonotary ANDREAS SBADACHIA, on which each cordon of the black hat is terminated by six *houppes*, arranged 1. 2. 3. A similar arrangement appears on the seal of CHRISTOPHER HILINGER, Protonotary, appended to a deed dated 1651. I noticed, in the Church of S. JACQUES at Antwerp, the monument of EMMANUEL VAN HORENBEECK, Canon and Protonotary, who died in 1719. His escucheon, which bears : *Azure, three bars argent, on a chief . . . three hunting horns, . . .* is timbred with a hat, the cordons of which end on either side in six houppes, 1. 2. 3. In the same church I observed a more modern example on the monument of J. M. DE MOOR, who died in 1841. His arms, which were : *Or, a chevron gules between three Moor's heads proper,* are surmounted by a helmet and lambrequins, while above the whole is the Protonotary's black hat with only three *houppes* on either side. In the Church of S. MARIE at Bruges I noted the following example. The monument of the Protonotary WARNER DOMINIC DE MONGET, who died in 1725, bears his arms : *Vair, a fess or; over all an escucheon azure, three storks argent.* The hat has six *houppes* on either side.

The pretentious book-plate of M. DUBUT, Curé de VIROFLAY, Protonotaire Apostolique, Commandeur de l'Ordre de Christ, in 1782, is engraved in *French Book-Plates* (by W. HAMILTON, 1892, London), and bears on an oval cartouche his *armes parlantes* (I suspect a mere assumption)—*Argent, on a mound in base two butts or targets (?) proper. On a chief gules a cross argent*—for the Order of Christ. The escucheon is surrounded, first by a motto band with the words CRUX CHRISTI GLORIA

MEA, and then by the red ribbon of the Order with its pendant cross. The escucheon, which is surmounted by a count's coronet, is placed upon an eight-pointed cross with balls at the end (which Mr Hamilton calls the "*Cross of S. Louis*," but I think is only intended as the Commander's Star), a staff is placed behind the shield, and a small mitre and the head of a key appear on either side of the coronet. The whole is surmounted by a protonotary's black hat, of which the six *houppes* on either side are tinctured green. (We pass by the other non-heraldic adjuncts of clouds and sunbeams, and the *quasi* supporters "Faith" and "Charity.")

That of PHILIPPE ALEXIS DE BAILLY, who is described as Noble graduate, Protonotary, and Canon of the "ci-devant Cathédrale de S. DONATIEN à Bruges," and who died in 1810, has the shield charged with his arms : *Azure, three crescents or*, and timbred with a hat resembling the preceding. It may be noted that the thirty-two quarters of this canon are arranged on the monument in four columns of eight escucheons, two rows on either side of the main shield.

The book-stamp of JEAN GENEST, Apostolic Protonotary and Archdeacon of NEVERS, in 1614, bears a shield of his arms : *Sable, a chief argent*, surmounted by a mitre, and the head (turned inwards) of a pastoral staff; all beneath a hat each of the cordons of which terminates in three tassels, 1. 2. (GUIGARD, *Armorial du Bibliophile*, tome i., p. 235.)

With regard to Canons and Canonesses, we have already observed that on the continent very many of the chapters were entirely closed against those persons who were unable to furnish the requisite proofs of gentle blood. Aspirants to admission were only received after their genealogical proofs of noble descent had been submitted to the most rigorous scrutiny. These *preuves de noblesse* varied at different times and in different places, and lists of these noble chapters and their genealogical requirements will be found in Part II. of this book. In several of these chapters the possession of a stall conveyed the right to the rank and title of Count, or Baron. In France, for example, the Canons of the Chapters of S. JEAN at Lyons; S. JULIEN at Brioude; and S. PIERRE at Macon; were all Counts by Royal Grant in right of their Stalls; as were the Canonesses of ALIX, BAUME-LES-DAMES; POULANGY; and S. MARTIN DE SALLES, en BEAUJOLAIS. At EVREUX the Canons had the title of Baron; in Germany the members of several noble Chapters had similar privileges. All these placed the coronet of their rank above their shields of arms, and the shields were surrounded by a *cordon* or ribbon of silk to which was attached a badge, or eight-pointed cross of enamel, somewhat resembling the Cross of the ORDER OF S. JOHN, but with variations in the colour of the ribbons, and the details of the badge. (*V.* Plate III., fig. 3.) Similar crosses and ribbons were worn, both at religious services, and in civil life, by the members of other chapters besides those whose names are given above, and fuller descriptions are given later in Part III. of this work. They are still worn by the Canons of several Continental Cathedrals and Collegiate Chapters, as at S. DENIS, TOULOUSE, LUCERNE, etc., etc.

The Canons of S. VICTOR also placed their shields upon the cross or badge, so that the arms of the latter projected on all sides, after the fashion originally adopted by the members of the ORDER OF ST. JOHN OF JERUSALEM, or MALTA (Plate XIII., fig. 2). The Dean and Canons, Counts of LYONS, also used supporters to their arms; these were the same for all, viz., on the dexter side a griffin argent, on the sinister a lion or.

On Plate III., fig. 3, I have engraved the arms and supporters of TOUSSAINT-JOSEPH PIERRE de BOISSEL, Abbé de BOIS-BOISSEL, Canon and Count of LYON, 1779, which are :—*Ermine on a chief gules a fess of mascles conjoined or.* The shield is timbred with the coronet of a Count, and supported by a griffin argent on the dexter side, and by a lion or, on the sinister. The shield is further ornamented with the ribbon, from which is pendant the badge of a Canon-Count as appointed by the King, Louis XV., in 1745.

The Canons of the Chapter of S. DENIS, near Paris, place in the shield above their paternal coat a chief charged with the arms of the Chapter (*v. ante*, p. 17). Similarly the Canons of S. VICTOR added to their arms a chief of the arms of the Abbey : *Azure, an escarbuncle or.* The Canons of the Church of S. DONAS, or S. DONATIEN, at Bruges, placed *en cimier* above the shield of their arms, a badge representing a chandelier, or *corona*, bearing eight lighted tapers, which was the conventional emblem of the Saint to whose honour the church was dedicated. (*See* Plate V., fig. 4.)

At TRENT the arms of the Canons are placed upon their fur amesses, which are extended like mantlings around their escucheons. In the Cathedral more than forty tombs dating from about the middle of the sixteenth century are adorned with the arms of Canons thus represented. I have observed several instances of the same usage on monumental slabs in the nave of the Cathedral of SANTA MARIA at Verona. The figures 7 and 8 on Plate V., engraved from my rough sketches taken on the spot, will sufficiently explain this curious disposition.

The amess, otherwise called *aumusse*, or *almuce*, was a kind of tippet and hood, of silk or stuff lined with costly grey fur, and was worn by Canons during the choir offices in the winter months of the year. The amess of the minor canons, vicars, or chaplains, was lined with *calabre*, a brown fur of a less expensive kind. The academic hood which has become a quasi-ecclesiastical vestment in the Church of England originated in the use of the

Gloria Deo

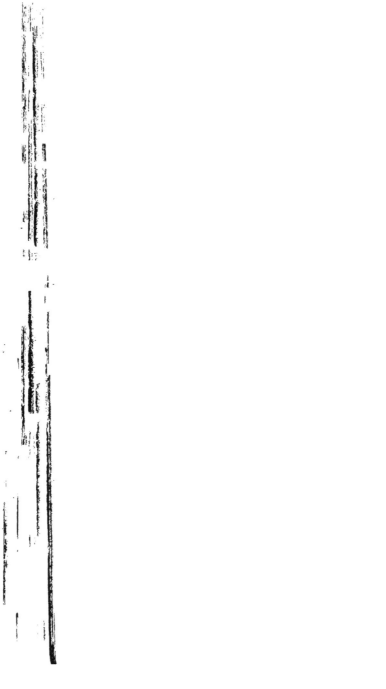

amess. The material of that worn in England by canons was of black cloth, but that of a doctor in any·faculty was everywhere of scarlet. At EXETER the amess was of black stuff, doubled and lined with red or green sarcenet. At STRASSBURG it appears to have been of red velvet lined with *ermine;* at BESANÇON of blue silk lined with red taffeta. (*Cathedralia*, p. 90.) In the Cathedrals of Southern Italy and Sicily there was' considerable variety in the colour and material ·of the amesses worn by the canons. Mr MACKENZIE WALCOT tell us (*Sacred Archæology*, pp. 14, 15) that it was of "violet at MONTE REGALE, CEFALU, MAZZANA, and MESSINA ; and black with violet edges and ends at OTRANTO and PALERMO. [This was, however, used by the *minor* canons.—J.W.] At LANGADOC (*sic*) "the canon's amess was purple in honour of martyrs, with a hood (*pænula*) of lamb's fur. At SETABIS it was of ermine ; at SYRACUSE, black or violet, according to the season ; at NETI, of black silk ; at VIENNE, in summer of green material; and at OTRANTO, violet, with crimson edges." ·At the present day it is seldom worn, at least I have hardly ever so seen it, but in Italy it is habitually carried over the left arm, with the fur outside, as a mark of their dignity by Canons, and minor-canons, on their way to and from the choir. Dr ROCK, however, says that though this is the general custom yet "in some churches it is still worn sewed to the canon's cope like a hood, and spread all about the shoulders." And in the appended note he adds :—" Such is the practice at ST. PETER'S, ST. MARY MAJOR'S, and ST. JOHN LATERAN'S at Rome. But in some of the smaller collegiate churches of the Holy City, the canons carry upon the left arm their almucia, which is neither ermine, like that of the upper canons, nor grey, as is the one given to the minor-canons of the great basilicas, but of brown skins." (*Church of Our Fathers*, vol. ii., pp. 88, 89. A great deal of interesting information as to the use of the "amice grey" will be found in Dr ROCK's learned work, vol. ii., pp. 52-60. *See* also *Cathedràlia*, by MACKENZIE WALCOT, pp. 89, 90.) The amess was also used armorially in rather a different manner from that depicted in Plate V., figs. 7 and 8, and described above as in use at Verona. The book-plate of PIERRE SÉGUIER, Comte de GIEN, and eventually Chancelier de France, has his arms: *Argent, seiné of fleurs-de-lis, on a mount in base a Paschal-Lamb regardant proper;* timbred by the coronet of a Marquis, surmounted by a biretta. A folded amess of fur is stretched above the coronet, and behind the biretta, and depends on either side of the shield. (See *French Book-Plates*, p. 123.) Two instances are given in GUIGARD, *Armorial du Bibliophile;* one of the arms of HENRI FRANÇOIS DE BARADEAU, Canon of NOTRE DAME at Paris, about the year 1722. Here the arms: *Azure, a fess between three roses or*, are surmounted by a biretta, and by an amess which seems to be placed behind the cap, and hangs unequally on either side (Plate III., fig. 1). A similar example, but with the inequality less marked, is that of GIRARD, Chanoine de SAINT SYMPHORIEN, which is not dated but is apparently of the seventeenth century. The arms are: *Argent, a stag's head caboshed sable.* (*See* tome i., pp. 71, 236.)

The Canons of several important Cathedrals have, by Papal Grant, the right to use the mitre (*mitra simplex* only, *vide post*, p. 67), and some other episcopal insignia, upon certain occasions. I have seen it thus used at MILAN, PAVIA, PISA, NAPLES, etc. At BAMBERG (where the privilege dates from 1053, having been granted by Pope LEO IX., *Acta Sanctorum*, Junii, t. iii., p. 871), BRAGA, BESANÇON, BRIOUDE, LISBON, LUCCA, MESSINA, PUY, RODEZ, SALERNO, etc., all the Canons are thus mitred. But in other Cathedral Chapters only the "dignitaries," or a limited number of the Canons have the right to the use of the mitre; this is the case at COLOGNE, COMPOSTELLA, MACON, MAGDEBURG, MAINZ, SEVILLE,, TOLEDO, TRIER, and VIENNE. At REGENSBURG (RATISBON), GHENT, LAVANTZ, and ST. DIÉ in the Vosges (granted by LEO IX. *ante* 1054) only the Provost; at SALZBURG the Provost and Dean, have this privilege. In all such cases we may be sure that the mitre was not omitted as an external ornament to the arms of those thus privileged. (We may mention here that some of the Canons of COLOGNE, MAGDEBURG, MAINZ, and TREVES, had the right to use the full robes of a Cardinal at Divine Service ; at MILAN, LISBON and PISA all the Canons had this privilege. (*See* ROCK, *Church of Our Fathers*, vol. ii., p. 112.)

The privileges of the Canons of ST. STEPHEN'S Cathedral at VIENNA are worthy of note. They precede in dignity all mitred Provosts and Prelates, but are inferior in rank to Suffragan Bishops. All the Dignitaries have the right to use the mitre. This privilege has belonged to the Provost since the foundation of the Chapter ; it was accorded to the Dean, Custos, and Cantor, by Pope CLEMENT XII.; and the Scholasticus received the same right from Pope BENEDICT XIV.

At MAINZ in 1580 WOLFGANG D'ALBERG, Provost (afterwards Archbishop); GEORGE SCHONENBERG, Dean, and HENRY STOCKHEIM, Chanter, each timbred his shield of arms with two helms, the dexter being surmounted by a mitre ; the sinister by the personal crest. Sometimes the helmet beneath the mitre is omitted. PHILIP VON SCHWALBACH, Chanter of MAINZ (who bore the arms : *Sable, three annulets in bend argent*), timbred his shield with a single helm bearing his crest, two buffalo horns with scalp and ears.

In the great Chapters of Germany, such as MAINZ, WÜRZBURG, and BAMBERG, during the vacancy of the See, the coins, medals, and seals bore the shields of arms

E

(often helmed and crested), of *all* the Dignitaries and Canons, arranged in a circle around a central escucheon of the arms of the Chapter, or the device of the patron Saint of the Church (*see* ZEPERNIK, *Die Capitels, und Sedis vacans, Münzen der Reichsstifter*, etc., Halle, 1822). In 1719, a medal of the Chapter of PADERBORN, *sede vacante*, bears on the obverse the figure of CHARLE- MAGNE, its reputed founder, and on the reverse that of a bishop in pontificals, holding a church. Each of these effigies is surrounded by a series of twelve shields of arms, one for each of the twenty-four Canons (KÖHLER, *Münz-Belustigung*, xi., p. 339). Similarly, in 1724, the Chapter of HILDESHEIM, *sede vacante*, struck a medal with the effigies of the Emperors CHARLEMAGNE, and LOUIS (der Fromme). On its obverse are seventeen, and on the reverse sixteen, shields of the arms of the Canons, each surmounted by their coronet. (*See* KÖHLER, *Münz-Belustigung*, xi., p. 409.)

Sovereign Princes and Nobles of high rank had sometimes the rank of Honorary Canons. Thus the Emperor was a Honorary Canon of ST. PETER'S and ST. JOHN LATERAN at Rome, and of the Chapters of CÖLN, SPEIER, REGENSBERG, BAMBERG, STRASSBURG, AACHEN, UTRECHT, LÜTTICH, etc. The King of France was Canon of ST. JOHN LATERAN at Rome ; and the stall has since been assigned to the head of the State for the time being, to the Emperor NAPOLEON III., and the Presidents of the Republic, MM. MACMAHON, THIERS, etc. The King of Spain is Honorary Canon of the Basilican Chapter of STA. MARIA MAGGIORE at Rome, as well as at TOLEDO, LEON, and (as Señor de VISCAYA) at BURGOS. The King of England was Honorary Canon of the Basilica of SAN PAOLO FUORI LE MURE ; and even in our own country the Sovereign has the rank of first Cursal Canon in the Chapter of ST. DAVID'S. The Dukes of BURGUNDY

had a stall at LYONS; the Dukes of BRABANT at
UTRECHT; the Marquis of ASTORGA at LEON; the
Counts of ANJOU at TOURS; and the Counts and
Seigneurs of CHASTELUS at AUTUN and AUXERRE. The
stall at AUXERRE was acquired in 1423 by CLAUDE DE
BEAUVOIR, Seigneur de CHASTELUS, Vicomte D'AVALON,
etc., Maréchal de France, in a rather interesting way.
During five weeks he defended against the English the
town of CREVANT, which belonged to the Chapter of
AUXERRE, and in recognition of its preservation the
Chapter accorded to him, and to his successors in the
Seigneurie, the dignity of *Chanoine-honoraire*, with the
right to occupy a stall during the offices, vested in a surplice. His arms: *Azure, a bend between seven billets or*,
(*en bannière*) remained in the crypt of the Cathedral at
AUXERRE when MENESTRIER wrote in 1673. (*L'Usage
des Armoiries*, pp. 73-74.)

PRIORS AND PRIORESSES.

It was customary for Priors to place a *bourdon* (*i.e.*, a
knobbed staff) of silver, in pale behind the shield of arms.
The black ecclesiastical hat, with three *houppes* on either
side, sometimes surmounts the shield, which is often placed
between two palms or branches of laurel, or olive. The
Prior de SENNETERRE of S. SAUVEUR in Velay, in 1540,
thus bore his arms: *Azure, five fusils in fess argent.* In
MAGNENEY'S *Recueil des Armes* (Paris, 1633) are several
examples. Thus, on plate 32, are the arms of M. BOUTON
DE CHAMILLY, Prieur et Seigneur de DANZY, who bore:
Gules, a fess or; and of M. DE PUGET, Prieur de la
Plastrière de Lyon, who carried: *Or, three pallets gules,
on a chief argent an eagle displayed sable.* In both
instances a *bourdon* is placed behind the shield, which is
accosted by two branches of olive in the former case,
by two palms in the latter. There are no hats in these

examples. JEAN BAPTISTE BOISOT, Prieur de la Loye de Lachaux, etc., who died in 1694, used his arms (*Sable, three annulets argent, on a chief Or three pallets azure*) with a prior's bourdon in pale behind the escucheon, and a rosary, with its pendant cross, encircling it. (Plate III., fig. 5 ; and *see* GUIGARD, *Arm. du Bibliophile*, tome i., p. 101.)

At S. ANDREWS, Priors ALEXANDER STUART and JOHN HEPBURN placed the pastoral staff, instead of the bourdon, in pale behind the shield. The remarkable seal of EUPHEMIA LESLIE (Countess of ROSS, Prioress of ELCHO) shows a crosier, or pastoral staff, behind the escucheon (LAING, *Scottish Seals*, vol. ii., p. 200). But abroad prioresses often used only the *bourdon*, like priors and surrounded the shield, or lozenge of their arms, with branches of olive or palm, or with a rosary, at their discretion. The Abbé SCARRON as Prior placed the *bourdon* behind his shield, which bore : *Azure, a bend bretessé or.*

Occasionally the Prior had the right, by special Papal grant, to use the mitre at the sacred offices. Thus among the MSS. of the Dean and Chapter of ELY is a letter of Pope MARTIN V. (1417-1431) to the Prior and Convent, in which permission is granted to the Prior and his successors to use the "mitre, ring, staff, amice, gremial, gloves, and other pontifical insignia, not only in the Church of ELY, but in whatever place they may give the solemn benediction after Mass, except in the presence of the Legate of the Holy See." It appears that Pope JOHN XXII. had previously conferred the same privileges on Prior WILLIAM POWCHER, but that after the deposition of the pontiff in 1415, an application was made to Rome for a new licence, or an authoritative confirmation of the old one. (*Historical MSS. Commission*, Twelfth Report, Appendix ix., p. 395.) LEO IX. granted to the Provost of the Collegiate Church of

S. Dié in the Vosges, the use of the mitre and other pontifical ornaments as early as 1050.

· Pope CLEMENT VI. granted to the Prior of WORCES-TER in 1351 the right to use the mitre ; this privilege was confirmed in 1363 by URBAN V. It was stipulated that even in the Bishop's presence the Prior might wear the *mitra simplex* or even *mitra aurifrigiata* (*v.i.* p. 67) ; but the *mitra pretiosa* (jewelled) only in his absence. (The grant is given in WILKINS' *Concilia*, t. iii., 201, and is also printed in ROCK'S *Church of our Fathers*, vol. ii., pp. 115-117.) In 1386 the Prior of WINCHESTER wore the *mitra simplex* in the presence of the Bishop, and the jewelled mitre in his absence. In all these cases the mitre would also be assumed as one of the external adornments of a shield of arms.

On the book-plate of HECTOR POMER, last Prior of ST. LAWRENCE at Nürnberg, which was designed by ALBERT DÜRER, and engraved in 1591, the arms of the Priory : *Argent, a grate, or gridiron* (on which S. Lawrence was martyred), are quartered with the personal arms of the Prior : *Per bend, in chief bendy of four gules and argent, in base sable plain* (*see* the plate engraved in Mr EGERTON CASTLE'S excellent work on *English Book-Plates*, p. 32, 1892). The shield is helmed and crested, and there is no mark of ecclesiastical dignity, but ST. LAWRENCE with palm and grill stands in the background—a *quasi*-supporter.

BARTHOLOMÆUS CATANEUS, Provost of HERZOGEN-BURG (a house of the Regular Augustinian Canons, dedicated to ST. GEORGE), bore on his seal in 1552 two shields—one of the arms of his house : *Argent, a cross patée gules ;* the other charged with his personal arms. The whole was surmounted by the effigy of S. GEORGE slaying the dragon. In 1561 his seal bears the coats quartered in one shield, but still surmounted by the figure of S. GEORGE, as above.

JOHN SCHACK, Provost of S. CROSS at Augsburg, used two shields *accolés* — one of the arms of his church: *Azure, a cross patée-throughout or;* the other of his personal arms: *Gules, three roses argent;* a mitre was placed above the conjoined shields, and a pastoral staff in bend-sinister behind them (MENÊTRIER, *Pratique des Armoiries,* p. 21). On the seal of MATTHEW WERTWEN, Provost of the Cathedral of. ST. STEPHEN at Vienna, the arms are surmounted by a mitre enfiling a pastoral staff (HUEBER, *Austria Illustrata ex Archivis Mellicensibus,* plate xxxv.). The seal of CHRISTOPHER POTINGER, Dean of the same church in 1538, has simply the personal arms with a crested helm (*ibid.,* plate xxxiv.).

FRANÇOIS RAPINE, Prior of S. PIERRE LE MOUSTIERS, in Nivernais, aumônier to Queen MARIE DE MEDICIS, bore a rather singular arrangement of his arms, thus: *Per pale: the dexter coupé* (a) *Argent, a chevron* (*engrailed?*) *between three escallops gules;* (b) *Barry of four azure and argent, over all three hearts gules crowned with open crowns or* (so that the hearts are on the argent bars, the crowns on the azure). The sinister half of the escucheon is occupied by the arms of his Priory: . . . *a key in pale with its double wards in chief.* (GUIGARD, *Arm. du Bibliophile,* tome ii., p. 176.)

The arms of M. CHARRON D'ORMEILLES, Dean of S. GERMAIN L'AUXERROIS, at Paris (*Azure, a chevron between two mullets in chief and a wheel in base or*), are represented in MAGNENEY'S *Recueil des Armes,* planche xxviii., with a pastoral staff in pale behind the shield, which is surmounted by a (black) hat with six *houppes* on either side (*see* Plate VI., fig. 2). SEGOING gives, in the *Armorial Universel,* planche 75, the arms of Dean DE LA HAYE: *Quarterly,* 1 and 4. *Azure, a fleur-de-lis or;* 2 and 3. *Azure, an unicorn's head couped, in base a crescent argent.*

1. Charron d'Ormeilles, Déan of S. Germain l'Auxerrois.

2. Chateaubriand, Abbé de Trisay.

CHARLES DE BECEREL, de la Bastie en Bresse, Doyen et Comte de Lyon, in 1650 only used his personal arms : *Argent, on a bend gules three cinquefoils of the first,* timbred with his countly coronet, and without any other indication of his dignity (GUIGARD, *Arm. du Bibliophile,* tome i., p. 82). The shield is accosted by palm branches, and a pastoral staff is placed in pale behind it, but there is no hat.

At EXETER the Dean, Precentor, Chancellor, and Treasurer had official arms which they might impale with their personal ones. These were as follows :—

The Dean : *Azure, a stag's head caboshed, between the horns a cross patée fitchée argent.*

The Precentor : *Argent, on a saltire azure a fleur-de-lis or.*

The Chancellor : *Gules, a saltire argent between four crosslets or.*

The Treasurer : *Gules, a saltire engrailed between four leopard's heads or.*

At BRISTOL Cathedral is a coat, unrecorded in the armorials and hitherto unidentified : *Azure, a saltire argent, in chief a portcullis or,* this may be, as I suspect, the official coat of a dignitary. (*See* my *Heraldry of Bristol Cathedral,* in the *Herald and Genealogist,* vol. iv., p. 289.)

The arms of English Deaneries are printed in Part II. of this book.

The Dean of WINDSOR, as Register of the Most Noble ORDER OF THE GARTER ; and the Dean of WESTMINSTER as Dean of the ORDER OF THE BATH ; append to their shields of arms the ribbons and badges worn by them as the ensigns of their respective offices in those Orders. In Scotland the Dean of the Chapel Royal, as Dean of the ORDER OF THE THISTLE, had the right to do the same. In Ireland, before the disestablishment of the Irish Church, the Dean of S. PATRICK'S Cathedral in Dublin was Registrar of the ORDER OF S. PATRICK, and was entitled to use similarly the ribbon and badge of his office.

The Clerical Members, or Chaplains, of the great ORDER OF S. JOHN OF JERUSALEM, equally with the Knights of Justice, added to their paternal arms a chief of the arms of the Order (*Gules, a cross argent*), and placed the whole escucheon upon the Cross of the Order with, or without, its surrounding chaplet and cross. Thus, LOUIS DE FOURBIN DE LA MARTHE, Abbé-Commendataire d'Ardenne, bears on his seal in 1672, the following arms :—*Or, a chevron azure between three leopard's heads sable ; a chief of Religion, Gules, a cross argent.* The whole escucheon is surrounded by a chaplet; and is placed upon the eight-pointed cross of the Order. (DEMAY, *Sceaux de la Normandie*, No. 2733.) Similarly, RÉNÉ FRANÇOIS DE FROULLAY DE TESSÉ, Abbé-Commendataire d'Aunay in 1725, "Chevalier non profés de l'Ordre de S. Jean," bore his arms (*Argent, a saltire gules, bordured engrailed sable*) arranged in the same manner (DEMAY, *Sceaux de la Normandie*, No. 2741).

. Even the female religious of the ORDER OF S. JOHN used the "chief of the religion" and placed their arms on the Cross of the Order. *See* the arms of Saint UBARDESQUE DES UBARDINI (*Argent, the attire of a stag gules*) engraved in GOUSSANCOURT, *Martyrologe des Chevaliers de Saint Jean de Hierusalem*, folio, Paris, 1643, tome ii., p. 230. Those of Saint ROSELINE DE VILLENEUVE (*ibid.*, tome ii., p. 246), and GALIOTE DE GOURDON DE GENOUILLAC (*ibid.*, tome i., p. 317), are other examples of the same custom ; and the idea that only the Knights and Grand Crosses of the Order had the privilege of placing their shield of arms upon the eight-pointed cross, or badge, is thus clearly shown to be quite without foundation.

The clerical members and officials of any Order of

Knighthood are entitled to use its ribbon and badge as an external ornament of their shield of arms. If they belong to the lower classes of the Order, and so are only entitled to wear the ribbon and badge at the button-hole, or on the left breast—then the cross is suspended by its ribbon from the base of the shield. But if they have higher rank which entitles them to wear the ribbon and badge *en sautoir*—that is by a ribbon passing round the neck and supporting the badge at the neck or middle of the breast—then they have also the right to surround the escucheon with the ribbon of the Order supporting its pendant badge, and (according to circumstances) to place their escucheon upon the Cross of the Order.

Before the disestablishment of the Irish Church, the Dean of S. Patrick's Cathedral in Dublin held the office of Registrar of the Order of S. PATRICK, and used its ribbon and badge both as a personal and as a heraldic decoration. (*See* also under ARMAGH and DUBLIN.)

One of the Colonial Bishops (at the present time Archbishop MACHRAY of RUPERT'S LAND) holds the office of Prelate of the Colonial Order of S. MICHAEL and S. GEORGE, and wears its insignia. He also surrounds his arms with the ribbon and pendant badge.

The Canons of S. GEORGE'S Chapel, Windsor, wore in grand ceremonies of the ORDER OF THE GARTER mantles of murrey taffeta having on the right shoulder an escucheon of the arms of the Order (*Argent, a cross gules*) in a roundle embroidered with gold and silk, but they had no other badge at any time.

CHAPTER IV.

ABBOTS AND ABBESSES.--The Crosier, or Pastoral Staff—
Its History—The Celtic Staff—The *Bachul More*, and S.
FILLAN'S *Quigrich* — The Crutch, or Tau-headed Staff —
Mediæval Crosiers—The Mitre—Its History—Anglo-Saxon
Mitres—Different kinds of Mitres—Their Colour—*Abbés-com-
mendataires—Custodinos—Abbés Réguliers*—The *Sudarium*—
The Abbatial Hat — Ensigns of Temporal Jurisdiction —
Ecclesiastical Princes and Princesses—The *Cordelière*.

IN ancient times the only external ornament by which
the dignity of Abbot, or Abbess, was heraldically denoted,
was the crosier, or pastoral staff with a crook-head, which
was placed in pale behind the shield of arms.

Even in later times some abbots were content to use
the crosier only as a mark of their office, thus JEAN DE
MONTENAY, "Supérieur général des Chanoines Réguliers
de la Congrégation de France," and Abbé de S. Geneviève
in 1691, bore : *Azure, three fleurs-de-lis or,* in a cartouche,
behind which is a crosier in pale (GUIGARD, *Armorial du
Bibliophile,* ii., 124). JEAN DE LA ROCHEFOUCAULD, Abbé
de MARMOUTIERS (d. 1583), used his shield (*Burelé argent
and azure over all three chevrons gules, the first écimé*) with
a simple crosier behind the shield, the whole surrounded
by a wreath of two palm branches. (*Ibid.,* ii., 32.)

Those who are interested in the ecclesiastical origin
and use of the crosier will find abundant information in
the 2nd vol. of SMITH'S *Christian Antiquities ;* in
MARTIGNY, *Dictionnaire des Antiquités Chrétiennes ;* and
especially in a Monograph on *Le Baton pastoral* by
l'Abbé BARRAULT, and ARTHUR MARTIN, Paris, 1856,
which is declared by the writer in SMITH'S *Dictionary* to

be the most elaborate treatise on the subject. The limits of the present work preclude more than a few brief notes. The pastoral staff, or crosier, was employed as early as the fourth century as a sign of the episcopal dignity; a century or so later it appears to be used by abbots. PUGIN seems to think that the use by abbots is coeval with that by bishops.

In the life of ST. CÆSARIUS, Bishop of ARLES, written by one of his own clergy in 502; we find that on some public occasions his staff was carried by a cleric. "Cum vir Dei . . . ad aliam ecclesiam pergeret clericus cui cura erat baculum illius portare, quod notariorum officium erat, oblitus est, in quo ministerio ego serviebam, etc. (Quoted from his life in the *Acta Sanctorum*, August, tom. vi., p. 79, by Dr ROCK, *Church of our Fathers*, vol. ii., p. 182.) We learn also from S. ISIDORE of Seville, that a staff was delivered to a newly consecrated bishop as a sign of authority; and the *Pontifical* of EGBERT of York, as well as an Anglo-Saxon Pontifical preserved at Rouen, give an identical exhortation,—" *Cum datur baculus hæc oratio dicitur*: Accipe baculum pastoralis officii, et sis in corrigendis vitiis sæviens," etc. (*See* MARTENE, *De Antiq. Eccl. Rit.*, tom. ii., lib. i., cap. viii.; and ROCK, *loc. cit.*).

The right to use the staff as a symbol of office does not appear to have been conceded to abbesses until a much later period. In comparatively modern times its heraldic use *per abusum* has passed to ecclesiastics of lower rank as will be shown later. No doubt the pastoral staff was originally only the walking staff of the venerable bearer, which supported his steps in his peregrinations, and on the crutch head of which his body rested somewhat in the long offices of religion. But it soon became the symbol of spiritual authority.

The earliest type of the Episcopal crosier represented

in the catacombs is a much shorter staff than that which
is familiar to us as an ecclesiastical instrument in the
present day. The original *baculus pastoralis* probably
had only a boss or a simple bend at its top like an ordinary
walking stick. This form of a simple bend, having sometimes at a later period a slight pendant in a direction
nearly parallel to the main staff, was retained for the
staves of the old Celtic Bishops and Abbots long after
the more appropriate (as directly symbolical) form of the
shepherd's crook had come into general use in other
countries. The *Bachul More*, the old crosier of S. MOL-
UAG of LISMORE, is now at INVERARY in the possession
of the Duke of ARGYLL. It is a simple curved staff
about three feet in length with a simple bend at the top.
It was formerly ornamented with metal. A still more
notable crozier, the Coygerach, or Quigrich of S. FILLAN,
is now preserved in the Museum of the Society of Antiquaries, in EDINBURGH, having been carried to Canada
by the representatives of its ancient hereditary bearers,
who held their lands by its tenure. A full and very
interesting account of its history is given in the *Proceedings of the* (Scottish) *Society of Antiquaries*, 1st series,
vol. xii., from the pen of its secretary the late learned
and accurate antiquary JOHN STUART, LL.D., whose
writings on archæological subjects have been a quarry
out of which later writers have very liberally dug
materials for their own books and lectures, often with
very slight (if any) acknowledgement of their obligations. The head of the Quigrich was originally of
bronze inlaid with *niello*, and out of reverence was afterwards enclosed by S. FILLAN'S successors in a silver gilt
case of beautiful and elaborate design. It is described
at length, and with the help of all the illustrations of
Dr STUART'S paper, in Dr J. ANDERSON'S *Scotland in
Early Christian Times*, p. 216, *et. seq.*, but without the
very smallest acknowledgement of any indebtedness

1. de Lorraine

2. d'Espinay

3. de Souvré

4. d'Albert

5. de Vassé

6. de la Porte

to his predecessor's *Historical Notices of S. Fillan's Crozier.*

In the Eastern Churches the pastoral staff of the Bishops, Abbots, etc., terminates not in a crook, but in a crutch, or tau, usually of the precious metals, but occasionally of ivory, and of elaborate workmanship and expensive adornment. In the lengthy Ecclesiastical offices of the Eastern Church the sitting posture is very rarely permitted, and the original crutch would be a sensible support to its user when weary. In the West the Tau was the badge of the Order of S. ANTHONY (*v.* p. 75, and Plate V., fig. 10), and accordingly was used by the Abbots of that Order. But its use was not confined to them. In the tomb of MORAND, Abbot of S. GERMAIN DES PRÉS in 990, there was found a pastoral staff, six feet long, topped with a Tau of perforated ivory joined to the hazel shaft by a copper ferrule. (LABARTE, *Handbook of the Arts of the Middle Ages*, p. 382. A Tau-headed crosier is also represented on the sculptured slabs at Ipswich described and figured in Mr J. ROMILLY ALLEN'S *Early Christian Symbolism*, p. 319, and fig. 116.)

Dr ROCK in *The Church of our Fathers* gives much information about the early pastoral staves in use in Britain. They were at first of wood, cypress, ebony, cedar, elder, or pear, with heads or crooks of ivory, horn, or metal. Later they came to be constructed entirely of ivory (this necessitated the introduction of rings or bands), or of silver gilt, while the heads were resplendent with gold, gems, and costly enamels. This was the same in other countries and gave rise to the sneering rhymes of the old French jester :

> Au temps passé, du siècle d'or,
> Crosse de bois, évêque d'or.
> Maintenant, changeant les lois,
> Crosse d'or, évêque de bois.

Some finely carved crosier heads of ivory and others

of enamel are preserved in the South Kensington Museum, the Musée de Cluny, the Musée du Louvre, etc.

The crosiers which appear on early seals are drawn on too small a scale to afford us much information as to details but they at least preserve for us their general form. The most ancient one engraved in DEMAY (*Le Costume d'après les Sceaux*), is that of RICHARD, Archbishop of SENS, in 1067, which is a very short curved staff with a full volute. In the next century the staff is lengthened, and the volute springs from a knob, as on the seal of ACHARD, Bishop of AVRANCHES, 1161 to 1170. (Plate VIII., fig. 2.) Thereafter the staff is increased to the full height of a man; the volute becomes more elaborate and ends in a flower, or a serpent's head, and by degrees foliations, or crocketings, are added to its outline; then a figure, or a group of figures, is introduced in the volute; and finally the knob is developed into a series of pinnacles, and architectural niches, enclosing figures of saints and angels, culminating in such magnificent crosiers as that of WILLIAM of WYKEHAM, Bishop of WINCHESTER, which is preserved in NEW COLLEGE, OXFORD. It should be said that the crosiers on mediæval seals are almost invariably treated in the simplest way. Mr ST. JOHN HOPE tells us that it is only on the seal of ADAM DE ORLETON of HEREFORD, 1317, that we first meet with a richly wrought crook.

A fine early crosier of bone, with a triple volute ending in a dragon's head but having no boss, is to be seen in the Royal Museum of Northern Antiquities in COPEN-HAGEN, and it is figured (as well as the ivory head of a later one with a boss) in WORSAAE, *Nordiske Oldsager*, Nos. 542-543. The same work contains an engraving of what is called "En Abbeds Stav" of the early part of the sixteenth century; a disc of perforated metal consisting of a cross inscribed in a circle, and having in the angles the Evangelistic symbols (No. 617). The crosier of the Archbishop of LUND, of which the volute encloses a Paschal-Lamb, is No. 616 of the same collection. It is said by some that as early as the seventh century the use of the mitre and other Episcopal insignia had been conceded as a matter of favour to certain Abbots, but, as will appear later, this is extremely unlikely. When the custom arose of adding the insignia of ecclesiastical authority as external ornaments to the armorial escucheon, the mitre was naturally placed above the shield by those Abbots who had the privilege of wearing it. In more modern times instances are not wanting where it was used heraldically by those who had not the smallest right to it ecclesiastically, and examples will be found further on in this volume.

Those who are interested in the early use of the mitre as an ecclesiastical vestment are referred, as in the case of the pastoral staff, to the able article on the subject in SMITH'S *Dictionary of Christian Antiquities*, which is largely drawn from HEFELE'S Essay:—*Inful, Mitra und Tiara*, in his *Beiträge sur kirchen geschichte, Archäologie, und Liturgik ;* and other authoritative sources. It will be difficult for those who read it to dissent from the conclusion of the writer (which is against HEFELE'S argument) that " no case at all has been made out for a *general* use of an official head-dress of Christian ministers during the first eight or nine centuries after Christ. . . . The remains of Christian art, which can really be considered trustworthy, furnish no evidence whatever for the use of such a head-dress, but distinctly point the other way ; . . . we may still fairly say with MENARD — 'vix ante annum post Christum natum millesimum mitræ usum in ecclesia fuisse' (*Greg. Sacr.*, 557)."

I may add that there is no allusion to them in the ancient Sacramentaries, Liturgies, or Rituals. Pope

INNOCENT III. says that CONSTANTINE at the moment of quitting Rome for Constantinople desired to give his royal coronet to S. SYLVESTER, but the latter took for covering a round mitre with embroidery of gold (or as PLATINA says, a white mitre), but this had no distinctly official, or ecclesiastical, character. "Even a writer so late as IVO of CHARTRES (d. 1115) while describing the Jewish *mitra*, makes no mention of its Christian equivalent. There are grounds, however, for believing that the mitre was an ornament specially connected with the Roman Church, from whence its use spread gradually over Western Christendom, though its use had evidently not become universal in IVO'S time" (*Dict. of Christian Antiquities*, ii., p. 1216). PANUIN, who died in the pontificate of PIUS V., says — "Mitrarum usum in Romana ecclesia non ante sexcentos annos esse opinor." But after the year 1000 the references to their use become frequent. S. BERNARD tells us that Pope INNOCENT III. received S. MALACHI at Rome, taking off his own mitre to place it on the head of his saintly visitor.

I may here borrow from the Article in the *Dict. of Christian Antiquities* one or two of the instances used to illustrate the connection of the mitre with the Roman See. Archbishop EBERHARD of TREVES received from the hands of S. LEO in S. PETER'S at Rome on Passion Sunday 1049 the "Roman mitre." The POPE'S words in the charter are "*Romana mitra* caput vestrum insignivimus, qua et vos et successores vestri in ecclesiasticis officiis *Romano more* semper utamini." In a similar grant to ADALBERT, Bishop of HAMBURG, it is said of the mitre "quod est insigne Romanorum." PETER DAMIAN (*c.* 1070) writes an indignant letter to the Anti-Pope HONORIUS II. (CADALOUS, Bishop of PARMA) and says "habes nunc forsitan mitram, habes juxta morem Romani pontificis rubram cappam." In 1119

CALIXTUS II. grants the use of the mitre to GODEBALD, Bishop of UTRECHT. (*Dict. Christian Antiquities*, ii., 1216.) With regard to the Roman Court, BARONIUS under the year 1137 says :—" Mos erat non nisi mitratos romanos pontifices ad audientiam admittere petentes audiri." It is curious to find the privilege of using the mitre occasionally conferred upon laymen. ALEXANDER II. sent one to VRATISLAV, Duke of BOHEMIA, in token of esteem ; and INNOCENT II., did the same to ROGER, Count of SICILY.

But the shape of the mitre in those early days differed most materially from that of mediæval and modern times. Dr ROCK in his learned work on the *Church of Our Fathers*, vol. ii., speaks of a kind of handkerchief of linen, tied with fillets and having an enclosing circlet of gold, as being worn by Anglo-Saxon Bishops, but his plate of twelfth century Ecclesiastics derived from an Anglo-Norman manuscript (COTTON MS., Nero, c. iv.) in the British Museum, corresponds pretty closely with the descriptions we have of the *mitra Romana* which had been generally adopted by the Episcopate before that time. It was a round bonnet, usually white in colour, which was bound round the head by an embroidered band, fastened at first (as in the MS. referred to) at the sides, but afterwards these became the *vittæ* or *infulæ* which had a fringe of gold and sometimes little golden bells, and which still depend without any apparent use at the back of the modern mitre.

At the commencement of the twelfth century the round bonnet has begun to rise into a low lobe or horn above each ear. (We see the beginning of the fashion in the MS. already referred to.) These lobes rise higher until the effect produced is that of a low mitre of nearly the present shape, set on the head not with the points worn as at present, but with a point over each ear. It is thus that we find the mitre represented on the earliest

F

Episcopal seals known to us, as on those of PIERRE
LOMBARD, Bishop of PARIS in 1159; of GUILLAUME,
and ACHARD, Bishops of AVRANCHES, 1161, etc.; of
GUILLAUME, Archbishop of SENS, 1169; or in those of
ARNOULD, Bishop of LISIEUX in 1170, and of ROTROU,
Archbishop of ROUEN in 1175 (*see* our Plate VIII.,
where these are figured from DEMAY); in all of these
the fillets fall, one over each shoulder. On the seal
of Archbishop RICHARD of CANTERBURY (1174-1184)
the mitre, a fairly high one, has the horns or points
above the ears. (*See* also the seals of ALEXANDER and
ROBERT Bishops of LINCOLN, 1123 and 1148, *Catalogue
of Seals in British Museum*, Nos. 1655, 1688, 1699, etc.)

Towards the close of the twelfth century the mitre
undergoes a change of form. In the *Dictionnaire du
Mobilier Français*, tome ii., of M. VIOLLET LE DUC,
is a diagram showing how simple was its construction,
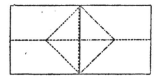 and I reproduce it. A piece of
damask, or other material, twice
as long as its breadth, was
creased down the middle, and
across it. Other creases were
then made from the shorter central crease to the middle
of the longer crease on either side, the edges were joined
with or without being bevelled off, and there roughly was
the mitre, to which were added a band of embroidery
(another vertical piece of the same pattern which concealed the seams); and then the "historical survival,"
the fringed *vittæ* at the back.

In England the first seal which gives us evidence of
the new fashion of wearing the mitre by which, as at
present, the points thereof are to the front and to the
back, appears to be that of HUGH PUDSEY, Bishop of
DURHAM in 1153, but it was not until the close of the
century that the new fashion became general here, and
on the continent, as will be seen by our plate, the horned

1. Guillaume, Abp. of Sens, 1169.

2. Achard, Bp. of Avranches, 1161-1170.

3. Guillaume, Bp. of Avranches.

4. Pierre Lombard, Bp. of Paris, 1159.

5. From Seal of the Abbey of S. Amand, 12th Cent.

6. Guillaume, Abp. of Bourges, 1201.

7. Jean, Bp. of Langres, 1296.

8. Arnoul, Bp. of Lisieux, 1170.

9. Rotrou, Abp. of Rouen, 1175.

10. Henri, Abp. of Rheims, 1233.

11. From Seal of Paris Officiality, 1250.

12. Guillaume, Abp. of Sens, 1262.

mitre continued in use up to a later date, though until the commencement of the thirteenth century there was no uniformity of practice. The seal of HUGH, Bishop of AUXERRE shows us that he had adopted the new fashion as early as 1144; and that of the Abbey of S. AMAND also affords evidence of its use in the later portion of the twelfth century. In the thirteenth the custom of wearing the mitre as at present was firmly established (*see* Plate VIII., composed from the sketches in DEMAY).

The material of the mitre had originally been simple white linen, orphreyed with embroidery; then it was made of silk damask, or cloth of gold or silver; finally it was adorned as at present with plates of the precious metals, and set with pearls and uncut precious stones.

In the Western Church there are now in use three kinds of mitres—the *mitra simplex, mitra aurifrigiata,* and *mitra pretiosa.* The *mitra simplex* is made of plain white linen, or white silk damask, with red fillets. The *orphreyed mitre, mitra aurifrigiata,* is composed of silk damask, or cloth of silver or gold, orphreyed or embroidered but without plates of metal, or any jewels except seed pearls. The *precious mitre, mitra pretiosa,* is adorned with jewels (properly uncut) and the precious metals. In the Museum at Stockholm I recently observed a *mitra pretiosa* of the fourteenth century from Linköping Cathedral, adorned with circular plates of silver gilt enamelled with half-length figures of Saints; of these both the circular and palar bands are composed. The mitre has two shields of arms; one of KETTIL KARLSSON (VASA), who was Bishop in 1400: (*Or, the* vase *sable*); and the other of the See. The upper edges of the mitre have also pipings of gilt metal. As a general rule, which however has exceptions, the *mitra pretiosa* should be worn by none who are not of at least episcopal rank. Pope CLEMENT IV. in 1267 permitted the use of the *mitra aurifrigiata* by exempt abbots, that is by the abbots whose monasteries were by papal rescript exempted from the canonical jurisdiction of the Bishop in whose diocese they were situated ; and he allowed the *mitra simplex* to all others who were present in council and synod ; elsewhere the exempt abbot used whatever might be granted to him by the Papal See. So on the memorial brasses of Abbot DELAMERE of ST. ALBANS, and of Abbot ESTENEY in Westminster Abbey the mitre represented is the *mitra pretiosa*, to which they probably had a right by papal grant. But in synod, and in the presence of the diocesan Bishop, abbots were ordinarily only allowed the use of the *mitra simplex*. To the present day this mitre alone is ordinarily worn in the presence of the Pope ; and is, for Cardinals, of white silk damask ; that of Bishops is of plain white linen ; both have red orphreys.

As to the colour of the ancient mitres Dr ROCK asserts that "excepting when made from hard gold, beaten into thin plates, or of cloth of gold, its colour was invariably white." His note adds, " All the old known mitres still in existence have a white ground." He instances the mitre of S. THOMAS of CANTERBURY preserved at Bruges, and that of WILLIAM of WYKEHAM of which there are remains at New College, Oxford. The LIMERICK mitre was of thin plates of solid silver studded with many precious stones. Dr ROCK tells that the *Ordo Romanus* drawn up by Pope GREGORY X. in 1271 prescribes the white colour for the mitre, and directs the kind to be worn at the various times. This his extract certainly does so far as the Pope is concerned, but any one who is familiar with the works of the early Italian painters (for instance those in the Brera at Milan, or in the Uffizi Gallery at Florence) must have a pretty clear recollection of many fine pictures in which the episcopal mitre is coloured (usually crimson, or red), and the writer must confess that he is not altogether con-vinced by Dr ROCK'S argument, presently to be quoted,

that these contemporary pictures of ecclesiastics, and
of ecclesiastical ceremonies, are inaccurate ; or that a red
mitre was never worn in ancient times but ·is a mere
modern pictorial invention. Dr ROCK says, " I am aware
that examples, though few and far between, of red mitres,
can be pointed out. In a sixteenth century stained glass
window at S. JACQUES, Liège, and upon a late tomb in
Maidstone Church, Kent, a crimson tinted· mitre edged
with gold appears. Let not, however, the young student
in ecclesiastical antiquities· be led astray upon this or
another question, touching the colour of vestments, by
such weak authority." His objections are, in brief, that
the window is " *cinque cento* " or " *renaissance*," and not to
be trusted, he says, because works of that epoch were
done, not by men who were ecclesiastics, but by artists·
uncontrolled by the clergy, men who cared not for the
rules and symbolism of ritual, but aimed solely at artistic
effect. How far Dr ROCK'S examples may be fairly open
to this criticism I cannot say ; but I am sure it does not
apply to the works of art to which I have made reference,
which belonged to an earlier age, and which, being in
many cases painted for the decoration of churches, can
hardly be suspected of the inaccurate or. careless treat-
ment of important details. In the Ecclesiastical Section
of the Mediæval Collection of the National Museum in
Stockholm, I have recently seen a mitre of the fourteenth century from the Cathedral of Vesterås. It
has no central band but is ·of two colours, light blue
and red, divided quarterly by a central, and by a horizontal dancetty line. The whole is embroidered with
seed pearls representing the Tree of Life supporting at
the top a pelican in piety, between in base two unicorns,
turned towards the tree. The fanons also are *goboné* of
the two colours and embroidered with seed pearls. But
so far as concerns late mediæval and modern usage, no
doubt the learned Doctor is accurate in his statements.

In England the arms of Abbots were frequently differenced from those of Bishops by a slight modification of the position of the mitre and pastoral staff. The Episcopal mitre was made to look straight to the front, while that of an Abbot was placed a little in profile. Again, the pastoral staff of a Bishop was represented with the crook turned away from the mitre, while that of an Abbot had the crook turned inwards to denote that his jurisdiction extended only to his monastery and its dependencies. Probably in this custom we find the origin of the old erroneous idea, not yet quite extinct, that the Abbot or Abbess *carried* the pastoral staff in a different manner from the Bishop. Dr ROCK (in *The Church of our Fathers*, vol. ii., pp. 207-210) adduces a quantity of incontestible evidence in disproof of this mistaken idea. There is, however, no doubt that the custom heraldically was as stated above (*vide infra*, under BISHOPS, pp. 79, 80, 92).

This was also the case originally in France. MENÊTRIER says :—" Les Abbés portent la crosse et la mitre comme les Evêques, mais leur mitre doit être tournée de pourfil, et la crosse devroit estre tournée en dedans, n'ayant jurisdiction spirituelle que dans leurs Cloistres. On n'y regarde pas de si prés, et il est peu qui ne mettent l'une et l'autre comme les Evêques."

The same writer in his *Art du Blason justifié*, p. 220, says (in 1661) " Les Abbes portent une crosse, les Abbez mitrez y ajoutent la mitre mais un peu tournée ;" but in 1718, *La Nouvelle Méthode du Blason*, published under his name, declares " aujour d'hui par abus tous les Abbez-commendataires qui n'ont nulle jurisdiction portent l'une et l'autre."

An *Abbé-Commendataire* was one who had a Royal grant out of the revenues of an abbey which he was supposed to administer, but who was neither resident in it nor even a member of the monastic fraternity. In fact the office was usually granted as a court favour to courtiers or poets whom it was desired to reward without expense to the royal revenues. The actual administration of the abbey was confided to ecclesiastics who were called *custodinos ;* and in the eighteenth century the *abbés-commendataires* no longer assumed any monastic dress, " un petit collet et une robe noire indiquaient seul qu'ils appartenaient à l'ordre ecclésiastique."

Hence arose the custom of giving the honorary title of *abbé* to all French ecclesiastics, who were flattered by the delicate suggestion it conveyed that their merits must have procured them a benefice. The abuse by which the king took possession of the monasteries which became vacant, and held them *en commende*, until he chose to nominate a titular abbot, was of ancient standing, going back as far as the ninth or tenth centuries. The title of abbot was then given to powerful persons who received the revenues of a monastery and exercised its seigneural rights, but left its spiritual administration in the hands of a monk who had the title of dean, or prior. Thus HENRI II., Duc de GUISE (1614-1664), was made by LOUIS XIII. *Abbé-Commendataire* of S. DENIS, and S. RÉMY ; and accordingly placed the crozier in pale behind the coroneted shield of his quartered arms. It sometimes bore only :—Quarterly of eight, in two horizontal rows each of four quarters, in chief, 1. HUNGARY, 2. NAPLES, 3. JERUSALEM, 4. ARRAGON ; — in base, 5. ANJOU, 6. GUELDERS, 7. JULIERS, 8. BAR. Over all LORRAINE. The whole escucheon was differenced by a label gules. But sometimes these quartered arms occupied the first and fourth grand-quarters ; the second and third grand-quarters being ; Quarterly, 1 and 4. CLEVES impaling MARK ; 2 and 3. BURGUNDY-MODERN. (Both examples are given from his books in GUIGARD, *Armorial du Bibliophile*, ii., 80.) The arms of CHRISTOPHE PAGOT, Seigneur de LAULNOY, Abbé-Commendataire of the

Abbeys of SAINT JACQUES de Provins, and of VALSAINTE, are :· *Argent, a chevron azure between three eagle's heads sable.* The shield is timbred with the coronet of a Marquis, to the dexter of which is a small mitre, and to the sinister the head of a crozier turned inwards. The supporters are two eagles. These lay-abbots were known as *abbés comtes (abba-comites)*, in opposition to the *abbés réguliers.* HUGH THE GREAT, father of HUGH CAPET, is often designed by early writers *Hugues l'Abbé* because he had the administration of the rich abbacies of SAINT DENIS, SAINT MARTIN de Tours, SAINT GERMAIN des Prés, and SAINT RICQUIER. It was doubtless in memory of these ancestral functions that in later times the kings of France had the title and prerogatives of Abbé de SAINT MARTIN. (*See* CHERUEL, *Dictionnaire Historique des Institutions, Mœurs, et Coutumes de la France*, tome i., p. 5. Paris, 1855.)

In the *Méthode du Blason* are two examples, one of the arms of the Abbé de CAMPS (*Azure, a lion rampant or, holding a shield argent*, this has the mitre on the dexter half of the escucheon full-faced and above the sinister half the head of the pastoral staff, turned outwards. The other shows the arms of the Abbé BOCHU "un Abbé régulier" (who bore *Azure, a chevron Or between two crescents in chief argent and a lion rampant of the second in base*). This has the mitre a little in profile and the pastoral staff with its head turned inwards.

So also the arms of GUILLAUME DE LA FAY ("Abbé, et chef général de l'Ordre de S. Ruf") (*Gules, three trefoils or*) are surmounted by the mitre and pastoral staff both turned inwards, to denote "un Abbé régulier." In this case the staff has attached to it the *sudarium*, a small scarf or veil, attached just below the crook. This was considered by some a distinction between the staves of a Bishop and Abbot. MENÊTRIER says :—

"Les Abbez d'Allemagne attachent à leurs crosses une petite écharpe ; ce qu'on ne pratique pas ailleurs. Néanmoins Tamburin en fait la marque de distinction entre les Evêques et les Abbéz. Baculus pastoralis quem gestare debet Abbas, orario aut sudario ornetur quia abbatialis est, et per longitudinem rectam cubitorum trium et unciarum duodecim protrahatur." (*De Jure Abbat.*, i., disp. 22, quæst. 2.) Dr ROCK (*Church of our Fathers*, vol. ii., pp. 210, 212) tells us that the only formal sanction given for such an ordinance came from S. CARLO BORROMEO, and that, whatever may have been the practice in Italy, it was not observed in England ; "neither the Roman Pontifical, nor the *Ceremoniale Episcoporum*, nor any decree of the Congregation of Rites, says one word upon the subject." The *sudarium* was used by bishops and abbots, simply for the sake of cleanliness, and to keep the burnished staff from being tarnished by the clamminess of the hand. The *sudarium* is attached to the staff on the tomb of Bishop BRANSCOMBE in Exeter Cathedral ; and Dr ROCK'S position may easily be fortified by reference to many mediæval seals. Mr MACKENZIE WALCOT is therefore incorrect in assuming that the *sudarium* was not employed by exempt Abbots (*Sacred Archæology*, p. 4).

LE PLAINE in *L'Art Héraldique* says : "Les Abbez portent une Mitre posée en profil, et une crosse tournée en dedans vers la Mitre, sans Chapeau ; et accolent leur écu ordinairement de deux Palmes, ce qui est néanmoins arbitraire, plusieurs mettans des supports ou tenans." "Ce que nous venons de dire des Abbez qui mettent une Mitre et une Crosse au dessus de leurs Armoiries se doit entendre de ceux qui sont crossez et mitrez, soit qu'ils soient commendataires ou Réguliers, les autres n'ayant pas le droit de porter la mitre ni la crosse." So, in SEGOING'S *Armoriel Universel*, two instances are given of the arms of *Abbés Réguliers ;* in both the head of the staff is turned inward, and the palm branches are placed around the base and flanks of the shield.

If the ecclesiastical hat were used, either in addition to the mitre and pastoral staff, or above the pastoral staff alone, it was black in colour and had six *houppes* (1. 2. 3.) on either side. In the Gallery of Pictures at Antwerp I noticed the portrait of the famous CÆSAR ALEXANDER SCAGLIA, Ambassador of Spain at the Congress of Münster, painted by ANTONY VAN DYCK. It bears the SCAGLIA arms : *Argent, a cross between four lozenges sable.* The shield is surmounted by a coronet (he is styled " *ex. com. Verrucæ, Abbas Stephardiæ et Mandanicis* ") and the black hat, with its six *houppes* on each side, surmounts the whole. When the coronet is used with the mitre and staff, either in abbatial or episcopal arms, it runs along the whole top of the escucheon ; the mitre and head of the staff appear above or on either side of the coronet. (*See* Plates VI., IX., XI.) SEBASTIEN GALIGAI, Abbé de MARMOUTIERS, in 1617, was content to use a hat with only three *houppes* on either side (1. 2.). His shield of arms bore : *Or, a chain in saltire azure,* and was surmounted by a mitre to the dexter, and a crosier is placed in pale behind the shield so that its crook, turned inwards, appears above the shield to the sinister. The black hat is above all. (GUIGARD, i., 231.) The arms of BENOIT BÉTHUNE DES PLANQUES, Abbot of S. BERTIN at S. Omer in 1677, are: *Argent, a fess gules, in dexter chief a small escucheon of the arms of* SAVEUSE, viz., *Gules, a bend between six billets or.* These are in a cartouche surmounted by the coronet of a count, above which are visible a small mitre, and the head of the crosier. (GUIGARD, i., 94.)

In GLAFEY'S *Sigilla* is engraved the seal of the Polish Abbot KRASINSKI. On it the arms are timbred with a coronet; above which is placed the crest without a helmet,

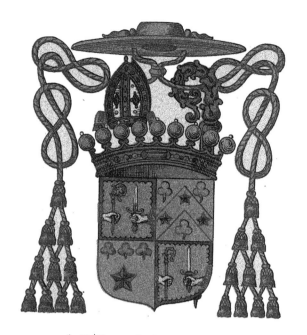

1. De Serres, Bishop of Puy, 1631.

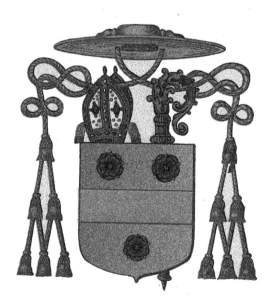

2. Malier, Bp. of Troyes.

and the whole is surmounted by the ecclesiastical hat with its six *houppes*, on either side. ·

It may be noted that occasionally the official arms of an Abbot differed from those of his Monastery. Thus the Abbé de MARMOÛTIER bore: *Azure, three sceptres, or bourdons, in pale and saltire or ;* while the arms of the Abbey were: *Vert, the mounted figure of S. Martin, dividing his cloak with a beggar, all proper.*

In Part II. of this work will be found a list of those Abbots and Abbesses who were temporal Princes and Princesses of the Holy Roman Empire. All these timbred their arms with the coronets, of their princely rank. The shields were frequently surmounted by several crested helmets (*vide ante*, p. 35), and the mitre itself was usually placed, with or without an intervening crimson cushion, upon one of the helmets (*cf.* Plate XVI.). The naked sword of temporal authority and the pastoral staff were placed by them in saltire behind the shield.

After this fashion the Abbots of S. PETER, in *Monte Blandino*, at Ghent, used to place the sword as well as ·the pastoral staff behind their arms to denote their temporal jurisdiction over a portion of the city. The Abbot of the Premonstratensian Monastery of S. MICHAEL at Antwerp placed in saltire behind his mitred shield his pastoral staff, and a long shafted cross, such as S. MICHAEL is represented as wielding in his conflict with Satan. The Abbot-General of the OLIVETAINS at Bologna, and the Abbot of SAN GEORGIO MAGGIORE at Venice, had a similar custom ; the former substituting a branch of olive, the latter the lance of S. GEORGE, for the cross.

The Abbots and Commanders of the ORDER OF S. ANTHONY either added to their arms the tau-shaped cross, the badge of the saint (Plate V., fig. 10), or (in more recent times) placed their shield upon the *tau* so that its arms projected beyond the shield, just as in the case of the members of the ORDER OF S. JOHN OF JERUSALEM (*cf.* Plate XIII., fig. 32).

In France, in the seventeenth and later centuries, Abbots frequently ensigned their arms with the coronets of their families ; as well as with the insignia of their ecclesiastical rank. Thus, GABRIEL DE CHATEAU-BRIAND, Abbé de TRISAY, in 1630, placed above his arms (*Gules, semé de fleurs-de-lis or*) the countly coronet, showing nine pearls ; above which are the mitre and the head of the pastoral staff, the point of the latter of course appears at the base of the shield. Two palm branches surround the base and sides of the shield, being tied together at its foot. (*See* Plate VI., fig. 2.) Abbesses placed their pastoral staff in pale behind the lozenge, or shield, of their arms, which was usually surrounded by a *cordelière* of knotted black, or black and white, silk, or sometimes by palms, or a crown of thorns. Those who were of great families usually added the coronet, and if of ducal rank sometimes also the mant-ling around the shield (*see* the arms of the Abbesses DE LORRAINE, D'ESPINAY, DE SOUVRÉ, D'ALBERT, DE VASSÉ, and DE LA PORTE, on Plate VII.).

According to FORD, the Abbess of LAS HUELGAS, near Burgos, was a Princess-palatine, and inferior in dignity to no one but the Queen. She was mitred, and possessed the rights of a *señora de horca y cuchillo* (*i.e.,* she had the rights of life and death, "pit and gallows"). She was styled "Por la gracia de Dios" and the monastery was exempt and extra diocesan. (I have only visited las Huelgas on ferial days, and so have missed seeing the mitre.)

As an example of the German use, I add here the description of the armorial insignia of the Abbess of BUCHAU, Princess of the Empire, of the house of KÖNIGSECK-ROTENFELS. *Per fess :*— A. *Per pale* I.

Quarterly, 1 and 4. *Argent three lions passant gules ;* 2 and 3. *Lozengy argent and gules ;* II. *Vert, a cross gules, in the dexter chief canton the sun in splendour, in the sinister a crescent figured or* (BUCHAU). B. *Lozengy bendy sinister or and gules* (KÖNIGSECK). The shield is supported by two golden lions rampant. The pastoral staff, and temporal sword are in saltire behind the shield, and the whole is surmounted by a princely hat, or coronet, of crimson velvet turned up with ermine, and adorned with gold.

Often the German Prince-Abbots quartered their official with their personal arms ; thus in 1688 PLACIDUS VON DROSTE, Abbot of FULDA, bore ; *Quarterly*, 1 and 4. *Argent, a cross sable* (FULDA); 2 and 3. *Per bend nebulé (crénélé ?) or and gules* (VON DROSTE). (*See* KÖHLER, *Münz-Belustigung*, xiv., p. 241.) The Abbots of WERDEN appear to have generally preferred another arrangement. In 1698, FERDINAND, Baron of EHREVILLE, bore a shield in which the quarters are separated by a plain cross throughout *Quarterly*, 1 and 4. *The arms of the Empire;* 2 and 3. *Barry . . . and . . . over all a lion rampant . . . crowned . . .* ; and placed the arms of the Abbey:—*Gules, two croziers in saltire proper, en surtout* on the centre of the cross. The main shield is mitred, and the temporal sword (head to the dexter) and crosier are in saltire behind it. Similarly one of his successors, Abbot THEODORE, in 1724 used exactly the same arrangement except that the second and third quarters are charged with his personal arms ; . . . *a saltire between four annulets* . . . (KÖHLER, xiii., pp. 193, 201). But ANSELM VON SONIUS, Abbot of WERDEN and HELMSTADT, bore:—*Quarterly of six;* 1 and 6. *Azure, a cross argent ;* 2 and 5. *Azure, a double-headed eagle displayed or ;* 3 and 4. *Gules, two croziers in saltire proper* (WERDEN). *Over all, Azure, a sun in splendour* (SONIUS). (GATTERER, *Heraldik*, p. 45.)

In France the regular Abbots sometimes used only their personal arms, at others they either impaled or quartered with them the arms of the Abbey. Thus, AUGUSTIN LE SCELLIER, Abbot of PRÉMONTRÉ in 1656, and CLAUDE HONORÉ LUCAS, Abbot in 1709, both impaled the arms of the Abbey with their own, but an intermediate Abbot, MICHEL COLBERT, in 1672, quartered them with his personal coat:—*Or, a serpent wavy in pale azure.* (DEMAY, *Sceaux de la Normandie*, Nos. 2848, 2849.)

CHAPTER V.

THE usual external ornament by which the arms of Bishops are distinguished is the mitre placed full-faced upon the shield, and in Great Britain the use of any other ensign of authority is very infrequent; though occasionally, but it seems improperly, two crosiers are placed in saltire behind the shield. (This can only fitly be done in the case of conjoined dioceses.) The book-plate of Bishop GILBERT BURNETT of Salisbury shows a shield bearing the arms of the See (Plate XXV., fig. 1) impaling his personal coat (*Argent, a hunting-horn sable stringed gules, in the bow a mullet* for difference, *in chief three burnet*—apparently not holly—*leaves vert*). The shield is encircled by the Garter, of which Order the Bishop of SALISBURY was then Chancellor. Above the Garter is a full-faced mitre, and a crosier and key are placed in saltire behind the shield.

Abroad, the mitre and the pastoral staff are generally employed, the former is placed full-faced, the crosier has its head generally, but not invariably, turned outwards. On the arms of French Bishops the mitre is placed above the top edge of the shield to the dexter, the head of the crosier occupying a similar position to the sinister. As to the direction of the crook we find that, whatever the strict rule may be, it is frequently disregarded. Plate IX. contains the arms of two French Bishops: DE SERRES, Bishop of Puy, to which allusion will be made later ; and MALIER, Bishop of Troyes, the latter bore:— *Argent, a fess azure between three roses gules, barbed and seeded proper*, in these and the other numerous examples of the arms of French Bishops given in MAGNENEY'S *Recueil des Armes*, the head of the staff is turned one way and the other indifferently, just as it was by Abbots (*v.* preceding chapter, p. 70).

On some mediæval seals the Bishop is represented holding a book, but without the mitre and pastoral staff. It may be well to remember that when this is the case the person represented was Bishop-elect, but had not received consecration. "Es de avertir que la falta de mitra y de baculo . . . denotan constantamente en el sello de un obispo la calidad de electo y no conse-grado." *Sellos Reales y ecclesiasticos : reinados de Don Alfonzo X. y Sancho IV.* in DORREGARAY'S *Museo Español de Antiguedades*, vol. ii., p. 541. Madrid, 1863. The example there given is of a Bishop-elect of Toledo. The Seal of FLORENCE, Bishop-elect of Glasgow in 1202, bears the figure of the Bishop without pontificals seated before a lectern, holding a palm branch in his hand as if teaching (LAING, *Scottish Seals*, vol. i., p. 163, plate xv., fig. 3, and *Reg. Episc. Glasg.*, plate i., fig. 3). This Bishop-elect was never consecrated, and he resigned his See in 1207. ROGER, Lord-Chancellor of Scotland in 1178, elected Bishop of S. ANDREWS (*circa* 1188), bore his seated effigy holding a rod and a book. A seal in 1193 shows that he had by that time been consecrated, as on it he is represented in pontificals. In GLAFEY, *Specimen Decadem Sigillorum*, Lipsiæ, 1749, tab. ii., fig. 15 represents the seal of ALBERTUS "Electus Cenetensis," which I take to be Cerreto in Naples. The Bishop is simply habited in a gown, and holds a book before his breast. On the seals of RICHARD KELLAW, 1311, and LOUIS DE BEAUMONT, 1318, both Bishops-elect of Durham, they are represented without pontificals, kneeling in prayer (*Brit. Mus. Cat.*, vol. i., Nos. 2456, 2458).

In the Introductory Chapter I have alluded to the practice by which a Bishop who possessed no armorial bearings by inheritance, generally assumed for himself either a coat borne by a family of the same name, from which he supposed he might be descended ; or, and with much greater propriety, an entirely new coat, and this is the custom still both among Anglican Bishops, and those of the Roman obedience.

Mgr. PIE, Bishop of POITIERS in 1863 assumed the following personal arms : *Azure, on a pedestal argent, the effigy of Nôtre Dame de Chartres proper.* The charge is the representation of the effigy of the Blessed Virgin and Holy Child, both black in colour, just as it exists in the shrine in the Cathedral of CHARTRES. Mgr. ANGEBAULT, Bishop of ANGERS, about the same time assumed : *Azure, a Passion-Cross and a fouled anchor in saltire argent.* (Both coats are engraved in *Le Héraut d'Armes*, pp. 362, 406. Paris, 1863.) FRANÇOIS BOUSSEN, Bishop of BRUGES (1834-1849) bore : *Argent, the figure of the Good Shepherd proper ;* and the present venerated Bishop JEAN JOSEPH FAIET (consecrated in 1864) bears : *Argent, a cross gules, on the centre point a heart of the last irradiated or.* In 1891 the arms of the Bishop of LIMOGES were : *Argent, on a cross sable the monogram XP combined or.* The shield was timbred with a ducal coronet, between a mitre and crosier. A (legatine ?) cross is in pale behind the shield and a hat with ten houppes (1. 2. 3. 4.) surmounted the whole.

The arms of the Spanish Cardinal LOUIS, BELLUGA Y MONCADA (b. 1663, created Cardinal in 1719) appear to

G

be a curious example of an assumed coat of faulty heraldry : *Purpure, rising from and wedged into a mount in base a long cross botonnée vert, the upper part irradiated, surmounted in fess point by a large heart pierced on either side by three swords proper.* (*Roma Sancta,* No. xlviii., ROSSI i., 289.)

Very generally (and especially in those southern countries where many of the Sees appear to have no fixed official arms) the personal arms, whether inherited or assumed, are alone used by foreign ecclesiastics with the external ornaments of their rank.

On the earliest Episcopal Seals in England in which both arms of the See and the personal arms of its occupant appear they were not at first combined, but were represented in separate escucheons. But although as early as 1396 the seal of THOMAS ARUNDEL, Archbishop of CANTERBURY, bears an escucheon on which the arms of the See are impaled with his personal quartered coat of FITZALAN and WARREN, I do not think the custom of impalement was generally adopted until *at least* a century later. EDMUND LACY, Bishop of EXETER, 1420, impaled the arms of the See with his personal coat. *Azure, three shoveller's heads erased* (*Brit. Mus. Cat.*, i., 1566) but this is exceptional. After the Reformation the present use became general. The seal of Bishop WREN of ELY (1638 - 1667) bears four escucheons in cross which contain the arms of the three Sees to which he had been successively preferred :—ELY, NORWICH, and HEREFORD, and, in base, his personal coat ; a curious example, but not worthy of imitation.

We may remark that in a few cases the personal arms of a Bishop were eventually adopted as the bearings of the See, and as such used by his successors. Examples will be found later under the Sees of MAINZ, HEREFORD, and WORCESTER; ALBI has already been mentioned at p. 18.

Abroad there is considerable variety of usage with regard to the use of official arms when any exist.

FABRITIUS PAULUTIUS, of FORLI, Bishop of PRATO gave the place of honour to his personal arms :—(*Or, three bars sable, on a chief gules a rose argent*), when he impaled them with those of his See : *Per pale* (a) *Gules, semé of fleurs-de-lis or* (usually with the Angevin chief, *Azure, three fleurs-de-lis, and a label gules of four points*). (b) *Or, an eagle dimidiated sable.*

The Bishops of BRUGES in Flanders usually quartered the arms of the See with their personal arms, but placed the official coat in the 2nd and 3rd quarters. Those of the See are : *Or, a lion rampant sable, collared argent, and having a plain cross of the same pendant.* But Bishops who were already entitled to bear quartered coats by descent, placed the arms of the See *en surtout.* For example Bishops HENDRIK VAN SUSTEREN (1716-1743) bore : *Quarterly, 1 and 4. Gules, a chevron between two stag's heads in profile and a leopard's head in base or ; 2 and 3. Azure, a wheel argent; over all an escucheon of the arms of the See.* JEAN ROBERT CAIMO, Bishop (1753-1771) bore : *Quarterly, 1 and 4. Argent, a fess azure; 2 and 3. Or, three canettes sable,* with the arms of the See *en surtout.*

These notes are taken from the interesting series of Episcopal arms, from 1512 to the present time, which are painted around and beneath the great west window of the Church of ST. SAUVEUR at Bruges.

In the MS. *Armorial du Héraut Gueldre* of the fourteenth century the arms of the then Bishop of BEAUVAIS are emblazoned : *Quarterly, 1 and 4. The Arms of the See : Or, a cross between four keys paleways wards in chief gules ; 2 and 3. . . . three leopard's heads ; 2 and 1. . . . the personal arms of the Bishop.* The Bishop of BEAUVAIS was one of the six great Ecclesiastical peers of France. The *Pairs de France* were originally only twelve in number ; six lay peers who were the great feudatories ;—1. The Duke of NORMANDY ; 2. The Duke of BURGUNDY ;. 3. The Duke of GUIENNE or AQUITAINE ; 4. The Count of FLANDERS ; 5. the Count of CHAMPAGNE ; 6. The Count of TOULOUSE :—and six ecclesiastical peers, who were originally the immediate vassals of the Duchy of France, a fact which explains how it came to pass that with the exception of the Archbishop of REIMS they were all simple bishops, inferior in the ecclesiastical hierarchy to the Metropolitans of LYON, BOURGES, TOULOUSE, BOURDEAUX, etc. These twelve great vassals, holding their lands immediately from the King, formed a High Court, or special tribunal for the trial of causes affecting any of their number, and took a special part in the coronation of the King. The six Ecclesiastical *Pairs de France* were then ;—1. The Archbishop-Duke of REIMS ; 2. The Bishop-Duke of LAON ; 3. The Bishop-Duke of LANGRES ; 4. The Bishop-Count of BEAUVAIS ; 5. The Bishop-Count of CHÂLONS (*sur Marne*); 6. The Bishop-Count of NOYON.

I. Père ANSELME makes the *Pairie* of the Archbishops of REIMS (who were also *legati nati* of the Holy See, and Primates of Belgian Gaul) to ascend to the year 1179 when GUILLAUME DE CHAMPAGNE, Cardinal-Archbishop of REIMS, crowned King PHILIP AUGUSTUS. This right of coronation was the special privilege attaching to this peerage. In the absence of the Archbishop the honour of officiating devolved upon the Bishop of SOISSONS, who was not a peer. He actually officiated at the coronation of LOUIS XIV., the See of REIMS being then vacant. (We may note in passing that the Provost, Dean, Dignitaries, and Canons of REIMS, made an energetic protest against the supposition, and assertion in a certain *Procés Verbal*, that the Bishop of SOISSONS had any right whatever so to officiate without their formal

1 de Nemours, Abp. and Duke of Reims   2. Sabastien Zamet, Bp. and Duke of Lang

Augustin Potier, Bp. Count of Beauvais 4. Philibert de Brichanteau, Bp. Duke of Lao

5. Felix de Vialard, Bp. Count of Chalons   6. Henri Barradat, Bp. Count of Noyon

permission (which as a matter of fact the said Bishop had thought it prudent to obtain), and they claimed for themselves and for the fabric of the Church the offerings made at the ceremony. 2. The Bishop-Duke of LAON bore in the coronation procession *La Sainte Ampoule*, the vessel in the form of a dove, containing the sacring oil—his *pairie* dated from 1174. 3. The Bishop-Duke of LANGRES carried at the coronation the Royal Sword, having been successful in a dispute for precedence with ; 4. The Bishop-Count of BEAUVAIS, whose *pairie* appeared to date only from 1189, he carried and presented the Royal Mantle at the coronation. The other two peers carried respectively the Royal Signet ring ; and the Royal scarf and belt. If any of these ecclesiastical Peers were unable to be present at the coronation their places were supplied in order of seniority by their juniors. Thus at the coronation of LOUIS XIV., the Bishop of BEAUVAIS represented the absent Bishop-Duke of LAON ; the Bishop-Count of CHÂLONS represented the Bishop-Duke of LANGRES, the Bishop of NOYON represented the Bishop-Count of BEAUVAIS, while the Archbishops of BOURGES and ROUEN filled the places of the Bishops of CHÂLONS and NOYON who were officiating for their absent seniors.

The official arms attaching to these Pairies were as follows :—

REIMS : FRANCE-ANCIENT (*Azure, semé of fleurs-de-lis or*) *a cross gules.*

LAON : FRANCE-ANCIENT, *a crozier in pale gules.*

LANGRES : FRANCE-ANCIENT, *a saltire gules.*

BEAUVAIS : *Or, a cross between four keys paleways gules.*

CHÂLONS : *Azure, a cross argent between four fleurs-de-lis or.*

NOYON : FRANCE-ANCIENT, *two croziers addorsed paleways argent.* (These are engraved on Plate X., and are impaled with the arms of the *occupants* of the Sees in 1679.)

These arms were borne impaled or quartered at pleasure with the personal arms, and were surmounted by the coronet of duke or count according to the dignity attached to the *pairie*, and surrounded by the *manteau armoyé* and ermine lined, which was the privilege of the Peers. The archi-episcopal, or episcopal, hat was placed above the whole. The Archbishop of REIMS placed his cross in pale behind the shield.

It is worthy of notice that when these ecclesiastical peers impaled or quartered their official coats they did not give them precedence over their personal arms. Thus CHARLES DES CARS, Bishop-Duke of LANGRES in 1614, bore his personal arms, *Gules, a pale vair in the first and fourth quarters ;* so also BENJAMIN DE BRICHANTEAU, Bishop-Duke of LAON in 1619 bore his arms, *Azure, ten plates 3. 2. 1. in the first and fourth.* (See MAGNENEY'S, *Recueil des Armes, planche* 12. The official arms are impaled in our Plate X.)

The Archbishop of SENS quartered the arms of his See (*Azure, a cross argent between four pastoral staves or*), with his personal arms. In the treasury at SENS is a silver reliquary bearing the arms of Archbishop GUIL-LAUME DE MELUN in 1339. They are, curiously, *en bannière*, and are :— *Quarterly*, 1 and 4. *Azure, seven bezants three, three, one, and a chief or ;* 2 and 3. *The arms of the See.* The Archi-episcopal cross is placed in bend over all, extending over the first and fourth quarters, an arrangement worthy of remark. (MENÊT-RIER, *Recherches du Blason*, pp. 252-3.) I have noticed the same practice of quartering in the second and third the arms of other French Sees when these were used at all ; but the arms of JACQUES DE SERRES, Bishop of Puy, and Comte de Velay in 1631, engraved on Plate IX., fig. 1, appear to be an exception.

In Germany the use of official coats is very much more general, and they are borne with considerable variety of use. The arms of the See and the personal arms of the Bishop are sometimes placed in two shields *accolés* under a single mitre or hat. Thus in the Carmelite Monastery of FRANKFURT AM MAYN are the arms of MATTHEW LANG VON WELLENBURG, Archbishop of SALZBURG (1519-1540) who had filled the office of coadjutor since 1514, and was made Cardinal in 1511. He used two shields *accolés*, the dexter contained the arms of his See: *Per pale* (a) *Or, a lion rampant sable* (b) *Gules a fess argent;* the sinister was occupied by his personal arms: *Per pale argent and gules, a rose and a fleur-de-lis dimidiated, conjoined, and counter-changed.* The archi-episcopal cross stands in pale behind the shields, and the hat of that dignity surmounts the whole. JOSEPH, Landgrave of HESSE-DARMSTADT, Prince-Bishop of AUGSBURG (1740-1768) in 1744 arranged his arms in two oval cartouches, the dexter of his See (p. 88) the sinister of his family. *Quarterly of six in three horizontal rows of two coats :*—1. *Argent, a cross patriarchal gules.* (Abbey of HIRSCHFELD, secularised at the Peace of Westphalia.) 2. *Per fess sable and or, in chief an estoile of the second* (often *argent*). (County of ZIEGENHAIN.) 3. *Per fess* (a) *Or a lion rampant gules, armed and crowned azure.* (County of CATZENELLNBOGEN); (b) *Per fess sable and or, in chief two estoiles of the first.* (County of NIDDA.) 4. *Per fess* (a) *Gules, two lions passant in pale or.* (County of DIETZ). (b) *Or, three chevrons gules.* (County of HANAU.) 5. *Gules, an escucheon per fess of the first and argent, between three Passion nails in pairle, and as many demi-nettle leaves alternately of the second.* (SCHAUMBURG.) 6. *Argent, two bars sable.* (County of ISENBURG.) Over all an escucheon of HESSE, *en surtout : Azure, a lion rampant double queuè barry of ten gules and argent crowned or.* Both escucheòns are crowned, the first with the princely hat of crimson turned up with ermine ; the second with a landgrave's coronet and cap. Between and above both is a single plain mitre, while the pastoral staff and the temporal sword are placed in saltire behind them (this arrangement is also found on a medal engraved in KÖHLER, *Münz-Belustigung*, vol. xix., p. 369).

Sometimes the coat of the See was quartered with the personal arms ; thus JOHN CHRISTOPHER VON FREY-BURG, Prince-Bishop of AUGSBURG (1665-1690) bore : *Quarterly*, 1 and 4. *Per pale gules and argent* (See of AUGSBURG) ; 2 and 3. *Per fess argent and azure in base three bezants* (VON FREYBURG) with the usual additions of external ornaments. So JOSEPH MORS, Bishop of CHÜR in 1628 quartered the arms of his See (*Argent, a steinbock rampant sable*), in the first and fourth places. His personal coat *Argent, a demi-Moor sable*, being in the second and third. (KÖHLER, *Münz-Belustigung*, vol. xii.)

Another common arrangement in Germany when several Sees were held by the same prelate, was that by which the arms of the Sees, and of their dependent Lordships, were quartered, and the prelate's personal arms placed on an escucheon *en surtout*. So also PETER PHILIP, of the Counts von DERNBACH, Prince-Bishop of BAMBERG (1672-1683) and of WÜRZBURG in 1675, as such Duke of FRANCONIA (*v.* p. 93), arranged his arms thus: Quarterly, 1. and 4. (BAMBERG) *Or, a lion rampant sable, over all a bend argent.* 2. (FRANCONIA) *Per fess indented gules and argent.* 3. (WÜRZBURG) *Azure, a banner quarterly gules and argent flying towards the chief from a lance in bend or.* Over all, DERNBACH : *Azure, billetty three hearts in pale or.* In 1661, FREDRICK WILLIAM, Count von WARTENBERG, Cardinal-Bishop of REGENSBURG, OSNABRÜCK, MINDEN, and VERDEN, quartered the arms of his Sees (for which *see* the respective names in Part II.). Over all an escucheon of WARTENBERG : *Argent, on a fess between three torteaux, a hunting-horn stringed or.* The pastoral staff and temporal sword are, as usual, in saltire behind the shield and a cardinal's hat surmounts the whole. (KÖHLER, *Münz-Belustigung*, xi., 25.) CHARLES of LORRAINE, Elector, and Prince-Bishop of TREVES in 1715, used an escucheon ; Quarterly of six, 1 and 4. OSNABRÜCK; 2 and 5. TRIER ; 3 and 4. Abbey of PRUM. Over all a quartered escucheon of his personal arms (*v.* p. 71). (KÖHLER, *Münz-Belustigung*, vol. xiii.) FRANZ CONRAD, Baron von RÖDT, Cardinal and Bishop of CONSTANZ (1750-1775) bore : Quarterly, 1 and 4. *Argent, a cross gules* (See of CONSTANZ) ; 2 and 3. *Per pale Or, and gules a fess argent* (. . .). *Enté en pointe Or, two hands and arms in chevron issuing from clouds in base of the flanks and holding together a key with double wards in pale* (Provost of EISGARN in Austria?) Over all an escucheon surtout *Argent, a cross gules.* The shield is supported by two lions rampant double-tailed. The external ornaments are as usual. (GATTERER, *Heraldik* 25.)

On many of the seals of the Prince-Bishops of HILDESHEIM given in HARENBERG (*Hist. Eccl.*), the escucheon of the personal arms of the prelate is placed *en surtout* upon that of the See :—*Per pale argent and gules*, so that the latter has at first sight the appearance of *a bordure divided per pale.*

Sometimes the disposition described above was reversed, and the arms of the See occupied the escucheon *en surtout* above the personal quarterings. Thus MARQUARD II. SCHENCK VON CASTELL, Prince-Bishop of EICHSTÄDT (1637-1685) bore : *Quarterly*, 1 and 4. *Argent, a stag's attire gules* (SCHENCK VON OBERBEVERN); 2 and 3. *Argent, two lions passant in pale double queués gules, crowned or* (SCHENCK VON LANDECK)

and over all the arms of the See of EICHŚTÁDT, *Gules,*
the head of a crosier in pale argent.

. Occasionally the arms of the See were placed in chief
above the personal arms, whether these were a plain or
a quartered coat. Thus PAULINUS MEYR, Prince-
Bishop of BRIXEN (1677-1685) bore : Quarterly of six,
1. *Gules, a Paschal-Lamb proper* (for the See of BRIXEN) ;
2. *Argent, an eagle displayed crowned or, over all a*
pastoral staff in fess of the last (Chapter of BRIXEN) ;
3 and 6. *Gules, a pelican in piety or ;* 4 and 5. *Azure, an*
arrow in bend argent, flighted, or between two mullets of
the last. Here the four lower quarters contain the
personal arms. So also BALTHAZAR VON PROMNITZ,
Prince-Bishop of BRESLAU in 1551 bore his official arms
in chief above his personal ones, thus :—*Per fess* (A) *per*
pale (*a*) BRESLAU (p. 272) and (*b*) SILESIA (p. 272) both
for his principality. (B.) *Per pale* (a) *Gules, an arrow in*
bend between two estoiles argent. (b) *Argent, two bends*
sable. On a champagne azure two lions passant in pale or.
Similarly, the Archbishops of SALZBURG usually placed
in chief above their personal bearings, the two impaled
coats which formed the arms of their See (*vide* p. 87).
Other examples of this arrangement will be found
recorded in later pages of this book.

An exceptional arrangement, affording an example of
the rare quartering per saltire, was adopted by ADAM
FRIEDRICH of the Counts von SEINSHEIM, Prince-
Bishop of WÜRZBURG (1755-1779, and of BAMBERG in
1757). *Quarterly per saltire,* 1 and 4. See of BAMBERG ;
2. FRANCONIA ; 3. WÜRZBURG (these are all given on
p. 88). Over all a coroneted shield of SEINSHEIM, viz. :
Quarterly, 1 and 4. *Paly of six argent and azure ;*
2 and 3. *Or, a bear rampant sable.* The Supporters were
two BAMBERG lions rampant sable, each debruised by
a bend argent. The usual external ornaments are used,
the princely hat, sword, and crosier.

With regard to the external ornaments employed heraldically to denote Episcopal rank we find that at first the crozier or pastoral staff was alone employed. GUIL-LAUME DE BRIE, Bishop of DOL in 1387, has on his seal, his arms ;—*Argent three bars crenelés sable ;* a crosier is placed behind the shield. (MORICE, *Histoire Ecclésias-tique et Civile de Bretagne*, Paris, 1742, tome ii., 16.) GEOFFROI, Bishop of QUIMPER in 1365, whose arms *Argent on a chief . . . three fleurs-de-lis . . .* used the same (*ibid.*, tome ii., cxxxiv.). [We may notice that in 1298 GEOFFROI, Bishop of TREGUIER, used a counter-seal on which in a quatrefoil is an eagle displayed between two croziers of which the crooks are turned inwards, there is no shield. (*Ibid.*, tome i. cxxiii., and our Plate XXXVI., fig. 2)]. The learned herald Père MENESTRIER observes that in his time (1673) the Italian Bishops timbred their shield of arms with the mitre only, and that the French Bishops often placed the pastoral staff alone behind the escucheon. But he adds that both mitre and staff were used and cites as an early example the arms upon the tomb of Bishop BUCCAPADULI (*c.* 1414) in the Church of SAN MARCELLO, at Rome. In MAGNENEY'S *Recueil des Armes*, Paris, 1633, we find a large store of Episcopal arms, which show clearly what were the usual external ornaments employed in France at that date. Many Bishops were content to use only the green Episcopal hat above the shield, but even here the tendency to assume a little more than was right is evident, the hat instead of having, as it had originally only, *six* houppes on either side (1. 2. 3.) has invariably ten (1. 2. 3. 4.) like that of an archbishop. This tendency to assumption went on increasing among the clergy (just as among the lay nobles of the time the coronet of a higher grade was continually assumed) until it became—and I may add that in Great Britain it still is—extremely difficult in many cases to determine the exact ecclesiastical rank of a Roman Catholic prelate from the bearings employed upon his seal, etc. If the Bishop was a member of a family who used a coronet, this was interposed between the shield and the hat ; and this was the case also when a temporal dignity such as that of prince, duke, or count was attached to the See (*vide* pp. 33 and 34). Other Bishops who did not use a coronet, placed the full-faced mitré on the top edge of the shield to the dexter, and the head of the crosier, turned indifferently outwards or inwards, appears on the sinister, a small portion of the staff is visible in base. In MAGNENEY'S book these Bishops have their proper hat with the six *houppes* only. Again there were others who used the mitre and crosier, and a coronet, beneath the hat. In this case the coronet immediately surmounts the shield, the mitre and crosier appear above it. Here again the head is turned indifferently in or out. We may repeat what has already been said in the case of abbots, that bishops and abbots used the crosier ritually in exactly the same way. There is no solid foundation for the idea that it is improper to represent a bishop with the crook of the pastoral staff turned inward, or an abbot with the crosier head turned outward. As a matter of fact on the earliest seals the staves of the bishops generally have the head turned inwards, an arrangement which was almost necessitated by the contraction of the *vesica* towards the top. But I have already noticed (pp. 70, 80) that heraldically there was in early times a custom of differentiating the insignia as above ; which, however, had nearly passed away so far as the crosier was concerned, before the seventeenth century. CHARLES DE BALZAC, Bishop-Count of NOYON, who died in 1642, has his arms (*Azure, three saltires couped argent two and one ; on a chief or, as many saltires couped of the first*) surmounted by his coronet of nine pearls ; to the right of it is a small mitre, to the left the head of the crosier turned inwards, the whole is beneath the green Episcopal hat (but with *ten houppes* on either side). HENRI BARADAT, Bishop of NOYON, *d.* 1600 (*Azure, a fess argent between three roses or barbed vert*) omitted the coronet, and used the full-faced mitre and crosier (head turned inward) beneath the same hat (GUIGARD, i., 71). The Bishop of MENDE in France had the title of Count de GEVAUDAN and claimed its sovereignty. The Royal letters patent of LOUIS VII. to the Bishop AUBERT, in 1160 are in FAVYN (pp. 161-162 English edition). A sceptre of gold was carried before the Bishop, who used the coronet of a Count.

THE USE OF THE TEMPORAL SWORD.

Examples have been already given in which the sword of temporal authority was added by Abbots and Bishops to the pastoral staff and mitre as an external ornament of the shield. ERLANG, Bishop of WÜRZBURG (1106-1121) is said to have originated this use. The Emperor HENRY V. desired to obtain possession of the Duchy of FRANCONIA (which belonged to the See of WÜRZBURG), in order to bestow it on his nephew the Duke of SWABIA. But the prelate desiring to show his determination to defend the possessions of his Church, caused a naked sword to be borne before him when he officiated, and this custom was retained by his successors (NOLDENIUS, *De Statu Nobilium*, cap. xvii., § 31 (1619); and PRAUN, in BURGERMEISTER, *Bibl. Equestr.*, ii., 889.) However this may be, many Bishops and Abbeys held their lands by military tenure, being bound to render personal service to the Suzerain in time of war. There is a formal *Ordonnance* relating to this military service in the Capitularies of CHARLES THE BOLD. It is the eighth in order of those which were drawn up "*in verno palatio*" under the presidency of EBROIN, Bishop of

POITIERS, in the first year of CHARLES' reign, and is here subjoined :—

"VIII. Quoniam quosdam Episcoporum ab expeditionis labore corporis defendit imbecillitas, aliis autem vestra indulgentia cunctis optabilem largitur quietem, præcavendum est utrisque, ne per eorum absentia res militaris dispendum patiatur. Itaque si vestra consentit sublimitas homines suos reipub. profituros cuilibet fidelium vestrorum, quem sibi utilem judicaverint committant, cujus diligentia ne se ab officio subtrahere valeat observetur."

"Les Evêques, chapitres, religieux, et clercs, qui tenaient terres en fief, étaient soumis au ban et arrière-ban, et devaient *l'ost* et *la chevauchée*." [*La chevauchée* était un service féodal dû par le vassal à son seigneur dans les guerres privées. Elle se distinguait ainsi de *l'host* ou *ost*, qui était le service militaire dû au roi pour les guerres générales. (CHÉRUEL, *Dictionnaire Historique des Institutions, etc., de la France*, tome i., p. 151.)] "Ils n'étaient point forcés d'aller eux-mêmes à la guerre, mais ils se faisaient représenter par leurs tenanciers." "Quand les ecclésiastiques entrèrent par la possession des terres nobles dans la hiérarchie féodale, ils furent, comme tous les vassaux, tenus du service militaire envers leurs suzerains. Le plus souvent ils s'en acquittaient par procureurs, de là l'institution des avoués et des vidames. Plus tard les évêques et les monastères se contentèrent d'envoyer leurs tenanciers à l'ost du roi, ou de payer une somme proportionnée à l'importance de leurs fiefs. Au XVIe siècle le clergé obtint la dispense du service moyennant une contribution d'hommes ou de l'argent ; cette dispense devint encore plus générale au siècle suivant, l'Église de France s'engageant, par contrat passé avec le roi, à payer une somme fixe pour subvenir aux frais de la guerre. Néanmoins pendant toute la durée du moyen âge, les ecclésiastiques parurent dans les

armées, ils prenaient même souvent une part active à la
guerre. - Les Évêques-Comtes de Beauvais portaient la
cotte d'armes au sacre du Roi, en souvenir de l'un d'eux,
Philippe de Dreux, qui était représenté sur les vitraux
de la Cathédrale en surplis avec la cotte d'armes. Ce
belliqueux prélat fut emené prisonnier de guerre en
Angleterre, et à la bataille de Bouvines, il se servait
d'une masse d'armes pour se conformer aux préceptes
de l'Eglise qui défend aux clercs de verser le sang."

La Roque has given (in his *Traité du ban et arrière-
ban*, Paris, 1676) many ancient rolls in which were
inscribed the names of all who owed military service to
the King. One of these was drawn up in 1214, at the
time of the battle of Bouvines. The names of Archbishops and Bishops figure in these lists, as well as those
of the lay-nobles, from all parts of France.

The Abbeys, independently of the contingent of men-
at-arms which they were bound to contribute to the
King for the fiefs which they held from him, were also
his debtors for *le droit de charroy*. This obligation
bound them to supply "*à leurs* frais, missions et despens,
un certain nombre de charrettes couvertes, de chariots, de
chevaux, et de sommiers, pour aider à chargier, conduire
et mener en ledict ost et armée, harnois de guerre, artil-
leries, vivres, et autres choses nécessaires pour icelle
armée." In 1431 the clerics in the Duchy of Burgundy
endeavoured to get quit of this obligation, but the Duke
Philippe *le Bon* enforced it in the case of all who
would not make a liberal pecuniary composition (see
L'Héraut d'Armes, pp. 280, 281, Paris, 1863). Clement
Vaillant in his treatise, *De l'Estat Ancien de la France*,
has seven entire chapters on the military duties which
Bishops and Abbots were obliged to perform by reason
of the fiefs which they held by military tenure.

In the eighteenth century the arms of some of the
Bishops of Durham (Bishops Trevor, 1750; and

EGERTON) are represented with the sword, and crosier in saltire behind their arms (*Herald and Genealogist*, vol. viii., 166-7), but these do not appear on their seals. The sword was of course allusive to their Palatinate jurisdiction.

MENÊTRIER remarks (*Méthode du Blason*, p. 209) that certain of the French Bishops were accustomed to place a helmet on one side of the shield, and a sword on the other. These were the Bishops of CAHORS, DOL, and GAP. He adds that the Bishop of MODENA did the same thing. In MAGNENEY'S *Recueil des Armes* (planche 13) the arms of RÉVEL, Bishop and Count of DOL, viz., *Argent, three trefoils vert*, have the Archi-episcopal cross placed in pale behind the shield, its head appearing above and between a mitre, and a coroneted helmet (with its lambrequins) both resting on the upper edge of the shield. The Episcopal hat, of six tassels on either side, surmounts the whole. The arrangement for the arms of Bishop DE LA ROCHE of CAHORS (*ibid.*, planche 16) is, that the coronet of a count rests on the whole upper edge of the shield, and above it is placed a plumed front-faced helm, between a mitre on the dexter, and the head of the pastoral staff on the sinister. Both examples are engraved in our Plate XI. I have not, myself, met with an instance of the arms of the Bishop of GAP adorned with the helmet of which Père MENÊTRIER speaks above; but in another work of the same author (*l'Abrégé Méthodique*, p. 95) there is a different arrangement. The arms are those of ARTUS DE LIONNE, Bishop and Count of GAP (*Gules, a column argent, on a chief cousu azure a lion passant of the second*). (Plate XIII.) This escucheon is surmounted by the count's coronet, over which is the green Episcopal hat; the pastoral staff and the naked sword are placed erect on either side of the shield upon the tassels of the hat, instead of being in saltire behind the shield, as is the

1. Révol, Bishop and Count of Dol.

2. De la Roche, Bishop of Cahors (1630).

more usual disposition. This latter mòde was used, as
we have already seen, by the Prince-Bishops and Abbots
of the Roman Empire; it was also employed by some
Italian Bishops; *e.g.,* the Bishops of VERONA, and (I
think) of REGGIO. A sword and helmet were certainly
borne before the Bishop of REGGIO, and placed on the
altar when he celebrated Mass. In the account of the ceremonies which took place on Nov. 10, 1505, on the occasion
of the translation of the Image of Notre Dame di Reggio,
we read (*Prima parte della relatione di Alfonzo Joachi*)
"In ultimo sene usci di Chiesa con maesta decente
Monsignor Vescovo, inanzi il quale era portato dal
Signor Conte Paolo Manfredi, Cavaliere di S. Jago, con
magnifica pompa, l'Elmo e lo Stoco pererogativa di
Vescovi di Reggio, per lo titolo che conservano l'autorità
che habevano di Principe. Posto- lo stocco e Elmo
su'l'altare secondo'l solito suo, M. Vescovo di richissimi
habiti Pontificali adorno s'en venne a dar principio al
Santo Sacrificio de la Messa."

The Bishops of LUCCA had, by Imperial concession,
granted in 1121, the *jus gladii et sanguinis* in VILLA
BASILICA, and to this the arms of that place very probably allude. They are: *Argent, in chief a sprig of basil, and
in base a scorpion, both between two swords erect paleways,
all proper.* (*Le Armi dei Municipij Toscani;* ccxliv.
Firenze, 1864.) A sword was borne before the Bishop
of ELY as Chief Justice of the Isle of Ely until the close
of the Episcopate of Bishop SPARKE in 1835.

In the Introductory Chapter are recorded many
instances in which the mitre has been introduced into
the arms of English Bishops as a mark of difference.
The following examples of the use of the mitre, or the
pastoral staff, within the shield, are from continental
practice, though the first is that of an Englishman. At
the English College in Rome on the tomb of JOHN
SHIRWOOD, Bishop of DURHAM (1485-1494) were the

H

following arms ". .. . . *à un chevron chargé d'une croisette sur la pointe, et accompagné de trois etoiles de . . . , à un chef . . . rempli de la mitre.*" Bishop SHIRWOOD'S arms, as given in BEDFORD'S *Blazon of Episcopacy*, on the authority of COLE'S MSS., are . . . *a chevron between three estoiles* . . . Here both the chief with its mitre and the crosslet are omitted. It is, then, possible that the introduction of the mitre on the chief may be an indication that this mode of marking the Episcopal dignity was in use in Italy at that time.

At VITERBO in the Monasterio del Paradiso, founded by the Cardinal-Bishop of PORTO (MENÊTRIER says "PORTO," but I think PRATO was the See) the arms of JOHN DE TOLET (?) an Englishman, are emblazoned thus : *Gules, five fleurs-de-lis in saltire or; impaling Or, three bendlets azure.* On the partition line is placed a pastoral staff in pale argent.

At Paris on the gate of the Collége d' Harcourt were the arms of the founder, ROBERT D' HARCOURT, Bishop of COUTANCES : *Gules, two bars or, over all a pastoral staff in pale proper* (Plate I., fig. 3).

The seal of JEAN, Bishop of NANTES in 1419, bears his arms (*Argent, five bendlets . . .*) supported by three angels, one standing behind the shield, the others kneeling each on one knee on either side. A pastoral staff is placed upon the shield, with its head projecting above it upon the breast of the angel *tenant* (MORICE, *Mémoires pour Servir à l'Histoire Civile et Ecclésiastique de la Bretagne*, cxc.). The seal is engraved in our Plate XXXVI.

In the Duomo at ALESSANDRIA is an Episcopal tomb with these arms : *Bendy . . . on a chief . . . three estoiles. In another chief over all is a mitre.* AYMER CHAT, Bishop of BOLOGNA, added to his family arms (*. . . two cats passant . . .*) *a chief charged with* *two shin bones in saltire between a mitre and a pastoral staff.*

Above shield, mitre, and pastoral staff we generally find in modern times the flat ecclesiastical hat with its fretted and tasselled cords. This is, for bishops, of a green colour, and the number of tassels is properly six on either side, arranged 1. 2. 3. In the eighteenth century we constantly find another row of tassels assumed on each side, but properly this arrangement is the distinctive mark of the archi-episcopal hat, and in modern times there is a tendency in some places (it has not reached Great Britain) to revert to the old and proper custom.

Le Père MENÊTRIER speaks of this use of the hat as a modern invention :—" Le chapeau vert que les Archeveques et les Eveques mettent à present sur les Armoiries est un invention de ce siécle, on n'en verra des exemples aux precedens. C'est une imitation des Chapeaux des Cardinaux." But in *l'Usage des Armoiries* (p. 248) he corrects this statement to some extent :—" L'usage du Chapeau pour les Archeveques et Eveques vient de l'Espagne, ou il est en pratique depuis long temps, et plus frequent que la crosse et la mitre. Les Armoiries de Don Rodrigue Fernand de Narvaez, Evesque de Jaen, sont à Baëça de cette sorte depuis l' an 1400." The hat appears above the arms of Bishop SHERBORNE at CHICHESTER.

When, for any of the reasons already mentioned, the coronet is used by an ecclesiastic it is usually placed directly upon the upper edge of the shield, and along the whole of it. I have already referred to the use of their coronets by the ecclesiastical *Pairs de France*, and I have now to subjoin some other instances in which the coronet was used to denote a temporal dignity attached to the See. The Bishop of GENEVA had the rank of Prince, and bore the ducal coronet above his shield, under the episcopal hat. S. FRANÇOIS DE SALES, Bishop and Prince of GENEVA in 1625, bore : *Quarterly,* 1 *and* 4. *Gules, three bends argent and a lion entravaillé (or); 2 and 3. Azure, a cross argent between four fleurs-de-lis (or). Over all : Azure, two bars or, voided gules, between a crescent in chief, and two estoiles of the second, in centre and base.* (MAGNENEY, *Recueil des Armoiries,* planche 12.) The Bishops of GRENOBLE and VIVIERS also had the title of Prince. ALPHONSE DE LA CROIS, Bishop and Prince of GRENOBLE in 1616, bore : *Azure, a horse's head couped at the neck or, on a chief cousu gules, three crosslets argent.*

The Bishops of CAHORS, VALENCE, GAP, LE PUY, DIÉ, ALETH, LISIEUX, LIMOGES, AGEN, TULLE, and VELAY used the coronet of the dignity of count attached to their Sees. The seal of the Polish Bishop ZALUSCKI of SUCKAU bears his arms : *Gules, on a mount vert a ram passant argent* (JUNOZSA), surmounted by a coronet which is placed between the head of the pastoral staff and the hilt of the temporal sword ; above the coronet is the mitre, and, crowning all, is the hat, the cordons of which have ten tassels 1. 2. 3. 4. on either side.

In Italy ROBERTO ADIMARI, Bishop of MONTEFELTRO, to whose See the Emperor FREDERICK annexed the County of S. LEON, has, upon his tomb in the Abbey Church of SANT' ANASTASIO, his arms surmounted by a tiara, like the Papal one, but with only a single coronet.

The Bishop of PISTOJA often placed his arms on a kind of square mantling, charged with the arms of the city of PISTOJA (*Chequy argent and gules*); impaling those of PRATO (*Gules, semé of fleurs-de-lis or*) (*ante,* p. 90). (This coat has now the Angevin chief ; *Azure, three fleurs-de-lis or, between the four points of a label gules. Armi de Municipj Toscani,* p. 321. Firenze, 1864.) They are thus represented on the gate of the Episcopal palace at PRATO, and Dr RICCIULLI informs us that the custom originated in disputes between the Bishops and the Provosts of the Monastery of PRATO. The latter claimed to be exempt from the Episcopal jurisdiction, and to exercise episcopal rights in PRATO. The custom referred to appears to have originated at the beginning of the sixteenth century.

The mitre of the Bishops of DURHAM is represented as rising out of a ducal coronet, assumed in memory of their Palatinate jurisdiction which has now passed away. It is not at all probable that such a mitre was ever *worn* at DURHAM in the offices of the church, although I should not deem Mr W. H. ST. JOHN HOPE'S objection fatal—"the mitre was usually made to shut flat for portability, which the presence of a rigid metal circlet would effectually prevent being done" ("Paper on Seals of English Bishops." *Proceedings, Soc. Antiq. Lond.,* xi.). Such things as "standing mitres" were known even in England. Hear the learned Dr ROCK :—"he (the gold-smith) wrought those two thin, though solid sheets of which it was to be made up, out of the precious metal in such a way that they not only opened and shut with utmost readiness by means of gimmels, or hinges, light though strong in their frame, and nicely adjusted at the sides, but so bent themselves upon the wearer's venerable brow as to sit with ease upon it." (*Church of our Fathers,* ii., 106, and *see* the notes on his preceding page. There is no allusion to the DURHAM mitres ; the remarks are on the general subject.)

But on the seals of their secular office as Princes-Palatine the Bishops of DURHAM were represented as was customary in the case of great feudatories. The obverse of the seal had the effigy of the bishop seated ; on the reverse he was represented in armour on horse-back. The earliest known seal of this kind is that of Bishop THOMAS HATFIELD, 1345. (*Catalogue of Seals in the British Museum*, No. 2486.) On it he is seen in full armour with sword, and shield charged with his arms (*Azure, a chevron between three lions rampant or*) on his head is a helm coroneted, and surmounted by a mitre adorned with a panache. The bishop is mounted on a horse galloping to the sinister and caparisoned with his arms as above. His successor Bishop JOHN FORD-HAM (1381) is similarly represented, but the figure is turned to the dexter and is vested in a coat of his arms. The helmet is coroneted, and bears the mitre out of which issues the crest of an eagle rising. (*Brit. Mus. Cat.*, No. 2488.) In the MS. *Armorial de Geldre* of the fourteenth century, his arms are given as " L' Evêque de Durham " (*Sable, a chevron between three crosses moline or*). The helmet above the *couché* shield has mantlings of sable lined with ermine, and supports a coronet of the usual size, of six floriations (two whole flowers and two halves being visible) out of which rises a mitre. Between the two points is a ball, on which stands the crest : an eagle rising, in its beak an escroll with the words " *Gloria Deo.*" (I have engraved it on Plate V., fig. 1.) The mitre is omitted from the crested and coroneted helms of his successors Bishops SKIRLAW, LANGLEY, and NEVILLE. (SKIR-LAW'S crest is a demi-angel, that of LANGLEY a panache, that of NEVILLE a bull's head. (*Brit. Mus. Cat. of Seals*, Nos. 2489, 2491, 2492.) The subsequent bishops used on their palatinate seals a plumed mitre with a coroneted helm. But though this is so, it must be observed that on his *ecclesiastical* seals the bishop is never represented as wearing any but the ordinary mitre without a coronet ; and I incline to the opinion that we may, therefore, consider the coronet rather as being an adjunct to the helmet (in fact the ordinary crest - coronet), than as a portion of the mitre. The only evidence in the opposite direction which appears to me of any value, is afforded by the seals of the sheriffs of the palatinate,

JOHN DE MENEVILLE, 1339 (notice that this is anterior to the date of Bishop HATFIELD), and ROBERT LATON, in 1385 ; on both of these a mitre issuing from a coronet (above an initial or initials) is the sole charge ; they are engraved in Mr LONGSTAFFE'S paper on the " Old Official Heraldry of DURHAM," in the *Herald and Genealogist*, vol. viii., p. 136.

It is worthy of remark that in the *Armorial de Geldre*, referred to above, the next achievement is that of HENRY DESPENSER, the warlike Bishop of NORWICH, 1370-1406, whose helmet is surmounted by a mitre out of which rises his crest of a griffin's head and wings (Plate V., fig. 3). There is no coronet in this case, though one was used about this time with the DESPENSER crest (THOMAS, Earl of GLOUCESTER used it in 1397, but HUGH LE DESPENSER in 1385 used only a wreath (see the *Cat. of Seals, Brit. Mus.*, ii., No. 9280).

The German Prince-Bishops, who used many helmets and crests with their shield of arms, frequently made the central one, or the first in dignity, to be a golden helm bearing a mitre for the See ; but I think I have rarely, if ever, seen the helm coroneted under such circumstances, though usually a cushion of crimson velvet with golden tassels is interposed between the helmet and the mitre. (For an example see Plate XVI.) But in Germany some of the most ancient and noble families use a mitre as a crest, and in that case the crest-coronet is sometimes found interposed. Thus the Princes of FÜRSTENBERG used as the crest of their County of WERDENBERG, a mitre gules, the orphreys or, set upon a coroneted helm of gold with its lambrequins of *red* and *white*. In this, and in other like cases, the arms to which a mitre-crest belongs will generally be found to contain as the charge a gonfanon, or church-banner. In the FÜRSTENBERG coat quoted above, the arms of WERDENBERG are : *Gules, a gonfanon argent.*

Similarly the Counts of VELDKIRCH, or FELDKIRCH,
bore : *Or, a gonfanon gules*, with a mitre *gules* as crest.
The Counts of MONTFORT (whose possessions were
bought as early as 1375 by LEOPOLD of AUSTRIA)
bore : *Argent, a gonfanon gules ringed or*, with the
same crest. (Plate V., fig. 6.) The Counts of TETT-
NANG, of the same stock as the Counts of VELDKIRCH
and MONTFORT, used the same arms and crest as
the latter. Sometimes the crest is the demi-figure
of a man, or a woman, mitred. These bearings admit
of a simple explanation. They were originally
assumed to denote that the families using them were
the hereditary *advocati, vogts,* or *avoués,* who held
certain seigneuries as fiefs from Bishoprics and monasteries by military tenure, with the obligation of
leading to war the contingents which the ecclesiastical
princes were bound to furnish. The mitres in such
crests are easily distinguished from those borne by
ecclesiastics, being usually of the tinctures of the arms ;
or, as in some cases, charged with the arms of the
bearers, and moreover the peaks are often surmounted
by the tufts of feathers which are so frequently found
ornamenting early German crests. (*See* the crest of
SAARWERDEN, Plate V., No. 2.) Similar officials in
France were the *vidames ;* the officers generally of high
nobility, to whom was committed also the duty of
exercising certain of the other temporal powers of the
Bishopric or Abbey to which temporal *seigneuries* were
attached. This was considered an office of high dignity,
and was usually hereditary in a noble family. A special
coronet of gold ornamented at equal intervals with four
crosses *patées* was, or might be, used by the *vidames.*
I think it possible that the introduction of the cross
patée into the Royal Crown of England by the pious
HENRY VI. may have been intended to denote his
devotion to and desire to protect the Church. The most

important of the Vidames (Vice-domini) were those of REIMS, AMIENS, CHARTRES, CHÂLONS, CAMBRAY, and LAON. The family of DE PREUILLY, in Touraine, of which the head was "*avoué, et chanoine-honoraire*" of the Chapter of S. MARTIN DE TOURS, bore for arms : *Or, between four alerions azure a man's arm couped, in fess, vested gules, the hand clenched proper; pendant from the wrist a maniple ermine, fringed and bordered argent, and charged with a cross patée of the third.* (Plate II., fig. 2.) The dignity of "Vidame d'Amiens" was held by the family of AILLY, Marquesses of ANNEBAUT.

The arms of "Le Vidame DE CHARTRES," JEAN I. DE VENDÔME (ancient), are given in the MS. *Armorial de Gilles le Bouvier, dit le Héraut Berry ;* (France No. 90.) *Argent, a chief gules over all a lion rampant azure.* (It will be remembered that this title was afterwards held by the Ducs de ST. SIMON who claimed a descent from the old Counts of VERMANDOIS. The author of the gossiping *Mémoires* was known by this title during the life-time of his father). The arms of "Le Vidame DE LAON" are given in the *Roll of Arms* of the fourteenth century, known as PLANCHÉS *Roll*, as follows : *Chequy, argent and azure, on a chief or, three pallets gules* (No. 448 of Mr GREENSTREET'S reprint in the *Genealogist*, 2nd series, vol. iv.).

The dignity of Advocate, or Valvasor, of the Bishopric of STRASSBURG was vested in the four noble families of ANDLAU, HOHENSTEIN, LANDSPERG, and TREGER, out of which one person was elected to fill the office. (SCHILTER, *de Feudo Militari*, § 20. *See* also the curious treatise of ANT. MATTHÆUS, *De Nobilitate ;* . . . *de Advocatis Ecclesiæ*, 1686. There is an "Elenchus Capitum" thereof in BURGERMEISTER, *Bibliotheca Eques- tris*, vol. ii., p. 1123. Ulm, 1720.)

In England the Lords of BERKELEY, great benefactors of the Church, and (*circa* 1142) founders of the Monastery

of S. AUGUSTINE at BRISTOL, used the mitre as a crest.
As in many German instances, it is charged with the
family arms (*Gules, a chevron between ten crosses patées
argent*), and this mitre is still the crest of the Earls of
BERKELEY, and of the Barons FITZHARDINGE of
BERKELEY. On the carved stalls in Bristol Cathedral
the arms of the family are supported by two mermaids,
and surmounted by a mitre (without helmet or wreath)
but the mitre is not charged with arms (*see* my
" Heraldry of Bristol Cathedral," in the *Herald and
Genealogist*, vol. iv., p. 289).

Except as a heraldic ornament, the use of the mitre
by the Bishops of the Anglican Communion had become
obsolete ; but of late years, it, with the use of the
pastoral staff has undergone a revival which is gradually
spreading. The majority of the English, Scottish, and
Colonial Bishops use at this date the pastoral staff.
Several English, many Colonial, and all the Scottish
Bishops use the mitre ; some also use the cope and
pectoral cross as well as the Episcopal ring.

The time that has elapsed between the discontinuance
and the resumption of these Episcopal ornaments is much
less than is supposed. It is said that the coronation of
George III. was the last at which the mitre was actually
used. The use of the full wig led to its discontinuance, as
it did to that of the cope, at DURHAM. But the effigies of
several of the English sixteenth and seventeenth century
Bishops are mitred on their tombs. Mitres of silver gilt
were suspended over the tombs of Bishops MORLEY, and
MEWS (1684 and 1706), in WINCHESTER CATHEDRAL.
The mitre worn by Bishop SEABURY, the first Bishop of
the now large and flourishing Episcopal Church in the
United States of America, is still preserved in TRINITY
COLLEGE, HARTFORD.

The heraldic mitre is often extremely ill drawn ; and
most of those worn in the Roman Church have diverged

greatly from the ancient and better shape. When revived by Bishops of the Anglican Communion there has usually been a reversion to the lower and more artistic, as well as more ancient form, instead of to the often bulbous, and nearly always much too high, shape adopted by prelates of the Roman obedience.

The mitre of S. THOMAS, Archbishop of CANTERBURY, formerly in the Treasury of the Cathedral of SENS, was presented by the Archbishop of that See to Cardinal WISEMAN. "It is low and angular; composed of white silk, embroidered with golden flowers and scroll work, with a broad band of red silk down the centre and round the margin." This mitre is engraved in DE CAUMONT, *Abécédaire d'Archéologie;* and in VIOLLET LE DUC, *Dictionaire du Mobilier Français.* Another still at SENS is of silver tissue with scroll work, and orphreys of gold tissue. The mitres referred to above as existing in the Museum at Stockholm, are moderate in height, and of the usual mediæval type.

CHAPTER VI.

ARCHBISHOPS, LEGATES, PRIMATES, PATRIARCHS

—The *Pallium*—Exceptional uses of it—The Archi-episcopal Cross—Legates—Temporal Dignities—Primates and Patriarchs—The Double-traversed Cross—The Archi-episcopal Hat—The Patriarchal Tiara, etc.

AN Archbishop is usually a metropolitan prelate having under his jurisdiction one or more suffragan diocesan Bishops whose Sees form his province. (In the Roman Catholic Church an archbishop has sometimes, chiefly in Central Italy and Sicily, no suffragans; *e.g.*, UDINE, FERRARA, LUCCA, and PERUGIA have none. The Roman Catholic Archi-Episcopal See of GLASGOW has no suffragans.) Our present use of the title seems to correspond with that of very early times. But later the title appears to have been appropriated to the patriarchal dignity, and the Council of CHALCEDON in 451 applied it to S. LEO, Patriarch of ROME, as they had already given it to the Patriarch of CONSTANTINOPLE. Afterwards it was applied to the Bishops in most of the capital cities of the Empire. Among the Latins, ISIDORE of SEVILLE is the first who mentions it, and hence it is concluded that the dignity did not exist in the West before the time of CHARLEMAGNE.

It is the privilege of an Archbishop to confirm the election of his suffragans; and either himself to consecrate them, or to entrust that office to prelates of his nomination. He has the right to convoke a Provincial Council (with the Royal Licence in countries where the Church is not free from State control) and to preside over, and regulate, its deliberations. In later times

Archbishops (and a few Bishops by special privilege, *v.* p. 116) have alone the right to wear the *pallium* conferred by the Papal See (as to which hereafter). In their Province the archi-episcopal cross is borne before them, as a sign of their dignity, except in the few dioceses which are specially privileged, and of which the bishops themselves have by grant from the Papal See the same right of using the cross. For instance, the Prince-Bishop of BAMBERG was exempt from any archi-episcopal control. As himself "Primate of Germany" he had the right to the use of the Archi-episcopal or Primatial cross; and also to the *pallium*, for which he paid fifty thousand livres into the Papal Exchequer; the Bishop of DOL in Brittany had the privilege of using the cross in his own diocese, unless the Archbishop of TOURS, or a Papal Legate, were present. (The privilege was conferred by Pope ALEXANDER VI. on Bishop THOMAS JARNY in 1402, in memory of the fact that the See of DOL had been archi-episcopal until reduced by Pope INNOCENT III.) The Bishops of PAVIA and LUCCA had also the privilege of using the cross; and it is employed by the Bishop of FUNCHAL in MADEIRA, as a memorial that his See was once archi-episcopal. The cross was, after the ninth century, the distinguishing mark of the Papal Legates; later it was granted as a personal favour to certain Primates; about the twelfth century its use was permitted to all Metropolitans, and the privilege was extended finally to all archbishops by Pope GREGORY IX. as a distinguishing mark of their dignity, and it is placed in pale behind their shields of arms. Long before this, however, both in Britain and on the continent it was the custom for archbishops to use a staff headed with a small cross instead of the ordinary pastoral staff. This is the staff which appears in the shields of the arms of the Sees of CANTERBURY, YORK (ancient), ARMAGH, and DUBLIN. (Plates XX. and XXVI.) According to modern usage the cross borne before an archbishop is a crucifix placed on the summit of a staff, and in processions the figure of the Saviour is turned towards the prelate. It must be remarked however that the archiepiscopal cross is not borne by, but *before*, the archbishop ; and that in the sacred offices the archbishop uses the ordinary crozier, or pastoral staff, like any diocesan bishop. But it became the custom, in and after the thirteenth century, to represent the archbishop as holding in his left hand the cross. After the year 1250 the Archbishops of CANTERBURY are always so represented. In the Province of YORK, Archbishop GEOFFREY LUDIIAM (1258-1265), is the first on whose seal we find the archi-episcopal cross. The Pope, though Bishop of ROME, does not at any time use the pastoral staff, or the archi-episcopal cross. At pontifical offices and consecrations he bears a *ferula*, or staff of gold, surmounted by a small cross *patée*. (MONTAULT, *l'Année Liturgique à Rome. See* also ROCK'S *Church of Our Fathers*, ii., 205, *et seq.*, and *see* below in Chapter on Popes.) Some archbishops had the special privilege of using their cross even beyond the limits of their province. Thus the Archbishop of NAZARETH had the right to use it everywhere ; the Archbishop of TOLEDO throughout Spain ; and the Archbishop of RAVENNA within three miles of Rome.

The Archbishop of CANTERBURY, as " Primate of all England," had the right of using his cross even within the bounds of the Province of YORK. The Archbishop of YORK claimed, but vainly, to have equal rights in the Province of CANTERBURY ; and in the continual contentions for the primacy between the two archi-episcopal Sees this matter of the right to use the cross is continually cropping up. In 1279 Archbishop PECKHAM excommunicated all who should supply provisions to the Archbishop of YORK, if the latter persisted in using

Henri Charles de Cambout-Coislin, Prince-Bishop of Metz, 1697-1732.

the crosier during his stay in the Province of CANTER-BURY. The contest for precedency, which first became acute in the reign of HENRY I. and gave rise to much unseemly disputing, sometimes led even to acts of personal violence between the occupants of the respective Sees. We read of both claiming the same seat of honour, and of one sitting down in the lap of the other. An interesting summary of these early contests for precedence between the Archbishops of CANTERBURY and YORK, will be found in that invaluable store-house of facts (*Notes and Queries*, 2nd series, xi., pp. 64, 176).

The contest was finally settled in 1353, the place of honour on the right hand of the King being accorded to the Archbishop of CANTERBURY ; while the Primate of YORK was allowed the seat on the left hand. In procession their crosses were to be carried together if the road was wide enough ; that of CANTERBURY on the right, that of YORK on the left hand side of the way. If the road became narrow, or if on entering a building there was not room for both to pass together, CANTER-BURY had the right of precedence ; as also in all provincial councils, and public ceremonials throughout the Kingdom. The Archbishop of CANTERBURY has the title of "*Primate of all England*," while the Archbishop of YORK is styled "*Primate of England.*" The title "Angliæ primas" first appears on a seal (circa 1181) of RICHARD, Archbishop of CANTERBURY (1174-1184). In the other province the earliest known seal with the same inscription is that of Archbishop WALTER GIFFARD (1266-1279). (*See* the *Catalogue of Seals in the British Museum*, vol. i., Nos. 1184 and 2308). A like distinction is made in the case of the archi-episcopal Sees of Ireland ; the Archbishop of ARMAGH being the "*Primate of all Ireland*," the Archbishop of DUBLIN, "*Primate of Ireland*;" but both Archbishops have the right to use the primatial cross over the whole of Ireland.

In the preceding chapter instances have been given in which, in early times bishops placed the mitre and pastoral staff, the ensigns of their dignity within the shield upon their personal arms. A like custom obtained with regard to the archi-episcopal cross. HUMBERT DE VILLARS, Archbishop of LYONS in 1340, bore: *Bendy of six or and gules over all a crozier in pale azure.* Archbishop PHILIP DE TUREY of the same See in 1400 bore: *Gules, an archi-episcopal cross in pale behind a saltire or* (Plate I., fig. 1). This cross is also represented *within* the shield of arms of BALTHAZAR DE GERENTE, Archbishop of EMBRUN, in 1550, as may be seen in his Cathedral.

Recently I observed a curious instance of archiepiscopal arms in the cloister of the Church of the AUGUSTINS at TOULOUSE, now used as a Museum of Antiquities, where are sculptured the arms of BERTRAND DE ROUERGUE, Archbishop of TOULOUSE, who died in 1474; they are: . . . *on a bend . . . three roses all within a bordure . . . thereon six roses . . .* Behind the shield stands the archi-episcopal cross with a single traverse; and above, and on either side of it, is a doctor's biretta. The three birettas denote the Archbishop's degrees as Doctor of Civil Law; Doctor of Canon Law; and Master (Doctor) of Theology.

In the Latin Church the distinguishing vestment of an archbishop is the *pallium*, or pall. This corresponded with the *omophorion* of ecclesiastics in the Greek Church, and both alike were probably derived from a reduced survival of the old Roman *toga* worn as an official badge by civil magistrates. In the Greek Church the *omophorion* formerly consisted of a long band of woollen stuff; it is now usually of silk, embroidered with crosses, and passes once round the neck, its ends falling both before and behind to at least the level of the knees. Originally worn by Patriarchs, it is now a vestment common to all of the Episcopal order. It was a recognised vestment as early as the sixth century; and among the mosaics of that date in the Church of St. Sophia at Constantinople may still be seen representations of bishops of the fourth century wearing *omophoria* with coloured crosses. Dr Rock, in his learned work *The Church of Our Fathers*, vol. ii., p. 127, *et seq.*, tells us that the pall in use in the West in the sixth century was of the same shape, viz., "a long straight band, in width somewhat broader than now, and so put on, that being thrown loosely about the neck of the bishop, it hung half-way down his breast and back, and met upon the left shoulder in a manner that allowed one end to droop before, the other behind, his person, as may be seen on SS. Maximianus and Ecclesius, each in his day Archbishop of Ravenna." Dr Rock's reference here is to the mosaics (*c.* 547) which still remain in the Church of S. Vitale at Ravenna, and they are figured by him in his vol. i., p. 319. The writer on the subject in the *Dictionary of Christian Antiquities* considers it open to doubt whether the vestment here represented is a *pallium;* but a personal inspection of the mosaic satisfied me that it is. (I do not know what else it could be.) Each has, however, but a single cross visible. But in any case, just such a *pallium* is worn by Pope Paschal in the ninth century mosaic in the Church of Sta. Maria in Trastevere (*see* Didron, *Christian Iconography*, i., p. 77, fig. 26). "By the beginning of the ninth century the pall, though it still kept its olden shape of a long stole, began to be put on in a way slightly different from its first fashion; for instead of both ends falling at the side from the left shoulder, they fell down at the middle, one in front from the chest to the feet, the other just as low behind on the back of the archbishop; this we perceive from an interesting mosaic still at Rome. (The allusion here is to one of the mosaics in the apse of S. John Lateran. In it S. PETER gives a *pallium* to Pope LEO III., who, however, has one on already.) . This mosaic is engraved in DIDRON, *Christian Iconography*, vol. i., p. 82, fig. 28. S. PETER himself is represented as wearing the *pallium* and having three keys in his lap. With the left hand he gives the standard to CHARLEMAGNE. That the mosaic was contemporary with the Pope and Emperor represented, is proved by the fact that both wear the rectangular nimbus ; not the circular one which was reserved for the departed. (Pope PASCAL, who wears the *pallium*, has the square nimbus in a mosaic in STA. CECILIA in Trastevere. DIDRON, i., p. 26.) Dr ROCK goes on to explain how this arrangement, and a subsequent one, were practically carried out. But eventually, instead of being made in one long straight band like a stole, necessitating much arranging and pinning, the *pallium* was woven in its present shape— "a flat circular band, some three inches in breadth. from which hung down two straight bands put opposite each other, about a yard in length and as broad as the circle." At the present day the pendants scarcely exceed a foot in length, but formerly reached nearly to the feet of the wearer ; each of the pendants is weighted at the end with lead covered with black silk. It bore on it at first two crosses *patées* usually of bright purple colour, but sometimes red, at the extremities of the pendants ; afterwards it had four, now it has six, of black silk edged with cord. (The number, however, varies considerably, as will be seen by any good series of archiepiscopal seals ; five are *visible* on the pall of Archbishop WILLIAM WICKWANE of YORK (1279-1285), many more on that of Archbishop ALEXANDER NEVILLE, 1374 (*see* Mr PORTER'S paper on the "York Seals," in *Proceedings of the Soc. of Antiq. of London*, 1890). I counted no less than thirteen crosses incised on the visible portion of the *pallium* represented on the statue of Archbishop CAPPONI (1681) in the Campo Santo at Pisa. The statue of S. GREGORY at Chartres has a *pallium* with five visible crosses.

In the arms of CANTERBURY, YORK - ANCIENT, ARMAGH, and DUBLIN, the crosses are *patée-fitchées*. The pall was fastened to the chasuble with pins of gold with jewelled heads, and it has been thought that the *crosses patée-fitchées* originated in them. This is, however, doubtful, and is not referred to by Dr ROCK. A curious survival of the ancient shape of the *pallium* is to be found in the fact that one side of the pall is single, the other double, which was the result of the original manner of folding the straight stole-like vestment.

Much curious information as to the manner of conferring the *pallium* may be found in MONTAULT, *L'Année Liturgique à Rome*, and in Dr ROCK'S valuable work, and to these I refer the curious reader. The *pallium*, which was at first only given as a honorary distinction, became after the seventh century a badge the acceptance of which implied the acknowledgement of the supremacy of the See of Rome (see *Dictionary of Christian Antiquities*).

In the decree of the somewhat doubtful council said to have been held at Rome in 679, under Pope AGATHO, to consider the affairs of the English Church, the following words occur — " quos Archiepiscopus, qui pro tempore ab hac apostolica sede pallii honore decoratur, provehat," etc. (Given in HADDAN and STUBBS, vol. iii., p. 113.)

On St. Agnes' Day in each year two purely white lambs are laid on the high altar of the church of S. AGNES *fuori le Mure*, near Rome, and solemnly blessed ; they are then carried with scrupulous care and much ceremony to the Vatican, where they receive the Pope's blessing ; after which they are entrusted to the charge of some

nuns, who carefully rear them, and of their wool manu-
facture the *pallia*. These again are solemnly blessed in
S. PETER'S, and rest in a casket for a while on the tomb
of the Apostles, after which they are laid up in a reliquary,
ready to be sent "de corpore beati Petri" to the objects
of Papal favour, to be worn by them on certain high
festivals in the performance of Divine service.

The *pallium* is conferred upon each prelate succeeding to the archi-episcopal dignity, and (formerly at
least) in return for the compulsory offering of a large
sum of money (*vide* p. 109). By special privilege the
right to use the *pallium* has been conferred on a few
Bishoprics :—in BAMBERG, AUTUN, DOL, LE PUY
(CLERMONT?), MARSEILLES, LUCCA, PAVIA, VERONA,
and the suburban Bishopric of OSTIA (the Cardinal-
Bishop of which See always consecrates the newly-
elected Pope). In the case of a perpetual privilege the
occupant of the See assumes the *pallium* on consecration, but in all other cases personal application has to
be made for it by each successive archbishop. According
to the regulations of the Holy See its possession is now
necessary in order to the validity of many archi-episcopal
acts. An archbishop who has not received the *pallium*
is not entitled to perform any pontifical function, to use
the archi-episcopal cross, to confer Holy Orders, to
consecrate churches, or to summon a council, even
though translated from a diocese where he previously
had the right to wear it. Except by special privilege,
rarely accorded, an archbishop can only wear the
pallium within the limits of his province ; and its use is
limited to the mass of the greater Festivals, consecrations
and ordinations, and the anniversaries of the wearer's
birth and consecration. If an archbishop die within
his province he is buried with the pall round his shoulders ;
if elsewhere it is folded up and placed beneath his
head.

The *pallium* is now conferred upon rare occasions upon simple bishops, as a special mark of Papal favour, and recognition of long and good service in the Episcopate. It was so conferred on August 8, 1892 on the good Bishop of BRUGES, JOHN JOSEPH FAIET, who had filled that See for a quarter of a century. The ceremony took place in the Cathedral, and the Bishop received the *pallium* from the hands of the Papal nuncio. A French Bishop, the Bishop of CLERMONT, similarly received it some years ago.

The *pallium* appears as the principal charge in the arms of the archi-episcopal Sees of CANTERBURY, YORK (ancient), ARMAGH, and DUBLIN. (*See* Plates XX. and XXVI.) In all these cases the crosses are *patées fitchées.*

The arms of the French See of EMBRUN are, *Gules, a pallium between a mitre and a pastoral staff proper* (Plate I., fig. 12). The present Roman Catholic Archbishop EYRE of GLASGOW has assumed as the arms of his See : *Gules, a pallium argent fimbriated or, thereon four crosses patées sable.* These impaled with his Grace's personal coat : *Argent, on a chevron sable three quatrefoils or,* are engraved from his book-plate, on Plate XIII., fig. 1. The external ornaments are the Cross of the ORDER OF S. JOHN ; the primatial cross (with a double traverse) and the archi-episcopal hat, of its ancient shape.

The arms assumed by the late ENGELBERT (STERCKX), Cardinal-Archbishop of MECHLIN (MALINES), and Primate of Belgium, are a curious, perhaps unique, instance of the use of the *pallium* as a personal bearing. They are, *Or, a pallium accosted by two hearts proper. Over all, on a fess azure, the words "* PAX VOBIS," *of the field* (Plate I., fig. 10).

By modern custom the *pallium* is very frequently used as an external ornament of the armorial bearings of archbishops. I noticed this use in several cases among the arms of the contributors to the cost of the mosaics of the tomb of Pope PIO IX. in the Basilica of SAN LORENZO *fuori le Mure* at Rome. In the FRAUEN-KIRCHE at Munich I noticed the monument of LOTHAIR, Baron VON GEBSATTEL, first Archbishop of the See of MUNICH-FREISING (1818-1846). His shield of arms (*Gules, the head of an ibex couped at the neck argent horned sable*) has the *pallium* so placed as to lie along the top of the shield with a pendant on either side (Plate XIII., fig. 3). The legatine cross (with *double* transverse) is placed behind the shield, and the archi-episcopal hat, with ten tassels (1. 2. 3. 4.) on each side, surmounts the whole. On the tomb of PHILIP FONTANA, Archbishop of RAVENNA, in the Church of SAN BARTOLOMEO at FERRARA, the *pallium* is arranged round the shield like the collar, or *cordon*, of an Order of Knighthood. (The archi-episcopal cross is placed in pale behind it, accosted by a mitre and by the head of the pastoral staff.)

Usually, the *pallium* is placed in the chief of the oval cartouche (in which the arms of ecclesiastics are generally depicted) with a pendant falling over the central line of the shield. The arms of the present Archbishop (BAUSA?) of FLORENCE (*Azure, on a fèss or, three roses gules in chief an estoile of the second*) are thus depicted in the Duomo, with the *pallium* over all in chief. The cartouche has as external ornaments the double-traversed cross and the archi-episcopal hat. At MILAN the arms of the Archbishop (*Gules, three hunting horns, 2. 1. and a bordure or*) similarly ornamented with the *pallium*, are depicted on the front of the palace in the Piazza Fontana. The cartouche also bears the double-traversed cross, mitre, and green archi-episcopal hat.

In the Church of SS. GIOVANNI E PAOLO at Rome I observed the tomb of Cardinal MACELÚ, Bishop of OSTIA, who died in 1860. His arms (*Per fess in chief . . . a hand erect proper, and in base Chequy argent and gules*) are placed within á shield; the *pallium* is

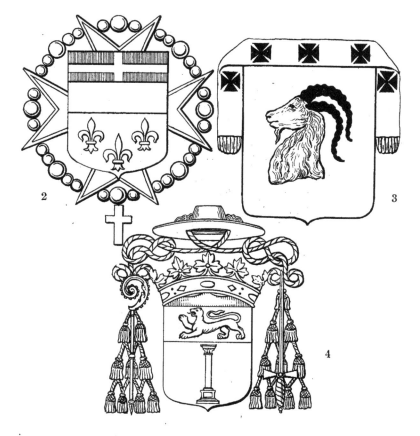

1. Archbishop Eyre (of Glasgow).   2. Knight of S. John (Chevalier d'Estaing).
3. Archbishop Gebsattel of Freysing and Munich.
4. de Lionne, Bp. of Gap.

spread along the top, and the centre pendant falls as usual on the central part of the chief. The cross, with double traverse, is placed behind the shield, and the red hat surmounts the whole. The visitor to Rome will find numerous examples of the like custom. But I notice that there are several recent examples in which the *pallium* is placed, somewhat like a motto band, *beneath* the shield of a modern prelate. (I think there was in 1892 an example in the arms of a Cardinal fixed outside his titular church, STA. PRASSEDE.) The new arrangement is not one worthy of imitation.

Except in Rome, where the use of coronets is forbidden to ecclesiastics, archbishops who have the rank of prince, count, etc., place the coronet above the shield of arms. When MENÊTRIER wrote in 1673 this, so far as France was concerned, was a modern innovation. He says : " On ne trouvera pas avant cent ans qu' aucun Prélat en France ait mis la couronne sur ces Armoiries, non pas mesme les princes " (*l'Usage des Armoiries*, p. 193).

In France, as we have already seen the Archbishop was also Duke of REIMS, and " Pair de France." The Archbishop of PARIS has had, since its conference in 1674, the title of Duc de S. CLOUD, and accordingly timbres his shield with the ducal coronet. Under the old *régime* the possession of this duchy entitled him as " *Pair de France*," to use around his shield the ermine-lined mantle *armoyée* which was the privilege of the *Pairie*.

The Archbishops of EMBRUN, ARLES, and TAREN-TAISE—(the last is no longer Archi-episcopal, and the two former are united to AIX), had the title of Prince, and used the ducal coronet. As an example we may cite the arms of GEORGES D'AUBUSSON DE FEUILLADE, who was made Archbishop and Prince of EMBRUN in the year 1649. In 1668 at the request of King LOUIS XIV. he resigned his See. The King to repay the obligation made him Bishop of METZ, "et lui donna le brévet du nom et du rang d'Archévêque ;" (I presume with the sanction of the Holy See, but?). He was Ambassador of France in Spain, and received there the ORDER OF THE ST. ESPRIT. (*See* LA POINTE, *Chevaliers de l'Ordre du St. Esprit*, plate 4' where his shield of arms : *Or, a cross ancrée gules*, is ensigned with the ducal coronet, the archi-episcopal cross and hat, and surrounded by the grand-cordon of the ORDER OF THE ST. ESPRIT.

I may here mention that while the lay members of the ORDER OF THE ST. ESPRIT were entitled to surround their arms with the *collars* of the ORDERS OF ST. MICHAEL (nearest the shield) and of the ST. ESPRIT with their pendant badges—the clerical members used only the *grand-cordon* of the ST. ESPRIT, the ribbon with its badge. Plates XIV., fig. 1., and XVIII., fig. 1. There are, however, in LA POINTE two instances in which the collars are substituted for the *cordon*, or ribbon. One is the case of LOUIS LE BARBIER, Chancellor of the Order in 1645, Bishop and Duke of LANGRES in 1655. His arms (*Azure, a chevron between three crosses patée-fitcheés or*) are surrounded by the collars of both Orders, and have the ducal coronet and mantle as well as the Episcopal hat. (LA POINTE, *Chevaliers de l'Ordre du St. Esprit*, plate *c.*) The other case is that of HARDOUIN DE PÉRÉFIXE DE BEAUMONT, Bishop of RODEZ in 1648, and Chancellor of the Order in 1661. He held the Archbishopric of PARIS from 1662-1671. His arms are given in LA POINTE, plate *h*, and are : *Azure, nine estoiles of five points* (3. 3. 2. 1.) *argent*. The shield is surrounded by both collars, with their badges. The archiepiscopal cross is behind the shield, and the archiepiscopal hat surmounts the whole. In GUIGARD, (*Armorial du Bibliophile*, ii., 156), his arms are thus represented from his book covers. The only difference

1. Descoubleaux, Archbishop of Bordeaux.

2. Harlay, Archbishop of Rouen (1633).

is that, in these latter, the ends of the cross are represented properly as ending in *fleurs-de-lis*, a privilege of
the See of PARIS. (It will be noticed that he has not the
coronet and mantle, as his tenure of office was anterior
to the creation of the Duchy of ST. CLOUD, *vide supra*,
p. 119). We may mention here that *le grand Aumônier*
was the first ecclesiastical dignitary of the kingdom in
France, and Bishop of the Court ; and that the dignity of
Commandeur des Ordres du Roi was inseparable from his
office. He therefore might use both collars.

The Archbishops of LYONS and VIENNE were Counts,
and used the coronet of that rank. The Archbishop of
ROUEN placed above his shield of arms two coronets,
that of a duke to the right, that of a count to the left of
the shaft of the cross, whose head, double-traversed,
appeared above them (MAGNENEY, plate 8, and our own
Plate XIV., fig. 2). FRANÇOIS DE HARLAY so bore them
in 1633, with the device " *Deo Medio.* "

The Archbishop of LUCCA, as Count of the Empire,
used the coronet of that rank. The Bishops of LUCCA
became Archbishops in 1726 ; but even as Bishops, they
were privileged to use the *pallium* and the cross (*v. ante*,
p. 109). The Archbishops of MAINZ, CÖLN, and
TRIERS, as Prince-Electors of the Holy Roman Empire,
used the electoral hat, or princely crown, above their
shield of arms, and at times added the princely mantle
around it (*see* Plate XV., fig. 2), and the arms of the
Prince-Bishop of Metz, HENRI CHARLES DE CAMBOUT-
COISLIN in 1697 have the princely coronet and crest in
our Plate XII.

The seal of MAURICE ADOLPHUS, Duke of SAXONY,
Archbishop of PHARSALIA *in partibus*, and Bishop of
LEITMERITZ in Bohemia (1733-1759), bears the Saxon
arms surmounted by the princely coronet between the
mitre and the head of the pastoral staff. The archi-
episcopal cross is placed in pale behind the shield, and

the whole is surmounted by the archi-episcopal hat
(GLAFEY, *Sigilla*, tab. ·i., fig. 3). A rare Thaler of
FRANCIS ANTONY, Count von HARRACH, Prince-Archbishop of SALZBURG (1709-1727), bears, in 1723, a cartouche of the following arms :—*Per fess ; in chief the
arms of* SALZBURG (*ante* p. 87) ; *in base those
of* HARRACH : *Gules, three ostrich feathers in pairle
argent, their stems united in a golden ball.* The shield is
crowned with the closed crown of a Prince of the
Empire, above which rises the head of the cross ; the
naked sword of the temporal power, and the pastoral
staff are in saltire behind the shield, and the archi-
episcopal hat above all. (KÖHLER, *Münz-Belustigung*,
iv., 121.)

I have observed a peculiar arrangement of personal
and official arms employed by Archbishop BERESFORD.
The personal arms and supporters are used, and
above the shield is an oval cartouche containing the
arms of his See, impaling the personal arms ; this
is surmounted by an " Archi-episcopal " mitre (that is,
according to a custom which has grown up in these
kingdoms since the seventeenth century, and is unknown
elsewhere, a mitre rising out of a ducal coronet, or open
crown). It is hardly needful to say that as a mark of
ecclesiastical dignity there is properly no difference whatever between the mitre of an Archbishop and that of a
Bishop, and that this assumption of a coronet has
really no sufficient authority to justify it. There is not
the slightest authority, so far as the seals go—nor, in fact
any other mediæval evidence, in support of the commonly
received notion that Archbishops are entitled to wear a
coronet round the mitre. Throughout the whole series
of seals and monuments, from the Norman Conquest
to the Reformation, and beyond, the archi-episcopal
mitre in no way differs from that of an ordinary bishop.
(Mr W. H. ST. JOHN HOPE, Assistant-Secretary, S.A.

Paper on the "Seals of English Bishops," *Proceedings of Soc. Antiq.*, London, 1887, xi., p. 271.) The helms upon which mitres are sometimes placed in German heraldry are often timbred with the usual crest coronet. Usually when this is so, a cushion is interposed between the coronet and the mitre ; but even where it is omitted the coronet is *an adjunct to the helmet*—not an integral portion of the mitre itself (*cf. ante* pp. 102, 103).

METROPOLITAN.

The dignity of Metropolitan appears to have arisen, as some other ecclesiastical dignities did, out of the civil organisation of the Empire. As in each political province there was a metropolis, a head city, to which resort was had for justice and other important affairs, and which usually possessed a Christian Church excelling the rest in opulence and ability to promote the common interest, it was natural that the prelate whose See was in the metropolis should become the president on occasions when Bishops were assembled in his metropolis. The civil metropolis became also the ecclesiastical metropolis, and thus (as we see from the canons of the Council of CHALCEDON), CÆSAREA, not JERUSALEM, was the seat of the Metropolitan in Palestine. When, as in the middle of the second century, Synods became matters of necessity, they would be naturally held in the metropolis and under the presidence of its Bishop. This however was not the invariable rule. EUSEBIUS tells us that at a Synod in PONTUS, the senior Bishop presided. In Africa, CARTHAGE was the Metropolitan See for the province ; but elsewhere, as in NUMIDIA and MAURETANIA, the senior Bishop presided, although CARTHAGE appears to have had some primacy over them. In the West the development of Metropolitan authority was of later date. Even in the East, the title was not in recognised use before the fourth century.

When the position and dignity became established the canonical arrangement was that the Metropolitan should be elected by the Bishops of the province, with the assent of the clergy and laity. In the East he was consecrated by the Exarch, or Patriarch; in the West by the provincial Bishops. When the See of ROME asserted its patriarchal authority over the whole of the West, the Pope claimed to sanction the appointment of Metropolitans by sending them the *pallium;* and as early as the sixth century the Pope sent to the Bishop of ARLES a *pallium* as Vicar of the Holy See in Gaul. (The Metropolitans did not however need its authorisation; and it was only at the Synod of FRANKFÜRT, in 742, that BONIFACE, as Legate of Pope ZACHARY, obtained a decision that all Metropolitans should request the *pallium* from the Pope, and obey his lawful commands. This grew into a promise of obedience, as a preliminary condition of receiving the *pallium*. (Condensed from the *Dictionary of Christian Antiquities*.)

PRIMATES AND PATRIARCHS.

INNOCENT III. declared : " Primas et Patriarcha, pene penitus idem sonant, cum Patriarchæ et Primates teneant unam formam, licet eorum nomina sunt diversa."

PATRIARCH. I have condensed below from the *Dictionary of Christian Antiquities*, the needful information regarding this title. The five Sees to which in its primary signification the title of Patriarch was attached were those of JERUSALEM, ANTIOCH, ALEXANDRIA, CONSTANTINOPLE, and ROME. " This use grew out of the general tendency to frame the higher organisation of the Church on the lines which were furnished by the Empire. The gradations in rank between Bishop and Bishop which corresponded to the gradations of rank between city and city of the same province, came to exist between metropolis and metropolis of the greater

Clement-Augustus, Duke of Bavaria,
Prince-Archbishop, and Elector, of Cologne (Cöln) 1723-1761

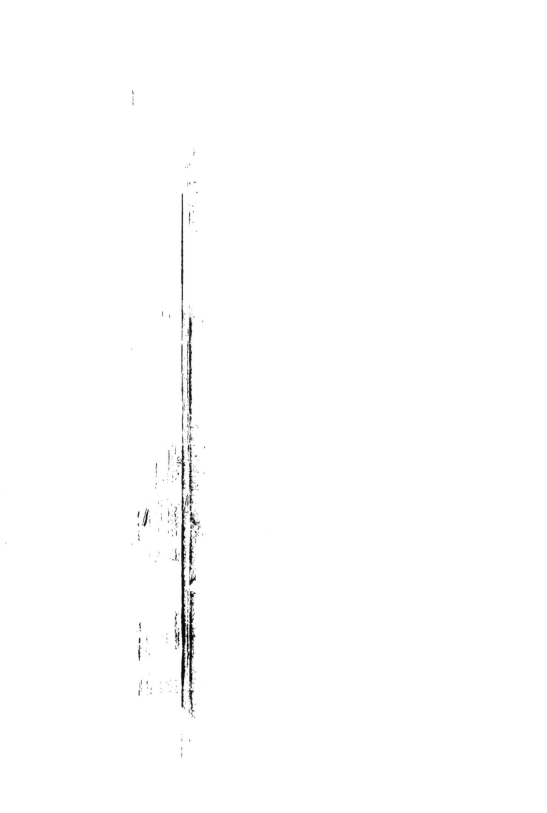

divisions of the Empire." At the time of the Council of NICÆA the great divisions of the éast were the-four *dioeceses*, ORIENS, PONTICA, ASIANA, THRACIÆ, each of which was divided into provinces, or eparchies, and each of these had one metropolis or more. Egypt was originally part of the *dioecesis Orientis*, but was made independent by the Council; the Bishops of PENTA-POLIS and LIBYA being subjected to the See of ALEXANDRIA. "There were thus in the East five great confederations of Churches, each of which was inde-pendent of the others; in the West the See of ROME stood alone in its supremacy." In the following century the Council of CHALCEDON took away the independence of the *dioecesis* of PONTUS, ASIA, and THRACE, sub-jecting them to the See of CONSTANTINOPLE.

By a later use the title of Patriarch was "given to the Bishop of the metropolis of a civil *dioecesis, i.e.*, of a division of the Empire consisting of several provinces; *e.g.*, to EPHESUS. It was also sometimes given to Metropolitans, who had other Metropolitans under them, *e.g.*, to the Bishop of THESSALONICA; and to the Bishop of BOURGES (as having beneath him not only his proper province of AQUITANIA-PRIMA, but also NARBONENSIS, with its metropolitan NARBONNE, and AQUITANIA-SECUNDA with its capital BORDEAUX); as also to the Bishop of LYONS; but its use in this sense was ultimately superseded in the west by the title 'Primate.'"

Outside the limits of the Catholic Church of the Roman organisation, it was adopted for the designation of their chief Bishop by the Vandals; and similarly it was adopted by the Lombard Kings of Italy, hence the Bishops of AQUILEIA, and afterwards of GRADO, were called "Patriarchs." The titular Patriarchate of GRADO was transferred to VENICE in 1451.

Primates (whether they have the patriarchal title or not) have the right to use as the emblem of their dignity a cross with two bars (a double traverse). RODERIC DA CUNHA, Archbishop of BRAGA and Primate of PORTU-GAL, thus describes this cross in the Sixth Chapter of his treatise on the Primacy of his See :—

"Ea differentia inter Primates et Archi-episcopos circa crucis ante se delationem reperitur, quia Primates eam deferunt ante se argenteam sive auream gemino hastili transverso compositam, quorum inferius longius est, summum vero brevius, insignum majoris potestatis et eminentiæ ; Archi-episcopi vero unico tantum bacillo transverso crucem gestant ; et eodem modo formatam crucem gemino scilicet bacillo ante se archi-prœsules Bracharenses gestant in signum Primatialis dignitatis, quam obtinere est notissimum."

This Primatial, or Patriarchal, cross is supposed to indicate the union of two powers in the same person ; the Primate being not only Metropolitan in his own pro-vince but also possessing authority over other Metro-politans. The use of the double cross is of considerable antiquity.

The *Armorial bearings* of the Patriarchs of CON-STANTINOPLE, VENICE, DAMASCUS, and JERUSALEM are depicted in the Book of the Council of CONSTANCE as accompanied by the cross with a double traverse, the cross patriarchal. The arms of the Patriarchate of JERUSALEM are said to be : *Azure, a cross patri-archal or between two estoiles in chief and a crescent in base argent.* Those of the Patriarchate of CONSTANTI-NOPLE : *Argent, a cross patriarchal between four estoiles gules* (FAVYN, *Théatre d' Honneur et de Chevalerie ;* and NISBET, *System of Heraldry,* vol. i., p. 116). I have considerable doubts as to the authenticity of these coats. The arms of the Archbishops of MAINZ and CÖLN, who had Primatial authority, are also thus dignified ; while ordinary Archbishops like TRIER have only the single-barred cross.

The four ancient Patriarchates were those of ANTIOCH, CONSTANTINOPLE, ALEXANDRIA, and JERUSALEM (Bishop BECK, of DURHAM, was made titular Patriarch of JERUSALEM) ; but the patriarchal dignity is attributed to the Archbishops and Primates of VENICE, and LISBON.

The Patriarchate of LISBON and the INDIES, was instituted by CLEMENT XI. in 1716.

The Archbishops of TOLEDO, BRAGA, LYONS, and BOURGES, all claim the Primatial dignity, and use the double cross. Since 1085 the Archbishop of TOLEDO has been Primate of SPAIN ; but the Archbishop of BRAGA in PORTUGAL claims the Primacy of the whole Peninsula, and as we have already seen, uses the cross with the double traverse.

Primates are properly Archbishops who preside over more than one Metropolitan Province, and to whom an appeal lies from the sentence of the Provincial Arch-bishops. Thus an appeal lay to the Archbishop and Primate of LYONS from the Archi-episcopal Sees of SENS, PARIS, TOURS, and ROUEN.

In France the Primates anciently were ; the Arch-bishops of ARLES (Primates of Gaul), LYONS, BOURGES, NARBONNE, and TRÈVES. In course of time most Metropolitans took the title of Primate. In the ninth century HINCKMAR, Archbishop of REIMS, claimed this rank ; which had been accorded to the See by ADRIAN I. The Archbishop of ROUEN styled himself Primate of NORMANDY. In 1079 GREGORY VII. made the Arch-bishop of LYONS "Primat des Gaules," but several Metropolitans, amongst others those of ROUEN and SENS, protested.

Over the west door of every church in VENICE is an oval cartouche containing the arms of the Patriarch. Behind the shield stands the patriarchal cross, accosted by a mitre, and the head of a pastoral staff. Above the shield is placed the *pallium*, so that the pendant falls as already described upon the top of the shield, and the whole is surmounted by the archi-episcopal, or as at present by the cardinal's hat. I remember that formerly all the church porches bore the arms of the then Patriarch Cardinal TREVISINATO: *Per bend sinister or and azure, over all a mullet pierced argent, thereon a rose proper, a chief per pale charged to the dexter with the arms of the French Empire; to the sinister, argent, a lion of S. Mark or.* The hat was that of an Archbishop, the arms having been put up before the Patriarch was created Cardinal in 1863.

The arms of the late Archbishop DARBOY of Paris, assassinated under the Commune in 1871, are thus arranged upon his seal. The shield (*Azure, a cross argent*) is surmounted by the coronet of his dignity as Duc de ST. CLOUD (*v. ante*, p. 120), and placed upon a mantle lined with ermine fringed gold. Behind it rises the primatial cross with its double traverse, and the whole is surmounted by the green archi-episcopal hat with fifteen tassels, 1. 2. 3. 4. 5. on either side.

It should be noticed that the Episcopal hat had formerly only six *houppes* or tassels, and the archi-episcopal ten tassels, on either side, while the cardinal's hat had fifteen. But in an age of assumptions, when almost everybody took something more than, according to the rules of strict heraldic propriety they were actually entitled to (witness the general assumption of coronets, or of coronets of higher rank than the title warranted), the custom grew up of depicting the archi-episcopal hat with fifteen instead of ten tassels on each cordon, the colour being thus the sole distinction between it and the hat of a cardinal. So also, many Episcopal hats were painted with the number of *houppes* (ten on each cordon) properly belonging to that of an archbishop. Of late years there has been a tendency to revert to the old and more correct rule, so far at least

Friedrich Carl, Count von Ostein,
Prince-Archbishop, and Elector (Mainz) 1743–1763

as ecclesiastical insignia are concerned, but the hat of the excellent Archbishop DARBOY is drawn after the less correct fashion.

Very similar remarks might fitly be made with regard to the use or abuse of the cross, whether simple or doubly-traversed. It has been shown that in former times bishops were content to denote their dignity simply by the addition of the mitre and crook-headed pastoral staff to their arms. At the present day there is hardly a Roman Catholic Bishop in Great Britain, etc., who has not replaced these by the ten *houpped* hat, and the (formerly) archi-episcopal or legatine cross. There were plenty of assumptions in France, but I do not think that this particular one occurred frequently. What did happen, however, with too great frequency, was the substitution of the cross with the double traverse (*i.e.*, the primatial or patriarchal cross) for the single-traversed cross which was their due, by Archbishops, some of whom had no claim whatever to Primatial or Metropolitan authority.

The Sees which had this claim, or possessed this right, have been named above. It may be interesting to give some examples which will mark the rise of assumptions. At Paris PIERRE DE MARCA, Archbishop of PARIS (d. 1672), bore the arms : *Quarterly,* 1 and 4. *Gules, a horse saliant or* (MARCA) ; 2 and 3. *Argent, three ermine spots sable* (TRESCENS) in a cartouche. Behind rises the archi-episcopal cross in pale, between a small mitre, and the head of the crosier. Above all the archi-episcopal hat of ten *houppes*. Then comes JEAN FRANÇOIS DE GONDI (the celebrated *coadjuteur* of the Fronde), second Archbishop of PARIS (afterwards known as the Cardinal de RETZ, he died 1679). He impaled the arms of his Church (*France-ancient, over all the effigy of the Virgin and Child or*), with his personal arms (*Or, two maces in saltire sable, tied in base gules*). Over this

K

he .placed the coronet of his dignity as Duc de St. Cloud ; the archi-episcopal cross with a single traverse, its ends being fleurs-de-lis, is in pale ; and the hat of ten *houppes* is above all.

Archbishop FRANÇOIS DE HARLAY-CHANVALLON, who died in 1695, did not impale the arms of his See. He used the ducal coronet and mantle, the cordon and badge of the ORDER OF THE ST. ESPRIT ; the fleur-de-lisée archi-episcopal cross, and the ten houpped hat.

Archbishop LOUIS ANTOINE, Duc de NOAILLES, Cardinal-Archbishop of PARIS, used the same external ornaments for his arms :—(*Gules, a bend or.*)   He died in 1729.   CHARLES VINTIMILLE DU LUC, Archbishop of PARIS, who died in 1746, used with his arms (*Quarterly*, 1 and 4. *Gules, a chief or;* 2 and 3. *Gules, a lion rampant or*) the ducal coronet (no mantle) ; the archi-episcopal cross and hat.   The hat has now fifteen *houppes* on each side.   This is retained by CHRISTOPHE DE BEAU-MONT, who died in 1781.   His arms (*Gules, on a fess argent, three fleurs-de-lis azure*) are ensigned with the ducal coronet and ermine-lined mantle, and the cordon of the ST. ESPRIT ; and for the first time ,the fleur-de-lisée cross of the Archbishop of PARIS gives place to the assumption of the double-traversed cross.   Omitting the *cordon* of the ST. ESPRIT the same arrangement is followed by Archbishop ANTOINE LE CLERC, Marquis de JUIGNÉ, Archbishop from 1781 to 1811. (*Argent, a cross engrailed gules, between four eagles, displayed sable.*) Archbishop AFFRÉ, who died on the barricades in the Revolution of 1848, retained the hat and double cross, but does not seem to have used the coronet or mantle. His arms were : *Azure, on a sea in base a dolphin blowing argent, on a chief cousu gules three estoiles of five points of the second.*

CLAUDE D'ACHEY, Archbishop of BESANÇON (d. 1637), assumed the double-traversed cross, and hat with

fifteen *houppes* as the external ornaments of his arms :—
Quarterly, 1 and 4. *Gules, two axes addorsed paleways*
(ACHEY) ; 2 and 3. *Vairé or and gules* (BAUFFREMONT).
While BERTRAND D'ESCHAUX, Archbishop of TOURS
before 1618, ensigned his coat (*Azure, three bars or*) with
a marquess' coronet, the double-traversed cross and the
hat of (only) ten *houppes* (GUIGARD, *Armorial du Bibliophile,* vol. i., pp. 52, 203). GILES DE SOUVRÉ, Bishop
of AUXERRE (d. 1631), used the double-traversed cross,
as well as the mitre and crozier, and the hat with
ten *houppes* above his arms :— *Azure, five cotices or*
(*ibid.*, ii., 209). This seems an extraordinary case of
assumption.

It is perhaps desirable to state that Primates and
Archbishops are not allowed the use of the cross in the
presence of a Papal Legate.

A Legate is the Pope's deputy for certain purposes.
Legates were of three kinds ; *legati a latere; legati nati;*
and *legati dati*. *Legati a latere* are cardinals with
almost Papal authority, such were WOLSEY and POLE.
Legati nati are prelates who are legates *ex officio* without
a special creation. The Archbishops of CANTERBURY
from 1195 to the "Reformation" were *legati nati*. The
power of conferring degrees in all faculties, which take
precedence of ordinary University ones, is a remnant of
the Papal privilege attaching to the legatine office.
Legati dati are prelates appointed for some special
purpose, such as the representation of the Pope on some
great occasion ; the holding of a council, or the trial of
some important ecclesiastical cause. All Legates had
the right to the use of the cross like archbishops.

A Patriarch is, it is said, entitled to wear, and
surmount his arms with a tiara, differing from the Papal
one in having only two crowns. I have not seen an
instance of this use ; but a writer in *Notes and Queries*
(3rd series, ii., 160), himself a respected dignitary of

the Roman Church, states the fact from actual inspection.

NAPOLEON I. attached the dignity of Count to the Archi-episcopal Sees, and that of Baron to the Episcopal ones. The following were the regulations for the use of the ensigns of their dignities, COMTES ARCHEVEQUES. "Toque de velours noir,[1] retroussée de contre hermine, avec porte aigrette or et argent, surmontée de cinq plumes, accompagnée de quatre lambrequins, les deux supérieurs en or, les deux autres en argent, surmontés d'un chapeau *rouge*[2] à larges bords, avec des cordons de soie de même couleur, entrelacés l'un dans l'autre, pendants aux deux côtés de l'écu, et terminés par cinq houppes chacun. Franc quartier d'Azur à la croix patée d'or.

BARONS EVÊQUES. Toque de velours noir, retroussée de contre vair, avec porte aigrette en argent; surmontée de trois plumes; accompagnée de deux lambrequins d'argent ; surmontée d'un chapeau vert aux larges bords avec des cordons de soie de même couleur entrelacés l'un dans l'autre, pendants aux deux côtés de l'écu, et terminés par quatre houppes chacun. Franc quartier de *Gueules à la croix alaisée d'or.*"

These "*Franc quartiers*" were distinctive marks to be borne within the shield. All official ranks were thus severally distinguished in the brief period of the " First Empire."

---

[1] The *toque de velours noir*, was the hat substituted for the ancient coronets by Napoleon I. when regulating the marks of dignity for his new *noblesse*. The number of the plumes, and the lining varied for each rank. The use lasted only a very short time. Under the " *Second Empire* " coronets replaced the hats.

[2] *Rouge* is printed in the directions, and was correct for the Archbishop of PARIS, who was a Cardinal. But it seems to have been forgotten, or unknown to the person responsible for the regulations, that *verte* was the colour for ordinary archbishops.

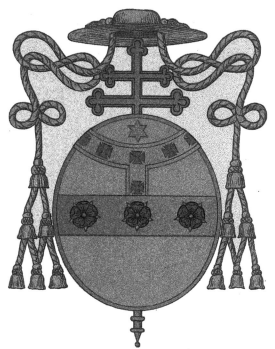

1. Archbishop (Bausa ?) of Florence.

2. Cardinal Medicis.

The Cardinal de BELLEY, Archbishop of PARIS under NAPOLEON I. thus bore : *Gules, four lozenges argent, 3 and* 1, *on a canton azure a cross patée or.* Bishop de FAUDOAS of MEAUX bore : *Azure, a cross or ; on a canton gules a cross alesée or.* These examples, with the regulations given above, are taken from the official authority, SIMON'S *Armorial Général de l'Empire Français,* tome i. In it these arms are engraved on Plates 25 and 53, with the external ornaments as ordered above. In the case of a bishop the *toque* was placed between a mitre on the dexter, and the head of a pastoral staff or crosier on the sinister side.

CARDINALS.— The Red Hat, *biretta*, and *calotte* — Use of Coronets—Cardinals from Regular Orders—Arms of Patronage—Composed Arms.

THE Cardinals were originally the incumbents of the principal churches in Rome. In later times they were divided into three classes; Cardinal-Bishops, Cardinal-Priests, and Cardinal-Deacons; and were appointed respectively from the Suffragan Bishops of the Roman patriarchate; the priest-incumbents of the city; and the deacons of the chapels of the hospitals.

In 1585 SIXTUS V. fixed the number of Cardinals, previously unlimited, at seventy; in allusion to the number of the Jewish elders. Accordingly, when the Sacred College is complete, which rarely happens, it consists of six Cardinal-Bishops; fifty Cardinal-Priests, and fourteen Cardinal-Deacons.

This distinction, is, however, a merely nominal one, and is the cause of much misapprehension among those who are not fully informed. There have been instances of Cardinal-Bishops who were only in Deacon's Orders; and of Cardinal-Priests who were not in Holy-Orders at all (except perhaps minor ones). On the other hand the class of Cardinal-Priests always includes many Archbishops and Bishops; and the higher rank of the priesthood is often found among the Cardinal-Deacons. In fact the rank of Cardinal is not, strictly speaking, an ecclesiastical one; it is merely a dignity of the Court of Rome. (On the dignity of Cardinal *see* CARTWRIGHT'S admirable book "*On the Constitution of Papal Conclaves*," Edinburgh,

1868.). Celibacy is the only absolutely indispensable qualification for it, though a lay Cardinal requires the Papal sanction before he can divest himself of his ecclesiastical character and return to secular life. Ignorance of the facts stated above has led Protestant controversialists to make unfounded charges of licentiousness and debauchery against men like the late Cardinal ANTONELLI, because they had sons and daughters. No doubt these were, strictly speaking, " illegitimate," but their existence was no proof of the grave charges of immorality often most unscrupulously made. No Cardinals who have not taken Orders can, however, vote in a conclave, except they have a special Papal dispensation; and, though there have been exceptions (or at least one), all Cardinals who have not previously taken Orders do so as a matter of course in modern times before being admitted to a conclave. At the request of Pope PIUS IX., all the lay Cardinals (among whom was his chief Secretary of State the famous ANTONELLI) took Deacon's Orders before his death: and I believe that at present there are no lay Cardinals at all. Cardinal-Deacons, although in Priests' Orders, cannot publicly celebrate mass. Cardinal-Priests, even if they be not Bishops, use all the Episcopal ornaments : mitre, pastoral staff, and pectoral cross, when officiating in the Church in Rome which gives to each his "title." The use of the mitre was permitted to Cardinal-Priests before 1130, and to Cardinal-Deacons in the year 1192. A Cardinal-Deacon, even if he be a layman, has precedence of all Bishops. In solemn ceremonies the Cardinal-Deacons wear the dalmatic; Cardinal-Priests the chasuble; and Cardinal-Bishops the cope; all are mitred, but in the Papal presence only the *mitra simplex* may be worn. Pope BONIFACE VIII. in 1299, conferred on the Cardinals the right to wear the princely purple, as Princes of the Church and participating in the regal power of the Supreme Pontiff.

The title of *Eminence*, still used, was given them by SIXTUS V. in 1586.

The use of the red *biretta* was granted at LYONS in 1245 to the Cardinals who were not members of Regular Orders ; and in 1592 the privilege was extended to those Regulars, who previously had worn the head-dress of their respective Monastic Orders. When a new Cardinal is resident in a foreign country he usually receives the *biretta* from the hands of the Sovereign, or Chief of the State, to whom the Pope sends it. The red *calotte*, or skull cap, is, under these circumstances, sent direct to the new Cardinals. In Rome the ceremonies are much more elaborate. The flat red hat which is now so intimately associated with the Cardinal's dignity is very rarely sent to a new Cardinal ; it is usually conferred by the Pope himself in a Consistory. This hat is said to have been first given by INNOCENT IX. to the Cardinals at the Council of LYONS in 1245, to remind them of their duty to be ready to shed their blood if needful in defence of the Catholic faith ; a warning considered appropriate in a time when the Roman Church was menaced by the hostility of the Emperor FREDERICK. This idea is maintained in the address given by the Pope to the new Cardinal when he places the hat upon his head. " Ad laudem omnipotentis Dei, et Sanctæ sedis Apostolicæ ornamentum, accipe galerum rubrum, insigne singularis dignitatis Cardinalatûs ; per quod designatur quod usque ad mortem et sanguinis effusionem, pro exaltatione Sanctæ Fidei, pace, et quiete populi Christiani, augmento et statu Sacrosanctæ Romanæ Ecclesiæ, te intrepidum exhibere debeas. In nomine Patris, et Filii, et Spiritûs Sancti. Amen." Contrary to popular notions, this hat is never again *worn* by a Cardinal ; it is only placed upon his bier at his funeral, and is afterwards suspended to the vault of the chapel or church, above, or near, the place where his body is interred. These are the

red hats so often seen dependent from the roof in
Italian churches. The red hat, however, with its
knotted cords each ending in a pyramidal fret of
fifteen tassels (1. 2. 3. 4. 5.), is always placed above
the representations of the arms of a Cardinal, as an
ensign of his dignity. This custom appears to date from
the early part of the fourteenth century. On the tomb
of BERNARD, Cardinal de LONGUISEL, who is interred
at ORVIETO, having died in 1290, neither hat nor mitre
is represented above his shield of arms; and on the
tombs of Cardinals who died at an earlier date their
effigies are mitred only. On the tomb of JACOPO,
Cardinal COLONNA, in the basilica of SANTA MARIA
MAGGIORE at Rome, about the close of the thirteenth
century, the mitre only is placed by the side of the
armorial shield. At SIENA, the hat is placed *within* the
shield of RICHARD, Cardinal PETRONI (d. 1313). The
tomb of MATTEO, Cardinal ORSINI (d. 1341), bears three
escucheons, two of the personal arms of the cardinal,
the third (which is placed between the other two)
contains a cardinal's hat, with plain strings knotted
together, without tassels. The earliest known examples
of the use of the hat surmounting the shield are
to be found on the tombs of ARMAND, Cardinal
de VIAS, nephew of Pope JOHN XXII. at Avignon,
date 1328; of AUDOIN, Cardinal D'ALBERT; and
PIETRO, Cardinal de MONTERONE, nephews of Pope
INNOCENT V.

At first the number of *houppes*, or tassels, of the strings
of the hat, now settled at fifteen on either side, was
varied at pleasure; sometimes, as in an instance recorded
above, none were used. This was the case also on the
monument at Rimini of Cardinal BONITO, Archbishop
of PISA, where the hat has two simple strings. But in
the case of his contemporary, WILLIAM, Cardinal
PHILASTIER, of Mans (1427-8) whose tomb is in the

church of S. CHRYSOGONUS, the hat has fifteen tassels on each side arranged as at present (1. 2. 3. 4. 5).

In the church of STA. MARIA in Trastevere, the arms of PHILIP, Cardinal d'ALENÇON (d. 1402); and WILLIAM, Cardinal de STAGNO (d. 1455) were surmounted by hats having on each side only six tassels (1. 2. 3). On the pavement before the choir of the Cathedral of Verona, I noticed that the slab which covers the grave of AUGUSTINUS VALERIUS, Cardinal-Bishop of VERONA bears his arms beautifully inlaid in marble mosaic ; viz., *Per fess or and gules an eagle displayed counter-changed, crowned of the first.* The cardinal's hat above this shield has only six tassels on each of its cords.

The seal of ZACARIAS, Cardinal DELFINI, 1565, bears his arms (*Azure*) *three dolphins naiant in pale* (*or*) timbred by a hat which seems to have six tassels on one side, seven on the other, probably an error of the artist.

Between the red hat and the shield is placed the coronet, if the Cardinal has a right to one, and the head of the cross which is placed behind the shield if the Cardinal is an Archbishop, or has been a Papal legate. This was the strict rule in former times but amid the assumptions of later ones, the double-traversed, or patriarchal, cross is frequently assigned to Cardinals. JEAN, Cardinal de BELLEY (d. 1560) appears to have used the double cross and cardinal's hat with his arms : *Argent, a bend fusilly gules between six fleurs-de-lis azure.* JEAN, Cardinal de FLEURY, minister of LOUIS XV., who bore : *Quarterly,* 1 *and* 4. *Azure, three roses or ;* 2 *and* 3. *Per fess gules and azure, in chief a lion naissant or,* used in France, the ducal coronet, the double-traversed cross, and the cardinal's hat.

Cardinal LA GRANGE D'ARQUIEN (d. 1707) bore in France the same external ornaments to his arms : *Azure, three stags trippant or ; En surtout, Sable, three leopard's heads or,* a brisure for the branch of ARQUIEN.

FRANÇOIS, Cardinal de BERNIS, Secretary of State, 1760, bore : *Azure, a bend and in chief a lion rampant or*, the escucheon ensigned with the double cross and cardinal's hat.

ARMAND DE ROHAN, Cardinal de SOUBISE, Prince-Bishop of STRASBURG (d. 1756) used an abbreviated form of his arms (ROHAN, *Gules, nine mascles conjoined 3. 3. 3. or; impaling* BRITTANY, *Ermine plain*) surrounded by the cordon of the ST. ESPRIT and the ducal mantle, and ensigned by the ducal coronet and the double-traversed cross ; the temporal sword and spiritual crosier are in saltire behind the shield, and the cardinal's hat surmounts the whole.

On the other hand, Cardinal MAZARIN was usually content with the cardinal's hat alone, though sometimes his arms (*Azure, the Consular fasces and axe in pale or, banded and bladed argent ; on a fess gules three stars of five points of the second*) are also surmounted by the ducal coronet. Cardinal TALLEYRAND DE PÉRIGORD, who was also Archbishop of REIMS, bore : *Gules, three lions rampant crowned or*, the cartouche crowned with the coronet of a marquis only, and surrounded by the ducal mantle ; the double-traversed cross is in pale behind the shield, and the cardinal's hat above all.

In Rome itself, the use of coronets is strictly forbidden to Cardinals by a bull of INNOCENT X. There, whatever be their birth, all are equal as Princes of the Church, and no secular dignity is allowed to give even an appearance of superiority to one over another. The cross of the ORDER OF S. JOHN, the badge of an Order which is religious, as well as military, is used even in Rome as involving no breach of the rule. Away from Rome the case is different ; the Cardinal apart from his brethren may add to his arms any coronet, or other mark of dignity, to which he is entitled. Thus the great Cardinal-Duke de RICHELIEU (ARMAND DU

PLESSIS) bore his arms (*Argent, three chevrons gules*)· surmounted by his coronet, and surrounded by the ducal mantle charged with his arms, and lined with ermine. The anchor, which was the badge of his office as "Grand Amiral de France" was placed in pale behind the escucheon, around which also was disposed the *cordon bleu* with the badge of the ORDER OF THE ST. ESPRIT. (*See* MAGNENEY, *Recueil des Armes*, planche i. and our Plate XVIII., fig. I.) Ecclesiastics who were *Chanceliers de France* placed the maces of their office in saltire behind the shield.

We have already remarked that the *collars* of the ORDERS OF THE ST. ESPRIT, AND OF S. MICHAEL, were not generally used by ecclesiastics who were members of either of those Orders. But LOUIS DE VENDÔME, Duc de MERCŒUR, Cardinal in 1667, appears to have used both collars around his shield, just as the lay knights did. His shield is also ensigned with the coronet of fleurs-de-lis, and the princely mantle of France. Other examples of the use of the collars are the following, LOUIS DE BARBIER, Bishop and Duke of LANGRES, *Pair de France* in 1645 (d. 1670) and HARDOUÌN DE BEAUMONT, Archbishop of PARIS in 1662 (*see* DE LA POINTE, *Ordre du St. Esprit*, planches *c*, and *n*). The Cardinal-Dukes of MAZARIN, and BOUILLON, similarly used the mantle *armoyé*, the ducal coronet, and the cordon of the ORDER OF THE ST. ESPRIT. ANTONIO, Cardinal BARBERINI, Archbishop of REIMS in 1667, bore his escucheon (*Azure, three bees or*) upon the white Cross of the Order of S. JOHN OF JERUSALEM, and ensigned with a ducal coronet. The *cordon bleu* of the ORDER OF THE ST. ESPRIT, with its badge, surrounds the shield; behind which rises the double-traversed cross. The cardinal's hat and a mantle *armoyée* enclose the whole (LA POINTE, planches *c*, and *n*). The arms of GEORGE, Cardinal d'ARMAGNAC, and Legate in 1580,

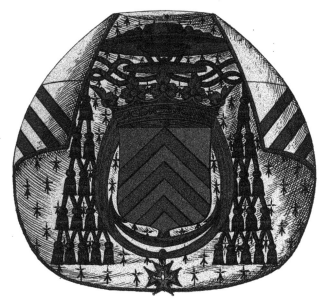

1. Richelieu.

2. Berulle.

are at Avignon, with the mantle *armoyée*. (*l'Usage des Armoiries*, p. 239.)

Cardinals who belong to those Spanish or Italian families which by custom or grant surround their shields of arms with banners, or other military trophies, do not cease to use them as ecclesiastics. Curious instances of this custom are afforded by the arms of GIROLAMO, Cardinal COLONNA ; and later by those of CARLO, Cardinal COLONNA (created 1796). They placed the arms of their family (*Gules, a column argent crowned or*) surmounted by the crest (*a mermaid with two tails proper*), but without a supporting helm, and with six banners on each side of the shield, upon a larger escucheon gules. The whole beneath the cardinal's hat. *See* also the COLONNA medals in LITTA, *Famiglie Celebri Italiane*. A medal of GIROLAMO, Cardinal COLONNA, Archbishop of BOLOGNA, has the shield surrounded by eight swallow-tailed flags charged with crescents. The same arrangement appears on his tomb in San Barnabo. (*See* CONLIN, *Roma Sancta*, lviii.; and ROSSI, *Effigies, Insignia, etc., Pontificum et S. R. E. Cardinalium defunctorum, ab anno* MDCVIII., pl. 11 and 105, 2 vols., fol. Romæ, n.d.) LOUIS, Cardinal PUERTO-CARRERO, 1669-1709, has thirteen flags around his shield.

Cardinals taken from a regular Order usually quarter, or impale, the arms of that Order with their personal arms ; or else place its device on a chief, or oval escucheon, either within the shield, or above and outside it. Of these customs examples are sufficiently numerous. The earliest which has come under my notice is that of Cardinal BONA, of the Order of the Reformed Bernardins in Italy (1669-1674). He quartered the arms of the Cistercian Order (FRANCE-*ancient*, an escucheon of BURGUNDY - *ancient*), with his personal ones :— *Gules, a lion rampant or, on a chief azure three roses argent*, and over all, on an escucheon of pretence, the

ROSPIGLIOSI arms as "arms of patronage," being those of CLEMENT IX. (ROSSI, i., 108).

JUAN EVERARD, Cardinal NIDARDUS (1672-1681) bore : *Quarterly*, 1 and 4. *Per pale or and argent, an eagle displayed sable ;* 2 and 3. *Gules, on a chevron argent, a rose of the first.* Over all an escucheon of pretence, crowned, and charged with a long cross standing on a mount of three coupeaux. In the chief of the main shield is a small escucheon, *Or, charged with the monogram* (I.H.S.?) (ROSSI, i., 121). GIOVANNI BAPTISTA, Cardinal PTOLOMÆI (1712-1726) of the Society of Jesus, placed the badge of the Jesuit Order (the sacred monogram I.H.S. in chief, and three passion nails pileways in base) on a roundel, or oval, in the chief of his shield above his personal arms, *Azure, a fess between three crescents argent.* (CONLIN, *Roma Sancta*, xxxii. ; and ROSSI, 261.)

But GIOVANNI BAPTISTA, Cardinal SALERNO, created 1719 ; and his contemporary ALVARO, Cardinal CIENFUEGOS, both of the Society of Jesus, placed the badge just described in a roundel, or oval, above the top line of the shield (not within it), below the cardinal's hat (*Roma Sancta*, Nos. li. and liii. ; also in ROSSI, i., 292). In 1628, the French Cardinal BERULLE (who bore *Gules, a chevron between three mullets of six points pierced or*), placed between his shield and the hat of his dignity the badge of the Congregation of the Oratory, founded by him in 1611, viz. a small crown of thorns encircling the words "JESUS MARIA." (*See* our Plate XVIII., fig. 1, and MAGNENEY, *Recueil des Armes*, planche 5.) In the same work (pl. 13) are engraved the arms of Bishop LE CLERC of GLANDEVEZ ; and d'ATICHY of RIEZ, who both, in 1630, made a similar use of the badge of the Minimes, the word *Charitas* within the crown of thorns.

ANTONIO, Cardinal BARBERINI, brother of URBAN VIII., bore above his personal arms (*Azure, three bees,*

2 and 1, *or*) a chief charged with the device of the Franciscan Order (*Argent, the Saviour's cross surmounted by two human arms in saltire, both bearing the stigmata (the one in bend being that of the Saviour naked ; the sinister that of S. Francis habited proper*). (Plate I., fig. 7.)

The like device was used on an escucheon in chief above his personal coat (*Azure, two barrulets between three mullets of six points or*) by FRANCISCO MARCO, Cardinal CASINO (ROSSI, i., 258).

LORENZO, Cardinal COZZA, General of the Franciscan Order, created Cardinal-Priest in 1726, bore : *Per pale*, 1st *the full arms of Pope* BENEDICT XIII., as arms of patronage. 2nd. His personal arms viz. *Per fess, in chief . . . a bird . . . ; and in base Barry of ten . . . and . . .* He also placed a small escucheon of the arms or device of the Franciscan Order above the shield and partly upon it (*Roma Sancta*, lxiii.). Similarly, LORENZO, Cardinal PORZIA, so created in 1728, Abbot of MONTE CASSINO, used the following arms : Per pale 1. *The full arms of* BENEDICT XIII. (*vide infra*, p. 165). 2. His paternal coat, *Azure, six fleurs-de-lis, and a chief or.* In chief, above and partly upon the shield, a small escucheon of the arms of MONTE CASSINO, viz. . . . *a mount of six coupeaux* 1. 2. 3. *in base, surmounted by a double cross, with the word* PAX *upon the lower traverse* (*Roma Sancta*, lxxxvii.). As the arms of Patronage included the arms of the Dominican Order, and those of BENEDICT XIII., these two examples are worthy of special notice.

AGOSTINO, Cardinal PIPIA, General of the Dominican Order, created Cardinal in 1724, used a shield per fess, in chief the arms of the Order of S. Dominic (*Argent, chapé sable, on the first a dog holding in its teeth a torch with which it illuminates an orb crossed proper*) in base his personal arms. In like manner VINCENZO LUDOVICO,

Cardinal GOTTI, created in 1728, bore the Dominican arms on a chief above his personal coat.

Cardinals, and other Ecclesiastics, who are members of the ORDER OF S. JOHN OF JERUSALEM, have the right to place in chief, above their personal coat the arms of the Order: *Gules, a cross argent.* The shield itself is placed upon the white eight-pointed cross of the Order (*cf.* Plate XIII., figs. 1 and 2). The arms of FRANÇOIS and ANTOINE, Cardinals BARBERINI (nephews of URBAN VIII.) are thus given in *L'Armorial Universel*, pl. 201 (*vide ante*, p. 40). (But in modern times the chief is usually omitted, and in the *Roma Sancta* there is no instance of its use. *See* the arms of Cardinal PAMFILI, *infra*, p. 148, and those of Archbishop EYRE on Plate XXXVI.)

The cross of the Teutonic Order was similarly used by German Ecclesiastics ; an example may be cited ;— DAMIANUS HUGO, Cardinal SCHÖNBORN, placed the shield of his arms upon the *white cross patée fimbriated sable*, of the Teutonic Knights. (*Roma Sancta*, No. xxxiv.)

SECTION B.

Arms of Patronage used by Cardinals.

The Cardinals of the Roman Church very frequently join to their personal arms those which were borne by the Pope to whom they owe their elevation. (Some examples of this custom have been already given in the previous pages.) This, it will appear presently, was done in a variety of ways, but the ordinary and original way of bearing these " arms of patronage " was that of *impaling* the two coats ; the dexter half of the shield, as the more honourable, being assigned to the Papal arms.

The earliest instances of this custom which have as yet come under my notice are the following :—ARMAND,

Cardinal de VIAS (1334); and PIERRE, Cardinal de MONTERONE, *impaled* with their personal arms those of their maternal uncles Popes JOHN XXII., and INNOCENT VI. (The arms of the Popes are in Part II.) RODERIGO, Cardinal LENZUOLO (1456), nephew and adopted son of CALIXTUS III., took the name of BORGIA, and *impaled* the Papal arms with his own. GIOVANNI SALEFENATI, Archbishop of MILAN, being created Cardinal by SIXTUS IV. (FRANCESCO DELLA ROVERE) in 1484 added to his personal arms the Papal oak tree *on a point in chief* (a "*point in chief*" is a triangle formed by the top line of the shield, and two lines drawn diagonally from the ends of the same until they meet each other). Of the Cardinals created by JULIUS II. (GUILIANO DELLA ROVERE, 1503-13) FRANCESCO ALIDOSI *quartered* the Papal arms, and FACCIUS SANCTORIUS, Bishop of VITERBO, *impaled* them.

The arms of LEO X. (MEDICI 1513-22) were *impaled* by Cardinals PUCCI, RUBEI, CAJETAN, CESI, and RANGONI ; by SERIPANDI to the sinister (*v.* CIACONIUS, p. 1181); *quartered* by Cardinals TARLATI, SALVIATI, and RODOLFI ; placed on " *a point in chief*" by Cardinal SYLVIO PASSERINO, and *compounded* with their family coats by Cardinals NUMANI, and ARMELLINI.

Under Pope PAUL III. (1534-1550) the FARNESE arms were added to their personal bearings by no less than seventeen Cardinals (GAMBARA, SFORZA, PUCCI, CACCI, MAFFEI, etc.). Of these UMBERTO, Cardinal GAMBARA, who bore the arms: *Or, a crayfish in pale gules, and a chief of the Empire,* placed the *six azure fleurs-de-lis* of the Pope around the crayfish of his own coat. GIOVANNI, Cardinal GAMBARA, nephew of the preceding, created in 1565 by PIUS IV., made a similar use of the Medicean *palle.* In general this manner of " compounding " the Papal and personal coats was only employed when the field of the two coats was of the same metal or tincture. (The arms of Cardinal GEORI, to be given presently, form an exception to the rule.)

The arms of MAXIMILIAN, Cardinal VON HOHENEMS, Bishop of CONSTANCE (1561-1589), appear on a coin struck by him in 1573, and are an interesting example. *Quarterly*, 1 and 4. *The arms of Patronage* (those of his uncle, PIUS IV., MEDICI); 2 and 3. . . . *a cross . . . impaling, Azure, a steinbock rampant or, horned sable* (HOHENEMS). *Over all, on an escucheon Argent, a cross gules* (See of CONSTANCE). The whole shield *enté en pointe* of the arms of the Abbey of REICHENAU . . . *a cross flory* . . . The shield is surmounted by the Cardinal's hat ; and the temporal sword and pastoral staff are placed in saltire behind the whole. (The escucheon is engraved in KÖHLER, *Münz-Belustigung*, xi.) The arms of PIUS IV. were also added to their own by Cardinals BORROMEO, GESUALDO, etc. ; those of JULIUS III. (1550) by Cardinals DE LA CORNE and SIMONCELLI ; those of PIUS V. (1566-1572) by Cardinals MAFFEO, SANTORIO, CESI, GALLO, and BONELLO. GREGORY XIII.(BUONCOMPAGNI, 1572-1585) similarly gave his arms to Cardinals LA BAUME, VASTAVILLANO, BIRAGUE, and RIARIO.

On the tomb of Cardinal GADDI in the Church of SANTA MARIA NOVELLA at Florence, I noticed that the arms of Pope PIUS IV. were quartered as arms of patronage in the first and fourth quarters, with those of GADDI : *Azure, a cross flory or*, in the second and third.

Under CLEMENT VII. (ALDOBRANDINI, 1592-1605), GIOV. BAPT. PORTUENSIS, Cardinal Deacon in 1599, *impaled* the ALDOBRANDINI arms with his own, *three crescents ;* GYMNASIUS DE CASTRO BONONIENSE, 1604, placed the Papal arms in the upper part of a shield *per fess*, above his personal arms (. . . *a hand holding compasses, beneath the Angevin-rastrello and fleurs-de-lis*);

while CARLO, Cardinal PIO, Bishop of ALBANO, used a still more remarkable arrangement : *Quarterly*, 1 and 4. *Gules, a cross argent, thereon a saltire of the first ; 2* and 3. *Gules, two bars argent.* These quartered coats are separated by a pale of the Papal arms (thus making the shield tierced in pale), and the whole is surmounted by a chief of the Empire, a portion of the paternal coat.

The arms of the Cardinals created by URBAN VIII. (BARBERINI, 1623-1644) afford instructive examples of the varied modes in which arms of patronage were borne. By GIOVANNI, Cardinal ALTIERI (who bore, *Azure, six estoiles,* 3. 2. 1. *or*), the Papal arms are placed on *a circular plate,* half within half without the shield (Plate I., fig. 4). FRANCESCO, Cardinal RAPACCIOLO, *quartered* the Papal arms (*Azure, three bees or*), his own (*Azure, a turnip leaved proper*) being in the second and third places (Plate I., fig. 5). Cardinal ROCCIUS *impaled* the Papal coat with his own : *Per fess, in chief or, an eagle displayed in base, three bunches of grapes proper.* The Spanish Cardinal LUGO placed above his own arms (*Or, issuant from waves of the sea in base, three isolated mounts argent, out of each a laurel branch proper,* the Papal arms *on a segmental chief*). (Plate I., fig. 6.) Lastly, ANGELO, Cardinal GEORI, sometimes *impaled* the Papal arms (Plate I., fig. 9), but sometimes *compounded* them with his own (*Or, a laurel wreath in chief, in base a mount of three coupeaux proper*) the Papal bees being placed within the laurel wreath in the latter case.

Under INNOCENT X. (PAMFILI, 1644-1655) Cardinals NICOLO LUDOVISI (d. 1688) and FRANCISCO MAIDAL-CHINI, *impaled* the Papal arms with their personal ones ; CAROLO, Cardinal GUALTIERI (d. 1673) placed the Papal coat above his personal arms in a shield divided *per fess.* (For LUDOVISI arms *see* GREGORY XV., p. 169). Those of MALDALCHINI were : *Azure, a wall embattled, masoned sable, in chief three estoiles or ;* and of GUALTIERI bore : *Barry azure and or, in chief three bezants* (otherwise, *Azure, three bars or, in chief as many bezants*).

Of the Cardinals created by ALEXANDER VII. (CHIGI, 1655 - 1667) GIROLAMO BUONCAMPAGNI (d. 1672), ANTONIO BICHI (d. 1691), CESARE RASPONI (d. 1765), JACOPO NINI (d. 1680), and CŒLIO PICCOLOMINI (d. 1664) *impaled* the Papal arms (DELLA ROVERE quartering CHIGI) with their own. VOLUMNIO BANDINELLI (d. 1667), *quartered* this Papal coat with his own (*Or plain, differenced by a roundle in chief, thereon a mounted knight*).

The arms of Cardinal BONA, created by CLEMENT IX. (ROSPIGLIOSI, 1667-1670) have already been given on p. 141 *ante*, and afford an instance of the Papal arms as arms of patronage being placed *on an escucheon of pretence.* ÆMILIO, Cardinal ALTIERI (d. 1676) similarly placed the ROSPIGLIOSI arms *in chief* on a small escucheon. (The ALTIERI arms here have the bordure.) But Cardinals SIGISMUNDO CHIGI (created in 1667), and FRANCISCO NERLI (1669-1670) *impaled* the Papal arms.

Of the Cardinals created by CLEMENT X. (ALTIERI, 1670-1676) three :—FELICE ROSPIGLIOSI, and FRANCESCO NERLI, both created in 1673 ; and ALLESSANDRO CRESCENCI created in 1675, *impaled* the ALTIERI arms ; but MARIO ALBERICI added them in a small *escucheon in chief* to his paternal coat.

Under INNOCENT XI. (ODESCALCHI, 1676-1689) his arms were *impaled* by Cardinals RAIMONDO CAPIZUCCHI (d. 1691) ; GIOVANNI BAPTISTA LUCA (1681-1683), and STEFANO FORLI (d. 1883.) But the arms of BENEDICT, Cardinal PAMFILI, created in 1683, afford a very curious example : *Tierced in pale ;* 1 PAMFILI ; 2 (*patronage*) ODESCALCHI ; 3 ALDOBRANDINI. The shield is placed upon the cross of the ORDER OF S. JOHN OF JERUSALEM, of which he was a member. Two Cardinals created by ALEXANDER VIII., (OTTO-

BONI, 1689-1691) *impaled* his arms; FERDINAND, Cardinal ABDUA, Archbishop of MILAN; and GIOVANNI BAPTISTA, Cardinal RUBINI, both created in 1690.

I have no note that the Cardinals created by INNOCENT XII. (PIGNATELLI, 1691-1700) and CLEMENT XI. (ALBANI, 1700-1721) used the Pontifical arms as arms of patronage, and had any done so I think the fact could hardly have escaped my observation. But under INNOCENT XIII. (CONTI, 1721-1724), ALESSANDRO, Cardinal ALBANO, *impaled* the Papal arms; and under his successor BENEDICT XIII. (ORSINI 1724-1730) besides the Cardinals COZZA, and PORZIA, whose arms have been given already (p. 143) the Papal arms were *impaled* by nearly all the Cardinals of his creation, *e.g.*, Cardinals PROSPER MAREFUSCO, VINCENZO PIETRA, NICOLO COSCIA, and NICOLO JUDICE (created 1725).

These arms of Patronage appear to have been often discarded (one would think somewhat ungratefully) after the decease of the Pope in honour of whom they had been assumed.

It may be added that these assumptions or grants were not always confined to Cardinals or other Ecclesiastics. In 1621 GREGORY XV. by a Papal Bull permitted Counts of the Lateran, and other Roman nobles thus to use his arms (MENÊTRIER, *Origine des Armoiries*, p. 305). The Major-Domo of the Papal Household still always assumes the Papal arms, and conjoins them with his own in one or other of the ways already described, and retains them after his elevation to the rank of Cardinal. (MONTAULT, *L'Année Liturgique à Rome*, p. 268). So far as my own observation goes I think that in the case of other Cardinals the custom is falling into abeyance.

The arms of the Cardinal "Camerlengo," *sede vacante*, are referred to in the following Section.

CHAPTER VIII.

POPES.

The Tiara — The Keys — The Triple-Cross — The *ferula* — The *Pavillon de l'Eglise*—" Cardinal Camerlengo" *sede vacante* — Popes from Regular Orders—Supporters of Papal Arms.

THE external ornaments with which the escucheons of the Popes are ensigned are :—the Tiara ; the "keys of S. PETER," and sometimes the cross with triple bars.

Usually the Tiara is placed above the escucheon ; and the keys (of which the dexter is of gold, and the sinister of silver), are placed in saltire behind the shield which bears the Pope's personal arms.

The tiara is a cap, or mitre, of thin metal, or cloth of gold and silver. It is not cleft like the present form of Episcopal mitre, and it is encircled with three open crowns of gold, foliated, and adorned with pearls, so as to resemble somewhat the coronets used by Marquesses in the British Peerage. The top is surmounted by an orb, or mound, on which is set a cross *patée*.

The principal tiaras are four in number. The first was given to Pope PIUS VII. by NAPOLEON I. in 1805, and weighs nearly eight pounds. It is richly jewelled. The emerald which supports the cross is valued at over £600, and the whole tiara is said to be worth above £9000. The second tiara dates from the pontificate of Pope GREGORY XVI. It weighs about three pounds, and is valued at about £380. The third tiara, and the most valuable, was the gift of Queen ISABELLA of SPAIN in 1854 ; it is of about the same weight as the last, but is thickly strewn with diamonds, to the number it is said of 18,000; its estimated value is over £12,500. The fourth was the gift of the Palatine Guard in 1860, and is worth about £850. I saw at least one other of very great value among the Jubilee presents in the Vatican in 1888, but I have no note of its donor or value. The tiaras are ranged on the altar when the Pope pontificates. A curious picture by DES PREZ in the Gallery at Stockholm represents the Pope (BENEDICT XIV.?) officiating at Mass at the High Altar in S. PETER'S at Rome, in the presence of a Swedish Prince (King FREDERICK of Sweden?) in 1740. The tiaras are arranged on the altar upon raised stands.

There is much uncertainty as to the time when the coronets were added to the original *infula*, the simple mitre of the Bishops of Rome. The usual account is that the first was sent to Rome by CLOVIS, King of the FRANKS; the second added by Pope BONIFACE VIII. (1294-1303); and the third either by BENEDICT XIII. or URBAN V. I recently remarked that on the tomb of Pope BONIFACE in the basilica of S. JOHN LATERAN the tiara has but one coronet. This is so far as I am aware the first appearance of it in connection with the Papal arms. The statue of Pope GREGORY the Great at Chartres represents him as wearing a high conical cap or mitre, surmounted by a ball. The border, or rim, is a circlet with very small floriations. (DIDRON, *Christian Iconography*, vol, i., p. 448. The statue is said to be of the thirteenth century.)

The pictures of early Popes by CIMA DI CONEGLIANO, in the Brera Gallery at Milan, show that the tiara was not originally ornamented with a floriated coronet, the border being quite different in shape. The colour is sometimes white, sometimes red; but much importance must not be attached to this variety of colour, which may have been, and probably was, at least in some cases, dictated by artistic considerations.

Various mystical meanings have of course been attached to the triple crown. When even the *fanons* of an ordinary mitre, by which it was originally tied on the head, were supposed to refer to "the literal and spiritual interpretations of Holy Scripture," it is certain that so important an object as the tiara of the Supreme Pontiff would give rise to many mystical suggestions (*de Insig.*, cap. 3, sect. 5.) SPENER says, " Perhibetur vero hæc ipse corona esse quam Imper. Anastasius cum titulo Patritii, Regi Franciæ Clodoveo, jam converso, misit. Hic vero non magni donum faciens Symmacho Papae obtulit. Ne vero mysterium in triplici corona desideretur cavit, M. GILBERT DE VARENNES, 4, p. 330, allegans eam triplicitatis rationem, quia potestatem acceperit super ecclesiam militantem, laborantem (in purgatorio), triumphantem." (*Opus Heraldicum*, pars gen., cap. vi., p. 314.) The coronets are considered by some to allude to a union in the Pope of the Royal, Priestly, and Prophetical Offices. Others think that they have merely a secular bearing, and denote the old kingdom of the HERULI, the Exarchate of RAVENNA, and the kingdom of LOMBARDY. Most probably the view expressed in the exhortation of the officiant as he places the tiara on the head of the new Pope is the correct one, and the crowns (if they symbolise anything of a religious character at all) allude to the triple character of Father, King, and Vicar of Christ. "Accipe tiaram tribus coronis ornatam ; et scias te esse Patrem Principum et Regum, Rectorem Orbis, in terrâ Vicarium Salvatoris nostri Jesu Christi, Cui est honor et gloria, in sæcula sæculorum, Amen." (For further information on the tiara and its mystical meaning *see* DUCANGE; FERRARIO ; and FESCH.)

It seems probable that many of the early Popes made

little if any use of their family arms. The tomb of Pope
CLEMENT IV. (d. 1271) at Viterbo has a shield charged
with *fleurs-de-lis*, but these do not appear to have been
his personal arms, and may have been allusive to his
French origin ; though, probably by error, the tinctures
are inverted. (*See* the List of Papal Arms from 1144
to the present day, in the following Chapter.)

The keys, the symbol of S. PETER, seem to have been
first employed heraldically upon Papal banners. FROIS-
SART, speaking of the militant Bishop of Norwich, says :—

" Faisoit l'Evesque de Nordwic devant luy porter les
Armes de l'Eglise: la Banniere de Saint Pierre de gueulles
à deux Clefs d'Argent en sautoir, comme Gonfalonier du
Pape Urbain, et en son Pennon estoient ses Armes."

In the Chapel of S. MARTIAL, built by Pope CLEMENT
VI., at Sens, remain two escucheons, on one of which are
the keys, on the other the *triregno*, or tiara. (MENÊTRIER,
l'Usage des Armoiries, p. 253. Paris 1673.) LEO III. is
said to have sent keys (in which were filings from those
of S. PETER), and a banner to CHARLEMAGNE, as *Avoué*
of the Church, and Protector of Rome. (MENÊTRIER,
de l'Origine des Armoiries, p. 292-4.) Escucheons of the
keys also remain at AVIGNON of this date. In 1357 the
Papal Legate ALBORNOZ put them up in the com-
munes of the Papal States.

When employed in conjunction with the Personal
arms of the Pope they (like other ecclesiastical insignia
of which we have seen examples in previous chapters)
were often in early times included in the shield. In the
Basilica of SAN GIOVANNI IN LATERANO, I noticed that
on DONATELLO'S splendid bronze tomb of Pope MARTIN
V. (1417-1431), the arms of the COLONNA are surmounted
by a chief bearing the cross keys beneath the tiara.
Popes URBAN V. and VIII. and ALEXANDER VII.,
also thus used them at times. NICOLAS V. seems
to have used only the cross keys in an escucheon

crowned with the tiara. MENÊTRIER says that examples of this Pope's escucheon were to be seen on the gates of the Churches of S. PAUL, S. THEODORE, and ST. LAURENT, in Rome. Later it became the custom to place the keys *en cimier*, beneath the tiara, and above the shield. INNOCENT VI., PAUL III., and PAUL IV., thus used them. They are thus represented on the tomb of Pope PIUS III. (PICCOLOMINI) in SANTA MARIA DELLA VALLE at Rome ; and on his picture by PINTURIC-CHIO in the Duomo at Siena. (*See* also LITTA, *Celebri Famiglie Italiane*, vol. iv.) The keys and tiara are thus represented on the tomb of Pope SIXTUS IV., in the Church of SANTA MARIA MAGGIORE at Rome. Similarly the arms of Pope JULIUS II. (DELLA ROVERE), are depicted on the tomb of ASCANIO, Cardinal SFORZA, in SANTA MARIA DEL POPOLO, the keys being in saltire beneath the tiara, above the shield. So are they on the tomb of Pope LEO X. (MEDICI), in SANTA MARIA MINERVA ; and on those of Popes CLEMENT VII. and LEO XI. in S. PETER'S, at Rome. [*See* SPENER, *Opus Heraldicum*, p. gen., p. 315 (who quotes from FESCH, *de Insig.* c. 3, n. 5), and MENÊTRIER, *Pratique des Armoiries*, cap. 8. *See* also the gold coins of Pope PIUS II. (PICCOLOMINI); of ALEXANDER VI. (BORGIA) ; and the medals of CALIXTUS III., 1455 ; and INNOCENT VIII., 1484.] An early example of this usage was to be seen in the case of the arms of Pope INNOCENT VI. (1352-1362), which were thus arranged at the Chartreuse de Villeneuve, near Avignon. Many modern examples of this custom could be cited. I recently saw the arms of Pope PIUS VI. thus depicted in the church of SAN GIOVANNI IN LATERANO. Pope ADRIAN VI. (1522) placed the keys in saltire behind the shield ; and this usage, and the precedent, are those which have been retained by his successors up to the present date.

It appears to be the custom at the funeral ceremonies

of a deceased Pope to represent the Papal arms crowned with the tiara, but without the keys; and the same custom appears to have been followed in the case of deposed Popes. The keys are not represented on the tombs of GREGORY XII. at Siena, and of JOHN XXII. at Florence. At the head of the latter monument is a circle containing the COLONNA column. Over this is a tiara, above the crossed keys, for Pope MARTIN V. As the keys are omitted from the escucheon of a dead Pope so they appear in saltire above the shield and beneath the *pavillon de l'Église* upon the coins struck by the "Cardinal Camerlengo," the chief depository of the Papal authority, during the vacancy of the Papal throne. The *pavillon de l'Église*, is a canopy, or umbrella, usually of red and yellow silk in alternate stripes.

For instance, in 1667, on the *scudi* of ANTONIO BARBERINI, "Cardinal Camerlengo" *sede vacante*; his arms are placed in an oval cartouche upon the eight-pointed cross of the Order of S. JOHN OF JERUSALEM of which he was a member (the small cross of the Order is pendant beneath the base of the shield); the legatine cross is placed in pale behind it, and the Cardinal's hat surmounts the whole. Immediately above the hat are the Papal keys in saltire, the cordons of the hat being brought (according to custom) through the bows of the keys; and the large open *pavillon de l'Église*, surmounts the whole. (KÖHLER, *Münz-Belustigung*, vol. x., p. 49.) Other examples are on the gold five scudi pieces, *sede vacante* in 1846; the silver scudi of the same date; and the gold "*doppia*" of 1823. In Italy at the present day families which have produced a Pope often place the keys and *ombrello* above the shield, or sometimes in a little escucheon within it, in memory of the fact. Thus the OTTOBONI (whence came Pope ALEXANDER VIII.) place the Papal keys and *ombrello* above the escucheon, beneath the mantling.

These cases must be distinguished from those in which the Papal arms have been granted as an augmentation, as in the case of the ESTES, Dukes óf FERRARA, MODENA, etc.

It should be noticed that some of the Popes have retained after their accession to the Papal throne, the arms or devices of the Regular Order to which they belonged, and which as Cardinals they had combined with their own. Thus BENEDICT XIII. bore in chief above his personal arms, those of the Dominican Order (*vide supra*, p. 143). The arms of (p. 165) BENEDICT XIII. thus arranged were impaled as arms of Patronage (*see* preceding Chapter) by PROSPER, Cardinal LAMBERTINI, who had been raised by him to the Cardinalate, and who was elected Pope under the title of BENEDICT XIV. on the decease of Pope CLEMENT XII. in 1740. It is curious to observe that even as Pope he retained the use of the full arms borne by BENEDICT XIII., and impaled them in the place of honour with his own. Popes CLEMENT XIV., PIUS VII., and GREGORY XVI., all combined with their personal arms those of the Regular Order to which they belonged (*vide infra*, Chap. IX.).

The Papal arms are frequently depicted with angel supporters, each of which bears in its exterior hand the Papal cross with triple bars.

. On a gold coin of Pope PIUS II. (PICCOLOMINI, 1458-1464) the Papal arms are supported by figures of the Apostles SS. PETER and PAUL. The shield is surmounted by the tiara, above which is also a cross potent perhaps the head of the *ferula*, p. 110. (KÖHLER, *Münz-Belustigung*, vol. xviii., p. 385.)

On the seal of the Dominicans in Newark, Leicester (15th century) S. CLEMENT, Pope, is represented holding in his hand the triple-barred cross. (*Cat. of Seals in B. Mus.* i., No. 3453.) The Pope does not use the ordinary

crosier, or crook-headed pastoral staff, unless he happen
to be in the Diocese of TRIER, or TRÈVES. The reason
assigned for this on the authority of Pope INNO-
CENT III., is the legend that "S. PETER the Apostle
sent his staff to EUCHARIUS, Bishop of TRÈVES, whom
he appointed with VALERIUS and MATERNUS to preach
the Gospel to the German race. He was succeeded in
his bishopric by MATERNUS, who was raised from the
dead by the staff of S. PETER. The staff is, down to
the present day, preserved with great veneration by the
Church at TRÈVES." But the Jesuit writer CAHIER
shows that there is some reason to think that the Popes
did use the pastoral staff up to the eleventh century,
and gives a figure of GREGORY THE GREAT thus represented from a miniature of the thirteenth century.

Other representations of S. GREGORY however, depict
him as bearing a staff surmounted by a cross ; one from
the *Hierolexicon* (which as well as that referred to from
CAHIER is to be found *sub voce* "pastoral staff," in the
Dictionary of Christian Antiquities, ii., 1556, shows S.
GREGORY bearing a staff with a head resembling a cross
patée. The saint is represented with the rectangular
nimbus, which shows that he was alive at the time the
drawing was made. (*See* DIDRON'S *Christian Iconography*, vol. i., p. 76, *et seq.*)

On a statue of the thirteenth century at CHARTRES
Pope GREGORY THE GREAT is represented holding in
his hand a staff surmounted by a long cross, archi-
episcopal as we should now term it. (DIDRON, vol. i.,
p. 448.)

MIGNE, *Dictionnaire de l'Orfèvrerie*, denies that the
Popes ever used the pastoral staff properly so called, *i.e.*,
one having a crook. But we have already remarked that
the crook was not essential to the pastoral staff, and
that the earliest had simply a knob or a crutch.

CHAPTER IX.

POPES.

Arms of the Popes from 1144–1893.

1144. LUCIUS II. (CACCIA-MEMINI).
Gules, a bear rampant proper.

1145. EUGENIUS III. (PAGANELLI).
Argent, a crescent azure, in chief a label gules.

1150. ANASTASIUS IV. (SUBURRA).
Per fess, in chief, Or, two lions rampant affrontés vert ; in base, Bendy or and vair. Over all a fess gules.

1154. ADRIAN IV. (BREAKSPEARE).
(*Arms unknown.*)

1159. ALEXANDER III. (BANDINELLI).
Or, plain. (This coat is often diapered, as in S. John Lateran.)

1181. LUCIUS III. (ALLUCINGOLA).
Lozengy, azure and argent.

1185. URBAN III. (CRIVELLI).
Quarterly gules and argent, in the centre point a sieve in profile or.

1187. GREGORY VIII. (MORRA).
Gules, two swords argent in saltire, the hilts in chief or, between four mullets of the last.

1187. CLEMENT III. (SCOLARI).
Chequy argent and gules, a chief of the Empire (but ?).

1191. CELESTIN III. (ORSINI).
Bendy gules and argent, on a chief of the second a rose of the first ; the chief soutenu by a divise or, thereon an eel naiant azure.

1198. INNOCENT III. (DEI CONTI DE SEGNI).

> *Gules, an eagle displayed chequy or and sable, crowned of the second.*

1216. HONORIUS III. (SAVELLI).

> *Per fess argent and or, over all a fess vert; in chief a rose surmounted by a martlet, and supported by two lions rampant gules, in base three bends of the last.*

1227. GREGORY X. (DEI CONTI DE SEGNI, *vide supra,* INNOCENT III.).

1241. CELESTIN IV. (CASTIGLIONE).

> *Gules, a lion rampant argent, holding a castle triple-towered or.*

1243. INNOCENT IV. (FIESCHI).

> *Argent, three bends azure* (or *Bendy argent and azure*).

1254. ALEXANDER IV. (DEI CONTI DE SEGNI, *vide supra,* INNOCENT III.).

1261. URBAN IV. (LANGLOIS).

> *Quarterly,* 1 and 4. *Or, a fleur-de-lis azure;* 2 and 3. *Azure, a rose or.*

1261. CLEMENT IV. (GROS)..

> *Or, six fleurs-de-lis azure, in orle.* (His family arms were : *Or, an eagle displayed sable, on a bordure gules ten bezants* (RIETSTAP, i., 835).

1271. GREGORY X. (VISCONTI).

> *Per fess embattled gules and azure* (but ?).

1276. INNOCENT V. (TARENTAISE ?).

> *Azure, three pallets or, on each as many fleur-de-lis of the field.* (?)

1276. ADRIAN V. (FIESCHI, as INNOCENT IV. above).

1276. JOHN XXI. (JULIAN ?).

> *Quarterly,* 1 and 4. *Argent, three crescents gules;* 2 and 3. *Sable, two pallets or.*

1277. NICOLAS III. (ORSINI, *vide supra,* CELESTIN III.).

1281. MARTIN IV. (MOMPITIÉ).

> *Per fess gules and or, in chief a human arm, issuant from the sinister flank proper, vested and manipled ermine.*

1285. HONORIUS IV. (SAVELLI, *vide supra*, HONORIUS III.).

1287. NICOLAS IV. (MASCI D'ASCOLI).

> *Argent, a bend between two (or three) estoiles azure ; on a chief of the last three fleurs-de-lis or.*

1292. CELESTIN V. (ANGELARIO DEL MORRONE).

> *Or, a lion rampant azure over all a bend gules (?)*

1294. BONIFACE VIII. (CAETANI).

> *Argent, two bends wavy azure.*

1303. BENEDICT XI. (BOCCASINI).

> *Gules, a pale embattled counter-embattled argent, a chief azure (?)*

1305. CLEMENT V. (COUTH, or DE GOT).

> *Barry argent and gules (?)*

1306. JOHN XXII. (D'EUSE).

> *Quarterly,* 1 and 4. *Or, a lion rampant azure between six hurts ;* 2 and 3. *Barry gules and argent (?)*

1334. BENEDICT XII. (NOVELLI).

> *Azure, an escucheon argent.*

1342. CLEMENT VI. (ROGER DE BEAUFORT).

> *Argent, a bend azure between six roses in orle gules.*

1352. INNOCENT VI. (AUBERT).

> *Gules, a lion rampant argent, debruised by a bend azure ; on a chief of the field, soutenu by a divise of the last, three escallops of the second.*

1362. URBAN V. (GRIMOARD).

> *Gules, a chief dancetty or.*

1370. GREGORY XI. (ROGER DE BEAUFORT, *vide supra*, CLEMENT VI.).

1378. URBAN VI. (PRIGNANI).

> *Or, an eagle displayed azure.*

1389. BONIFACE IX. (TOMACELLI).

> *Gules, a bend chequy argent and azure.*

1404. INNOCENT VII. (MILIORATI).

> *Or, on a bend coticed azure an estoile irradiated of the field (?)*

1406. GREGORY XII. (CORRER).

> *Per fess, azure and argent, a lozenge counter-changed.*

1409. ALEXANDER V. (FILARGI).

> *Azure, a sun in splendour between eight estoiles in orle or.*

1410. JOHN XXIII. (COSSA).

> *Per fess, in chief Gules a human leg proper ; in base, Argent, three bends (sinister ?) vert ; all within a bordure or ;* (or *indented argent and azure*).

1417. MARTIN V. (COLONNA).

> *Gules, a column argent crowned or.*

1431. EUGENIUS IV. (CONDOLMIERI).

> *Azure, a bend argent.*

1447. NICOLAS V. (PARENTUCCELLI).

> *Argent, two bends wavy, the one in chief gules, the other azure.*

1445. CALIXTUS III. (BORGIA).

> *Or, on a mount in base vert, a bull statant gules ; on a bordure of the third eight flames of the first.*

1458. PIUS II. (PICCOLOMINI).

> *Argent, on a cross azure five crescents or.*

1464. PAUL II. (BARBO).

> *Azure, a lion rampant argent, over all a bend or.*

1471. SIXTUS IV. (DELLA ROVERE).

> *Azure, an oak tree eradicated or, its four branches interlaced in saltire.*

1484. INNOCENT VIII. (CIBO).

> *Gules, a bend chequy argent and azure ; on a* *chief the arms of* GENOA : *Argent, a cross* *gules.*

1492. ALEXANDER VI. (BORGIA, *vide supra*, CALIX-TUS II.).

> BORGIA, *impaling* LENZUOLO ; *Barry or and* *gules.* ISABELLA BORGIA, sister of CALIX-TUS III. married LOFFREDO LENZUOLO, and their son RODERIGO assumed the BORGIA name and used the arms of his mother's family conjoined with his paternal coat. He became Pope as ALEX-ANDER VI.

1503. PIUS III. (PICCOLOMINI, *vide supra*, PIUS II.).

> (Cardinal TODESCHINI took the name and arms of his uncle PIUS II.)

1503. JULIUS II. (DELLA ROVERE, *vide supra*, SIX-TUS IV.).

1513. LEO X. (DE' MEDICI).

> *Or, five balls in orle gules, in chief a larger one of* *the arms of* FRANCE (*viz., Azure, three fleurs-* *de-lis or ;* granted by LOUIS XI. in 1465).

1522. ADRIAN VI. (DEDEL).

> (Arms doubtful. *Quarterly,* 1 and 4. *Or, three* *tent hooks vert.* 2 and 3. *Sable, a lion rampant* *azure* (? *argent*) *crowned or.* (*N. and Q.,* 6th S., vi., 82, 354.) Sometimes the hooks are *sable,* and the lion *or.*

1523. CLEMENT VII. (DE' MEDICI, *vide supra*, LEO X.).

> Though of illegitimate birth he used the full arms of the MEDICI.

1534. PAUL III. (FARNESE).

> *Or, six fleurs-de-lis azure,* 3. 2. 1 (this coat has a bordure on the monument in the Church of the Ara Cœli).

1550. JULIUS III. (DEL MONTE).

Azure, on a bend gules, fimbriated and between two olive wreaths (sometimes of *laurel,* but still) *or, three mountains, each of as many summits, of the last.*

1555. MARCELLUS II. (CERVINI).

Azure, on a terrace in base vert, a stag lodged argent, between six wheat-stalks or. (RIETSTAP says *bulrushes,* and is probably right ; *cf.* Ps. xlii.)

1555. PAUL IV. (CARAFFA).

Gules, three bars argent.

1559. PIUS IV. (DE' MEDICI, *vide supra,* p. 162).

He appears to have assumed the unaugmented coat : *Or, six balls in orle gules.*

1566. PIUS V. (GHISLIERI).

Or, three bends gules. (Sometimes depicted as *Bendy of six or and gules.*)

1572. GREGORY XIII. (BUONCOMPAGNI).

Gules, a dragon issuant from the base, winged or.

1585. SIXTUS V. (PERETTI).

Azure, a lion rampant or, holding a pear branch fruited proper ; over all on a bend gules, a comet in chief of the second, and a mount of three coupeaux in base argent.

1590. URBAN VII. (CASTAGNA).

Bendy of six or and azure, on a chief gules, soutenu by a divise argent, a chestnut leaved of the first.

1590. GREGORY XIV. (SFONDRATI).

Quarterly, 1 and 4. *Argent, a bend embattled counter-embattled, between two mullets of six points azure.* 2 and 3. *Or, on a mount in base a tree vert, between a flash of lightning in bend issuing from the dexter chief ; and in the sinister chief the conventional symbol of the wind in bend-sinister proper.* (See *N. and Q.,* 6th S., xii., 142.)

1591. INNOCENT IX. (FACCHINETTI).

> *Argent, a nut tree eradicated and fruited proper.*

1592. CLEMENT VIII. (ALDOBRANDINI).

> *Azure, a bend embattled counter-embattled between six estoiles or.*

1605. LEO XI. (DEI MEDICI, *vide supra*, LEO X.).

1605. PAUL V. (BORGHESE).

> *Azure, a dragon* (sometimes a *demi-dragon*) *or, a chief of the Empire.*

1621. GREGORY XV. (LUDOVISI).

> *Gules, three bends rétraites in chief, or.* (These are sometimes wrongly drawn *embowed ;* but the mistake only arises from the appearance of the bends on the common convex cartouche.)

1623. URBAN VIII. (BARBERINI).

> *Azure, three bees or,* 2 and 1. (Usually the bees are not *volant*, but close.)

1644. INNOCENT X. (PAMFILI).

> *Gules, a dove argent, in its beak an olive branch proper ; on a chief cousu azure two pallets gules between three fleurs-de-lis or.* (The chief is a survival of the Angevin bearings so common in the coats of the Guelphic families of FLORENCE, BOLOGNA, etc.)

1655. ALEXANDER VII. (CHIGI).

> *Quarterly,* 1 and 4. *Azure, an olive tree eradicated its four branches interlaced in saltire argent* (DELLA ROVERE) ; 2 and 3. *Gules, in base a mount of six coupeaux or, and in chief an estoile of the same* (CHIGI). Sometimes the CHIGI coat is used alone.

1667. CLEMENT IX. (ROSPIGLIOSI).

> *Quarterly or and azure, in each quarter a lozenge counter-changed.*

1670. CLEMENT X. (ALTIERI).

> *Azure, six estoiles argent.* A bordure, indented of the tinctures, is sometimes added. There is no bordure on the tombs of the ALTIERI. Chapel in STA. MARIA SOPRA MINERVA (*See* my paper, "Arms of the Popes," *N. and Q.*, 6th S., xii., 142), but it appears on the papal escucheon in S. PETER'S, and was so borne in the contemporary arms of patronage used by his cardinals (*vide ante*, p. 147).

1676. INNOCENT XI. (ODESCALCHI).

> *Vair, on a chief gules, a lion passant argent, this chief abaissé under another of the Empire.* (On the variations of this coat as given on the Pope's monument in S. PETER'S, etc., *see* my paper in *N. and Q.*, 7th S., vi., 205.)

1689. ALEXANDER VIII. (OTTOBONI).

> *Per bend azure and vert, over all a bend argent. A chief of the Empire.*

1691. INNOCENT XII. (PIGNATELLI).

> *Or, three pignate* (drinking pots with handles) *sable, 2 and 1.*

1700. CLEMENT XI. (ALBANI).

> *Azure, a fess between an estoile in chief, and in base a mount of three coupeaux, all or.*

1721. INNOCENT XIII. (CONTI).

> *Gules, an eagle displayed chequy argent and sable, crowned or.*

1724. BENEDICT XIII. (ORSINI).

> *Per pale ;* 1. ORSINI (*vide ante,* p. 158) *impaling* 2. *Vert, a castle argent the port azure* (Duchy of GRAVINA). *Over all in chief the arms of the* DOMINICAN ORDER (*vide* p. 143).

1730. CLEMENT XII. (CORSINI).

> *Bendy argent and gules, over all a fess azure.*

1740. BENEDICT XIV. (LAMBERTINI).

> *Per pale, two coats ;* 1. *The full arms of* BENE-
> DICT XIII. as above, (borne as arms of
> Patronage) ; 2. *Or, four pallets azure.*
> (LAMBERTINI of Bologna.)

1758. CLEMENT XIII. (REZZONICO).

> *Quarterly,* 1. *Gules, a cross argent ;* 2 *and* 3.
> *Sable (? azure) a castle with a central tower
> argent ;* 4. *Gules, three bends sinister argent
> (over all on an escucheon Or, a double-headed
> eagle sable crowned proper).*

1769. CLEMENT XIV. (GANGANELLI).

> *Azure, a fess between three estoiles in chief, and
> a mountain of three coupeaux in base or. In
> chief the arms of the* FRANCISCAN ORDER
> (*vide* p. 143).

1775. PIUS VI. (BRASCHI).

> The full arms of the Pope were : *Quarterly,* 1
> and 4. *The Empire ;* 2 *and* 3. *Azure on a fess
> between two fleurs-de-lis argent three estoiles
> proper. Over all on an escucheon, Gules, a
> lily slipped proper, in dexter chief the con-
> ventional symbol of the wind blowing on the
> lily ; on a chief argent three estoiles or.* This
> escucheon was often used alone.

1800. PIUS VII. (CHIARAMONTI).

> *Per pale, two coats ;* 1. *Azure, a mountain of three
> coupeaux in base, thereon a patriarchal cross,
> its arms patées or ; over all the word* PAX *in
> fess sable* (for the BENEDICTINE ORDER).
>
> 2. *Per bend or and azure, on a bend argent three
> Moor's heads couped sable wreathed of the
> third ; on a chief of the second three estoiles
> argent,* 1 *and* 2.

1823. LEO XII. (DELLA GENGA).

> *Azure, an eagle displayed argent.*

1. Pope Leo XIII

2. Pope Pius IX

1829. PIUS VIII. (CASTIGLIONE).

Gules, a lion rampant argent holding a castle triple-towered or.

1831. GREGORY XVI. (CAPPELLARI).

Per pale, two coats ; 1. *Azure, two doves argent drinking out of a chalice or, in chief an estoile of the second* (being the arms of the CAMALDOLI ORDER). 2. *Per fess azure and argent, over all on a fess gules three mullets or, in chief a hat sable* (CAPPELLARI).

1846. PIUS IX. (MASTAI-FERRETTI).

Quarterly, 1. and 4. *Azure, a lion rampant crowned or, its hind foot resting on a globe of the last* (MASTAI). 2 and 3. *Argent, two bends gules* (FERRETTI.) (Plate XIX., fig. 2.)

1878. LEO XIII. (PECCI).

Azure, on a mount in base a pine tree proper ; between, in sinister chief a comet, or radiant star, argent, and in base two fleurs-de-lis or. Over all a fess of the third (Plate XIX., fig. 1.) (The rays of the comet are usually in *bend-sinister.* The pine tree is generally drawn like a cyprus. For an account of the variations of the PECCI arms *see Notes and Queries,* 6th Series, vii., pp. 488, 489.)

PART II.

CHAPTER I.

Arms of English, Scottish, and Irish Sees blazoned, with
Historical and Heraldic Notes.

THE earliest Episcopal seals bore only an effigy of the
Bishop usually standing vested *in pontificalibus*, holding
his pastoral staff, and with his right hand raised in the
act of benediction.

Later the seal often included representations of the
patron saints of the Bishop, or those of his cathedral
church, arranged under an architectural canopy; the
bishop himself being represented on his knees in the base
of the *vesica*-shaped seal. In the beautiful and elaborately
engraved seals of the Middle Ages, the effigies of the
patron saints were inserted in the niches of the architectural canopy under which the bishop was represented
standing or seated, while shields bearing the assumed
arms of the See, and those of the bishop's family were
added upon either side of his effigy, or were placed in
the lower angle of the *vesica*.

Remains of the architectural canopy, mutilated almost
beyond recognition, may still be traced in the armorial
bearings of several Sees; *e.g.* TUAM, SODOR and MAN,
MORAY, and ABERDEEN. In others the canopy has
disappeared, and the effigy of the saint alone remains,
e.g. SALISBURY, CHICHESTER, LINCOLN, and ROSS.

In England the use of armorial bearings appropriated
to the See is of considerable antiquity. These were, as
all other armorial bearings were originally, assumptions
only, and at very varying dates, although after the
institution of the College of Arms the arms in use

were authoritatively confirmed ; and in the case of Sees of later erection a regular armorial grant was made.

The use by which the arms of the See were impaled in the place of honour, with the personal arms of the Bishop has been noticed elsewhere (Part I., pp. 19 and 82).

PROVINCE OF CANTERBURY.

CANTERBURY.

Azure, a crosier or Episcopal staff in pale argent ensigned with a cross patée or, surmounted by a pall-throughout of the second, edged and fringed gold, and charged with four crosses formées-fitchées sable (Plate XX., fig. 1).

These arms appear first on the seal of Archbishop SIMON ISLIP (1349-1366). (*Cat. of Seals in Brit. Mus.,* No. 1223.) On the seal of a successor SIMON of SUD-BURY (1375-1381), a pastoral staff, with the crook turned towards the edge of the shield, is added on each side of the *pallium ;* but this arrangement appears to be unique. (*Ibid.,* No. 1225). On the *pall* or *pallium, vide ante,* pp. 112-119. His personal arms were impaled with those of the See by Archbishop THOMAS FITZALAN, son of ROBERT, thirteenth Earl of ARUNDEL (1397-1414). (*Ibid.,* No. 1238.)

The See of CANTERBURY was founded by S. AUGUS-TINE in 596, the city being the capital of the dominions of ETHELBERT, King of KENT. Precedence over the more ancient archi-episcopal See of YORK was granted to it by the Pope GREGORY VII. in 1073. In spite of this, disputes for precedency continued for some centuries and sometimes resulted in personal conflicts between the attendants of the archbishops (*vide ante,* p. 111). After the conquest of Ireland the Archbishops of CANTERBURY who had already asserted authority over the remains of the ancient church in Wales claimed jurisdiction over the Irish Sees ; but this ceased on the creation of the Archbishoprics of ARMAGH, DUBLIN, CASHEL, and TUAM, at the Synod of KELLS in 1151-1152. The Archbishop is now Primate and Metropolitan "of all England," and the first peer of the Realm. He has precedence of all the great Officers of State, and of all Dukes who are not of the blood-royal. He has the title of "*His Grace.*"

The following is a list of the Suffragan Sees of the Province of CANTERBURY :—

LONDON, WINCHESTER, BANGOR, BATH and WELLS, BRISTOL, CHICHESTER, ELY, EXETER, GLOUCESTER, HEREFORD, LICHFIELD, LINCOLN, LLANDAFF, NORWICH, OXFORD, PETERBOROUGH, ROCHESTER, ST. ALBANS, ST. ASAPH, ST. DAVIDS, SALISBURY, SOUTHWELL, TRURO, WORCESTER.

LONDON.

> *Gules, two swords in saltire argent, the hilts in base or* (Plate XX., fig. 4).

The arms are allusive to the dedication of the Cathedral to the great Apostle S. PAUL, whose effigy first appears on the seal of Bishop FITZNEAL (1189-1198). The coat as given above is found for the first time on the seal of Bishop RALPH STRATFORD in 1348.

LONDON was the chief of the three Archbishoprics which existed in early British times. Its Bishop RESTITUTUS was present at the Council of ARLES, in the year 314. On the re-introduction of Christianity into England by the Roman mission under S. AUGUSTINE, it was made the See of a Bishop in 596. It now has precedence next to CANTERBURY among the Sees of the southern province, and next to YORK among those of all England.

WINCHESTER.

> *Gules, two keys endorsed in bend, the upper or, the lower*

argent, their rings interlaced in base ; between them a sword in bend sinister of the third, the point in chief, hilted gold (Plate XX., fig. 6).

The division of the WESSEX diocese into the Sees of DORCHESTER and WINCHESTER was attempted unsuccessfully by King CENWALCH about the year 660. Its division into WINCHESTER and SHERBORNE took place in 704-705.

The Cathedral of WINCHESTER, founded by KENEGIL, King of WESSEX, appears to have been originally dedicated to S. AMPHIBALUS. It was afterwards placed successively under the invocation of S. PETER and S. SWITHIN.

The effigies of SS. PETER and PAUL appear on the seal of Bishop RICHARD TOCLIVE (1174-1188), of Bishop WILLIAM of WYKEHAM (1367-1404) and (with S. SWITHIN) on that of Bishop WILLIAM of WAYNFLETE (1447-1486). In these facts we may find the origin of the arms as at present borne, which combine the sword of S. PAUL with the keys of S. PETER.

Bishop WAYNFLETE'S seals have a shield charged with a sword in bend, and with a key (or keys) in bend sinister ; and in the chief a mitre. In the hall of NEW COLLEGE, Oxford, is a similar shield in painted glass with the field of the shield *azure*. This may possibly be of earlier date than WAYNFLETE'S seal, but the tincture of the field is, so far as I am aware, unique. Whether the keys be drawn in bend or in bend-sinister the one which lies above the blade of the sword (be it higher or lower than the other) is the golden one. On the shields which adorn the vaulting of the nave of WINCHESTER Cathedral ; on a doorway in the south aisle of the nave ; and in the vaulting of the south aisle ; all of the early part of the fifteenth century, the keys are in bend. Similar examples occur in the Lady Chapel (*c.* 1490), and others in the vaulting of the choir (*c.* 1525). A like

1. Canterbury.   2. York (Ancient).

3. York (Modern).   4. London.

5. Durham.   6. Winchester.

shield in TROMOND'S Chantry in WINCHESTER College (c. 1425) has the addition of a mullet in the base point.

But there are two shields in the vaulting of the nave which bear the sword, not the keys, in bend. Several like examples impaling Bishop LANGTON'S arms, are in his chapel (1505) and there are others of the time of Bishop FOX, and in Bishop GARDNER'S Chantry. The same arrangement is also apparent on a shield in the vaulting of the College tower (c. 1480).

The Bishop of WINCHESTER is Prelate of the Most Noble ORDER OF THE GARTER ; as such he places the Garter round his shield of arms. His badge is worn at the neck by a ribbon of garter-blue, and is of gold enamelled with the arms of the Order (*Argent, a cross of* ST. GEORGE *gules*) ; surrounded by the Garter, and surmounted by a mitre of gold. He has precedence next to the Bishop of DURHAM. The County of Hampshire, the Isle of Wight, West Surrey and the Channel Islands (formerly part of the Diocese of COUTANCES in Normandy) are in the jurisdiction of this See.

BANGOR.

Gules, a bend or, gutté de poix between two mullets pierced argent (Plate XXI., fig. 1).

This is the present, but probably not quite correct, blazon of these arms. Older blazons make the bend argent ; and both the Parliament Roll of 1512, and COLE'S MSS., charge this bend with *larmes*, or *azure drops*. The origin of the coat appears to be quite unknown ; it is found on the seal of Bishop MERRICK (1559-1566) impaled with his personal arms. The jurisdiction of this See includes Anglesey, and parts of Carnarvon, Merioneth, and Montgomery.

The Cathedral is dedicated to S. DANIEL, or DEINIOL, who was Bishop of the Principality of GWYNEDD in 516, and died in 584. HERVEUS, a Breton, was the first foreign bishop forced upon the See in 1092, but in 1109 he was driven from it, and translated to ELY (*see* HADDAN and STUBBS, i., p. 299, 304 et seq.). In 1120, DAVID, a Welshman from the Scotch Abbey at WÜRZBURG, was presented to the See by GRIFFITH, Prince of GWYNEDD, and was consecrated at WESTMINSTER, being the first Bishop of this See professing canonical obedience to the See of CANTERBURY. Between 1161 and 1177 BANGOR probably had a bishop yielding allegiance to the Irish Church (*see* HADDAN and STUBBS, i., 345, 375, etc.).

BATH and WELLS.

 Azure, a saltire quarterly-quartered or and argent (Plate XXI., fig. 2).

These are the arms of the See of WELLS alone, and are a modern variation of the cross of S. ANDREW, to whose honour the Cathedral of WELLS was dedicated.

The arms of the Abbey of BATH are, *Azure, two keys endorsed in bend-sinister, the upper argent, the lower or, their wards in chief; enfiled by a sword in bend of the second, the hilt in base gold.* This should properly be impaled with the coat of WELLS; unless there be a reversion to the old coat described below. The original dedication of the Abbey was probably to S. PETER, as his name alone appears on its first seal (1159-1175), but the effigy of S. PETER is accompanied by that of S. PAUL on the Chapter seal of 1530, and, as in the case of WINCHESTER, the arms are allusive to both saints. The seal of Bishop ROBERT BURNELL (1275-1292) has on one side of the Bishop's effigy the keys of S. PETER; on the other the saltire of S. ANDREW. Bishop MONTAGU (1608-1616) placed *a saltire or* for WELLS between the keys and sword of BATH; and in so doing appears to have partially followed the example of Bishop BEKINGTON (1443-1465), who placed a

1. Bangor. 2. Bath and Wells.

3. Bristol. 4. Carlisle.

5. Chester. 6. Chichester.

pastoral staff in pale behind the saltire, the keys in the *dexter*, and the sword in the *sinister* flank. This coat appears frequently in WELLS Cathedral. (*See* Appendix.)

The WESSEX Bishopric was divided in the year 705 into the Sees of WINCHESTER and SHERBORNE. (*See* HADDEN and STUBBS, iii., 275.) The Diocese of SOMERSET, with WELLS as the cathedral city, was separated from SHERBORNE in 909. The Bishop's throne was removed to BATH in 1122, without the consent of the Chapter of WELLS, and much strife arose between the monks of BATH Abbey and the Canons of WELLS in consequence. But in 1137 Bishop ROBERT got the controversy settled by arranging that both parties should have a voice in the Episcopal election, and that a Bishop's throne should be in both churches. Thus the title of the diocese became "BATH and WELLS," but the Cathedral of BATH was suppressed under HENRY VIII., and since 1542 the Chapter of WELLS has been the sole chapter of the Bishop, though the title of the See remains unchanged. The See comprises all Somersetshire, except the parish of Bedminster which is attached to BRISTOL.

BRISTOL.

Sable, three open crowns in pale or (Plate XXI., fig. 3).

The origin of these arms is unknown to me. MR MACKENZIE WALCOT'S suggestion that they are the coat of King EDMUND THE ELDER, buried at PUCKLE-CHURCH, near BRISTOL, is entirely without foundation. Possibly they may refer remotely to the dedication of the Cathedral to the Ever-Blessed Trinity. The same charges appear on a field *azure* on old stained glass in the choir. (*See* p. 198.)

The See of BRISTOL was erected by Henry VIII. in 1541, and was united to GLOUCESTER in 1836. It is now awaiting division therefrom, but the separation had

N

not taken place at the date of the publication of this book, and the arms of both the Sees are borne impaled by the present Bishop.

CHICHESTER:

Azure, Our Blessed Lord in glory seated on a throne proper, vested argent, girdled or, his dexter arm raised in the act of benediction. Issuant from his mouth fessways towards the sinister a sword proper. (The whole between two golden candlesticks with candles illuminated proper). (Plate XXI., fig. 6.)

These bearings occur as the devices on the seals of Bishops RICHARD DE LA WICH (1245-1253), and JOHN CLIPPING (1253-1262) ; Bishop SEFFRID II. (1180-1204) appears also to have used them, but his seal is not described in the *Brit. Mus. Catalogue.* They are evidently derived from the Book of the Revelations (i., 16. ; ii., 12-16 ; xix., 15-21) ; and were adopted from the early seals as the regular arms of the See.

On the seal of Dean WILLIAM GRENEFIELD (1296-1299) the figure is evidently that of the Blessed Saviour, though the sword is omitted (*Cat. of Seals in Brit. Mus.,* No. 1478). On the Chapter seal *ad causas,* in 1422, the Saviour is represented with the sword, but the candlesticks and candles are replaced by the letters Alpha and Omega. (*Ibid.,* No. 1473.)

In more modern times the origin of the arms was entirely forgotten ; and, as a consequence, the blazon has undergone a perversion almost unique in its absurdity, and unparalleled even in the history of Heraldry. The coat is still blazoned, I regret to say, with the authority of the College of Arms (and although its true meaning has been pointed out independently by the late Precentor of CHICHESTER, the Rev. MACKENZIE WALCOT, and myself) as follows :

"*Azure, a Presbyter-John sitting on a tombstone, his*

right hand extended, all or, with a linen mitre on his head
and in his mouth a sword proper."

As so blazoned it was a puzzle to heraldic students,
and many suggestions were made as to the reason of the
selection of the mythical mediæval personage known
as "Prester John" for the arms of the South Saxon
Bishopric ; for the "tombstone" on which he is seated ;
and for the sword, wrongly drawn as piercing the jaws
instead of issuing from the mouth. A quarter of a
century has elapsed since the true explanation was
pointed out, but so great is the vitality of error that
probably another quarter of a century may elapse before
the correction is authoritatively adopted ! It seems to
be the business of nobody at the Heralds' College to
put right an error, however patent, if only it be consecrated by precedent. Meanwhile seal-engravers and
compilers of heraldic manuals go on doing their best
to stereotype the error, in spite of its incongruity and
absurdity.

"PRESTER JOHN," once regarded as a mythical King
of Ethiopia, or Abyssinia, seems now to be thoroughly
identified with YELIN TASHI, the founder of the realm
of Kara Kitai, who after his conquest of Eastern and
Western Turkistan, became known by the title of
Gurkhan, and had his capital at BALA SAGUN (in the
valley of the Tchu). A full account of the legend of
Prester John, and of the modifications which it underwent, will be found in the interesting work of Dr
AUGUSTIN OPPERT, "*Der Presbyter Johannes in Sage*
und Geschichte." (*See* also YULE'S *Cathay*, pp. 173,
182 ; and his second edition of *Marco Polo*, vol. i., pp.
229-233; and ii., pp. 539-543.) Professor BRUUN of
Odessa, in his article on "*The Migrations of Prester*
John" (Odessa, 1870), propounds with some force a
theory that he was Prince ORBELIAN of Georgia.
(*See* SCHUYLER, *Turkistan*, vol. ii., p. 122, note.)

The jurisdiction of the See extends over the County of Sussex.

ELY.

Gules, three open crowns, two and one, or (Plate XXII., fig. 1).

These arms, which appear on the seal of Bishop WILLIAM DE LUDA (1290-1298) are those attributed to the foundress of the original monastery in the Isle of Ely, S. ETHELREDA, wife of EGFRID, King of Northumbria ; and to her, in conjunction with S. PETER, the present Cathedral is dedicated. The coats of arms assigned to the Saxon Kings are inventions of a very much later age than the date 673 assigned to the foundation of the monastery.

The See was created by HENRY I. in 1109. The Bishops had the jurisdiction and rights of Counts Palatine, but the Act of Parliament 27, HENRY VIII., cap. 35, swept away nearly the whole of their privileges. The present jurisdiction of the See comprises Cambridgeshire, the counties of Huntingdon and Bedford, and a small piece of Suffolk.

EXETER.

Gules, a sword erect in pale argent, the hilt in base or, surmounted by two keys endorsed in saltire of the last (Plate XXII., fig. 2).

The present dedication of the Cathedral is to S. PETER only, but the figures of SS. PETER and PAUL occur on the seal of Bishop WALTER BRONSCOMB (1258-1280), and were continued by several later Prelates, and in the seals of other diocesan officials. The arms are a combination of the emblems of both Apostles. The first instance of the use of a regular coat armorial for the See seems to be found in the seal of Bishop STAFFORD (1395-1419) on which two keys are represented in saltire

with an indistinct object in the base of the shield.
On the seal of his successor, Bishop EDMUND LACY
(1420-1455) the keys and sword were placed in saltire,
as in the arms of BATH and WINCHESTER.

The present arrangement appears first on the seal of
Bishop JOHN BOOTHE (1465-1478).

In Exeter Cathedral the arms of the See are represented with considerable variations. In the ancient east
window of the north aisle the keys appear endorsed and
erect, the bows being interlaced. Elsewhere a single
key and sword are placed in saltire ; two keys in saltire
without the sword, are also used ; and in Bishop
OLDHAM'S chantry the keys are in saltire, with a sword,
either in pale or in fess.

It is worthy of note that the arms of EXETER
COLLEGE, Oxford, are those of its founder WALTER
DE STAPELDON, Bishop of Exeter (1306-1329), who
added to his paternal arms (*Argent, two bars nebulée
sable*) *a bordure of the last charged with eight keys or.*
This bordure is sometimes blazoned *gules*, sometimes
azure, and the latter form is that employed at Oxford.
(*Vide post*, p. 231.) The jurisdiction of the See extends
over the whole of Devon, except five parishes which
belong to Truro.

GLOUCESTER.

Azure, two keys in saltire, wards in chief or (Plate
XXII., fig. 3).

The Abbey Church at GLOUCESTER was originally
dedicated to S. PETER, but afterwards to SS. PETER
and PAUL. (*See* Seals of fifteenth century, *B. Mus. Cat.*,
Nos. 3195, 3202.) The Pauline sword was then added in
pale to the keys of S. PETER (*New Monasticon*, i., 542),
but in later times has dropped out of use in the armorial
bearings of the See. It remains, however, with the hilt
in chief, upon a shield which is sculptured on the south

porch; upon the bells; and upon encaustic tiles of the Cathedral, as well as upon the Conventual Seal.

It is to be hoped that it may be restored to its old place ere long.

The See of GLOUCESTER was founded by HENRY VIII. in 1541. It was united to BRISTOL in 1836, but preparations are making for the dissolution. At present its jurisdiction consists of the County of Gloucester, Bristol, and portions of Somersetshire and Wiltshire; and the arms of the United See at present are those of GLOUCESTER impaling BRISTOL.

HEREFORD.

Gules, three leopard's faces reversed, two and one, jessant de lis or (Plate XXII., fig. 4).

These are derived from the personal arms of S. THOMAS DE CANTILUPE, who was Bishop from 1275 to 1282. The See was originally subject to the British Bishopric of S. DAVID'S. The dedication of the Cathedral is to S. ETHELBERT.

The original arms of CANTILUPE were: *Gules, three fleurs-de-lis* only. Bishop CANTILUPE bore *three leopard's heads jessant fleur-de-lis;* the reversal for the See may have been intended as a "difference." The jurisdiction of the See comprises the County of Hereford, and parts of the counties immediately adjacent thereto.

LICHFIELD.

Per pale gules and argent, a cross potent and quadrated between four crosses patées all counter-changed (Plate XXII., fig. 5).

The origin of these arms is unknown, but they have a certain resemblance to the arms of Jerusalem. This resemblance was stronger when, as formerly, the *crosses patées* on the *argent* half of the shield were painted *or*. As a mere conjecture I suggest that there may be a

1. Ely.

2. Exeter.

3. Gloucester.

4. Hereford.

5. Lichfield.

6. Lincoln.

connection between the cross which was worn by the Knights of the *Holy Sepulchre*, and the supposed derivation of LICHFIELD from an ancient field of the dead, or cemetery. The earliest seal on which the bearing appears (at least in the British Museum collection) is that of Bishop WILLIAM BOOTH (1447-1452) in which it is described as a "cross potent," only. Mr MACKENZIE WALCOT thinks the coat may have been given by Bishop CLINTON, the Crusader, in memory of his visit to the Holy Land. (*N. and Q.*, 5th S., ii.; p. 462.) In FROISSART'S *Chronicles*, tome iv., cap. lxiii., a banner borne by RICHARD II. on his expedition to Ireland, is said to have been " Une croix potencée d'or et de gueules à quatre colombes blanc au champ de l'escu." (PLANCHÉ, *Pursuivant at Arms*, p. 213.)

I notice that the seals of Bishops RICHARD SCROPE (1386-1398), and WILLIAM SMITH (1493-1496) have on them a shield charged with an eagle, the charge in the reputed arms of the kingdom of MERCIA. This would refer to the See of COVENTRY. (*Cat. of Seals in the British Museum*, Nos. 1640, 1643.) The eagle also appears on the seal of Bishop RICHARD SAMPSON (1543-1554), but is not included in an escucheon (*ibid.*, No. 1645).

The variations of the See are briefly as follows : See of MERCIA, founded 656. Bishopric of LICHFIELD, 669. Archbishopric, 786. (HIGBERT was the only Archbishop of Lichfield.) Bishopric only, 799. Throne removed to CHESTER, 1075; to COVENTRY, 1085. United Bishopric of COVENTRY and LICHFIELD, 1385 ; of LICHFIELD and COVENTRY, 1661 ; of LICHFIELD alone, 1836. The dedication of the cathedral is to the Blessed Virgin (whose effigy carrying the Holy Child appears upon the early seals) ; and to S. CHAD. The jurisdiction of the See comprises Staffordshire, and part of Shropshire.

LINCOLN.

Gules, two lions passant guardant in pale or ; on a chief azure the effigy of the Blessed Virgin, seated, crowned, and sceptred, and holding the Holy Child, all of the second (Plate XXII., fig. 6).

Up to 1496 the Episcopal seals usually contain the effigy of the Blessed Virgin · with . the Child ; but on the seals of Bishop WILLIAM SMITH (1495-1514) the shield of arms at present used appears. As the throne of the Bishop of the See, formed by the union of the ancient Bishoprics of DOR-CHESTER and SIDNACESTER, was placed at LIN-COLN in 1075 by WILLIAM the Conqueror, the arms borne by him (or at least by his successors, kings of England and dukes of Normandy) may have been used to commemorate the founder. The suggestion that the arms may have originated in the fact that GEOFFREY PLANTAGENET (natural son of King HENRY II. by FAIR ROSAMOND) was Bishop-elect, though without consecration, from 1173 to 1182, does not now appear to me so probable as at one time it did. The dedication of the Cathedral is to the Blessed Virgin, and All Saints. The jurisdiction of this See consists of the County of Lincoln.

LLANDAFF.

Sable, two pastoral staves endorsed in saltire, the dexter or, the sinister argent. On a chief azure three mitres, with their infulæ, or. (Plate XXIII., fig. 2.)

On the seal of an early bishop (whose name I am unable to give) in my cabinet, the arms are : *A sword in bend, above a key in bend-sinister.* Bishop MARSHALL (1478-1496) bore *two keys in bend sinister enfiled by a sword in bend,* with the chief charged as at present.

1. Liverpool.

2. Llandaff.

3. Manchester.

4. Newcastle.

5. Norwich.

6. Oxford.

The Cathedral is dedicated to S. DAVID. The See was founded for the principality of GWENT by DUBRICIUS (d. 612), perhaps even earlier by S. TEILO. The counties of Monmouth and of Glamorgan, excepting the district of Gower, are in the jurisdiction of this See.

NORWICH.

Azure, three mitres, two and one, or (Plate XXIII., fig. 5).

These arms appear in 1351 on the seal of Bishop WILLIAM BATEMAN (1344-1355), and may possibly refer to the union in the See of NORWICH of the Bishoprics of THETFORD, DUNWICH, and ELMHAM. The dedication of the Cathedral is to the Ever-Blessed Trinity.

OXFORD.

Sable, a fess argent, in chief three ladies crowned with open crowns proper, vested of the second, couped below the breasts. In base an ox of the second passing a ford barry wavy argent and azure. (Plate XXIII., fig. 6.)

This See was founded by HENRY VIII. in 1541. The base contains the punning arms of the city. (The ox and ford appear in the base of the thirteenth century Seal of the Carmelites at Oxford. (*Cat. of Seals in Brit. Mus.*, No. 3812.) Probably the heads in chief should be rather of kings than of queens, and they, like the crowns in the University arms, may refer to the Royal Founders of the University. Since the Royal Castle of Windsor with the Chapel of S. GEORGE has been included in the Diocese of OXFORD, the Bishop has held the high office of Chancellor of the Most Noble ORDER OF THE GARTER. As such he surrounds the shield of his arms with that illustrious ensign; and wears the badge of his office:—a golden medal surrounded by the Garter, and enamelled on the one side with the arms of the Order (*Argent, a cross gules*), on the other with a red rose. The badge is worn at the neck from the ribbon of garter-blue. This office was originally attached to the See of SALISBURY, in which diocese Windsor was situated. The present jurisdiction of the See comprises the counties of Oxford, Berkshire, and Buckinghamshire.

PETERBOROUGH.

Gules, two keys addorsed in saltire, between four crosslets fitchées or (Plate XXIV., fig. 1).

The See was founded by HENRY VIII. in 1541. The dedication of the Cathedral is to S. PETER, and the keys are allusive thereto. The seal of the Abbey (consecrated in 664) appears to have borne only the Petrine keys, without the crosslets, in the thirteenth century (*Catalogue of Seals in the Brit. Mus.*, No. 3830. *See* also the seal of RICHARD ASHTON, Abbot (1438?), *ibid.*, No. 3838.) The counties of Northampton, Leicester, and Rutland are in the jurisdiction of this See.

ROCHESTER.

Argent, on a saltire gules an escallop or (Plate XXIV., fig. 3).

The Cross of S. ANDREW in these arms alludes to the dedication of the Cathedral to that saint. The *escallop* may possibly refer to the oyster fisheries of the diocese. (The early seals of the Priory bear the effigy of S. ANDREW on the cross, *v. Brit. Mus. Cat.*, Nos. 3919, 3920.) ITHAMAR, of this See, consecrated in 664, was the first *English* Bishop in the land. The jurisdiction of the See consists of parts of the counties of Kent and Surrey.

ST. ALBANS.

Azure, a saltire or, surmounted by a sword in pale proper, above the point thereof in chief a celestial crown of the second (Plate XXIV., fig. 4).

At the erection of the See in 1877 the arms blazoned

1. Peterborough.

2. Ripon.

3. Rochester.

4. St. Albans.

5. St. Asaph.

6. St. Davids.

above were granted to it. They are composed from the old arms of the Abbey: *Azure, a saltire or;* and the sword and celestial crown refer to the martyrdom of the patron saint. (*See* the following letter from the Bishop of ROCHESTER, first Bishop of S. ALBANS to me. "Henley, Feb. 12, 1877. Dear Sir,—We take for the coat of the See of St. Alban's the old arms, the saltire cross, and pass through the centre of it the sword with the point upwards and the celestial crown over it. This I think is what you would recommend.—Yours faithfully, T. L. ROFFEN.")

The jurisdiction comprises the counties of Essex, and Hertfordshire, and North Woolwich.

ST. ASAPH.

Sable, two keys endorsed in saltire wards in chief argent (Plate XXIV., fig. 5).

These arms appear on the seals of Bishops ROBERT LANCASTER (1411-1433) and WILLIAM HUGHES (1573-1600). But on the seals of Bishop JOHN TREVOR (1395) and in the Procession Roll of 1512, the key in bend is surmounted by a pastoral staff in bend-sinister. This arrangement also appears on the seal of Bishop JOHN WYNNE (1715-1727). S. KENTIGERN probably founded this See of LLANELWY for the Principality of POWYS, early in the seventh century, and left it in charge of his disciple S. ASAPH. It was the last British See which held out against submission to the See of Canterbury.

The jurisdiction of this See comprises the counties of Denbigh, and Flint, with parts of Carnarvon, Montgomery, Merioneth, and Shropshire.

ST. DAVIDS.

Sable, on a cross or, five cinquefoils of the field (Plate XXIV., fig. 6).

The origin of these arms is unknown to me. It has often been asserted that in British times there were three Archi-episcopal Sees, London, York, and Caerleon, and that on the advance of the Saxon power the See of CAERLEON was removed to MENEVIA by S. DAVID (d. 601), from whom the place takes its present name.

Although a kind of primacy was claimed for the Bishop of S. DAVIDS in the eighth and ninth centuries "there is no real evidence for the existence of any Archi-episcopate at all in Wales during the Welsh period, if the term is held to imply jurisdiction admitted or even claimed (until the twelfth century) by one See over another." (HADDEN and STUBBS, vol. i., p. 148.)

The claims to Archi-episcopal authority first advanced by BERNARD, Bishop of S. DAVIDS (1115-1148), and afterwards by GIRALDUS, were made with the object of gaining not rule over Wales, but freedom from CANTERBURY, and in the latter case, from English nominees to Welsh Bishoprics. (HADDEN and STUBBS, vol. i., pp. 149-150.)

The jurisdiction of ST. DAVIDS consists of the counties of Pembroke, Cardigan, Caermarthen, Brecknock, with parts of Radnor and Glamorgan.

SALISBURY.

> *Azure, the Blessed Virgin standing crowned, vested and holding in her arms the Holy Child all or* (Plate XXV., fig. 1).

The Cathedral is dedicated to the Blessed Virgin, and to this dedication the arms allude. The figure of the Virgin and Child at full length but seated, appears first on the seal of Bishop RICHARD MITFORD (1395-1407). And in this manner it had been previously represented on the seals of officials of the See, the Dean and Chapter, and Archdeacons of Berkshire; the earliest example being found in the counter-seal of Adam, the Chancellor in 1239 (*Brit. Mus. Cat. of Seals*, No. 2233). But a half-length figure of the Virgin and Child appears on the small counter-seals of Bishop ROBERT BINGHAM (1229-1246), and of Bishop ROBERT WICKHAMPTON (1274-1284.) The seated figure is the main device on the seals of Bishops ROBERT HALLAM (1407-1417), and RICHARD BEAUCHAMP (1450-1481); and, but half length only, in the upper portion of that of LORENZO, Cardinal CAMPEGGI (1525-1534).

The earliest seal in the British Museum Collection which contains the figures enclosed in a shield as heraldic charges is that of Bishop BENJAMIN HOADLEY (1723-1724), where the coat is impaled to the dexter with his personal arms: Quarterly, *Azure and or, in the first quarter a pelican in piety argent.* The shield is encircled with the Garter and badge of the ORDER OF THE GARTER, the office of Chancellor of that Illustrious Order being at that time attached to the See of SALISBURY (*vide ante*, p. 79). The See has jurisdiction over the whole of Dorsetshire, and the greater part of Wiltshire.

SOUTHWELL.

> *Sable, three fountains proper* (i.e. *barry wavy azure and argent*), *a chief tierced per pale ; (a) Or, a stag couchant proper; (b) Gules (? Azure), the figure* (or *demi-figure*) *of the Blessèd Virgin and Child* (as *in the arms of* LINCOLN) ; *(c) Or, two staves raguly in cross, vert* (Plate XXV., fig. 3).

This See, which has under its jurisdiction the counties of Derby and Nottingham, was founded in the year 1884.

TRURO.

> *Argent, on a saltire gules a key, wards upward in bend ; surmounted by a sword, hilt in chief, in bend-sinister, both or ; in base a fleur-de-lis sable. All within a bordure of* CORNWALL, *viz., Sable fifteen bezants.* (Plate XXV., fig. 4.)

The red *saltire*, the cross of S. PATRICK, is taken as

the heraldic symbol (in modern times only) of the ancient Celtic Church. The sword and key in saltire are taken from a shield in the church of S. GERMANS, the old Episcopal seat. The *fleur-de-lis* is assumed to denote the transference of the See to the church of ST. MARY at Truro. The bordure is composed from the arms of the Duchy of CORNWALL. The See was founded in 1877. Its jurisdiction is the County of Cornwall, the Scilly Isles, and a few parishes of Devonshire.

WORCESTER.

Argent, ten torteaux in pile (Plate XXV., fig. 6).

The arms of the See of WORCESTER, like those of the See of HEREFORD, are assumed from the personal arms of one of its bishops. Bishop GIFFARD (1268-1302) bore the arms given above.

The first known Episcopal Seal on which these appear as Diocesan arms is that of Bishop THOMAS PEVERELL (1407-1419). They are there impaled with his personal coat. The jurisdiction of the See comprises the counties of WORCESTER and WARWICK, and some small enclaves in the counties of STAFFORD and OXFORD.

THE PROVINCE OF YORK.

comprises the following Sees :—

YORK, DURHAM, CARLISLE, CHESTER, LIVERPOOL, MANCHESTER, NEWCASTLE, RIPON, SODER AND MAN, and WAKEFIELD.

YORK.

Gules, two keys addorsed in saltire, the wards upwards argent, in chief a royal crown proper (Plate XX., fig. 3).

The old arms of the Archi-episcopal See of YORK seem to have been identical with those now borne for CANTERBURY ; but the present bearings appear as

1. Salisbury.

2. Sodor and Man.

3. Southwell.

4. Truro.

5. Wakefield.

6. Worcester.

early as the seal of Archbishop ROBERT WALDBY (1397-1398), though the crown is more properly the Papal tiara. Another seal of the same Archbishop has, however, the ancient arms impaling his personal coat. The seal of Archbishop BOWET (1407-1423) bears the modern arms, although on a window in the Cathedral his arms appear impaled with the ancient coat, of which curiously the field is *gules*, not *azure*.

Both coats appear, on separate shields, upon the seal of Archbishop SAVAGE (1501-1507); but it is the ancient one which is impaled with the personal arms of the prelate (Plate XX., fig. 2). The seal of Archbishop EDWARD LEE (1531-1544), is, so far as I am aware, the latest upon which the ancient coat is found. On the seals of Archbishops WALDBY and LEE, the *pallium* is charged with *five* crosses *patées fitchées*, and this may have formed a distinction between the arms of the Sees of YORK and CANTERBURY, as it does in the parallel case of DUBLIN and ARMAGH.

The arms at present borne refer to the dedication of the Cathedral to S. PETER.

The Archbishopric of YORK is the most ancient in England, and dates from the first introduction of Christianity into this land. "Eborius Episcopus de civitate Eboracensi provincia Britannia," was one of the three British Bishops present at the Synod of Arles in 314; and a Bishop of YORK was present at the councils of Nicæa, Sardica, and Ariminum, after the conquest of Britain by the Pagan Danes and Saxons, and the consequent obliteration of Christianity in all but the mountain lands of Wales, Cumberland, etc. (where the original British Church still survived under bishops owning no allegiance to the See of ROME). On the reintroduction of Christianity by the Roman Mission under Saint AUGUSTINE, it was again made an Archiepiscopal See, and claimed jurisdiction over the Scottish Sees. (*Vide infra*, pp. 216, 224.)

The precedence of CANTERBURY was long contested by the Archbishops of YORK, but the claim of the latter was established by Papal authority, though the Archbishop of YORK was permitted to bear the title of "Primate of England," which he still retains, and he, also, is designated "*His Grace.*" In the Table of Precedency the Lord High Chancellor alone intervenes between him and his brother of CANTERBURY.

DURHAM.
> *Azure, a cross or between four lions rampant argent*
> (Plate XX., fig. 5).

The earliest *Episcopal* seal in the British Museum Collection on which this coat appears, seems to be that of Bishop ROBERT NEVILLE (1438-1457), but on the shield · representing the arms of this prelate in the east window of Leek Church (a liberty belonging to him) the cross is the cross patonce, which also appears on the seal of Bishop LAWRENCE BOOTH, official for the sequestrator, in 1474 (*Catalogue of Seals in British Museum*, i., No. 2510).

This bearing, cantoned with the four silver lions, is commonly known as the "Arms of S. CUTHBERT;" and is attributed to the monastery of DURHAM. The plain cross appears on the seals of Bishops DUDLEY (1476-1483) and WILLIAM SEVER (1502-1505), but on that of Bishop RUTHALL (1509-1523) it is replaced by the cross patonce. This form, impaling RUTHALL, is in the dining-room of Auckland Castle, though on his palatinate seal the coat with the plain cross is similarly used. (*Herald and Genealogist*, viii., 156.) The plain cross is the one impaled by TUNSTALL, in Auckland Castle (*ibid.*, p. 160). Bishop WILLIAM DUDLEY made the lions *passant*. (*Cat. of Seals, Brit. Mus.*, No. 2477.) It may be noticed that the plain cross with the lions is to be seen on a fifteenth century seal of the Vicar-General of the diocese.

On a seal of Bishop TUNSTALL (1530-1559) the Cuthbertine coat is impaled with his personal arms, but on another seal (in the *Brit. Mus. Collection,* No. 2483) I gather that the plain cross was used. The plain cross is employed by both Bishops RUTHALL and TUNSTALL on their Palatinate seals ; and this was the form used pretty generally by the later bishops. Instances are to be found in which, but probably by mistake only, the lions are blazoned *or.* As Counts Palatine the Bishops of DURHAM used seals on which they are represented in full armour, and mounted, brandishing a sword, and wearing a coroneted helmet surmounted either by a plumed mitre, or by their personal crests (*vide ante,* pp. 101, 102). Their personal arms are borne upon the shield and the caparisons of the horses. The mitre rising from a coronet is still used as a heraldic ornament, although the palatinate jurisdiction was finally abolished (1835-1836) by the Act of Parliament (6 WM. IV., cap. 19). The union of the temporal and spiritual power was also sometimes indicated, as in Germany, by the sword and pastoral staff being placed in saltire behind the shield. The Bishop has precedence next after the Bishop of LONDON.

CARLISLE.

Argent, on a cross sable, a mitre with labels or (Plate XXI., fig. 4).

These arms are said by Mr MACKENZIE WALCOT (*N. and Q.,* 5th S, ii., 462) to be those of the Priory. In the Parliament Roll of EDWARD VI. (1553) the arms of the See appear impaling the personal arms of Bishop ROBERT ALDRICH (1537-1556), and a royal crown replaces the mitre on the centre of the cross (*see* BEDFORD, *Blazon of Episcopacy,* p. 115). The See was founded by HENRY I. in the year 1133, and then consisted of the lands won from Scotland in 1092, which had previously been under the jurisdiction of the See of

o

WHITHORN, or GALLOWAY. The northern portion of Lancashire, "beyond the sands," was added to CARLISLE in 1847, when the Diocese of CHESTER was divided, and the See of MANCHESTER created.

CHESTER.

> *Gules, three mitres with labels, two and one or* (Plate XXI., fig. 5).

The coat is said to have been borne for the Priory before the erection of the Post-Reformation See.

This See was one of the six founded by King HENRY VIII. in 1541. Before this the County of CHESTER had had been included in the Diocese of LICHFIELD, but the throne of the Bishop of the See was at CHESTER from 1075 to 1085 (*v. ante*, LICHFIELD, p. 182).

The County of Lancaster, and portions of Yorkshire, with Cumberland and Westmoreland, were originally included in the See, which now consists simply of the County of Chester.

LIVERPOOL.

> *Argent, the eagle of* S. JOHN *the Evangelist, with its wings expanded sable ; beaked, armed, and nimbed or, holding in its dexter claw an ancient ink-horn of the second. A chief per pale azure and gules, on the first an open book or, inscribed with the words* " Thy Word is truth ;" *on the second an ancient ship of three masts gold.* (Plate XXIII., fig. 1.)

The arms of the See of LIVERPOOL, founded in 1880 contain the Eagle of S. JOHN which appears on the ancient seal of the borough. This in modern times has been wrongly considered to represent the mythical " liver," a bird of the cormorant species, with a sprig of laver (or seaweed) in its beak, from which the city was erroneously supposed to derive its name. The ship on the chief is a fitting hieroglyphic of the immense commerce of the port. The open book was introduced at the urgent request of the first Bishop (RYLE); but these texts in minute characters rather complicate, and so spoil, what would otherwise have been a simple and appropriate design (*cf.* KILDARE, p. 209).

The eagle holds the penner and ink-horn of the Evangelist, in accordance with the old legend which declares that S. JOHN was constantly attended by an eagle bearing his writing materials. The real cause of the attribution of the eagle to S. JOHN as his peculiar symbol was, of course, widely different. The first charter of the borough was given by King JOHN.

MANCHESTER.

Or, on a pale engrailed gules three mitres labelled of the field. On a canton of the second three bendlets enhanced, also of the field. (Plate XXIII., fig. 3.)

The canton in this coat is allusive to the bearings of the city of MANCHESTER, which are: *Gules, three bendlets enhanced or, on a chief argent a ship in full sail proper.* These arms (without the chief) were borne by the family of GRESLET, GRELÉ, or GRELLEY, feudal barons of MANCHESTER in Norman times. The *engrailed pale* in the arms of the See is said also to be allusive to the name of this family. The See was founded in 1847, and consists of the southern portion of Lancashire, formerly comprised in the See of Chester.

NEWCASTLE.

Gules, three castles argent, on a chief azure the cross of S. CUTHBERT *or* (Plate XXIII., fig. 4).

The base of the arms contains the bearings of the city of Newcastle. The chief commemorates the fact that the See was formed out of the ancient Diocese of DURHAM. The cross of ST. CUTHBERT is that which was found on the breast of the saint in 1827.

RIPON.

Argent, on a saltire gules, two keys in saltire wards up-
wards or. On a chief of the second a Paschal-
Lamb proper. (Plate XXIV., fig. 2.)

The Paschal-Lamb on the chief is probably derived
from a seal of the Abbey of Saint WILFRID at RIPON,
in the twelfth century. The keys are probably from the
arms of the See of York, out of which the new See took
its origin in 1836; it includes also the Yorkshire portion
of the old Diocese of Chester. RIPON seems to have
been a Bishop's See for a few years in Anglo-Saxon
times, but was merged in York on WILFRID'S restoration in 686. (HADDAN and STUBBS, iii., 165.)

SODOR AND MAN.

Gules, between two pillars argent, the Blessed Virgin
standing with arms extended, vested crowned and
nimbed, holding in her right hand an ancient
church all proper. In the base of the shield the
charge of the arms of the Island of MAN ; *three*
legs in armour, flexed and conjoined in pairle, proper,
garnished and spurred or. (Plate XXV., fig. 2.)

The figure in these arms is more probably that of
S. GERMANUS, who was left as Bishop in MAN by
S. PATRICK, in 447. The pillars are only the remains
of the architectural canopy under which on the ancient
seals the effigy of the bishop, or patron saint, was
placed. (*See* the Seals of Bishops MARK, 1275, JOHN,
1408, etc., *Cat. of Seals in Brit. Mus.*, Nos. 2529-2531.)

The See originally included the Hebrides, as well as
the island of MAN. The old Norse name for the
Hebrides was the Sudreys, or Sudreyar, the southern
islands; and from this word is derived the title of SODOR,
which is still retained, although the Hebrides now form the
Scottish diocese of " THE ISLES," having been separated
from MAN for some centuries. While under Norwegian

rule the See was suffragan to the Archbishop of
NIDAROS or TRONDHJEM, by whom the bishops were
for the most part consecrated from the time of the
erection of the Metropolitan See of NIDAROS in 1154
up to about the middle of the fourteenth century. The
Archbishop of YORK, however, always protested that
MAN was under his jurisdiction, and sometimes consecrated the Bishop up to 1226. (See *The Chronicle of Man—
Chronica Regum Manniæ et Insularum*, edited by Professor
MUNCH, Christiania, 1860.) ALEXANDER of Scotland
subdued MAN in 1266; in 1314 it became subject to the
crown of England, and EDWARD III. gave the title of King
of MAN to MONTACUTE, Earl of SALISBURY. In 1341
the Earl of NORTHUMBERLAND had this dignity, but on
his attainder King HENRY IV. granted it to Sir JOHN
STANLEY. It was long held by the Earls of DERBY,
from whom it came by descent to the Duke of ATHOLL
in 1735. From him the Sovereign rights were purchased
by the State in 1765 ; and all claims on the revenue, etc.,
were extinguished by a further payment in 1829. The
Bishop of SODOR and MAN has a seat, but no vote, in the
House of Lords, because the Isle of MAN has a separate
legislature of its own in which the Bishop has a share. The
jurisdiction of the See consists only of the Isle of MAN.

WAKEFIELD.

*Or, a fleur-de-lis azure, on a chief of the same, three
celestial crowns of the first* (Plate XXV., fig. 5).

The arms of the See (created in 1888) are based on
the arms of the city of WAKEFIELD which are : *Azure,
a fleur-de-lis or.*

The jurisdiction of the See comprises parts of the
West Riding of Yorkshire.

" Suffragan Bishops " (or *Chorepiscopi*), appointed
under the Acts, 26 HENRY VIII., and 1 ELIZABETH,
use only their personal arms, ensigned with the mitre.

ARMS OF ENGLISH DEANERIES.

CANTERBURY. *Azure, on a cross argent, the monogram* ⟨monogram⟩ *sable.*

LONDON. *The arms of the See ; in chief the letter* D *or.*

WINCHESTER. *The arms of the See, in chief the letter* D *or.*

BANGOR. *Argent, an abbot in pontificals proper.*

BRISTOL. *Sable (but ? Azure), three open crowns in pale or (v.* p. 177).

CHICHESTER. In 1422 the seal of the Dean and Chapter *ad causas* bears the figure of the Saviour, as in the arms of the See, but between the Greek letters A and Ω. In 1428 and 1523 these are omitted, but the Saviour holds an open book (*Cat. of Seals in Brit. Mus.*, Nos. 1473, 1469, and 1478).

ELY. *Gules, three keys erect or.* In S. ANDREW'S Church, Ely (*v. Gent. Mag.*, April 1860). Brass to Dean TYNDALL, Ely Cathedral. Glass in East window, S. Andrew's Church, Cambridge. Seal of PATRICK, fifteenth century (*B. Mus. Cat.*, No. 1585).

EXETER. *Azure, a stag's head caboshed, between the horns a cross patée-fitchée argent (vide ante,* p. 55.)

GLOUCESTER. *Argent, three chevrons gules between ten torteaux.*

HEREFORD. *Gules, five chevrons or (Cat. of Seals, B. Mus.*, Nos. 1618, 1620).

LICHFIELD. *The arms of the See, on the cross the letter* D *sable.*

LINCOLN. *The arms of the See, in chief the letter* D *or.*

NORWICH. *Argent, a cross sable.*

PETERBOROUGH. *Gules, two swords in saltire, between four crosses patées argent (B. Mus. Cat.*, No. 2144).

SALISBURY. *The arms of the See, the letter* D *in chief.*

ST. DAVID'S. *The arms of the See, but with reversed tinctures (v.* p. 187).

WELLS. Probably, *Azure, a saltire or,* only (as on tomb of Dean HUSEE in 1305); but the keys of S. PETER, and the sword of S. PAUL are generally placed erect in either flank (*cf.* the arms of the See, p. 176, *ante.*)

WORCESTER. The arms of the See, and (?) *on a canton gules the* BLESSED VIRGIN *with the* HOLY CHILD *proper.*

YORK. *The modern arms of the See, but with a mitre in chief or. Gules, two keys addorsed argent, between in chief a royal crown, or; in base and flanks three plates.* (These may possibly be Hosts. *See* the elaborate work on the *Heraldry of York Minster,* by Dean PUREY-CUST.)

DURHAM. *Arms of the See, with the letter* D *sable in centre.*

CARLISLE. *Argent, a cross sable* (?).

RIPON. *Argent, on a saltire gules the letter* D *of the field.*

ARMS OF CERTAIN ECCLESIASTICAL FOUNDATIONS.

THE CHAPEL-ROYAL OF S. GEORGE AT WINDSOR.

The arms of the Order of the Garter, viz.: *Argent, a S. George's cross gules.* The shield is encircled by the blue Garter, with its motto—"*Honi soit qui mal y pense.*"

THE SEE OF WESTMINSTER (1540-1550). (Now often used for the Abbey.)

Azure, the reputed arms of EDWARD THE CONFESSOR, viz.: *A cross patonce between five martlets or, on a chief of the same, between two double roses of Lancaster and York, barbed and seeded proper, a pale charged with the Royal arms* (viz., Quarterly of FRANCE and ENGLAND).

THE ABBEY OF WESTMINSTER (modern).

Azure, on a chief indented or, the head of a pastoral staff and a mitre gules.

THE COLLEGE OF MIDDLEHAM.

The Royal Arms: *Quarterly,* 1 and 4. ENGLAND; 2. FRANCE-ANCIENT; 3. IRELAND.

THE CHAPEL-ROYAL, SAVOY.

*Argent, on a cross gules an ostrich feather, its escroll of
the first thereon the motto* ich dien, *between in chief a
sword, in base a fleur-de-lis above an ink-moline, in
dexter flank a house, and in sinister flank a lion passant, all or. On a chief paly of four azure and of the
second a Paschal-Lamb couchant proper, between two
bezants, each ensigned with an Imperial crown, and
charged with a double rose of* YORK *and* LANCASTER.
This escucheon is supported on the breast of an
eagle displayed sable, quilled, beaked, and crowned
with an Imperial crown, or. (*N.B.*—The eagle
should not be placed in an escucheon, it supports
the shield *by the guige* held in its beak.)

IRELAND.

At the creation of the four Archbishoprics of ARMAGH,
DUBLIN, CASHEL, and TUAM, by the Synod of KELLS
in 1151-1152, Ireland had thirty-two dioceses. The inde-
pendence of the Irish Church was acknowledged at this
Synod; and the jurisdiction previously claimed by the
Archbishop of CANTERBURY over Ireland was given up.

In later times several of the Sees were held together.
At the time of the passing of the "Church Temporalities
Act" in 1833, there were four Archbishoprics and
eighteen Bishoprics existing. But by that Act the
Archbishops of CASHEL and TUAM were to be abolished
on the decease of the then Archbishops, and the number
of the Suffragan Sees was similarly to be reduced to ten
by the union of certain of them to other existing Sees.

The Irish Church was disestablished by Act of Parliament in 1871, and since then the Bishopric of CLOGHER
has been restored as a separate See, having been separated in 1886 from ARMAGH, to which it had been
united on the death of Lord ROBERT TOTTENHAM, in
1850, according to the provisions of the Act of 1833.

It must be noted that most, if not all, of the arms at present used for the Irish Sees are of Post-Reformation assumption ; most of the old Irish Episcopal seals bear simply the effigy of the Bishop, or of the Patron saints of the diocese (*v. ante*, p. 171).

ARMAGH. Archbishopric.
Suffragan Sees :—MEATH ; CLOGHER ; DERRY and RAPHOE ; DOWN, CONNOR, and DROMORE ; KILMORE, ELPHIN, and ARDAGH ; TUAM, KILLALA, and ACHONRY.

DUBLIN. Archbishopric.
Suffragan Sees :—OSSORY, FERNS, and LEIGHLIN ; CASHEL, EMLY, WATERFORD, and LISMORE ; CORK, CLOYNE, and ROSS ; KILLALOE, KILFENORA, CLONFERT, and KILMACDUAGH ; LIMERICK, ARDFERT, and AGHADOE.

ARMAGH.
Azure, an Episcopal staff in pale argent, ensigned with a cross patée or, surmounted by a pall-throughout argent, edged and fringed gold, charged with four crosses formée-fitchées sable (Plate XXVI., fig. 1).

It will be seen that these arms are identical with those of CANTERBURY. The seal of Archbishop OCTAVIAN DE PALATIO (1480-1513) (*see* WARE'S *Irish Bishops, sub voce*) bears two shields ; one charged with two keys in saltire, which was probably borne for the See ; the other bearing a fess, perhaps the personal arms of the prelate.

The See was founded by S. PATRICK about the year 444, and became archi-episcopal under Bishop GELASIUS, who received the *pallium* from Pope EUGENIUS IV. in 1152. The Archbishop is "Primate of all IRELAND." The office of Prelate of the most Illustrious ORDER OF

S. PATRICK was attached to the See on its institution in 1783; and the light blue ribbon of that Order, with its motto "*Quis separabit*," placed round the archi-episcopal arms, served as a sufficient difference from the arms of the Archbishopric of CANTERBURY. Since the dis-establishment of the Irish Church the office of Prelate of the Order of S. PATRICK has ceased.

MEATH.

> *Sable, three mitres argent, two and one* (Plate XXVI., fig. 3).

This diocese is composed of several ancient Sees (TRIM, KELLS, ARDBRACCAN, SLANE, etc.), which were consolidated with the Bishopric of CLONARD before 1152.

CLONARD was founded by ST. FINIAN as a school of the prophets about the year 520, but, though WARE calls him Bishop, it is probable that he was only of Abbatial rank. To the Bishopric of CLONARD the Sees of KELLS and DULEEK were afterwards conjoined. The three mitres may thus be allusive to these three Sees.

The field of these arms has sometimes been tinctured *vert* (see KENT'S *Banner Displayed*, p. 578). WARE blazons the arms : *Sapphire (azure) three mitres with labels Topaz (or)* but his cut is *sable*. (*Irish Bishops*, p. 135.)

The Bishop of MEATH has precedence over all Irish Bishops, and the title of "Most Reverend" is borne by him as a mark of this dignity. The Bishopric of CLAN-MACNOIS, founded by S. KIARAN (a pupil with S. COLUMBA of S. FINIAN at CLONARD), but in his time (he died in 549) probably only an Abbacy, was united to MEATH in 1568.

CLOGHER.

> *Azure, a Bishop seated in full pontificals proper, in the act of benediction, and holding his pastoral staff in the left hand* (Plate XXVI., fig. 5).

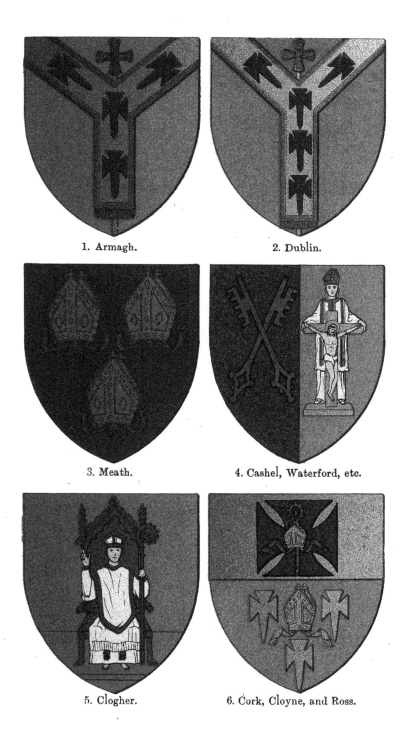

1. Armagh.

2. Dublin.

3. Meath.

4. Cashel, Waterford, etc.

5. Clogher.

6. Cork, Cloyne, and Ross.

This is probably a survival of the device on the old Episcopal seal, and not properly speaking a heraldic charge. (*See* my remarks on pages 216, 217.) The See, united to ARMAGH in 1850, was restored to a separate existence in 1886. It was originally founded by S. MACARTIN (?) who was a disciple of S. PATRICK, and died in 506.

DERRY and RAPHOE.
> *Gules, two swords in saltire proper, the hilts in base or ; on a chief* the arms of IRELAND : *azure, a harp or, stringed argent.* DERRY.
> *Ermine, a chief per pale azure and or ; the first charged with a sun in splendour of the last ; the second with a cross patée gules.* RAPHOE.

These coats are usually borne impaled (Plate XXVII., fig. 1).

In the last edition of BURKE'S *General Armory*, 1878, the ancient arms of the See of DERRY are said to have been *a church proper*. This appears to be only the remains of the architectural porch, or canopy, under which the bishop, or patron saint, was represented on ancient seals. *Sable, three mitres or*, were the arms confirmed to the See by CARNEY, " ULSTER ; " but, apparently in consequence of their similarity to those of MEATH, Bishop KING, of DERRY (1690-1702) had the arms changed to those at present borne.

The second half of the chief of RAPHOE is often blazoned *argent*, but I now think wrongly. WARE in his *Irish Bishops*, p. 269, makes this half *gules* and the charge *or* in his blazon, but his cut is correctly as above.

The See of DERRY was originally founded at ARD-FRATH, but was removed to MAGHERA, and thence in 1158 to DERRY, where the Abbot FLAITHBHEARTACH is said to have built the Cathedral in 1164, and to have been consecrated Bishop.

The See of RAPHOE, united to DERRY in 1834, appears
to have been founded before the close of the ninth century,
as in 885 MOEL BRIGID, its Bishop, was translated to
ARMAGH.

DOWN, CONNOR, and DROMORE.

*Azure, two keys in saltire the wards in chief or, sur-
mounted in the fess point by a lamb passant proper.*
DOWN.

*Argent, two keys in saltire the wards in chief, gules ;
surmounted by an open book in fess proper, between
two crosses patées-fitchées in pale sable.* DROMORE.

These arms are usually borne quartered (Plate XXVII.,
fig. 2).

The See of DOWN, of uncertain foundation, was
restored by ST. MALACHI I. (Morgair), who resigned the
Archbishopric of ARMAGH in 1134, to become Bishop of
DOWN. It was enlarged by JOHN DE COURCY, the
Conqueror of ULSTER, in 1183. He substituted regular
Monks of the Benedictine Order from the Abbey of
S. WERBURGH at CHESTER for the secular Canons, and
dedicated the church to S. PATRICK, instead of the Holy
Trinity. The tomb of S. PATRICK was in the Cathedral ;
and to it, according to COLGAN, the bodies of S. BRIDGET
and S. COLUMBA were afterwards brought. (*See* also
Bishop REEVES, *Ecclesiastical Antiquities of* DOWN *and*
CONNOR, p. 224.)

The See of CONNOR, having been united to DOWN
in 1441, long before armorial bearings were used on
the seals of Irish Bishops, has no special arms of
its own.

On an old seal found in 1789 in the County of CLARE,
is the figure of the Blessed Virgin MARY and the Holy Child.
Under this is the bust of the Bishop, and at the foot is a
shield charged with a cross between four quatrefoils.
The legend reads ; " Sigillu . . . enecs (?) dei. gra.

dromorenc. epi. ;" probably it was the seal of Bishop FLORENCE, MAC DONEGAN (1309-1369) (?)

The arms given above for DROMORE were borne by Bishop LAMBERT (1717-1726); but Bishop MAULE (1731-1744) used : *Argent, semé of trefoils slipped vert, a cross patée gules ; on a chief azure the sun in splendour or.* (Sometimes the trefoils are in *orle* only.) DROMORE was annexed to DOWN and CONNOR in 1842. It was founded by S. COLMAN, *circa* 556. Bishop JEREMY TAYLOR held it with DOWN and CONNOR (1661-1667).

KILMORE, ELPHIN, and ARDAGH.

Argent, on a cross azure a pastoral staff enfiling a mitre, all or. KILMORE.

Sable, two pastoral staves in saltire or, in base a lamb couchant argent. ELPHIN.

Or, a cross gules between four trefoils slipped vert, on a chief sable a key erect of the first. ARDAGH.

These arms are usually combined thus. The shield *Per fess*, in chief KILMORE ; in base, ELPHIN *impaling* ARDAGH. (Plate XXVII., fig. 4.)

In consequence of the ignorance of painters and engravers, and of a laxity with regard to the proper registration of changes in Episcopal arms in " ULSTER'S " office, there is very considerable difficulty in determining the correct blazon of the arms of the Irish Sees, and this is the case with regard to all of the three coats above given. The bishops varied their arms at pleasure. With regard to KILMORE I have adhered to the blazon I gave in my original volume, and have made the cross *azure* (although in the last edition of BURKE'S *General Armory* I find it blazoned *sable*). In so doing I have followed Archbishop BERESFORD'S opinion, and the arms are thus represented in old *Peerages*, etc. I have in my possession a letter from the Lord Primate Archbishop BERESFORD to the Bishop of KILMORE ; as follows : " My dear Lord,—In WARE'S *Bishops* the arms both of ARDAGH and KILLALOE are given as somewhat different from what they now are. Instead of five they have only one trefoil *Emerald* in each quarter. In KILLALOE the cross is *Ruby*, in ARDAGH *Sapphire*. The cross-of KILMORE is *Sapphire*. The arms were changed by Bishop GODWIN (1713-1727), before that KILMORE bore, *Pearl, a cross Ruby between twenty trefoils slipped Emerald.*[1] Of KILLALOE and ARDAGH the arms now appear to be the same.—Yrs. truly, M. G. ARMAGH."

The beautiful seal of THOMAS, Bishop of ELPHIN (1581), the matrix of which is now in the Royal Irish Academy, bears the then arms of the See : . . . *three mitres, two and one* . . . In the *General Armory* in 1878, a mitre is placed in chief above the pastoral staves ; but this appears to be quite a modern addition. With regard to ARDAGH I have departed from my former blazon in favour of that given in the *General Armory*. If "*Arma sunt distinguendi causa*," it is surely undesirable that there should be duplicate bearings in so small a group as that formed by the arms of the Irish Episcopate, though I doubt whether the arms given by Sir BERNARD BURKE after the disestablishment had anything of official authority. In any case it would be better that ARDAGH and KILLALOE should not have identical bearings. (*Vide infra*, p. 214.)

The See of ARDAGH is said to have been founded by S. PATRICK about the year 450. The See was united to that of KILMORE at the Restoration of CHARLES II. in the year 1660. In 1692 the Sees were again separated, and Bishop BURGH was appointed to ARDAGH, but as he died very shortly after, the See was in the same year reunited to KILMORE. ARDAGH was disjoined in 1742, and was held *in commendam* by the Archbishop of TUAM

[1] *See* Seal of Bishop WETENHALL (1699-1713).

1. Derry and Raphoe.

2. Down, Connor, and Dromore.

3. Killaloe, Clonfert, and Kilfenora.

4. Kilmore, Elphin, and Ardagh.

5. Limerick.

6. Ossory, Ferns, and Leighlin.

until 1841, when it went back to KILMORE. The See of KILMORE was at first near a place called BREFINE; but in 1454 Bishop ANDREW MACBRADY, "Bishop of TRIBURNA" erected the Cathedral and from it, the KILMORE or great church, the See took its name. The See of ELPHIN is one of those which claim S. PATRICK as its founder, but its early history is unknown. It was united to KILMORE and ARDAGH in the year 1841.

TUAM, KILLALA, and ACHONRY.

Azure, beneath a triple architectural canopy three figures, in the centre the Blessed Virgin MARY *holding in her arms the Holy Child, between on the dexter the figure of a Bishop* (S. JARLATH) *in pontificalibus and in the act of benediction; and on the sinister S.* JOHN *supporting with his left arm a lamb argent, each in proper vestments or, the hands, feet, and faces proper.*

Here again is evidently a reproduction of the old unheraldic Episcopal seal to which allusion has frequently been made. At present no other coat is borne. (Plate XXVIII., fig. 1.) ACHONRY has never had any arms. Those of the See of KILLALA, are : *Gules, a crosier, or pastoral staff, in pale, over it in the fess point an open book all proper* (Plate XXVIII., fig. 2). The tincture of the field in this coat is frequently represented *azure.*

The See of TUAM is reputed to have been founded by S. JARLATH early in the sixth century, and to him the Cathedral was dedicated. The See of MAYO founded by S. GERALD, a monk of LINDISFARNE about 668 was annexed to TUAM in the year 1559.

TUAM was raised to the dignity of an Archbishopric in the twelfth century, and EDAN O'HOISIN received the *pallium* from Cardinal PAPARO, the Papal Legate, in the year 1152; but it is probable that some of his predecessors had already held the dignity without receiving the pall. The Archbishop was Primate of CONNAUGHT.

In 1839 TUAM ceased to be an Archi-episcopal See, and the Diocese of ARDAGH reverted, as has been stated before, to its old sister See of KILMORE. The United See of KILLALA and ACHONRY was then joined to TUAM ; an union which continues. The See of KILLALA was founded by S. PATRICK, who, about the year 440, made his disciple MURDOCH its first Bishop, The Diocese of ACHONRY is of uncertain foundation, but the Church of ACHAD, its old name, seems to have been founded by S. FINIAN of CLONARD (*q.v.*). The old Bishops were often called Bishops of LINY from the Barony in which ACHONRY was situated. MILER MACGRATH, Archbishop of CASHEL, who had been a Franciscan monk, was made Archbishop of CASHEL in 1571 by Queen ELIZABETH, and held *in commendam* the Sees of ACHONRY and KILLALA from 1607 until his death in 1622. Thereafter the last-named two Sees remained united until in 1834, when they were united to TUAM, by the provisions of the *Church Temporalities Act.*

DUBLIN.

> *Azure, an Episcopal staff in pale argent ensigned with a cross patée or, over all a pall-throughout argent, bordered and fringed or, thereon five crosses patées fitchées sable* (Plate XXVI., fig. 2).

These arms are only distinguished from those of CANTERBURY and ARMAGH by the number of the crosses *patées*. Sometimes as a slight difference the staff of DUBLIN is all *or.* Until the disestablishment of the Irish Church the Archbishop (who has the title of Primate of IRELAND) was Chancellor of the ORDER OF ST. PATRICK, and surrounded his arms with the ribbon and motto of the Order (*v. ante*, p. 201). This office is now held by the Chief Secretary for Ireland.

The See of KILDARE was united to DUBLIN in 1846. Its arms are : *Argent, a saltire engrailed gules on a chief azure, an open book proper.* (The text thereon is "The Law was given by Moses, but grace and truth came by Jesus Christ" (John, i., 17), but usually the shield blazoned is too small in size for these words to be legible.)

The arms appear on the seal of Bishop COBBE (1731-1742). On the seal of Bishop LANE, in 1495, one shield bears *a pastoral staff and key in saltire*, presumably for the See. The *saltire* is sometimes blazoned *sable*, but erroneously. The saltire of the FITZGERALDS of KILDARE is *gules;* and probably that of the See is related to it.

The See of DUBLIN was founded by S. PATRICK in, or about, the year 448, and was raised to the rank of an Archbishopric in the year 1152, at the same time as ARMAGH, CASHEL, and TUAM. The See of GLANDALAGH, founded by S. KEVIN early in the seventh century, was united to DUBLIN in 1214 ; and that of KILDARE, as mentioned above, in 1846. KILDARE is said to have been founded about the close of the fifth century. The Cathedral was dedicated to S. BRIDGET, who received the veil at KILDARE from S. PATRICK in the year 467, and who founded a nunnery here before 484. It is doubtful when the regular succession of Bishops began.

OSSORY, FERNS and LEIGHLIN.

Azure, a Bishop in pontificals between two pillars argent, in his left hand a pastoral staff, in his right a closed book, the Bible, or. OSSORY.

(Gules) a ciborium, or closed chalice, between five crosses patées fitchées or. FERNS.

Sable, two pastoral staves addorsed in saltire surmounted on the fess point by a mitre or. LEIGHLIN.

There is considerable doubt with regard to these coats

(Plate XXVII., fig. 6). That attributed to OSSORY is obviously derived from the old unheraldic Episcopal seal, and the columns (as in the case of SODOR and MAN, *ante*, p. 196), are the remains of the architectural canopy. The coat given above seems to have been quite disused in modern times, and was only resumed by Bishop WALSH in 1887, or 1888. The second coat with the tincture *gules*, is assigned to OSSORY as its modern arms in BURKE'S *General Armory ;* but I think on no better authority than that of WARE, whose cuts and blazons are seldom in accord. WARE gives, *Azure, two keys in saltire and in fess point a mitre or*, for FERNS ; and says that no arms have been borne for LEIGHLIN since the union of the Sees.

But on the seal of Bishop MAGUIRE of FERNS (1490-1512), beside the Annunciation, two angels support a chalice and host in chief, and I am not sure at all that here we may not have the origin of the *ciborium ;* or that I am wrong in attributing the coat in which it appears to FERNS. The idea that the *ciborium* is a cup assumed from the BUTLER arms seems to me void of any probability. The seal of Bishop COMYN of FERNS (1509 - 1519), bears two shields, one of which is charged with a key and pastoral staff in saltire. Mr MACKENZIE WALCOT gives the arms of LEIGHLIN as I have blazoned them ; and attributes to FERNS, *Azure, two keys in saltire surmounted by a mitre (in fess point) argent.*

By this time the reader is in a position to understand the force of my remark on p. 205. I do not expect my own blazons to escape criticism ; but there is absolutely no certainty attainable, and those given are probably as correct as any others which exist.

The See of OSSORY was founded before the coming of S. PATRICK ; probably about the year 400. It was at first situated at SAIGER, and in the eleventh century was removed to AGHAVOE, and thence to KILKENNY. The united diocese of FERNS and LEIGHLIN was joined to OSSORY in the year 1835. FERNS and LEIGHLIN were united in the year 1600. The early history of the See of FERNS is obscure, but LEIGHLIN is said to have been founded as early as 628.

CASHEL, EMLY, WATERFORD, and LISMORE.
Gules, two keys addorsed in saltire, the wards in chief or. CASHEL.
Azure, a Bishop in pontificals holding before him a crucifix argent, thereon the figure of the Redeemer proper (sometimes the whole is *Or*). WATER-FORD. (Plate XXVI., fig. 4.)

There can be no doubt whatever that the coat given for WATERFORD is derived from a not uncommon way of representing the Ever - Blessed Trinity, such as occurs on the Seal of the Priory of the Blessed Trinity, DUBLIN, as well as on many Scottish Seals: —the Eternal Father seated, in front of Him the crucified Son ; the Holy Spirit overshadowing both. (*See* DIDRON, *Iconographie Chrétienne*, vol. ii., pp. 69-72. BOHN'S Edition.) The dedication of WATERFORD Cathedral is to the Trinity. Bishop TRENCH in 1802, changed the position of the " Bishop from the sitting to the standing posture." Bishop FRY of WATERFORD (1691-1707) had a grant of these arms: *Vert, two keys in saltire or, between in chief a lion passant gardant argent ; in the dexter flank a bible open ; in the sinister an annulet of the second, and in base six cloven tongues proper.* These were not used after 1802. Bishop TRENCH resumed the older and simpler bearings.

No arms are used for EMLY (united to CASHEL in 1568) ; or for LISMORE (united to WATERFORD in 1363). Archbishop EDMUND BUTLER (1527-1550) natural son of the Earl of ORMONDE, bore on his seal a pastoral staff and cross in saltire, for CASHEL. (On the seal of the Bishop of EMLY in 1380, one of the shields bears a plain cross.)

The date of the foundation of the See of CASHEL, and the succession of its early Bishops, are shrouded in great obscurity. It became an Archbishopric in 1152, and the Primacy of MUNSTER belonged to it. The See of EMLY, which claimed S. PATRICK as its founder, was united to it in 1568 ; and the conjoined Sees of WATERFORD and LISMORE were added by the provisions of the *Church Temporalities Act.* Of these Sees LISMORE was founded in the former half of the seventh century, and included the ancient Bishopric of ARDMORE. But WATERFORD does not appear to have been the seat of a Bishop until towards the close of the eleventh century. WATERFORD and LISMORE were united, under Bishop THOMAS LE NEVE of WATERFORD, in the year 1363.

CORK, CLOYNE, and ROSS.

Argent, a cross patée gules, thereon a mitre enfiling a pastoral staff or. CORK.

Azure, a mitre proper labelled or, between three crosses patées fitchées argent. CLOYNE.

These arms are generally borne on a shield divided *per fess ;* CORK *in chief,* CLOYNE *in base* (Plate XXVI., fig. 4).

No arms are borne for the See of ROSS, which was united to CORK in 1582-1583.

The cross in the arms of CORK appears rather to be a *plain cross coupé with the ends patées.* This cross seems to be intended for that of the Templars. The lands of their preceptory of S. JOHN in CORK were incorporated with the Cathedral lands for choral purposes. On the quartered arms of Bishop STEPHEN BROWN of ROSS in

1402, a mitre appears as a charge, and Dr CAULFIELD suggests that this is the origin of the mitre on the cross of CORK. (*See* Dr CAULFIELD'S paper in *The Proceedings of the Royal Historical and Archæological Association of Ireland*, 4th S., vol. ii., p. 329, 1875.)

The date of the establishment of the See of ROSS is doubtful, but it appears to have originated in a monastery founded by ST. FACHNAU, or FACHTNA (who may have been of the Episcopal order) in the Isle of Dar Enis near Youghal, and who probably died about the close of the sixth century.

The See was united under Bishop WILLIAM LYON in 1583, to the conjoined Sees of CORK and CLOYNE. Of these CLOYNE is said to have been founded by ST. COLMAN, a follower of S. FINBAR, Bishop of CORK, at the close of the sixth century. In 1430 CORK and CLOYNE were united under Bishop JORDAN, and remained so until 1638. During this period of Union ROSS was added, as above stated, but in 1678 CLOYNE was disjoined and remained a separate See until 1835 when it was once more united to CORK and ROSS. As to CORK, the foundation of the See is attributed to S. FINBAR (or FINNBHAR, otherwise BARRY), whose Christian name was LOCHAN, and who established a school at Corcach-Mohr of Munster, the " marshy place where Cork now stands." After an Episcopate of seventeen years he died in 630, or 633 (Bishop FORBES, article in the *Dictionary of Christian Biography*).

KILLALOE, KILFENORA, CLONFERT, and KILMAC-DUAGH.

> *Argent, a cross azure* (or *gules*) *between four* (or *twelve*) *trefoils slipped vert, on a chief of the second a key in pale or.* KILLALOE.
>
> - *Azure, two pastoral staves addorsed in saltire or.* CLONFERT.

*Argent, a rose gules barbed and. seeded proper, on a
chief sable three mullets or.* KILFENORA. (Plate
XXVII., fig. 3.)

The arms generally used at present are arranged thus :
Per fess ; in chief KILLALOE, *in base* CLONFERT. I do
not know why KILFENORA is omitted. No arms are
known for KILMACDUAGH, which was united to CLON-
FERT in 1602.

The arms borne by Bishop WITTER of KILLALOE
(1669-1674) were: *Quarterly,* 1 and 4. . . . *a
chevron (gules) between three crescents . . . ;
2 and 3. . . . on a saltire engrailed . . . five
fleurs-de-lis.*

DR CAULFIELD suggests that the last quartering may
be the true arms of the See, since on a chapter seal of
1697 the charge is *a plain saltire coupé . . . thereon
five fleurs-de-lis.* The former identity of the arms of
KILLALOE with those of ARDAGH has been already
noticed (*ante* p. 205). But in 1713-1716 Bishop CARR
bore *the red cross between four trefoils,* and thus avoided
confusion. In 1839 Bishop TONSON used three *trefoils* in each *canton ;* but in 1801 the seal of the
Dean and Chapter reverts to the type of Bishop
CARR. In the last edition of BURKE'S *General
Armory* the tincture of the cross has been changed to
azure.

The See of KILLALOE is said to have been founded
by S. MOLNA as a monastery over which he presided ; and he was succeeded by his pupil ST.
FLANNAN, who obtained the Episcopal dignity, being
consecrated at Rome by Pope JOHN in 639. He is
called *Episcopus Luanensis,* but all this appears only very
doubtful. The ancient See of ROSCREA, which is said
to have arisen in the seventh century, was joined to
KILLALOE about the close of the twelfth. The See of
KILFENORA, as to the foundation of which we know

1. Tuam.   2. Killala.

3. St. Andrews.   4. Aberdeen and Orkney.

5. Argyll and Isles.   6. Brechin.

nothing with certainty (although ST. FACHNAN, to whom the Cathedral is dedicated, may have been its founder), was held *in commendam* by the Archbishops of TUAM after 1660 until its union with KILLALOE. The See of CLONFERT grew out of an abbey founded there in 558 by ST. BRENDAN, who probably was its first bishop, though that honour is sometimes attributed to ST. MOENA, who died in 571. The See of KILMAC-DUAGH, founded by S. COLMAN in the seventh century, was held *in commendam* by Bishop ROBERT LYNCH after his translation to CLONFERT in 1602, and never again had a separate existence.

LIMERICK, ARDFERT, AND AGHADOE.

> *Azure, two keys endorsed in saltire the wards upwards ; in the dexter chief a crozier paleways, in the sinister a mitre, all or.* LIMERICK. (Plate XXVII., fig. 3.)

The arms were thus borne by Bishop SMYTH in 1695. The blazon given in BURKE'S *General Armory* is slightly different ; the keys are there described as being *in base ;* an arrangement by which more room is made in chief for the other charges. No arms are recorded for the other Sees.

The Cathedral, and probably the See, of LIMERICK had as founder DONALD O'BRIEN, about the commencement of the twelfth century. At the beginning of the next century the old See of INIS SCALLERY founded by S. PATRICK, or at least a portion of it, was united to WATERFORD. The Sees of ARDFERT and AGHADOE, which had been combined from very ancient times, were handed over to LIMERICK in 1667. AGHADOE near KILLARNEY, had an ancient Cathedral, dedicated to S. FINNAN, of which some remains are still extant. ARDFERT was formerly known as the Bishopric of KERRY.

SCOTLAND.

There are fourteen Sees in Scotland which are now governed by seven Bishops:. ABERDEEN, ARGYLL, BRECHIN, CAITHNESS, DUNBLANE, DUNKELD, EDINBURGH, ₂GALLOWAY, GLASGOW, THE ISLES, MORAY, ORKNEY, ROSS, ST. ANDREWS. These are thus united: ABERDEEN and ORKNEY; BRECHIN; ARGYLL and THE ISLES; EDINBURGH; GLASGOW and GALLOWAY; MORAY, ROSS, and CAITHNESS; ST. ANDREWS, DUNKELD, and DUNBLANE.

The Archbishop of YORK formerly claimed primatial authority over the Scottish Bishops (the province of YORK certainly extended to the Forth, as the kingdom of Northumbria did; and since the churches of Lothian were under the See of ST. ANDREWS, as those of Teviotdale were claimed by the See of GLASGOW, there was so far some ground for the assertion of supremacy by the See of YORK (SKENE, *Celtic Scotland*, ii.), but this ceased when the Sees of ST. ANDREW'S and GLASGOW were raised to the archi-episcopal rank in₋ 1470 and 1491 respectively. The Papal Bull of INNOCENT III. which acknowledged the independence of the Scottish Church names only nine Sees, no mention is made of ARGYLL, THE ISLES, EDINBURGH, GALLOWAY, and ORKNEY. ARGYLL was at that time included in DUNKELD; EDINBURGH was not founded; GALLOWAY (or WHITHERNE) was suffragan to YORK; while ORKNEY and THE ISLES yielded obedience to the Norwegian See of NIDAROS, or TRONDHJEM. The adherence of the bishops and clergy to the House of Stuart resulted in the formal abolition of Episcopacy in Scotland by WILLIAM of ORANGE; but in spite of Penal Laws (which made the assembly of more than five Episcopalians for worship an offence punishable, on the first conviction by imprisonment, and if repeated by transportation) the old attachment to the Church was not extinguished in considerable districts, and the Sees above-named have (with the exception of ARGYLL and THE ISLES), retained a regular succession since the early part of the eighteenth century, although the dioceses have been from time to time differently arranged.

The arms of the Sees, like those of the Irish dioceses and of the Sees of the old foundation in England, originated for the most part in simple assumption. The successive occupants of the Sees varied the figures upon their seals at pleasure, and several of the coats now used can scarcely be said to belong to the Sees.

Before the Reformation the seals of British and Irish Bishops bore at first only the figure of the Bishop in pontificals, and in the act of benediction. In process of time to this was added a representation of the Blessed Trinity, or of the patron saints of the Bishop and his Cathedral church. These were usually arranged under an elaborate architectural canopy, and the Bishop himself was often represented kneeling in the base of the *vesica*-shaped seal.

Remains of this canopy, although mutilated almost beyond recognition, may be traced in the arms now used for the dioceses of SODOR and MAN, MORAY, and TUAM, and in the old arms of OSSORY. The present arms of the See of WATERFORD are evidently derived from a seal which, like those of many of our early Scottish Bishops, bore simply a representation of the Ever-Blessed Trinity; while the effigies of the saints which appear on the present arms of the Sees of MORAY, ROSS, GALLOWAY, ORKNEY, and THE ISLES are no doubt remains of the custom to which I allude.

In Scotland, as in Ireland, the arms used upon Episcopal seals of a date anterior to the Reformation are, ordinarily, the personal arms only of the bishop to whom the seal belonged ; and in both countries the arms now assigned to, or assumed for, the Sees are for the most part of a date posterior to the Reformation.

·Several of the Scottish Episcopal seals of the thirteenth and fourteenth centuries bear, however, shields which do not contain the personal arms of the bishop ;˙ but which, though not regular diocesan arms, were yet obviously borne to indicate the territorial district over which his authority extended. Thus the seal of Bishop PILMORE of MORAY (1326-1362) bears two shields, one of the arms of Scotland ; the other charged with the arms of the Earldom of MORAY. ˙(LAING, *Scottish Seals*, i., No. 905, p. 506.)

The seal of Bishop ROGER of ROSS (1284-1304) has two shields of the arms of that Earldom ; and a similar arrangement is to be found on the seal of Bishop ALEXANDER (1357-1370) (LAING, ii., p. 182 ; and i., 161).

On the seal of Bishop THOMAS MURRAY of CAITHNESS and THE ISLES (1348-1360) are two shields ; one of his personal arms, the other charged with a lymphad within the Royal *Tressure ;* this latter LAING assigns to the See of the Isles but I think it much more likely to represent ORKNEY, or CAITHNESS. (LAING, ii., p. 184.) In all these cases the arms of the territorial Lordship in which the See was situate, are borne as *quasi* diocesan arms ; and this happened when, as was afterwards the case, the arms of the temporal Lordship of BRECHIN were assumed as the arms of the See, though the Episcopal seal still bore the old representation of the Trinity. It was only in the time of Sir CHARLES ERSKINE, Lyon King of Arms (the framer of the Act of 1672, by which the Lyon Register was made " the unrepealable rule of all arms and bearings in Scotland ") that the practice was introduced into Scotland by which the arms of the See are impaled, according to the custom long obtaining in England, with the personal arms of the bishop who presided over the diocese. In the Lyon Register in 1672 the arms of most of the Scottish Sees are recorded (it is not stated that a formal grant was given, but the previous assumption was authorised). BRECHIN, ABER-

DEEN, and GLASGOW, however, do not appear there, and the arms used for them were perhaps thought those of the cities rather than of the Sees. It seems nearly certain that a regular grant was made to EDINBURGH on the establishment of that See.

ABERDEEN and ORKNEY.

Azure in the porch of a church S. NICOLAS *in pontificals, his right hand raised over three children in a cauldron surrounded by flames, in the left hand a pastoral staff all proper.* ABERDEEN.

Argent, the figure of S. MAGNUS *in royal robes, crowned and sceptred proper.* ORKNEY. (Plate XXVIII., fig. 4.)

The coat borne of late years for ABERDEEN, originated in the seal of that Royal Burgh. The representation of S. NICOLAS restoring to life the three children boiled at Myra, appears on its fine common seal of the date 1420.

It is curious that in the grant, or rather confirmation, of arms made to the Royal Burgh of ABERDEEN by Sir CHAS. ERSKINE of Cambo, Lyon King of Arms, in 1674, the reverse of the seal is ordered to bear: *Azure, a Temple, Argent*, ST. MICHAEL (NICHOLAS) *standing in the porch mitered and vested propper* (sic) *with his Dexter hand lifted up to Heaven, praying over three children in a boyling cauldron of the first, and holding in the sinister a Crozier Or.* (In the patent it is "S. NICHOLAS," Sir G. MACKENZIE is, therefore, in *error*, and was copied by SETON, NISBET, LAING, and myself.) "MICHAEL" is of course a slip of the pen. The "temple" is a vestige of the old architectural canopy above the saint. (*See* the Burgh Seals, engraved in GORDON'S "*Description of Aberdeen,*" Spalding Club, 1842 ;—and LAING'S *Scottish Seals,* vol. i., plate 29.)

The figure of S. NICOLAS appears on a seal appended

to a document in 1357, the legend of the seal being " signum beati Nicolai Aberdonensis." S. NICOLAS, as the patron saint of sailors, was naturally associated with the important seaport of ABERDEEN. In England most of the churches dedicated to him are in seaport towns. But the figure of S. NICOLAS does not appear on the seals of the pre-Reformation Bishops; while the effigy of the Blessed Virgin Mary and the Holy Child does repeatedly. For this reason the late Bishop SUTHER of ABERDEEN and ORKNEY (1857-1883) placed on his seal the effigy of the Virgin and Child, and in the base a mitred shield of the arms of the city of ABERDEEN (*Gules, three castles triple-towered, two and one, within a Royal tressure, all argent*).

On the seal which I had the pleasure to design for the present Bishop (DOUGLAS) I reverted to the old ecclesiastical type, placing the Blessed Virgin and the Holy Child in the centre compartment of an architectural canopy, the side niches of which have the figures of S. COLUMBA, and S. MAGNUS, who (as on the old Episcopal and other seals) bears a long sword. The Bishop's paternal arms are, mitred, in the base of the seal.

The earliest notice of the See of ABERDEEN is found in a memorandum in *The Book of Deir*, in which the refoundation of the Church of DEIR by the Mormaer of BUCHAN is declared in a charter which is witnessed by NECTAN, Bishop of ABERDEEN. The tradition which placed the Bishop's seat originally at Murthlac is only supported by some spurious documents in the Chartulary of ABERDEEN ; the date of the removal is said to be 1125, which is pretty clearly false. The Diocese of ORKNEY was anciently attached sometimes to Scotland, sometimes to Norway. In 1396 the Bishop of ORKNEY was present at the coronation at CALMAR of ERIC, King of Norway, Sweden, and Denmark. The See was made suffragan to ST. ANDREWS in 1472.

It was dormant from 1757 to 1864 when it was revived and united to ABERDEEN.

ARGYLL, and THE ISLES.

Azure, two pastoral staves addorsed in saltire, beneath a mitre in chief, all or. ARGYLL.

Azure, on waves of the sea in base S. Columba kneeling in · a coracle (sometimes holding in his hand a dove), *all proper, and looking towards a blazing star in the dexter chief or.* THE ISLES. (Plate XXVIII., fig. 5.)

The arms of ARGYLL as here given only appear, so far as I am aware, on the seal of Bishop ARTHUR ROSS (1675-1679) impaling his personal arms. (LAING, *Scottish Seals* i., p. 169.)

On the seal of Bishop ANDREW KNOX of SODOR (*i.e.* THE ISLES) (1606-1622) the figure in the boat holds a book in his left hand and points over the sea with his right. On that of Bishop WALLACE (1661-1669) the bishop is rowed in a boat by three men. (LAING, i., pp. 169, 170.)

It has been thought probable that the coat really contains the arms used for MAN, not for SODOR ; and that the saint is S. MAUCHOLD, not S. COLUMBA, with reference to the legend of his committing himself to the waves to find a sphere for his mission work under the guidance of God. (BARING-GOULD, *Lives of the Saints*, April.)

I have already spoken of SODOR under the heading of SODOR and MAN (*ante*, p. 196). With regard to ARGYLL, the diocese is said to have been separated from DUN-KELD in 1200. Dr SKENE assents (*Celtic Scotland*, vol. ii., p. 408), but adds that Canon MYLNE of DUNKELD tells us that the diocese was divided by JOHN "THE SCOT" elected Bishop of DUNKELD in 1167. The seat of the Bishopric seems to have been at first at MUCKAIRN on the south side of Loch Etive. About 1235 it was removed to LISMORE. In 1236 the Bishop of MORAY received the Papal mandate, directing the separation of the Church of LISMORE from the See of THE ISLES in order that a new bishopric might be formed there, and the LISMORE Cathedral Chapter was created (*c.* 1249). After the Revolution the See of THE ISLES was united to MORAY and ROSS, but in 1845 was joined to ARGYLL.

BRECHIN.

Or, three piles in point gules. BRECHIN. (Plate XXVIII., fig. 6.)

In the introductory remarks to these arms of Scottish Sees (*ante,* p. 218), I have mentioned that the arms of the See of BRECHIN are the arms of the temporal Lordship of that name. They are undoubtedly the arms borne by DAVID, Earl of HUNTINGDON (1199-1219), on whom his elder brother King WILLIAM the LION, conferred the Lordship of BRECHIN ; and they appear on the seals of DAVID, and on that of his legitimate son JOHN "le Scot," Earl of CHESTER (1231-1244). Sir DAVID LINDSAY'S Manuscript of 1542 gives to "The Lord BRECHIN of Old," the coat, "*Or three piles gules,*" the piles not being arranged in point ; but at plate 606, in which the arms of the Lordship of BRECHIN are quartered by the ERSKINES, the piles are depicted in point.

DAVID, Earl of HUNTINGDON and GARIOCH, gave the Lordship of BRECHIN to his natural son HENRY, who was accordingly styled of that place, and bore the arms, *Or, three piles in point gules.*

At the forfeiture and execution of his descendant DAVID, Lord of BRECHIN, in 1321, King ROBERT the BRUCE gave the Lordship of BRECHIN to Sir DAVID BARCLAY who had married a daughter of the forfeited lord. From the BARCLAYS the Lordship passed to their heirs the MAULES of PANMURE, who accordingly quartered in their shield the arms of BRECHIN.

(DOUGLAS, *Peerage of Scotland*, i., 245 ; ii., 351.) At the latter reference the tincture of the field is erroneously changed from *Or* to *Argent*, a change which made the coat identical with that borne by the family of WISHART. But NISBET correctly observes that "the similitude of the Lord BRECHIN'S bearing with that of the name of WISEHART has led Sir GEORGE MACKENZIE" (*Science of Heraldry*, p. 3) (and through him more recent writers), "into the mistake of calling the Lords BRECHIN the WISHARTS . . . whereas none of that name ever were concerned with the Lordship of BRECHIN, or used that title." I was therefore quite wrong when, in my *Introductory Notice of the Arms of the Episcopates of Great Britain and Ireland*, I wrote " The arms are those borne by WISHARTS, formerly lords of BRECHIN." This fact was pointed out to me, immediately on the publication of my little book, by my dear friend and diocesan the late Bishop FORBES, who had become convinced of the error into which Sir GEORGE MACKENZIE'S mistake had led us. He had however used the arms, *Argent, three piles gules*, for so long a time on his Episcopal seal, and caused them to be carved and emblazoned on stained glass, etc., so frequently, that he was unwilling himself to revert to the correct blazon, but expressed the hope and belief that his successors would do so. The older blazon is now pretty frequently used.

The See of BRECHIN was founded by King DAVID I. towards the end of his reign, about 1150, probably out of the remains of the old Pictish See of Abernethy. It was in Stratherne, in the northern part of Angus, and in the Mearns, that the Pictish population remained longest distinct from the Scots. SAMSON, Bishop of BRECHIN, witnessed the charter granted to the Church of DEIR in the last year of DAVID'S reign. (SKENE, *Celtic Scotland*, ii., 396, 397. *See also the Book of Deir*, edited for the Spalding Club, by the late JOHN STUART, LL.D.)

EDINBURGH.

Azure, a saltire argent, in the centre chief point a mitre
· of the last garnished or (Plate XXIX., fig. 1).

These arms, impaling his personal ones, appear on
the seal of Bishop ALEXANDER ROSE, 1688. .(LAING ii.,
170.) The See was founded by King CHARLES ·I. in
1633, and its Bishop, as Chancellor of the Metropolitan
See of ST. ANDREWS, was to have precedence next to
the two Archbishops.

The Counties of Peebles, Roxburgh, and Selkirk
were transferred from the See of Glasgow to that of
Edinburgh in the year 1888.

GLASGOW and GALLOWAY.

Argent, in base a tree issuing from a mount, an old church
bell pendant from a bough on the sinister side, on the
top of the tree a robin ; upon the trunk of the tree a
salmon lying fessways back downwards, all proper,
holding in its mouth an annulet or. GLASGOW.

Argent, S. NINIAN *in pontificals, holding a pastoral staff*
proper. GALLOWAY. (Plate XXIX., fig. 2.)

The See of GLASGOW was founded in the sixth century
by S. MUNGO, or KENTIGERN.· It was restored by Earl
DAVID, brother of King ALEXANDER, about 1115. In
the See thus reconstituted was included the district of
Teviotdale, which had been part of the Diocese of
DURHAM. This was one of the grounds upon which
was based the claim of supremacy made by the Archbishop of YORK ; which was firmly resisted.

The rights of the See of York were, however, admitted
in the case of the See of GALLOWAY, or CANDIDA CASA,
which had been founded by the English Kings of Northumbria in the eighth century. GALLOWAY, though civilly
part of Scotland, thus belonged ecclesiastically to England.
In 1491 GLASGOW was raised to the dignity of an Archbishopric, and GALLOWAY was made suffragan to it.

1. Edinburgh. 2. Glasgow and Galloway.

3. Moray, Ross, and Caithness. 4. Dunkeld.

5. Dunblane. 6. St. Andrews, Dunkeld, Dumblane.

The arms of the See of GLASGOW, are really those of the city, and first appear in their present form on the seal of Archbishop CAIRNCROSS, 1684. His successor Archbishop PATERSON bore them with the head of S. MUNGO on a *chief*. The bird, the fish, and the ring had, however, been used as accessories on the seals of the ancient Bishops. They relate to the miracles attributed to S. MUNGO, who was said to have restored to life the pet robin of. S. SERF after its head had been wrung from its body. The salmon and ring refer to a story of the recovery by S. MUNGO of a lady's ring the loss of which had caused her chastity to be impugned.

The arms assumed for GALLOWAY appear on the seal of Bishop PATERSON (1674-1679), impaling his personal arms.

MORAY, ROSS, and CAITHNESS.

Azure, S. GILES *mitred; standing within a church porch; holding in his dexter hand a Cross, and in the sinister a book, all proper*. MORAY.

Argent, S. BONIFACE, *proper, habited gules; and a Bishop in pontificals proper, vested purpure*. ROSS.

Azure, a crown of thorns or, between three crosses of S. ANDREW *couped argent*. CAITHNESS.

At present these bearings are usually borne thus: *In chief* MORAY *impaling* ROSS; and CAITHNESS *in base* (Plate XXIX., fig. 3). This is an unusual arrangement, and hardly so satisfactory as quartering would be. The first two coats afford good illustrations of the remarks which I have already made in the introductory paragraphs to the arms of the Scottish Sees (p. 217). The saints and the "church porch" are all derived from the non-armorial seals of mediæval times. The charges on the so-called arms of MORAY are without any authority, and are simply derived from the Burgh seal of ELGIN. (LAING, *Scottish*

Q

Seals, i., p. 211.)   S. GILES does not, I believe, appear on the old Episcopal seals.

The seal of Bishop PILMORE of MORAY (1326-1362) bears the usual representation of the Blessed Trinity, and two shields, one charged with the Royal arms of SCOTLAND, the other bearing the arms of the Earldom of MORAY, doubtless to indicate the territorial extent of the See (*ibid.*, i., 506.)   Generally the personal arms of the Bishop are alone represented, with the effigies of the Trinity.

On the seal of ROSS the saints are probably S. PETER, and S. BONIFACE.   The seals of Bishop ROGER (1284-1304) (LAING, ii., 182) and Bishop Alexander (1357-1370). (*Ibid.*, i., 161, No. 931), both bear two shields charged with the arms of the Earldom of ROSS, used as in the previous case of MORAY to indicate the extent of the See.

The arms of CAITHNESS are a modern assumption.

On the Seal of Bishop THOMAS MURRAY of CAITHNESS and THE ISLES (1348-1360) (LAING, ii., p. 184) are two shields, one of his personal arms, the other bearing a *lymphad*, or *galley, within the Royal Tressure.*   This latter LAING attributes to THE ISLES, but it may have been borne for CAITHNESS.   It may be remarked, however, that the Earls of ROSS, who were Lords of THE ISLES, *quartered a lymphad in the first and fourth quarters, with* ROSS *in the second and third*, both coats without the tressure.   (*Ibid.*, ii., Nos. 536, 540).

The See of MORAY is said to have been founded by King ALEXANDER in 1115.   A charter granted by King DAVID to the Monks of DUNFERMLINE between 1128 and 1130, is witnessed by (among others) GREGORY, Bishop of MORAY, and MAKBETH, Bishop of ROSSMARKYN. (SKENE, *Celtic Scotland*, vol. ii., p. 377.)   DORNOCH was organised as a Cathedral chapter soon after the appointment of GILBERT MURRAY to the See, *circa* 1190. (*Ibid.*, vol. ii., p. 384.)

St. Andrews, Dunkeld, and Dunblane.

Quarterly, 1 and 4. *Azure, a saltire argent.* St. Andrews.

    2. *Argent, a Passion-Cross sable between two passion-nails gules.* Dunkeld.

    3. *Argent, a saltire engrailed azure.* Dunblane. (Plate XXIX., figs. 4, 5, 6.)

The See of S. Andrews is said to have originated with the introduction of Christianity into this country, and the legend relates that some relics of the saint were brought from his grave at Patræ by a Greek monk. The ship which bore them being driven ashore near the site of the present city, the Pictish chief of the district founded a church under the invocation of the Apostle, and S. Andrew thus became the patron saint of the Picts, while the saltire cross which was the instrument of his martyrdom became the badge of the realm. As a matter of fact the Scottish Church founded by Kenneth M'Alpin, was placed under the rule of the Abbot of Dunkeld (878-889) by King Giric. In 908 the primacy was transferred to St. Andrews from Abernethy, the Culdees of which Church had had the right of electing the Abbot of Dunkeld. The line of ancient Bishops of Alban at St. Andrews ended in Fothad in 1093, and the See remained vacant for fourteen years. In 1107 Turgot, Prior of Durham, was appointed by King Alexander, and in his days all the rights of the *Keledei* throughout the whole kingdom passed to the Bishopric of St. Andrews. The appointment of Turgot brought about the claim of the Archbishop of York to supremacy over the Scottish Church ; a claim founded on Pope Gregory's commission to S. Augustine, by which all churches north of the Humber were placed under the rule of the See of York ; and this was fortified by the convention between the Archbishops of York and Canterbury in 1072. But the right had never been recognised ; and the only substantial ground on which it could be based was very similar to that on which the claim of the English King to exercise civil supremacy over Scotland was founded. But, as has been noticed, the province of YORK certainly extended to the Forth, as did the kingdom of Northumbria ; and since the churches of the Lothians were subject to the See of ST. ANDREWS, as those of the English See of GALLOWAY or WHITHERN were (so it was asserted) to the See of GLASGOW, there was so far some ground for the assertion of the claim of supremacy by the See of YORK (SKENE, *Celtic Scotland*, vol. ii., p. 376). ST. ANDREWS became an archbishopric in 1472. Since 1842 it has been held in union with the See of DUNBLANE and DUNKELD.

DUNBLANE was founded towards the close of King DAVID'S reign. LAURENCE, Bishop of the See, witnesses a charter granted by MALCOLM IV. (between 1160-1162) to the monks of DUNFERMLINE. (SKENE, *Celtic Scotland*, vol. ii., p. 396.) It, with the See of BRECHIN, was probably formed out of the remains of the old Pictish Bishopric of ABERNETHY. The arms assumed for DUNBLANE are ·borne quartered in the second and third places, with those of DOUGLAS (simply a heart) in the first and fourth, by Bishop ROBERT DOUGLAS in 1684. Another seal of the same bishop has the coat impaling the full arms of DOUGLAS (LAING, *Scottish Seals*, vol. ii., Nos. 1062, 1063).

A church was built at DUNKELD by KENNETH MACALPIN, and a portion of the relics of S. COLUMBA was transferred to it. The abbot became the first Bishop of the Pictish Kingdom. His office passed into the hands of a line of lay abbots from which descended the Royal line of Scotland. King ALEXANDER founded the See in 1107. The credit of this is erroneously assigned to DAVID I., who according to SKENE, superseded the *keledei*, and created a Bishop with a college, or chapter, of secular Canons. (*Celtic Scotland*, vol. ii., p. 368.)

CHAPTER II.

ARMS OF COLONIAL SEES.

THE arms assumed for Colonial Sees, and even those which were the subjects of regular grants from the Heralds' College, are not for the most part remarkable for heraldic beauty, or propriety. The inventive powers of the designers did not reach further (as regards the early colonial seals at least) than the juxta-position of a key and a pastoral staff; a bible and a crown. Some of the assumptions in which landscapes are introduced are striking examples of heraldic impropriety; and are, we would hope, to be replaced at an early date (say at the next vacancy, or subdivision of the diocese), by compositions in better armorial taste.

The establishment of Ecclesiastical provinces with Metropolitan Sees, which has become pretty general of late years, has in the case of several provinces led to the adoption in the arms of the suffragan Sees of a charge indicative of this common bond of union, and this deserves commendation. At the First General Synod of the Canadian Church, held at Toronto in September 1893, under the Presidency of the Metropolitan, the Bishop (MACHRAY) of RUPERT'S LAND, the Provincial Organisation of that Church was formally completed. It was decided that a Primate of all CANADA should be elected, and that two provinces should be at once formed (a third, to be composed of the Sees of BRITISH-COLUMBIA, being for the while in abeyance) the Metropolitans of which should be Archbishops of the Provinces. Accordingly, Bishop MACHRAY was elected by the House of Bishops, Primate of all CANADA, and Metropolitan of the Province of RUPERT'S LAND, with the title of Archbishop; and Bishop LEWIS of ONTARIO, Metropolitan of that Province, also with the archi-episcopal title and dignity.

PROVINCE OF LOWER CANADA.

FREDERICTON; NOVA SCOTIA; QUEBEC; TORONTO; MONTREAL; HURON; ONTARIO; ALGOMA; and NIAGARA.

FREDERICTON.

Arms: *Gules, a pastoral staff in pale surmounted by two keys addorsed in saltire or; on a chief of the last a Paschal-Lamb with its flag, all proper* (Plate XXX., fig. 1).

The See was formed out of the Diocese of NOVA SCOTIA in the year 1845. It comprises the whole of the Civil Province of NEW BRUNSWICK, an area of 27,174 square miles.

NOVA SCOTIA.

Arms: *Or, a Paschal-Lamb bearing its flag (the Jack thereof azure a saltire argent); on a chief azure a pastoral staff and a key in saltire of the first* (Plate XXX., fig. 2).

This, which is among the earliest of Colonial Sees, was founded in 1787. It includes Nova Scotia, Cape Breton, and Prince Edward's Island.

QUEBEC.

Arms: *Gules, a lion of ENGLAND supporting a key erect or; on a chief cousu wavy sable an open book, across it a pastoral staff in bend proper. On a canton argent, a cross between four crosses patées gules.* (Plate XXX., fig. 3.)

The Diocese of QUEBEC was founded in the year 1793. Its territories are Quebec, the districts of Gaspé S. Fráncis, and Three Rivers.

TORONTO.

Arms : *Azure, a pastoral staff and key in saltire, between in chief an Imperial crown or ; in flanks two open books ; and in base a dove with an olive branch in its mouth, all proper* (Plate XXX., fig. 5).

The Bishopric of TORONTO was founded in 1839 ; and though it still has an area of over 9000 miles in the Province of Ontario, five dioceses have been carved out of the original See.

MONTREAL.

Arms : *Azure, a pastoral staff and key in saltire or, surmounted by an open book in fess point, between in chief a star of six points, and in base an anchor argent* (Plate XXX., fig. 6).

This See was formerly included in Quebec, and was divided from it in the year 1850. Its area is about 44,000 square miles.

HURON.

Arms : *Gules, two swords in saltire argent, hilted or ; in chief an Imperial crown proper* (Plate XXX., fig. 7).

The dedication of the Cathedral is to S. PAUL. The See was founded in the year 1857. Its territory includes the southern part of the Province of Ontario, and contains an area of over 1200 miles.

ONTARIO.

Arms : *Argent, on a cross gules an open book proper* (Plate XXX., fig. 8).

The Cathedral is dedicated to S. GEORGE, to this the arms are allusive. The Diocese of Ontario was created in 1862, and includes an area of about 20,000 square miles of the Province of Ontario.

ALGOMA.

> Arms : *Azure, a pastoral staff and key in saltire or, surmounted in fess point by an open book, between in chief an Imperial crown and in base a sprig of maple of three leaves proper* (Plate XXX., fig. 9).

Until lately this was a missionary district but it has now become a settled diocese. It includes an area of about 50,000 square miles in the civil districts of Algoma, and Thunder Bay, Muskoka, and Parry Sound.

NIAGARA.

> Arms: *Tierced in fess :* (a) *A representation of the Falls of Niagara ;* (b) *Argent, a cross gules ;* (c) *Vert, three maple leaves conjoined proper* (Plate XXX., fig. 10).

The See of Niagara was founded in 1875, it comprises six counties in the Civil Province of Ontario.

NEWFOUNDLAND.

> Arms: *Argent, on a cross between four crosses patées gules an Imperial crown or. On a chief azure a Paschal-Lamb couchant, with its flag proper.* (Plate XXX., fig. 4.)

The dedication of the Cathedral is to S. JOHN THE BAPTIST, who is often figured with the Lamb.

This is an independent Diocese not included in the Province of Canada. It was formed out of the See of NOVA SCOTIA in 1839. Besides the Island of Newfoundland (which is about 42,000 square miles in area),

1. Fredericton.   2. Nova Scotia.   3. Quebec.

4. Newfoundland.   5. Toronto.   6. Montreal.

7. Huron.   8. Ontario.   9. Algoma.

10. Niagara.   11. Columbia.   12. Caledonia.

the See also includes the Island of Bermuda, in the Atlantic ; and about 160,000 miles of Labrador.

PROPOSED PROVINCE OF COLUMBIA.

(As yet independent Dioceses.)

COLUMBIA (Metropolitan), 1849.   CALEDONIA, 1879.
NEW WESTMINSTER, 1874.

COLUMBIA (hereafter to be called VANCOUVER).

Arms : *Argent, a cross patée quadrate in the centre gules ; on a chief the arms of* COUTTS *quartering* BURDETT (*viz., Quarterly,* 1 *and* 4. *Argent, a stag's head erased gules, between the attires a pheon azure ; all within a bordure embattled of the last charged with four buckles or,* COUTTS.   2 *and* 3. *Azure, two bars or, on each three martlets gules,* BURDETT). (Plate XXX., fig. 11.)

The See was founded in 1859, by the munificence of Miss ANGELA BURDETT-COUTTS (created Baroness BURDETT-COUTTS, 1871).   (*See* CAPE TOWN, p. 244.)

The territory includes Vancouver, and the adjacent islands.

CALEDONIA.

Arms : *Azure, a saltire argent, surmounted by a pastoral staff or, over all in the fess point an open book proper.   On a chief barry wavy of the first and second, a salmon naiant proper.* (Plate XXX., fig. 12.)

The arms are allusive to the title of the See (*vide ante,* ST. ANDREWS, p. 227).

The chief refers to the natural products of the diocese. The See was formed out of the preceding in 1879.   It includes the north part of the mainland of British Columbia, and the Queen Charlotte Islands.

New Westminster.

Arms : *Azure, a cross flory between five martlets or ; On a chief dancetty or, between two roses gules a pale ermine, thereon a mitre proper* (Plate XXXI., fig. 1).

The arms are composed from those of Westminster (*vide infra*, p. 199). The diocese, which includes the southern mainland of British Columbia, was founded in the year 1879.

Province of Rupert's Land.

Rupert's Land (Metropolitan) ; Moosonee ; Saskatchewan ; Mackenzie River ; Athabasca ; Qu'Appelle ; Calgary ; Selkirk.

Rupert's Land.

Arms : *Ermine, a cross gules, on a chief azure a pastoral staff in bend, surmounted by an open book proper* (Plate XXXI., fig. 2).

This great diocese includes a district of over 200,000 square miles, comprising the Province of Manitoba, and parts of the territories of Ontaria and Keewatin.

Moosonee.

Arms : *Per fess in chief azure the aurora borealis ; in base on waves, in front of two islands each bearing a pine tree, a canoe manned by three rowers, all proper* (Plate XXXI., fig. 3).

This is one of the landscape coats in bad heraldic taste, to which allusion was made in the introductory remarks on p. 229. The district was separated from the See of Rupert's Land in the year 1872. It contains the eastern division of Rupert's Land, including the whole basin of Hudson's Bay, and reaches northward to the Pole !

MACKENZIE RIVER (formerly called ATHABASCA).

> Arms : (*Azure ?*) *Argent, semé of ears of maize slipped, in chief an open book, and in base a pair of snow-shoes in saltire, all proper* (Plate XXXI., fig. 7).

The former Diocese of ATHABASCA was divided in 1883 into two parts of which the southern retains the original name of the See, but the northern part was thenceforth to be known by the name of MACKENZIE River.

SASKATCHEWAN.

> Arms : *Vert, on a fess wavy argent, between in chief a key and a pastoral staff in saltire, and in base a garb, an Indian in a canoe, all proper.*

The arms allude to the situation of the diocese upon the River SASKATCHEWAN, the garb in base to the cornlands of the district (Plate XXXI., fig. 5).

The See of SASKATCHEWAN was divided from that of RUPERT'S LAND in 1872, and is united at present to the See of CALGARY which is as yet unendowed. Its own district is the Province of SASKATCHEWAN and a piece of territory being to the north-east thereof in North-West Canada.

QU'APPELLE.

> Arms : *Ermine, a Passion-Cross gules ; on a chief azure the sun rising irradiated proper* (Plate XXXIV., fig. 11).

This See which comprises the District of ASSINIBOIA in the North-West Territory, with an area of 96,000 miles, was founded in 1884 out of parts of the Dioceses of RUPERT'S LAND, and SASKATCHEWAN.

ATHABASCA.

> Arms : *Or, a tuft of rushes between three sykes proper; On a chief wavy azure, a dove volant argent holding in its beak an olive sprig vert* (Plate XXXIV., fig. 10).

The See of ATHABASCA contains only the southern portion of the original diocese of that name. In 1883 the northern portion became the independent See of MACKENZIE River (*vide supra*). The present See has an area of 250,000 square miles in the North-West Territory.

CALGARY.

(Arms at present undecided.)

This See contains an area of about 100,000 square miles. It was separated formally from the See of SASKATCHEWAN in the years 1887-1888 ; but being as yet unendowed it is still administered by the Bishop of that See. Its territory is the District of ALBERTA, in the North-West Provinces.

SELKIRK.

Arms : *Per fess vert and argent, over all an open book between in fess pine trees, and in base a bear passant, proper (?).*

This See was founded in the year 1891.

PROVINCE OF CALCUTTA.

CALCUTTA (Metropolitan); MADRAS; BOMBAY; COLOMBO; RANGOON; LAHORE; TRAVANCORE; CHOTA NAGPORE.

CALCUTTA.

Arms : *Per fess indented ermine and gules ; in chief a mitre in front of a bunch of palm leaves ; in base a crosier in bend, surmounted by an open book, all proper* (Plate XXXI., fig. 6).

This See was founded in the year 1814, and comprised all India. It now consists of Bengal ; the North-West, and Central Provinces ; Assam ; Central India ; and parts of Rajputana and Oude now handed over to the See of CHOTA NAGPORE.

MADRAS.

> Arms : *Argent on a champagne in base a banyan tree beneath it a tiger and lamb (? leopard and kid) couchant proper. On a chief azure a dove volant, bearing an olive sprig proper, between two crosses patées ermine.* (Plate XXXI., fig. 4.)

(The arms are obviously allusive to Isaiah, xi. 6.)

The diocese was founded in 1835. It includes the whole Presidency ; and also Mysore, Coorg, Hyderabad, and Berar.

BOMBAY.

> Arms : *Sable, a crosier and key in saltire, between two Eastern crowns in chief and base or* (Plate XXXI., fig. 8).

(Bishop DOUGLAS used only his personal arms). Separated from Calcutta in 1832 this See comprises all the Presidency (except Sinde) ; parts of Central India and Rajputana ; as well as Aden on the Red Sea.

COLOMBO.

> Arms : *Argent, a serpent coiled in base and transfixed by a Passion-Cross proper. On a chief azure, a dove volant bearing in its beak an olive sprig proper* (Plate XXXI., fig. 9).

The arms are allusive to the triumph of Christianity over heathenism ; while the dove in chief refers to the name of the See. The Island of Ceylon was constituted a separate diocese in 1845.

RANGOON.

> Arms : *Argent, on a champagne a palm tree proper. Affixed thereto is a shield bearing the arms of the* See of WINCHESTER. (Plate XXXI., fig. 10 ; and Plate XX., fig. 6, for the escucheon.)

This See, which includes the whole of BURMAH, as well as the NICOBAR and ANDAMAN ISLES, was established in 1877, chiefly by the liberality of persons resident in the English Diocese of WINCHESTER.

LAHORE.

Arms : *Azure, on a fess ermine (between in chief the sun rising behind a snowy mountain chain ; and in base five bars wavy argent) a sword and pastoral staff in saltire proper* (Plate XXXI., fig. 11).

The arms are intended to allude to the position of the diocese, beneath the Himalayas, and in the district of the Punjaub, *i.e.*, the five rivers. A little heraldic knowledge might easily have been employed to make a good coat out of this landscape. The See was founded in 1877 for the Punjaub and Scinde.

TRAVANCORE.

Arms : *Azure, a saltire or, over all an Indian spear paleways, the blade argent, beneath an Eastern crown in chief of the last.*

This See was founded for the States of TRAVANCORE and COCHIN in the year 1879 (Plate XXXI., fig. 12).

CHOTA-NAGPORE.

The Arms of this See are not yet settled.

PROVINCE OF AUSTRALIA., (NEW SOUTH WALES).

SYDNEY (Metropolitan) ; TASMANIA ; NEWCASTLE ; MELBOURNE ; ADELAIDE ; PERTH ; BRISBANE ; GOULBURN ; GRAFTON AND ARMIDALE ; BATHURST ; BALLAARAT ; NORTH QUEENSLAND ; and RIVERINA. The original Diocese of AUSTRALIA, originally an Archdeaconry of CALCUTTA, was founded in 1836, and included NEW ZEALAND and TASMANIA.

1. New Westminster. 2. Rupert's Land. 3. Moosonee.

4. Madras. 5. Saskatchewan. 6. Calcutta.

7. (Athabasca.)
now Mackenzie River. 8. Bombay. 9. Colombo.

10. Rangoon. 11. Lahore. 12. Travancore.

SYDNEY.

> Arms : *Azure, four stars of eight points in cross argent* (Plate XXXII., fig. 8).

These stars represent the famous constellation of the Southern Cross, and appear in several of the coats of arms of the Sees of this province. This See was founded in 1847; and the Bishop created by Letters-Patent Metropolitan of Australia and Tasmania.

TASMANIA.

> Arms : *Azure, a pastoral staff and key, in saltire or, between four stars of eight points argent* (Plate XXXII., fig. 9).

This See was created in 1842. · It includes the whole island of Tasmania.

NEWCASTLE.

> Arms : *Azure, an open crown enfiling a pastoral staff in pale or. On a bordure sable twenty-four billets argent.* (Plate XXXII., fig. 10.)

This See was formed out of the Diocese of Australia in 1847. It contains about 14,000 square miles, and includes the central part of the east coast of New South Wales.

MELBOURNE.[1]

> Arms : *Azure, on a chevron argent, between in chief a crosier and a palmer's staff and scrip paleways; and in base four stars of eight points in cross of the second, an open book proper* (Plate XXXII., fig. 11).

[1] The arms assumed for the Roman Catholic Archdiocese of MELBOURNE were : *Per fess azure and argent, in chief four estoiles (mullets) argent; in base a crosier bendways behind an open book which supports a heart inflamed proper.*

The arms assumed for the Roman Catholic See of SANDHURST were identical with the base of the previous coat, but the crosier was in bend-sinister, in saltire with an arrow in bend. (*Notes and Queries*, 5th S., xii., 63, 64.)

This See was founded in 1847. It has an area of over 43,000 square miles, and includes the eastern half of the colony of Victoria.

ADELAIDE. ·
> Arms :⁓ *Argent, on a cross between four estoiles gules, a mitre enfiling a pastoral staff in pale or* (Plate XXXII., fig. 12).

This bishopric was formed out of part of the Diocese of Australia, and includes the colony of South Australia. The Episcopal charge of the Territory of North Australia is also at present included in it as a temporary arrangement ; so that the See extends right across Australia from north to south.

PERTH.
> Arms : *Azure, two pastoral staves in saltire argent, headed or, between four estoiles of the second* (Plate XXXIII., fig. 1).

This diocese was divided from the See of AUSTRALIA in 1857. It embraces the colony of West Australia, having an area of over a million of square miles.

BRISBANE.
> Arms : *Azure, the figure of the Saviour (as the Good Shepherd), proper* (Plate XXXIII., fig. 2).

The See was founded in 1859, on the separation of QUEENSLAND from NEW SOUTH WALES. A new diocese, that of ROCKHAMPTON, is in process of formation out of its territories.

GOULBURN.
> Arms : *Gules, a Paschal-Lamb passant upon a mount, above it an open book with seven seals proper. On a chief or, between two doves each holding a sprig of olive in its beak proper, a pale azure charged with four estoiles in cross argent.* (Plate XXXIII., fig. 3.)

This See was formed out of that of SYDNEY in 1863. It includes the south-eastern part of New South Wales.

GRAFTON AND ARMIDALE.

Arms: *Azure, at the intersection of the arms of a Passion-Cross argent; an open book, in chief a dove volant beak downwards proper* (Plate XXXIII., fig. 4).

This See, which contains the north-east part of New South Wales, was formerly contained in the Diocese of SYDNEY. Part of it was included in NEWCASTLE in 1847; but the present See was created in 1865.

BATHURST.

Arms: *Azure, two pastoral staves in saltire proper between four estoiles argent; in chief a Paschal-Lamb of the second* (Plate XXXIII., fig. 5).

The Diocese of BATHURST was formed out of portions of the Dioceses of SYDNEY, NEWCASTLE, and GOULBURN. Its territory is the west part of New South Wales.

BALLARAT.

Arms: *Ermine, a mill-rind sable; on a chief azure a celestial crown or* (Plate XXXIII., fig. 6).

This See was formed out of that of MELBOURNE in 1875. Its territory is the western division of the colony of Victoria.

NORTH QUEENSLAND.

Arms: *Azure, a Paschal-Lamb proper, between three cross-crosslets fitchée argent* (Plate XXXIII., fig. 7).

As its name indicates, the See includes the northern division of the colony of Queensland, an area of 250,000 square miles.

R

RIVERINA.

Arms : *Azure, four bars wavy argent, over all a Passion-Cross or; on a canton of the second, a lymphad sable* (Plate XXXIV., fig. 10).

This See was founded in 1884 by the munificence of Mr CAMPBELL (commemorated in the canton of the arms). It contains the western part of New South Wales, an area of 70,000 square miles.

PROVINCE OF NEW ZEALAND.

CHRISTCHURCH (Metropolitan); AUCKLAND; NELSON; WAIAPU; WELLINGTON; MELANESIA; and DUNEDIN.

CHRISTCHURCH.

Arms : *Azure, on a cross argent the monogram* $\frac{\iota}{x}$ *sable ; in the first canton three estoiles, one and two, of the second* (Plate XXXII., fig. 1).

This See was founded in the year 1856. Its Bishop was in 1868 elected Primate of the Province. Its territory includes CHRISTCHURCH, and part of WESTLAND, an area of 20,000 square miles.

AUCKLAND.

Arms : *Azure, three estoiles, one and two, argent* (Plate XXXII., fig. 2).

AUCKLAND was the first of the New Zealand Sees; and its arms (three of the stars of the Southern Cross) appear in most of the other provincial coats. This, founded in 1841, was the original Diocese of NEW ZEALAND, out of which the other Sees have been carved. It includes the northern part of the North Island of New Zealand.

1. Christ Church, M. 2. Auckland. 3. Nelson.

4. Wellington. 5. Waiapu. 6. Melanesia.

7. Dunedin. 8. Sydney, M. 9. Tasmania.

10. Newcastle. 11. Melbourne. 12. Adelaide.

NELSON.

> Arms : *Or, a cross-Calvary azure; on a canton the arms of* AUCKLAND (as above) (Plate XXXII., fig. 3).

This diocese was founded in 1857. It consists of the north part of the Southern Island of New Zealand.

WELLINGTON.

> Arms : *Argent, a cross gules, in the first quarter the arms of* AUCKLAND ; *Azure, three stars, one and two, of the first* (Plate XXXII., fig. 4).

The Diocese of WELLINGTON was founded in 1858 ; and contains the province from which it takes its name, and a portion of the district of Taranaki.

WAIAPU.

> Arms : *Azure, a saltire argent, on a canton the arms of* AUCKLAND (Plate XXXII., fig. 5).

(The arms allude to the fact that the See is a district originally settled by Scottish colonists.)

The See includes the eastern district of the West Island of New Zealand, and some outlying islands. It was founded in 1858.

MELANESIA.

> Arms : *Azure, a Passion-Cross or, in chief three estoiles, one and two, of the second* (but ? *argent*) (Plate XXXII., fig. 6).

The Diocese was founded in 1861 for the Western Islands in the South Pacific Ocean.

DUNEDIN.

> Arms : *Gules,* S. ANDREW *holding his cross before him proper. On a canton the arms of* AUCKLAND (Plate XXXII., fig. 7).

The See, founded out of CHRISTCHURCH in 1866, includes OTAGO, and SOUTHLAND. (The district, like WAIAPU, was settled by colonists from Scotland.)

Province of South Africa.

Capetown (Metropolitan); Grahamstown; St. Helena; Bloemfontein; Maritzburg; Zululand; St. John's, Kaffraria; Pretoria.

Capetown.

Arms: *Quarterly, azure and sable, in the first and fourth a lion rampant argent, in the second and third three open crowns paleways or; over all on a cross of the last an anchor of the second in the fess point; and in the honour point an escucheon of the arms of* Burdett-Coutts (*vide ante,* p. 233), (Plate XXXIII., fig. 8).

This rather complicated coat was composed out of the arms of the Sees of Durham and Bristol, with which the first Bishop Gray was connected. The anchor is the symbol of good hope, and the escucheon. records the munificence of Miss Burdett-Coutts, the founder of the See. This was the first South African Bishopric, and was founded in 1847. It now includes only the western district of the Cape Colony.

Grahamstown.

Arms: *Argent, a cross gules, thereon a sword in pale the blade wavy proper, in the dexter canton an anchor sable* (Plate XXXIII., fig. 9). The arms formerly used were: *Argent* (sometimes *azure*), *a saltire gules, over all an anchor sable.*

The Cathedral is dedicated to St. George. The anchor refers to the Metropolitan See.

St. Helena.

Arms: *Azure, in base on waves of the sea, wherein are fishes, an ancient galley of three masts, sails furled, all proper. In chief a crescent, and a star of eight points argent.* (Plate XXXIII., fig. 10.)

1. Perth. 2. Brisbane. 3. Goulburn.

4. Grafton and Armidale. 5. Bathurst. 6. Ballarat.

7. North Queensland. 8. Cape Town. 9. Grahamstown.

10. St. Helena. 11. Bloemfontein. 12. Maritzburg.

This See was founded in 1859, and includes the islands of ST. HELENA, ASCENSION, and TRISTAN D'ACUNHA.

BLOEMFONTEIN.

Arms : *Azure, a saltire argent, over all a flaming sword erect in pale proper* (Plate XXXIII., fig. 11).

The dedication of the Cathedral is to SS. ANDREW and MICHAEL ; so the Cross of the Apostle, and the sword of the Archangel compose the arms. The See was founded in 1863. It comprises the Orange Free State, Basutoland, Bechuanaland, and Griqualand West.

MARITZBURG.

Arms : *Per fess; in chief, Azure, a saltire argent, above it an estoile or; in base, Argent, on waves of the sea a ship proper* (Plate XXXIII., fig. 12).

The first coat is that of the original Diocese of NATAL, founded in 1853.

ZULULAND.

Arms : *Sable, a wooden cross proper, on a champagne in base vert an anchor (or ?). In chief on a canton azure an estoile argent.* (Plate XXXIV., fig. 1.)

A piece of false heraldry. The cross is said to represent that which was erected over the grave of Bishop MACKENZIE of Central Africa, in whose memory the See was founded in 1870.

ST. JOHN'S, KAFFRARIA.

Arms : *Azure, the figure of the Apostle and Evangelist S. JOHN* (Plate XXXIV., fig. 2).

The See was constituted in 1873 out of the Dioceses of GRAHAMSTOWN and MARITZBURG.

MASHONALAND.

(No arms are recorded at present.)

PRETORIA.

Arms : *Tierced in fess gules, argent, and azure. In chief the lion of* ENGLAND *supporting a banner of* ST. GEORGE ; *in base an anchor of the second.* (Plate XXXIV., fig. 3.)

These arms I composed for the See out of the old Dutch colours ; with the lion of ENGLAND in chief, and the anchor of CAPETOWN in base. As given in CROCK-FORD, it appears to be borne with *a bordure vert ;* if it be so used the later addition has not improved the coat.

PROVINCE OF THE WEST INDIES.

GUIANA (Metropolitan) ; JAMAICA ; BARBADOS and WINDWARD ISLES ; ANTIGUA ; NASSAU ; TRINIDAD ; and HONDURAS.

GUIANA.

Arms : *Argent, on a cross azure a Passion-Cross or. On a chief gules a lion of* ENGLAND *holding a pastoral staff.* (Plate XXXIV., fig. 4.)

This See was separated from that of BARBADOS in 1842.

JAMAICA.

Arms : *Gules, a pastoral staff and key in saltire surmounted by an open book in fess point or, between a lion of* ENGLAND *in chief, and a pineapple in base proper* (Plate XXXIV., fig. 5).

This diocese was created in 1824. It formerly included the Bahamas, now in the See of NASSAU ; and the mainland settlements of Honduras.

BARBADOS.

Arms : *Azure, a pastoral staff and key in saltire, between in chief the Imperial crown or, and in base an estoile argent* (Plate XXXIV., fig. 6).

This See was founded in 1824. It was divided in 1842, and the Dioceses of GUIANA and ANTIGUA separated from it. It consists of the Island of BARBADOS.

WINDWARD ISLES.

> Arms: *Azure, three galleys under sail, two and one, argent ; on a chief of the last a cross gules* (Plate XXXIV., fig. 7).

This See was formerly part of that of BARBADOS, and is temporarily administered by the Bishop of that See.

ANTIGUA.

> Arms: *Argent, a Passion-Cross gules between a serpent erect, and a dove proper ; on a chief of the second a pastoral staff and key in saltire beneath the Imperial crown, or* (Plate XXXIV., fig. 8.)

This See was formed out of that of BARBADOS, as stated above, in the year 1842.

NASSAU.

> Arms: *Argent, a landscape, in base on a rock an open bible at the foot of an Iona Cross ; behind it the open sea, thereon a ship sailing to the sinister, and a palm-covered land.*

The Archdeaconry of the Bahamas was separated from the See of BARBADOS in 1861. The See includes the Turks and Caicos Isles.

TRINIDAD.

> Arms: *A device composed of a long cross flory incorporated with the ancient triangular symbol and legend of the Blessed Trinity : in base the letters Alpha and Omega.*

This See, founded in 1872, includes the Islands of Trinidad and Tobago; the latter was recently transferred from the Windward Isles.

DIOCESES, NOT COMPRISED IN PROVINCES, BUT HOLDING
MISSION FROM THE SEE OF CANTERBURY.

NEWFOUNDLAND (and BERMUDA).

Arms : *Argent, on a cross between four crosses patées
gules an Imperial crown ; on a chief azure a
Paschal-Lamb couchant proper* (Plate XI., fig. 4).

The dedication of the Cathedral is to S. JOHN THE
BAPTIST, who is often figured with the Lamb.

This is an independent diocese not included in the
Province of Canada: It was formed out of the See of
NOVA SCOTIA in 1839. Besides the Island of Newfoundland (which is about 42,000 square miles in area),
the See includes the Island of Bermuda, in the Atlantic ;
and about 160,000 miles of Labrador.

JERUSALEM.

Arms : *Argent, a Hebrew inscription between two
estoiles in chief, and a dove with its olive branch in
base, all proper. On a chief (per pale) gules (and
argent, in the first) the lion of* ENGLAND *(in the
second, the* PRUSSIAN *eagle).*

The original chief referred to the united foundation
of the See by Great Britain and Prussia in 1841 ; but
the See has no present connection with Prussia, and the
chief, of gules only, contains the British lion.

GIBRALTAR.

Arms : *Per fess indented gules and argent; in chief a
pastoral staff and key in saltire or, upon them a cross
patée* (or *Maltese cross*) *of the second. In base, on
a rock proper, a lion of* ENGLAND *holding a Passion-
Cross of the first.* (Plate XXXV., fig. 1.)

The See of GIBRALTAR, founded in 1842, includes
Malta; so probably the original *cross-patée* in the chief was
intended by the designer to represent the eight-pointed
cross of the ORDER OF S. JOHN of JERUSALEM, which
is not a *cross-patée.*

1. Zulu Land

2. St. John's, Ka.

3. Pretoria

4. Guiana

5. Jamaica

6. Barbados

7. Windward Isles

8. Antigua

9. Riverina

10. Athabasca

11. Qu'Appelle

12. E. Equatorial Af·

is

VICTORIA (CHINA).

Arms : *Gules, between in chief an Eastern crown, and in base an escallop shell, all argent, a pastoral staff of the second headed or, and a key in saltire, surmounted in the fess point by an open book* (Plate XXXV., fig. 7).

This See which includes the island of Hong-Kong, and the South China Missions, was founded in the year 1849.

SIERRA LEONE.

Arms : *Argent, a lion couchant in front of a serrated rock proper; on a chief gules two trumpets in saltire mouths upward, of the first* (Plate XXXV., fig. 3).

The Bishopric was founded in the year 1852. Its territories are : Sierra Leone, the Settlements on the Gambia River, and on the Gold Coast.

MAURITIUS.

Arms : *Barry wavy of ten argent and azure, a pastoral staff and key in saltire thereon an open book in fess point, between in chief a celestial crown and in base an anchor, all proper* (Plate XXXV., fig. 2).

The See of MAURITIUS, which includes the Seychelles and adjacent islands, was founded in the year 1854.

SINGAPORE, LABUAN and SARAWAK.

Arms : *Per fess, in chief a saltire (?). In base a pastoral staff in pale surmounted by two keys addorsed in saltire.* (Plate XXXV., fig. 5, but doubtful.)

The arms borne for the See of LABUAN in Borneo were : *Or, a cross per pale gules and sable,* derived from the arms of the Rajah (BROOKE) of SARAWAK. The See of LABUAN and SARAWAK was created in 1855 ; and in 1869 the British Colony of the Straits-Settlement (including Singapore, Malacca, and Penang) was placed under its jurisdiction, and the name of the See was accordingly modified.

CENTRAL AFRICA, 1861.

Arms : *Sable, on a cross argent a .roundle of the same, thereon the .monogram,* CA. (Plate XXXV., fig. 12).

This missionary See was founded by the Universities of England in 1861, for Zanzibar Island, and the adjacent mainland.

HONOLULU.

Arms : *Per fess gules and azure, in chief two keys in saltire addorsed argent ; in base a cross-moline of the same* (Plate XXXV., fig. 10).

This See embraces the Hawaian, or Sandwich Isles ; and was founded in the year 1861.

NIGER DISTRICT.

A landscape in base ; to the dexter a rock, thereon a palm tree, on the sea, out of which the sun is rising, a ship in full sail—*all im*proper. (This See was founded in 1864.)

EAST EQUATORIAL AFRICA.

Arms : *Sable (? Gules) a cross patée-fitchée argent; on a chief wavy ermine a tent of the second, between two mill-rinds sable* (Plate XXXIV., fig. 12).

This diocese was founded in 1884.

LEBOMBO. ·

Arms : *Gules, two keys in saltire, wards downwards, argent ; on a chief of the last an anchor sable.*

The See was founded in (1891 ?).

MADAGASCAR.

Arms : *Azure, a cross-Calvary or* (Plate XXXV., fig. 4).

The See was established in the year 1874.

1. Gibraltar 2. Mauritius 3. Sierra Leone

4. Madagascar 5. Singapore, &c. 6. Japan

7. Victoria 8. North China 9. Mid-China

10. Honolulu 11. Falkland Islands 12. Central Africa

FALKLAND ISLES.

Arms : *Per fess; in chief, Argent a plain cross gules; in base, Azure a map of S. America* (Plate XXXV., fig. 11).

This Diocese, which has the charge of the English churches in S. America, was founded in 1869.

NORTH-CHINA.

Arms : *Gules, a cross-moline or* (Plate XXXV., fig. 8).

The Diocese of NORTH-CHINA, as at present constituted for the six northern provinces of China, was founded in 1880.

MID-CHINA.

Arms: *Azure, on a fess wavy argent (out of which in chief emerges the rising sun) a dove volant holding in its beak a sprig of olive proper; in base a pastoral staff and key in saltire or* (Plate XXXV., fig. 9).

The See was founded in 1880.

JAPAN.

Arms : *Argent, a cross gules; on a chief barry wavy of six of the first and azure the sun rising or* (Plate XXXV. fig. 6).

The See was established in 1887.

COREA.

Arms: *Gules, semé of leaves a cross-moline or, all within a bordure wavy argent* (*cf.* N. CHINA).

This See, which embraces the Kingdom of Corea, and the Province of Shing King in Manchuria, was founded in the year 1889.

CHAPTER III.

Archbishops and Bishops, Electors and Princes of the Holy
Roman Empire and Central Europe.

MAINZ (MAYENCE).

Arms : *Gules, a wheel of six spokes argent.*

The Elector, and Prince-Archbishop of MAINZ, was Arch-Chancellor of the HOLY ROMAN EMPIRE in Germany ; he was also Dean of the Electoral College, and presided over it on the occasions when it deliberated upon the choice of a prince to fill the vacant Imperial throne. He had the titles of *Obrister Churfürst* (which appears in a diploma of the Emperor MAXIMILIAN I.), *Kur-Erzkanzler, Metropolit, und Primas von Deutschland.* According to MEGENFRIED, a monk of FULDA, who wrote in the tenth century, the See is said to have been founded by CRESCENS, a disciple of the Apostle S. PAUL. It was originally suffragan to TRIER. The first really historical personage who occupied the See was S. BONIFACE, who held it from 747 to 755, being placed over it by Pope ZACHARIAS, who confirmed its authority over the cities of CÖLN, SPEIER, TONGERN, UTRECHT, and WORMS, and indeed over all the district in which S. BONIFACE had laboured. The Pope also conferred on the See the Metropolitical dignity. Under Pope JOHN XXII. (1316-1334) the See of MAINZ had fourteen suffragan Sees :—AUGSBURG, CHUR, CONSTANZ, EICH-STADT, HALBERSTADT, HILDESHEIM, OLMÜTZ, PADER-BORN, PRAG, SPEIER, STRASBURG, VERDEN, WORMS, and WÜRZBURG, thus about half of the whole German Empire was subject to it.

Of these it lost in 1343 OLMÜTZ and PRAG, the latter of which became at once an Archbishopric, a dignity which OLMÜTZ also attained in later times. The Sees of HALBERSTADT and VERDEN were lost, and their possessions secularised, at the Peace of Westphalia.

The Bishopric of FULDA was made suffragan to MAINZ in 1752, and that of CORVEY in 1785. The Archbishop WILHELM (954-968) a natural son of the Emperor OTTO, received from his father the dignity of Arch-Chancellor of the German Empire for himself and his successors. His predecessors, since LULLUS the successor of S. BONIFACE, had held the title of *Archicapellan.* As Elector, and Arch-Chancellor of the Empire in Germany, the Archbishop had precedence over all Princes and Prelates of the Empire. If the coronation of the Emperor, as King of the Romans, took place in his Arch-diocese he was the officiant; and when it took place else-where, even in the Arch-diocese of CÖLN, he had the right to officiate alternately with the Archbishop of CÖLN. This right, which seems to contravene the pro-visions of the *Aurea Bulla,* was established in 1657.

Like the Emperor himself the Elector had his heredi-tary great officers of state. The Landgrave of HESSE was his Grand-Marshal; the Count of VELDENTZ, the Grand-Master of his Household; the Count of SCHÖN-BORN, his Grand-Steward; and the Count of STOLBERG, his Grand-Chamberlain. These great personages dis-charged the duties of their offices by hereditary deputies, who in the eighteenth century were respectively the Counts of HEUSENSTAM, and the Barons of GREIFFEN-KLAUEN-VOLRATH, CRONBERG, and METTERNICH. For the better maintenance of their great dignity the Electors in later times often held the Prince-Bishopric of WÜRZBURG *in commendam.* (*Vide post,* p. 331.)

The many privileges attaching to the dignity of Arch-Chancellor are set out at length in SPENER, *Opus Heraldicum*, pars spec., pp. 265-268 ; among them was the office of Postmaster-General of the Empire. Among the possessions of the See was the County of KÖNIG-STEIN, given in 1581 by the Emperor MAXIMILIAN to Archbishop DANIEL BRENDEL VON HOMBURG.

After the French Revolution the territories of the Electorate were overrun by the French invaders, and a great portion of its possessions were incorporated by NAPOLEON in the short-lived Confederation of the Rhine. The then Archbishop and Elector, CARL THEODORE VON DALBERG (elected in 1802) ceased to be Arch-Chancellor of the German Empire in 1810. He had been made Prince of REGENSBURG in 1804, and Archbishop of the same place in 1806. NAPOLEON made him Primate of the Confederation of the Rhine in 1810, and he became Grand-Duke of FRANKFÜRT-AM-MAYN in 1813 ; he died in 1817. NAPOLEON reduced the See of MAINZ to the rank of a bishopric ; and it is now suffragan to the Archbishopric of FREIBERG in Breisgau.

The arms refer to the well-known story of Archbishop WILLIGIS (975-1011), whose father was a millwright. That he might find in the constant remembrance of his humble parentage a protection against the temptation to arrogance, the Archbishop is said to have had the walls of his chamber painted with the device of a mill-wheel and the motto " *Willigis recolas, quis es, et unde venis.*" • Of this the common versions in Germany are

"Willigis ! Willigis ! gedenck von wannen du kommen bist ;"
or
"Willigis ! Willigis ! deiner Ankunft nicht vergiss."

The device in later times became the charge of the Archi-episcopal arms. It must however be noted that the arms of the City of MAINZ are : *Gules, two wheels connected by a cross argent.* These are said to be derived from those of the Archbishopric. This may possibly have been the case. On the other hand the reverse has been thought equally probable; and it has been supposed that the charges had a more prosaic origin in the floating mills which still utilise the current of the turbid Rhine at MAINZ. But "Herr Hofrath ESTOR will mit der gemeinen Erzehlung von des Willigis Rade in Mayntzischen Wapen nicht zufrieden seyn, sondern hält es vielmehr mit dem Herrn geheimden Justitien Rath GRUBERN vor das *Typarium*, oder Reichs-Siegel." (TRIER, *Einleitung zu der Wapen-Kunst*, pp. 334, 335.)

The Elector quartered the arms of the See of MAINZ in the first and fourth places, with his personal arms in the second and third; but when, as was frequently the case in the seventeenth and eighteenth centuries, other Sees were held *in commendam*, their arms, and those of their dependencies, were borne quartered with those of the Archi-episcopal See, and the personal arms of the Elector were placed in an escucheon *en surtout*.

The shield was surmounted by golden helmets, of which the central one bore a mitre on a crimson cushion; the others were timbred with the crest of the See of MAINZ (*on a princely hat of crimson, turned up ermine, a wheel argent*, as in the arms); the crest or crests of the other Sees held by the prelate; and his personal crest or crests. But the shield was often adorned with a mantle of crimson velvet lined with ermine, and surmounted by the Electoral hat, or crown; the helmets and crests were then omitted. But in either case the primatial cross with a single traverse was placed in *pale* behind the shield; while the union of temporal with spiritual authority was denoted in the usual manner by the naked sword (point downwards), and the crozier or pastoral staff, placed in saltire behind the escucheon.

The examples given by SPENER (tab. xi.) are as
follows:—

JOHN PHILIP VON SCHÖNBORN, Archbishop and
Elector, 1647-1673, also retained the See of WÜRZBURG,
to which he was elected in 1642, and that of WORMS,
which he acquired in 1663.   He bore : *Quarterly of
six, in two horizontal rows,* 1. Duchy of FRANCONIA
(*v.* p. 331) ; 2 .and 5. MAINZ ; 3 and 4. See of WORMS
(*v.* p. 330) ; 6. See of WÜRZBURG (*v.* p. 267).   Over all
the personal arms, *Gules, a lion passant crowned or, upon
three rocks, or points, in base argent.*   Six helmets and
crests were used.   Beginning from the *dexter* side, they
were arranged, 1. WÜRZBURG ; 2. FRANCONIA (p. 267) ;
3. MITRE ; 4. See of MAINZ ; 5. WORMS ; 6. SCHÖN-
BORN (*between two horns per fess gules and argent a demi-
lion rampant crowned or*).

To him succeeded LOTHAIR FRIEDRICH VON MET-
TERNICH (1673-1675), who also held the Sees of SPEIER
and WORMS.   His arms were : *Quarterly,* 1 and 4.
WORMS ; 2 and 5. MAINZ ; 3. SPEIER (*v.* p. 322) ;
4. Abbey of WEISSENBURG (*v.* p. 322).   Over all the
personal arms : *Argent, three escallops sable.   Crests,*
1. WEISSENBERG ; 2. WORMS ; 3. MITRE, etc. ; 4.
MAINZ ; 5. SPEIER ; 6. The personal crest : *Out of a
coronet the head and neck of a swan proper.*

His successor, DAMIAN HARTARD VON DER LEYEN
(1675-1678), was also Prince-Bishop of WORMS, and
accordingly bore : *Quarterly,* 1 and 4. MAINZ ; 2 and 3.
WORMS ; over all his personal arms, *Azure, a pale
argent.*   The *crests* were four :—1. WORMS ; 2. MITRE,
etc.; 3. MAINZ ; 4. LEYEN. *The head of a greyhound
argent, between two wings azure semé of silver linden
leaves.*   This Elector used *Supporters,* two white greyhounds.   (He and his predecessors had also the usual
arrangement of the primatial cross, the sword and
pastoral staff.)   After another METTERNICH (1679),

ANSELM FRANZ VON INGELHEIM held the See from 1679 to 1695. His sixty-four quarters are given in SPENER, *Op. Her.*, p. spec., p. 745. He bore: *Quarterly*, 1 and 4. See of MAINZ; 2 and 3. INGELHEIM, *Sable, a cross counter-componé gules and or.* The *helms* and *crest* are three; 1. MAINZ; 2. the MITRE; 3. *Two wings each charged as the Ingelheim quarter;* being the personal crest.

On our Plate XVI. we give from TRIERS, *Einleitung zu der Wapen-Kunst*, the arms of JOHAN FRIEDRICH, Count von OSTEIN, who was elected in 1743, and died in 1763. (He held the See of WORMS *in commendam* from 1756.) The arms are:—*Quarterly*, 1 and 4. The See of MAINZ; 2 and 3. The arms of OSTEIN: *Azure, a greyhound springing or, collared gules.*

The crests are three, on golden helms. The centre supports the mitre on a crimson cushion. The dexter bears the silver wheel of the See upon an Electoral hat; and the sinister, the personal crest a demi-greyhound as in the arms. The archi-episcopal cross is in pale, and the temporal sword and crosier, in saltire, behind the shield, which is surrounded by an ermine-lined mantle of crimson velvet fringed with gold.

TRIER (TREVES).

Arms: *Argent, a cross gules.*

According to ecclesiastical legend the See of TRIER derived its foundation in the year 66 from SS. EUCHARIUS, VALERIUS, and MATERNUS, disciples of S. PETER, and successively bishops of the See. This tradition has no solid foundation, and the earliest historical bishop appears to be AGRITIUS, or AGROETIUS, on whom the archi-episcopal dignity is said to have been conferred by Pope SYLVESTER, and who flourished in the early part of the fourth century. The title of Archbishop really appears for the first time two centuries later.

s

LUDOLF of SAXONY, Archbishop from 994 to 1008, is said to have been the first Elector of TRIER, but the secular eminence of the See as an Electoral principality appears to date from the times of Archbishop BALDWIN, Count of LÜTZELBURG (who held the See from 1307 to 1354), since there is some doubt as to the exact time when the right of electing the Emperor became restricted to the seven princes, three ecclesiastical and four secular.

The Archbishop of TRIER held the second place in the Electoral college, and voted first at the Imperial elections held under the presidency of the Elector of MAINZ. He used the titles, "Von Gottes Gnaden Erzbischof·zu Trier, des heil. röm. Reiches, und des Königreiches Arelat, Erzkanzler und Kurfürst;" "S. Romani Imperii Archi-Cancellarius per Galliam et Regnum Arelatense." As to the empty title of Arch-Chancellor of the Empire in Gaul, etc., we find that the Archbishops of VIENNE had the office of Arch-Chancellor in the Burgundian kingdom at Arles, during the reign of the Emperors of the house of SUABIA.

The Elector had his principal residence at COBLENZ. To him belonged the strong fortress of EHREN-BREITSTEIN, which commands the Rhine at this point, and is said to have been founded by Archbishop HILLIN, who held the See from 1152 to 1169.

The Abbacy of ST. MAXIMIN near TRIER was an adjunct of the Archi-episcopal See ; and in his quality of Abbot the Archbishop was Arch-Chaplain of the Empress. The princely Abbey of PRUM in the Ardennes, which had been long coveted by the Archbishops, was finally united to the See in the year 1576, as the Provostship of WEISSENBURG had been in 1545. The three Bishoprics of METZ, TOUL, and VERDUN were suffragan to TRIERS until the conquest of the territory by the French. At the Peace of LUNEVILLE France was left in possession of the territories on the left bank

of the Rhine, those on the opposite bank were given to NASSAU, and the Elector was indemnified by a pension of 100,000 florins. The Concordat of 1801 established a new ecclesiastical organisation, in consequence whereof TRIER lost its Archi-episcopal dignity and was made suffragan to MECHLIN. In 1815 TRIER became a possession of the Prussian Crown, and the See was vacant until 1824. It is now suffragan to CÖLN.

CHARLES CASPAR VON DER LEYEN, who filled the See from 1652 to 1676, bore (according to FURST, *Wappenbuch*, iii., 3), the arms following: *Quarterly*, 1 and 4. *Argent, a cross gules* (TRIER); 2 and 3. *Azure, a pale argent* (his personal coat); *Over all, on an escucheon, the arms of the* Abbey of PRUM: *Gules, on a mount in base vert a Paschal-Lamb passant regardant argent, holding a banner of the last charged with a cross of the first*. (SIEBMACHER in the *Wappenbuch*, i., plate 13 assigns to PRUM a different coat: *Per fess azure and gules, in chief three fleurs-de-lis or ;* but the reason does not appear, and the coat previously given is certainly that usually borne for the princely abbey.) The Elector CHARLES CASPAR used three crested helms of gold ; of these the central one bore on a crimson cushion the archi-episcopal mitre. The helm on the dexter side was surmounted by the Electoral hat, and bore the crest of the See, an octagonal fan charged with the arms thereof, and bearing in the centre an escucheon of the arms of LEYEN. The points of the fan are ornamented as usual with small tufts of peacock's feathers. The helm on the sinister side is *timbred* with an open crown, out of which rises the LEYEN crest already described at p. 256.

His successor the Elector JOHN HUGO VON ORSBECK, who filled the See from 1676 to 1711, was also Prince-Bishop of SPEIER (elected in 1675) and retained that See with his Electorate. Accordingly he bore the following arms: *Quarterly*, 1. TRIER, as above; 2. PRUM, as above; 3. WEISSENBURG (*v.* p. 322); 4. SPEIER, *Azure, a cross argent*; and over all an escucheon of his personal arms: *Or, a saltire gules between four nenuphar leaves vert.* The helms and crests are five in number; the central one bears the mitre, those next on either side have respectively the crests of TRIER and SPEIER (*see* p. 322), the outside helm to the dexter bears the crest of WEISSENBURG, *Out of a crest-coronet or, a pair of eagle's wings gules, charged as the arms; v.* p. 322; and that to the sinister the personal crest of ORSBECK, *the head of a horse argent bridled gules.* Here, as in all other German examples, the helmets have lambrequins of the chief metal and colour in the coats to which they belong. The arms of the Elector CHARLES of LORRAINE, in 1715, are at p. 89, *ante.* The Archbishops of TRIER employed the usual arrangement of their archi-episcopal cross, temporal sword, and spiritual crosier, as external adjuncts to their shield of arms. It is worthy of notice that in the *Wapenrolle von Zürich*, taf. xxv., the banner of TRIER is depicted as *Sable, a cross argent*, of which the reason is not evident.

The Electors of TRIER had a splendid nominal list of great officials: The Dukes of LUXEMBURG, Marshals; Barons of ISENBURG, Marshals of the Palace; the Electors of BRANDENBURG, Cupbearers; the Barons of HELFEN-STEIN, Stewards, etc. The actual officials were, the Barons of ELZ, Marshals; the Stewardship was hereditary in the family of LEVEN; the Chamberlainship in that of SOTERN; the Butlership in that of SCHENCK, all of Rhenish nobility.

The arms of the DOM-CAPITEL of TRIER were the arms of the See with the addition of a demi-figure of S. PETER issuing from clouds, holding in the dexter hand two keys in saltire and in the sinister an open book.

CÖLN (COLOGNE).

Arms : *Argent, a cross sable.*

The authentic list of occupants of the See of CÖLN appears to commence with S. MATERNUS, who was present at the Council held at ROME in 313. His successor EUPHRATES was a member of the Council of SARDICA thirty years later. S. CUNIBERT who held the See for about forty years (623-663 ?) appears to have held the title of Archbishop as a personal distinction, and the See was not really an archi-episcopal one until the time of HILDEBRAND (785-819) though some writers place its erection in the times of S. AGILOLF who was martyred in 717. Under Archbishop HILDEBRAND the suffragans of CÖLN were BREMEN, LÜTTICH (LIÈGE), MIMIGARDEFORD (afterwards MÜNSTER), MINDEN, OSNABRÜCK, and UTRECHT. Of these BREMEN was united later to the Archi-episcopal See of HAMBURG (*v.* BREMEN, p. 271) ; UTRECHT became itself a Metropolitan See in 1559, while MINDEN was secularised in 1648. The Emperor OTTO III. is said to have added the dignity of Elector to the archbishopric in the time of HERIBERT, Count of ROTHENBURG, who held the See from 999 to 1021. The Archbishop also claimed the dignity of Arch-Chancellor of the Holy Roman Empire throughout Italy (*Erzkanzler des Apostolischen Stuhles und des heiligen römischen Reiches deutscher Nation*), which is said to have been first held by PELEGRINUS, Archbishop from 1021 to 1036 ; though others consider that FRIEDRICH, Marquis of FRIULI, who held the See from 1099 to 1131, was the first who possessed this dignity. At the Imperial Elections CÖLN voted second. The Archbishop had the honour of crowning the Emperor if that ceremony took place in his diocese; otherwise he claimed to exercise the right alternately with the Archbishop of MAINZ (*v. s.* p. 253). Like the other great Ecclesiastical Princes of Germany the Elector had a grand official Household in which the principal places were held by the Prince of AREMBERG, Grand Cupbearer ; the Count of MANDERSCHEID-BLANCKENHEIM was Grand-Master of the Household ; and the Count of SALM-REIFFERSCHEID, Marshal.

The arms borne by the Elector were as follows : *Quarterly*, 1. *Argent, a cross sable*, for the See of CÖLN ; 2. *Gules, a horse salient argent*, for the Duchy of WESTPHALIA. This part of Saxony was seized and held by Imperial authority by PHILIP VON HEINSBERG (Archbishop and Elector from 1167 to 1191) when HENRY THE LION was put under the ban of the Empire by the Emperor FREDERICK (BARBAROSSA) in 1180. 3. *Gules, three (heart-shaped) nenuphar leaves or*, for the Principality, or Duchy, of ENGERN, which came to the See under the same circumstances as WESTPHALIA. 4. *Azure, an eagle displayed argent, armed or*, for the County of ARNSPERG. This county was sold in 1368 by its last possessor GOTTFRIED VON ARNSPERG (who had no longer hope of posterity by his wife ANNE of CLEVE), to CUNO, administrator of the See of CÖLN, for behalf of the church. Upon this quartered escucheon the personal arms of the Archbishop and Elector were placed *en surtout*. The archi-episcopal cross *in pale*, with the naked temporal sword and spiritual crosier *in saltire*, appeared in the usual manner behind the shield, which was further supported by two golden lions rampant, or by a golden griffin on the dexter side, and the lion on the sinister. (*See* Plate XV., fig. 1.)

In the sixteenth and following two centuries the Electors often held other Sees *in commendam* with their own, and their arms were therefore combined with those of the Archbishopric of CÖLN.

As a notable example we give (Plate XV., fig. 2) the arms of CLEMENT AUGUSTUS, Duke of BAVARIA, Archbishop and Elector from 1723 to 1761. He also held at the same time the Sees of HILDESHEIM, MÜNSTER, OSNABRÜCK, and PADERBORN, and the Grand Mastership of the TEUTONIC ORDER. The oval shield is separated into four Grand Quarters by the cross of the TEUTONIC ORDER, *Sable, bordered argent* (slightly *patée* at the ends), *thereon a cross flory or.*

I. The arms of the See of CÖLN and its dependencies, as already given above, viz. : *Quarterly,* 1. CÖLN ; 2. WESTPHALIA ; 3. ENGERN ; 4. ARNSPERG.

II. The See of HILDESHEIM, *Per pale argent and gules,*

III. *Per fess* (a) (*in chief*) *Quarterly,* 1 and 4. *Gules, a cross or* (See of PADERBORN); 2 and 3. *Argent, a cross-moline argent* (County of PYRMONT, *vide post,* p. 309); (b) (*in base*) *Argent, a wheel of six spokes gules* (See of OSNABRÜCK).

IV. *Quarterly of six* (in two horizontal rows each of three quarters); 1 and 6. *Per fess argent and gules in chief three martlets sable* (Burg-gravate of STROMBERG); 2 and 5. *Azure, a fess or* (See of MÜNSTER); 3 and 4. *Gules, three balls, two and one, or* (Lordship of BORCKELOHE).

On the centre of the Cross of the TEUTONIC ORDER, and forming a part of it, is a shield of the arms of GERMANY : *Or, a single-headed eagle displayed sable.* On its breast is placed an escucheon of the personal arms of the Elector, viz. : *Quarterly,* 1 and 4. *Fusilly in bend-sinister argent and azure,* BAVARIA ; 2 and 3. *Sable, a lion rampant or, crowned and armed gules,* Palatinate of the RHINE. The archi-episcopal cross in pale, conjoined with the naked temporal sword, and spiritual crosier in saltire, are placed behind the shield, which is mantled with crimson velvet, lined with ermine, and surmounted by the Electoral hat.

MAXIMILIAN FRIEDRICH, Count of KÖNIGSECK-ROTHENFELS, Prince-Archbishop and Elector of COLOGNE, Bishop of MÜNSTER, 1761-1784, bore :

Quarterly of eight (in four horizontal rows each of two quarterings) ; 1. *Argent, a cross sable* (CÖLN) ; 2. *Gules, a horse saliant argent* (WESTPHALIA) ; 3. *Gules, three hearts or* (ENGERN) ; 4. *Azure, an eagle displayed argent* (ARENSBERG or ARNSPERG) ; 5. *Azure, a fess or* (MÜNSTER) ; 6. *Per fess argent and gules, in chief three birds sable* (STROMBERG) ; 7. *Gules, three balls or* (BORCKELOHE) ; 8. *Argent, three fleurs-de-lis gules* (. . .?). *Over all* (KONIGSECK) : *Lozengy in bend sinister or and gules.* The shield is surmounted by the Electoral hat ; and the crosier and temporal sword are in saltire behind the escucheon. The Supporters are the usual griffin and lion (*v.* p. 262).

ARCHBISHOPS AND BISHOPS, PRINCES OF THE EMPIRE, ETC.

1. AUGSBURG.

Arms : *Per pale gules and argent.*

The traditional origin of this See ascends to the third century when S. NARCISSUS and his dèacon S. FELIX are said to have preached the gospel in the neighbouring country. The list of the early Bishops of the See goes back to the sixth century ; but S. WICTERP, or WIGBERT, who occupied the throne from about 737 to 768, is the first really historical personage connected with the See. Its possessions appear to have been largely increased by Bishop SIMPERT (778-809) ; he was a Prince of LORRAINE, nephew of the Emperor CHARLEMAGNE, and had been Abbot of MURBACH. The See, at first suffragan to MILAN, was afterwards under SALZBURG, and in the ninth century was transferred to MAINZ. Bishop BRUNO, a duke of BAVARIA, who occupied the See from 1006 to 1029, was the first of the Prince-Bishops of AUGSBURG.

The principality, which included the counties of GEISENHAUSEN and WITZLINGEN with many lordships, was secularised in the year 1802, and on its restoration by the Concordat of 1817 the See became suffragan to the new Archbishopric of MÜNCHEN-FREYSING.

The arms of JOHN CHRISTOPHER VON FREYBERG, Prince-Bishop from 1665 to 1690, are given by SPENER, (*Opus Heraldicum*, p. spec.; plate xxxii.) They are: *Quarterly*, 1 and 4. *Per pale gules and argent* (See of AUGSBURG); 2 and 3. *Per fess argent and azure, in the last three bezants* (otherwise balls of gold), (Barons von FREYBERG). The Episcopal mitre on a crimson cushion is placed on a golden cherub's head above the centre of the shield. On either side is a golden helmet, properly mantled, of these the dexter bears the crest of the See: *On an open crown or, a fan crest* (of twelve points) *of the arms of the See, with the usual little balls and tufts of peacock's feathers at the angles.* The sinister is the crest of FREYBERG, *In a crest-coronet or, a panache of five ostrich feathers argent.* The temporal sword, and the spiritual crosier, are placed in saltire behind the escucheon.

JOHN FRANCIS SCHENK VON STAUFENBERG, was Prince-Bishop of AUGSBURG from 1737 to 1740 (he had been coadjutor of AUGSBURG since 1714, and of CONSTANZ since 1694). He bore the following arms: *Quarterly*, 1. *Argent, a cross gules* (CONSTANZ); 2. (AUGSBURG); 3. *Argent, a cross gules* (Abbey of REICHENAU); 4. *Argent, two hands issuing from clouds in flanks and holding in pale a key with double wards* (Abbey of . . .). Over all an escucheon of his personal arms: *Argent, a fess gules between two lions passant azure.*

The shield has the usual crosier and temporal sword placed in saltire behind it, and is also supported by *two lions regardant;* the whole is surrounded by a mantle surmounted by the crown of a Prince of the Empire.

FRANZ CONRAD, FREIHERR VON RÖDT, was Bishop of CONSTANZ from 1750 to 1775. He bore: *Quarterly*,

1. *Per pale: Argent (? Or) and gules, a fess argent,* the personal arms of the Barons RÖDT ; 2 and 3. *Argent, a cross gules* (See of CONSTANCE) ; 4. *Or, two hands issuing from clouds in flanks and holding in pale a key with double wards* (Abbey of EISGARN (?) *v.* p. 89).

The arms of the DOM-CAPITEL are : *Per pale gules and argent, over all the effigy of the Blessed Virgin holding the Infant Saviour.*

2. BAMBERG (Prince-Bishopric).

Arms : *Or, a lion rampant sable, over all a bend argent.*

This See was founded in the year 1007 by the Emperor HENRY II. at the request of his wife CUNEGUNDA. The Emperor endowed the new See with the entire County of BAMBERG, which had lapsed to the Crown ; LAUENTHAL and VILLACH in Carinthia ; and other possessions, including ABACH, near Ratisbon, the place of his birth. The first bishop of the See was the Chancellor EBERHARD, nephew of the Emperor, who held it until his decease in 1041. The Bishop had archiepiscopal honours, being entitled to use the archi-episcopal cross and *pallium,* and he held his See immediately from the Pope. He ranked as the first Prince-Bishop of Germany, and claimed precedence over the Grand Master of the TEUTONIC ORDER. His dignity may be estimated by the fact that the four secular Electors did not disdain to hold the honorary hereditary offices of his household. The Elector of SAXONY was Grand-Marshal ; the Elector of BAVARIA, Grand-Steward ; the King of BOHEMIA was Grand-Cupbearer ; and the Elector of BRANDENBURG his Grand-Chamberlain. LYMNŒUS says " Hesitavi aliquando affirmare Electores esse Officinarios Episcopatûs Bambergensis ; nunc autem dubio plane solutus sum, legi enim in literis investituræ datis anno 1475 die Martii post Festum Michaelis, a Philippo

Episcopo Bamb. Albertum Electorem Brandenb. inves-
titum fuisse de officio supremi Camerarii Episcopatûs
Bamberg. et omnibus ejusdem pertinentiis, etc." (*See*
PRAUN, *von den Heer Schilden des Teutschen Adels, etc.*)

The Electors however discharged their duties by
deputies who were respectively members of the families
of EBNET, POMMERSFELDEN, AUFSÄSS, and ROTEN-
HAN.· (BURGERMEISTER, *Bibliotheca Equestris*, Pars.
II., p. 832.)

The possessions of the See were secularised in 1802,
and BAMBERG became an Archbishopric with EICH-
STÄDT, SPEIER, and WÜRZBURG, as its suffragans.

The arms, etc., of PETER PHILIP VON DERNBACH,
Prince-Bishop from 1672 to 1683, are given in SPENER,
Op. Her. p. spec., p. 387, tab. xv., and have been
blazoned already at p. 88. Over the escucheon (which
has the usual accompaniments of archi-episcopal cross,
temporal sword and pastoral staff) are arranged five
crests—the centre (which is placed on the escucheon
without the intervention of a helm) consists of the
Imperial Crown. (This according to TRIERS, *Einleitung zu der Wapen-Kunst*, p. 394, was an Imperial
Augmentation.) The other crests have golden helms
and proper mantlings. Next to the centre on the
dexter side is the crest of BAMBERG: *On a crimson
cushion an octagonal fan charged with the arms and
tufted ;* to the sinister the crest of FRANCONIA : *Out of
a crest-coronet or two horns per fess indented gules and
argent.* The external crests are, to the dexter WÜRZ-
BURG : *Out of a princely hat a panache of three ostrich
feathers, a white one between two others, blue and red, the
whole placed between two lances with their banners as in
the arms.* The last helm on the sinister side bears the
personal crest of DERNBACH : *Two eagle's wings charged
with the personal arms.*

The arms of ADAM FRIEDRICH, Count of SEINSHEIM,

Prince-Bishop of BAMBERG, etc., in 1757, have been blasoned at p. 90, *ante.*

Bishop FRIEDRICH SCHREIBER, elected Bishop of BAMBERG in 1875, bore: *Quarterly,* 1 and 4. *Or, a lion rampant sable, over all a bend argent* (See of BAMBERG); 2 and 3. *Azure, two pens in saltire between four stars of six points argent.* Upon the top edge of the shield (*cf.* Plate XIII., fig. 3) lies the *pallium* which is the great privilege of the See. It is *charged with nine crosses patées sable.* The head of the patriarchal cross with its double traverse appears behind the shield between the mitre and the head of the crosier, and the whole is surmounted by the Episcopal hat. (The crosses of the Bavarian Orders of MERIT, of the CROWN, and of S. MICHAEL are appended by their ribbons beneath the shield.)

BASEL (BASLE).

Arms: *Argent, the head of an ancient crosier gules.*

This See was originally situated at AUGST (*Augusta Rauracarum*) but in 450 that place was destroyed by the Huns, and the See was removed to BASEL, which is in the same neighbourhood. The first really historic Bishop was RAGNACHAR, who lived at the commencement of the seventh century, though the first Bishop JUSTINIAN is said to have been present at a reputed synod held at CÖLN in 346 against the Arians; and at the Council of ORLEANS held July 11, 511, by command of CLOVIS, ADELPHIUS Bishop of BASEL is said to have been present. After RAGNACHAR, WALAN who lived in the time of GREGORY II. (*circa* 715-731) is the next in the list who has a certain existence. In 1004 the Emperor HENRY II. conferred on the Bishop ADALBERO II. the right of hunting in the Forests of ELSASS, etc., a permission which was extended four years later to other districts in Switzerland. In 1271, the Counts of PFIRT sold to the See of BASEL nearly the whole of their county ; but in 1361 Bishop JOHN SENN VON MÜNSINGEN again sold the county to RODOLPH, Duke of AUSTRIA, who had married the daughter of ULRIC, last Count of PFIRT. Apparently some rights were reserved to the See, inasmuch as when by the Treaty of MÜNSTER the County of PFIRT and the rest of the Suntgau were ceded to France, the then Prince-Bishop made energetic protests in the Diet, but in vain.

The See of BASEL was made suffragan to BESANÇON at the commencement of the eighteenth century. At the Reformation the Chapter of the Cathedral, which had fallen to the Protestants, had removed to FREIBURG IM BREISGAU; since 1677 it has shifted to ARLESHEIM and DELLEMONT. After the French Revolution BASEL was included in the Confederation of the Rhine, but at the Restoration in 1815 the territories were for the most part included in the Canton of BERN. By the Concordat and Papal Bull of 1828 the See of BERN is declared to be held immediately from the Roman See, and the seat of the Bishop is in the Chapteral church of SS. URS and VICTOR in Solothurn.

As concerns the arms of the See (Plate V., fig. 5), there was long much uncertainty as to what the charge really was. The very learned German Herald SPENER, has the following paragraph in his *Opus Heraldicum ; pars generalis*, p. 302. "Anchoram etiam vocat Basiliensium δεῖγμα Freherus, ob piscatoris munus quod ab imperio teneat ; sed Cl. Seb. Feschius, *de Insig.*, c. 8, n. 14, mavult esse nauticum instrumentum seu *fahr-stachel*," by which I suppose is meant a boat-hook. But an examination of the fourteenth century manuscript known as the *Wapenrolle von Zürich*, taf. xxv., fig. 568, shows that the ancient banner of BASEL was charged with a crosier, or pastoral staff, gules on a white field. The staff has been shortened till nothing remains but the crook and the socket by which it was attached to the staff. I have myself carefully examined the seals of the early bishops, and the tombs which remain in the Minster at BASEL, many of which bear in sculpture the arms of the See, and I have come to the conclusion that the charge is certainly as I have blazoned it above. The German Heralds usually give the tincture of the charge as *sable*. This is its tincture in the arms of the City and Canton, but not (anciently at least) in those of the See.

The arms of JACOB SIGISMUND VON REINACH-STEIN-BRUNN (1737-1743) were : Quarterly of six, in two horizontal rows :—I. and VI. The arms of the See ; II. and V. *Or, a lion rampant double queué gules, and hooded azure ;* III. and IV. *Or, two bends gules* . . . There are four golden helms, of which the two in the centre support respectively the mitre and the princely hat. The outer helm to the dexter bears, Out of a crest-coronet of gold a demi-lion or, whose back has a ridge, or crest *échancré*, tufted with peacock's feathers. The sinister helm bears, Out of a coronet or a demi-wolf proper.

BISANTZ (BESANÇON) (Archbishopric).
Arms : *Gules, an eagle displayed or.*

The line of Bishops of BISANTZ is said to commence with S. FERREOLUS towards the close of the second century. S. CELIDONIUS, or CHELIDONIUS, was certainly set over the See by S. HILARY in 444. BERNUINUS, or BERNOUIN, is said to have been its first Archbishop in about the first quarter of the ninth century. As the See with the rest of the Burgundian kingdom was absorbed by the Empire under HENRY I. the Archbishop became Arch-Chancellor of Burgundy, and Prince of the Holy Roman Empire. The Suffragan Sees were AVENCHES, now LAUSANNE ; AUGUSTA-RAURACARUM, now BASEL; WINNICH, now CONSTANCE ; and NION, now BELLEY. With regard to the last-named See we may note here that it was transferred to BELLEY about the

middle of the sixth century. The date of its erection at
NOŸON is unknown .VINCENTIUS ".episcopus Belli-
censis" was present, in 555, at the second Council of
Paris. Among the later occupants of the See was
BONIFACE of SAVOY, elected in 1233, who in 1240 became
Archbishop of CANTERBURY. In 1802 METZ, VERDUN,
and TOUL were made suffragan to BESANÇON. After
the French Revolution there was a long vacancy in the
See; but it was called back into life by the Concordat
of 1817.

BISANTZ fell under Hispano-Burgundian rule in 1651;
but LOUIS XIV. seized the Franche-Comté in 1674, and
the Treaty of NIMEGUEN in 1679 confirmed France in
its possession. Despite the change of Sovereigns the
Archbishops continued to hold the title of Princes of
the Holy Roman Empire.

As to the arms, it is doubtful whether they were
assumed with reference to those borne by BYZANTIUM;
or whether they are allusive to the Apostolic symbol of
the Evangelist S. JOHN, who, with S. STEPHEN, appears
to have been co-patron of the church.

BRANDENBURG (Bishopric).

Arms : *Gules, two keys in cross argent.*

This See, founded by the Emperor OTTO the Great
in 949, was first a suffragan of MAINZ, and later of
MAGDEBURG. The last Catholic Bishop, JOACHIM,
Duke of MUNSTERBERG, resigned the See in 1560 to the
Elector JOACHIM II. of BRANDENBURG. The crest of
the See was: *Out of a mitre two crosiers, each having a
bannerol of the arms of the* See.

BREMEN (Archbishops of BREMEN and HAMBURG).

Arms : *Gules, two keys addorsed in saltire, and in chief
a crosslet patée-fitchée argent.*

The Bishopric of BREMEN was founded on July 14, 788, by the Emperor CHARLEMAGNE, who appointed S. WILLEHAD its first Bishop. It was made suffragan to CÖLN.

The Emperor LOUIS (*der Fromme*) in 834 (May 15), erected the Archbishopric of HAMBURG, and set over it S. ANSGAR, a monk of CORVEY, who in the year 849 also became Bishop of BREMEN. In 858 Pope NICHOLAS I. formally united the Sees. ANSKAR and his successors took up their residence at BREMEN, but it was only in 1223 that the definite removal of the archiepiscopal throne to BREMEN took place, and that the See took the name of that city alone. The See reached its greatest extent in the years between 936 and 1072. Under the Archbishop CHRISTOPHER of BRUNSWICK-LÜNEBURG (also Bishop of VERDEN), who filled the See from 1511 to 1558, the Chapter became Protestant. Thereafter, the See was nominally filled by five German princes, under the last of whom, FRIEDRICH, Prince (afterwards King) of DENMARK, its possessions were finally secularised in 1648, and pledged to the Swedish Crown in payment of a war indemnity.

BRESLAU (WRATISLAV, or WROCLAW)(Prince-Bishopric).
Arms : *Quarterly*, 1 and 4. *Gules, six fleurs-de-lis argent* (BRESLAU); 2 and 3. *Or, an eagle displayed sable, having on its breast a crescent argent* (SILESIA).

Founded probably about the commencement of the eleventh century its first historical Bishop was JEROME who held the See from 1051 to 1062. At the close of the thirteenth century its possessions were so extensive that the lands were erected into a Principality of the Empire, and its Bishops received the titles of Prince of NEISSE, and Duke of GROTTKAU. The See was at first suffragan to GNESEN, but in 1354 it was relieved from this subordination, and was held immediately from the Roman

See as it is at present. Political changes have occasioned the division of its possessions, and, though most of the lands are included in the Prussian monarchy, a portion is still under Austrian dominion. The See was under a Vicar-apostolic from 1817 to 1823 when the bishopric was reconstructed. (The tinctures of the coat quartered in the 1st and 4th, are sometimes given as *Azure* and *Or.*) The arms of BALTHASAR VON PROMNITZ, Prince-Bishop in 1551, are given at p. 90, *ante*.

JOSEPH CHRISTIAN, Prince HOHENLÖHE-WALDEN-BURG-BARTENSTEIN, who had been coadjutor-Bishop since 1789, held the See of BRESLAU from 1795 to 1817. His shield was, *Quarterly of six, in two horizontal rows each of three quarters ;* 1 and 6. *Argent, two lions passant gardant sable* (HOHENLÖHE) ; 2 and 5. (*Azure?*) *six fleurs-de-lis or*, 3. 2. 1. (BRESLAU) ; 3 and 4 *Per fess :* (a) *Sable, a lion passant crowned or ;* (b) *Or, four lozenges conjoined four and four in two rows sable* (LANGENBERG). *Over all an escucheon, Azure, a lion rampant argent, crowned or* (GLEICHEN). (This coat is sometimes omitted.)

The escucheon is surmounted by a princely hat between the head of a crosier and a mitre ; and is supported to the dexter by *a lion rampant or, crowned with a princely crown ;* and to the sinister by *a lion rampant sable, crowned with an Eastern crown or*. The whole is surrounded with a princely mantle, and surmounted by a princely hat.

BRIXEN (Prince-Bishopric).

Arms: *Gules, a Paschal-Lamb passant regardant argent diademed or, and holding by a golden cross staff its banner of the second charged with a cross of the first*. (It is sometimes depicted improperly as standing on a terrace *vert in base*, as in SIEBMACHER, *Wappenbuch*, vol. i., plate ii., where also the lamb is not *regardant*. Some have seen in the arms of the See an allusion to S. AGNES, whose head was said to be included among the relics of the Church of BRIXEN.)

This See was originally founded at SEBEN (*Sabiona*), where S. CASSIAN is said to have been its first Bishop about the middle of the fourth century, and it was primarily suffragan to the patriarchal church of AQUILEIA. A more probable first Bishop is S. INGENUIN, who lived at the close of the sixth century; but the series of bishops becomes historical only towards the close of the eighth century, in ALIM, or ALTHEUS, who was living about 804. About the year 798 the Bishopric was made suffragan to SALZBURG. It is not quite clear at what date the transference of the See to BRIXEN took place, but in all probability it was during the Episcopate of S. ALBUIN, who lived at the close of the tenth century and died in 1006. The See had the honour of furnishing a Pope to the Roman Church in the person of POPPO, or WOLFGANG, elected Bishop about 1039, Patriarch of AQUILEIA in 1042, and Pope in 1047, when he took the title of DAMASUS II. The possessions of the See were secularised in 1802, but the title of Prince-Bishop in the Austrian Empire was restored to it in 1818. It had as its hereditary officials the Dukes of BAVARIA, CARINTHIA, MERAN, and SUABIA, as Marshal, Chamberlain, Butler, and Carver.

With the arms as given above those of the Cathedral Chapter are often borne impaled; they are : *Argent, an eagle displayed gules, crowned and armed or, across its breast a pastoral staff in fess of the last.* (TRIERS, *Einleitung zu der Wapen-Kunst*, p. 397.) These are evidently the arms of TIROL differenced by the addition of the crosier.

The banner of BRIXEN depicted in the *Wapenrolle von Zürich*, taf. xxiv., has the eagle placed with its head towards the staff, and the crosier is of *azure* not *or*.

The crest used was, Out of a crest-coronet of gold a pentagonal (? hexagonal) fan crest, its points ornamented in the usual way with little tufts of peacock's feathers; the fan is of silver and charged with the eagle and crosier of the Chapteral arms. (*See* TRIERS, *Einleitung zu der Wapen-Kunst*, p. 398.) SPENER, *Opus Heraldicum*, p. spec., plate xxvi., gives the arms of Bishop PAULINUS MAYR, 1677-1685. These have already been described at p. 90, *ante*.

CAMIN (or POMMERN) (Bishopric).
Arms : *Gules, a cross-moline argent.*

This See was founded in 1133 by Pope INNOCENT II. who made the See of STETTIN and POMMERN suffragan to the Archbishopric of MAGDEBURG. The Pomeranian See was first situated at JULIN, in the island of Wollin; and its first Bishop was ADALBERT, the coadjutor of OTTO of BAMBERG, by whom Pomerania had been won to Christianity. In 1176 Bishop CONRAD removed his throne to CAMIN, and the See became suffragan to the Polish Archbishopric of GNESEN. Pope CLEMENT III. made it one of the bishoprics held immediately from the Papal throne.

ERASMUS MANTEUFFEL, 1522-1544, was the first bishop to favour the opinions of the Reformation. His successor BARTHOLOMEW SWAWE resigned his See in 1540 on entering into the married state.

In 1648, after the See had been nominally filled by six Dukes of POMERANIA in succession, it was finally secularised, and by the Treaty of OSNABRÜCK became a secular Principality of the Electorate of BRANDENBURG. The coat above given contains the arms as now blazoned among the quarterings of the great shield of PRUSSIA. In SIEBMACHER'S *Wappenbuch* i., 12, they are: *Azure, a digamma or.*

CAMMERICH (CAMBRAY) (Prince-Bishopric, afterwards Archbishopric).

The first authentic Bishop of CAMBRAY whose name appears in the list of the occupants of the See seems to be S. VEDAST, who was first set over the Church of ARRAS (*Atrebatum*) by S. REMIGIUS in the year 510. In 1093 ARRAS was separated from CAMBRAY. CAMBRAY was suffragan to REIMS up to 1559, in which year Pope PAUL IV. raised it to the rank of an archbishopric.

On the extinction of the old line of the Counts of CAMBRESIS, the Emperor HENRY I. gave the county to the See, and with it the rank of Prince of the Holy Roman Empire. Bishop JAMES of CROY was created Duke of CAMBRAY in 1510. The arms of the See were, *Argent, three lions rampant, two and one, gules*, to these there was often added *a chief of the Empire*, which sometimes was attached to the personal coat.

WILLIAM DE BERGHES, fourth Archbishop of CAMBRAY, who died in 1609, bore his personal arms : *Per fess ;* A (in chief), *Per pale* (a) *Sable, a lion rampant or*, BRABANT. (b) *Or, three pallets gules*, MECHLIN. B (in base), *Vert, three mascles or*, BAUTERSEM. *The whole beneath a chief of the Empire, the eagle charged on the breast with a label gules.* The only external ornaments were the archi-episcopal cross and hat. JOSEPH DE BERGAIGNE, Archbishop (1645-1647), quartered CAMBRAY (*Argent, three lions rampant gules*) in the first and fourth ; with, in the second and third, his own coat : *Azure, on a bend gules, bordered argent, three roses of the last*). *Above the quartered coats a chief of the Empire.* This is a remarkable arrangement, and there is apparently no label. The ornaments are a ducal coronet ; and the archi-episcopal cross and hat. CHARLES DE ST. ALBIN, *Bâtard d'Orléans*, son of the Regent PHILIPPE, filled the See of CAMBRAY from 1723-1764. He bore on an oval cartouche the arms of the EMPIRE, and on the breast of the Eagle his personal coat: ORLÉANS (FRANCE-MODERN, *a label argent*) *debruised by a baton gules péri en barre.* The cartouche is ornamented with a princely crown of fleurs-de-lis alternating with strawberry leaves ; the sword and crosier are in saltire, and the archi-episcopal cross with a double traverse, in pale, behind the escucheon, which is mantled ; and the hat with fifteen *houppes* on each side, surmounts the whole. His successor LÉOPOLD CHARLES DE CHOISEUL (d. 1774) bore his personal coat : *Azure, a cross between twenty billets or* (five in saltire in each quarter); *augmented with the Chief of the Empire.* On the cross an escucheon *en surtout* of CAMBRAY. The external ornaments were the sword and archi-episcopal cross in saltire behind the mantling, which is surmounted by the Crown of a Prince of the Empire.

CAMBRAY has since become an Archbishopric of France, with ARRAS as its suffragan.

CHIEMSEE (Bishopric).

> *Per pale:* 1. *Or, a lion rampant sable.* 2. *Gules, a crosier in pale argent.*

The first bishop of this See, which was suffragan to SALZBURG, was RUDIGER VON RODECK, Provost of the Monastery of S. HIPPOLYTUS at ZELL in the Pinzgau, who was nominated by Archbishop EBERHARD at the division of the See of SALZBURG in 1215.

The Bishop and his successors lived in the monastery in the Isle of Herren-Chiemsee, and in Salzburg ; but in 1446 the Archbishop FRIEDRICH TRUCHSESS appointed the parish church of S. JOHN in the Leukenthal to be the Cathedral of the diocese. In 1805 the portion of Tirol in which CHIEMSEE was situated became part of the possessions of Bavaria. The See was suppressed, and the Bishop SIGMUND, Count of ZEIL and TRAUCH-

BURG, pensioned at the foundation of the See of MUNICH-FREYSING.

SIGMUND CHRISTOPH, Count of WALDBURG-ZEIL, Prince-Bishop of CHIEMSEE, 1797-1805, bore the arms of his See on a chief *per pale* (a) *Or, an eagle displayed sable;* (b) *Gules, the head of a pastoral staff, or.* Beneath this chief were placed his personal arms : *Quarterly*, 1 and 4. *Or, three lions passant in pale sable* (SUABIA) ; 2. *Azure, three fir cones or* (WALDBURG) ; 3. *Azure, a sun in splendour above a mount in base or* (SONNENBERG).

In the *Wapenrolle von Zürich*, taf. xxv., the banner of CHIEMSEE is : *Per pale*, 1. *Or, an eagle displayed dimidiated gules.* 2. *Argent, a pastoral staff in pale azure.*

CHÜR (COIRE) (Prince-Bishopric).

Arms : *Argent, a steinbock springing sable.*

The foundation of this Bishopric is of great antiquity, and is by some carried back even to Apostolic times, and ascribed to S. PETER. S. ASIMO, its Bishop, was present at the Council of CHALCEDON in 450. It was originally suffragan to MILAN, but in the year 843 was transferred to MAINZ. Since about 1171 the Bishops had the title of "Fürsten des heil. römischen Reiches deutscher Nation" (which Bishop EGINO received from the Emperor FREDERICK BARBAROSSA), and sat in the Swabian circle. In 1404 MODESTUS VISCONTI of MILAN gave the Valtelline to the See.

The possessions of the See were secularised in the year 1802-1803, and the bishop removed his residence to MERAN. Pope PIUS VII. made the See to depend only on the Chair of S. PETER. In 1823 the Catholic portion of the Canton of ST. GALL was united to CHÜR, under the title of the See of CHÜR and ST. GALL ; but in 1836 they were again divided, and in 1846 ST. GALL was refounded as an independent See.

The arms of ST. GALL were formed from those of the

Abbey: *Argent, a bear rampant sable, collared of the field;* and were, *Or, a bear erect sable, on its shoulder a raguly staff proper.*

The Cathedral is dedicated to S. LUCIUS, who is said to have been a British prince. In it I noticed the following examples of Episcopal arms. First, on the gravestone of JOHANNES FLUG VON ASPERMONT (elected 1601, resigned the See in 1627); the arrangement is as follows: *Quarterly,* 1 and 4. The arms of the See, as above (the *steinbock* is *contourné* in the first quarter); 2 and 3. *Per fess* (a, *in chief*) *Sable, a fess argent* (ASPERMONT); (b, *in base*) *Azure, three heads and necks of swans argent, beaked gules* (FLUGI). On the tomb of his nephew of the same name, elected 1636, died in 1661, the arrangement is different, and somewhat curious: *Quarterly,* 1 and 4. FLUGI; 2 and 3. ASPERMONT; *Over all, in an escucheon en surtout the arms of the* See of CHÜR. Beneath in a smaller escucheon are the arms of WERDENBURG: *Gules, a gonfanon argent, ringed or* (this coat was usually borne by the family *en surtout* above the quartered coats of ASPERMONT and FLUGI).

The shield is surmounted by a mitre and behind is placed the pastoral staff *in pale.* On either side of the mitre is a helm, crested and mantled. The dexter crest is that of the See: *A hexagonal fan, having the usual tufts of peacock's feathers, and charged with the arms of the See;* the sinister is the crest of ASPERMONT; *Out of a crest-coronet or, two horns sable, each charged with a fess argent.* The arms of Bishop JOSEPH MOHR (1627-1635) have already been printed at p. 88.

CONSTANZ (CONSTANCE) (Prince-Bishopric).

Arms: (*Argent, a cross gules*).

The first Bishops resided at WINDISCH (*Vindonissa*) in the Aargau, where the See was erected, it is said, in the fourth century. MAXIMUS was Bishop *circa* 580, and in his time CLOTHAIR transferred the See to CONSTANZ from WINDISCH which had been destroyed in a German invasion. It was originally suffragan to MAINZ, and the Bishop held the rank of Prince of the Holy Roman Empire, having his seat between the Bishops of STRASBURG and AUGSBURG. It seems probable that the princely dignity was attached to the possession of the great Benedictine Abbey of REICHENAU. This was founded in the year 724 by S. FIRMIN, and after much disputation united to the See in 1538, by MARK DE KNORINGEN the fifty-ninth abbot, JOHN VON WESA being at that time the occupant of the See. In spite of some diminution at the Reformation, the See was so vast in extent that it included three hundred and fifty religious houses, seventeen hundred and sixty parishes, and seventeen thousand priests and religious. In 1802 the possessions of the See were secularised, and incorporated either in the Grand-Duchy of BADEN, or in SWITZERLAND. Thereafter the diocese was administered by a Vicar-general. (The arms of REICHENAU also were : *Argent, a cross gules.*)

CORVEY (Prince-Bishopric).

Arms : *Per fess or and gules.*

The celebrated Benedictine Abbey of CORVEY on the Weser (not to be confounded with the French Abbey of CORBIE near AMIENS), was founded under LOUIS *le Debonnaire* in 822. In 844 the Emperor LOTHAIR endowed it with the island of RÜGEN. In 1783 Pope PIUS VI. converted the Abbacy into a See ; and, in 1793, the Emperor FRANCIS II. confirmed it. It had but a short existence. The Prince-Abbot THEODORE VON BRABECK was preconised as its first Bishop in 1792 ; the second and last was FERDINAND VON LÜNING in 1795. In the general upturning in 1802 the possessions of the See were secularised, and given to the Princes of NASSAU (*vide post*, FULDA, p. 285). The diocese was included in that of PADERBORN in 1821. .The crest of the Abbacy was, *Out of a coroneted helm two* (sometimes *three*) *crosiers proper.*

CUJAVIA (LESLAU, or WLADISLAW) (Bishopric).
Arms :
In the tenth century the first seat of the CUJAVIAN Bishopric is said to have been at KRUSCHWITZ. Pope INNOCENT II. in 1133 made it suffragan to MAGDEBURG. Bishop ONOLD, who lived *circa* 1160, transferred his seat to LESLAU, and it, later, became suffragan to GNESEN, the Polish Archbishopric. The See in the twelfth century included all the eastern part of Pomerania. In 1806 there commenced a long interregnum, and in 1818 a portion of the See was united with the Diocese of CULM.

The Bishop, styled of WLADISLAW, was, in 1818, placed under the Metropolitan See of WARSAW.

CULM (LÖBAU) (Bishopric).
Arms : *Argent, within a narrow ring gules touching the edges of the shield, a cross couped sable, bordered argent.*
In 1243, the "Prussian Bishopric" was divided by Pope INNOCENT IV. into the four .Sees of CULM, ERMELAND, POMESANIEN, and SAMLAND. In 1245 the Pope appointed ALBERT (Archbishop of ARMAGH in Ireland, and administrator of the Diocese of LÜBECK) to be Archbishop of PRUSSIA, LIVONIA, and ESTHONIA, with the oversight of the new Sees. Later CULM, under the designation of LÖBAU, was suffragan to RIGA, and afterwards to GNESEN.

DORPAT (Bishopric).
Arms : *Gules, a sword in pale traversed by a key in fess argent.*
ALBERT VON BUXHÖVEDEN, Bishop of RIGA in 1210, appointed THEODORIC, Abbot of the Cistercian Mon-

astery at DÜNAMÜNDE, Bishop of ESTLAND, and his act
was ratified by Pope INNOCENT III. But the lands
were overrun by King WALDEMAR of DENMARK, and
the Bishop slain. Bishop ALBERT filled up the See by
the appointment of his brother HERMAN, who had been
Abbot of S. PAULI in BREMEN, and placed his residence
in the town of LEAL. After the Teutonic Order had
firmly established itself in Livonia, HERMAN, in 1224,
removed to DORPAT. The See was suffragan to RIGA.
Its existence ended in 1558, on the seizure of DORPAT
by the Russians.

EICHSTÄDT (Prince-Bishopric).

Arms : *Gules, a crosier in pale argent* (usually with the
sudarium entwined around the staff).

This See was founded in 746 by S. BONIFACE, Archbishop of MAINZ, who placed over it S. WILIBALD, son
of his sister BONA. WILIBALD had, at first, only his
monastery, and the half of the County of HERSCHBERG,
which, with the permission of the Duke of BAVARIA, had
been given to it by the Count SUITGAR, a donation confirmed by Count GEBBARD the last of his line. The
monastery was built on the banks of the river Altmuhl ;
around it there soon grew up a little town, which took
its name of EICHSTÄDT from the oak forest in its neighbourhood. The Bishop of EICHSTÄDT held the first
rank among the suffragans of the See of MAINZ, and
was Chancellor of its Cathedral. In the fourteenth
century the dignity of Prince of the Holy Roman
EMPIRE was attached to the See ; and the Bishop took
the ninth place on the bench of Spiritual Peers in the
College of Princes of the Empire, having his seat
between the Bishops of WORMS and SPEIER.

In 1802 the Principality was secularised ; the then
Bishop, JOSEPH, Count von STUBENBERG, was elected
Archbishop of BAMBERG in 1821, and held it with his

See which was reconstituted by the Concordat of 1817.

Like the other great bishops, the Prince-Bishop of EICHSTÄDT had his hereditary court officials. The Count of CASTELL was Marshal; the Count of SCHAUM-BURG, Chamberlain ; the Count of LEONRODT, Master of the Household ; and the Baron of EYB, Steward. Several princes held fiefs from the See ; among them the Duke of SAXE-GOTHA. The Bishop was *ex-officio* Chancellor of the University of INGOLSTADT.

FRANZ LUDWIG SCHENK, Baron von CASTELL, was Prince-Bishop of the See of EICHSTÄDT from 1725 to 1736 ; and his arms were thus arranged : *Quarterly, 1 and 4. Argent, two attires of a stag united by the scalp gules ; 2 and 3. Argent, two lions passant in pale gules, crowned or.* Over all in an escucheon en surtout the arms of the See of EICHSTÄDT, *Gules, the head of a crosier argent* (*cf.* p. 89, *ante*). The escucheon was surmounted by four crested helms :—1. (to the dexter) *Out of a crest-coronet the charge of the first and fourth quarters ;* 2. *A mitre upon a cushion proper* (for the Seè).; 3. *A princely hat, from which rises an arm habited argent, the cuff or, the hand holding a crosier in bend-sinister, proper* (Provostship of OENINGEN); 4. *Out of a crest-coronet the bust of an old man habited gules, turned up and buttoned argent* (this and the first crest belong to the personal arms of the Prince-Bishop).

The crosier and temporal sword were arranged in saltire behind the shield, which was also supported by two lions rampant, crowned or.

The arms of the DOM-CAPITEL were : *Gules, three lions passant in pale or.*

ERMLAND (Bishopric).

Arms : *Azure, a Paschal-Lamb passant proper.*

The Bishopric of ERMLAND was constituted by Pope JOHN VI. in 1250, and made suffragan to RIGA. (*See*

under CULM.) After the Reformation the former
Diocese of SAMLAND was included in its jurisdiction;
and in 1821 some portions of the former Diocese of
POMESANIA were added to it.

FREIBURG (Archbishopric).
Arms: *Or, a cross gules.*

The Arch-diocese of FREIBURG IM BREISGAU was
created in 1827, in some sort as a successor to the See
of CONSTANZ (*vide ante*, p. 280). Its jurisdiction is
composed of fragments from the former Sees of BASEL,
MAINZ, SPEIER, STRASBURG, WORMS, and WÜRZBURG.

FREISING (Prince-Bishopric).
Arms: *Argent, the bust of a Moor sable, habited gules,
and crowned with an Eastern crown or.*

The See of FREISING was established by Pope
GREGORY III. in 730, for the Regionary Bishop S. COR-
BINIAN, one of the coadjutors of S. BONIFACE. It was
suffragan to SALZBURG. The Bishop was a Prince of
the Empire, having the fourteenth place on the bench of
spiritual princes. This dignity probably dates from about
the year 1140 when the Diet of RATISBON confirmed the
purchase for the church by the then Bishop, OTTO,
Markgrave of AUSTRIA, of the rights of government of
the lands surrounding FREYSING which had belonged
to the Count of SCHIREN and WITTELSBACH. In 1802
the possessions of the See were secularised, and after the
death of the Bishop, JOSEPH CONRAD VON SCHROFFEN-
BERG in 1803, there ensued an interregnum which lasted
until 1818 ; when a new See—to be known as that of
MUNICH, or MÜNCHEN-FREYSING—was created with
archi-episcopal rank, having as its suffragans the Sees
of AUGSBURG, PASSAU, and REGENSBURG (RATISBON).

FULDA (Prince-Bishopric).
Arms: *Argent, a cross sable.*

This celebrated abbey was founded in 744, being one of the four erected by S. BONIFACE ; the others were FRITZLAR (afterwards a bishopric), HARNEMBURG, and ORDORF. After several translations the body of S. BONIFACE found its last resting-place at FULDA in Hesse.

The abbey was one of the greatest of the early schools of learning in Germany. It had the title of *Primas*, or first of all abbeys, which was conferred on it by Pope JOHN XIII. about the year 968. In 1133 the Emperor LOTHAIR II., gave to the Abbot, BERTHOLOMEW DE SCHLIZ, the dignity of Arch-Chancellor of the Empress, with the right to place the crown on her head at a coronation. The Abbot also used the title of "Primate of Germany and Gaul," and claimed precedence immediately after the Archbishop of MAINZ, before all other prelates. But in 1184, Archbishop PHILIP VON HEINSBERG of CÖLN, at the head of four thousand armed men, vindicated his own precedence at a Diet at MAINZ, and the Emperor FREDERICK conceded his claim. In the Imperial Diet the Abbot had place and voice after the Bishop of CHÜR. The abbacy was raised to the rank of a bishopric, Oct. 5, 1752, and the eighty-first Abbot, AMAND VON BUSECK, who had been Prince-Abbot since 1737, became the first Bishop of the See in 1752. He held it for the brief period of four years. The See was one of those suffragan to the Archbishopric of MAINZ. In 1802 the possessions of the See were secularised, and handed over to the princes of ORANGE-NASSAU, as compensation for the loss of the hereditary office of Stadthalter of the Netherlands ; and the Bishop-Abbot received a pension until his death in 1814. From this time up to the year 1829 the See was governed by a Capitular and Apostolic Vicar, who had the spiritual oversight of the Electorate of HESSEN-CASSEL. Thereafter the See was newly constructed, and it is now suffragan to the Metropolitan Church of FREIBURG IM BREISGAU.

The crest of FULDA was: *On a crest-coronet or, the sable cross of the arms.* The DOM-CAPITEL of FULDA impaled a coat the reverse of that borne by the See (viz., *Argent, a cross. sable*), with *Argent, on a mount in base three lilies proper.* Sometimes the arms were placed in two escucheons *accolés.*

GENF (GENEVA) (Prince-Bishopric).
Arms: *Per pale* (a) *the arms of the Empire dimidiated;* (b) *Gules, a key paleways argent, wards in chief.*
The arms of the modern See are: *Gules, two keys in saltire argent, wards in chief.*
The list of Bishops of GENEVA goes as far back as the latter part of the fourth century, but the earliest names have no historical support. In the year 450 the Pope, LEO I., made the See suffragan to VIENNE. It was in the year 1154 that the Emperor FREDERICK II. (*Barbarossa*) raised the Bishop to the rank of Prince of the Holy Roman Empire. At the Reformation the Prince-Bishop, PIERRE DE LA BAUME, removed his throne, first in 1534 to GEX, and a year later to ANNECY. In 1802 the possessions of the See were completely secularised. In 1819 the spiritual jurisdiction was transferred by the Pope to the Bishop of LAUSANNE, resident at FREIBERG (Switzerland), with the title of LAUSANNE-GENEVA. In 1864 the district around the city was again erected into a distinct See, and M. MERMILLOD became its Bishop.

GNESEN (Archbishopric).
Arms: *Azure, a sword in pale, hilt in chief, and two keys in saltire, wards in chief, argent.*
The archbishopric is said to have been erected in 966 and WILIBALD is named as the first occupant of the See, but it is only in the year 1000 that we find in authentic history the name of GAUDENTIUS as archbishop. GNESEN had as suffragans the Sees of BRESLAU,

CAMIN, COLBERG, CUJAVIA, CRACOW, and LEBUS. In the year 1133 GNESEN with BRESLAU came under German rule, and was made for a while suffragan to the Archi-episcopal See of MAGDEBURG. At the beginning of the thirteenth century the Archbishop HENRY obtained for himself and his successors in the archbishopric the dignity of "*legati nati*" of the Holy See. In 1416 Archbishop NICOLAS TROMBY became Primate of POLAND with the right to crown the king. Later on the archbishops had the office of administrators of the kingdom in the interregnum between the death of one king and the election of his successor.

The fall of the kingdom of Poland necessitated new ecclesiastical arrangements. After 1809 the archbishops had the title of GNESEN-POSEN, but resided at the latter place, and administered GNESEN with the assistance of a coadjutor-Bishop. The present Polish Sees are WARSAW (Archbishopric); KIELCE; LUBLIN; PODLACHIA; PLOTZK; SANDOMIR; SEYNA; WLADISLAW. CRACOW is directly subject to the Holy See.

GÖRZ (Prince-Archbishopric).

Arms : *Per pale:* (a) *Sable, a cross with three traverses botonny argent ;* (b) *the arms of the County of* GÖRZ *viz. : Per bend ;* (1) *Azure, a lion rampant or ;* (2) *Argent, two bends sinister gules. On a chief Or, a single-headed eagle displayed, sable, on its breast the arms of* AUSTRIA, *on the wings the letters* M. T., *and* F. I., *gold.*

In 1751 the Patriarchate of AQUILEIA was divided by the Pope into the Archbishoprics of GÖRZ and UDINE, with COMO, PEDENA, TRIENT, and TRIEST as suffragan Sees. But changes were soon made, GRADISCA being erected into a bishopric, and LAIBACH into an archbishopric (*vide infra*, p. 291). GRADISCA had the rank of co-Cathedral with GÖRZ. The arms of GRADISCA

are : *Per fess Or and azure, over all a cross-moline argent.*
But though the title of the See is still GÖRZ and
GRADISCA the Bishop's throne is at the former place,
which is now the Metropolitan See of the Illyrian kingdom ; and its occupant has the title of Prince-Archbishop of the Austrian Empire. The suffragan Sees at
present are LAIBACH, VEGLIA, PARENZO and POLA,
TRIEST and CAPO D'ISTRIA. (Arms of VEGLIA: *Argent,*
S. QUIRINUS *in pontificals proper.*)

GURK (Prince-Bishopric).
Arms : *Per pale :* (a) *Or, a lion rampant sable crowned
of the field ;* (b) *Per fess gules and argent.*
The See was erected in 1071 by the Emperor HENRY
IV. and Pope ALEXANDER II. ; it was, and is, suffragan
to SALZBURG. Since 1787 the bishop has had his
throne at KLAGENFURT. He is a Prince of the Austrian
Empire. The arms are obviously derived from those of
the See of SALZBURG (*q.v.*, and *cf.* LAVANT, p. 292).

HALBERSTADT (Prince-Bishopric).
Arms : *Per pale argent and gules.*
The date of the erection of this Bishopric is unknown.
It was probably founded by CHARLEMAGNE, and its
original seat was at OSTERWIK, where he erected a fine
church from which the place took its name of SELIGEN-
STADT. Thence it was removed to HALBERSTADT. It
was suffragan to MAINZ.
In 1542 the reformed doctrines began to find favour
here, and the See was administered by a succession of
Princes of the houses of BRANDENBURG and BRUNS-
WICK. At the Peace of Westphalia the Principality with
its dependencies (part of the County of HOHNSTEIN,
and the Lordships of LORA and KLETTENBERG), was
finally given to the Electorate of Brandenburg.
The crest of the Bishopric, as born by the Princes of
the Brandenburg house, was : *Out of a golden crest-coronet*

an arm embowed in armour holding a palm-branch ; but this may very possibly be a late assumption, and not really attached to the See.

HAVELBERG (Bishopric).

Arms : *Azure, two crosiers in saltire, in chief a cross couped fitchée argent ;* but some authorities give the arms : *Sable, a cross argent,* and SIEBMACHER, *Wappenbuch* i., plate 11., makes this cross slightly *patée* at the ends.

On the conversion of the Wends to Christianity OTTO THE GREAT founded this See, May 9th, 946. It was at first suffragan to the Archi-episcopal See of MAINZ, but was transferred in the year 968 to the Archbishopric of MAGDEBURG. After the death of the last Bishop, BUSSO VON ALVENSLEBEN, in 1522, the Elector of BRANDENBURG took possession of the temporalities of the See, in disregard of the protestations of the Chapter.

HILDESHEIM (Prince-Bishopric).

Arms : *Per pale argent and gules* (*v. ante,* p. 89).

The original seat of this bishopric was at ELZE, where CHARLEMAGNE is said to have founded a church in the year 796, and dedicated it to S. PETER. In 814 LUDWIG *der Fromme* transferred the See to HILGENSCHNEE, which afterwards took the name of HILDESHEIM. GUNTHAR who ruled from 815 to 834 appears as its first authentic bishop. The new See included the whole of OSTPHALIA, and was suffragan to MAINZ. The twentieth bishop, BERNHARD VON ROTHENBURG acquired, "per revelationem ac admonitionem familiaris cujusdam spiritûs (quem Chronica Saxonum à rustico pileo, quo tectus incedebat, Hudikin vocant)," the County of WINZENBERG, deserted by its Count, who suddenly disappeared, after having slain a Saxon. (*See* LUCÆ, *Graffen-Saal,* pp. 780, 781.)

U

The Counties of HOMBURG and BEYN, with other
lordships, were acquired by succeeding bishops ; and its
possessions and wealth were so great that in 1519 Bishop
JOHN, Duke of SAXE-LAUENBURG, had the temerity to
make war on the Dukes of BRUNSWICK, and the Prince-
Bishop of MINDEN. On this account he was put under
the ban of the Empire by the Emperor CHARLES V., and
the See was denuded of a great portion of its possessions
which was transferred to BRUNSWICK by the Treaty of
QUEDLIMBURG in 1523.

In 1629, FERDINAND, Prince-Bishop and Elector of
CÖLN, who also held the See of HILDESHEIM *in
commendam* (he was brother of MAXIMILIAN, Elector
of BAVARIA), obtained from the Diet of SPEYER a
sentence restoring to the See its former possessions.
The Princes of BRUNSWICK had at first to yield, but
later a compromise was effected, and confirmed by the
Treaty of MÜNSTER in 1648. The Prince-Bishopric,
which for nearly two hundred years (from 1573-1761)
had, with the exception of a single Episcopate, been
held *in commendam* by the Elector of CÖLN, was finally
secularised in 1802. Its possessions fell first to France ;
then, in 1813, to Hanover ; and finally, in 1886, to
Prussia. The See was restored, so far as spiritualities
are concerned, in 1824. The Bishop of HILDESHEIM
also administered the Diocese of OSNABRÜCK from 1824
to 1857 (*vide infra*, p. 308). HILDESHEIM is now
exempt from any archi-episcopal jurisdiction, being held
immediately from the Holy See.

The crest of the See is : *Out of a crest-coronet the figure
of the Blessed Virgin holding in her arms the Holy Child—
between two lances with banners of the arms.* SIEBMACHER,
Wappenbuch i., plate 10, gives as arms to HILDESHEIM :
Quarterly, gules and or, but wrongly.

To the Deanery, or DOM-PROPSTEI the following arms
are attributed : *Per bend, argent and gules* (a difference

from the arms of the See), and the crest, *Out of a crest-coronet six lances with banners* (of the arms?) *proper.*

KÖNIGGRÄTZ (Prince-Bishopric).
Arms:
This See comprises a portion of the Bishopric of LEITOMISCHL erected by the Emperor CHARLES IV. in 1344. In 1660 the Emperor LEOPOLD I. made MATTHEW FERDINAND ZOUBEK, Abbot of S. NICOLAS in Prague, first Bishop of a new See of KÖNIGGRÄTZ; this was confirmed by the Pope in 1664, and the Emperor conferred on the occupant of the See the title of " Prince of the Holy Roman Empire," but without seat or vote in the Imperial Diet. KÖNIGGRÄTZ was, and continues to be, a suffragan See to the Archbishopric of PRAGUE.

LAIBACH (Prince-Bishopric).
Arms : *Or, the eagle of the Austrian Empire, dimidiated, and conjoined with the azure eagle of CARNIOLA having on its breast a crescent gobonny argent and gules ; a crosier or upon the palar line.*
This See was founded by the Emperor FREDERICK III. in 1462. It was to be held immediately from the Holy See, the Emperor reserving to himself the right of Patronage. For a short time LAIBACH had the status of an Archbishopric and Metropolitan Church ; dignities conferred on it in 1787 by Papal Bull, and the Sees of ZENGG, MODRUS, GRADISCA, and TRIESTE were suffragan to it. Twenty years later changes were made by which LAIBACH reverted to its old position of a bishopric holding immediately from the Holy See. Since 1830 it has been suffragan to the Archbishopric of GÖRZ and GRADISCA (*q.v.*). The title of Prince, which was conferred by the Emperor FERDINAND I. in 1533 on the second Bishop, CHRISTOPH RAUBER, and his successors in the See (and which was lost in 1807 when the See was

reduced from the archi-episcopal rank), was again conferred on it by the Emperor FRANCIS I. of Austria in
1826.

LAUSANNE (Prince-Bishopric).
Arms: *Per pale gules and argent two* ciboria *in fess
counter-changed.*

The legend that this See was founded by S. BEATUS,
who was sent by S. PETER to preach the gospel in
Switzerland, is unhistorical; but there is no reason to
doubt that as early as the first half of the fourth century
an Episcopal See existed at WIFFLISBURG, or AVENCHES
(*Aventicum*), and that it was removed to LAUSANNE by
Bishop MARIUS towards the end of the sixth century
(593 or 594). It was suffragan to BESANÇON. SEBASTIAN
DE MONTFAUCON, who occupied the See from 1517 to
1560, was the last prelate who resided at LAUSANNE.
In consequence of the spread of Protestantism in his
diocese he had to remove to FREIBERG. In 1819 a new
diocese was formed by Papal Authority under the title
of LAUSANNE-GENEVA, which was to be held immediately
from the Roman See.

Since the year 1125 the Bishops of LAUSANNE had the
title of " Fürsten des h. römischen Reiches deutscher
Nation."

LAVANT (Bishopric).
Arms: *Per bend;* (a) *Or a lion rampant sable;* (b)
Gules, a bend-sinister argent.

This was one of the Sees into which Archbishop
EBERHARD of SALZBURG divided his diocese (*see*
CHIEMSEE, and SECKAU), it was founded in 1228. In
the year 1786, when the dioceses were re-arranged, the
Bishop's throne was removed to ST. ANDREAE in
Carinthia, and a portion of its jurisdiction was transferred
to the Bishopric of SECKAU. The boundaries of the See

underwent a further re-arrangement in 1859, and at present it is suffragan to SALZBURG. The arms are, obviously, only a different arrangement of those of SALZBURG. (But *Per pale sable and or, over all a fess gules*, also appears in my notes; perhaps for the Chapter.) MARBURG is the present place of the See.

LEBUS (Prince-Bishopric).

Arms: *Or, the heads of two boat-hooks (?) in saltire and, in chief an estoile argent, the whole within a bordure gules.* (SIEBMACHER, *Wappenbuch*, vol. i., plate 12.)

The arms are somewhat doubtful. The charges are two staves in saltire, each headed with a fleur-de-lis of which the interior leaf is wanting. Towards the lower end of each of the staves is an annulet on the exterior side. I suspect that these boat-hooks are only a depravation of two crosiers (*cf.* BASEL).

The town of LEBUS, where this Bishopric had its original seat, is in the Prussian Province of BRANDEN-BURG, a little to the north of FRANKFÜRT on the Oder. BERNHARD, who died a little before 1150, is the first historical name on the roll of bishops. The last was JOHN of HORNBURG who died in 1555. His quasi-successor was JOACHIM FREDERICK, Markgrave of BRANDENBURG, who laid aside the title of "Prince-Bishop of LEBUS" on his succession to the Electoral dignity in 1598.

LEITMERITZ (Bishopric).

Arms:

LEITMERITZ is situated in Bohemia, on the river Elbe. The See was founded by the Emperor FERDINAND III. in 1655, with the approval of Pope ALEXANDER VII. Its boundaries have since undergone a re-arrangement. The See is suffragan to the Archbishopric of PRAG.

LEITOMISCHL (Bishopric).

Arms :   .

The Abbey was founded 1098, but this Bohemian See was erected in 1344 by Pope CLEMENT VI. and the Emperor CHARLES IV. At the same time the See of PRAG was made archi-episcopal, and to it LEITO-MISCHL was suffragan. The See came to an end in the Hussite troubles of the fifteenth century, and is now comprised in KÖNIGGRÄTZ.

LEUBEN (or LEOBEN) (Bishopric).

Arms :   .

This bishopric, situated in Styria, was founded in 1786 by the Emperor JOSEPH II. with the sanction of Pope PIUS VI. It had only one bishop, ALEXANDER, Count VON ENGEL, who died in 1800. Thereafter the Prince-Bishop of SECKAU united the See to his own.

LIMBURG (Bishopric).

Arms :

The See of LIMBURG-on-the-Lahn (in the Prussian province of HESSE), was only erected in the year 1821 by the Bull "*Provida solersque.*" It is suffragan to the Metropolitan See of FREIBURG IM BREISGAU.

LINZ (Bishopric).

Arms : *Per fess:* (a) *Azure, a cross botonny argent ;* (b) *Gules, two pallets argent.*

This See was erected in 1784 by the Emperor JOSEPH II. with the approval of Pope PIUS VI. Its territories were taken out of the Bishopric of PASSAU, and include the Archduchy of Upper Austria. The See is suffragan to the Metropolitan Archbishopric of VIENNA. The arms given above may possibly be those of the DOM-CAPITEL.

LÜBECK (Prince-Bishopric).

Arms :

These as given by SPENER, *Opus Heraldicum*, p. spec. lib. iii., cap. xii., are : *Azure, a cross couped or, the upper arm surmounted by a mitre of the last*, and to this agrees TRIERS, *Einleitung zu der Wapen-Kunst*, Leipzic, 1744, p. 403. The Crest is three banners charged with these arms. SIEBMACHER wrongly makes the coat to be *Or, a cross gules* (see *Wappenbuch*, vol. i., plate 11., where the arms of the cross are slightly *patées* at the ends).

This See was originally placed by the Emperor OTTO I., its founder, at ALDENBURG, or OLDENBURG, in Holstein, in the year 967. The Bishop REGINBERT moved his throne to MECKLENBERG. In 1052 Archbishop ADALBERT of HAMBURG divided the See of OLDEN-BURG into three bishoprics ; OLDENBURG, RATZEBURG, and MECKLENBURG. In the Slavonic uprising of 1066 Bishop ESSO of OLDENBURG had to flee, and the See was void until the consecration of VICELIN in 1149.

In 1163, at the entreaty of Bishop GERALD, the See was transferred to the new and flourishing city of LÜBECK by HENRY THE LION, with consent of the Emperor FREDERICK I. HENRY THE LION endowed the See with possessions given to it under his pressure by ADOLF, Count of HOLSTEIN. Lutheranism began to make itself felt under the fortieth Bishop, HEINRICH BOCKHOLT (1523-1535) who discouraged it ; but his successor, DETLEW VON REVENTLOW favoured it, and so did the following six bishops up to JOHAN ADOLF, Duke of HOLSTEIN-GOTTORP, who was also Archbishop of BREMEN, and was nominated Bishop in 1586. He was succeeded by his youngest brother, JOHN FREDERICK, whose influence averted the secularisation of the See, when that fate befell so many ecclesiastical foundations, by the Treaty of MÜNSTER. In recognition of his good offices, the Chapter elected to the Bishopric six princes of Holstein in succession. Bishop JOHAN ADOLF (1586-1607) was the first married prelate. The See was finally secularised in 1802. In the Diets of the Empire, the Prince-Bishop of LÜBECK sat next to the Prince-Bishop of OSNABRÜCK; but, after the establishment of the Reformation, neither had place on the bench of the Spiritual Princes.

LÜTTICH (LIÈGE) (Prince-Bishopric).
  Arms: *Quarterly,* 1. *Gules, a column standing on a quadrangular base argent, its capital or,* Bishopric of LIÈGE; 2. *Gules, a fess argent,* Duchy of BOUILLON; 3. *Argent, three lions rampant vert (armed gules),* Marquisate of FRANCHIMONT; 4. *Or, four bars gules,* County of LOOS.

The See of LIÈGE was originally founded at TONGERN; it is said that S. MATERNUS was its first bishop in the year 130. The original See comprised both TRIER and CÖLN. In the fourth century we find S. SERVATIUS as Bishop, a name which appears to be authentic. The See was first transferred to MAESTRICHT, and then to LIÈGE, by its Bishop S. HUBERT, in the year 709; but the title of TONGERN was not at once relinquished. Up to the time of CHARLEMAGNE TONGERN was the only See suffragan to the Archbishopric of CÖLN.

The bishopric was a Principality of the Holy Roman Empire; and the Prince-Bishop belonged to the Circle of Westphalia. In the Diet he and the Prince-Bishop of MÜNSTER had alternately precedence one of the other.

The Prince-Bishop had also the titles of Duke of BOUILLON, Marquis of FRANCHIMONT, and Count of LOOS, the reasons of which will be stated presently. In 1794 the French seized the principality; in 1815, the Congress of VIENNA confirmed its secularisation, and handed over its territory to the kingdom of the Netherlands; but the

Revolution of 1830 transferred it to the new kingdom of
Belgium. Since 1801 it has been suffragan to the
Archi-episcopal See of MECHLIN, but the See was
vacant between 1801 and 1829.

The Duchy of BOUILLON in the Ardennes was sold
by Duke GEOFFREY, with the consent of his brothers
EUSTACE and BALDWIN, to Bishop OBERT, or OSBERT
(1092-1117), for the sum of six thousand marks of pure
silver, in order to raise his equipment for the Crusade in
the course of which he became King of JERUSALEM. (He
reserved the right of redemption on his return, but this
never took place.) The ducal title appears to have
been first used by Bishop JOHN VON HEINSBERG, who
occupied the See from the year 1419 to his resigna-
tion in 1455. This adoption was probably less a
piece of ecclesiastical pride (as would probably be
at once assumed in modern times) than a means of
asserting strongly the undoubted rights of his See. For
we find it stated that in the fifteenth century "ce Duché
entra dans la Maison de la Marck en 1552 par la protection du Roi de France." TRIERS says (*Einleitung zu
der Wapen-Kunst*, p. 405) " Im funfzehenden *Seculo* ward
Bouillon Roberto, Grafen zu der Marck, wegen eines
gethanen Vorschusses versetzet." It seems difficult to
ascertain the truth about the matter. SPENER, who is
generally full of information, says : " Quo jure vero
delatum sit Bullionum ad Marcanos non æque expressum
ullibi legi." I conclude that the "right of the strong
hand" was all that the Counts of MARCK had ; for by
the Treaty of CAMBRAY the Duchy was restored to the
Bishop of LIÈGE, but only to be again seized by the
King of France, and given with FRANCHIMONT and
LOOS to the house of LA TOUR D'AUVERGNE, as representatives of the Counts of MARCK.

The Marquisate of FRANCHIMONT appears to have
been in possession of the See in the eleventh century,

when the Bishop vindicated his right to it against the claim of the Duke of LORRAINE.

The County of LOOS is said to have been granted to the See by its Count LOUIS in 1202, to be held therefrom by his successors as a fief of the Church, and to revert to it on the extinction of his male line ; this took place in 1336. Others say that it was pawned to the See by VINCENT, its last Count, apparently in *articulo mortis.* But the county was claimed and occupied by THIERRY, sister's son of the last Count ; and a strife ensued which lasted until 1361, when a pecuniary payment was made by the bishop in satisfaction of any claims possessed by the Counts of HEINSBERG, as heirs of THIERRY ; and the See entered into full possession of the county. The County of HORN was also claimed by the See ; and in 1568, at the death of the last Count, was handed over to it by the Duke of ALVA, Governor of the Netherlands for PHILIP II. of Spain.

Of the arms borne by the Prince-Bishops of LIÈGE (LÜTTICH) some examples may be given. The quartered arms of the See were usually arranged in an oval escucheon : 1. *Gules, a column on a stepped quadrangular base argent crowned or,* See of LIÈGE ; 2. *Gules, a fess argent,* Duchy of BOUILLON ; 3. *Argent, three lions rampant vert,* Marquisate of FRANCHIMONT ; 4. *Or, four bars gules,* County of LOOS. The last two coats are *enté en pointe* of the arms of the County of HORN, *Or, three hunting horns gules virolled argent.* Upon the main escucheon is the personal coat of the bishop. (Thus FRANZ ANTON, Count of MÉAN DE BEAUVIEUX, Prince-Bishop (1792-1795) bore : *Argent, on a mount in base an oak tree proper ; an eagle sable, crowned with an antique crown and supported by a trangle held in its claws, is brochant over the stem of the tree.*) The main escucheon has the spiritual crosier and temporal sword in saltire behind it, and is adorned with an ermine mantle and a princely hat. The supporters are two lions regardant. (His personal supporters were griffins holding banners.)

In the case of Bishop GEORGE LOUIS, Count von BERGHEM (1724-1743), the supporters are two lions rampant, and his personal arms are included in the escucheon *en surtout*. An earlier Prince-Bishop, JOHAN LUDWIG VON ELDEREN (who held the See from 1688-1694), used a similar arrangement; the main shield is quartered, but the *enté en pointe* of the County of HORN was not at that time included in the escucheon. The personal arms of this Prince-Bishop were; *Argent, a fess haussé or, between nine pieces of vair, four in chief, five in two rows* (3 and 2) *in base*. (A briefer blazon would be *Beffroi, a fess haussé vair*.) The main shield has neither sword nor staff, but is supported by two ibexes collared, and is surmounted by a princely hat.

EBERHARD VON DER MARK (de Sedan) Prince-Bishop (1506-1538), used two white griffins as supporters to the quartered coat, on which the personal arms, *Or, a fess chequy argent and gules*, are placed *en surtout*.

SPENER (*Opus Heraldicum*, pars specialis, lib. iii., cap. viii.), tells us that on the coins of the bishopric the column was surmounted by a cross.

MAGDEBURG (Prince-Bishopric).

Arms : *Per fess gules and argent.*

The Archbishopric of MAGDEBURG was a foundation of the Emperor OTTO I. The first Archbishop was ADALBERT (who had been a monk of WEISSEMBERG, and a missionary in Russia), elected to fill the See in 968. The Pope sent him the *pallium* in 970; and conferred on him equal religious rights and privileges with those enjoyed by the Archbishops of CÖLN, MAINZ, and TRIER. Like them, he was a Prince of the Holy Roman Empire, but he did not attain to the dignity of

Elector. The Sees suffragan to MAGDEBURG were : BRANDENBURG, HAVELBERG, MEISSEN, MERSEBURG, POSEN, and ZEITZ. S. NORBERT, Bishop from 1126 to 1134, followed the Emperor LOTHAIR into Italy, and received the title of Primate of Germany. In 1539 the Archbishop was ALBERT, Markgrave of BRANDEN-BURG, who also held the Bishopric of HALBERSTADT, and the Electorate of MAINZ. He permitted the exercise of the Reformed religion to his subjects at MAGDEBURG and HALBERSTADT. He was succeeded by two other princes of the line of BRANDENBURG; of whom the latter, FREDERICK, elected in 1551, died in 1552 without having received the *pallium* (the price of which was thirty thousand pieces of gold). To him succeeded three other BBANDENBURG princes: SIGISMUND, JOACHIM FREDE-RICK, and CHRISTIAN WILLIAM. The first of these embraced Protestantism, and the second handed over the cathedral and monastery to the Reformers. On the death of the Markgrave CHRISTIAN WILLIAM in 1631, there was a vacancy in the See until 1638, when AUGUSTUS, Duke of SAXONY, was made "administrator" of the diocese. At his death in 1680, the possessions of the See, with the rank of a duchy, were incorporated with those of the Elector of BRAN-DENBURG.

The crest borne by the Princes of the House of BRANDENBURG for MAGDEBURG was : *Out of a golden crest-coronet a pelican in her piety argent.* This, however, does not appear in the achievement of Duke AUGUSTUS of SAXONY as Administrator of the Diocese (*vide supra*) which is given by SPENER in the plate accompanying the "*Prolegomena*" of his *Opus Heraldicum* (pars specialis). It is probable, therefore, that the crest was assumed somewhat later on the incorporation of the Duchy with the BRANDENBURG possessions. The arms of the Cathedral Chapter are : *Per bend gules and argent.*

1. Bishop Wilkinson (R.C.) of Hexham.   2. Seal of Bishop of Treguier.
3. Medal of the Cardinal Camerlengo, *sede vacante*, 1836.
4. Seal of Jean, Bishop of Nantes, in 1419.

MEISSEN (Prince-Bishopric).

Arms: *Gules, on a mount in base a Paschal-Lamb holding its banner proper.*

The See of MEISSEN was founded October 19, 967, by the Emperor OTTO THE GREAT, who appointed his chaplain BURCHARD as its first bishop. Its erection was confirmed by Pope JOHN XIII. in the following January. It was at first held immediately from the Holy See, but was soon made suffragan to the Archbishopric of MAGDEBURG. The Bishop had the rank of. Prince of the Empire. The Reformation caused the destruction of the See; the last bishop was JOHANN VON HAUGWITZ, elected in 1555. He resigned his office in 1581. The possessions were secularised, and are included in Saxony.

On the seal of Bishop NICOLAS ZIEGENBOCK (1379-1392) are two shields, one of the See; the other of his personal arms: . . . *an open pair of tailor's shears in bend having a pair of wings attached.* (GLAFEY, *Specimen*, tab. xii., fig. 9.) On the seal of Bishop JOHANN VON KITTLITZ, elected in 1393, the arms of the See are in the first and fourth quarters; the others contain the personal arms of the Bishop, which appear to be the head and bust of a man, looking to the sinister; the head conjoined with that of a beast, perhaps a wolf. The Bishop died in 1408, having resigned his See in 1398. He was succeeded by THIMO VON KOLDITZ, whose arms appear to have been: *Bendy of six, sable and argent, on a chief or a lion naissant gules.* These arms (without tinctures) appear on one of three shields which are engraved on his seal. The others contain, one the arms of the See, and the other a *lozengy* coat.

On all these seals (which are engraved in GLAFEY, *Specimen Decadem Sigillorum*, plates iii. and xii., Leipsic,

1749) the *Paschal-Lamb is regardant*, and is not placed on *a mount;* but on two other seals of Saxon princes who administered the possessions of the See (*ibid.*, figs. 19, 20), the Lamb looks forward, and stands on a mount in base. SIEBMACHER'S blazon: *Per pale Or and azure, a fleur-de-lis counter-changed* (*Wappenbuch*, i., 12) appears to be quite without authority.

MERSEBURG (Bishopric).

Arms: *Or, a cross sable.*

The first Bishop of this See, founded by the Emperor OTTO, about 967, was BOSO, a monk of S. EMMERAN'S in REGENSBURG, who was consecrated in 968. His successor was GISELER, consecrated in 971. GISELER was also Archbishop of MAGDEBURG, and under him a new distribution of jurisdiction took place, the diocese being split up into the Sees of HALBERSTADT, MAGDEBURG, MEISSEN, and ZEITZ. HENRY II. renewed the See about the year 1004.

At the time of the Reformation, SIGISMUND VON LINDENAU (1535-1544) was the last prelate who combined the ecclesiastical and temporal jurisdictions. At the last date, AUGUSTUS, Duke of SAXONY, assumed the administration of the temporalities, and they were soon absorbed in that state. The Congress of VIENNA, in 1815, transferred a large portion to Prussia.

METZ (Prince-Bishopric).

Arms: *Argent, a lion rampant sable, crowned or.*

The coat: *Gules, a cross argent*, is sometimes given, and may be the arms of the Chapter.

This See has a double traditional origin, being said to owe its foundation to S. CLEMENT, disciple of

S. PETER, and to PATIENS, a scholar of S. JOHN. The first of the long list of bishops to whom we can assign a historical date is HESPERIUS, who was present at the Council of Clermont in 535. The bishop had the title of "*Fürst des heiligen römischen Reiches deutscher Nation.*" In 1552 the French under HENRY II., conquered its territory, and "the three Bishoprics" (METZ, with the adjacent Sees of TOUL and VERDUN) were ceded to France by the Treaty of CHÂTEAU CAMBRESIS ; though they remained suffragan to TRIÉR. In 1802 they were made suffragan to BESANÇON. Since the Franco-German War the See of METZ has been held immediately from the Papal throne.

MINDEN (Prince-Bishopric).

Arms : *Gules, two keys in saltire argent, the wards in chief.*

This See was founded early in the ninth century. Its first bishop HERUMBERT, or ERKANBERT, the traditional baptiser of WITEKIND, filled the See from 803 to 813. From the first it was suffragan to CÖLN. Under Bishop LUDWIG, Duke of BRUNSWICK-LÜNEBURG, the Emperor LUDWIG IV. in 1339 raised the possessions of the See to the rank of a free Duchy of the Empire. It was secularised in 1648, and by the Treaty of MÜNSTER came into possession of the House of BRANDENBURG, as an equivalent for VOR-POMMERN ceded to Sweden along with HALBERSTADT as a war indemnity. In 1807 MINDEN was included in the new kingdom of WESTPHALIA ; and in 1810 formed part of the French department of Haut-Ems ; but in 1814 it was won back by Prussia. The district is now included in the See of PADERBORN. The crest used, since it came to the House of Brandenburg, is : *Out of a golden crest-coronet, a demi-lion rampant gules, holding two keys in saltire argent.*

MÜNSTER (Prince-Bishopric).

Arms : *Azure, a fess or.*

The tradition that this See was founded in 784 or 791 by the Emperor CHARLEMAGNE is inexact. S. LUDGER the first bishop was not consecrated before 802. The name of the See was at first taken from MIMEGARDEVORD, or MIMIGERNAFORDE. The name MÜNSTER (*Monasterium*), first appears under the seventeenth Bishop, ERPHO, or ERPO, who ruled the See from 1084 to 1097. The See was, and remains, suffragan to the Archbishopric of CÖLN. HERMANN, Count VON KATZENELLNBOGEN, who appears in the list as twenty-fourth bishop, and who ruled the diocese from 1174 to 1203, obtained from the Emperor OTTO IV. the rank of Prince-Bishop of the Empire, for himself and his successors in the See. His successor, OTTO, Count of OLDENBURG, appears to be the first Bishop elected by the Chapter, the foregoing prelates having been nominated by the Emperor. At the Reformation the city of MÜNSTER came into the hands of the Anabaptists, but the Chapter remained Catholic. In 1802 the possessions were seized by Prussia, and secularised. The Bull " *De salute animarum*," created a new Diocese of MÜNSTER in 1821.

With the arms given above were often quartered those of its chief possessions, thus :—

Quarterly of six (in two horizontal rows, each of three quarters) :—

1 and 6. *Per fess argent and gules, on the fess line three blackbirds sable* (Burg-gravate of STROMBERG).

2 and 5. *Azure, a fess or* (the arms of the See).

3 and 4. *Gules, three bezants* (Lordship of BORCK-ELOHE). The personal arms of the Prince-Bishop were placed *en surtout.*

The Burg-gravate of STROMBERG was united to the See, with the consent of the Emperor CHARLES IV., when the last Count of STROMBERG was put under the ban of the Empire. In 1553, on the decease of JOSSE, last of the Counts of BRONCHORST, and Lords of BORCKELOHE, the last-named Lordship was claimed by the Bishop, on the ground that Count GISBERT of BRONCKHORST had, in 1406, pawned it to the See, which was to have the right of actual succession in the event of the extinction of his male heirs. But it was claimed and retained by the Count of LIMBURG-STIRUM, whose wife ERMENGARDE was the daughter of a brother of the last Count JOSSE. The pretensions of the Count were sustained by the States of the Netherlands, on the ground that BORCKELOHE was a dependence of the Duchy of GUELDERS. (*See* SPENER, *Op. Her.*, p. spec., pp. 645, 647.)

The County of VECHTE was also acquired by purchase in 1247, in the Episcopate of OTTO, Count of LIPPE. FRANZ, Count of WALDECK, Prince-Bishop of MÜNSTER from 1532 to 1553 (who also held the Sees of OSNABRÜCK and MINDEN), bore the following arrangement : *Quarterly*, 1 and 4. *Azure, a fess or* (MÜNSTER) ; 2. *Argent, a wheel gules* (OSNABRÜCK) ; 3. *Gules, two keys in saltire argent* (MINDEN.) Over all the arms of WALDECK : *Or, a star of eight points sable.* The whole is surmounted by the crowned helm of WALDECK, with its crest, *a star sable between two golden wings.*

The crest of the See of MÜNSTER, was : *On a crowned helm a pair of horns between which is a shield charged with the arms of the See.* The crest of the Burg-gravate of STROMBERG was : *On a crowned helm an eagle's wing charged with the arms of the Burg-gravate.* That of BORCKELOHE was a similar wing, bearing the arms of that Lordship. The arms borne by the DOM-CAPITEL appear to have been ; *Or, a fess gules.*

NAUMBURG (ZEITZ) (Bishopric).

Arms : *Gules, a sword in bend-sinister proper, hilt in base, traversed by a key in bend, wards in chief or.*

This See was founded by the Emperor OTTO I. in the year 968, at ZEITZ ; whence it was removed to NAUMBURG between the years 1028 and 1032, on the re-arrangement of the See of MERSEBURG (*vide ante*, p. 302).

The bishopric came to an end on the death of Bishop JULIUS PFLUG, consecrated in 1541, but dispossessed in 1546, and again restored in 1547. The administration of its temporal possessions afterwards passed to the House of SAXONY. Since 1815 the territories have been included with those subject to the Prussian Crown.

OESELL (Bishopric).

> Arms : *Quarterly*, 1 and 4. . . . *the eagle of S. John rising ; 2 and 3. . . . a Paschal-Lamb; on a champagne in base two Passion crosses, one in bend the other in bend-sinister.*

This island was conquered, and its inhabitants forcibly converted to Christianity, by an army which crossed the frozen sea at the instigation of Archbishop ALBERT VON BUXHÖVEDEN, of RIGA, on Jan. 27, 1227.

The island was made into a bishopric under GOTTFRIED, elected in 1227. In 1238 King WALDEMAR of Denmark seized it, but confirmed the Bishop in his office. Somewhat later it came under the dominion of the Teutonic Order. At the time of the Reformation Bishop JOHN MÖNCHHAUSEN sold his rights to FREDERICK, King of DENMARK, for 30,000 thalers, and it was thereafter administered by MAGNUS, Duke of SCHLESWIG-HOLSTEIN, FREDERICK'S brother, In 1721 OESELL was united to Russia by the Treaty of NYSTAD.

OLMÜTZ (Prince-Bishopric, Archbishopric).

> Arms : *Per fess :* (a) *Gules, four piles issuing towards the chief argent ;* (b) *Gules, two piles issuing towards the chief argent.*

After the introduction of Christianity into Moravia by

its apostles CYRIL and METHODIUS, the latter was, in the year 868, appointed by the Pope Archbishop of MORAVIA and PANNONIA, with his throne at WELE-HRAD, the then capital of MORAVIA. After the extinction of the See in the tenth century the Archbishop of LORSCH had the spiritual oversight of the country. But the See was refounded about the year 960, and SYLVESTER, who died in 966, was its first Bishop, and placed his throne at OLMÜTZ. After the foundation of the Archbishopric of PRAG that See had the ecclesiastical supervision of the territory from 911 to 1063 ; but Pope ALEXANDER III. refounded the See of OLMÜTZ, and gave it as suffragan to MAINZ. In 1344 it was again made subject to PRAG. In 1777-OLMÜTZ was raised to the rank of an archbishopric, and the newly erected bishopric of BRUNN was given to it as a suffragan See ; an arrangement which is still operative.

The Bishop was temporal Prince of OLMÜTZ and its vicinity, with seat and vote in the Diet. His title was, " Herzog des heiligen römischen Reiches, Fürst und Graf der Königlichen böhmischen Kapelle."

The arms of the See as given in SIEBMACHER'S *Wappenbuch*, appear above. They are differently given in later times ; as by JACOB ERNEST, Count of LICHTENSTEIN, elected Bishop in 1778. He bore : *Quarterly*, 1 and 4. *Gules, a fess from which proceed four piles towards the chief and as many towards the base, argent* (See of OLMÜTZ); 2 and 3. *Or, an eagle displayed sable, on its breast a crescent argent* (SILESIA); Over all his personal arms. (*See* KÖHLER, *Münz-Belustigung*, xiv., 107.) The arms now used appear to be : *Quarterly*, 1 and 4. THE EMPIRE, *on the fess of the Austrian escucheon the letters* M. T. ; 2 and 3. The coat as given by SIEBMACHER above. (The DOM-CAPITEL *use a key and a sword in saltire, the hilt of the sword in chief, the wards of the key in base.*

OSNABRÜCK (Prince-Bishopric).

Arms: *Argent, a wheel of six spokes gules.*

Many ecclesiastical writers make WIHO, the first Bishop of this See, and place his nomination about the year 783, but this is very doubtful. The first authentic Bishop appears to be MEINHART, who died in the year 829. JOHN HOET, who fills the forty-first place in the list of bishops, and who governed the See from the year 1349 to 1366, was raised to the dignity of Prince-Bishop of the Empire by the Emperor CHARLES IV.

In 1625 the Chapter of OSNABRÜCK, elected the Cardinal FRANCIS WILLIAM, Count of WARTENBURG. But the Swedes, having seized the territories, made GUSTAVUS, Count of WASABURG, a natural son of King GUSTAVUS ADOLPHUS, (nominal) bishop in 1633. This dignity he appears to have retained until his death in 1648. Then FRANCIS WILLIAM was restored, by the provisions of the Treaty of MÜNSTER, on payment of 160,000 livres ; and it was arranged that, for the future, the See should be possessed alternately by a Catholic and by a Protestant prince. The latter was always to be the youngest prince of the line of Duke GEORGE of BRUNSWICK-LÜNEBURG, at that time general of the Swedish troops. On the failure of this line the right was to pass to that of AUGUSTUS, Duke of WOLFFENBÜTTEL. It was in consequence of these provisions that FREDERICK (afterwards Duke of YORK) the newly-born son of King GEORGE III. of Great Britain and Ireland, was made Prince-Bishop of OSNABRÜCK on February 26, 1764, and held what seemed to English Protestants that very odd title until the final secularisation of the See in 1802. After that time the spiritual administration of the diocese was generally in the hands of the Bishop of PADERBORN (but *see* pp. 290 and 305). In 1858 the Bishopric was formally reconstructed, and it is now held immediately from the Papal See.

PADERBORN (Prince-Bishopric).

> Arms: *Quarterly*, 1 and 4. *Gules, a cross or*, See of
> PADERBORN ; 2 and 3. *Argent, a cross ancred
> gules*, County of PYRMONT.

The church at PADERBORN was founded by CHARLE-
MAGNE about the year 777, and erected into an Episcopal See, with the spiritual oversight of a portion of
Middle Saxony, in the year 795. In 1187, WITIKIND,
Count of SCHWALENBURG and WALDECK (being in need
of money for his outfit as one of the Companions of
FREDERICK BARBAROSSA on the projected Crusade)
sold to the Bishop the temporal lordship of PADERBORN,
which his ancestor had received from the Emperor
CHARLEMAGNE as "advocate" of the See. The price
paid was 300 marks of pure silver. The temporal
possessions of the See, which already included the town
and district of Warpurg, increased greatly after this
time. In 1312 at the death of the Count of STOPPEL-
BERG that county was divided between the See of
PADERBORN and the Counts of LIPPE.

The Bishop was a Prince of the Empire, with seat
and vote in the Diet, and precedence between the
Bishops of HILDESHEIM and FREYSING. He had the
first place in the Circle of Westphalia. Like other
ecclesiastical princes he had a large household of
hereditary officials.

The See was suffragan to MAINZ up to the year 1803.
On 23rd November 1802 the possessions of the Bishopric
were secularised, and given to the Kingdom of Prussia as
a hereditary Principality. A Papal Bull re-founded the
See in 1821, and made it suffragan to CÖLN.

As to the arms of PYRMONT, which are quartered with
those of the See, the following is the explanation of their
assumption. On the death of PHILIP VON SPIEGEL-
BERG, last of the Counts of PYRMONT (who had acquired
PYRMONT from the Counts of SCHWALENBERG-WAL-

DECK), HERMAN SIMON, Count of LIPPE, husband of PHILIP'S sister, URSULA, claimed the succession to PYR-MONT ; though REMBERT VON KERSSENBROCK, Bishop of PADERBORN (1547-1568) declared that the right of succession in default of male heirs had been transferred by purchase to his See. But his successor in the bishopric was JOHN, Count of HOYA ; who being a cousin of HERMAN SIMON of LIPPE, arranged that the latter should hold the county as a fief of the See of PADERBORN, to which it should revert if the direct male line failed. Accordingly, on the death without issue of PHILIP, Count of PYRMONT (son of HERMAN SIMON) in 1583 the county should have reverted to PADERBORN ; but the Counts of GLEICHEN, as heirs in the female line, claimed it, and with the assistance of PHILIP, Duke of BRUNSWICK-GRUBENHAGEN, repelled the efforts of the then Prince-Bishop, HENRY of SAXE-LAUENBURG, to occupy the county with his troops. On the extinction of the GLEICHEN line, the Counts of WALDECK took possession of PYRMONT. In 1629 the See of PADER-BORN was held *in commendam* by a very powerful prince, FERDINAND of BAVARIA, Prince-Archbishop and Elector of CÖLN, who invaded the county. After much fighting, in which each party was alternately victorious, an agree-ment was made by which the Counts of WALDECK were left in possession of PYRMONT, with a reservation to the See of PADERBORN of the right of succession thereto, if the male line of the Counts of WALDECK should fail.

The crest of PADERBORN is, *On a princely helm* (without a coronet), *a red cushion supporting a plain black cross.* That of PYRMONT is : *On a coroneted helm a column topped with a coronet or, out of which rises a panache of peacock's feathers ; the column is pierced in bend-sinister by an arm of the Cross of* PYRMONT, *having a pointed lower end.* The "column" of the crest of PYRMONT, though generally so described, is really nothing but a tall *hat* as in the cases of the crests of SAXONY, BRUNSWICK, etc.

PASSAU (Prince-Bishopric).

Arms: *Argent, a wolf springing gules.*

This See was an outcome of the Bishopric (or Archbishopric) of LORCH. About the year 738, in consequence of an invasion of the Avars, Bishop VIVILO transferred his throne to PASSAU, and it was in 739 designated by S. BONIFACE as one of the four Sees into which Bavaria was to be divided. For some time the See was suffragan to SALZBURG, but, in 1728, Pope BENEDICT XIII. decided that it should be held immediately from the Papal throne.

The bishop's title accordingly was thenceforth "Exemter Bischof und des heiligen römischen Reiches Fürst zu Passau." In the Imperial Diet he sat between the Bishops of REGENSBURG and TRIENT. On February 22, 1803, the possessions of the See were secularised, and transferred to the Electorate of Bavaria. At the present day the See is suffragan to the modern Archbishopric of MÜNCHEN-FREISING.

JOSEPH DOMINICK, Cardinal and Count of LAMBERG, who had been Bishop of SECKAU in 1712, became Bishop of PASSAU in 1723, and held the See until 1761. His arms were: *Quarterly*, 1 and 4. *Per pale :* (a) *Barry of four argent and azure ;* (b) *Gules plain* (LAMBERG) ; 2 and 3. *Or, a hound salient sable collared of the field* (POTWEIN) ; *over all two escucheons accolés en surtout ;* I. PASSAU SEE (the wolf *contourné*) ; and II. *Gules, on a mount in base vert two greyhounds rampant argent supporting between them a ladder of four bars or* (SCALA), both these escucheons are ensigned with the same mitre. The main escucheon was surmounted by a princely hat, and placed on the breast of a double-headed *Imperial eagle sable, armed, beaked, and diademed or; over the heads is the Imperial crown proper.*

The arms of the See of PASSAU (*the wolf contourné*) were placed on a chief above his personal arms by the Prince-Bishop, THOMAS, Count VON THUN und HOHENSTEIN, who filled the See in 1795-1796. He bore: *Quarterly, 1 and 4. Azure, a bend or; 2 and 3. Per pale:* (a) *Argent, an eagle dimidiated gules;* (b) *Sable, a fess argent; Over all, on an escucheon en surtout, Gules, a fess argent* (CALDES).

The DOM-CAPITEL of PASSAU used as arms: *Out of a coronet an arm in pale holding in the hand a ball or loaf.*

POMESANIA (Bishopric).

Arms· . . .. *the Evangelistic symbol of* S. JOHN, *an eagle rising, between two pastoral staves erect paleways, heads turned inwards.* Sometimes the .arms are . . . *the eagle, and a chief thereon a plain cross* . . .

The cathedral of this See was at MARIENWERDER in the province of East Prussia. The Bishopric was founded in 1243, and was suffragan to the archi-episcopal See of RIGA. After the defection of Bishop ERHARD VON QUEIS, in 1524, the Bishops of CULM assumed the title and jurisdiction of POMESANIA, which were confirmed to them by Papal Bull in 1601.

POSEN (Bishopric).

Arms :

This See was founded by Duke MIECISLAUS of POLAND (d. 992). Its first bishop was JORDANUS, elected in 968. The Emperor OTTO I. made the See suffragan to the Archbishopric of MAGDEBURG ; but it afterwards in the eighteenth century, came under GNESEN (*vide ante*, p. 287).

PRAG (PRAGUE) (Prince-Bishopric, and Archbishopric).
Arms : *Sable, a fess or.*

The first Bishop of PRAG was DIETMAR, a Benedictine of MAGDEBURG, who was nominated by the Emperor OTTO, in the year 973. The See was at first made suffragan to the Archbishopric of MAINZ ; but in the year 1344 Pope CLEMENT VI., at the request of the Emperor CHARLES IV., erected the See into an archbishopric, with the new Sees of OLMÜTZ and LEIT-OMISCHL as suffragans. During the Hussite troubles the See was vacant from 1431 to 1561. The Archbishop had the rank of Prince of the Holy Roman Empire, and used the title :—"Legatus natus per Bohemiam, Bambergensem, Misnensem, et Ratisbonensem dioec : Primas regni Bohemici ; Cancellarius perpetuus Universitatis Pragensis, necnon studiorum protector."

The Sees which are now suffragan to this archbishopric are BUDWEIS, KÖNIGGRÄTZ, and LEITMERITZ.

WILHELM FLORENTINE, Prince of Salm, held the Archbishop of PRAG from 1793 to 1810 ; and placed its arms : *Sable, a fess or,* in chief above his personal coat ; *Quarterly,* 1 and 4. *Sable, a lion rampant gardant argent* (WILDGRAVE) ; 2 and 3. *Or, a lion rampant gules, crowned azure* (RHEINGRAVE) ; *Over all an escucheon, Quarterly,* 1. *Gules, three lions rampant or* (County of KYRBURG) ; 2. *Gules, two salmon embowed and addorsed between four cross-crosslets argent* (County of SALM) ; 3. *Azure, a fess argent* (Lordship of HINSTINGEN) ; 4. *Gules, a column argent, crowned or* (Lordship of ANHOLT). The whole escucheon, which has the usual marks of spiritual and temporal dignity, was supported by two savages wreathed and bearing clubs proper.

The arms of the Archbishop of PRAG : *Sable, a fess or,* have usually the *pallium* included in the shield in chief. Above the escucheon appears the head of a patriarchal cross between a mitre and the head of a crosier. This is surmounted by the green archi-episcopal hat, and the whole is surrounded by a mantle topped by the princely crown. FREDERICK JOSEPH, Prince of SCHWARZEN-BERG, and Duke of KRUMAN, who had been Bishop of SALZBURG since 1835, was elected Archbishop of PRAG 1849-1850, and was cardinal in 1842. He bore the arms of PRAG (*Sable, a fess or*), with the *pallium* arranged in the chief of the shield. On an escucheon *en surtout*, surmounted by a princely crown, were his personal arms : *Quarterly*, I. *Paly of eight argent and azure* (SEINS-HEIM) ; 2. *Per fess dancetty argent and gules.* (*Coupé emanché d'argent sur gueules, le gueules brochant par trois pièces sur l'argent*, is a more accurate blazon) (SULZ) ; 3. *Argent, a staff raguly in bend sable, inflamed at the top proper* (BRANDIS) ; 4. *Or, a raven perched on the head of a Turk and picking out his eye, all proper.* The head of a patriarchal cross appears in pale behind the shield, between a mitre and the head of a pastoral staff. This is surmounted by the mantling, and princely hat ; and the cardinal's hat and tassels surmount the whole.

RATZEBURG (Prince ?) (Bishopric).

> Arms : *Gules, a fess dancetty the centre point conjoined with a cross argent.* Another coat bears *a tower surmounted by a mitre and having behind it a crosier and sword in saltire.*

This See was formed by Archbishop ADALBERT of HAMBURG, who, in 1052, divided the Diocese of ALDEN-BURG into the three Sees of ALDENBURG, MECKLEN-BURG, and RATZEBURG.

The last Catholic Bishop, CHRISTOPH VON SCHU-LENBERG, resigned his See in 1544, embraced Pro-testantism, and became the ancestor of the line of Counts of that name. The lands of the See were appro-priated by the Dukes of MECKLENBURG ; but in 1864,

RATZEBURG, as capital of LAUENBURG, was ceded to the Crown of Prussia. In the first coat described above I have given the arms attributed to the See by SIEBMACHER (*Wappenbuch*, vol. i., plate 11), but in the MECK-LENBURG quarterings the arms of the secularised principality are given as: *Gules, a cross couped argent* (to this some of the Dukes added *à mitre or* upon the upper arm). The same quartering was borne in the eighteenth century in the full shield of the Prussian monarchy, along with the other MECKLENBURG quarterings, to denote the "*jus expectationis,*"—the right of eventual succession.

As borne by the House of MECKLENBURG the crest of RATZEBURG was: *Out of a golden crest-coronet seven lances, with banners floating, three to the dexter, four to the sinister.* (According to general use, these crest-banners are charged as the arms.)

REGENSBURG (RATISBON) (Prince-Bishopric).

Arms: *Gules, a bend argent.*

The traditional date of the foundation of this See is about the latter part of the fifth century, but the first authentic name in the list is that of GAUBALD, or GERI-BALD, appointed about the year 739, by S. BONIFACE of MENTZ. Up to the year 1817 REGENSBURG was suffragan to the Archi-episcopal See of SALZBURG, and its Bishops were Princes of the Empire, with precedence next to the Prince-Bishop of FREYSING, and above him of PASSAU. In 1805 the See was raised to the rank of an Archbishopric, under Bishop CARL THEODORE VON DALBERG, but its tenure of that rank was brief; the Archbishop died in 1817 (*see* mention of him under MAINZ, *ante* p. 254) and had no successor in the dignity; and the See, reduced to its former rank, became one of the suffragans of the newly-created Archbishopric of MÜNCHEN-FREISING.

For the arms of WILHELM, Cardinal WARTENBERG, Bishop of REGENSBURG, etc. (1649-1661) *see* pp. 88, 89.

SPENER gives (*Opus Heraldicum*, p. spec., p. 678), and Plate XXX., the arms of ALBERT SIGMUND, Duke of BAVARIA, who was Bishop from 1668 to 1685. He was also Bishop of FREISING, and his arms are therefore: *Quarterly, 1 and 4. The See of* FREISING (*ante* p. 284) ; 2 and 3. See of REGENSBURG (as above), *Over all an escucheon of his personal arms: Quarterly, 1* and 4. *Fusily-bendy argent and azure* (BAVARIA); 2 and 3. *Sable, a lion rampant or, crowned and armed gules* (Palatinate of the RHINE). The shield has as external ornaments a (legatine?) cross in pale, and also the pastoral staff and temporal sword in saltire behind the shield. There are no crested helms ; but on the top of the shield is placed, to the dexter, a mitre ; to the sinister, a ducal hat, one on either side of the head of the cross.

REVAL (Bishopric).

> Arms: . . . *two Passion-crosses in saltire argent ;* but the coat, as given in SIEBMACHER (*Wappenbuch*, i., 12), is : *Gyronny of sixteen or and azure, over all an escucheon argent.*

The creation of this See probably took place about the close of the twelfth century. FULCO, Bishop of ESTHONIA, is said to have been the first to fill the Episcopal throne. Others consider WESCELIN, who appears in the list as his successor, really the first bishop. In 1347 REVAL came with ESTHONIA under the dominion of the Teutonic Order. Originally the See was suffragan to LUND, but in 1374 it was transferred to the Arch-diocese of RIGA. Towards the close of the sixteenth century the Bishopric came to an end in consequence of the spread of Protestant opinions in the Baltic lands.

RIGA (Archbishopric).

> Arms : *Gules, a sword and pastoral staff in saltire or.* (Sometimes quartered with (2) *a cross couped ; and* (3) *a fleur-de-lis ;* the arms of the DÖM-CAPITEL).

Towards the middle of the twelfth century Christianity made its way into Livonia, and the Augustinian Monk MEINHARD was appointed Missionary-Bishop about the year 1190. He and BERFOLD, his successor in that office, both resided at Uexhüll, but the third Bishop, ALBERT VON BUXHÖVDEN, transferred his seat to the new city of RIGA. Under his successor NICOLAS, the See of SEMI-GALLEN was united to RIGA ; which two years later was made an archbishopric by Pope ALEXANDER IV. Archbishop SCHÖNUNG was the prelate (1528-1539) under whose primacy the doctrines of the Reformation spread in Livonia ; and the last of the holders of the dignity was WILHELM, Margrave of BRANDENBURG, who had been his coadjutor since 1529, and succeeded in 1539.

ROTTENBURG (Bishopric).
    Arms : *Sable, a cross or.*
    This See was founded in 1821, and embraced in its jurisdiction the whole kingdom of WÜRTTEMBERG. It is suffragan to the Metropolitan See of FREIBURG IM BREISGAU.

S. POLTEN (Bishopric) *vide infra*, WIENER-NEUSTADT.

SAINT GALL (Bishopric) *vide* CHUR, *ante* p. 278.

SALZBURG (Prince-Archbishopric).
    Arms: *Per pale :* (a) *Or, a lion rampant queue fourchée sable ;* (b) *Gules, a fess argent* (the arms of AUSTRIA).
    S. RUPERT, Bishop of WORMS, is the traditional founder of the See of SALZBURG, and has the title of "Apostle of Bavaria." At the desire of the Prince THEODON, whom he had converted to Christianity, RUPERT is said to have built a church in the town of

JUVAVIA (the Roman Colony of *Juvavum*), which, from its situation on the river Salza was afterwards known as SALZBURG. The first of RUPERT'S successors having regular diocesan authority was Bishop JOHN, who was set over the See by S. BONIFACE in the year 739. Bishop ARNO, Bishop in 787, was the first to attain the dignity of Archbishop, being so created in 798 by Pope LEO III., with the consent of CHARLEMAGNE, and held the See until his death in 821. Towards the close of the eleventh century Archbishop GEBHARD, Count of HELFENSTEIN in Suabia, in consideration of the services he had rendered to Pope GREGORY VII. in opposition to the Emperor HENRY IV, obtained for himself and his successors the dignity of *Legatus natus* of the Holy See throughout the whole of Germany.

Archbishop EBERHARD VON TRUCHSEN created the Bishoprics of CHIEMSEE, LAVANT, and SECKAU (which *see*) out of the See of STRASBURG, early in the thirteenth century. At the close of the fifteenth century the Sees suffragan to SALZBURG were : BRIXEN, since 798 ; CHIEMSEE, since 1215 ; FREISING, since 724 ; GURK, since 1070 ; LAVANT, since 1221 ; PASSAU, since 737 ; REGENSBURG, since 697 ; and SECKAU, since 1218.

The possessions of the See were secularised in 1803. In 1812 the district came into possession of the Bavarian crown, and in 1816 it was restored to AUSTRIA. Its present suffragans are BRIXEN, GURK, LAVANT, SECKAU, and TRIENT.

Under the Empire the Archbishop of SALZBURG and the Elector of BAVARIA had alternately the presidency of the Circle of BAVARIA. At the court of the Emperor the Archbishop dined at the Imperial table even in the presence of the Empress. Other princes only had that honour when the Court was absent from Vienna, and when the Empress was not present. The Emperor

FRANCIS I., conferred on the Archbishop in 1750 the title of Primate of Germany.

The Archdukes of AUSTRIA were the hereditary advocates or protectors of the See of SALZBURG; and the hereditary officials of the Archbishop's court were Counts of KHUENBURG, Cupbearers; the Counts of THANHAUSEN, Stewards; the Counts of LADRON, Marshals; the Counts of THÖRING, Chamberlains.

The arms of LEOPOLD ANTONY, Baron VON FIRMIAN, who held the See from 1727 to 1744, are given by GLAFEY (*Specimen Decadem Sigillorum*, Leipsic, 1749) and are: On a chief the arms of the See as given above. The rest of the shield is: *Quarterly*, 1 and 4. *Barry of six gules and argent, on the bars of gules six crescents reversed, three, two, one, of the second, their points touching the bars of argent* (FIRMIAN); 2 and 3. *Azure, a demi-stag's attire in bend, with four points each supporting an estoile or* (METZ). *Over all, Argent, an open crown or on a cushion gules, tasselled of the second* (CHATEAU of LEOPOLDSKRON). Behind the shield are the archi-episcopal cross in pale, and the crosier in saltire with the naked temporal sword. The Archi-episcopal hat with six tassels on either side surmounts the whole.

SAMLAND (Bishopric).

Arms: . . . *a crozier and sword in saltire (hilt in chief) proper.*

This bishopric was founded in the thirteenth century. Its first prelate was HENRY VON STRETBERG. Its cathedral was at Königsberg, and the See was suffragan to RIGA. The last Bishop GEORGE VON POLENTZ, elected in 1518, embraced Protestantism and gave up the possessions of the See to Duke ALBERT of Prussia in 1525.

SCHLESWIG (Bishopric).

Arms : *Per pale gules and azure, two keys in saltire argent, wards in chief.* (SIEBMACHER, *Wappenbuch* i., 11., gives the arms, *Gules, a beetle* (?) *in bend or.*)

S. ANSKAR built a church in HADEBY, the port of SCHLESWIG, early in 848, but it was a century later that the Emperor, OTTO the Great, founded a bishopric here by the advice of Archbishop ADALDAG of HAMBURG. Up to 1104 SCHLESWIG was suffragan to the last-named See, but it was then transferred to the Archbishopric of LUND. The last Catholic Bishop was GOTTSCHALCK VON AHLEFELDT, who governed the See from 1507 to the year 1541.

SCHWERIN (MECKLENBURG) (Bishopric).

Arms : *Per fess gules and or, over all two pastoral staves azure, headed argent.* (The arms given by SIEBMACHER, i., 12, *Azure, a griffin segreant or,* are rather those of the County of SCHWERIN.)

First of the bishops of the See of MECKLENBURG (composed out of the See of ALDENBURG, *vide,* LÜBECK) was JOHN, nominated in 1052 and murdered in 1066. Thereafter the See was vacant, but in 1158 Duke HENRY THE LION of SAXONY refounded it. Its first bishop was BERNO, and the See was removed to SCHWERIN in 1167. It was always suffragan to HAMBURG. Bishop MAGNUS, Duke of MECKLENBURG, who filled the See from 1516 to 1520, was the last Catholic Bishop. After him the See was administered by Princes of MECKLENBURG or of HOLSTEIN up to 1648, in which year the possessions were completely secularised, and transferred as a temporal Principality to the House of MECKLENBURG. Its crest is, *Out of a crest-coronet a griffin issuant or.* (To the See of MECHELBURG, SIEBMACHER assigns : *Azure, a lion rampant crowned or, Wappenbuch,* i., 12.)

SECKAU (Prince-Bishopric.)

Arms: *Gules, a dextrochere issuing from sinister flank proper, habited argent turned up or* (SIEBMACHER, *Wappenbuch*, i., 12). (Sometimes the field is argent, sometimes gules, sometimes per fess of these tinctures.)

The Bishopric of SECKAU was erected out of the Diocese of SALZBURG by Archbishop EBERHARD in the year 1218. It was not a Prince-Bishopric of the Holy Roman Empire, as it held from the Dukes of AUSTRIA; but it has now that title in the Austrian Empire. It is still suffragan to SALZBURG. The arms of the DOM-CAPITEL are: *Gules, a chief of fur au naturel.*

SEMIGALLEN (or CURLAND) (Bishopric.)

Arms: (. . .) *a Paschal-Lamb passant proper.*

In the year 1217 BERNHARD, Count of LIPPE (father of Archbishop GEBHARD of BREMEN) was made Bishop of SEMIGALLEN, having his seat at SELBURG. It was transferred to CURLAND in 1246. The bishopric became extinct at the Reformation. Its last bishop was MAGNUS, Duke of HOLSTEIN, who was also Bishop of REVAL and OESELL, and died in 1583.

SITTEN (or SION) (Prince-Bishopric.)

Arms: *Azure, a trefoil on a spray in base gules, in chief two stars each of six points or.*

This See was founded in commemoration of the martyrdom of the Theban Legion in 302. Its original seat was *Octodurum*, the present town of MARTIGNY, in Switzerland. It was thence removed to S. MAURICE, then back to MARTIGNY; and finally in 580 to SITTEN, or SION, where its bishops resided in an unbroken succession in the old Castle of MAJORIA until its destruction by fire in the year 1788. The first regular bishop was THEODORE whose exact date is uncertain. He appears to have died about the year 390. CHARLEMAGNE bestowed on the See the County of WALLIS (VALAIS) with full sovereign rights, which it exercised until the occupation of the VALAIS by the French in 1798, but the title of Prince-Bishop of the Holy Roman Empire is still retained.

SION was originally suffragan to MILAN, then to LYON, thence it was transferred to VIENNE EN DAUPHINÉ, and about the middle of the eighth century to MOUTIERS EN TARENTAISE. Since 1513 it has held immediately from the Holy See.

SPEIER (SPIRES) (Prince-Bishopric).

> Arms : *Quarterly,* 1 and 4. *Azure, a cross argent,* the arms of the See ; 2 and 3. *Gules, a castle with two towers argent, pierced by a pastoral staff in bend of the second, in chief an open crown,* Abbey of WEISSENBERG.

The origin of this See is lost in the obscurity of antiquity. It was probably founded by King DAGOBERT who died in 638, and who is said to have nominated ATHANASIUS as its first bishop. It certainly existed as an Episcopal See in the middle of the seventh century, when the names of PRINCIPIUS and DAGOBODO appear as successive and authentic bishops. The occupants of the See have held the rank of Prince-Bishops of the Holy Roman Empire since the twelfth century. They occupied the fifth place on the bench, sitting between the Bishops of EICHSTÄDT and STRASBURG. The See was formerly a suffragan to the Archbishopric of MAINZ, but afterwards was transferred to BAMBERG. Its possessions were lost at the Reformation, and their secularisation completed in the year 1802. The See was restored in spirituals in 1818.

The Benedictine Abbey of WEISSENBURG founded by DAGOBERT in 629, and of which the abbot was made Prince of the Empire by CHARLES IV., was incorporated with the See of SPEIER by Abbot PHILIP VON FLERS-HEIM. He was elected Bishop of SPEIER in 1529, and obtained the consent of the Pope PAUL III. and the Emperor CHARLES V. to this incorporation. The Chapter of SPEIER bore : *Azure, a cross patée-throughout argent ; over all the Blessed Virgin Mary with the Holy Child proper, issuant from a crescent of the second.*

DAMIAN AUGUST PHILIP CARL, Count of LIMBURG. STYRUM, filled the See of SPEIER from 1770 to 1797.

His arms were rather curiously arranged in a series of three oval escucheons, two and one. The first contains the arms of the See : *Azure, a cross argent ;* the second those of the Abbey of WEISSENBURG : *Gules, a castle argent, masoned sable, through the gate of which passes a crosier in bend or, an open crown of the last in chief.* The lowest oval contains the personal arms of the Prince-Bishop : *Quarterly,* 1. *Argent, a lion rampant gules, crowned or* (LIMBURG) ; 2. *Gules, a lion rampant crowned or* (BRONCKHORST) ; 3. *Or, two lions passant-gardant in pale gules* (WISCH) ; 4. *Or, three torteaux* (BORCULO or BORCKELOHE, *v. ante,* p: 303) ; *Over all, Or, on a fess gules three pallets argent* (GHEMEN).

A princely hat is placed above the group of escucheons, behind them are the crosier and temporal sword in saltire ; and the whole arrangement has as supporters a savage man, and a savage woman, wreathed and resting on clubs held in the exterior hands all proper. (These supporters were those of the personal arms of the Counts of LIMBURG.)

STRASBURG (Bishopric).

Arms : *Quarterly,* 1 and 4. *Gules, a bend argent,* for the See of STRASBURG ; 2 and 3. *Gules, a bend having at either edge an engrailure of small trefoils* (resembling the adornments of the *Crancelin* of SAXONY) Landgravate of LOWER ELSASS.

The earlier portion of the long catalogue of the early Bishops of STRASBURG is quite untrustworthy. Out of the first score of names only two or three are to be recognised as those of historical persons; of these the first is probably that of S. ARBOGAST who lived before the middle of the seventh century. It is only with WINGERN, or WITGERN, who lived about a century later (*c.* 728) that the succession becomes continuously historical. Originally the See was suffragan to MAINZ, then to TRIER, then again to MAINZ. In modern times the See as included in France has been under BESANÇON ; since 1802 under FREIBURG IM BREISGAU, and is now (since the reconquest of Elsass by Germany) held immediately from the Holy See. The bishops had the title of " Fürst-bischöfe von Strasburg, Landgrafen vom Elsass, und des heiligen römischen Reiches Fürsten.

The Landgravate of LOWER ELSASS was acquired for the See by Bishop JOHANN, Baron von LICHTENBERG, who in 1357 purchased from JOHN, last Count of OETTINGEN, the upper portion of the Landgravate, and re-united to it the other fiefs which the Count held from the Chapter.

The crests used were (1, in the centre) *On a princely helm of gold the Episcopal mitre.* To the dexter (2) *A like helm, thereon a princely hat of crimson velvet, doubled with ermine and surmounted by a wing gules charged with a bend argent*; this was the crest of the See. To the sinister (3) *a crowned helm, thereon a mitre out of which rises a female figure vested gules, crowned and holding in the dexter hand a ring or,* the crest of the Landgravate of ELSASS.

The cathedral establishment of STRASBURG was one of the most famous in Christendom. It consisted of two parts, the High Chapter and the High Choir. The High Chapter was composed of twenty-four *Dom-Herren*, or Canons. The High Choir had at first seventy-two Capitular Prebendaries (afterwards reduced to twenty-two), they had their own lands and corporate seal.

TARENTAISE (Archbishopric).

Arms:

The date of the foundation of this Archbishopric, the seat of which was MOUTIERS EN TARANTAISE, in Savoy, is unknown. Bishop SANCTUS, or SANCTIUS, was, however, present at the council of EPAONE in the year 517, at that time the See was suffragan to VIENNE. CHARLEMAGNE made it archi-episcopal, and the name of ANDREAS appears in 828 as that of its first archbishop. SION was suffragan to it, as was later the See of AOSTA. Formerly the Archbishops had secular jurisdiction as Counts of TARENTAISE. In 1792, the archbishopric came to an end, but a new bishopric was created in 1825; it is now suffragan to CHAMBÉRY.

TOUL (Prince-Bishopric).

Arms: *Azure, a stag's head caboshed, having a cross between its antlers or, all within a bordure gules.*

The first historical Bishop of this See known to us is S. AUSPICIUS, who lived in the middle of the fifth century, but it is only a couple of centuries later that we have the commencement of a regular and authentic list of the succession of bishops.

From the middle of the twelfth century the Bishop held the title of " Prince of the Holy Roman Empire, and Count of TOUL." Pope PIUS VI. in 1777 divided the See into three: S. DIÉ, NANCY, and TOUL, and made the two latter suffragan to TRIER; they were, however, held together by the succeeding prelates, and in 1821 were formally united as the See of NANCY-TOUL.

This, with the Sees of S. DIÉ and VERDUN, was made suffragan to BESANÇON.

TRIENT (Prince-Bishopric).

Arms: *Argent, an eagle displayed sable armed or, semé of flames proper, and having on its wings Klee-Stengeln of the third.*

Christianity, it is said, was first propagated in the district of the Tridentine Alps by the teaching of S. HERMAGORAS, Bishop of AQUILEIA in the first century, when the ancient city of TRENT was made the seat of a bishopric. But the first historical holder of the See is ABUNDANTIUS who was present at the council of AQUILEIA in 381. CHARLEMAGNE endowed the See with considerable possessions, to which the Emperor CONRAD in 1207 added the town of BOTZEN, and made its district a Principality of the Empire. The Bishops retained the princely title until the close of the Germanic, or Holy Roman, Empire ; and are still Princes of the Austrian Empire. When the Dukes of Austria became Counts of TIROL they accepted the office of Advocates of the See of TRIENT. The Counts of THUN were its hereditary Cupbearers ; the Barons of FIRMIAN held the office of its Marshals.

As to the arms, SPENER makes the eagle, *gutté de sang* instead of *semé of flames* (*Opus Heraldicum*, pars spec., cap. xxxviii., p. 717) ; and SIEBMACHER substitutes *à crescent gules* for the *Klee-Stengeln* (*Wappenbuch*, i., 15). Up to 1751 TRIENT was a See suffragan to AQUILEIA. It was then, in 1752, transferred to GÖRZ. Later it was held immediately from the Roman See, but it is now suffragan to SALZBURG.

TRIESTE (Bishopric).

Arms :

Traditionally the See of TRIESTE was founded in the

first century by HYACINTHUS, a disciple of HERMA-
GORAS, patriarch of AQUILEIA. FRUGIFER, who filled
the See about the year 524, appears to be the first
historical bishop. TRIESTE was a See suffragan to
AQUILEIA until the extinction of the latter in 1752. It
was then made suffragan to the newly-founded Archbishopric of GÖRZ. Later it was held immediately from
the Holy See, but is now suffragan to the united See of
GÖRZ and GRADISCA.

UTRECHT (Archbishopric).
Arms : *Per fess or and gules, a cross flory counter-
changed.*
The first authentic Bishop of the See of UTRECHT
was S. WILLIBROD who was consecrated in the year 696,
and ruled it for forty-three years. In 748 Pope ZACHA-
RAIS made the See suffragan to the Archbishopric of
MAINZ, from which it was transferred to CÖLN (*See*
Appendix). The Emperor CONRAD III. in 1145 gave
to the Chapter of UTRECHT the right of electing the
bishop. In 1559, PAUL IV. made the See an arch-
bishopric, and gave to it the five newly-created Sees of
DEVENTER, GRONINGEN, HARLEM, LEUWARDEN, and
MIDDLEBURG, as suffragans.
The arms of these Dutch Sees were, of—
HARLEM : *Gules, a sword in pale surmounted by a
plain cross couped in chief, all between four estoiles, one in
each canton of the shield argent.*
DEVENTER : *Or, the Imperial eagle beneath a crown.*
GRONINGEN : *Or, the Imperial eagle sable, on a chief
azure three mullets argent.*
MIDDLEBURG : *Gules, a large castle or.*
LEUWARDEN : *Azure, a lion rampant within a narrow
bordure argent.*
But the revolt of the Netherlands from the yoke of
Spain (1573-1579) and the establishment of Protestantism

in the United Provinces, caused the extinction of this arrangement, and from 1602 until 1718 the spiritualities of the Dutch Sees were administered by a Vicar-Apostolic. CORNELIUS STEENHOVEN, consecrated in 1724, was the first Jansenist Archbishop; and the succession has been maintained up to the present day in independence of the See of ROME.

There is also a modern Roman Catholic Archbishopric of UTRECHT, with the four suffragan Sees of BOIS-LE-DUC, BREDA, HARLEM, and ROERMOND.

VERDEN (Bishopric).

Arms: *Azure, a bend counter-compony gules and argent.*

Of this See, founded about the close of the eighth century, the first authentic bishop appears to be HARUCH, who was present at a Synod in MAINZ in 829. The See of VERDEN was originally suffragan to HAMBURG, but later was placed under the Archbishopric of MAINZ. The Reformation early found a footing in this See, and the Catholic succession ended in 1631. In 1644 Sweden took possession of the bishopric, and, by the provisions of the Peace of Westphalia, retained it as a secular Duchy of the Empire. In 1720 VERDEN fell to Hanover; in 1810 it was incorporated with the kingdom of Westphalia; in 1813 it reverted to Hanover, and since 1866 it has been included in the possessions of the Prussian monarchy.

VERDUN (Prince-Bishopric).

Arms: *Sable, a cross argent* (SIEBMACHER, *Wappenbuch*, vol. i., p. 12, makes it slightly *patée* at the ends).

The first authentic bishop of this See (of which the traditional foundation goes back to the early part of the fourth century) was S. FIRMIN, who filled the throne from

486 to 502. The bishops had the title of Prince of the ·
Holy Roman Empire, and Count of VERDUN. The for-
tunes of the See resembled those of the other Austrasian
Bishoprics of METZ and TOUL ; at one time it belonged
to the Empire, at another it was incorporated with
France. In the latter case it was suffragan to BESAN-
ÇON, and so remains at the present time.

VIENNA (WIEN) (Archbishopric).

Arms : *Gules, a fess argent ensigned with a cross patée
of the same conjoined to the upper edge of the fess.*
(The arms are sometimes blazoned, but erroneously, as, *Gules, a cross argent, thereon an escucheon
of the arms of* AUSTRIA ; *Gules, a fess argent.*)

In 1468 Pope PAUL II., at the desire of the Emperor
FREDERICK, erected the Collegiate Chapter of VIENNA
into a bishopric and severed the city and district from
the See of PASSAU. LEO, Count of SPAUR, was nominated by Pope SIXTUS IV. first bishop of the new See in
1471. It was always an exempt See, holding immediately from the See of ROME. In 1722 Pope INNOCENT
XIII., raised the See to the archi-episcopal rank,
and gave to it as suffragans the Sees of St. PÖLTEN
(otherwise known as WIENER-NEUSTADT) and LINZ,
and this arrangement still continues.

The Archbishops of VIENNA sometimes impale the
arms of the See in the first place, with their personal
arms in the second, according to English custom.
Thus, JOSEF OTHMAR, Cardinal RAUSCHER (Bishop
of SECKAU in 1849, Archbishop of VIENNA in 1853, and
Cardinal in 1855), bore the arms of the See, impaled
with, *Per bend, azure and or, a river wavy in bend argent,
between two estoiles counter-changed.* A predecessor,
Archbishop CHRISTOPH ANTON, Count VON MIGAZZI,
VON WAITZEN UND SONNENTHURN ; elected 1757,
created Cardinal in 1761, died 1803, placed the arms of

the See on a chief above his personal arms :—*Quarterly sable, and argent, on a bend azure three fleurs-de-lis or, in the first and fourth quarters (respectively above and below the bend) a sun of the third; in the third and fourth quarters a castle sable.* Both used the escucheon mantled, and crowned with a princely crown ; behind it the archiepiscopal cross; the whole surmounted by the proper hat, with its cordons on either side.

WIENER-NEUSTADT (Bishopric) (ST. PÖLTEN).

> Arms : *Gules, a castle with two towers argent, in chief a cross-crosslet or.* (The arms of S. PÖLTEN are, *Azure, a letter Y of ancient shape or.*)

Pope PAUL II. founded this See by a Bull dated Jan. 18, 1468, but which only came into operation in the year 1476. It was originally held immediately from the Holy See ; but, on the creation of the Archbishopric of VIENNA in 1722, it was made suffragan to that See. In 1784 Pope PIUS VI. at the desire of the Emperor JOSEPH II. transferred the See to the town of ST. PÖLTEN.

WORMS (Prince-Bishopric).

> Arms : *Sable, a key in bend argent, between eight plain crosses-crosslets or (four in chief, as many in base, arranged fess-ways, two and two).*

Bishop RUPERT, who was living in the year 697, appears to be the first historical bishop of this See. Nothing is certainly known of his successors until the name of EREMBERT appears. He was consecrated in 770, and held the See for nearly a quarter of a century. There is however a weird legend that originally MAINZ itself was suffragan to WORMS, and that GEROLD, Archbishop of WORMS was slain in battle by a Saxon Prince. GEROLD'S son, GEWILIEB or GERVILIUS, who succeeded his father in the See, is said to have avenged his death by the assassination of the Saxon Prince with his own hand. Thereupon he was deposed by GREGORY III., and the archbishopric transferred to MAINZ, to which WORMS was made suffragan.

The See was early made a Principality of the Holy Roman Empire, and in the seventeenth and following· century was usually held *in commendam* by the Arch-bishop-Elector of MAINZ. It had very considerable possessions, but its position on the frontier exposed it to continual dangers. In 1688 it was overrun by the French armies, and never recovered the ruin they brought in their train. In 1792 it was again seized by the French republicans. In 1803, being thoroughly secularised, it fell to Hesse Darmstadt ; and, after a brief possession by France in 1814, was restored to that principality by the Congress of Vienna. In spirituals it appears· now to be included in MAINZ.

The crest of the See was : *On a princely helm a crimson cushion supporting a fan-crest of hexagonal shape, charged with the arms of the See, and adorned at the points with little golden knobs whence spring small tufts of peacock's feathers.*

WÜRZBURG (Prince-Bishopric).

Arms : *Quarterly*, 1 and 4. *Per fesse dancetté gules and argent*, Duchy of FRANCONIA ; 2 and 3. *Azure, a lance in bend or, with its banner Quarterly gules and argent floating towards the chief*, See of WÜRZBURG.

This See was founded by S. BONIFACE, Archbishop of MAINZ, who, with the consent of the Pope, and of CARLOMAN, Duke of AUSTRASIA, nominated as its first. bishop his relative the Englishman S. BURCHARD, in the year 741. PEPIN considerably augmented the possessions of the See; and (as the Bishops in later times asserted) even conferred upon it the whole Duchy of

FRANCONIA, in recognition of BURCHARD'S assistance in placing him on the throne. The Bishop had the rank and title of Prince of the Holy Roman Empire as early as the twelfth century; but the first who appears to have assumed the title of Duke of FRANCONIA, and put it on his coinage, etc., was Bishop GOTTFRIED, Count of LIMPURG, who filled the See from 1443 to 1445. This title was disputed at the Diet of WORMS in 1521 by the Electors of MAINZ, SAXONY, and BRANDENBURG, and by the Bishop of BAMBERG, all of whom held portions of the Duchy of FRANCONIA, but the Emperor CHARLES V. accorded *the title* to the Bishop of WÜRZBURG alone. (*See* the Imperial Confirmation in UNRATH'S Treatise " *de Jurisdictione Ecclesiastica Nobilium Immediatorum*, Sec., xx-xxvi., 1646; and NOLDENIUS, *de Statu Nobilitatis*, § 32, "Episcopi non habent plenarium Franconiæ Ducatus jus, sed tantum nomen et inscriptionem Ducis.") But as early as the commencement of the twelfth century Bishop ERLUNG, Count of CALW (1106-1121), had caused the naked sword to be borne before him in processions, to indicate his temporal jurisdiction in the Duchy of FRANCONIA. This Duchy the Emperor HENRY IV. had seized, and wished to give to his nephew CONRAD, Duke of SWABIA, in order to punish the bishop for his adherence to Pope PASCHAL II. Thenceforth when the Bishop of WÜRZBURG celebrated Mass the naked sword was held upright during the office by the Grand-Marshal, an office hereditary in the Counts of DERNBACH. The Counts of STOLBERG were Hereditary Grand-Chamberlains; the Counts of WERNBURG Grand-Stewards; and the Counts of CASTEL, Grand-Cupbearers of the See; but except on great state occasions they all performed their duties by deputy.

The arms of PETER PHILIP, Count of DERNBACH, Prince-Bishop of WÜRZBURG, etc., in 1675, are given at p. 88; and those of ADAM FRIEDRICH, Count of

SEINSHEIM, Prince-Bishop in 1755, are described at p. 90.

The crests borne by the Prince-Bishops of WÜRZBURG in addition to the mitred helm, and their own personal crest or crests—were, for the Duchy of FRANCONIA ; *Out of a golden crest-coronet two horns, each per fess dancetty gules and argent ;* and for the SEE : *A princely hat thereon a plume of three ostrich feathers blue, white, and red, between two golden lances with banners* (as in the arms of the See).

The WÜRZBURG crests vary somewhat at different times. In 1519 the following was used : *Out of a crest-coronet or, two horns with banners of the arms of the See in their mouths, and behind them three ostrich feathers, gules, argent, gules.* In 1540, the crest, *arising from a crest-coronet or, is the bust of a man vested gules, the hat turned up argent and bearing the feathers as above; the whole between two horns per fess indented, alternately gules and argent.* In 1544 this crest is divided into two ; one helm bears the *horns ;* the other the *banners without a crest-coronet.*

The possessions of the See were secularised in the year 1802, in the Episcopate of GEORGE CHARLES, Baron VON FECHENBACH. Before this the See was suffragan to MAINZ, but since its resuscitation in 1817 it has been made suffragan to the Archi-episcopal See of BAMBERG.

CHAPTER IV.

ABBEYS AND OTHER PRINCELY FOUNDATIONS OF THE EMPIRE.

BERCHTESGADEN (Provost. Prince of the Empire).
Arms: *Gules, two keys addorsed in saltire argent.*

This monastery of Regular Augustinian Canons was founded in the Diocese of SALZBURG by BERINGER and CUNO, Counts of SULTZBACH, and by their mother ERMENGARDE. They built it in 1008 and richly endowed it. Its first Provost was EBERHARD, afterwards Bishop of SALZBURG. The monastery is exempt from all jurisdiction, ecclesiastical or secular, that of the Pope and the Emperor alone excepted. The Prior had the sixth place among the Abbots and the Princes of the Empire.

As to the arms, TRIERS (*Einleitung zu der Wapen-Kunst*, p. 396), notices that in the *Nürnbergische Wapen-Kalendar*, No. xxvii., p. 13—the key in bend-sinister is of gold. TRIERS thinks this a mistake. He also notices that the then Provost and Prince, CAJETAN ANTON, Baron VON NOTHAFT, elected 1732, bore the following arms :—*Quarterly*, 1 and 4. *The arms of the Provostship*, as above ; 2 and 3. *Azure, six fleurs-de-lis argent ;* 3. 2. 1., the arms of the Founders, the old Counts VON SULTZBACH. (The field is *gules* in SIEBMACHER, ii., 11.) *Over all, Or, a fess azure*, the personal arms of the Counts and Barons NOTHAFT (SIEBMACHER, *Wappenbuch*, i., 78, etc.).

CORVEY (Princely Abbacy) (*vide ante*, p. 280).

EINSIEDELN (Princely Abbey).

Arms : *Or, two eagles rising (to sinister) in pale sable.*

This ancient and celebrated abbey, in the Swiss canton of SCHWEIZ, was founded near the hermitage of S. MEINRAD by a monk of the Abbey of REICHENAU near Constance. HILDEGARDE, granddaughter of LOUIS *le debonnaire*, built a chapel for the hermit who received the crown of martyrdom in 863. EBERHARD, Provost of STRASBURG, retired to the Hermitage in 934, and was followed by others. Thus the hermit's cell became the nucleus of the large and flourishing monastery. PRAUN asserts that the abbot first received the title of Prince in the year 1274. (PRAUN, *von Adelichen Europa, und dem Heer-Schilden des Teutschen Adels;* in BURGERMEISTER, *Bibliotheca Equestris*, ii., p. 835.) As, since the acknowledgement of the independence of Switzerland, EINSIEDELN was beyond the limits of the Empire, I suppose that (as in the case of S. GALL), the princely rank was merely titular, and conferred no right to a voice in the Diets of the Empire.

AUGUSTAN, Abbot in 1618, bore : *Quarterly,* 1. EINSIEDELN (as above) ; 2. *Gules, on a mount in base of three coupeaux vert edged or, a plain cross argent between two estoiles of six points of the third ;* 3. *Azure, two boat poles* (for punting), *in saltire proper, the head* (like a cronel) *argent ;* 4. *Or, a cockatrice vert.* Above the shield, in place of the crest, is an irradiated oval containing the effigy of the BLESSED VIRGIN MARY, and the HOLY CHILD. This coat is in the collection of painted glass in the South Kensington Museum. As borne by Abbot HENRY (1846-1874) the arrangement differs somewhat : *Quarterly,* 1. *Gules, on a mount in base vert a hammer (or pick ?) argent, between two fleurs-de-lis, and surmounted by an estoile or ;* 2. *Or, three lions passant gules ;* 3. *Or, a cockatrice vert ;* 4. *Azure, the boat staves* (as in No. 3 above). *Over all the arms of* EINSIEDELN.

ELWANGEN. (Provost. Principality of the Empire).
Arms: *Argent, à mitre or.* (This is not "false heraldry," gold being the *proper* colour of the *mitra preciosa.*)
This was a Benedictine Abbey in Suabia, in the Diocese of AUGSBURG. It was founded about the year 764 by two brothers, HARIOLPHUS and ERLOLPHUS, who were consecutively Bishops of LANGRES. The Duke of WÜRTTEMBURG was its Protector, or Advocate ; and the Provosts were made Princes of the Holy Roman Empire, by the Emperor HENRY II. In 1460, in the time of the 48th Provost JOHAN VON HERNHEIM, the Provostship was secularised with the approval of Pope PIUS II. (It appears to have been held *in commendam* by one of the Prince-Bishops.) It held the third place among the "Abbots and Princes."

FULDA (Princely Abbacy, afterwards Bishopric) (*vide ante*, pp. 77, and 284).

HEIDERSHEIM (Principality).
This was held by the JOHANNITER MEISTER; the Master of the ORDER OF S. JOHN in Germany. His arms were: *Quarterly*, 1 and 4. *Gules, a cross argent*, the arms of the ORDER OF S. JOHN ; 2 and 3. His personal arms. The shield was placed upon the eight-pointed cross of the Order (known as the Maltese Cross) of gold enamelled white (*vide ante*, p. 144).
GATTERER (*Heraldik*) gives the following example:—
FRANZ JOSEF VON SCHAUEMBERG ZU HERLESHEIM, Bailiff, and Commander of BILLINGEN, etc., Master of S. JOHN in Germany, Prince ZU HEIDERSHEIM, etc., bore: *Quarterly*, 1 and 4. The "arms of the Religion"

as above ; 2 and 3. *Per fess;* (a) *Chequy argent and gules;* (b) *Or, plain.* *Over all an escucheon, Argent, two bars azure (? Azure, three bars argent,* SIEBMACHER, *Wappenbuch*).

The Grand Prior, or Master, of S. JOHN, had his seat in the Diet next after the Prince-Bishops since the time of the Emperor CHARLES V. The escucheon was usually surmounted by three princely helms, of which the central one bore the princely hat, the dexter one was timbred with a fan-crest of the arms of the Order, the sinister with the *personal* crest of the JOHANNITER-MEISTER.

The Meister VON MERVELDT bore: *Quarterly,* 1 and 4. *The arms of the Order;* 2 and 3. His personal coat: *Azure, three chevrons interlaced or, two issuant from the base, the other from the chief.* The escucheon, placed on the white eight-pointed cross of the Order, had three crested helms; the dexter, *a fan-crest, Gules, a cross argent ;* the central one was surmounted by a princely hat; the sinister (the personal crest of the Prior), *an escucheon of the arms between two ostrich plumes azure, on the dexter three bends-sinister, on the sinister as many bends or).* The arms were supported by two ostrichs. The Count VON REINACH, Master 1777-1796, used a golden lion, and a wolf proper as supporters ; these were derived from the crests of his personal arms.

HIRSCHFELDT (Abbey).

Arms : *Argent, a cross patriarchal* (slightly *patée*), *the bottom point flory, gules.*

This celebrated Benedictine Abbey was founded about the year 763 by S. LULLO, on the site of the hermitage which had been the home of S. STURM.

It was one of the four monasteries which had the title of Imperial, viz., MURBACH, WEISSEMBURG, FULDA, and HIRSCHFELDT. Its possessions were increased by PEPIN, and CHARLEMAGNE. The abbey was secularised at the Peace of Westphalia ; and handed over to the Landgraves of Hesse-Cassel as a compensation for their losses in the " Thirty years " war.   Thereafter it had the rank of a Principality (*v. ante*, p. 87.)

The crest borne for it by the Hessian princes is : *Out of golden crest-coronet a panache of peacock's feathers proper.*

KEMPTEN (Princely-Abbey).

Arms : *Per fess gules and azure, the bust of a woman issuant from the base, habited sable, veiled argent, and crowned with an Imperial crown proper.*

The Benedictine Abbey of KEMPTEN in Suabia was, it is said, founded in the year 777, by HILDEGARDE, daughter of HILDEBRAND, Duke of SUABIA, and wife of the Emperor CHARLEMAGNE, who endowed it so munificently as to have the credit of its foundation.   It owed its origin really to AMELGAR, daughter of CHARLE-MAGNE'S sister, who founded it in the year 752.   The abbacy was held immediately from the Roman See and was one of the four " Imperial Abbeys." Its abbot had not only princely rank (which was originally conferred by the Emperor CHARLES IV. in 1380 on the then abbot HEINRICH VON MITTELBERG), but held the office of Grand-Marshal of the Empress, an office confirmed after a long desuetude by the Emperor LEOPOLD in 1683. The Abbot wore the Ecclesiastical habit only up to noon ; thereafter he appeared as a Secular Prince.   He had a splendid court, and included among his hereditary officials the Elector of BAVARIA, as Grand-Master of the Household ; the Elector of SAXONY, as Grand-Cupbearer; the Count of MONTFORT, Grand-Marshal ; and the Count of WERDENSTEIN as Grand-Chamberlain ; offices which were of course discharged by deputies.   (The last-named office was, it was said, rightly attached to the Dukes of AUSTRIA by reason of the Landgravate of NELLENBURG,

held by them as a fief of KEMPTEN.)' The possessions
of the abbacy extended to three hundred and thirty-six
square miles, including the County of KEMPTEN, in
right of which we may presume the princely rank was
conferred. But the city of KEMPTEN purchased its
freedom from the Abbot SEBASTIAN BREITENSTEIN, in
1523, for sixty-four thousand livres, and embraced
Protestantism.

The female figure which is the charge of the arms is
said to represent the Empress HILDEGARDE.

In the Diets of the Empire the Prince-Abbot had the
second place on the bench of his Order, having seat and
vote immediately after the Prince-Bishop of FULDA.
ANSELM, Baron VON MELDEGG, was elected Prince-Abbot
in 1728, and bore : *Quarterly*, 1 and 4. (The arms of the
abbey as given above) ; 2 and 3. *Gules, on a fess argent
three annulets of the field.* Over the shield are three
princely helms of gold. The dexter bears, *on a crimson
cushion, the abbatial mitre enfiling a crosier in bend.* On
the centre is, what is presumably the Crest of the Abbey
—*the figure of a Moor in a long black cloak, bordered and
girdled with silver and semé of silver flames ; holding in
the right hand a sword and in the left a sceptre.* (This
seems to have been originally simply the figure of the
princely founder.)

The third helm is surmounted by the personal crest of
the then Abbot, *two horns gules on each a fess charged with
an annulet of the first.* (*See* TRIERS, *Einleitung zu der
Wapen-Kunst*, p. 403, and SIEBMACHER, *Wappenbuch*, v.,
plate 178.)

KREUTZLINGEN (Abbey).

Arms : *Per pale, Argent a cross gules ; impaling, Gules,
a pastoral staff with its sudarium argent.*

This Augustinian monastery, which is in proximity
to the city of CONSTANZ, was founded in the year 1120

by IDALRIC, Count of KYBURG ; and ULRICH, Count of
DILLIGEN, Bishop of CONSTANCE.

MURBACH AND LUDERS (United Princely-Abbacies).

Arms : *Per pale :* (a) *Argent, a hound saliant sable,
collared or, ringed gules,* Abbey of MURBACH ; (b)
*Gules, issuing from the base a cubit arm in pale,
habited in a sleeve of ashen grey, the hand proper
in the Act of Benediction,* Abbey of LUDERS.

The Benedictine Monastery of MURBACH in UPPER
ELSASS (one of the four " Imperial " Abbeys, *v.* p. 337),
is said to have been founded by EBERHARD, Duke of
SUABIA, ancestor of the family of the GUELPHS. The
dignity of Prince of the Empire appears to have been
conferred on the Abbot by the Emperor FERDINAND in
the year 1548. Although the Treaty of MÜNSTER
handed over Elsass to the French Monarchy, it was
expressly stipulated that the Abbeys of MURBACH and
LUDERS should continue to be fiefs held immediately
from the Empire.

The Abbey of LUDERS was founded by Queen BERT-
HILDIS, of Burgundy, and enriched by CLOTHAIR of
France.

Since the union of the abbeys, though both retained the
princely title, the Abbot, or administrator, had only a
single vote in the Diet. The precedence of the Abbot was
next to the Provost of ELWANGEN (who had the third
seat on the abbatial bench), and above the Provost of
BERCHTESGADEN. The precedency claimed (futilely)
was next after FULDA.

The crests, borne with the arms above given (which
were frequently quartered instead of being impaled),
were as follows:—Three princely helms of gold properly
mantled, on the central one *the abbatial mitre upon a
crimson cushion ;* on the dexter (for MURBACH) *out of a
crest-coronet or, a demi-hound saliant sable* (according to

German custom both in the crest and the arms, the hound faces the centre helm, or the central line of the shield (see *A Treatise on Heraldry*, pp. 220, and 604.) The sinister crest is, *Out of a golden crest-coronet an arm and blessing hand*, as in the arms of LUDERS.

OCHSENHAUSEN (Abbey).

Arms : *Or, on a mount vert an ox gules issuant from a house on the sinister proper, roofed of the third.*

This Benedictine Abbey in the old Diocese of CONSTANCE was originally founded by three brothers, Barons of WOLFHARTSCHWEND, as a cell of the Abbey of S. BLAIZE. In 1420 Pope MARTIN V. made it an independent Abbey. The Abbot occupied the third place among the prelates who voted in the Swabian circle, but the Abbey was not princely.

PETERSHAUSEN (Abbey).

Arms : *Per bend, azure and argent, in the first a key, in the second a fish, both bendways and counterchanged.*

The Benedictine Abbey of S. GREGORY at PETERSHAUSEN, near CONSTANCE, was founded in 983 by GEBHARD, Bishop of that See. The Abbot had the twelfth seat among the prelates who voted in the circle of SUABIA ; but was not a Prince.

PRUM (Princely-Abbey).

Arms : *Gules, on a mount in base vert a Paschal-Lamb regardant and holding its banner proper.*

The Benedictine Abbey of PRUM in the Ardennes was founded by the widowed BERTRADE, and her son CARIBERT, Count of LAON, in 720. King PEPIN married CARIBERT'S daughter, also named BERTHE, or BERTRADE ; and he and his successors largely endowed it. The Abbots were Princes of the Empire, but in the year 1579 the Abbey was united to the Electoral and Archi-episcopal See of TRIER (*vide ante*, p. 258).

ROGGENBERG (Abbey) (or ROCKENBURG) (not Princely).
Arms : *Gules, on a mount in base vert, a distaff in pale or, entwined with flax argent.*

The Premonstratensian Abbey of ROGGENBERG (or ROCKENBURG) was founded in the year 1226 by BERT-HOLD, Count of BIBERICH ; and his wife, a Countess of ZOLLERN. It was a Daughter-House of the great Abbey of WISPERG, and was situated near to Ulm.

SALMANSWEYER (or SALMONSCHWEILER) (Abbey).
Arms : *Sable, a bend counter-componé gules and argent bordered or (Orig. Cist.*, i., p. 50).

This Cistercian Abbey, a Daughter-House of MORI-MOND, was founded in the year 1137 by GONTRAN, Baron of ADELSREUTTE. Its possessions were much augmented by the splendid benefactions of the Emperors CONRAD III. and FREDERICK II. BURCHARD, Arch-bishop of SALZBURG and Papal-Legate, was counted its second founder. This was not a Princely abbey.

STABLO AND MALMEDY (united) (Princely Abbeys).
Arms : *Per pale, (a) Or, on a mount in base, and in front of a tree vert, a lamb passant argent, holding with its foot a crozier, or pastoral staff, in bend gules*, Abbey of STABLO. [But *see* RUDOLPHI, *Heraldica Curiosa*, p. 32, folio, Nürnberg, 1698 : " Die Abtey de Stablo führt einen beladenen Wolffe, welcher von dem Erbauer solches Closters, an statt des Esels, der bey solchem Bau gebraucht, und von dem Wolff verzehret worden, der Bau *Materialien* zuzutragen soll verdanunt, und auch deswegen zum Wappen solcher Abtey angenom-

men werden seyn" (BECHMAN, *Exerc. ii., de Insignibus*, § 68)]; (b) *Argent, on a mount in base vert, a dragon wings expanded sable.*

The Benedictine Abbey of STABLO, or STAVELOT, in the Diocese of LIÈGE, and forest of Ardennes, was founded about the year 650 by SIGEBERT, King of AUSTRASIA. He was also founder of the sister abbey of SS. PETER and PAUL at MALMEDY, distant from it only about two leagues. The Abbeys, which were sometimes distinct, sometimes under one head, were finally united in 1128; although STABLO was in the Diocese of LIÈGE, and MALMEDY in that of CÖLN. The Abbot was a Prince of the Empire; having, however, only one vote for the conjoint abbeys. He had also the title of Count DE LOGNE. The Monks of MALMEDY had abundance of oak bark from the forest of the Ardennes, and possessed some of the most flourishing tanneries in Europe.

WEINGARTEN (Abbey) (Princely-Abbey).
Arms: *Azure, semé of nenuphar leaves argent, over all a lion rampant or.*
The Benedictine Abbey of S. MARTIN was founded in the year 1053 by GUELPH I., Duke of BAVARIA.

WEISSEMBURG (Princely-Abbey).
Arms: *Gules, a castle reaching across the shield argent.*
The Benedictine Abbey of SS. PETER, PAUL, and STEPHEN in Lower Elsass, was founded about the year 623 by King DAGOBERT. It was one of the four abbeys (with FULDA, KEMPTEN, and MURBACH) which had the title of "Imperial." Its Abbots were created Princes of the Empire by the Emperor CHARLES IV.; and it is said were counted of ducal rank—but this appears doubtful. The abbey was secularised in the year 1526.

MONASTERIES FOR WOMEN.

ANDLAU (Princely-Abbacy).

Arms : *Argent, a bend wavy couped sable.* . (Plate II., fig. 3.)

The famous Benedictine Abbey for women was founded about the year 880, by the Empress RICHARDA of Scotland, the repudiated wife of CHARLES *le Gros.* She retired to it, and died there in 894. Pope LEO IX. visited it in 1049 and consecrated the church, newly built by the Abbess MATHILDA, sister of the Emperor CONRAD. The Abbess, who was a member of the circle of the Upper Rhine, received from the Emperor CHARLES V. in 1521, the title of Princess of the Holy Roman Empire, and voted by her deputy in the Diets. (On the Chapter, *vide infra*, Appendix B.) The charge of the arms is described in French blason as "*un crochet de sable.*"

BAINDT (Princely-Abbacy).

Arms : *Or, a bend wavy couped sable.*

The Cistercian Abbey of the Holy Trinity of BAINDT was founded in the year 1241 by CONRAD SCHENCK of WINTERSTETTEN, nephew of HEINRICH of TANNE and KÜSSENBERG, Bishop of CONSTANZ, in whose diocese it was situated, not far distant from the Abbey of WEINGARTEN. The Abbess had the rank of Princess of the Empire, occupying the last place on the Roll of Abbesses.

BUCHAU (Princely-Abbacy).

Arms : *Vert, a cross cousu gules, in the dexter canton the sun, in the sinister a crescent figured, both or.*

The Benedictine Abbey of BUCHAU in Suabia was founded at the close of the ninth century by ADELINDA, daughter of HILDEBRAND, Duke of SUABIA, and sister of CHARLEMAGNE'S second wife HILDEGARDE. ADE-

LINDA built the monastery near BIBERICH on the Lake of Constance in memory of her husband OTTO, Count of KESSELBURG, who, with his three sons, was slain in battle with the Huns. The Abbess had the rank of Princess of the Empire. She had a vote among the abbesses of the Circle of the Rhine, though the abbey was in Suabia. In · public ceremonials the naked sword of temporal dominion was borne before the abbess. (On the Chapter, *vide infra*, Appendix B.) The proof required was of sixteen quarters of Princely or Countly Nobility.

ELTEN, in the Duchy of Cleves, was founded in 970. The abbess had the title of Princess, and the proof required was of sixteen quarters.

ESSEN (Princely-Abbacy).
Arms : *Argent, a bend wavy couped sable.*
The Benedictine Abbey of ESSEN, or ASSINDE, in the Duchy of BERG and Diocese of CÖLN, was founded in the year 860 by ALTFRIED, who had been a monk at FULDA and CORVEY, and was Bishop of HILDESHEIM from 847 to 874. The Abbess was a Princess of the Empire. In its palmy days the abbey was so rich that it supported fifty-two nuns, and twenty canons. Subject to it were the daughter convents of RELINCKHAUSEN and STOCKEM-BERG. (On its Chapter, *vide infra*, Appendix B.) The proof was of sixteen quarters of Countly or Princely Nobility at ESSEN ; but at RELINCKHAUSEN and STOCKEMBERG, though sixteen quarters were shown, only eight of *Noblesse Militaire* had to be proved.

GANDERSHEIM (Princely-Abbacy).
Arms : *Per pale sable and or.*
This Benedictine Abbey for women, situated in the Duchy of Brunswick, was founded in the year 852 at BRUNSHAUSEN ; and was thence removed to GANDERS-

HEIM in the See of HILDESHEIM, by LUDOLPH, Duke
of SAXONY, and his wife ODA. Their three daughters
consecutively held the office of abbess. The Abbess
had the rank of Princess of the Empire. At the
Reformation the abbey became a noble Chapter of
Protestant canonesses (*vide infra*, Appendix B.). The
proof required was sixteen quarters of Princely or
Countly families.

GUTENZELL (Princely-Abbacy).
> Arms : *Argent, a bend counter-compony of the first and
> gules.*

This Cistercian House was founded in the year 1330,
near the city of Ulm, by two sisters, Countesses of
SCHLOSSBERG. It had at one time a population of
nearly two hundred choir-sisters, and as many serving-
sisters. By the eighteenth century these had dwindled
to under a dozen of each. The Abbess was Princess of
the Empire, and was included in the Circle of Suabia.
(On the Chapter *see* Appendix B.) (*Orig. Cist.*, i., p. 57.)

HEGGENBACH, or HECKBACH (Princely-Abbacy).
> Arms : *Sable, a bend counter-compony argent and gules.*

The Cistercian Monastery for women at HEGGEN-
BACH in the Diocese of CONSTANCE was founded by two
Béguines, one of the family of ROSEMBURG, the other
of that of LAUDENBURG, in the year 1233. At one
time it had as many as a hundred and twenty nuns.
The Abbess, who had a seat in the Circle of Swabia, was a
Princess of the Empire.

HERFORD (HERVORDEN) (Princely-Abbey).
> Arms : *Argent, a fess gules.*

The foundation of this Benedictine monastery, which
is situated in the County of RAVENSBERG, is attributed
to LOUIS *le Debonnaire* about the year 822. Others

ascribed it to VALDGER of DORENBERG who descended from a secretary of WITEKIND. The Abbess had the rank of Princess of the Empire, and a vote among the Prelates of the Circle of the Rhine. At the Reformation in the sixteenth century the abbey (which apparently had ceased for some centuries to be governed by the strict Benedictine rule) became a Protestant noble Chapter (*vide post*, Appendix B.). The proofs required were sixteen quarters of Princely or Countly families.

LINDAU (LINDAW) (Princely-Abbey).
   Arms : *Gules, a right hand appaumé in pale proper.*

This abbey followed the Benedictine rule for nuns, and was originally built in the year 841 at NONNEN-HORN on Lake Constance. Its founders were the Counts ADALBERT, MANGOLD, and UDALRIC. The original foundation was for an abbess and twelve nuns. The monastery at NONNENHORN was ruined by the Huns in the tenth century; and a new home was found on one of the islands at LINDAU, around which a town soon sprung up. The Abbess had very early the rank and prerogatives of a Princess of the Holy Roman Empire, and the naked sword of temporal jurisdiction was borne before her on solemn occasions. The arms are usually represented with the figures of the BLESSED VIRGIN and HOLY CHILD above the shield. (On the Chapter of LINDAU *vide post*, Appendix B.)

QUEDLIMBURG (Princely-Abbacy).
   Arms : *Gules, two pruning knives in saltire argent handled or.*

This Benedictine Abbey for women was founded by the Emperor HENRY, *the Fowler*, in recognition of his successes over the Huns. It was completed by his wife MATILDA. Their son the Emperor OTTO largely endowed it, and his sister MATILDA became its first abbess. The Emperors of the Saxon line were ·its advocates or protectors ; a dignity which probably passed on their extinction to the house of ANHALT-BRANDENBURG.

The Abbess had the rank of Princess of the Empire, and held immediately from the Emperor. The confession of Augsburg was adopted by the then Abbess ANNA VON STOLBERG. (On the Chapter, *vide infra*, Appendix B.)

The Abbess SOPHIA, a Princess of the Palatinate, who ruled the abbey from 1645 to 1680, bore her arms in a lozenge : *Quarterly, per saltire :* 1. (In chief) *Sable, a lion rampant or, crowned gules* (the PALATINATE) ; impaling BAVARIA, *Fusilly bendy argent and azure.* 2 and 3. (In flanks) *Argent, a lion rampant azure, crowned or* (County of VELDENTZ). 4. (In base) *Chequy argent and gules* (County of SPANHEIM). *Over all, in an escucheon en surtout the arms of* QUEDLIMBURG, as above. The crosier is placed in pale behind the shield.

NIEDER-MUNSTER (Princely-Abbey).

> Arms : *Gules, a crosier in pale argent surmounted in fess by the letter* N.

This monastery at RATISBON (which must be distinguished from the NIEDER-MUNSTER, or BAS-MOUSTIER, in the Diocese of STRASBURG) is said to owe its foundation to JUDITH, daughter of ARNULF, Duke of BAVARIA, and wife of HENRY, Duke of BAVARIA, son of the Emperor HENRY, *the Fowler.* The Abbess had rank among the Prelates of the Lower Rhine.

OBER-MUNSTER (Princely-Abbey).

> Arms : *Azure, nine fleurs-de-lis or, three, three, three.*

The Upper Monastery at RATISBON was founded about the middle of the ninth century, by EMMA, wife of the Emperor CHARLES, *le Gros*, and of LOUIS, *the German.* Like the Abbess of NIEDER-MUNSTER, the

Abbess of this foundation had a seat among the prelates in the Circle of the Lower Rhine.

ROTHEN-MÜNSTER (Princely-Abbey).

Arms: *Gules, a column or between two horns of a stag paleways, each of six points* (the scalp sometimes appears below the column).

This Cistercian Abbey for women took its origin from a small religious house named HOHENMAUREN, near ROTWEIL in the Black Forest, where some pious women lived in community under the authority of an abbess, who is variously named WILLIBURGA, and EMMA, wife of a Baron of WILDENWERCK. About the year 1126 she was warned by a heavenly voice to remove her house; and committing herself to the guidance of the ass on which she rode, they finally stopped at HOLBEINS-BACH, where she purchased the site for a new religious house from the Canons of ST STEPHEN of Constance. The Abbess had her place among the prelates of the Bench of Suabia.

REMIREMONT (Princely-Abbey).

Arms:

This abbey was founded in the year 620 by S. ROMA-RIC, a noble of the Court of CLOTHAIR. He had divided nearly all his possessions between the poor and the Abbey of LUXEUIL; and finally consecrated to the service of GOD his own chateau in the Vosges, which he converted into a double monastery, under the Rule of S. COLUMBAN. It became Benedictine in the reign of LOUIS *le Debonnaire*. The nuns were divided into seven courses, each of twelve sisters, and they kept up a perpetual service. The abbey was afterwards converted into a Noble-Chapter of *chanoinesses*, to the number of ninety-eight, who were only bound by vows so long as they were resident. The Abbess had the rank of Princess of the Empire since the year 1290. (On the Chapter, *vide infra*, Appendix B.) REMIREMONT is in the Vosges on the river MOSELLE in the Diocese of ST. DIÉ.

S. HAIMERAN, OR S. EMERAN (Abbey).

Arms : *Quarterly of eight* (in two horizontal rows each of four quarters) ; 1 and 8. *Or, an eagle displayed dimidiated and conjoined to the palar line sable ;* 2 and 7. *Azure, three fleurs-de-lis argent ;* 3 and 6. *Argent, a palm branch in pale vert ;* 4 and 5. *Gules, a key in pale, wards in chief* (and turned to the exterior of the shield) *argent.* (SIEBMACHER, *Wappenbuch*, i., 12.)

The Monastery of S. HAIMERAN at RATISBON was founded about the close of the seventh century in honour of the patron saint of the city. A small chapel which contained the relics of the martyr was converted by Duke THEODORE of BAVARIA into a church, around which the monastery gradually grew up. Here the seat of one of the four Bavarian Bishops was originally placed, but it was afterwards transferred to the Church of S. STEPHEN. The possessions of the monastery were held immediately from the Emperor ; and consequently PRAUN appears to assign to the Abbot the dignity of Prince of the Empire ; SIEBMACHER places S. HAIMERAN among the " Befürste und Befreÿte Abteyen."

The same plate contains the arms of two Commanderies, the first those of FÜRSTENFELD VON MÖLLING. *Per pale ;* (a) *Gules, a plain cross argent*, the arms of the ORDER OF ST. JOHN ; (b) *Sable, a cross-moline argent* (perhaps *intended* for the cross of the Order).

The other is the coat borne for the Commandery of LECH VON SONTAG in the TEUTONIC ORDER. It consists of the full arms of the Order, viz. ; *Argent, a cross sable, thereon a narrow cross flory or, on an escucheon en surtout of the last, an eagle displayed of the second* (the arms of the German KINGDOM).

ECCLESIASTICAL PRINCIPALITIES IN POLAND.

CRACOW (Principality) AND SÉVÉRIE (Duchy).

In 1243 BOLESLAS V. conferred the rank of Prince on the Bishops of CRACOW, as a reward for the services rendered by Bishop PRANDOTA DE BIALOCZEW during the invasion of Cracow and Sandomir by CONRAD, Duke of MASOVIE. In 1443 ZBIGNIEW OLESNIÇKI, Cardinal and Prince-Bishop of CRACOW, bought for his See the Duchy of SÉVÉRIE from the Duke of TESCHEN.

The County of KOZIEGLOWY was also the property of the Bishops of CRACOW.

LOWICZ.

The Principality of LOWICZ was conferred on the Archbishop of GNESEN, and his successors, by Duke CONRAD II. of MASOVIE, as an expiation of the murder of the Chancellor JEAN CZAPLA in 1240.

PULTUSK.

The Bishops of PLOÇK were Princes of PULTUSK.

SIELUN.

This Principality was the appanage of the senior Canon of the Cathedral of PLOÇK.

VARMIE.

This Bishopric, erected in 1241, held the secular Principality of the same name.

CHAPTER V.

ARMS OF ABBEYS AND OTHER RELIGIOUS HOUSES IN GREAT BRITAIN.

THE list of arms here subjoined, as borne by Monastic Institutions in England, makes no pretence to completeness.. In the case of many of the less important foundations no satisfactory evidence of their use of regular arms can be adduced.

ABBOTSBURY (Dorsetshire) (Benedictine Abbey).
  Founded *c.* 1026, dedicated to S. PETER.
  Arms : *Azure, three sets of two keys addorsed paleways, bows interlaced, wards in chief.*

ABINGDON (Berkshire) (Benedictine Abbey).
  Arms : *Argent, a cross patonce between four martlets sable.* (Seal of WILLIAM, Abbot in 1371. On that of JOHN SANTE, D.D., Abbot, Ambassador from England to the Roman See, the cross in the arms is *patée.*) (*Cat. of Seals in Brit. Mus.*, Nos. 2544, 2545.)

The abbey was dedicated to S. MARY, and is said to have been founded by CISSA, as early as the year 675, at Shrovisham which afterwards was called after the abbey. In 947 King EDRED rebuilt CISSA'S Abbey and set over it S. ETHELWOLD, afterwards Bishop of WINCHESTER.

ALVINGHAM (Lincolnshire) (Gilbertine Priory dedicated to S. MARY).
  Arms : *Argent, three bars gules, over all a crosier in bend of the first headed or.*

AMESBURY (Wiltshire).

Benedictine Monastery for women, founded towards the close of the tenth century by Queen ELFRIDA, in expiation of the murder of her step-son EDWARD in 978. Arms.?

ASHBRIDGE (Bucks) (Augustinian Friars).

Founded by EDMUND, son of RICHARD Earl of CORNWALL, in 1283.

> Arms : *Gules, on an altar, a Paschal-Lamb proper resting its foot on an orb or; in base a lion rampant.* . . .
> (See *Cat. of Seals, Brit. Mus.*, No. 2569.)

ATHELNEY (Somerset) (Benedictine Abbey).

A seal of the abbey given in *Cat. of Seals in Brit. Mus.*, No. 2571 bears two shields of arms ; (a) . . . *a bugle horn between three crowns* . . . ; (b) *Quarterly*, 1 and 4. . . . *three crowns in pale* . . . ; 2 and 3. . . . *a cross patée-throughout.* . . . (DUGDALE, *Mon. Angl.*, vol. ii., p. 402.)

ATHERSTON (Warwickhire) (Friary).

> Arms : *Or, three piles in point gules, a canton ermine ;* the arms of BASSETT.

AXHOLM (Lincolnshire) (Carthusian Priory).

The seal of the house bore the arms of THOMAS MOWBRAY, Earl of NOTTINGHAM, afterwards Duke of NORFOLK, 1395 :—*Gules, a lion rampant argent.* In the base on a separate shield the coat of BROTHERTON :— ENGLAND, *a label argent* (*Cat. of Seals in Brit. Mus.*, No. 2574.)

AYLESFORD (Kent) (Carmelite Priory).

> Arms : Those of the founder RICHARD Lord GREY of CODNOR 1240, *Argent, three bars azure.* (Pro-

2 A

perly, *Barry of six argent and azure.*) (*Cat. of Seals in Brit. Mus.*, No. 2577.)

BANBURY (Leper Hospital of S. JOHN).
Arms: . . . *a cross-patriarchal fitchée.*

BARDNEY (Lincolnshire) (Benedictine Abbey).

This house was already existing in the seventh century. Its importance was increased by the enshrinement there of the body of S. OSWALD, killed in 642 in battle with the Mercian King PENDA. The relics were given by OSFRIDA, niece of S. OSWALD, and wife of ETHELRED, King of MERCIA, who, after a reign of twenty-seven years, himself embraced the monastic state and became Abbot of BARDNEY. The Abbey was sacked and destroyed in 870 by the Danes, who are said to have put to death 300 monks. The relics of S. OSWALD were removed to the Abbey of S. PETER at Gloucester. BARDNEY was rebuilt by WILLIAM the CONQUEROR.

The arms, which appear on several seals of the abbots of the fourteenth and fifteenth centuries, were : (*Gules*) *a cross patée* (or *flory*) *between four lions rampant* (*or*). (*Cat. of Seals in Brit. Mus.*, Nos. 2582, 2586.) These are attributed by mediæval Heralds to S. OSWALD, King of NORTHUMBERLAND. (They are those of NOSTELL.)

BARKING (Essex) (Benedictine Nunnery).

This house is said to owe its foundation to S. ERKONWALD, in the year 665, who made his sister S. ETHELBURGA its first abbess. In later times the house was a double foundation (for monks and nuns). It was suppressed by HENRY VIII.

Arms· *Azure, in chief three lilies, in base as many roses two and one, argent; all within a bordure gules semé of bezants* (or *plates*). (EDMONDSON, *Heraldry.*)

BARNSTAPLE (Devon) (Cluniac Priory of S. MARY MAGDALENE).
Arms : *Gules, a bend or, in chief a label argent.*

BASINGWERK (Flintshire) (Cistercian Abbey).
Founded in 1131 by RANULPH, Earl of CHESTER.
Arms : *Argent, on a cross engrailed vert five mullets or* (*Harl.* MS., 1928-35) (*Orig. Cist.* i., p. 99).

BATTLE (Sussex) (Benedictine Abbey of HOLY TRINITY).
Arms : *Argent, on a cross gules a mitre between two royal crowns in pale and as many orbs in fess proper.* (Four swords appear to have been sometimes substituted for the orbs.)

BEAULIEU, BEWLEY, BEAULY (Hampshire) (Cistercian Priory).
This monastery was founded in 1203 by King JOHN, and dedicated in the year 1249 to the honour of the Blessed Virgin Mary (*Orig. Cist.,* i., p. 210.)
Arms : *Gules, a crosier in pale enfiled with a royal crown or, all within a bordure sable, billetty of the second.*
It must be noted that the *bordure* does not appear on the seal of the priory in the fifteenth century (*Cat. of Seals in Brit. Mus.,* No. 2621). TANNER makes the field *Quarterly argent and gules;* and charges the bordure with bezants.

BEC (Norfolk) (Hospital of S. THOMAS at Billingford).
Arms : Those of WILLIAM DE BEC, its founder temp. HENRY III. (*Gules*), *a cross-moline* (*ermine*) (*Cat. of Seals in Brit. Mus.,* No. 2625.)

BEIGHAM, or BAŸHAM (Sussex) (Premonstratensian Abbey of S. MARY at Lamberhurst.).

Arms: A seal of Abbot JOHN CHETEHAM in 1426 bears a shield charged with *in chief a lion passant, in base a crosier, on the sinister side two lozenges in pale.* (*Cat. of Seals in Brit. Mus.,* No. 2630.)

BERMONDSEY (Surrey) (Cluniac Abbey of ST. SAVIOUR).

This house was founded by ALWYN in 1082.

Arms: *Per pale, gules and azure, a bordure argent.* Sometimes there is added to this: *Over all a lion passant (gardant) holding a pastoral staff enfiled with a mitre or, and the bordure is charged with eight letters P sable.*

BEVERLEY (Yorkshire) (Benedictine Abbey).

The Abbey was founded about the commencement of the eighth century by S. JOHN of BEVERLEY, who became Bishop of HEXHAM and Archbishop of YORK, and finally retired to the abbey where he died. It was a double foundation, *i.e.,* it had religious of both sexes. The abbey was largely enriched by the patronage of HENRY V., who attributed the victory of AGINCOURT (Oct. 25, 1415), to the aid of S. JOHN of BEVERLEY.

Arms: *Argent, a crosier in pale sable enfiled with a royal crown or; all within a bordure of the second billetty of the third* (EDMONDSON'S *Heraldry* makes the *bordure bezantée,* and probably correctly).

BILEIGH (Essex).

Arms: According to TANNER this priory bore: *Azure, six fleurs-de-lis, three, two, and one, argent.*

BINDON (Dorset) (Cistercian Abbey of S. MARY).

This house was founded about the year 1172 by WM. DE GLASTON; and, later, by ROBERT DE NEWBURGH (*Orig. Cist.*, i., p. 167).

Arms: *Or, a cross engrailed sable* (the arms of MOHUN).

BIRKENHEAD (Chester) (Benedictine Priory).

Arms: *Quarterly gules and or, over all a crosier erect proper, in the first quarter a lion of* ENGLAND.

BITLESDEN, BITTLESDEN, or BETLESDEN (Buckinghamshire) (Cistercian Abbey of SS. MARY and NICOLAS).

Founded by Sir ARNOLD DU BOIS in the year 1147.

Arms, those of the founder: *Argent, two bars and a canton gules*. (According to the *Cat. of Seals in Brit Mus.*, No. 2657), this coat is wrongly given on a fourteenth century seal as a *fess* and *quarter*.

BODMIN (Cornwall) (Benedictine Priory of SS. MARY and PETER).

Arms: On a seal of the priory in the fifteenth century the arms are: . . .. *three fishes naiant in pale* . . . (*Cat. of Seals in Brit. Mus.*, No. 2677), but the coat usually assigned to it is: *Or, on a chevron azure between three lion's heads vert* (*purpure* according to EDMONDSON) *as many annulets of the first*, which appear to have been borne by the Priory at S. GERMANS.

BOLTON (Yorkshire) (Priory of Carmelites).

Arms: *Gules, a cross patonce vair*.

BORDESLEY (Worcestershire) (Cistercian Abbey of S. MARY).

This abbey was founded in 1138 by the Empress MATILDA, daughter of King HENRY I., and widow of

the Emperor HENRY V. (She afterwards married GEOF-
FREY PLANTAGENET, Count of ANJOU.) RICHARD I.
increased its possessions.

> Arms : These are doubtful, but on a seal of Abbot
> WILLIAM HALFORD about the year 1465, appears
> a shield of arms described in *Cat. of Seals in Brit.*
> *Mus.*, No. 2684, as bearing : *Quarterly*, I and 4.
> *Five crosses-crosslets in saltire;* 2 and 3. ENGLAND.
> Another shield bears the arms of BEAUCHAMP :
> *Gules, a fess between six crosses-crosslets or.*

If this be correctly given the arms which appear in the
first shield may possibly be those of the foundation.
I have not myself seen the seal, but I have a suspicion
that the *crosslets* in the first and fourth quarters are
only badly drawn or worn impressions of *fleurs-de-lis*,
and that the shield may simply be, Quarterly of FRANCE-
ANCIENT and ENGLAND.

BOXLEY (Kent) (Cistercian Abbey).

> Founded (*c.* 1145) by WILLIAM D'YPRES, Earl of
> KENT (JANAUSCHEK, *Orig. Cist.*, i., p. 91).

> Arms : *Argent, three* (or *five*) *lozenges conjoined in bend-
> sinister gules, on a canton of the last a crosier in
> pale or.*

BRIDLINGTON (Yorkshire) (Priory of Augustinian
Canons dedicated to S. MARY).

> Arms : *Per pale sable and argent, three letters* B *counter-
> changed, two and one.*

BROMER, BROMERE or BROMME (Hampshire) (Priory of
Augustinian Canons).

> Arms : *Gules, a sword in pale proper, hilt in base or,
> surmounted by two keys in saltire, wards in chief,
> the dexter of the second, the sinister argent.*

BROMHOLME (Norfolk) (Cluniac Priory of S. ANDREW).
  Arms: *Argent, on a cross (patriarchal) within a
  bordure or, a similar cross sable.*

BRUTON (Somerset) (Augustinian Abbey).
  Arms: *Gules, a maunch ermine, issuant therefrom a hand
  proper holding a fleur-de-lis or.* (Otherwise, *Or, a
  cross engrailed sable*, MOHUN.)

BUCKENHAM (Norfolk) (Priory).
  Arms: *Argent, three escallops sable.*
  This house was founded about 1146, by WILLIAM
  D'ALBINI, Earl of ARUNDEL, and his wife Queen
  ADELINA, widow of King HENRY I.

BUCKFASTRE, or BUCKFASTLEIGH (Devon) (Cistercian
  Abbey of S. MARY).
  This house was founded in 1136 (*Orig. Cist.*, i., p. 103).
  Arms: *Sable, a pastoral staff in pale or, enfiled by a
  buck's head caboshed argent* (or *of the second*).

BUCKLAND (Devon) (Cistercian Abbey of SS. MARY
  and BENEDICT) (*Orig. Cist.*, i., p. 261).
  Arms: *Per pale* (otherwise *Quarterly*) *argent and gules,
  a crosier in bend or.*
  On a fifteenth century seal (*Brit. Mus. Cat.*, No. 2749),
  the shield bears: *Or, a lion rampant azure*, being the
  arms of AMICIA DE REDVERS, Countess of DEVON, who
  founded the abbey in 1278. (She was the daughter of
  GILBERT DE CLARE, Earl of GLOUCESTER). Her
  daughter ISABELLA DE FORTIBUS, Countess of ALBE-
  MARLE, enlarged in 1291 her mother's foundation.

BURCESTER (Oxford) (Augustinian Priory of ST.
  EDBURGA).
  Arms: *Barry nebuly of six . . . and . . .* (See
  Cat. of Seals in Brit. Mus., No. 2773.)

BURNHAM (Buckinghamshire) (Augustinian Abbey of
S. MARY).
Arms: *Or* (or *gules*), *on a chief argent three lozenges
gules.* (See. *Cat. of Seals in Brit. Mus.,* No. 2776.)

BURSCOUGH (Lancaster) (Priory of Augustinian Canons).
Arms: *Per fess indented . . . and . . . in chief
two crosiers between three annulets . . .*

BURTON-ON-TRENT (Staffordshire) (Benedictine Abbey).
This house was founded about the middle of the
eleventh century by WILFRIC, servant of King
ETHELRED.
Arms: *Or, on a cross engrailed azure five mullets
pierced sable.*

BURTON ST. LAZARUS (BURTON LIZARS) (Leicestershire).
This was the chief Hospital of the Order of S. LAZARUS
in England.
Arms: *Per pale* (a) *Gules, a lion rampant argent;*
(b) *Argent, a cross gules.* The dexter impalement
commemorates the founder, ROGER DE MOWBRAY
(*Brit. Mus. Cat. of Seals,* No. 2789).

BURY ST. EDMUNDS (Suffolk) (Benedictine Abbey).
This abbey was founded about the year 1020 by King
CANUTE in honour of the martyred ST. EDMUND, King
of the East Angles; and replaced the little wooden
church which had been built over his grave.
Arms: *Azure, three open crowns, each enfiling a pair of
arrows in saltire, or.*
On the seal of RICHARD DE INSULA, Abbot (1223-
1234) only one crown enfiling a single arrow appears
(*Cat. of Seals in Brit. Mus.,* No. 2803). On that of
SIMON DE LUTON, Abbot, 1257-1279, No. 2804, there is

only a single arrow surmounted by a crown. On that of JOHN MELFORD, Abbot in 1517, is a shield with three crowns. On the seal of JOHN MUNK, Receiver of the Castle Ward in 1438, a shield of arms bears two arrows in saltire, enfiled by a coronet of fleurs-de-lis and pearls; while on that of Receiver THOMAS EDON in 1454 the shield is charged with the arms of ST. EDMUND, *three crowns* (without the arrows) *within an engrailed bordure* (*Brit. Mus. Cat. of Seals*, Nos. 2808, 2815).

BYLAND (Yorkshire) (Cistercian Abbey of S. MARY).

This Abbey was founded in the year 1134, by ROGER DE MOWBRAY (*Orig. Cist.*, i., p. 104).

Arms: *Gules, a lion rampant argent* (MOWBRAY) *debruised by a crutch, or pilgrim's staff, in bend.* (See *The Herald and Genealogist*, ii., p. 193.)

CALDER (Cumberland).

Arms: *Argent three escucheons ;* 1. *Or, a fess between two chevrons gules* (FITZWALTER) ; 2. *Gules, three luces hauriant argent* (LUCY); 3. *Sable, a fret argent* (FLEMING).

These coats are those of the families who contributed to the aggrandisement of the abbey (*See* MOULE, *Heraldry of Fish.*, p. 54 ; and Plate I., fig. 11, of this book).

CAMPSEY (Suffolk) (Augustinian Nunnery of S. MARY).

Arms: *Per pale:* (a) . . . *a cross lozengy* . . . (b) . . . (*diapered, or lozengy ?*) *a chief dancetty* . . . (See *Cat. of Seals in Brit. Mus.*, No. 2830.)

This Nunnery was founded in 1199, by THEOBALD DE VALOINES.

CANTERBURY (Benedictine Abbey of ST. AUGUSTINE).

Arms: (*Azure*) *two keys in saltire* (*or*). (See *Cat. of*

Seals in Brit. Mus., No. 2846.) Otherwise: *Sable, a cross argent, in the first quarter the* pallium *and staff from the arms of the See.*

CANTERBURY ; ST. GREGORY.
　Arms : *Per chevron sable and argent in chief two mullets pierced of the second ; in base an open crown proper* (otherwise *a chough proper*).

CANTERBURY ; BLACK-FRIARS.
　Arms : *Azure, on a cross argent between four mitres or the letters* ⅟x (but ?).

• CANTERBURY ; CHRISTCHURCH (now Cathedral) (Benedictine) (*v.* p. 198).
　Arms : *Azure, on a cross argent the letters* ⅟x *sable.*
　Founded in 597 by S. AUGUSTINE.

CARLISLE (Priory) (*See Bishopric* of CARLISLE, *ante* p. 193 ; and *Deanery,* p. 198).
　Arms : *Argent, a cross sable.*

CARMARTHEN (?) (Priory).
　Arms : *Azure, a dove holding an olive branch proper.*

CARTMEL (Lancashire) (Priory of Augustinian Canons).
　Arms : *Per pale or and vert, a lion rampant gules.*
　The arms of the founder, BIGOT, Earl MARSHAL.

CASTLE-ACRE (Norfolk) (Cluniac Priory of S. MARY).
　Arms : *Argent, a cross chequy of the field and azure, between twelve crosses-crosslets fitchées sable.*

CASTLE-HEDINGHAM.
　Arms : *Argent, two long billets in saltire, the one gules; the other azure.*

CERNE (Dorset) (Benedictine Abbey of SS. MARY, PETER, and BENEDICT).

Arms: *Azure, a cross engrailed or, between four garden lilies argent slipped proper.* (See *Cat. of Seals in Brit. Mus.*, No. 2893.)

CHARLEY (Leicestershire) (Priory).

Arms: *Azure, a saltire between two open crowns in chief and base, and as many mitres in flanks, labelled or.*

CHERTSEY (Surrey) (Benedictine).

Arms: *Per pale or and argent, two keys addorsed in bend-sinister, their bows interlaced in base, the upper gules, the lower azure, enfiling a sword in bend proper, hilted gold.*

CHICHE, or ST. OSYTH'S (Essex) (Priory of Augustinian Canons).

Arms: *Or, three open crowns gules.* (See *Cat. of Seals in Brit. Mus.*, No. 2949.)

CIRENCESTER (Gloucester) (Mitred Abbey of Augustinian Canons).

Arms: *Argent, on a chevron gules three lamb's heads argent.* EDMONDSON gives: *Gules, on a chevron argent three ram's heads couped and affrontés sable, armed or, in dexter chief canton two lions of* ENGLAND.

CLEEVE (Somerset) (Cistercian Abbey of S. MARY).

Arms: . . . *seven lozenges,* 3. 3. 1. (See *Cat. of Seals in Brit. Mus.*, No. 2960.) (*Orig. Cist.*, i., p. 202).

COBHAM (Kent) (College of S. MARY MAGDALENE).

Founded by JOHN DE COBHAM in 1362.

Arms: *Gules, on a chevron or, three lions rampant sable.*

The arms of the founder (*Cat. of Seals in Brit. Mus.*, No. 2970).

COGGESHALL (Essex) (Cistercian Abbey of S. MARY).
This Abbey owed its foundation to King STEPHEN in 1139 (JANAUSCHEK, *Orig. Cist.*, i., p. 105).
    Arms : . . . *three cocks* . . . (*Cat. of Seals in Brit. Mus.*, No. 2972).

COLCHESTER (Essex) (Mitred Abbey of Benedictines).
The Abbey was dedicated to S. JOHN the Baptist.
    Arms : On its seal in 1422 the arms are given thus: (*Argent*) *a cross* (*gules*) *within a bordure* (*or*), *over all an escarbuncle* (*sable*) (*Cat. of Seals in Brit. Mus.*, No. 2980, 2981).

COMBE (Warwick) (Cistercian Abbey of S. MARY).
Founded in 1150, by WILLIAM DE CAMVILLE (*Orig. Cist.* i., p. 121).
    Arms : ENGLAND, *in chief a label of five points.* On a thirteenth century seal the shield is supported by two lions (*Cat. of Seals in Brit. Mus.*, No. 2989).

COMBERMERE (Chester) (Cistercian Abbey of S. MARY and S. MICHAEL). Founded in 1133. (*Orig. Cist.*, i., p. 100.)
    Arms : *Quarterly or and gules, a bend sable, over all a crosier of the first in pale.*

COTTINGHAM (Yorkshire) (Priory of Augustinian Canons).
Founded by Sir THOMAS WAKE of LYDEL, in 1332, in honour of the BLESSED VIRGIN, and SS. PETER and PAUL. The seal (described in *Cat. of Seals in Brit. Mus.*, No. 3004), has on it three shields : One *Barry of twelve* . . . *and* . . . ; another of the arms of the founder : *Or, two bars gules, in chief three torteaux ;* and another ; . . ., *a cross patonce* . . .

COVERHAM (Yorkshire) (White Friars).
Arms : *Or, a chief indented azure* (BUTLER).

COVENHAM (Lincoln).
Arms : *Gules, a saltire argent* (NEVILLE).

CROXDEN (Staffordshire) (Cistercian Abbey of S. MARY).
Founded by BERTRAND DE VERDON about the year
1176, and endowed by HENRY II. (*Orig. Cist.*, i., p. 176).
Arms : (*Or*), *fretty* (*gules*) (*Cat. of Seals in Brit. Mus.*,
No. 3014).

CROXTON (Leicester) Premonstratensian Abbey of S.
JOHN the Evangelist.
Arms : *Or, a bend between six martlets sable* (LOTEREL).

CROYLAND (Lincoln) (Benedictine Abbey of S.
GUTHLAC).
This celebrated abbey was founded early in the eighth
century by ETHELBALD, King of Mercia, in honour of
the hermit S. GUTHLAC, who had predicted his attain-
ment of the regal dignity. The abbey was burnt by the
Danes in 870, but was restored by EDRED'S Chancellor,
THORKETIL.
Arms : *Quarterly*, 1 and 4. *Gules, three knives paleways in fess argent, handled or ; 2 and 3. Azure,
three scourges paleways in fess, each having three
lashes or. Or : Gules, a cross flory or, within a
bordure azure, thereon eight crosses-crosslets argent.*

DARLEY, or DERLEY (Derby) (Augustinian Priory).
Arms : *Argent, six horse-shoes sable, nailed or.*

DEREHAM, or West Deerham (Norfolk) (Premonstratensian Canons of S. MARY).
Arms : *Azure, three crosiers, two and one, each enfiled*

by a deer's head caboshed or. But the seal of
JOHN DE ROCHAM, Abbot in 1329, has on it two
or three shields (1) *Barry argent and azure an
orle of martlets gules, dimidiating* S. POL : *Gules,
three pallets vair on a chief or.* (2) *Or, a maunch
gules* (HASTINGS). In base (? in a shield) *a stag's
head caboshed* for DEERHAM. (*Cat. of Seals in
Brit. Mus.*, No. 3054.)

DIEULACRES (Staffordshire) (Cistercian Abbey of SS.
MARY and BENEDICT).
This abbey was founded, *circa* 1155, at PULTON, by
ROBERT THE BUTLER, in order that prayers might be
made for the deliverance of his master RANULF, Earl
of CHESTER, at that time held in prison by the King.
RANULF increased its possessions and transferred it to
DIEULACRES. (*Orig. Cist.*, i., p. 142.)
Arms : *Sable* (? *Azure*), *three garbs or, over all a pastoral
staff proper.*

·DOVER (Kent) (Benedictine Priory of S. MARTIN).
Arms : *Sable, a cross* (*argent*) *between four leopard's
heads or.* (*See* the seal of ROBERT, the Prior, in
1345, *Cat. of Seals in Brit. Mus.*, No. 3068.)

DRAX (York) (Priory of Augustinian Canons of S.
NICHOLAS).
Arms : *Argent, on a fess gules between three drakes
proper a rose of the first* (or *or*).

DUNKESWELL (Devon) (Cistercian Abbey of S. MARY).
Arms : (*Gules*), *two bendlets wavy* (*or*), for WILLIAM
BRIWERE, the founder, in 1201 (*Orig. Cist.*, i.,
p. 206) (*Cat. of Seals in Brit. Mus.*, No. 3078.)

DUNMOW (Essex) (Priory of Augustinian Canons of S. Mary).

Arms : *Sable, a cross argent between four mullets or (? argent).* (*Cat. of Seals in Brit. Mus.*, No. 3082.)

DUNSTABLE (Bedfordshire) (Priory of Augustinian Canons, dedicated to S. PETER).

Arms : *Argent, on a pile sable a horse-shoe fastened by a staple to its centre point or.*

EASBY (Yorkshire) (Premonstratensian Abbey of S. AGATHA).

Arms : *Azure, a bend or* (SCROPE) ; *over all a pastoral staff in bend-sinister proper* (Plate I., fig. 8).

EDINGTON or HEDINGTON (Wiltshire) (Priory of Augustinian Friars).

Arms : *Or, on a cross engrailed gules five cinquefoils (or roses) argent* (otherwise *of the field*).

EGLESTON.

Arms : *Gules, three escallops argent* (arms of DACRE).

ELSYNG (London) (Priory and Hospital, Cripplegate).

Arms : *Gules, a lion rampant barry argent and sable.*

ELY (Cambridge) (Benedictine Nunnery of S. ETHEL-REDA).

Founded in 672 by S. ETHELREDA, a Princess of the East Angles, as a double monastery (*i.e.* for both sexes). It was destroyed by the Danes in 870, but was rebuilt a century later by S. ETHELWOLD, Bishop of WIN-CHESTER. The See of ELY was founded in 1108. (*Vide ante*, p. 180.)

Arms : *Gules, three open crowns or.*

The arms of the Priory are given as : *Or, three keys erect azure, two and one, wards in chief* (v. p. 198).

EVESHAM (Worcestershire) (Benedictine Abbey of
S. MARY, and S. ECGWINE, Bishop).
This abbey was founded before the year 718 by
S. ECGWINE, Bishop of WORCESTER, whose name was
afterwards joined in the dedication.
Arms: *Azure, a chain in chevron couped and padlocked
at one end, between three mitres, all argent.*

EWELME (Oxford) (Hospital).
The common seal bore the impaled arms of the
founders: (a) *Azure, a fess between three leopard's
faces or,* for WILLIAM DE LA POLE, Duke of
SUFFOLK; and (b) . . *a lion rampant queue
fourchée* for (ALICE CHAUCER?) his wife, 1437.
(See *Cat. of Seals in Brit. Mus.*, No. 3120.)

FAVERSHAM, or FEVERSHAM (Kent) (Benedictine
Abbey).
Founded in 1148 by King STEPHEN, confirmed and
enlarged by HENRY II. and his successors.
Arms: ENGLAND *dimidiated, and impaling: Azure,
three ships without masts, also dimidiated argent*
(being together the arms of the CINQUE-PORTS),
differenced by a crosier proper on the palar line.

FLIXTON (Suffolk) (Augustinian Priory of SS. MARY
and CATHARINE).
Arms: *Azure* (or *Gules*), *a Catharine wheel with a
cross-Calvary projecting from it in chief argent.*

FOUNTAINS (Yorkshire) (Cistercian Abbey of S. MARY).
Founded about the year 1132 by S. ROBERT, and
other Benedictine monks of York. About ten years later
the Cistercian rule was adopted. (*Orig. Cist.*, i., p. 37.)
Arms: *Azure, three horse-shoes or.* (A chevron,
sometimes charged with crosses-patées, is occasionally inserted in the blasons of this coat.)

FRITHELSTOKE (Devon) (Augustinian Priory).
Arms : *Vairy argent and sable.*

FURNESS (Lancaster) (Cistercian Abbey of S. MARY).
Arms : *Sable, on a pale argent a crozier of the first.*
(Another coat, *Sable, a bend chequy argent and azure,* is given in TONGE, *Visitation,* etc. Surtees Society. The last tincture is probably *gules* (*cf.* p. 414).
The abbey was founded by King STEPHEN in 1127, when still Earl of MORTAGNE and BOULOGNE.

GARENDON (Leicestershire) (Cistercian Abbey of S. MARY).
Founded in 1133 by ROBERT DE MONTFORT, Earl of LEICESTER (JANAUSCHEK, *Orig. Cist.,* i., p. 30).
Arms : *Gules, a cinquefoil ermine* (the. arms of the County of Leicester), *over all a pastoral staff in bend or.* MONTFORT bore : *Gules, a lion rampant queue fourchée argent.*

GLOUCESTER (Mitred Benedictine Abbey of S. PETER).
Founded in 680 by ETHELBERT, King of MERCIA.
(*See* Bishopric, *ante* p. 181).

GRIMSBY (Lincoln) (Abbey of Augustinian Canons).
Founded by King HENRY I.
Arms : (*Gules*), *on a chevron between a royal crown, and a lion of* ENGLAND *in chief* (*or*), *and in base a crosier issuing from the base* . . . *three fleurs-de-lis* . . . (*Cat. of Seals in Brit. Mus.,* No. 3230.)

GLASTONBURY (Somerset) (Mitred Benedictine Abbey of S. MARY).
This monastery claimed JOSEPH of ARIMATHEA as its founder in the first century, but the date of its

2 B

foundation is lost in the mists of antiquity. It pretty certainly existed in the fourth century.

Arms: *Vert, a cross treflée (or flory) argent (between four open crowns or), on a canton of the second the* BLESSED VIRGIN, *holding the* HOLY CHILD, *proper.*

GUISBOROUGH (GISBORNE) (Yorkshire) (Priory of Augustinian Canons).

Arms: *Argent, a lion rampant azure, over all a bend gules.*

HALES-OWEN (Shropshire) (Premonstratensian).

Arms: *Azure, a chevron argent between three fleurs-de-lis or.*

HALTEMPRISE, or HALTEMPRICE (York) (Priory of Augustinians).

Arms: *Sable, a cross patonce (or flory) argent ;* otherwise, *Sable, a cross patonce quarterly argent and gules.*

HAVERFORD (Pembroke).

Arms: *Gules, a dragon argent winged or, on a chief azure three mullets of the last.*

HAYLES (Gloucester) (Mitred Cistercian Abbey of S. MARY).

Founded in 1246 by RICHARD, Earl of CORNWALL and King of the ROMANS (*Orig. Cist.*, i., p. 246). The chief relic, and the one which added to its fame and popularity, was a reputed vial of the Holy Blood, which was obtained for it in 1272 by EDMUND, Earl of CORNWALL, son of the founder.

Arms (those of the founder): *Argent, a lion rampant gules within a bordure sable bezantée, differenced by a crosier in bend or* (passing over the lion).

HEDINGHAM, *vide ante*, EDINGHAM.

HERTLAND (Devon) (Abbey of Augustinian Canons of ST. NECTAN).

Arms : *Gules, a bend between three pears or.* Another coat is : *Argent, a crosier in pale or, enfiled by a stag's head caboshed sable attired of the second.*

HOLLAND (Lincolnshire).

Arms : *Azure, fleury and a lion rampant argent* (the arms of HOLLAND) *debruised by a bend gules, thereon three keys or, wards uppermost.*

HOLME-CULTRAM (Cumberland) (Cistercian Abbey of S. MARY).

Founded in the year 1151 by DAVID I., King of Scotland. The English Kings, HENRY II., RICHARD, and HENRY III., confirmed the grants of land, and increased the possessions of the abbey (*Orig. Cist.*, i., p. 130).

Arms : *Azure, a cross-moline or ; impaling, Or, a lion rampant sable.*

HOLME, or HULME (Norfolk) (Mitred Benedictine Abbey of S. BENEDICT).

Founded by CANUTE in 1036.

Arms : *Sable, a crosier in pale, between two open crowns in fess or.* (See *Cat. of Seals in Brit. Mus.*, Nos. 3304, 3305.)

HULTON (Stafford) (Cistercian Abbey of S. MARY).

Founded by HENRY AUDELEY in 1223 (*Orig. Cist.*, i., p. 223).

Arms (those of its founder) : *Gules, a fret or.* (See *Cat. of Seals in Brit. Mus.*, No. 3306.)

HYDE (Hampshire) (Benedictine Abbey of S. PETER at Winchester).

Arms : *Argent, a lion rampant sable, on a chief of the last two keys addorsed paleways, the bows interlaced of the first.*

INGHAM (Norfolk) (Priory of Redemptorists, or Trinitarians).

Arms : (Those of the Order) *Argent, a cross patée, the pale gules, the fess azure ;* but the arms of the house appear to have been those of Sir MILES STAPLETON, its founder, *circa* 1360; *Argent, a lion rampant sable.* (See *Cat. of Seals in Brit. Mus.,* No. 3314.)

IXWORTH, or IKESWORTH (Suffolk) (Priory of Argentinians of S. MARY).

Arms : *Lozengy or and sable ;* being those of BLUND, its founder. (*Cat. of Seals in Brit. Mus.,* No. 3332.)

JERVAUX, or JOREVAL (Yorkshire) (Cistercian Abbey of S. MARY).

This abbey was founded in the reign of King STEPHEN (1135-1154) (*Orig. Cist.,* i., p. 119).

Arms : These appear to have been those of its founder, viz., *Or, three chevrons interlaced in base gules, a chief vair,* ST. QUENTIN. (See *Cat. of Seals in Brit. Mus.,* No. 3315.)

KENILWORTH (Warwickshire) (Priory, afterwards Abbey, of Augustinian Canons).

Arms : *Argent, on a chief azure two mullets or, pierced gules* (the arms of CLINTON).

KEYNSHAM (Somerset) (Abbey of Augustinian Canons).

Arms : (*Gules*) *six clarions or rests* (*or*) (See *Cat. of Seals in Brit. Mus.,* No. 3346.)

KIRKBY-BELLER (Leicester) (Augustinian Priory).

Arms : *Per pale gules and sable, over all a lion rampant argent crowned or,* the arms of BELLER. (*Cat. of Seals in Brit. Mus.,* No. 3358.)

KIRKHAM, or KYRCHAM (Yorkshire) (Priory of Augustinian Canons of the Holy Trinity).
Arms: *Gules, three water-budgets, over all a pastoral staff in pale, or.*

KIRKSTALL (Yorkshire) (Cistercian Abbey of S. MARY). Founded by HENRY DE LACY in 1147 (*Orig. Cist.*, i.,. p. 93).
Arms: *Azure, three swords points in base argent, hilted or.*

KIRKSTEAD (Lincoln) (Cistercian Abbey of S. MARY). Founded in 1139 by HUGH BRETON (*Orig. Cist.*, i., p. 55).
Arms: . . . *three crowns* . . . (*Cat. of Seals in Brit. Mus.*, No. 3377.)

KNARESBOROUGH (Yorkshire) (Priory of Trinitarians, or Redemptorists).
Arms: *Argent, a lion rampant gules, crowned or, a bordure sable bezantée* (CORNWALL).

KNOLL, or KNOLE (Warwick).
Arms: . . . . *a rose en soleil* . . . (*Cat. of Seals in Brit. Mus.*, No. 3381.)

LAMBOURNE (Berkshire) (Hospital).
Arms: *Bendy wavy of six argent and sable ;* for JOHN ESTBURY, the founder. (*Cat. of Seals in Brit. Mus.*, No. 3392.)

LANDE (Leicester) (Priory of Augustinian Canons).
Arms: *Or, three pales gules, a bordure azure bezantée ;* arms of RICHARD BASSET, the founder. (*Cat. of Seals in Brit. Mus.*, No. 3394.)

LANERCOST (Cumberland) (Priory of Augustinian Canons).
Arms: *Or, two flaunches gules.*

LANGDON (Kent) (Premonstratensian Abbey of S. MARY).

Arms : *Azure, two crosiers in saltire proper, the sinister headed sable.*

LANGLEY REGIS (KING'S LANGLEY) (Hertford) (Priory of Black Friars).

Arms : . . . *on a bend engrailed* . . . , *between six fleurs-de-lis* . . . , *three crosses-crosslets fitchées* . . . (*Cat. of Seals in Brit. Mus.,* No. 3408.)

LANGUEST (Denbigh), "VALLE CRUCIS" (Cistercian Abbey).

Founded at close of twelfth century by MADOC AP GRIFFITH (*Orig. Cist.,* i., p. 205).

Arms : *Gules, on a lion rampant between three crosses-crosslets fitchées argent as many bars sable.*

LATTON (Essex).

Arms : *Gules, five mullets,* 2. 2. 1. *or on a canton of last* (or *ermine*) *a griffin segreant sable.*

LAUNCESTON (Cornwall) (Augustinian Priory).

Arms : *Argent, gutté de sang, a cock* (*sable,* or *gules*), *on a chief gules three roses of the field* (or *or*).

LEDES (Kent) (Priory of Augustinians of SS. MARY and NICOLAS).

Arms : *Argent, a cross voided gules* (EDMONDSON says the field is *or*). *Or, a cross-moline gules.*

LEICESTER (S. MARY DE PRATIS) (Abbey of Augustinian Canons).

Arms : *Gules, a cinquefoil ermine.*

LEIGH or LEES (Essex) (Priory of Augustinians).
Arms: *Sable (or azure), three plates, on each as many piles in point wavy of the field (or gules).*

LENTON (Nottingham) (Clugniac Priory of S. SAVIOUR).
Arms: *Quarterly Or and azure, over all a cross-Calvary of the first, fimbriated and stepped sable.*

LINGFIELD (Surrey) (College of S. PETER).
Arms: (Those of COBHAM, the founder) *Gules, on a chevron or, three (lions rampant) sable.*

LLANTHONY (Gloucester) (Priory of Augustinians.)
Arms: *Argent, on a chevron gules between three Cornish choughs sable as many crosiers or* (the arms of DEANE).

LYNN (Norfolk) (Carmelite, or White Friars).
Founded by Bishop HERBERT DE LOSINGA, in the reign of WILLIAM RUFUS.
Arms: *Azure, three conger's heads erased and erect, each holding in the mouth a cross-crosslet fitchy or,* (the *congers* are sometimes called *sea-dragons*).

LONDON.

ST. ANTHONY'S.
Arms: *Or, a cross tau* (ST. ANTHONY'S Cross) *azure.*

S. BARTHOLOMEW'S HOSPITAL.
Arms: *Per pale argent and sable, a chevron counterchanged.*

CHARTER-HOUSE (the old Carthusian Monastery).
Arms: those of Sir WALTER DE MANNY, the founder, viz., *Or, three chevrons sable.*

CHRIST'S HOSPITAL.

Arms : *Argent, a cross, and in dexter canton: a sword in pale gules* (City of LONDON); *on a chief azure a double rose of* YORK *and* LANCASTER, *between two fleurs-de-lis or.*

S. KATHARINE'S HOSPITAL.

Arms : *Per fess gules and azure, in chief a sword fess-ways, in base a demi-Katharine's wheel argent.*

S. MARY'S HOSPITAL (without Bishopsgate).

Arms : . . . *a cross-moline voided* . . . *for the founder,* BRUNE (*Cat. of Seals in Brit. Mus.,* No. 3541), but S. MARY'S BISHOPSGATE is otherwise said to bear : *Per pale argent and sable; a cross-moline counter-changed, in the dexter canton a martlet of the second* (but *gules* according to EDMONDSON).

ST. MARY GRACES (Eastminster).

Arms : *Per pale,* (a) *Per fess,* . . . *in chief a lion's face; in base* . . . *a fleur-de-lis;* (b) . . . *a crosier in pale.*

S. MARY OVERY (Southwark).

Arms : *Argent, a cross lozengy gules, in dexter chief a mullet* (or according to EDMONDSON *a cinquefoil*) *of the last.*

ST. THOMAS OF ACRE (or of ACON).

Arms : *Azure, a cross patée per pale gules and argent.*

MAIDEN BRADLEY (Wilts. and Somerset) (Priory of Austin Friars).

Arms : . . . *an escucheon* . . . *within an orle of martlets.* . . .

MACCLESFIELD (Cheshire).
Arms : *Gules, a mitre between three garbs or.*

MAIDSTONE (Kent) (College of S. MARY).
Arms : *Azure, three bars or.*

MALMESBURY (Wilts.) (Mitred Benedictine Abbey of
SS. MARY and ALDHELM).
Arms : *Gules, two lions of* ENGLAND, *on a chief argent
a mitre between two pastoral staves azure* (?).
Founded before 675, in which year S. ALDHELM,
afterwards Bishop of SHERBORNE, became abbot. King
ATHELSTAN was buried here.

MALTON (York) (Gilbertine Priory).
Arms : *Argent, on three bars gules a pilgrim's crutch
in bend sable.* (See *The Herald and Genealogist,*
vol ii., pp. 192, 345, 406) (*cf.* SEMPRINGHAM).

MALVERN (Little) (Benedictine Priory).
Arms : *Argent, on a fess between three cock's heads
erased sable, wattled gules, a mitre or.* The arms
of Bishop JOHN ALCOCK, of Worcester and Ely,
a benefactor. (*Cat. of Seals in Brit. Mus.,*
No. 3605.)

MARGAM (Glamorgan) (Cistercian Abbey of S. MARY.)
Arms : *Gules, three clarions or,* and, *Or, three chevrons
gules,* CLARE. (Both shields are on the seal of
the abbey in 1525. (*Cat. of Seals in Brit. Mus.,*
No. 3608.)
The abbey was founded in 1147 by ROBERT DE CLARE,
Earl of GLOUCESTER (*Orig. Cist.,* i., p. 107).

MAXSTOKE (Warwick) (Priory of Augustinian Canons).
Arms : *Argent, on a chief azure two mullets or,*

pierced gules, the arms of CLINTON of MAX-
STOKE.

MELFORD (Suffolk) (Trinity Hospital).
Arms (of Sir WILLIAM CORDALL, Master of the Rolls,
founder, *temp.* Elizabeth). *Quarterly*, 1 and 4.
*Argent, a chevron ermine between three griffin's
heads erased gules ;* 2 and 3. . . . *a chevron
between three lions passant gardant.* . . . (*Cat.
of Seals in Brit. Mus.*, No. 3625.)

MENDHAM (Suffolk) (Clugniac Priory).
Arms : *Or, on a fess gules three plates* (arms of WILLIAM
DE HUNTINGFIELD, founder, on seal of 1307. (See
Cat. of Seals in Brit. Mus., No. 3626.)

MELSA or MEAUX (Yorkshire) (Cistercian Abbey).
Arms : *Gules, a cross patonce vair between four martlets
argent.*
Founded in 1150 by WILLIAM, Earl of ALBEMARLE,
or AUMERLE, Lord of HOLDERNESS ; and confirmed by
King JOHN (*Orig. Cist.*, i., p. 124).

MEREVALE, MURIVALLE—"DE MIRA VALLE". (War-
wick) (Cistercian Abbey of S. MARY).
Founded *c.* 1147 by ROBERT, Earl FERRARS (*Orig.
Cist.*, i., p. 114).
Arms : *Vaire or and gules* (arms of the founder). ·

MERTON (Surrey) (Priory of Augustinian Canons).
Arms : *Or, fretty azure ; on the joints six eagles displayed argent.*

METTINGHAM (Norfolk) (College of Secular Priests first
at RAVENINGHAM, then at NORTON SOUPECORS).
Arms: *Per pale azure and gules, a lion rampant argent.*

MILTON or MIDDLETON (Dorset) (Benedictine Abbey of S. MARY).
Founded by King ATHELSTAN in 933.
Arms : *Sable, three baskets of cakes argent.*

MISSENDEN or MESSENDEN (Buckingham) (Abbey of Augustinian Canons).
Arms : *Ermine, two bars wavy sable, over all a crosier, in bend or.*

MICHELNEY, or MUCHELNEY (Somerset) (Benedictine Abbey of SS. PETER and PAUL).
Arms : *Argent, two keys in bend enfiling a sword in · bend-sinister gules.*

MONK-BRETTON (York) (Clugniac Priory).
Arms : *Sable, in chief two covered cups, in base a cross patée argent.*

NANTWICH (Chester).
Arms : *Per pale azure and gules, two palmer's staves in saltire or.*

NEATH (Glamorgan) (Cistercian Abbey of the Trinity).
Arms : *Gules, three rests, or clarions, or.*
Founded in 1130, by Sir RICHARD GRANVILLE, and CONSTANCE, his wife (*Orig. Cist.*, i., p. 98).

NEWARK (Leicester) (College).
Arms : ENGLAND, *a label ermine* (?) for HENRY, Duke of LANCASTER. (See *Cat. of Seals in Brit. Mus.*, No. 3450.)

NEWBURGH (York) (Abbey of Augustinian Canons of S. MARY).
Arms : *Gules, a lion rampant or, debruised by a palmer's staff* (or *crosier*) *in bend-sinister of the last.* (See *The Herald and Genealogist*, vol. ii., p. 192.)

NEWCASTLE (Northumberland) (Carmelites).

Arms: . . . *crusily.* . . . *three lions passant in pale* . . . (? BYKER). (See *Cat. of Seals in Brit. Mus.*, No. 3686.)

NEWENHAM (Bedford) (Augustinian Prior of S. PAUL).

Arms: On the seal of WILLIAM DE WOKETON, Prior in 1427, are two shields, one . . . *a lion rampant* . . . ; the other . . . *a cross patonce* . . . (See *Cat. of Seals in Brit. Mus.*, No. 3693).

NEWENHAM (Devon) (Cistercian Abbey of S. MARY).

Founded in 1246 by REGINALD DE MOHUN (*Orig. Cist.*, i., p. 246).

Arms: The seal of Abbot LEONARD HOUNDALLER, about 1406, has two shields; one (*Or*), *a cross lozengy* (meant probably for the *engrailed sable cross* of MOHUN); the other . . . *three pierced mullets* . . . (See *Cat. of Seals in Brit. Mus.*, No. 3695.)

NEWSTEAD (Nottingham) (Abbey of Austin Canons).

Arms: Same as See of LINCOLN (*ante* p. 184).

NORTON (Chester) (Priory of Austin Canons).

Arms: *Gules, a pale fusilly or.* To this is sometimes added, *a bordure azure thereon eight mitres of the second.* (*See* LELAND, *Collectanea*, i., 53.)

NORTHAMPTON (Augustinian Priory of S. JAMES).

Arms: *Per pale argent* (?) *and gules, over all an escallop or.*

NORWICH (Benedictine Priory, afterwards Cathedral).

Arms: *Argent, a cross sable.* (See *Cat. of Seals in Brit. Mus.*, No. 3768.)

NOSTELL (Priory).

Arms: *Gules, a cross between four lions rampant or.* (See. *The Herald and Genealogist,* vol. ii., pp. 460-462.)

NOTTINGHAM (Carmelites, or White Friars).

Arms: *Barry of eight argent and azure, a label of five points gules,* for the founder, REGINALD, Lord GREY DE WILTON, 1276.

OLVESTON, OWSTON, or OSSULVESTON (Leicestershire) (Priory of Austin Canons).

Arms: *Argent, three bars azure, a bordure gules.*

OSENEY (Oxford) (Abbey of Augustinian Canons).

Arms: *Azure, two bends or.*

OTTERY (Devon) (Collegiate Church of S. MARY).

Founded by JOHN DE GRANDISON, Bishop of EXETER, in 1337.

Arms (Those of the founder): *Paly of six argent and azure, on a bend gules a mitre proper between two eagles displayed or.*

PENTNEY (Norfolk) (Priory of Augustinian Canons).

Arms: *Gules, three covered baskets or.*

PENWORTHAM (Lancaster) (Benedictine Priory).

Arms: *Argent, on a chevron between three water-bougets gules two pairs of keys in saltire or.*

PERSHORE (Worcester) (Benedictine).

Arms: *Sable, on a chevron between three ant-hills or, charged with ants proper; as many holly leaves vert.* (*Or . . . a cross raguly . . .*)

PETERBOROUGH (Medehampstead) (Benedictine Abbey
of S. PETER, now Cathedral).

Was founded, about the year 655, by PENDA, King of
MERCIA. It was rebuilt in the tenth century. The See
was founded by HENRY VIII. in the year 1541.

Arms: The arms of the abbey were: *Gules, two keys
in saltire or.* (*See* those of the Bishopric at
p. 186, *ante.*)

PIPEWELL (Northamptonshire) (Cistercian Abbey of
S. MARY, DE DIVISIS).

Founded in the year 1143 by RADULF, Earl of CHESTER;
and WILLIAM DE BUTEVILLE (*Orig. Cist.*, i., p. 76).

Arms: *Argent, three crescents gules; impaling, Azure, a
crosier in pale or.*

PLYMPTON (Devon) (Priory of Augustinian Canons of
SS. PETER and PAUL).

Arms: *Gules, two keys addorsed in bend or, enfiling a
sword in bend-sinister proper*

POLLESHOO, or POLSLOE (Benedictine Priory of S.
CATHARINE).

Arms: *Gules, a sword between three Catharine wheels
argent.*

POLLESWORTH (Warwick) (Benedictine Abbey of SS.
MARY and EDITH).

Founded near the forest of Arden, in the middle of the
ninth century, by King ETHELWOLF, for S. MODWENNA
the instructress of his daughter EDITH.

Arms: *Gules* (EDMONDSON says *Azure*), *a fess coticed
between six crosslets or.*

PONTEFRACT (Yorkshire) (Clugniac Priory of S. JOHN).

Arms: *Quarterly or and gules, a bend sable, over all a
label of five points in chief argent.*

RAMSAY (Huntingdonshire) (Benedictine Abbey of S. MARY, etc.).

Founded about the year 972 by S. OSWALD, Bishop of WORCESTER, and Archbishop of YORK. The dedication was to S. MARY, S. BENEDICT, and all Virgins.

Arms: *Or, on a bend azure three ram's heads couped argent.* (See *Cat. of Seals in Brit. Mus.*, Nos. 3876, 3878.)

READING (Berkshire) (Mitred Benedictine Abbey of SS. MARY, JOHN, and JAMES).

This Abbey was founded in 1126, by King HENRY I., who presented to it its chief relic the hand of S. JAMES; and who was himself buried within its walls. The monastery, one of the grandest in England, is said to have contained two hundred monks.

Arms: *Azure, three escallops or.* (See *Cat. of Seals in Brit. Mus.*, No. 3886; seal of Abbot JOHN THORNE.)

RICHMOND (Yorkshire) (Grey Friars, Priory of S. MARTIN).

Arms: *Gules, two bars gemels, a chief, and over all a crosier in pale or.*

RIEVAULX (Yorkshire) (Cistercian Abbey of S. MARY).

Founded *c.* 1127, by WALTER LESPEC (*Orig. Cist.*, i., p. 22).

Arms: *Gules, three water-budgets argent, over all a crosier in pale proper* (ROOS, differenced).

ROCHESTER (Abbey).

Arms: *Argent, a saltire gules.*

ROYSTON (Hertford) (Priory of Augustinian Canons of SS. NICOLAS, and THOMAS of CANTERBURY.

Arms: *Per pale two coats; (a) Argent, a fess gules; (b) Chequy argent and azure.*

RUFFORD (Nottingham) (Cistercian Abbey of S. MARY).
Founded in 1148 by GILBERT, Earl of LINCOLN.
Arms: *Azure, flory, a lion rampant or* (*Orig. Cist.*, i.,
p. 112).

RUSHEN (Isle of Man) (Cistercian Abbey).
Founded by OLAF I. in 1147 (*Orig. Cist.*, i., p. 101).
Arms: *Argent, a cross sable fretty or.*

RUSHWORTH (Norfolk) (Collegiate Church of S. JOHN,
Evangelist).
Arms: *. . . on a bend . . . three roses.*

ST. ALBANS (Hertford) (Mitred Benedictine Abbey).
This celebrated abbey was founded, about the year 793,
by OFFA, King of MERCIA, in expiation of the murder
of S. ETHELBERT, King of the East Angles. It was
built on the place of the martyrdom of S. ALBAN, the
protomartyr of ENGLAND, where a church had been
already raised to his honour, but destroyed by the
invading Danes. The abbey became a Cathedral
Church in 1877 (*vide ante*, p. 186).
Arms: *Azure, a saltire or* (*Cat. of Seals in Brit. Mus.*,
No. 3944).

ST. BEES (Cumberland) (Benedictine Priory).
Arms: (those of the Earls of NORTHUMBERLAND,
viz.): *Quarterly*, 1 and 4. *Or, a lion rampant
azure* (PERCY-ANCIENT, or LOUVAIN); 2 and 3.
Gules, three lucies hauriant argent (LUCY).

SALLAY, SAWLEY, SALLEY (Yorkshire) (Cistercian
Abbey of S. MARY).
Founded in 1147, by WILLIAM DE PERCY, under the
title of Mount Saint Andrew (*Orig. Cist.*, i., p. 109).
Arms (of the founder): *Azure, five fusils in fess or.*
Otherwise, *Argent, on a pale sable a crosier or.*

SALTREY, SAWTRE, or SOLTRE (Huntingdon) (Cistercian Abbey of S. MARY).
Founded in 1147, by SIMON ST. LIS, Earl of NORTHAMPTON ; and MALCOLM, King of Scotland (as Earl of HUNTINGDON) (*Orig. Cist.*, i., p. 95).
Arms : *Argent, two bars gules fretty or.*

SELBY (Yorkshire) (Benedictine Monastery of the BLESSED VIRGIN, and S. GERMAIN D'AUXERRE).
Founded by WILLIAM THE CONQUEROR.
Arms: *Sable, three swans close argent, two and one, beaked and membered or* (See *The Herald and Genealogist*, vol. ii., p. 193).

SELE (Sussex) (Benedictine Priory of S. PETER).
Arms : On the fifteenth century seal are two shields, one of ENGLAND with *a label;* the other bears *a fess nebuly with a demi-lion issuant in chief between two cross-crosslets.* (See *Cat. of Seals in Brit. Mus.*, No. 3986.)

SEMPRINGHAM (Lincoln) (Priory).
Arms : *Barry of six argent and gules, over all a palmer's crutch in bend (sinister) or.* (See *The Herald and Genealogist*, vol. ii., p. 345) (*cf.* MALTON).

SHAFTESBURY (Dorset) (Benedictine Abbey of SS. MARY and EDWARD).
Founded, in the tenth century, by ELGIVA, wife of King EDMOND, grandson of ALFRED THE GREAT.
Arms: *Argent, on a pale coticed sable three roses of the first.*

SHERBORNE (Dorset) (Benedictine Abbey of S. MARY).
Arms : *Gules, a cross argent, over all a crosier in pale to the dexter side of the shield proper.*

2 C

SHREWSBURY (Shropshire) (Benedictine Abbey of SS. PETER and PAUL).
Arms : *Azure, a lion rampant, debruised by a crosier in bend, all within a bordure argent* (or *or*).

SLAPTON (Devon) (College of S. MARY).
Arms: (*Or*), *three piles in point* (*gules ;* the arms of the founder, Sir GUY DE BRYAN). (*See Cat. of Seals in Brit. Mus.*, No. 4032.)

SOUTHWICK (Hampshire) (Priory of Augustinian Canons).
Arms : *Argent, on a chief sable two roses of the first.*

STANLEY (Wiltshire) (Cistercian Abbey of S. MARY).
Founded by the Empress MATILDA at LOKESWELL ; transferred to STANLEY by King HENRY II. (*Orig. Cist.*, i., p. 125).
Arms: . . . *crusily fitchy* . . . *a bend ermine* (?). (See *Cat. of Seals in Brit. Mus.*, No. 4082.)

STRATA FLORIDA (Cardiganshire) (Cistercian Abbey of S. MARY) (JANAUSCHEK, *Orig. Cist.*, i., p. 157).
Founded by RHYS AP GRYFFYDD in 1184, rebuilt under the patronage of EDWARD I., in 1288.
Arms: *Sable, a crosier in pale enfiled by a stag's head argent.*

ST. GERMAN'S (Cornwall) (Benedictine Priory).
Arms : *Or, on a chevron azure between three lion's heads erased purpure, as many annulets of the first.*

STRATFORD LANGTHORNE (Essex) (Cistercian Abbey).
Arms: *Or, three chevrons gules* (CLARE), *over all a crosier in bend argent* (founded *c.* 1135).

SUDBURY (Suffolk) (College).

Arms (of SUDBURY): *Gules, a talbot sejant within a bordure engrailed or.*

TAMWORTH (Stafford) (Collegiate Church of S. EDITH).

Arms: *Sable, on a fess argent between three pheons or, a stag's head caboshed of the field between two pellets* (the arms of PARKER).

TANREGGE (Surrey) (Priory).

Arms: *Gules, three bezants.*

TATESHALLE or TATTERSHALL (Lincolnshire) (Collegiate Church).

Arms: *Quarterly,* 1 and 4. *(Argent) a chief (gules) over all a baton* (for Sir RALPH CROMWELL the founder); 2 and 3. *Chequy (or) and (gules) a chief ermine* (TATTERSHALL).

TAVISTOCK (Devon) (Benedictine Abbey of SS. MARY and RUMON).

This abbey was founded in the tenth century (*c.* 961), by ORDGAR, Earl of DEVON, father of Queen ELFRIDA.

Arms: *Vairé or and azure, on a chief of the first two mullets* (sometimes *pierced*) *gules.* Otherwise, *Vair, on a chief or, two pierced mullets gules.*

TEWKESBURY (Gloucestershire) (Benedictine Abbey of S. MARY).

Founded by ODDO and DODDO, two pious nobles of Mercia, in the time of King ETHELRED.

Arms: *Gules, a cross engrailed or, within a bordure argent.* (Note, the *engrailure* takes the form of one large indentation on either side of each arm.)

THAME (Oxfordshire) (Cistercian Abbey of S. MARY).

Founded, in the year 1138, by Sir ROBERT GAIT, with the aid of ALEXANDER, Bishop of LINCOLN.

Arms : *Argent, on a chief sable two crosiers or.* Otherwise, *Sable, on a chief argent two crosiers* (?) . . . (*Orig. Cist.*, i., p. 46).

THETFORD (Norfolk) (Clugniac Priory of S. Mary).

Arms: *Per pale or and vert, a lion rampant gules* (arms of BIGOT, Earl of NORFOLK, Earl Marshall).

THETFORD (Norfolk) (Canons of the Holy Sepulchre).

Arms : *Chequy or and azure* (for WARENNE). (See *Cat. of Seals in Brit. Mus.*, No. 4162.)

THONESTON, or THOMPSON (Norfolk) (Collegiate Church).

Arms : *Argent, on a chevron gules between three cross-crosslets fitchées azure, an estoile for difference* (? *or*) ; for the founder, Sir THOMAS SHARDE-LOWE.

THORNEY (Cambridge) (Benedictine Abbey of SS. MARY and BOTOLPH).

Was founded early in the seventh century (*c.* 604) by SEBERT, King of the East Saxons. It was rebuilt in 970 by ETHELWOLD, Bishop of WINCHESTER, with the help of King EDGAR.

Arms : *Azure, three crosiers, two and one, between as many cross-crosslets, one and two, or.*

THORNHOLM (Lincoln) (Priory of Augustinian Canons of S. MARY).

Arms: . . . *fretty* . . . *a canton* . . . (See *Cat. of Seals in Brit. Mus.*, No. 4172).

THORNTON ON HUMBER, or TORRINGTON (Lincoln) (Abbey of Augustinian Canons of S. MARY).
Arms: *Azure, two crosiers addorsed in pale or* (or *argent*).

THURGARTON (Nottingham) (Priory of Augustinian Canons of S. PETER).
Arms: *Argent, three keys, two and one, sable, wards in chief* (EDMONDSON gives the reverse). But in the *Cat. of Seals in Brit. Mus.*, No. 4190, is the seal of WILLIAM BINGHAM, Prior 1471-1477, which bears a shield charged with the arms of the founder, RALPH D'AYNCOURT : *Azure, billetty, and a fess dancetty or.*

TILTEY (Essex) (Cistercian Abbey of S. MARY).
Founded in 1152 by ROBERT DE FERRERS and MAURICE DE TILTEY.
Arms: *Argent, on a cross gules five fleurs-de-lis or.*

TUTBURY (Stafford) (Benedictine Priory of S. MARY).
Founded, at the close of the eleventh century, by HENRY DE FERRERS, for the repose of the souls of WILLIAM THE CONQUEROR, and Queen MATILDA ; and for the souls of his own wife and parents.
Arms: The fifteenth century seal given in *Cat. of Seals in Brit. Mus.*, No. 4218, bears two shields ; one of *Azure, a saltire vairy or and gules, between four crescents argent*, for the Priory ; the other of *Vairy or and gules*, the arms of the founder.

TORRE (Devon) (Premonstratensian Abbey).
Arms: *Gules, a fess between three crosiers or.*

TYNEMOUTH (Northumberland) (Benedictine Priory of SS. MARY and OSWIN).
Arms: *Gules, three open crowns or.* (See *The Herald and Genealogist*, vol. ii., p. 192.)

TYWARDRET, or TREWARDRETH (Cornwall) (Benedictine Priory).

Arms : *Gules, a saltire between four fleurs-de-lis or.*

ULVERSCROFT (Leicester) (Priory of Augustinian Canons of S. MARY).

Arms : *Gules, seven mascles, 3. 3. 1., argent.*

"VALLE CRUCIS" (*vide ante*, p. 375).

VALE-ROYAL (Chester) (Cistercian Abbey.)

Arms : *Gules, three lions passant gardant or* (ENGLAND), *debruised by a crosier in pale gules, the head sable, all within a bordure of the last bezantée* (*Orig. Cist.*, i., p. 259).

WALEDEN (SAFFRON-WALDEN) (Essex) (Benedictine Abbey of the BLESSED VIRGIN MARY and S. JAMES).

Founded in the year 1136 by GEOFFREY DE MANDEVILLE, Earl of ESSEX.

Arms : *Azure, on a bend gules, coticed and between two mullets or, three escallops argent.*

WALSINGHAM (Norfolk) (Priory of Augustinian Canons of S. MARY).

Arms : *Argent, on a cross sable five billets* (otherwise *five garden lilies*) *of the field.*

WALTHAM (Essex) (Abbey of Augustinian Canons of Holy Cross).

Founded by TOVI and HAROLD in the ninth (?) century.

Arms : *Argent, on a cross engrailed sable five crosscrosslets fitchées or.* (*Cat. of Seals in Brit. Mus.*, No. 4250.)

WARDON, or DE SARTIS (Bedford) (Cistercian Abbey of S. MARY).

Founded in 1135 by WALTER L'ESPEC (*Orig. Cist.*, i., p. 43).

Arms : *Azure, a crosier between three warden pears or.* (*Cat. of Seals in Brit. Mus.*, No. 4259.)

WARE (Hertfordshire) (House of the Franciscans).

Founded by BALDWIN DE WAKE.

Arms : *Or, two bars gules in chief three torteaux*, the arms of the founder.

WARSOP (Nottinghamshire) (Abbey).

Arms : *Argent, on a bend between six martlets gules* (arms of FURNIVAL) *a crosier or.*

WELBECK (Nottingham) (Premonstratensian Abbey of S. JAMES).

Arms : *Gules, three lozenges conjoined in fess argent, on each a rose of the first.*

WENLOCK (Shropshire) (Clugniac Priory of S. MIL-BURGA).

Probably founded about the seventh century, rebuilt in the twelfth. The Abbess MILBURGA was niece of PENDA, King of Mercia.

Arms : *Azure, three garbs or, over all a crosier of the last.*

WENDLING (Norfolk) (Premonstratensian Abbey.)

Arms : *Azure, three crosiers or, over all on a fess gules as many Hosts, each stamped with the monogram* I. H. S.

WESTMINSTER (Mitred Benedictine Abbey of S. PETER).

Arms : *Gules, two keys in saltire, wards in chief or.* (See *Cat. of Seals in Brit. Mus.*, Nos. 4305, 4309, and 4311).

Founded in the seventh century by SEBERT, King of the East Angles) ; restored by EDWARD THE CONFESSOR.

WHALLEY (Lancashire) (Cistercian Abbey of S. MARY).
  Arms : *Gules, three whales hauriant, from the mouth of each the head of a crosier issuant or* (*Orig. Cist.,* i., p. 167).

WHITBY (Yorkshire) (Benedictine Abbey of SS. PETER and HILDA).
  Arms : *Azure, three snakes coiled argent.* (Ammonites, the fossils of S. HILDA).

WILTON (Wilts.) (Benedictine Abbey of SS. MARY and BARTHOLOMEW.
  Founded, in 800, by EGBERT, King of Wessex, and his sister ALBURGA, wife of WULSTAN. It was rebuilt by King ALFRED towards the end of the ninth century.
  Arms :

WINCHCOMBE (Gloucester) (Benedictine Abbey of SS. MARY and KENELM).
  Founded in the year 798 by KENULF, King of Mercia.
  Arms : Those of MORTIMER, *the inescucheon chargèd with a cross gules for difference.*

WINCHESTER (Hampshire) (Hospital of S. CROSS).
  Arms : *Argent, five crosses-patées argent,* 2. 2. 1.

WINGFIELD (Suffolk) (Collegiate Church of SS. MARY, ANDREW, and JOHN BAPTIST).
  Arms : *Argent, on a bend gules three pairs of wings conjoined in lure of the first,* the arms of THOMAS WINGFIELD.

WORCESTER (Priory).
  Arms : Those of the See (?) (*v. ante,* p. 190) *on a canton gules, the figure of the* BLESSED VIRGIN MARY *holding the* HOLY CHILD *proper.*

WOBURN (Bedfordshire) (Cistercian Abbey).
Arms: *Azure, three bars wavy argent.*
The abbey was founded in 1145, by HUGH DE BOLE-
BECK (JANAUSCHEK, *Orig, Cist.,* i., p. 83).

WORKSOP (Nottingham) (WIRKESOP, or RADFORD)
(Priory of Augustinian Canons).
Arms: *Or, a lion rampant per fess sable and gules* (the
arms of DE LOVETOT?).

WOOTTON-WAVEN, or WALWAYNES (Warwick) (Benedictine Priory.
Arms: *Quarterly,* 1 and 4. *Or, a chevron gules* (STAF-
FORD); 2 and 3. *Or, in a maunch a hand proper
gules, holding a rose of the second, slipped vert.*

YORK (S. Mary).
Arms: *Sable, three birds, two and one, argent;* otherwise, *Argent, on a cross gules a bezant figured or
(and in the dexter canton a key).* (See *The Herald
and Genealogist,* vol. ii., p. 193.)

YORK (Holy Trinity) (Benedictine Priory).
Arms: *Gules, a cinquefoil argent* (?), for RALPH PAY-
NELL, the founder.

YORK (College of S. WILLIAM, Archbishop).
Arms: *Gules, seven mascles,* 3. 3. 1. *or* (the arms of the
Archbishop) (otherwise *nine mascles*).

CHAPTER VI.

ABBEYS, MONASTERIES, ETC., IN GERMANY, SWITZERLAND, ETC.

THE monasteries of the Cistercian Order very generally use as part of their arms the reputed coat of S. BERNARD; *Sable, a bend counter-compony argent and gules* (but *see* p. 415). Sometimes the bend is converted into a *bend-sinister;* occasionally it appears as a *chevron.*

WÜRMSPACH (near Rapperschwyl).

Founded in 1259 by RUDOLPH IV., Count of RAPPERS-CHWYL.

> Arms : *Quarterly*, 1 and 4. *Gules, on a bend argent three serpents gliding azure;* 2 and 3. *Sable, a bend counter-compony argent and gules.*

RATHHAUSEN.

(Nunnery founded in 1245. Canton of Lucerne).

> Arms : *Quarterly*, 1 and 4. *Argent, a trefoil vert;* 2 and 3. *Sable, a bend-sinister counter-compony* (or *chequy*) *argent and gules.* Or, *Quarterly*, 1. *Argent, a demi-figure of the* BLESSED VIRGIN MARY *and the* HOLY CHILD *proper*; 2 and 3. *as above;* 4. *Argent, a trefoil vert.* (Or, *Or, a mullet sable.*)

MAGDENAU.

Nunnery founded in 1244 by RUDOLF DE GLATTBURG, and increased by the Counts of TOGGENBURG and HAPS-BURG.

> Arms : *Quarterly*, 1 and 4. *Azure, the* BLESSED VIRGIN MARY *with the* HOLY CHILD, *and lilies, all proper;*

2 and 3. *Argent, a dove volant with an olive spray in its mouth, proper. Over all, Sable, a bend counter-compony argent and gules.*

S. URBAN, in the Aargau in the Canton of Lucerne, founded about 1148 (*Orig. Cist.*, i., p. 200).

Arms: *Per pale;* (a) *Sable, a bend counter-compony argent and gules ;* (b) *Per fess, azure and argent, over all, a lion rampant* . . .

SALAMANSWEILER (near Oberlingen).

Founded in 1137 by GONTRAN, Baron VON ADELS-REUTE ; and increased by the piety of the Emperors CONRAD and FREDERICK (*Barbarossa*), and lastly by the gifts of BURCHARD, Archbishop of SALZBURG, which are commemorated by the inclusion of the SALZBURG arms in the coat of the abbey (*Orig. Cist.*, i., p. 50).

Arms: *Quarterly*, 1 and 4. The arms of the Cistercian Order ; 2 and 3. SALZBURG (*v.* p. 87).

AU.

Arms: *Argent, water in base proper.*

BANZ (near Lichtenfels) (Benedictine, founded 1096).

Arms: *Or, a cockatrice vert* (or *gules*) *crowned of the field.*

CÖLN (Mommersloch).

Arms: *Or, a fess dancetty sable.*

BEINWIL.

Arms: *Per fess gules and argent, in base two arm-bones fessways proper.*

BELLELAYE (Premonstratensian).

Founded about 1140, near Délémont.

Arms: *Argent, a capital letter B sable.*

CAMBERG.
Arms : *Azure, a chevron, engoulé in a lion's mouth, or.*

CREUZLINGEN (Augustinian).
Founded 1120, by IDALRIC, Count of KYBURG, and Bishop of CONSTANZ.
Arms : *Per pale;* (a) *Gules, a cross botonny argent ;* (b) *Sable, a crosier paleways argent.*

DALHEIM (Mainz) (Cistercian) ("*Sacra Vallis*").
Arms : . . . *a cross tau, in front thereof two keys in saltire, wards in chief* . . . (JANAUSCHEK, *Orig. Cist.*, i., p. 60).

ELTEN.
Arms : *Argent, two wings affrontés sable.*

ERLACH (Cistercian ?).
Founded by a Bishop of BASEL in twelfth century.
Arms : *Gules, a bend argent.*

ESCHENBACH, S. (Cistercian).
Founded in 1294 by WALTER, Baron of ESCHENBACH.
Arms : *Argent, a cross recercelée sable.*

FELDBACH (Cistercian).
Founded in 1152, near Constance.
Arms : *Sable, billetty (couchés) or, over all a lion rampant (? argent).*

FRAUBRUNNEN, or FRAUENBRUNN (Cistercian).
Founded in 1309, near Bergedorf.
Arms : *Gules, a bend between two lions rampant or.*

GALEN.
Arms : *Or, three crampons gules.*

GARSTEN.

Arms : *Gules, a fess argent; impaling Vert, a griffin rampant argent inflamed proper.* (AUSTRIA impaling STYRIA.)

GLEINCK.

Arms : *Gules, on a mount in base a trefoil vert.*

HERMETSCHING (Switzerland).

Arms : *Azure, a serpent ondoyant in pale argent, crowned or.*

HEILSBRONN (Cistercian).

Founded in 1132 (JANAUSCHEK, *Orig. Cist.*, i., p. 27).

Arms : *Gules, a fountain or, jetting water proper.*

GERAS.

Arms : *Chequy vert and gules* (!).

GOTTSTALT.

Arms : *Gules, on a pale or three chevrons sable.*

HEINRICHAU (Cistercian) (*Orig. Cist.*, i., p. 229).

Arms : *Argent, a cross-moline gules on the centre a plate charged with an eagle displayed sable.*

KAISERSHEIM (Cistercian) (*Cesarea*).

Founded in 1133 (*Orig. Cist.*, i., p. 32).

Arms : *Or, three bars azure, a lion rampant gules.* The shield is borne on the breast of an Imperial eagle crowned proper.

KATHARINEN KLOSTER (Frankfürt A. M.).

Arms : . . . *three frogs in bend.*

LIEBFRAUEN STIFT (Frankfürt A. M.).

Arms : . . *a river in bend.*

HEILIGEN KREUZ (Cistercian) (*Orig. Cist.*, i., p. 36).
Founded, *circa* 1134, by LEOPOLD, Markgrave of Austria.
Arms : *Azure, a cross argent, over all two crosiers in saltire proper.*

HUMILIMONT.
Arms : *Paly of six, argent and gules.*

INTERLACKEN or LAC DE JOUX (Premonstratensian). (Switzerland).
Founded in 1133 by SEILGER, seigneur d'Oberhoffen.
Arms : *Argent, a demi-ibex sable.*

KÖNIGSFELDEN.
Nunnery founded by ELIZABETH of CARINTHIA, widow of the Emperor ALBERT I.
Arms : *Gules, on a mount in base vert, a cross patriarchal patée argent.*

LAACH (Benedictine).
Founded in 1093, suppressed in 1802.
Arms : *Per pale ;* (a) *three tall towers fessways ;* (b) *a dimidiated eagle.*

LANDSTRASS.
Arms : *Argent, a wild man with an uprooted pine tree vert.*

LÜNEBURG (S. Michael).
Arms : *Gules, S. MICHAEL transfixing the dragon, all proper.*

LUTRY (Switzerland).
Arms : *Per fess gules and argent.*

LAMBACH.
Arms : *Gules, on an eagle displayed argent crowned or, four bars sable.* Also, *Argent, on waves proper, a boat gules therein a demi-girl naked affrontée.*

MUNSTERLINGEN (Switzerland).
Arms : *Argent, a cross gules.*

MARCHTHAL (Premonstratensian, an Imperial Abbey).
Founded in 1170 by HUGH, Count of TÜBINGEN.
Arms : *Gules, a key and sword in saltire, in chief a cross-crosslet argent.*

NEUSTADT (Cistercian) (*Orig. Cist.*, i., p. 276).
Founded by FRIEDRICH III., King of the Romans, 1442.
Arms : *Gules, a fess argent, a cross patée (sable ?) on the edge of the fess a mitre proper.*

ORBE.
Arms : *Gules, two dolphins embowed addorsed argent.*

LA PART DIEU (Carthusian, near Bulle) (Switzerland).
Arms : *Gules, a stork with its vigilance argent.*
Founded in 1307 by GUILLEMETTE DE GRANSON, widow of PIERRE, Count DE GRUYÈRE.

ROMONT.
Arms : *Gules, a* ciborium *or.*

REICHERSBERG (See *Orig. Cist.*, i., p. 87).
Arms : *Per pale gules and argent, two wings affrontés or.*

RUTI (near Rapperschweil, Premonstratensian).
Founded in 1208 by LUITPOLD, Baron DE ROGGENSBERG.
Arms : *Argent, a capital R sable.*

ST. BLAISIEN (Benedictine, near Basel).
Founded in 963 by the Emperor OTHO.
Arms : *Or, an ibex rampant sable.*

SALZBURG (S. PETER).
Arms : *Or, two keys in saltire sable.*

SCHAFFHAUSEN (Benedictine).
Founded in 1052 by EBERHARD, Count of NELLEN-BERG.
Arms: *Or, a ram proper, issuant from a house in sinister flank gules.*

SEITENSTELLEN.
Arms : *Gules, on a mount in base vert, a pole crossed by a staff raguly in bend argent,*

STEINFELD (Benedictine, afterwards Premonstratensian).
Arms : *Argent, a heart gules pierced by two arrows in saltire proper.*

TRAUNKIRCHEN.
Arms : *Gules, two "morning stars" in saltire or.*

WELTERHAUSEN.
Arms : *Barry of four gules, sable, or, gules.*

WORMS.
Arms : *Azure, three fleurs-de-lis or.*

WÜLZBERG.
Arms : *Azure, a crosier in pale or, traversed by a key and sword in saltire argent.*

ZÜRICH.
Arms : *Argent, a stag passant, having a lighted candle between its horns, all proper.*

NÜRNBERG (S. Sebald).
Arms : *Gules, a fess argent ; over all S. SEBALD as a pilgrim holding a church, all proper.*

LUOGK.

Arms : *Argent, a distaff proper.*

MAULBRONN (in Würtemberg, Cistercian).

Founded in 1138 (*Orig. Cist.*, i., pp. 56, 57).

Arms : *Or, a bend-compony of five pieces, three of gules, two of argent.*

WERDEN-HELMSTADT (Abbey).

Arms : *Quarterly, of six in two rows each of three quarters ;* 1 and 6. *Azure, a cross argent ;* 2 and 5. *Azure, a double-headed eagle argent ;* 3 and 4. *Gules, two crosiers in saltire argent.* On an escucheon en surtout the personal arms of the abbot. (These were, for Abbot SONNIUS, 1757-1774 ; *Azure, a sun in splendour or ;* and for Abbot BIRNBAUM, 1780-1797, *Argent, on a mount in base a tree vert.* (*See* also p. 77.)

The sword and crozier are placed in saltire behind the shield, and it is surmounted by three crested helms. Of these the dexter is ; *Out of a crest-coronet Or a double-headed eagle argent.* The central helm bears *a mitre on a crimson cushion ;* and the sinister helm is timbred with the personal crest of the abbot. (This for Abbot SONNIUS was, *Out of a crest-coronet the sun in splendour or, between two wings argent ;* for Abbot BIRNBAUM the crest was *Out of a crest-coronet or, a mount vert thereon a tree proper between two wings argent.*

S. VINCENT AU BOIS (Augustinian Abbey).

In the Diocese of CHARTRES, founded by GEOFFREY, Bishop of CHARTRES in 1066, enlarged by HUGHES DE CHÂTEAUNÉUF in 1130.

The arms of ALENÇON, viz., *Azure, three fleurs-de-lis or, on a bordure gules eight plates.*

2 D

FÉCAMP (Benedictine).

Founded in 658. It was the richest, and most magnificent in Normandy.

Arms: *Quarterly*, 1 and 4. FRANCE; 2 and 3. *Gules, two lions passant gardant or*, NORMANDY. *Over all . . . three mitres proper.* Sometimes the arms in the *surtout* are used alone.

JUMIÈGES (Benedictine).

Founded in 655 by S. PHILIBERT; rebuilt by ROBERT, Archbishop of CANTERBURY; consecrated in 1069 by the Archbishop of ROUEN in the presence of WILLIAM THE CONQUEROR.

Arms: . . . *a cross . . . between four keys . . .*

AMIENS.

Arms: *Argent, two bends gules; Or, three mallets gules; Argent, three mallets gules.*

ARRAS.

Arms: *Or, two crosiers addorsed in pale argent, within an orle of rats following exterior line of shield sable.*

ARRAS (S. VAAST D'ARRAS) (Benedictine).

Founded in 658.

Arms: *Or, a cross ancrée gules.* JEAN, Abbot in 1483, bore: *Quarterly*, 1 and 4. . . . *a crown* . . . ; 2 and 3. . . . *a bend* . . . The shield is *soutenu* by an angel, and supported by two rats (for Arras). (DEMAY, *Sceaux de la Normandie*, No. 2640.)

MONT ST. QUENTIN (Benedictine).

Founded *c.* 644.

Arms: . . . *a crosier in pale between on the dexter a crescent surmounted by a fleur-de-lis; on the sinister an estoile.* (DEMAY, *Sceaux de la Normandie*, No. 2695.)

ST. BERTIN (Benedictine).
Founded about 600 by S. WINNOCK, near St. Omer.
Arms : . . . *two crosiers in saltire* . . . *between four hunting horns.* Later it appears that the arms were *three lions rampant.* (DEMAY, *Sceaux de la Normandie,* Nos. 2704, 2711.)

NOTRE DAME D'ONAN (or D'ONNANS) at Dôle (Cistercian). Founded in 1595.
Arms : *Sable, a cross argent.*

MONT-BÉNOIT (Augustinian Abbey).
Founded in 1141.
Arms : *Azure, the figure of* S. AUGUSTINE *in pontificals or.*

BEAUME (Abbaie Royale de).
Arms ; *Azure, two keys in saltire or, and* S. PETER *seated proper.*

TROIS-ROIS, or LIEU CROISSANT (Cistercian Abbey in Franche Comté).
Arms : *Azure, three Eastern crowns, two and one, in chief a star of eight rays argent* (*Orig. Cist.,* i., p. 33).

AMBINAY (Abbey).
Arms : *Azure, a chevron or, between two crescents argent in chief, and a lion rampant of the second in base.*

S. ANDOCHE D'AUTUN (Benedictine Abbey).
Founded about the close of the sixth century under the patronage of Queen BRUNEHAUT.
Arms : *Azure, the* BLESSED VIRGIN *proper.*

NOTRE DAME D'AUTUN (Collegiate Chapter).
Arms : *Azure, three keys, two and one, wards in chief or.*

NOTRE DAME DE BOUS (Chazey) (Cistercian).
Founded *c.* 1155.
Arms : *Azure, the* BLESSED VIRGIN MARY *having in front of her a shield : Azure, on a chevron between three estoiles or, as many escallops gules.*

VARENBON (Chapter).
Arms : *Azure, a mitre or, between two ermine spots sable.*

BOURG EN BRESSE (Chapter of Notre Dame).
Arms : *Azure, two keys in saltire or.*

CHALONS (Cathedral Chapter of S. Vincent).
Arms : *Azure, fleury or, over all the royal sceptre gules.*

CLUNY (Chief Abbey of the Benedictine Order, near Mâcon).
Founded in 910 by WILLIAM IX., Duke of AQUITAINE, destroyed by the revolutionists in 1793.
Arms : *Gules, a sword in pale, point in chief, and two keys in saltire argent.*

LA CHASSAIGNE EN BRESSE (Cistercian Abbey). (N. D., DE).
Founded in 1145 and 1151 by ETIENNE DE VILLARS on setting out and returning from the Crusade.
Arms : *Bendy of six or and gules (Orig. Cist.,* i., p. 147).

MONTLUEL EN BRESSE (Collegiate Chapter).
Arms : *Gules, two keys in saltire, wards in chief argent.*

TOURNUS (S. Philibert de) (Benedictine Abbey between Mâcon and Chalons).
This is said to have originated in a small religious house founded in the second century.
Arms : *Gules, a crosier or, and a sword proper, accostés in pale.*

LUXEUIL (Benedictine).
Founded in 590 by the Irish Missionary COLUMBANUS.
Arms : *Azure, the figure of* S. BENEDICT *or.*

GRACE-DIEU (Besançon) (Cistercian) (*Orig. Cist.,* i., p. 57).
Founded *c.* 1139 by RICHARD DE MONTFAUCON.
Arms : *Or, three bars sable, on the first two cross-crosslets argent.*

ACEY (Notre Dame d') (Cistercian).
Founded *c.* 1137 by RENAUD III., Comte de BOUR-
GOGNE (JANAUSCHEK, *Orig. Cist.,* i., p. 40).
Arms : *Gules, a cross argent.*

S. VINCENT DE BESANÇON (Benedictine).
Founded in 1092 by HUGUES, Archbishop of
BESANÇON.
Arms : *Azure, a crosier in pale between the letters* S.
and V. *or.*

BUILLON (Notre Dame de) (Cistercian).
Founded in 1133 (*Orig. Cist.,* i., p. 110).
Arms : *Or, two roses in chief gules, and a trefoil in base sable.*

LA CHARITÉ (Cistercian Abbey, near Besançon).
Founded in 1133 by ALAYS DE TREVA (*Orig. Cist.,*
i., p. 30).
Arms : *Or, a pelican in its piety gules.*

CHERLIEU (Notre Dame de) (celebrated Cistercian
Abbey) (*Orig. Cist.,* i., p. 19).
Founded *c.* 1127 by S. BERNARD. It bore, like
MOLAISE, BUSSIÈRE, CITEAUX, MAIZIÈRE, DIJON, and
other Cistercian Abbeys, the old shield of FRANCE
charged with the arms of BURGUNDY-ANCIENT, *Bendy*

of six or and azure, a bordure gules. Sometimes BUR-
GUNDY alone is used by the Cistercians (*v.* p. 415).

GOAILLE (Notre Dame de) (Augustinian Abbey, near
Salins).
Founded in 1207.
Arms : *Or, a saltire gules.*

ST. CLAUDE (ancient and illustrious Benedictine Abbey
in Mt. Jura).
Arms : *Argent, two staves raguly in saltire gules, and a
bar coupé in fess vert, in chief a trefoil of the last,
in base a crescent of the second.* Otherwise :
Azure, the figure of S. CLAUDE *in pontificals or*
(but these were the arms of the Chapter).

LA FERTÉ SUR GRÔNE (Cistercian). (Notre Dame de.)
Founded about 1113 by the Counts of CHALONS).
Arms : *Per pale argent and gules, in the latter a castle
of the first, from its port a hand issues and holds a
crosier in pale upon the argent.* (Sometimes the
whole field is *gules*.) (*Orig. Cist.*, i., p. 3.)

PONTIGNY (Cistercian).
Founded about 1114 by THIBAUT, Count DE CHAM-
PAGNE (*Orig. Cist.*, i., p. 4).
Arms : *In base a bridge of three arches, out of it a tree
in pale between two fleurs-de-lis, on the tree a bird.*

GEMBLOUX (in Brabant) (Benedictine).
Founded in the tenth century.
Arms : *Sable, three keys argent.* (Its Abbots had title
of Count.)

AFFLIGEM, or AFFLINGHEM (Benedictine) (in Brabant).
Founded about 1085.
Arms : *Gules, two keys in saltire surmounted by a sword
in pale argent.*

VLIERBACH.

Arms: *Or, the seated figure of the* BLESSED VIRGIN, *holding the* HOLY CHILD, *all proper.*

CORSSENDONCK (Augustinian Nunnery).

Arms: *Or, the figure of the* BLESSED VIRGIN, *standing and holding the* HOLY CHILD *proper.*

DEN GROOTEN BIGARDE (Benedictine Nuns).

Arms: *Per pale* (à) *Gules, a crescent argent;* (b) *Or, three chevrons sable.*

ANTWERP (Premonstratensian Abbey of S. MICHAEL).

Arms: *Gules, a cross argent, angled with rods or sceptres, topped with fleurs-de-lis of the same.*

VILLERS (Cistercian) (*Orig. Cist.*, i., p. 87).

Arms: *Quarterly,* 1 and 4. *Vert, a Paschal-Lamb proper;* 2 and 3. *Or, a lion rampant sable.*

PUITS D'ORBE (Côte d'Or) (Benedictine Nunnery of the BLESSED VIRGIN MARY).

Founded by RAYNAUD, Sire DE MONTBAR, *c.* 1120.

Arms: *Azure fleury or, a bordure componé of six pieces argent and of the first, all within another bordure gules.* (HOZIER, *Armorial Général de* FRANCE; *Généralite de Bourgogne.*)

COMBERTAULT.

Arms: *Azure, two crosiers in saltire or.*

MARCILLY (Cistercian Nunnery known as Notre Dame de Bon-Repos).

Founded in 1239 by BURET DE PREIS, Chevalier, and MARIE D'ANGLURE, his wife. In 1460 the nuns were replaced by Cistercian monks (*Orig. Cist.*, i., p. 278).

Arms: *Sable, a bend or; impaling Azure, three roses argent.*

PRALON, NOTRE DAME DE (Côte d'Or) (Benedictine Nunnery).
Founded in 1149 by GUI DE SOMBERNON.
Arms : *Azure, three bars or.*

S. ROMAIN.
Founded in 1088.
Arms : *Azure, a crosier or.*

PALLEAU PRIORY (Burgundy).
Arms : *Per pale* (a) *Azure, three eagle's legs and claws, two and one, or ;* (b) *Gules, a crosier in pale, surmounted by a mitre argent.*

FLAVIGNY (Benedictine Mitred Abbey).
Founded in the eighth century, now Dominican.
Arms : *Azure, three towers argent, two and one.* (*Azure,* S. STEPHEN *or,* is also assigned to the " Abbaye de Flavigny " in HOZIER'S *Armorial Général de France.*)

MOUTIER-SAINT-JEAN (Benedictine Abbey of celebrity, styled " l'abbaye royale de " M. S. J.).
Arms : FRANCE-ANCIENT.

VAL-CROISSANT (Cistercian), near Valence.
Founded in 1188 (*Orig. Cist.,* i., p. 188).
Arms : *Gules, the figure of the* BLESSED VIRGIN MARY (Notre Dame de l'Assumption) *proper, cantoned with four crescents or.*

CHÂTILLON-SUR-SEINE (Augustinian).
Founded before 1138 in the Diocese of LANGRES.
Here S. BERNARD studied.
Arms : *Azure, the figure of the* BLESSED VIRGIN MARY *argent between two towers of the same.*

S. MARCEL (at Châlon-sur-Saône).
Founded about 580 by a son of K. CLOTHAIR. Here
ABÉLARD died in 1142.

> Arms: *Or, four bends sinister gules* (according to
> HOZIER, but ?).

S. MARTIN (at Autun).

> Arms: *Gules, a sword and a crosier accostés in pale
> proper, on a chief azure two fleurs-de-lis or.*

SEMÙR (en Brionnois) (Chapter of).

> Arms: *Azure, the figure of* S. NIZIER *in pontificals or.*

S. SULPICE EN BRESSE (Cistercian Abbey, originally a
Clugniac Priory).
It was given before 1140 to the Cistercians by
AMADEUS III., Count of SAVOY (*Orig. Cist.*, i., p. 27).

> Arms: (of SAVOY) *Gules, a cross argent.*

BAR-SUR-SEINE (Collegiate Chapter of).

> Arms: *Gules, a dragon or.*

FONTENAY, NOTRE DAME DE (Cistercian Abbey, near
Vezelay) (*Orig. Cist.*, i., p. 8).

> Arms: *Gules, three bends or; over all two barbel
> embowed and addorsed proper, in chief a fleur-de-lis
> of the second.*

FONTMOIS, also bore the same. (HOZIER, *Armorial de
FRANCE, Généralité de Bourgogne*).

NUITS (Chapter of S. DENIS at).

> Arms: *Azure, three cinquefoils or.*

BEAUNE (Chapter of the Collegiate Church).
Arms: *Azure, the* BLESSED VIRGIN MARY, *seated and holding in her arms the* HOLY CHILD.

DIJON (Collegiate Chapter of S. JOHN THE BAPTIST).
Arms: *Azure, the figure of* S. JOHN THE BAPTIST, *holding in his arms a lamb proper.*

TART, NOTRE DAME DE (celebrated Cistercian Abbey).
Founded in 1135, under the invocation of Notre Dame de l'Assomption, by ARNOLF CORNU and his wife EMMELINE, with the aid of HUGH, Duke of BURGUNDY.
Arms: .*Azure, " the Assumption " proper.*

RELIGIOUS HOUSES IN STYRIA.

SIEBMACHER gives in the *Wappenbuch* (vol. iii., 78), the following arms of religious houses in Styria.

FAHRA (Provostry) ; *Per fess ;* (a) *in chief. Azure, a group of The Incredulity of* S. THOMAS ; (b) *in base, Argent, an eagle's leg in fess conjoined with a wing sable.*

GÖSS (" Aptey des Frauen Closter zu Göss ") ; *Or, a horse-shoe sable.*

NEUBURG (Aptey) ; *Azure, a cross treflé-fitchée or, surmounted in base by a horse-shoe of the second.*

PÄLLA (Provostry) ; *Per fess ;* (a) *Tierced in pale :* 1. *Gules, the demi-figure of a saint (? The Saviour) ;* 2. *Argent, an eagle displayed gules ;* 3. *Gules, a demi-figure of the Blessed Virgin holding the Holy Child proper ;* . (b) *Sable, a horse (?) courant to the sinister argent.*

QUADMUNDT (Abbey) ; *Per pale argent and gules two fusils-throughout, conjoined and counter-changed.*

RHEIN (Abbey); *Azure, a large German letter* M *the centre lines in the form of a cross cantoned with* A.R.I.A., *making (with the enclosing* M) *the name of the Blessed Virgin Mary, the whole Or, and crowned with an open crown of the same.*

ROTTENMAN (Provostry); *Azure, three balls or,* 1 and 2·

SAINT LAMPRECHT (Abbey); *Azure, a capital letter* L.

SEGGAU (Provostry); *Gules, a chief of fur (au naturel) argent.*

STAINTZ (Provostry); *Gules, a heart-shaped leaf reversed argent.*

CHAPTER VII.

ARMS AND DEVICES OF REGULAR RELIGIOUS COMMUNITIES.

MENTION has been made of the custom by which Bishops, Cardinals, and Popes, sometimes retain, or combine with their armorial bearings, the arms, or devices of the religious orders or communities to which they have belonged. Accordingly, a notice of the chief of these is here given with a brief record of their foundation.

THE ORDER OF ST. BENEDICT.

This is the most ancient of the Monastic Orders of the west. It was founded in 530 by S. BENEDICT of Nursia. Its cradle was the celebrated Abbey of MONTE CASSINO in the kingdom of Naples. The majority of the French monasteries followed the rule of this Order. To it belonged the great Abbeys of ST. GERMAIN DES PRÈS, ST. DENIS, ST. MARTIN DE TOURS, JUMIÈGES, MARMOÛTIER, ST. WAUDRILLE, etc. The great Abbey of CLUNY, near MÂCON, was the chief house of the Order in France; and was founded in 910, by GUILLAUME IX., Duke of AQUITAINE, under the headship of BERNON, Abbé of Gigny. At his death S. ODO succeeded to the abbacy, and made it the head of a "Congregation" of dependent houses (*v.i.*). CLUNY was dedicated to SS. PETER and PAUL, and accordingly, its arms (adopted of course in later times) were allusive to this dedication. They were: *Gules, two keys in saltire wards in chief or, in front of a sword in pale proper, the hilt in base.* (Like those of the See of EXETER, Plate XXII., fig. 2.) But the Order of S. Benedict was never a united body under one head, so that it had no distinct arms (MENÊTRIER, *Recherches du Blason*, p. 177), and many of its houses simply used the effigy of the founder on their seals.

In England the Order was commonly known as "*the Black Friars*," and was the most important of the religious communities. To it belonged the Monasteries of CHESTER, GLOUCESTER, OXFORD, and PETER-BOROUGH, which afterwards became cathedrals; besides many others of almost equal splendour and importance, *e.g.*, BATTLE, CROYLAND, GLASTONBURY, MILTON, PERSHORE, RAMSEY, SELBY, SHERBORNE, and TEWKS-BURY. In Scotland we may mention COLDINGHAM, DUNFERMLINE, and TYNINGHAM.

THE CISTERCIAN ORDER.

This was a reformation of the Benedictine Order which originated with S. ROBERT, Abbé de MOLESME, in the Diocese of Langres. He with other monks seceded and in 1098 founded a monastery at CÎTEAUX, near Dijon in Burgundy. Its most noted daughter-abbeys were: CLAIRVAUX (of which S. BERNARD was the first abbot), LA FERTÉ, PONTIGNY, and MORIMOND. From these "les quatres premières filles de Clairvaux" originated an infinite number of abbeys; and certain semi-religious, semi-military, Orders of Knighthood, all under the Benedictine "rule." The celebrated Orders of ALCAN-TARA, AVIS, CALATRAVA, and MONTESA, established in the Peninsula to defend church and state against the Moorish invaders, were all of the filiation of the Cistercian Abbey of MORIMOND (JANAUSCHEK, *Orig. Cist.*, i., p. 5).

The Cistercians were often known as BERNARDINES from S. BERNARD who reformed the "rule." The arms adopted for all the Cistercian houses were: FRANCE-ANCIENT, thereon an escucheon of BURGUNDY-ANCIENT (i.e., *Azure, semé of fleur-de-lis or;* an escucheon *en surtout: Bendy of six or and azure, within a bordure gules*). The Bernardine houses used: *Sable, a bend counter-compony argent and gules;* probably the coat of the ancient Counts of TROYES, who founded and endowed CLAIRVAUX. These coats seem to be common to the whole of the Cistercian foundations. The Abbeys of CITEAUX, DIJON, LIEU-DIEUX, MOLAISE, etc., bore the former only. But other houses adopted different arms; *e.g.*, the Abbey of BUSSIÈRE, and the Priory of S. John the Evangelist at AUXOIS, near Semur, both bore the arms of BURGUNDY-ANCIENT only. At NÔTRE DAME DE BALERNE, near Besançon, the arms were: *Per pale* (a) *Azure, billetty a lion rampant or* (BURGUNDY-COUNTY); (b) *Gules, an eagle displayed or* (BESANÇON). The Abbeys of FONTMOIS, and NÔTRE DAME DE FONTENET, near Semur, both used: *Gules, three bends or, over all two barbel addorsed in pale proper, in chief a fleur-de-lis of the second.*

In England the first of the Cistercian houses was founded at Waverley, in Surrey in the year 1129. By the time of EDWARD I. there were no less than sixty-one. FOUNTAINS, TINTERN, KIRKSTALL, FURNESS, BEAULIEU, SCARBOROUGH, BYLAND, NETLEY, and RIEVAULX; in Scotland, MELROSE, BALMERINO, CUPAR, CULROSS, SWEETHEART, GLENLUCE, DEIR, KINLOSS, etc., all belonged to this Order.

In France, the FEUILLANTS and TRAPPISTS, are both reforms of the Cistercians. The FEUILLANTS originated in JEAN DE LA BARRIÈRE in 1578, and took their name from an abbey at Toulouse. The TRAPPISTS were so called from the Abbey of LA TRAPPE in which a reform was instituted by ARMAND JEAN LE BOUTILLIER DE RANCE, Abbè in 1663. The CONGRÉGATION DE S. MAUR (near Paris) was another offshoot. It had for its device the word PAX between a fleur-de-lis above, and three Passion nails beneath, all within a crown of thorns. *Les Filles Anglaises* of the Benedictine rule founded a house in Paris in 1620.

The CLUGNIACS were, as has been stated above, a reformed Order of Benedictines who, under S. BERNON, Abbé de Gigny, built a monastery at Cluny, on the Sâone in 912. Its first principal priories were LA CHARITÉ (sur Loire) ; S. MARTIN DES CHAMPS, at Paris ; SOUVIGNY, SOUCILANGES, and LEWES. MEAUX and VEZELAY, in France ; CASTLE-ACRE, BERMONDSEY, THETFORD, and WENLOCK in England ; CROSS-RAGUEL and PAISLEY in Scotland ; were all houses of this Benedictine reform.

The CARTHUSIAN ORDER (CHARTREUX).

This Order, a reformation of the Benedictine rule, was founded about 1086, by S. BRUNO, of Cologne, a Canon of Reims, who established himself with his six disciples in a wild and picturesque district near Grenoble, where he built the monastery, now known as *la Grande Chartreuse*, on land given by Bishop HUGUES DE CHÂTEAUNEUF. In 1170 Pope ALEXANDER took the Order formally under the protection of the Holy See. The arms of the Order, are : *Argent, an orb azure, banded and surmounted by a cross or.*

These seem to have been derived from the following story. Pope BENEDICT VIII. gave to the Emperor HENRY II., an Imperial orb, which he sent to the Abbey of Cluny, saying that it could not be in better hands than in those of men who had renounced the pomps and vanities of this wicked world. The Carthusians adopted it as the charge of their arms to denote a like renunciation. The Order was established in England where they had the foundation now known as the CHARTERHOUSE (a corruption of CHARTREUX), SKENE in Surrey, and MOUNT GRACE.

ORDER OF S. AUGUSTIN (AUSTIN FRIARS, or "EREMITES.")

This monastic Order dates from 1256, when Pope ALEXANDER IV. united into one "congregation" hermits of different institutions, under the name of "Hermits of St. Augustin." (These are not to be confounded with the "Regular Canons" of S. Augustin which follow.)

They were divided into four provinces: France, Germany, Italy and Spain. The monks were called "les grands Augustins" to distinguish them from "*les petits Augustins*, or *Guillemites* (an Order founded in Italy by a Frenchman, GUILLAUME DE MALAVAL, in 1157, and who had a monastery at Montrouge near Paris. These became extinct in 1680.) "*Les grands Augustins*" were one of the four mendicant Orders. In 1588 SIXTUS V., subjected them to reform, and the new Congregation was called "*les Augustins 'déchaussés'*" or "*Petits pères*" (*de la Mort*).

MENÊTRIER tells us that this Order had no fixed arms ; but that he had seen used in some places : *Argent, a chief sable, in base a heart gules, inflamed on the chief proper.* Sometimes the heart was pierced with two arrows azure. The convent of the Augustins at PONTARLIER, bore : *Or, a heart inflamed gules, pierced in bend by an arrow sable, the feathers and head argent ;* that at Saint AMOUR, in Franche Comté, did the same. At GRAY, the heart was pierced by two arrows in saltire or.

In Italy the arms were : *Per fess, sable and argent, over all a pastoral staff, round which in base was wrapped the cincture of S. Monica, sable.*

The convent of the *Augustins déchaussés* at BROU, in Burgundy, bore : *Gules, St. Augustin or.* Those at MONTCROISSANT : *Argent, a St. Augustin proper, habited, etc., purpure.*

Les Filles de la Conception, known as *les Dames Anglaises*, followed the rule of S. Augustin and had a house in Paris established in 1633.

THE AUGUSTINE CANONS.

Regular Canons of S. AUGUSTINE ; these, commonly called "*the Black Canons*," were an Order of conventual Canons who followed the rule of S. AUGUSTIN (less stringent than that of S. BENEDICT). They came into England in *c.* 1105, and were only second to the Benedictines in wealth and power. They possessed the Priory of CARLISLE, and the Abbey of S. AUGUSTINE at BRISTOL, both of which were made Cathedrals by HENRY VIII. They also had the mitred Abbeys of CIRENCESTER and WALTHAM.

THE PREMONSTRATENSIANS.

These, known in England as the "*White Canons*" from the colour of their habit and cloak, were Canons who adopted the rule of S. AUGUSTIN as revised by S. NORBERT of Cleves, Archbishop of Magdeburg. In 1120 he founded a monastery in the Diocèse of LAON known as Prémontré, from a legend that a certain meadow had been indicated by an angel as the site of the proposed building. HONORIUS II. gave them his sanction in 1126, and they were introduced into England about the year 1140. The Abbot of WELBECK was head of the Order here. TORRE, EAST DEREHAM, and HALESOWEN were English Monasteries. DRYBURGH and FERNE were the chief houses in Scotland. In France the arms of the Order (given, it was said, by S. LOUIS) were : FRANCE - ANCIENT, *over all two crosiers in saltire or ;* but the house at AUXERRE bore : *Azure, a crosier in pale between two fleurs-de-lis or.*

2 E

FRANCISCANS (Minorites).

This celebrated Order was founded by S. FRANCIS of Assisi, in 1206. Its monks were called *Cordeliers*, from the cord round their waists ; and "*Frères-mineurs*" because they claimed *inferiority* to other religious Orders. The Order was reformed in the fifteenth century by S. BERNARDINO of Siena : and became divided into two sections, OBSERVANTINS and CONVENTUELS; of whom the first adopted the reform, while the latter did not. About the close of the same century, another reform took place in Spain, where those who adopted it were known as *Recogidos ;* which, translated into French, gave another name to the reformed Order—*les Récollets.* Lastly, in 1525 the reform of MATTEO BASCHI, approved by CLEMENT VII. in 1528, produced the CAPUCHINS, so called from the long hood of their brown habit. The Franciscans were one of the four mendicant orders ; the others were the Augustins, the Carmelites, and the Dominicans.

The religious houses of the nuns known as CAPUCINES were under Capuchin direction. They followed the strict rule of SANCTA CLARA, and were also known as "*les Filles de la Passion.*"

The arms of the Franciscan Order are : *Argent, a cross of Calvary traversed by two human arms in saltire (sometimes issuant from clouds in base), one in bend naked, representing the arm of our Saviour, the other in bend sinister habited in the dress of S. Francis, both bearing the* stigmata. (The Franciscan *Cordeliére* is sometimes knotted round the shield.)

The arms were borne in chief above their own by Pope CLEMENT IV. and by ANTONIO, Cardinal BARBERINI, brother of Pope URBAN VIII. (*v. ante*, pp. 143, 166). The Franciscan monastery at BESANÇON made the field of the arms *gules*, the cross *or*. That at BOURG-EN-BRESSE had the field *azure*.

The *Tiercelins*, or *Penitents of the Third Order of S. Francis*, often bore as device the dove of the Holy Spirit above a heart inflamed, or dropping tears.

The DOMINICANS (" FRÈRES PRÉCHEURS," " FRIAR PREACHERS," " JACOBINS," " BLACKFRIARS ").

S. DOMINIC (DE GUZMAN), Canon of Osma in Old Castile, founded this Order in 1205. It was confirmed by Pope INNOCENT III. in 1216. It followed the rule of S. AUGUSTIN. In the year 1221 the first English house of the Order was founded at Oxford. In 1276 a large monastery was built at London, whence the locality of Black-Friars takes its name. Bishop CLEMENT of Dunblane, who was himself a Dominican, introduced them into Scotland in 1231. LAURENCE, ANDREW, DAVID, and FINLAY, Bishops of ARGYLL between 1261 and 1420, were of this Order. The Dominicans, as has been already said, were a mendicant Order.

In Paris their house was in the Rue S. JACQUES, whence they obtained the name of "*Jacobins*." (From their new house, built in the Rue St. Honoré, the celebrated political club which held its meetings in it at the time of the French Revolution, took its name). The well-known arms of the Order are : *Argent, chapé sable* (the colours of the habit). To this simple coat additions were afterwards made : *In base a hound couchant, holding in its mouth a torch blazing proper ; in chief a palm branch and a branch of lilies proper, issuing out of an open crown proper, and surmounted by an estoile or.* These arms were borne, with their own, by Popes BENEDICT XIII. and XIV. (*vide* pp. 143, 165, 166).

Mrs JAMESON says, in her *Legends of the Monastic Orders*, p. 376 :—" Before he " (S. DOMINIC) "was born his mother dreamed that she had brought forth a black-and-white dog, carrying in his mouth a lighted torch. When his godmother held him at the font she beheld a star of wonderful splendour descend from heaven and settle on his brow. The colours of the habit, black over white, which form the field of the arms, were said to have been determined by the BLESSED VIRGIN herself, in a vision seen at Orleans by a monk of the Order. It is black and white, the white denoting purity of life, the black mortification and penance. Hence, when the Dominicans are figured as dogs (*Domini canes*), a common allegory, they are always white, with patches of black."

The convent of Dominicans at MONBOSON, en Franche Comté, registered their arms as : " *d'Argent, chapé de sable, à deux étoiles d'or en chef, et un chien couché de sable en pointe, tenant en sa gueule un flambeau de même allumé de gueules.*"

The convent of Jacobine nuns in the town of CHALON-SUR-SAÔNE used as its arms : *Argent, S. Dominic, habited sable ;* those at SEMUR and BEAUNE : *Azure, S. Catharine of Siena* (*argent*, at BEAUNE ; *or*, at SEMUR): Those at AUTUN had *S. Catharine proper on a shield argent.* (HOZIER, *Armorial Général de France.*)

THE CARMELITES.

This Order took its name from Mount Carmel, where there was an Order of monks some of whom came into Europe during the Crusades. It was recognised by ALEXANDER III., 1170.

The nunneries of this Order were reformed by S. THERESA of Avila, in Spain, in 1568 ; and, under her counsels, the like reform was initiated among the monks of the Order by S. JEAN DE LA CROIX. Those who accepted the reform were known as *Carmes déchaussés*, because they went barefoot. The original arms of the Order were : *Sable, mantelé* (or *chapé*), *argent ;* to this were afterwards added *three estoiles counter-changed.* The *Carmes Déchaussés* made the sable point in base terminate in a cross *patée* on the argent chief. The CARMELITES were one of the four mendicant Orders.

MINIMES (BONSHOMMES).

This Order was founded by S. FRANCIS DE PAULE in 1440, and confirmed by Pope SIXTUS V. in 1473. Its device was the word "CHARITAS," usually divided into three syllables, on an azure field, and enclosed in an oval of golden rays. There were also at Abbeville nuns of this Order who took the name of *Minimesses*. They followed the Franciscan rule.

SERVITES (" Servi B. M. Virginis ").

The Order of the SERVITES, or SERVITEURS DE LA VIÈRGE. It was founded at Marseilles in 1252. They were commonly known as *les Blancs Manteaux*. Their device was on an azure field a monogram of the letters S.M., out of which springs a plant of seven lilies. They followed the rule of S. AUGUSTINE.

MATHURINS.

The Order of the MATHURINS, or TRINITARIANS, was founded in 1198, by JEAN DE MATHA, for the release of captives taken by the corsairs of the Mediterranean. Their name was derived from the Church of S. MATHURIN in Paris, which was granted to them. They bore : *Argent, a cross patée, the perpendicular gules, the traverse azure.*

THE JESUITS.

This Order, which has played so important a part in affairs both ecclesiastical and secular, was founded in 1534 (and approved by P. PAUL III. in 1540), by a Spaniard, INIGO LOPEZ DE RECALDE, better known as S. IGNATIUS LOYOLA. Its device was the golden name of JÈSUS, in an azure oval, surrounded by golden rays, as at

BOURG-EN-BRESSE and MÂCON ; or more commonly as at BESANÇON, PONTARLIER, GRAY, and VESOUL, the cypher I.H.S., the H surmounted by a cross ; and beneath it three passion nails, within the oval, and all surrounded by the rays. Examples of the use of this device, but without the rays of gold, by Cardinals of the Jesuit Order are given *ante*, p. 142).

A reference to HOZIER'S *Armorial Général de France* shows that some houses of the Order bore different devices ; at Dijon : *Azure*, the names JESUS, MARIA, *or ;* at PARAY : *Azure*, the name JESUS *or*. At SALINS the larger device was blazoned on a field gules.

THE NUNS OF THE VISITATION OF ST. MARY.

This Order was founded at Annecy by S. FRANCIS DE SALES, Bishop of GENEVA, and Madame JEANNE FRANÇOISE, widow of CHRISTOPHER RABUTIN, Baron DE CHANTAL. It was approved by Pope PAUL V. in 1619, and was very widely spread in France. It was under the rule of S. AUGUSTIN. Its device was : *Or, within a crown of thorns proper, a heart gules surmounted by a cross sable, and pierced by two arrows, feathered and pointed argent*. The heart is usually charged with the sacred name JESUS in golden letters. At AVALLON, BOURBON-LANCEY, and some other places, the field of the shield appears to have been azure.

THE GILBERTINES.

These were Canons instituted by S. GILBERT at SEMPRINGHAM in NORFOLK in the year 1148. The rule was in the main that of S. AUGUSTINE. (The nuns were Benedictine.) The arms of SEMPRINGHAM appear to have been : *Argent, two bars gules, over all a crutched staff in bend azure* (or *or*). These arms were borne on a chief above his personal coat ; *Or, a bend between two bull's heads couped sable ;* by ROBERT HOLGATE, Prior of WOTTON, Bishop of LLANDAFF in 1537, Archbishop of YORK in 1545. (*See* also ALVINGHAM, p. 353, and MALTON, p. 378.)

THE CELESTINES.

This was a Benedictine Order founded at Sulmone in 1254 by PIETRO DE MORONE, afterwards Pope as CELESTINE V. It was sanctioned by URBAN VIII. in 1264. The first monastery was at Monte Majella in Naples. PHILIPPE LE BEL introduced them into France in 1300. They were secularised in 1776 and 1778 by Popes CLEMENT XIV. and PIUS VI. Their arms were: *Azure, a Passion-Cross argent, entwined with the letter* S, for SULMONE. In France a fleur-de-lis was placed on either side of the cross.

ORDER OF CAMALDOLI.

This was an Order of Reformed Benedictines, founded by S. ROMUALD in 1012, at Camaldoli near Arezzo in the Apennines. Their arms were: *Azure, a chalice or, out of which drink two doves argent, in chief an estoile of the second.* (*See* the arms of Pope GREGORY XVI. *ante,* p. 167.)

The reformed Camaldolese of MONTE CORONA, near Perugia, bore: *Argent, a mountain of three coupeaux supporting an open crown proper.*

URSULINES.

These nuns who followed the rule of S. AUGUSTINE, established themselves in Paris in 1608. The Congregation was founded by MARIE L'HUILLIER, Dame de S. BEUVE, approved by Pope PAUL V. They occupied themselves chiefly in the education of young women, and had a great number of houses in all parts of the country. Their device consisted of the words JESUS MARIA in Roman letters, on a roundel, or oval. The tinctures varied in different places. That most frequently used was azure, with the words in gold ; as at AUXONNE, VITEAUX, MONTBARD, AUTUN, SEURRE, etc. At PONTARLIER this device was surmounted by a crown : at ORNANS the words were placed beneath a crown or, and above an estoile argent. At AVALON the field was gules, the words or ; this was reversed at PARAY. At SAULIEUX the field was argent, at FLAVIGNY or, the words in both cases sable. At MÂCON and BOURBON-LANCEY the field was azure, the names were surmounted by a cross, and in base were three passion nails. A number of houses bore the effigy of S. URSULA. At SEMUR-EN-AUXOIS, BEAUNE, BELLEY, etc., this was Or, on a field azure ; at NOYERS, Or, on a field gules ; at BOURG-EN-BRESSE, Argent, on a field gules.

The URSULINES at BEAUGENCY bore : *Azure, a golden lily among thorns ;* those of CHARTRES, the golden lily alone ; those of CLERVAL, ARBOIS, and NOZEROY used : *Azure, a lily proper issuing from golden thorns*, as did those of S. HIPPOLYTE but on a field gules.

· THÉATINS.

This Order was founded in 1524 at Chieti (otherwise called Theati, whence came the name) by Cardinal MACELLO GAËTANI of Vicenza; and PIETRO CARAFFA, Bishop of Chieti, who was afterwards Pope as PAUL IV. Their badge was a cross-Calvary on a mountain of three *coupeaux*.

ORATORIANS.

The "Congregation of the Oratory" was founded in Italy in 1558 by S. PHILIP NERI. Its device was a demi-figure of the BLESSED VIRGIN MARY, issuing from a crescent.

The Congregation of the Oratory in France was founded on the model of that in Italy by Cardinal DE

BÉRULLE in 1611, and had the sanction of Pope PAUL V. in 1613. Its badge was the names of "JESUS" and "MARIA," surrounded by a crown of thorns. The tinctures of these devices varied; for instance, at BEAUNE, DIJON, MÂCON, BEŞANÇON, and ORLÉANS, the ground was azure, the names and crown gold. At CHALON-SUR-SAÔNE the ground was argent, and the rest sable. At SALINS the ground was gold, the words azure, the crown vert. At POLIGNY the ground was gules, the words or, the crown vert. At PARIS the first house of the Congregation was in the Faubourg St. Jacques; it was afterwards removed to l'hôtel du Bouchage near the Louvre. Its chapel is now a Protestant meeting-house still called *l'Oratoire*.

In 1852 the Congregation was re-established at Paris under the title of *l'Oratoire de l'Immaculée Conception*.

CHAPTER VIII.

Arms of Universities and Colleges.

.THE UNIVERSITY OF OXFORD.

THE honour of founding the University of OXFORD is usually attributed to King ALFRED, but the arms seem to be based on those attributed in mediæval times to the Saxon King S. EDMUND, viz.: *Azure, three open crowns or.* This coat with the addition of an open book has been in use since the middle of the fifteenth century.

As now borne the arms are: *Azure, between three open crowns or, an open book proper having on the dexter side seven golden seals, and bearing the words " Dominus illuminatio mea."* The opening words of S. JOHN'S Gospel ; the motto " *Sapientia et Felicitate;*" and others, have sometimes been substituted for these. The shield is sometimes represented with the six University maces laid in saltire behind it, sometimes with angel supporters. The supporters in the east window of the Bodleian Library are: *Dexter, a lion rampant or ; sinister, a Paschal-Lamb, holding its banner, and having a key pendant from its sinister fore-foot.* I believe that the origin of these will be found in Rev. v. 5, 6. The "lion of the tribe of Juda ;" and the Lamb with its seven horns and eyes, which had the power to open the book with the seven seals.

The coats of arms now borne for the several Colleges are, as will hereafter appear, mostly assumed from those borne by their respective founders. It does not seem that they were ever the subjects of authoritative grants from the College of Arms, from whose jurisdiction the

University was exempted by a special Charter of HENRY IV., and accordingly in the several *Visitations of Oxford* in the years 1566, 1574, and 1634, no entries of these arms are to be found recorded. (This sufficiently accounts for many variations and irregularities.)

Mr BELL (writing in *Notes and Queries*, 6th S., xii., p. 446) tells us there is strong evidence that in the year 1574 no College bore arms as a corporate body ; for in the church notes compiled in that year by RICHARD LEE, *Portcullis*, though most of the arms now used are given from the stained glass of the chapels, etc., in each case it is the family name of the founder which is attached to the shield, and in no case that of the college. On the other hand it is distinctly stated in the late Dean BURGON'S notes on the *Arms of the Colleges at Oxford* (4to, 1855), that the arms of BRAZENOSE were confirmed by LEE in 1574 ; though Mr BELL says, and I incline to think correctly, that the mode of blazoning ." *Tierced in pale*" was not in use in England at that time.

UNIVERSITY COLLEGE

Is said to have been founded by King ALFRED, but really owed its origin to WILLIAM, Archdeacon of DURHAM, about the year 1249. The arms used are: *Azure, a cross patonce between five martlets*, or *doves, or.* This coat was traditionally ascribed by mediæval heralds to EDWARD THE CONFESSOR, but without the smallest foundation in fact. Dean BURGON suggests that the arms should rather be those of WILLIAM of DURHAM. And in the windows of the chapel the founder's coat appears to be : *Or, a fleur-de-lis azure, on each leaf thereof a mullet gules.*

BALLIOL COLLEGE

Was founded by JOHN BALLIOL of Barnard's Castle, Yorkshire, father of the claimant of the Scottish crown, and his wife DEVORGILLA, daughter of ALAN, Lord of GALLOWAY. BALLIOL died in 1269, but DEVORGILLA carried out his wishes.

The BALLIOL arms are : *Gules, an orle argent,* and these are sometimes represented as dimidiated, and impaled with GALLOWAY : *Azure, a lion rampant argent crowned or.* But if we refer to the counter-seal of DEVORGILLA as appended to the Foundation Charter of the College in 1282, we find, that the arms of GALLOWAY and BALLIOL (the latter dimidiated) are conjoined, GALLOWAY being to the dexter. This is quite in opposition to modern notions, according to which the arms of the husband occupy the place of honour on the *dexter* side. The seal and counter-seal of DEVORGILLA are described in LAING'S, *Catalogue of Scottish Seals,* vol. ii., p. 14, and depicted in Plate V. of the same excellent work. In ASTLE'S *Account of the Seals of the Kings, etc. of Scotland,* 1792, the seal is also engraved, and the *lion* of GALLOWAY appears to undergo a slight diminution (much less than dimidiation), but that this is incorrect seems clear from LAING'S plate.. If the College is not content with the arms of BALLIOL only, I think it would do well to use the conjoined coats as they appear on DEVORGILLA'S seal, and not correct (?) them to suit modern ideas.

MERTON COLLEGE

Was founded in 1264 by WALTER DE MERTON, Bishop of ROCHESTER, Chancellor of ENGLAND in the reign of Henry III. Its arms are : *Or, three chevrons, the first and third per pale gules and azure, the second per pale of the same tinctures inverted.* The patron of WILLIAM DE MERTON was GILBERT DE CLARE, who bore : *Or, three chevrons gules,* and the MERTON coat is, therefore, an instance of a differenced coat borne as a sign of dependence or patronage.

EXETER COLLEGE

Was founded in 1316, by WALTER STAPLETON, Bishop of EXETER (1306-1329). The arms are usually :—
Argent, two bendlets nebulé sable within a bordure of the second charged with eight pairs of keys addorsed and the bows interlaced or. The number of· the keys varies, and· the *bordure* has been sometimes depicted *azure*, sometimes *gules*, and the bends drawn *wavy*, but the coat as first given is said to have been "confirmed" in 1574 (? *vide ante*). The arms of Sir WILLIAM·PETRE, Secretary of State, temp. HENRY VIII., are sometimes impaled with the above, but are often incorrectly drawn. If used at all, the coat granted to Sir WILLIAM, which is described hereafter under WADHAM COLLEGE, is that which should be employed.

ORIEL COLLEGE.

The date· of its foundation is variously given as 1323 and 1326. The arms are the Royal arms of ENGLAND :—
Gules, three lions passant gardant or, differenced by the addition of *a bordure engrailed* (sometimes *invecked*) *argent* These were commemorative of King EDWARD II., to whom, and to ADAM DE BROME, the College owed its foundation. The name of the ·College is said to be derived "from the motto on the sign of a Spaniard's house, who taught Hebrew there when the College was founded, אוריאל, *Deus illuminatio mea*, from whence the University motto was afterwards derived," (Mr MACRAY in *Notes and Queries*, 8th S., iv., p. 405, from Bodl. MS., Rawlinson, D. 912, f. 249).

QUEEN'S COLLEGE

Was founded in 1340 by ROBERT DE EGLESFIELD, Confessor of Queen PHILLIPPA, wife of EDWARD III. The arms are : *Argent, three eagles displayed gules, armed or, on that in dexter chief a mullet of six points pierced of the third*, for difference (a mark of cadency which appears to be often forgotten).

NEW COLLEGE.

This College was founded by WILLIAM of WYKEHAM, Bishop of WINCHESTER, in the year 1375. The College bears the arms of the founder, viz., *Argent, two chevrons sable between three roses gules, seeded or, barbed vert*. The idea that these chevrons were made double to denote the Bishop's double foundations is unfounded ; they appear on the Bishop's seal as Archdeacon of LINCOLN. (See *Herald and Genealogist*, vol. v., pp. 226, 227.)

These arms are borne impaled on the sinister side, with those of the See of WINCHESTER (*vide ante*, p. 174). to the dexter. The whole is surrounded with the Garter, and ensigned with a mitre.

LINCOLN COLLEGE.

This College owed its original foundation to HUGH FLEMYNG, Bishop of LINCOLN in 1429. THOMAS SCOTT, Archbishop of YORK in 1479, is counted as its second founder. The arms borne by the College are commemorative of both its benefactors ; they are *Tierced in pale* (a) *Barry of six argent and azure, in chief three lozenges gules, on the second bar of argent a mullet pierced sable*, for Bishop FLEMYNG ; (b) *Or, on an escucheon the arms of the* See of LINCOLN (*vide ante*, p. 183) surmounted by a mitre proper; (c) *Vert, three stags trippant argent, attired or*, for THOMAS SCOTT or ROTHERAM, Bishop of LINCOLN in 1472, and Archbishop of YORK in 1480.

ALL SOULS COLLEGE

Was founded in 1437 by HENRY CHICHELY, Archbishop of CANTERBURY. The College accordingly bears the arms of the founder : *Or, a chevron between three cinquefoils pierced gules*.

MAGDALEN COLLEGE

Was founded in 1459 by WILLIAM of WAYNFLETE, Bishop of WINCHESTER, under the name of WINCHESTER COLLEGE. The arms are those of the founder. *Lozengy* (or rather *fusilly*) *sable and ermine; on a chief of the first three garden lilies argent, the stamens or.* (The chief contains the old arms of ETON College.)

BRAZENOSE, or BRAZEN NOSE.

The date of the foundation of this College is probably 1512, though some authorities say three years earlier, or as many later. Its first founder was WILLIAM SMITH, Bishop of LINCOLN, and its later benefactor Sir RICHARD SUTTON. The name is probably derived from *Brasinium*, mediæval Latin for a brew-house, which formerly occupied a portion of the site of the College.

The arms at present used are said by Dean BURGON to have been confirmed by LEE, *Portcullis*, in 1574, but as already pointed out, this seems very doubtful. They are :—*Tierced in pale* (a) *Argent, a chevron sable between three roses gules seeded or, barbed vert,* the arms of Bishop SMITH ; (b) *Or, on an escucheon surmounted by a mitre proper, the arms of the* See of LINCOLN (*vide ante*, p. 183); (c) *Quarterly,* 1 and 4. *Argent, a chevron between three bugle horns stringed sable,* for SUTTON. 2 and 3. *Argent, a chevron between three cross-crosslets sable,* SAINSBURY. (There appears to be some doubt if these coats were really borne by Sir RICHARD SUTTON ; but as used now they are intended to commemorate the benefactors of the College.)

CORPUS CHRISTI COLLEGE

Was founded by RICHARD FOX, Bishop of WINCHESTER in the year 1516, and afterwards enriched by Bishop HUGH OLDHAM. The arms are : *Tierced in pale* (a) *Azure, a pelican or, vulned proper,* for RICHARD

Fox, the founder; (b) *Argent, an escucheon charged with the arms of the* See of WINCHESTER (*vide ante*, p. 184), *and surmounted by a mitre proper;* (c) *Sable, a chevron or, between three owls argent; on a chief of the second as many roses gules, barbed vert, seeded gold.* These are the canting arms (*Owl*dham) of Bishop OLDHAM.

CHRIST CHURCH,

Founded by Cardinal WOLSEY, and completed by HENRY VIII. It was originally called CARDINAL'S COLLEGE, and on its seal as such are the arms (of WOLSEY) as at present borne, but supported by two silver griffins, each holding a golden column, or staff. (*See* DUGDALE'S *Monasticon*, p. 11, pl. 10.) The arms are: *Sable, on a cross engrailed argent a lion passant gules between four leopard's faces azure; on a chief or, a rose of the third, barbed vert, seeded gold, between two Cornish choughs proper.* Modern ingenuity has traced the origin of these bearings (which are very likely of WOLSEY'S own design), to his place of birth, and other circumstances. Thus the *cross engrailed on a sable field* may have been assumed allusively to his birth at IPSWICH in Suffolk. (The Earls of SUFFOLK bore: *Sable, a cross engrailed or.*) The *rose* of ENGLAND, etc., may be allusive to his office under the crown; and the *choughs*, derived probably from the arms of S. THOMAS of CANTERBURY (*Argent, three Cornish choughs sable, beaked and legged gules*), may have been allusive to his own Christian name, and patron saint.

TRINITY COLLEGE

Was the first founded after the REFORMATION, and owed its existence in 1554 to Sir THOMAS POPE. The arms used are those of the founder: *Per pale or and azure, on a chevron between three griffin's heads erased four fleurs-de-lis all counter-changed.* Dean

BURGON tells us, on the authority of the then President, that the *Azure* had been changed to *Vert;* but if this were so it appears that the original and proper tincture has been resumed.

ST. JOHN'S COLLEGE

Was founded by Sir THOMAS WHITE in the year 1557, and bears his arms: *Gules, on a canton ermine a lion rampant sable, all within a bordure of the last charged with eight estoiles or. On the honour point an annulet or.* Probably the annulet was originally a mark of cadency (as *e.g.* in the arms of Earl of BANTRY), but in some WHITE coats it is the principal charge.

JESUS COLLEGE

Owes its origin to Dr HUGH PRICE, or AP RICE, who obtained a charter for its foundation from Queen ELIZABETH in the year 1571. The arms now borne, and which were probably intended to commemorate the founder, are really those of Archbishop ROTHERHAM (*cf.* LINCOLN, p. 430). They are: *Vert, three bucks trippant argent, attired or,* and appear to be without any authority.

WADHAM COLLEGE

Was founded in 1612 by NICHOLAS WADHAM, and his design was carried out after his decease by his widow DOROTHY PETRE. The arms now used by the College are an impaled coat intended to commemorate both these persons: *Per pale* (a) *Gules, a chevron between three roses argent, barbed vert, seeded or.* WADHAM (b) *Gules, a bend or, between two escallops argent,* PETRE. There is, however, considerable doubt whether these arms were those borne by the lady. Dean BURGON says they are certainly not those used by her father. He had obtained from HENRY

2 F

VIII. an augmentation to the arms of PETRE which consisted of *a chief or, charged with a rose between two demi lilies gules*, and moreover the *bend* was charged with a *chough sable between two cinquefoils gules.* (It seems too that the tincture of the field of the coat borne by him was *azure*, while the *escallops* were *or*.) The arms *with the augmentation*, etc., appear on the lady's tomb in ILMINSTER CHURCH, Somersetshire, but as the escucheon has probably been repainted it cannot be appealed to as decisive of the question.

PEMBROKE COLLEGE (originally BROADGATES HALL)

Was founded by THOMAS TESDALE of GLYMPTON in the year 1624. The arms are a composition from the arms of the HERBERTS, Earls of PEMBROKE (WILLIAM HERBERT, Earl of PEMBROKE, being Chancellor of the University at the date of foundation), and are : *Per pale azure and gules, three lions rampant argent ; a chief also per pale or, and of the third, the dexter charged with a rose of* ENGLAND, *the sinister with a thistle vert.*

On this it is only necessary to remark that the thistle in chief should really be *a teazle*, being taken from the *armes parlantes* of the founder, which were : *Argent, a chevron between three teazles vert.*

WORCESTER COLLEGE

Was founded by Sir THOMAS COOKES, Baronet of Norgrove and Bentley in Worcestershire, under the title of GLOUCESTER COLLEGE, in the year 1714. The arms as now borne are : *Or, two chevrons gules between six martlets sable*, with the Baronet's badge of the arms of ULSTER : (*Argent, a hand paleways gules.*) But it appears from Mr GRAZEBROOK'S *Heraldry of Worcestershire* that the arms of the COOKES of Bentley were : *Argent, two chevrons gules between six martlets of the last.* EDMOND-SON attributes to COOKES of Norgrove : *Argent, two chevrons gules between six martlets sable ;* so that in any case the field of the arms now borne appears to be incorrect. The arms borne by COOKES seem to have been assumed from the JENNETTS, whose co-heiress ANNE had espoused WILLIAM COOKES. The original arms of COOKES were apparently : *Barry of six argent and sable, in chief three mullets gules.*

HERTFORD COLLEGE

Was incorporated as a College in 1874 having been previously known as MAGDALENE HALL. Its history appears to be that Bishop WAYNFLETE, the founder of MAGDALENE COLLEGE, erected the Hall as a provision for students previous to admission to the COLLEGE. HERTFORD COLLEGE, which dated from the times of EDWARD I., was originally and for many generations known as HART, or HERT, HALL (*Aula Cervina*). It was incorporated as HERTFORD COLLEGE in 1740, but was insufficiently endowed, and in 1805 there being no Principal and only one Fellow remaining, the College fell into decay. The corporation was dissolved by Act of Parliament in 1822, and the endowment was appropriated, in part to the foundation of the Hertford Latin Scholarship in 1834, and in part (in 1833 on the death of the surviving Fellow, Rev. Richard Hewett), to MAGDALENE HALL, a foundation which dated from 1602.

The arms used for HERTFORD COLLEGE are those which are said to be the original bearings of HERT HALL (and the arms of ELIAS DE HERTFORD), viz. : *Gules, a hart's head caboshed argent, attired or, between the attires a cross patée-fitchée of the last.*

KEBLE COLLEGE was founded in 1869.

The arms are those of the Rev. JOHN KEBLE, the author of the "*Christian Year,*" in memory of whom the

College was founded. They are: *Argent, a chevron engrailed gules, on a chief azure three mullets or.*

The University of Cambridge.

The thirteenth century is usually assigned as the date of the foundation of the University of CAMBRIDGE. Its senior College, PETER-HOUSE, dates from 1257, but it had probably been a place of learning long before that, though it is not necessary to endeavour to rival the antiquity of the sister University of OXFORD by carrying the date of the foundation back to 631, and assigning the honour of its institution to SIGBERT, King of the East Angles.

The arms borne by the University are: *Gules, on a cross ermine between four lions of* ENGLAND (*i.e., passant gardant or*) *a book of the first, edged and clasped gold.* This appears first on the present seal of the University which bears the date 1580. I may here say that for this piece of information, and for others incorporated below, I am indebted to the excellent papers read in 1885 by W. H. ST. JOHN HOPE, Esq., M.A., F.S.A., Assistant Secretary of the Society of Antiquaries, before that learned Society, and since printed in its proceedings.

The earlier seals, dating from before 1291 and 1420 respectively, are not armorial but bear representations of the Chancellor seated beneath a canopy, arrayed in academicals, and between two disputing scholars (compare these with seals described hereafter under S. ANDREWS, PARIS, and HEIDELBERG).

PETER-HOUSE.

This College was founded in 1257 by HUGH DE BALSHAM (Bishop of ELY, 1257-1286), and the arms are commemorative of the founder. They are *Or, four pallets within a bordure gules, thereon eight open crowns of the first.* This coat was granted by ROBERT COOKE, *Clarencieux,* King of Arms, in 1575. The arms of BALSHAM appear to have been *Or, three pallets gules:* the bordure is allusive to the arms of the See of ELY— *Gules, three open crowns or (vide ante,* p. 180). RANDLE HOLMES, in his *Store House of Armory and Blazon,* describes another seal which bears the effigy of S. PETER, holding a closed book which supports a church, and in the other his keys. These bearings may have been derived from an ancient seal, but no impression is known to exist.

CLARE HALL

Was founded in 1338 by ELIZABETH, daughter of GILBERT DE CLARE, Earl of GLOUCESTER and HERE-FORD, by JOAN, daughter of King EDWARD I. The arms of the College are *Per pale* (a) *Or, three chevrons gules;* (b) *Or, a cross gules; all within a bordure sable, guttée d'or.* They are thus the arms of CLARE, impaling those of ELIZABETH'S first husband JOHN DE BURGH, son of the Earl of ULSTER, who died *vitâ patris* in 1313. Mr HOPE plausibly suggests that the *sable bordure* bedewed with golden drops are allusive to ELIZABETH'S widowhood and grief for her first husband. It will be noticed that here, as in the arms of BALLIOL, the arms of the lady occupy the place of honour in an impaled coat, contrary to the practice of modern times. ELIZABETH'S seal, bearing the arms of CLARE, impaling DE BURGH, and having the *bordure guttée,* was used by her in 1353. It also bears roundels charged with the arms of her other husbands: THEOBALD, Lord VERDON and Sir ROGER DAMORY (See *Cat. of Seals in Brit. Mus.,* ii., No. 7940). ELIZABETH'S foundation occupied the place of UNIVERSITY HALL founded in 1326 by Chancellor RICHARD DE BADEW but burnt down some years later.

On the monument in the Church of S. EDWARD at CAMBRIDGE, of SAMUEL BLYTHE, D.D., Master of CLARE HALL, 1690, the arms of the College are placed in chief above his personal coat : *Argent, a chevron gules between three lions rampant sable.*

PEMBROKE COLLEGE

Was founded in the year 1347 by MARY DE ST. POL, wife of AMYER DE VALENCE, Earl of PEMBROKE, and the arms of the College are those of the founder, viz., DE VALENCE, *Burelé argent and azure, an orle of martlets gules;* impaling ST. POL-CHATILLON : *Gules, three pallets vair, a chief or,* both coats dimidiated and conjoined.

TRINITY HALL—"the Hall of the Holy Trinity of Norwich "—

Was founded in 1350, by WILLIAM BATEMAN, Bishop of NORWICH (1344-1355). The arms are : *Sable, within a bordure engrailed, a crescent ermine.* They were granted in 1575 by COOKE, *Clarencieux* (See *Archæologia Æliana,* May 1859). In S. EDWARD'S Church, Cambridge, TRINITY HALL impales DALLING : *Ermine on a bend sable three acorns or.*

CORPUS CHRISTI COLLEGE

Was founded in 1352 by the CAMBRIDGE guilds of CORPUS CHRISTI, and of the BLESSED VIRGIN. The arms, which were granted by COOKE, *Clarencieux,* in the year 1570, are : *Quarterly,* 1 and 4. *Gules, a pelican in her piety argent ;* 2 and 3. *Azure, three garden lilies argent, slipped proper.*

KING'S COLLEGE

Was founded by King HENRY VI., February 1440-1441, and enlarged by the same prince two years later, Mr St. JOHN HOPE tells us that its original coat, up to 1448, bore: *two garden lilies in chief, and in base a mitre enfiling a crosier; a chief per pale azure and gules, in the first a fleur-de-lis of* FRANCE, *in the second a lion of* ENGLAND. But in January 1448-1449 the King issued letters-patent under the Great Seal granting arms to his Colleges at CAMBRIDGE and ETON ; and of these the grant to KING'S COLLEGE, CAMBRIDGE, is a new one. The bearings in base are converted into: *Sable, three roses argent*, but the chief of FRANCE and ENGLAND is retained unaltered.

QUEENS' COLLEGE

Was founded in 1448 by Queen Margaret of ANJOU, to whom HENRY VI. gave the College of S. BERNARD and its possessions, with permission to refound it as a new College under the name of "Reginale Collegium Sancte Margarete et Sancti Bernardi." This was accordingly done on April 15, 1448. The arms are those of the Queen, viz.: *Quarterly of six;* (1) *Barry of eight, gules and argent* (HUNGARY); (2) *Azure, semé of fleurs-de-lis or, a label gules* (NAPLES); (3) *Argent, a cross potent between four crosslets or* (JERUSALEM); (4) *Azure, semé de fleurs-de-lis or, a bordure gules* (ANJOU); (5) *Azure, two barbels addorsed between four cross-crosslets or* (BAR); (6) *Or, on a bend gules three allerions argent* (LORRAINE); *the whole within a bordure vert, for difference.* This coat was granted by ROBERT COOKE, *Clarencieux*, in 1575. (In JERUSALEM the crosslets were wrongly made *potent*).

At the fall of the House of LANCASTER Queen ELIZABETH WIDVILE, wife of EDWARD IV., took the College under her patronage in 1465. Hence it is that by some the College is known as QUEENS', not QUEEN'S.

ST. CATHARINE HALL

Was founded in 1473 by ROBERT WOODLARKE,

Provost of KING'S COLLEGE. Its arms are, *Gules, a Catharine wheel or.*

JESUS' COLLEGE

Owes its foundation in 1496 to JOHN ALCOCK, Bishop of ELY (1486 to 1500). Its arms are, *Argent, on a fess between three cock's heads sable, crested and wattled gules, a mitre or, all within a bordure of the third, thereon eight (or ten) open crowns of the last.* These are the arms of the founder, with the addition of a *bordure* derived from those of the See of ELY, as in the case of PETER-HOUSE.

CHRIST'S COLLEGE.

A college known as GOD'S HOUSE was founded in 1442 by WILLIAM BYNGHAM, priest of the church of S. JOHN ZACHARY in Cambridge. This was refounded and enlarged in 1505 by MARGARET BEAUFORT, Countess of RICHMOND and DERBY, the mother of King HENRY VII. The arms are those of BEAUFORT, viz. :— *Quarterly,* FRANCE-MODERN *and* ENGLAND, *all within a bordure-compony argent and azure.*

ST. JOHN'S COLLEGE.

This College owes its foundation to the munificence of the same lady, by whom the old hospital of S. JOHN was in 1511 converted into a College under that dedication. The arms appear to be identical with those of CHRIST'S COLLEGE given above.

MAGDALENE COLLEGE

Was originally founded by EDWARD STAFFORD, Duke of BUCKINGHAM in 1512, under the name of BUCKING-HAM COLLEGE. It was refounded as MAGDALEN COLLEGE by THOMAS, Lord AUDLEY in 1542. Its arms are those of the later founder, viz. : *Quarterly, per pale*

*indented or and azure, in the second and third quarters
an eagle displayed of the first ; over all on a bend of the
second a fret between two martlets gold.*

TRINITY COLLEGE

Was founded in 1546 by HENRY VIII., who combined
for that purpose MICHAEL HOUSE (which had been
founded in 1324, by HERVEY DE STANTON, Chancellor
of the Exchequer, who held Canonries in the Cathedrals
of YORK and WELLS, besides the Rectories of East
Dereham and North Creke); KING'S HALL, a foundation of EDWARD III., dating from 1337, and some small
hostels.

Its arms are : *Argent, a chevron between three roses
gules, seeded or, barbed vert ; on a chief of the second a lion*
of ENGLAND *between two books paleways of the third*.

GONVILLE AND CAIUS COLLEGE.

GONVILLE HALL had been founded in 1348 by
EDMOND GONVILLE, Rector of Terrington and Rushworth as the Hall of the Annunciation of the Blessed
Virgin MARY. JOHN CAIUS, M.D., refounded and
enlarged it in 1558, desiring that it should henceforth be
known as GONVILLE and CAIUS COLLEGE.

The arms are those of the founders impaled, with
the addition of *a bordure-compony argent and sable ;*
thus : *Argent, on a chevron coticed (indented) sable,
three escallops or* for GONVILLE, *impaling : Or, semé
of gillyflowers (?) in the midst of the chief a sengreen
resting on the heads of two serpents in pale, their tails
nowed together all proper, and resting upon a square stone
vert, between them a book sable,* for CAIUS ; *the whole
within a bordure-compony argent and sable.* The latter
coat was a grant by DALTON, *Norroy* King of Arms,
who accompanied it with an elaborate explanation of
its symbolical meanings. (The curious will find it

given in BOUTELL'S *Heraldry, Historical and Popular,*
pp. 363, 364.)

EMMANUEL COLLEGE.

Sir WALTER MILDMAY founded this house in 1584.
Its arms are : *Argent, a lion rampant azure, holding in
the dexter paw a wreath of laurel vert ; in chief a scroll
sable inscribed with the name "*EMMANUEL*" or.*

SIDNEY-SUSSEX COLLEGE.

In 1595 this College was founded in accordance
with the will of FRANCES SYDNEY, widow of THOMAS
RADCLIFFE, Earl of SUSSEX. The arms borne by the
college contain the impaled coat of the Countess :
Per pale : (a) *Argent, a bend engrailed sable,* for RAD-
CLIFFE ; (b) *Or, a pheon azure,* for SIDNEY. (The
seal of the Master bears *a lozenge charged with the
eight quarters* of the Countess, and ensigned with her
coronet.)

DOWNING COLLEGE.

This College was founded in accordance with the will
of the Right Hon. Sir GEORGE DOWNING, Bart., who
died in 1749, but it only received its charter of incorporation in 1800.

Its arms are :—*Barry of eight (or ten) argent and vert,
a griffin segreant or, within a bordure azure, thereon
eight roses of the first, barbed and seeded proper.* These
are the arms of the founder, with the addition of a
bordure for difference.

SELWYN COLLEGE ·

This College was founded in 1882.

The arms are those of the late Bishop SELWYN
formerly Bishop of NEW-ZEALAND, afterwards of LICH-
FIELD. The arms of the latter See are represented

impaled with the arms of the Bishop, thus : *Per pale,*
two coats ; (a) *the arms of the See of* LICHFIELD (p.
182) ;. (b) *Argent, on a bend coticed sable, three annulets*
or ; all within a bordure engrailed gules, in chief a crescent.
of the last for difference (SELWYN).

Official Arms of the Regius Professors in the UNIVERSITY
OF CAMBRIDGE.

DIVINITY.

Gules, on a cross ermine between four martlets argent
a book of the first, garnished or.

LAW.

Purpure, a cross-moline or ; on a chief cousu *gules, a*
lion passant of the second, charged on the body with the
letter L *sable.*

MEDICINE.

Azure, a fess ermine between three lozenges or ; on a
chief cousu *gules, a lion passant of the third, on its body*
the letter M *sable.*

HEBREW.

Argent, the letter ℸ *sable, on a chief gules a lion*
passant or.

GREEK.

Per chevron argent and sable, in the first the letters
A *and* Ω *in the second a grasshopper, all counter-changed,*
on a chief gules a lion passant or, on its shoulder a text Ϭ
sable. (These arms are in S. Giles Church, Cambridge,
on a monument to NICHOLAS CARRE, Regius Professor
of Greek, 1569, they are impaled to the dexter, with
. . . to the sinister, viz.: *Per chevron . . . and*
. . . , *three unicorn's heads erased counter-changed,*
these, however, were not his personal arms, these, which
are on a separate escucheon, are (*Gules*) *on a chevron*

(*argent*) *three mullets* (*sable*); *in chief as many fleurs-de-lis* (. . .)

Note.—Though in all cases above the lion is blazoned as a *lion passant*, the lion of ENGLAND is intended, and it should probably be depicted *passant gardant*.

THE UNIVERSITY OF DURHAM.

The University of DURHAM as now constituted was founded in the year 1832. CROMWELL, as Lord Protector had previously founded an University there in 1657 but it was dissolved three years later. The arms now used are: *Argent*, S. CUTHBERT'S *cross* (*formée-quadrate*) *gules; on a canton the arms of* Bishop HATFIELD: *Azure, a chevron or, between three lions rampant argent.* (See *The Herald and Genealogist*, vol. viii.)

UNIVERSITY COLLEGE

Bears: *Azure, between four lions rampant argent a cross or* (being the arms of the See of DURHAM); *on a chief of the second a cross formée-quadrate gules between two mitres proper.* This College now includes Bishop COSIN'S HALL.

BISHOP HATFIELD'S HALL.

The arms are those described above as being in the canton of the University arms: (*Azure, a chevron or, between three lions rampant argent*).

BISHOP COSIN'S HALL (now included in UNIVERSITY COLLEGE)

Bore the arms of Bishop COSIN : *Azure, a fret or.*

THE COLLEGE OF MEDICINE AT NEWCASTLE-ON-TYNE

Is affiliated to the University of DURHAM, and bears: *Argent,* S. CUTHBERT'S *cross gules, a chief tierced in pale;* (a) *the arms of* Bishop HATFIELD, as above; (b) *Or, the rod of Esculapius in pale proper;* (c) *Gules, a castle argent*, derived from the arms of the city of NEWCASTLE.

UNIVERSITY OF LONDON.

The University of LONDON was founded in 1826, and had its home in Gower Street; it was known as UNIVERSITY COLLEGE from 1836 up to 1851. The governing body known as the University of LONDON had then its seat at Somerset House. As now constituted the University dates from 1851. Its arms are: *Argent, on a cross gules a rose of the first, crowned with an Imperial Crown, and irradiated, or ; on a chief azure a book open proper.*

KING'S COLLEGE, LONDON

Was incorporated in 1829. Its arms were those of the then reigning Sovereign, King GEORGE III. The motto is *Sancte et Sapienter.*

SION COLLEGE, LONDON.

Argent, on a chevron between three griffin's heads erased sable, a leopard's face or. Founded in 1630.

THE VICTORIA UNIVERSITY,

Situated at MANCHESTER, was founded in 1880. It includes OWEN'S COLLEGE, Manchester; UNIVERSITY COLLEGE, Liverpool ; and the YORKSHIRE COLLEGE, Leeds.

Its arms are : *Per pale argent and gules, a rose counterchanged between, in chief a terrestrial globe semé of bees volant, and a Golden-Fleece ; and in base a cormorant having in its beak a bunch of laver (seaweed) proper.* The motto is *Olim armis nunc studiis.* The charges in the arms are allusive :—the *red* and *white rose* to the counties of LANCASTER and YORK, for whose special benefit the University exists ; *the globe, bird*, and *Golden-Fleece* are derived from the arms of the cities of MANCHESTER, LIVERPOOL, and LEEDS.

UNIVERSITY COLLEGE, LIVERPOOL,

Incorporated in 1881, bears: *Azure, between three cormorants, each having in its beak a sprig of laver, an open book argent, thereon the words* FIAT LUX. The motto is: HAEC OTIA STUDIA FOVENT.

THE SCOTTISH UNIVERSITIES.

THE UNIVERSITY OF ST. ANDREWS

Was founded in 1411 by Bishop HENRY WARDLAW, and contains the Colleges of S. MARY (the original college of Bishop WARDLAW, enlarged by Archbishops JAMES and DAVID BEATON and Archbishop HAMILTON) and the now united Colleges of S. SALVATOR and ST. LEONARD. Of these, the former was founded by Bishop KENNEDY in 1458, the latter by Prior HEPBURN in 1532, and bears in the centre the figure of S. ANDREW on his cross, in the base.

The University seal bears beneath a canopy the seated figure of the Chancellor, or other instructor, lecturing to a class of eight students, of whom seven are seated at a table and one on the floor. Upon the canopy are three shields, the centre one *on a chief a crescent reversed* . . . supported by two angels ; the *dexter* bears the *arms* of SCOTLAND ; the *sinister* the personal arms of the founder, viz.: . . . . *on a fess between three mascles* . . . *three cross-crosslets* . . .

The seal of S. SALVATOR'S COLLEGE bears *the effigy of the Redeemer in the act of benediction and holding an open book*. A mitred shield contains the arms of Bishop KENNEDY : *Argent, a chevron between three cross-crosslets fitchée all within a double tressure flory-counter-flory, gules.*

THE UNIVERSITY OF GLASGOW

Originated with Bishop TURNBULL (1448-1454) who obtained a charter of foundation from JAMES II. in 1443 ;

and the Papal Bull of Pope NICHOLAS V. confirming it and establishing the University given in 1450.

The seal of the University is *vesica*-shaped and bears a *mace between the tree supporting a bird (robin) and fish (salmon)* which occur as charges in the arms of the city. In chief is a *dexter hand holding a book open and charged with the words*, Via veritas via (? vita) (LAING, *Scottish Seals*, vol. ii., p. 201, No. 1144).

THE UNIVERSITY OF ABERDEEN

Was founded by Bishop WILLIAM ELPHINSTONE (1483-1514), who obtained a Papal Bull from ALEXANDER VI. for that purpose in the year 1494, and himself obtained or provided the necessary endowment for the College erected almost under the shadow of his Cathedral in Old Aberdeen. The old common seal of the University bears *a vase or pot in which are arranged three garden lilies, the emblem of the Blessed Virgin; on the front of the vase are three fishes arranged in a fret. In chief a hand reaches downwards in pale and holds an open book.* KING'S COLLEGE was originally known as S. MARY'S COLLEGE, and this accounts for the assumption of the *lilies* of the Blessed Virgin MARY. From this seal were derived the arms of old KING'S COLLEGE ; *Azure, a bough pot or, containing three garden lilies slipped, the pot charged with as many fishes in fret ; from the centre chief issuing downwards in pale amid rays of the sun a hand holding an open book all proper ;* but these arms were not formally granted, or recorded in the LYON office. MARISCHAL COLLEGE was founded in New Aberdeen in the year 1593 ; and endowed by GEORGE KEITH, fifth Earl MARISCHAL, under the sanction of an Act of Parliament, with the status and privileges of an University. This position it maintained independently of the University of Old

Aberdeen until 1860, when, in accordance with the provisions of the "Universities (Scotland) Act" of 1858, the two were united in one University to be called thenceforth the University of ABERDEEN, and to take rank among the Universities of Scotland as from the date and erection of KING'S COLLEGE and UNIVERSITY, i.e. 1494.

In 1888 the *Senatus Academicus* under the presidency of the much honoured Principal (now Sir) WILLIAM GEDDES, LL.D., petitioned *Lyon* King of Arms for a grant of armorial bearings for the University, and on September 26 of the same year a formal grant was made of the following : *Quarterly,* 1. *Azure, a bough pot or, charged with three salmon fishes in fret proper, and containing as many lilies of the garden the dexter in bud, the centre full-blown, and the sinister half-blown, also proper flowered argent ; issuant downward from the middle chief amid rays of the sun a dexter hand holding an open book likewise proper ;* 2. *Argent, a chief paly of six or and gules ;* 3. *Argent, a chevron sable between three boar's heads erased gules, armed of the field and langued azure ;* 4. *Gules, a tower triple-towered argent, masoned sable, windows and port of the last.* In an escrol below the shield is placed this motto, "*Initium Sapientiæ Timor Domini.*" It will be seen that these four quarters contain : first, the arms assumed for the UNIVERSITY and KING'S COLLEGE, Old Aberdeen, as already given on the page preceding (the new blazon is not beyond criticism). The second quarter contains the arms of the founder of MARISCHAL COLLEGE and UNIVERSITY. In the third quarter are the undifferenced arms borne by Bishop WILLIAM ELPHINSTONE, who obtained the Papal Bull for the University of Old Aberdeen and endowed S. MARY'S (afterwards KING'S) COLLEGE therein. The fourth quarter contains a portion of the arms of the Royal Burgh of Aberdeen (*Gules, within a double tressure flory-counter-flory argent, three towers triple-towered of the last).*

EDINBURGH UNIVERSITY

Was founded by Royal Charter of JAMES VI. granted in 1582.

The arms borne by the University are :—*Argent, on a saltire azure an open book, in chief a thistle slipped proper; in base on a rock the castle of Edinburgh as represented in the arms of that city.*

IRELAND.

THE UNIVERSITY OF DUBLIN

Was founded in the year 1591 by Queen ELIZABETH, and a new charter was granted by JAMES I. in 1609.

The arms are: *Quarterly azure and ermine, in the first quarter a book open proper, clasped or; in the fourth quarter a castle argent, inflamed proper; over all in centre point the harp of Ireland royally crowned of the third.*

TRINITY COLLEGE

Was founded on the grant by Queen ELIZABETH of the Augustinian monastery of All Saints in 1591. It received a new charter in 1637.

Its arms are: *'Azure, a book closed, clasps to dexter, between in chief on the dexter a lion passant-gardant, and in the sinister a harp, all or. In base a castle with two towers domed, each surmounted by a flag floatant to the flanks of the shield, the dexter charged with the cross of* S. GEORGE ; *the sinister with that of* S. PATRICK.

THE ROYAL UNIVERSITY OF IRELAND

Was founded in 1880, and incorporates QUEEN'S COLLEGE, Belfast ; QUEEN'S COLLEGE, Cork ; QUEEN'S COLLEGE, Galway ; (all these were founded in 1845).

2 G

The arms granted to it are: *Per saltire ermine and ermines.* *In the centre point an open book surmounted by an Imperial Crown proper, between four escucheons:* (A, *in chief*) *Vert, a harp or, stringed argent ;* (B, *in base*) *Azure, three antique crowns or ;* (C, *in dexter flank*) *Or, a cross gules, thereon an escucheon argent charged with a dexter hand erect couped gules ;* (D, *in sinister flank*) *Per pale* (a) *Argent, an eagle displayed sable dimidiated and conjoined to the palar line ;* (b) *Azure, an arm embowed issuing from the dexter flank and holding a dagger erect proper.* Of these escucheons the first contains the modern arms of IRELAND ; the second, the ancient arms ; the third has the arms of ULSTER ; and the fourth those of CONNAUGHT.

UNIVERSITY OF MELBOURNE AND OF SYDNEY.

UNIVERSITY OF MELBOURNE.
Azure, between four mullets of eight points (argent), the figure of VICTORY, *winged and habited proper, holding in the extended right hand a laurel wreath or.* Motto: ·*Postera crescam laude.*

UNIVERSITY OF SYDNEY, N.S.W.
Argent, on a cross azure an open book between four estoiles of eight points argent, on a chief gules a lion of ENGLAND. Motto: *Sidere mens eadem mutato.*

UNIVERSITY OF HEIDELBERG.
The arms of the University are: *Sable, a lion rampant or, crowned gules, holding in its paws an open book inscribed* semper apertus proper. The University seal bears the effigy of S. PETER seated under an architectural canopy, between two figures of the Elector RUPERT, and his son, each kneeling on one knee and supporting a shield, the former bearing the arms of BAVARIA :

Fusilly in bend-sinister, argent and azure ; the latter those of the PALATINATE OF THE RHINE : *Sable, a lion rampant or, crowned gules.* The legend is S. universitatis studü heydelbergensis.

The seal of the Rector bears (within the cuspings of a sexfoil) the arms of the University. The legend is S. rectoratus studü heidelbergensis.

Each of the faculties in the University has its special seal. The seal of the FACULTY OF CATHOLIC THEOLOGY, founded in 1627, is oval in shape and *bears the seated effigy of* S. AUGUSTINE *in pontificals.* The legend is " Sigill. facult. theolog. univers. heidelberg."

The seal of the FACULTY OF PROTESTANT THEOLOGY is round, and *bears an open book inscribed* " Ad legem et testimónium." The legend is " Sigillum facultatis theologicæ Academiæ heidelb."

The circular seal of the FACULTY OF LAW *bears on a mount in base the Palatinate lion, not crowned, holding a pair of scales.* The legend runs "Sigill. facultatis juridicæ heidelbergensis."

The FACULTY OF MEDICINE has a circular seal *bearing a shield charged with the standing figure of the winged lion of* S. MARK. The legend is " Sigillvm facvltatis medicæ acad. heidelberg."

The seal of the PHILOSOPHICAL FACULTY OF PROTESTANTISM, founded in 1576, bears, under a baldachino, a figure in doctor's robes seated behind a table, before him is an open book each page bearing the letters SS. Below him are two demi-figures of students each having a book with the same letters. The seal has no legend.

The CATHOLIC FACULTY OF PHILOSOPHY, established in 1627, has a seal which bears the image of S. CATHARINE, with her attributes of martyrdom the sword and the wheel. It also has on it a shield charged with the arms of the University as before given. The legend is " Sigill. philosophicæ facultatis heidelberg."

The small seal of the University is charged with the arms, but the lion is uncrowned. There is no legend, but its place is filled by a close laurel wreath. (*See* HEIDELOFF. *Gedenk-blatter der Universitaten Heidelberg.* Nürnberg, *s.a.*)

UNIVERSITY OF PARIS.

The seal of the University in 1292 is a large circular one. The principal compartment is divided into three portions of which the upper one occupies the half of the compartment, and contains under an architectural niche the crowned figure of the Blessed Virgin, seated and having on her left knee the Holy Child. Beneath this the lower half is divided into four smaller niches; in the two upper ones, which are arched, are two doctors seated, in profile, reading their books; in each of the two lower ones are seated two scholars, similarly occupied. The smaller compartments on either side of the great central one, contain, on the dexter, the full length figure of a Bishop in pontificals, holding his crosier in both hands; in a small niche beneath his feet a seated female figure : on the sinister the compartment contains S. CATHARINE holding a palm branch in one hand and a book in the other. The small niche at the bottom is said by M. LECOY DE LA MARCHE to contain *un évêque à genoux*, but this I cannot make out. (The obverse of the seal is engraved in M. LECOY DE LA MARCHE'S *Sceaux*, Paris, n.d. p. 263.) The reverse of the seal contains a seated figure holding in one hand a dove, as the emblem of the Holy Spirit, and in the other a fieur-de-lis. The inscription appears to be: " S. Universitatis, magistror. et scolariv. parisius." The arms of the University in later times were those of FRANCE (*Azure, three fleurs-de-lis or*), *differenced by a hand issuing from clouds in chief and holding a closed book, all proper.*

The " Nation of England " in the University of PARIS had its special seal, on which, above the figures of a doctor teaching two scholars, is represented a group of saints in three stages ; the lower contains S. MARTIN of Tours dividing his cloak with the beggar ; above are two saints, S. CATHARINE and another ; and above all is the representation of the coronation of the Blessed Virgin, patroness of the University (LECOY DE LA MARCHE, *Sceaux*, p. 264).

UNIVERSITY OF (PRAG) PRAGUE.

Argent, the wall of a city having a gate flanked with two towers gules, in chief an arm issuant in pale, vested azure, holding a book (closed) proper.

This University was founded by the Emperor CHARLES IV. in 1348. Its seal bears *the effigy of* S. WENCESLAS *bearing a large curved heater-shaped shield charged with the Imperial Eagle, he holds in the right hand a square banner, with a pendant, similarly charged.* The Emperor is represented kneeling, and receiving a book from the saint. There are two small shields ; one *charged with the single-headed Eagle of* GERMANY, *the other with the rampant lion of* BOHEMIA. Each faculty has a special seal. That of the THEOLOGICAL FACULTY bears the double-headed eagle of the Empire (with the *" heiligenscheine "*) ; *on its breast is the figure of the Blessed Virgin* MARY *supporting the Holy Child.* Behind this is a large anchor, having no cross beam. Above the eagle's head is the monogram I.H.S. (with a cross above the H.) in a circle irradiated. The legend is, " Sigil. facultat. theologicæ Universitatis Pragensis."

The seal of the FACULTY OF LAW bears the Imperial double-headed eagle holding sword and sceptre, and having the *" heiligen scheine."* *On its breast is a shield charged with a female figure which holds a book and points upwards.* The legend is "Sigillum facultatis juridicæ Universitatis Pragensis."

The seal of the FACULTY OF PHILOSOPHY and ARTS is similar in character to that of the THEOLOGICAL FACULTY, but *on the breast of the eagle is the figure of* S. CATHARINE *with her wheel and a palm branch.* The legend runs :. (Sig) ".Facult. Philosophicæ et Artium Universitatis Pragen."

The seal of the FACULTY OF MEDICINE has the double-headed eagle as above but without the anchor, or the sword and sceptre. *On its breast is a shield charged with the figures of two saints bearing the palm branch of martyrdom.* Above the shield is a full-length figure of S. JOHN the Baptist. The inscription is "Sigillvm facvltatis medicæ Universitatis Pragensis."

UNIVERSITY OF (MENTZ) MAYENCE (1476-1798.)

Arms : Quarterly, 1 and 4. *Argent, a wheel gules* (arms of the See) ; 2 and 3. *Argent, two bars sable.*

· UNIVERSITY OF GREIFSWALD or GRYPHISWALD, (Pomerania) founded in 1456.

Arms : . . . *a griffin rampant to sinister* . . .

UNIVERSITY OF BASEL (BASLE), founded in 1460.

The seal of the Rector bears *an arm issuing from clouds in chief and holding a book in pale ; before the latter is a small shield of the arms of* BASEL · (*v.* p. 268).

Each faculty has a distinct seal with appropriate devices combined with the arms of BASEL.

UNIVERSITY OF GRÄTZ, in Styria, founded in 1585, by the Emperor FERDINAND I.

Arms : *Tierced in fess :* (a) (*Azure ?*) *the sacred mono-*

gram I.H.S. *ensigned with a cross, beneath it three passion nails in pile the whole irradiated ;* (b) *Argent, two arms, one issuing from either flank, the hands holding in the centre of the shield a closed book paleways ;* (c) *Vert, a griffin argent inflamed at its mouth and ears, proper ;* the arms of STYRIA.

UNIVERSITY OF SALZBURG, founded 1623, suppressed in 1810.

Arms : *Azure, on a mount in base a lion rampant double-tailed argent. On a chief the arms of* SALZBURG ; viz., *Per pale* (a) *Or, a lion rampant sable ;* (b) *Gules, a fess argent.*

UNIVERSITY OF NÜRNBERG.

The seal bears, *a female figure holding in one hand a laurel branch, in the other an open book.* It also contains two shields of the NÜRNBERG arms ; A. *Per pale* (a) *Or, the Imperial Eagle dimidiated proper ;* (b) *Bendy of six gules and argent.* B. *Azure, a harpy displayed crowned or, the face and breast proper.*

UNIVERSITY OF BRESLAU, founded 1702.

Arms : *Per pale* (a) *Gules, a lion contourné argent crowned or.* (b) *Or, an eagle dimidiated sable. Over all a chief charged with the Imperial Cypher* L. I. The shield is borne on the breast of an Imperial eagle, over the heads of which, on a *circular cartouche* is the Jesuit device of the *Sacred monogram* I.H.S. (the H. ensigned with a cross) *above three passion nails in pile.*

UNIVERSITY OF BESANÇON, founded in 1691.

Azure, an open book argent, between three fleurs-de-lis or.

UNIVERSITY OF CAEN, founded in 1437.

(*Gules*), *a hand issuing from the chief in pale holding a book ; on a chief fleury a lion passant gardant.* (DEMAY, *Sceaux de la Normandie,* No. 2571.) The shield is supported by an angel.

UNIVERSITY OF VALENCE, founded in 1452.

A book between a fleur-de-lis, and a dolphin, in chief the dove irradiated representing the Holy Spirit. (DEMAY, *Sceaux de la Normandie,* No. 2577.)

UNIVERSITY OF COLOGNE (CÖLN), founded in 1388.

Argent, an arm issuing from the sinister flank proper vested azure, holding a closed book gules ; on a chief of the last three open crowns or.

UNIVERSITY OF VIENNE (WIEN), founded in 1365.

Gules, a fess argent, thereon an arm issuing from the sinister flank and holding a book proper.

UNIVERSITY OF ERFURT, founded in 1379.

Gules, a demi-wheel argent, on a chief azure an arm issuing fessways from the dexter flank, vested of the second and holding a closed book in pale proper.

UNIVERSITY OF BOLOGNA, founded in 1088.

Gules, two keys argent in saltire. On a chief azure a closed book paleways or.

At the present day the Italian Universities appear to seal their diplomas, etc., with seals bearing only the Royal Arms of ITALY.

APPENDIX A.

ON THE USE OF SUPPORTERS BY ECCLESIASTICS.

ALTHOUGH the armorial use of supporters by Ecclesiastics appears to have become almost obsolete in Great Britain and Ireland, except in the very infrequent case of one who is also a secular Peer of the realm, an examination of a good series of Ecclesiastical seals will show that in the fourteenth and later centuries, down even to the last, it was sufficiently common both at home and abroad.

I am not able to say that the custom had its origin in decorative architecture, but at any rate when armorial shields were placed, as was not unfrequently the case, upon the bosses at the intersection of the vaulting, or to help in filling up the void spaces in spandrils, these shields were often supported by an angel. In mediæval times the arms of clerics are very frequently represented on their *secreta*, or private seals, with a single angel standing or kneeling behind the shield, and acting as its supporter.

The pretty counter-seal, or *secretum*, of GILBERT GREENLAW, Bishop of ABERDEEN (1390-1424) bears his shield of arms (. . .) *a chevron* (. . .) *between three water-budgets* (. . .) supported by an angel with expanded wings (LAING, *Descriptive Catalogue of Scottish Seals*, vol. i., p. 154). This is also engraved in the second plate of seals given in the second volume of the *Registrum Episcopatus Aberdonensis*, published by the Spalding Club, in 1845.

The seal of WILLIAM FOULER given in LAING'S second volume at p. 65 has a similar arrangement, the shield supported by the angel, bears . . . *a rose* . . . *between three crosses-crosslet fitchées* . . . At page 27 of the same volume is recorded the armorial seal of THOMAS BULLYN, Canon of GLASGOW, who in 1460 bore a shield charged with a *bull's head caboshed*, and supported by an angel. It does not appear to be positively certain that ROBERT GUTHRIE of Kimblethmont was an Ecclesiastic, although it is very probable that such was the case. On his seal (described in LAING, vol. ii., p. 77), the arms . . . *a bull's head caboshed, between three garbs* . . .) have an angel supporter.

Upon the seal *ad causas* of ROBERT NEVILLE, Bishop of DURHAM (1438-1457), an angel holds a shield charged with the personal arms of the prelate : [1] (*Gules*), *a saltire* (*argent*), *charged with two annulets interlaced in fess, for difference* (*Catalogue of Seals in the King's Library, British Museum*, vol. i., p. 406. London, 1887). The shield is in the base of the *vesica*-shaped seal. (*See* also SURTEES, *History of the County of Durham*, vol. i., plate iii., fig. 9.)

From this original use of a single supporter it was an easy and natural step to the adoption of double supporters ; and these were frequently, but as we shall see by no means invariably, angels. Bishop JOHN FORDHAM of DURHAM (1382-1388) has on his privy-seal a shield bearing his arms : (*Sable*), *a chevron between three crosses patonce* (*or*), thus supported. (*British Museum Catalogue of Seals.* vol. i., pp. 403-404 ; and SURTEES, *Durham,* vol. i., plate v., fig. 4.)

Archbishop HENRY BOWETT of YORK (1407-1423), has upon the base of his seal *ad causas* his own effigy, half-length, in the act of prayer, and bearing his crozier ; in front of him is the shield of his arms : (*Argent*), *three stag's heads caboshed* (*sable*), supported by two angels. (*British Museum Catalogue*, vol. i., p. 374.)

In Scotland early examples of the same use are not wanting. In 1360, JOHN DE GAMERY, Canon of CAITHNESS, has upon his seal, a shield charged with *a chevron between in chief a mullet, and a cinquefoil, and in base a lion's head affronté.* The shield has two angel supporters (LAING, *Scottish Seals*, vol. i., p. 175, from the Balnagowan Charters). The *secretum* of JAMES KENNEDY, Bishop of ST. ANDREWS (1440-1446) bears his arms : (*Argent*), *a chevron* (*gules*) *between three cross-crosslets fitchées* (*sable*) *the whole within a double tressure flory counter-flory* (*of the second*). The shield is timbred with a mitre, and is supported by two kneeling angels (LAING, vol. i., p. 146). Similarly the circular seal of ROBERT COLQUHOUN, Bishop of ARGYLE (1473-1495) bears a shield of his arms (*Argent*), *a saltire engrailed* (*sable*) with two kneeling angels for its supporters.

The seal affixed in 1477, used by JOHN LAING, Bishop of GLASGOW (1473-1482), has in its base a shield of his personal arms : Quarterly, 1 and 4. . . . *a pale* . . . *;* 2 and 3. . . . *three piles* . . . (LAING, vol. i., p. 166, plate xvii.,

---

[1] The tinctures are not indicated on mediæval seals ; here and elsewhere when they are supplied from other sources they are placed within brackets.

fig. 3. It is also engraved in Archbishop EYRE's Monograph on the *Episcopal Seals of the Ancient Diocese of Glasgow*, plate iii., fig. 11. Glasgow, 1891 ; and in the *Registrum Episcopatûs Glasguensis*, vol. ii., plate iii., fig. 3, published by the Maitland Club. In this last it is erroneously ascribed to Bishop CAMERON, who held the See from 1426 to 1446.)

Bishop ANDREW FORMAN who held the See of MORAY from 1501 to 1514, when he was translated to ST. ANDREWS, used in 1502, a circular seal in the base of which are engraved his personal arms : Quarterly, 1 and 4. (*Azure*), *a chevron or, between three fishes hauriant argent;* 2 and 3. *Sable, a camel's head erased and contourné or, collared and belled (of the last).* The shield is timbred with a mitre and is supported by two kneeling angels (LAING, *Scottish Seals*, ii., p. 176). The arms of THOMAS RUTHALL, Bishop of DURHAM, 1509-1523 (*Per pale azure and gules, a cross engrailed or, between four doves of the last collared sable; on a chief quarterly ermine and of the third, two roses of the second, barbed and seeded proper*) appear at Auckland Castle with the angel supporters (*Herald and Genealogist*, vol. viii., p. 165). The latest instance of angel supporters to Anglican Episcopal arms with which I am acquainted is afforded by the seal of Bishop WILLIAM KNIGHT, of BATH and WELLS (1541-1547), who was employed as Ambassador to the Emperor MAXIMILIAN, and Secretary of State. His arms, granted in 1514 by letters-patent, are a curious example of the overcharged style of the times, and are as follows : *Per fess, or and gules, in chief the double-headed eagle of the Empire sable, and in front thereof a rose of England gules, barbed and seeded gold, both dimidiated per fess; in base a sun in splendour proper dimidiated and conjoined to the charges in chief.* The shield is supported by angels. (See *British Museum Catalogue*, vol. i., p. 202, where the coat is wrongly blazoned.) I have followed the ordinary mode in which the Bishop's arms are depicted, but the blazon now given from BURKE's *General Armory*, 2nd Edition, p. 572, would lead us to believe that the Imperial Eagle should properly be borne whole, and not dimidiated per fess. "*Per fesse, or and gules, an eagle with two heads displayed sable, having on its breast a demi-rose and a demi-sun, conjoined into one, counter-changed of the field.*"

So far the choice of angelic beings as the supporters seem to lend an air of Ecclesiastical propriety to their assumption, but we soon find that the use of mundane creatures, birds, beasts, and even fishes, was not less frequent.

Bishop THOMAS DE HATFIELD of DURHAM (1345-1381) has on

his *secretum* his arms : (*Azure*), *a chevron* (*or*) *between three lions rampant* (*argent*). The supporters are two lions sejant-guardant, each beneath the base of a small tree. (Above the shield is a half-length figure of the Blessed Virgin crowned and holding in her right arm the Infant Saviour, in the left hand a sceptre topped with a fleur-de-lis. (See *British Museum Catalogue*, vol. i., p. 403 ; and SURTEES' *Durham*, vol. i., plate v., fig. 3.)

The *secretum* of JOHN DE BARNET, Bishop successively of WORCESTER 1361, BATH and WELLS 1364, and ELY 1366, bears his arms (*Argent*), *a saltire, and in chief a leopard's head* (?) (*sable*). The shield is supported by two griffins. BEDFORD in his *Blazon of Episcopacy*, p. 18, No. 14, gives the blazon as above on the authority of WHARTON'S *Anglia Sacra :* and with it agrees the description of a *secretum* or signet of Bishop BARNET in the *Catalogue of Seals in the British Museum*, vol. i., p. 201, No. 1425, in which, however, no mention is made of the existence of the supporters. But Mr W. H. ST. JOHN HOPE, Assistant Secretary of the Society of Antiquaries, in an excellent paper on the seals of the Bishops of BATH and WELLS, blazons the charge in chief of the Bishop's arms as a coronet with three fleurons. He considers that the saintly effigies which occupy the upper portion of the seal, indicate that it was engraved for JOHN DE BARNET, while he was yet Archdeacon of London, and before his election to the See of Worcester in 1361.

Two lions support the shield of arms (. . .) *on a fess* (. . .) *between three mascles* (. . .) *as many cross-crosslets* (. . .), which appears on the seal of WALTER WARDLAW, Bishop of GLASGOW in 1368-1387 ; Cardinal of the Holy See in 1385, died 1387 (LAING, *Scottish Seals*, vol. ii., plate x., fig. 4 and p. 185.)

The *secretum* of ALEXANDER NEVILLE, Archbishop of YORK (1374-1392), bears his shield of arms : (*Gules*), *a saltire* (*argent*), *differenced by a crescent* (*sable*). The shield is timbred with a helm bearing the crest of a bull's head, issuing from a crest-coronet ; and is supported by two griffins segreant. (*British Museum Catalogue*, vol. i., p. 373.)

The counter-seal of WALTER TRAIL, Bishop of ST. ANDREWS (1385-1401), has his personal arms : (*Azure*), *a chevron between two mascles in chief* (*or*), *and a trefoil slipped in base* (*argent*), surmounted by a figure of the Blessed Virgin with the Holy Infant, and is supported by two lions rampant gardant. (LAING, *Scottish Seals*, vol. i., p. 146, No. 869.)

On the Privy Seal of THOMAS ARÚNDEL (son of ROBERT FITZ-

ALAN, thirteenth Earl of ARUNDEL), Archbishop of CANTERBURY (1397-1414), his armorial bearings are finely engraved. The shield is *couché*, and bears the arms : Quarterly, 1 and 4. (*Gules*), *a lion rampant* (*or*), *armed, etc.* (*azure*), FITZALAN ; 2 and 3. *Chequy* (*or and azure*), WARREN ; *the whole within a bordure engrailed* (*argent*), *for difference.* It is surmounted by a helm which bears the crest, out of a crest-coronet a griffin's head or, between two wings sable. The supporters are *two lions sejant-gardant.* (*British Museum Catalogue*, vol. i., p. 168, No. 1239). The lions are seated on mounts, and at the fore feet of each is a trefoil on a stalk.

In the Collection of Seals in the King's Library of the British Museum there is also an imperfect impression (No. 2050) of the seal of RICHARD COURTENAY (son of Sir PHILIP COURTENAY of Powderham), and Bishop of NORWICH (1413-1415). On it the personal arms of the Bishop (*Or*), *three torteaux, in chief a label* (*azure*), *each point charged with three bezants for difference* are represented on a couché shield surmounted by a crest-coronet. The crest itself, and the dexter supporter have both been destroyed, but the sinister supporter is a lion. The coat of PETER COURTENAY, Bishop of EXETER, 1478, and of WINCHESTER, 1487-1492, is supported in Winchester Cathedral by two dolphins. (On another use *see* MOULE, *Heraldry of Fish*, p. 19.) In S. Alban's Abbey the Chapel of Abbot RAMRYDGE contains his arms, supported by rams. The arms are a saltire couped. The rams have collars charged with the letters *rydge*, making a rebus of the name. (Plate LXXVII.) (*See* BOUTELL, *Heraldry, Historical and Popular.*)

The *secretum* of JOHN STAFFORD, Bishop of BATH and WELLS (1425-1443), and afterwards Archbishop of CANTERBURY (1443-1452), bears his personal arms, *Or, on a chevron gules a mitre, proper, all within a border engrailed sable, for difference.* The shield is supported by two eagles. (*Catalogue of Seals, British Museum*, vol. i., p. 201.) Mr ST. JOHN HOPE considers that the eagles are borne in allusion to the Bishop's Christian name.

JOHN CAMERON, Bishop of GLASGOW (1426-1446), used on his fine round seal (the first of this shape in the Glasgow Series), a shield bearing his personal arms : (*Or*), *three bars* (*gules*) supported on either side by a salmon, holding in its mouth a golden ring. (For the origin of these, *see* p. 225, *ante.*) The seal is engraved in LAING, *Scottish Seals*, vol. ii., plate ix., fig. 2. (*See also* the Monograph on the *Seals of the Ancient Diocese of*

Glasgow, by Archbishop EYRE, p. 12. Glasgow, 1891.) The arms thus arranged, but with the addition of a mitre above the pastoral staff, were also sculptured on the tower of the Episcopal Palace at Glasgow.

The fine round seal of JAMES STUART (second son of King JAMES III.), Duke of ROSS, Archbishop of ST. ANDREWS (1497-1503) bears the Royal Arms of Scotland (*Or, a lion rampant, within a double tressure flory-counter-flory gules*) ensigned with a ducal coronet and the archi-episcopal cross, and supported by two unicorns, which are without collars and chains. This and the following are early examples of the use of unicorns as supporters by the Royal House of Scotland. (LAING, *Scottish Seals*, vol. ii., p. 169.) ALEXANDER STUART, natural son of JAMES IV., who was made Archbishop of ST. ANDREWS in 1509, Lord Chancellor in 1511, and was slain at Flodden in 1513, bore the same arms and supporters as the preceding, but omitted the coronet. (This seal is engraved in LAING, *Scottish Seals*, vol. ii., plate ix., fig. 5.)

The arms of GAVIN DUNBAR, Bishop of ABERDEEN (1518-1523): *Argent, three cushions within the Royal tressure gules*, are represented in one of the illuminated letters from the Episcopal *Epistolare*, engraved in the first volume of the *Registrum Episcopatûs Aberdonensis* published by the Spalding Club of Aberdeen, in 1845. The shield is timbred with a mitre, and is supported on either side by a dun bear, chained or, a canting allusion to the Bishop's family name. The Bishop does not appear to have employed the supporters upon his seal. The learned authors of the *Lacunar Bascilicæ Sancti Macarii Aberdonensis* (the Heraldic ceiling of S. Machar's Cathedral in Old Aberdeen), published by the *New Spalding Club* in 1888, say that the good Bishop does not seem to have had any right to supporters. It will, however, be admitted that our judgment as to this must depend, not on modern notions, but on the custom of the time. I think there is abundant evidence of what that custom was, and that the Bishop has a very good answer to the charge of "vain glory" made against him above, and elsewhere in the work referred to

On Durham Castle the arms (*Azure, three combs or*) of CUTHBERT TUNSTALL, who was translated from LONDON (which See he had filled from 1522) to DURHAM in 1531, are supported by cocks, a well-known badge of his family. At Auckland he appears to have used both angels and cocks. (*See* the interesting papers on the Old Official Heraldry of Durham, by W. H. DYER LONGSTAFFE, in *The Herald and Genealogist*, vol. viii.)

. Once more—Bishop DAVID CUNINGHAM of ABERDEEN (1577-

1603) bore his arms : (Quarterly, 1 and 4. *Argent, a shakefork sable, in chief a mullet for difference;* 2 and 3. . . . . *two garbs* . . . MURE of Rowellan), with the canting supporters two conies. (LAING, *Scottish Seals*, vol. ii., p. 175.)

Nor was this use of supporters by any means confined to such dignified Ecclesiastics as were of high rank, secular, or Ecclesiastical. This has already been shown in the use of a single supporter, and the *secretum* of JOHN DE BARNET, Archdeacon of LONDON, has been already referred to at p. 460.

The fine seal of THOMAS STUART, Archdeacon of ST. ANDREWS, natural son of King ROBERT II. of Scotland, and bears in 1443, a shield of the Royal Arms of Scotland : *Or, a lion rampant within a double tressure flory - counter - flory gules, debruised by a bend counter-compony (argent and azure?)* as a mark of illegitimacy. The seal affords an example of the use of triple supporters ; an angel with expanded wings stands behind the shield, while a *dragon sejant* supports it on either side. (LAING, *Scottish Seals*, vol. ii., p. 155, where it is engraved.)

WILLIAM CAIRNS, Vicar of GLAMIS, in 1455, bore his arms (. . . *a mullet of six points* . . . *on a chief* . . . *three birds* . . .) supported by *two lions sejant gardant;* while, according to a type of which we have already noted other examples, the Blessed Virgin holding her Holy Child appears standing behind the shield (LAING, *Scottish Seals*, vol. ii., p. 27). PATRICK HOME, Archdeacon of TEVIOTDALE, bore in 1454 upon his seal the quartered arms : 1 and 4. (*Argent*), *three popinjays* (*vert*) for PEPDIE ; 2 and 3. (*Vert*), a *lion rampant* (*argent*) HOME, supported by two parrots or *popinjays* (LAING, i., 76), and in 1478 JAMES LINDSAY, Dean of GLASGOW, used a seal on which his family arms : *Gules, a fess chequy argent and sable, differenced by a mullet in dexter chief,* are supported by *two lions sejant gardant.* (LAING, *Scottish Seals*, vol. i., p. 99, No. 519.)

CHICHELEY, Archbishop of CANTERBURY, 1414-1443, is said to have employed two silver swans, ducally gorged and chained, as his supporters.

The supporters used by Cardinal WOLSEY are given at p. 432, *ante.* On Plate XXXVI., fig. 1, are engraved the arms, etc., of the Right Rev. THOMAS WILKINSON, Bishop of the Roman Catholic Diocese of HEXHAM and NEWCASTLE : *Azure, a fess erminois between three unicorns passant argent.* The Bishop has resumed the use of angel supporters.

The Right Rev. J. R. ALEXANDER CHINNERY-HALDANE, as Bishop of ARGYLL and THE ISLES most properly retains the use of his supporters, two eagles proper. His arms are : *Quarterly*, 1 and 4. *Argent, a saltire engrailed sable*, HALDANE ; 2. *Argent, a saltire between four roses gules, barbed and seeded or*, LENNOX ; 3. *Or, a bend chequy sable and argent*, MENTEITH. *Over all an escucheon Azure, a chevron ermine between three lions rampant or. On a canton, Vert a harp of* IRELAND, CHINNERY.

FOREIGN EXAMPLES.

The use of supporters by Ecclesiastics was even more common on the continent, that is in those portions of it where supporters were used by lay nobles, for in Italy and the peninsula of Spain and Portugal supporters were not in general use at all.

I noticed recently in the cloister of the old Augustinian monastery at TOULOUSE which is now employed as an archæological museum, a boss from the vaulting of some large church which bears a shield finely carved with the quartered arms of FOIX and BEARN. (FOIX, *Or, three pallets gules*. BEARN, *Argent, two cows passant in pale gules clarinés or.*) The shield is supported by two angels, and its early date may possibly be deduced from the curiously shaped hat which surmounts it. This has no brim but curves outwards from the top to the rim. It may possibly be a souvenir of PIERRE DE FOIX, Archbishop of ARLES.

The seal of JEAN, Bishop of NANTES in 1409, bears his arms : (*Argent, five bendlets gules*), supported by three angels, one standing behind the shield, the others each kneeling upon one knee. A crosier is placed paleways *upon* the escucheon but its crook is projected upon the breast of the standing angel. This is a very curious and uncommon arrangement. (The seal is engraved in MORICE, *Mémoires pour servir de Preuves à l'Histoire Ecclésiastique et Civile de Bretagne*, tome ii., fig. 190, folio. Paris, 1742; and *see* our Plate XXXVI., fig. 4.)

REYNAUD, "*bâtard de Bourbon*," illegitimate son of CHARLES, Duc de BOURBON, used in 1472, as Archbishop of NARBONNE, the shield of his arms, *Argent, a wide bend of* FRANCE-ANCIENT (i.e., *Azure, semé de fleurs-de-lis or*) *charged with a filet in bend gules*. The shield was supported by two angels holding palm-branches, derived from the Royal supporters of France. (Père ANSELME, tome i., p. 310.)

In the choir of the beautiful and very interesting Cathedral of ALBI, in the south of France (very little known to or visited by English travellers, but most worthy of the trouble of a detour) I noticed in the marvellous choir several examples in which the arms of LOUIS I. of AMBOISE (Bishop of ALBI, 1473-1502, and Cardinal), which were : *Paly of six, or and gules*, are carved with two winged stags as supporters. (These were also used as supporters by Kings CHARLES VI., CHARLES VII., and LOUIS XI. of France, the last of whom died in 1483. We may therefore conjecture that as the Bishop held his See during the life of the last-named Sovereign, their use by him may have been a special mark of Royal favour).

On the seal of JEAN, *bâtard de Bourgogne*, Provost of ST. OMER in 1482 (afterwards of NOTRE DAME at BRUGES), natural son of Duke PHILIPPE LE BON of BURGUNDY, his arms are supported by *two rampant lions*. The arms are : *Or, on a very broad fess the quartered coat of* BURGUNDY :—Quarterly, 1 and 4. BUR-GUNDY-MODERN : *Azure, semé of fleurs-de-lis or* (this should be *within a bordure goboné argent and gules*, but the bordure is omitted, perhaps intentionally). 2. *Per pale* (a) BURGUNDY-ANCIENT : *Bendy of six or and azure, within a bordure gules :* (b) BRABANT, *Sable, a lion rampant or.* 3. *Per pale* (a) BURGUNDY-ANCIENT *as in 2;* (b) LIMBURG, *Argent, a lion rampant gules crowned or.* Over all, FLANDERS : *Or, a lion rampant sable.* The shield is ensigned with a priest's broad hat having only a single tassel on each side. (The seal is engraved in VREE, *Généalogie des Comtes de Flandre*, tome i., p. 128, see also tome ii., p. 406, folio. Bruges, 1642.) (On the modes of denoting illegitimate descent I may be permitted to refer the reader to my chapter on the Marks of Illegitimacy in vol. ii. of *A Treatise on Heraldry, British and Foreign*, by JOHN WOODWARD, and GEORGE BURNETT. Edinburgh, 1892.)

The tomb of Archbishop BRIÇONNET, at TOULOUSE, bears his arms : *Azure, a bend componé of five pieces or and gules, on the first compon of gules an estoile of the second; the same charge is repeated in the sinister canton of the shield.* The shield is supported by a single lion, and surmounted by a hat having six *houppes* or tassels on either side.

The arms of TRISTAN DE SALAZAR, Archbishop of SENS, on the Hôtel de Sens at Paris, were supported by two eagles ; and those of FRANÇOIS D'INTEVILLE, Bishop of AUXERRE (*Sable, two lions passant gardant in pale or*), were depicted over the gateway of his palace there, "dans un écu en bannière" (rather curiously), and supported by two mermaids.

The arms of CLAUDE DE SEYSSEL, Bishop of MARSEILLES (1509-1517), were supported by two griffins. His arms were : *Gyronny or and azure*, and were differenced by the addition of *a torteau in the centre point.* The pastoral staff was placed

2 H

in pale behind the escucheon, and a mitre surmounted the whole.
(The arms are thus represented in a manuscript edition of
THUCYDIDES, which formed part of the library of SEGUIER,
Chancellier de France.) Pere MENÊTRIER justly considers the
arrangement a singular one. (*L'Usage des Armoiries*, pp. 220, 221.
Paris, 12mo.) Writing in the year 1673, the same learned and
accurate herald says that a century earlier "la plus part des
Prelats et des Ecclesiastiques titrez mettoient des supports à leurs
Armoiries" . . . "Aujour d'hui il y a peu d'Ecclésiastiques
qui mettent des supports à leurs Armoiries." I suspect, however,
that at the date when MENÊTRIER penned these words the use of
supporters by the French nobility in general had begun to decline.
It certainly revived again later, as the examples presently to be
given will show very clearly.

Speaking of the use of angels as supporters to arms, he says,
"Celles de plusieurs Prelats et de plusieurs Ecclesiastiques sont de
cette maniere en diverses Eglises. Ainsi il est vray de dire qu'il
n'y a jamais eu de regle pour cela ; comme il est vray qu'il n'y a
jamais rien eu de fixe et de determiné pour les supports, que l'on a
changez autant de fois qu'on a voulu." (*L'Usage des Armoiries*,
p. 217.) He tells us also that the arms of CHARLES, Cardinal de
BOURBON, remained in the Cathedral at LYONS, and were thus
depicted :—the shield of arms (*Azure, three fleurs-de-lis or, over all
a bendlet gules*), was supported by a *lion rampant* behind it, and
the head of the Archi-episcopal cross also appeared above the shield.
All this was placed under a pavilion *semé* of cyphers of the
Cardinal's name, and surmounted by the tasselled red hat of his
dignity. The curtains of the pavilion were drawn back to allow
the shield to be visible, and were supported by two human arms,
each wearing a maniple, and issuing from clouds—each hand held
a fiery sword. The tassels of the Cardinal's hat were made to fall
over the lion's shoulders. (This very curious and interesting
example is engraved in MENESTRIER's little volume, *L'Usage des
Armoiries*, at p. 216.)

In the very interesting Church of S. BERTRAND DE COMMINGES,
near Luchon in the Pyrenees, I noticed carved on the stall of the
abbot an escucheon, charged with a lion rampant, and supported
by a man and a woman.

LEONOR D'ESTAMPES, Abbé of BOURGEUIL EN ANJOU, afterwards Bishop of CHARTRES, and who died as Archbishop of
REIMS in 1651, bore his arms (*Azure, two piles in chevron or, on
a chief argent, three open crowns gules*), supported by the lions
rampant of his family.

The Dean and Canons of the Cathedral Church of S. JEAN, at LYONS, all of whom were Counts in right of their canonries (*vide ante*, Chap. III., p. 45) not only used the coronet of that rank but added to their personal arms supporters ; on the dexter a *griffin segreant argent*, on the sinister a *lion rampant or*. These supporters were obviously derived from the arms of the Chapter, which were : *Gules, a griffin argent, and a lion or, rampant-combatant*. These Capitular arms had their own supporters, viz., two angels proper, but they were sometimes placed upon the breast of the single-headed eagle displayed (the Evangelistic symbol of S. JOHN, to whose honour their church was dedicated). A curious example is afforded by the book-stamp of ANTOINE DE FEURS, "doyen et chanoine-comte" of the Church of LYONS, about the year 1500. On it his arms (*Lozengy or and sable*) are supported, not in the usual manner by the *griffin* and lion, but by the eagle of S. JOHN on the dexter side, and by the lion on the sinister (GUIGARD, *Armorial du Bibliophile*, tome i., p. 214.)

CLAUDE DE FOUGÈRES, Dean and Count of the Church of S. JEAN at LYONS, in 1507 bore his arms : *Azure, a chief lozengy or and gules*, supported by the official supporters, a lion to the dexter, a griffin to the sinister, and timbred with the coronet of a count, but without any other indication of his Ecclesiastical dignity (GUIGARD, *Armorial du Bibliophile*, tome i., p. 224). So also, CHARLES-EMMANUEL FROULLAY DE TESSÉ, Canon and Count of LYON, who was also Abbé of SAINT MAUR, used the official supporters, the griffin to the dexter, the lion to the sinister. (GUIGARD, i., 228.)

MICHEL EDOUARD COLBERT, Dean of the Cathedral of ORLÉANS, in 1735, and Abbé-Commendataire of the Royal abbeys of SAINT MESMIN, and of S. MICHEL EN THIERACHE, used his escucheon (*Or, a serpent ondoyant in pale azure*), supported by two unicorns regardant, and timbred with a ducal coronet above which are the mitre and the head of the pastoral staff of the Abbé-Commendataire. (GUIGARD, *Armorial du Bibliophile*, tome i., p. 169.) The supporters are personal, not official.

In 1749, JACQUES DE ST. PIERRE, Abbé-Commendataire de TRÉPORT, bore on his seal an escucheon : . . . *a chevron between three cinquefoils* . . . with the external ornament of a coronet, mitre, and pastoral staff. The shield is supported by *two lions rampant*. A little later, in 1768, JEAN JACQUES, Comte de LIGNIVILLE, Abbé-Commendataire de TRÉPORT, bore on his seal his arms : *Lozengy or and sable*. The arms are ensigned with a coronet, and have the mitre and staff arranged above it in the usual manner. The supporters are the ordinary ones borne by the family, viz., two savages. (*See* DEMAY, *Les Sceaux de Normandie*, Nos. 2890, 2891.)

Another Ecclesiastic, RÉNÉ HENRI DES CARBONNIÈRES in 1781, sealed with the arms : *Azure, on three bends argent* (more properly *Bendy of eight argent and azure*) (*eight* or *eleven*) *glowing coals proper.* This escucheon was supported by two savages proper, and surmounted in the usual manner by coronet, mitre, and the head of the crozier. (DEMAY, *Sceaux de Normandie*, No. 2873.) On his book-plate, the escucheon of I. F. SEGURET, Canon of the Cathedral Church of ST. ALAIS (which bore his arms : Quarterly, 1 and 4. *Azure, a castle* . . . *on a chief* . , . *three estoiles* . . . . ; 2 and 3. *Gules, a chevron between two mullets in chief* . . . , *and a* . . . *in base*), is supported by a *lion passant-regardant en baroque*, and by another *contourné sejant-regardant.* (*French Ex-Libris*, by WALTER HAMILTON, p. 106, 1892.)

CHARLES D'ORLÉANS, Abbé de ROTHELIN, who was son of HENRI D'ORLÉANS, Marquis de ROTHELIN (a descendant of the celebrated JEAN, Comte de DUNOIS, *bâtard* D'ORLÉANS, born in 1403), bore the following arms : Quarterly, 1 and 4. *Or, a bend gules* (BADEN-HOCHBERG). 2 and 3. *Or, on a pale gules three chevrons argent* (NEUFCHÂTEL). *Over all, Azure, three fleurs or, a label argent, with a baton (gules) péri en bande* (ORLÉANS) ; used as supporters two angels (derived from the supporters of the Royal arms of France), and timbred the escucheon with the coronet of a French Prince (strawberry leaves alternating with demi fleurs-de-lis). JOHANNA, daughter and heiress of PHILIP, last Margrave of BADEN-HOCHBERG, Comte de NEUFCHÂTEL (who died in 1503), married LOUIS D'ORLÉANS, Duc de LONGUE-VILLE. Their younger son FRANÇOIS, Marquis de ROTHELIN, Comte de NEUFCHÂTEL, was father of an illegitimate son, also named FRANÇOIS, from whom descended the Abbé de ROTHELIN named above.

The student who is curious with regard to the ancient modes of distinguishing illegitimate descent by a change of tincture, will notice an example here in the NEUFCHÂTEL quarters. The proper arms of NEUFCHÂTEL as borne by the House of BADEN were : *Gules, on a pale or, three chevrons sable.* I may refer the reader to what I have already written on this subject in *A Treatise on Heraldry, Ancient and Modern*, vol. ii., chap. xvii.

If the use of supporters by Ecclesiastics was, as has been shown in the foregoing examples, sufficiently frequent in France for several centuries, it was even more general among Ecclesiastics of high rank in the Holy Roman Empire. By the three Ecclesiastical Prince-Electors, as well as by the other Prince-Bishops, and Abbots of the Empire supporters were habitually employed.

The official supporters of the Electors and Prince-Archbishops of CÖLN (Cologne) were formerly *two lions rampant or;* but commonly in more modern times a griffin was substituted for the lion on the dexter side. The arms of the Elector MAXIMILIAN of BAVARIA, who was the Prince-Archbishop from 1650 to 1688, are engraved in SIEBMACHER'S *Wappenbuch*, vol. i., plate iii., and are: Quarterly, 1. *Argent, a cross sable.* (See of COLOGNE); 2. *Gules, a horse saliant argent* (Duchy of WESTPHALIA); 3. *Gules, three nenuphar leaves or* (Duchy of ENGERN); 4. *Azure, an eagle displayed argent* (County of ARNSPERG). Over the whole an escucheon containing the personal arms of the Prince-Elector, viz.: Quarterly, 1 and 4. *Fusilly bendy argent and azure* (BAVARIA); 2 and 3. *Sable, a lion rampant or, crowned gules* (Palatinate of the RHINE). The shield is mitred, *in pale* behind it rises the archiepiscopal cross; the crosier or pastoral staff, and the naked temporal sword are placed in saltire. The supporters are the *griffin* and *lion rampant*, both *or*.

The arms of DAMIAN HARTARD VON DER LEVEN, Elector and Prince-Archbishop of MAINZ are given at p. 256 *ante;* the escucheon is supported by *two greyhounds argent*. (In this case, and in the following, the supporters are personal, and not appropriated to the See.) A similar arrangement was used by JOHN FREDERICK CHARLES, Reichsgraf VON OSTEIN, who was Elector and Prince-Archbishop of MAINZ. His personal arms: *Azure, a greyhound springing argent collared gules*, were placed upon the quartered shield of the arms of his Sees; and the supporters were two greyhounds collared as in the arms at p. 257. I have followed TRIERS in making the greyhound *or;* the Counts of OSTEIN at present bear the greyhounds *argent*.

In 1708 the Abbess of BUCHAU, Princess of the Empire, born Countess of KÖNIGSECK-ROTENFELS had her arms (*Fusilly in bendsinister, or and gules*) supported by two golden lions.

On the seal of JOSEPH, Abbot of LAMSPRING in 1730, are two shields, one containing the arms of the abbey: *Azure, on a terrace in base, a lamb passant, holding a crozier proper;* the other charged with the personal coat of the abbot: *Argent, a chevron between three birds sable*. The shields are supported by the figures of two saints, on the dexter by S. GEORGE (?), on the sinister by S. DENIS, decapitated and holding his head in his hand. (*See* HARENBERG,

Historia Ecclesiæ Gandersheimensis.) It is obvious that the use of supporters in this case is official, not personal.

The tomb of FERDINAND of BRUNSWICK-HARBURG (d. 1753), Canon of the Church of ST. BAVON, at Ghent, is adorned with his shield bearing the arms of LÜNEBERG : *Or, semé of hearts gules, a lion rampant azure* (BRUNSWICK); *Gules, two lions passant in pale or* (EBERSTEIN) ; *Azure, a lion rampant argent crowned or* (HOMBURG) ; *Gules, a lion rampant or, within a bordure goboné argent and azure;* etc. The shield is surmounted by his coronet, and priestly hat, and is supported by two lions regardant (*or ?*).

The arms of ADAM FREDERICK VON SEINSHEIM, Prince-Bishop of WÜRZBURG in 1755, who also became Bishop of BAMBERG in 1757, are given *ante* p. 90. The shield is supported by two of the BAMBERG *sable lions rampant, each charged with a bend passing from the head to hind feet argent.* This is a very curious example of the use of official as distinct from personal supporters.

The arms of RAIMUND, Count von STRASOLDO, Prince-Bishop of EICHSTÄDT from 1757 to 1781, on the other hand are supported by two Moors—derived from the personal arms—of these the dexter holds the temporal sword, the sinister the crosier of spiritual dignity. The arms are : Quarterly, 1. *Or, a double-headed eagle displayed sable, armed gules, each head crowned and diademed proper,* for the Empire ; 2 and 3. *Or, the bust of a Moor proper, wreathed argent, collared gules;* 4. *Or, a plume of five ostrich feathers alternately sable and argent.* Over these arms is usually borne an escucheon, *Barry of six sable and or,* but in the example before us this personal coat of STRASOLDO is replaced by an escucheon charged with the arms of the See of EICHSTÄDT : *Gules, a crosier or pastoral staff in pale* (usually with an entwined *sudarium*) *argent* (*v. ante,* p. 282).

Visitors to STRASBURG may still see on the pediment of the mansion erected by him in la Grande Rue de l'Église the finely sculptured arms of EMMANUEL THÉODOSE DE LA TOUR D'AUVERGNE, Cardinal de BOUILLON (d. 1715). These are : Quarterly, 1 and 4. *Azure, semé de fleurs-de-lis or, a tower argent, masoned sable* (LA TOUR); 2. *Or, three torteaux gules* (BOULOGNE) ; 3. *Coticé in bend, or and gules* (TURENNE) ; *Over all an escucheon, per pale;* (a) *Or, a gonfanon gules, fringed vert* (AUVERGNE) ; (b) *Argent, a fess gules* (BOUILLON). *A label, for cadency, runs in chief above the first two quarters.* The shield is surmounted by a ducal coronet, which is enfiled by the patriarchal cross with its double traverse. The cardinal's hat, with fifteen *houppes* on either side is placed above the coronet ; and the shield is supported by *two griffins regardant, each of which is charged upon the shoulder with the gonfanon,* the charge from the quarter of AUVERGNE.

The Papal arms are often represented with angel supporters, each holding the Papal cross with its triple traverse. On a gold ducat of Pope ALEXANDER VI. (BORGIA) the shield of arms (*v.* p. 162) is supported by two angels, issuing from clouds, and is surmounted by the keys crossed in saltire, beneath the Papal *triregno* or tiara. (*See* also p. 156 *ante.*)

Examples of the continental use of supporters might be multiplied almost indefinitely, but I have selected out of a much larger number examples which, for one reason or another, seemed to be interesting, and probably more than sufficient have been adduced to refute the statement which appears in some modern books of heraldry that Ecclesiastics have no right to supporters. Of these one of the most recent is the book of M. GOURDON DE GENOUILLAC, entitled *l'Art Héraldique,* published at Paris in 1892, and forming part of the Bibliothèque de l'Enseignement des Beaux Arts. At p. 160 the author says, "Cependant, retenons une règle qui a toujours été observée. Les femmes et les ecclésiastiques ne portent pas de tenants." I distinctly traverse both these statements, even as regards French armory; but it is curious to notice that, so far as Ecclesiastics are concerned, the assertion referred to is in distinct contradiction to one made on only the previous page where it is said (quite correctly, as we have shown in these pages), that "tous les Comtes de l'Église Cathédrale de Lyon ont pour supports un lion et un griffon qui sont les figures des armoiries du chapitre!"

The examples given of a heraldic usage, which we have shown to extend over five centuries, and which has not yet entirely died out, are probably authority sufficient for my statement that any Ecclesiastic at home or abroad, who would have the right as a layman to bear his arms with supporters, need not suppose that his ecclesiastical position deprives him of the privilege, or that there is any lack of precedent for his continuing the use of all that heraldically belongs to him. It seems to me, moreover, that any Bishops who now chose to assume supporters would be as fully entitled so to do as were their predecessors of centuries ago. A heraldic right does not appear to me to be lost, because (as a result of the ignorant misstatements of professional heralds, and heraldic books) it has fallen into abeyance.

APPENDIX B.·

CONTINENTAL CHAPTERS,· AND PREUVES DE NOBLESSE.

REFERENCE has already been made in these pages to the fact that admission to many of the continental Chapters was confined to persons of noble birth, who were required to produce proofs of their descent which were submitted to the most rigorous scrutiny. This was the case in the great religious houses.for either sex. The "*Preuves de Noblesse*" varied at different times even in the same Chapter, but the tendency was always to increase the strictness of their requirements.. Germany was the land where these requirements were exacted with the greatest rigour; but even there, as will be presently shown, there was considerable variety in the qualifications expected, both as regards the kind of nobility required, and as to the antiquity of it.·

First of all, it is necessary to say that the general British idea of nobility is a very different one from that which it obtains on the Continent of Europe. With us it is for the most part connected, most erroneously, with the dignity of the Peerage, and a seat, either present or prospective, in the House of Lords. The idea of the existence of an *untitled* nobility is one which has yet to dawn on the minds of a large portion of our people, who flatter themselves that they are well instructed.

Even in France in modern times our insular idea began to be adopted, and evoked the following protest :—

"La 'noblesse, on ne le sait pas assez, quoique ce soit une vérité aussi banale que possible, est parfaitement indépendante des titres, qui ne sont en quelque sorte qu'un ornement, une décoration ajoutée à la noblesse même. Leur défaut n'empêche pas une famille d'être d'une aussi ancienne extraction que celle qui a été. plus favoriseé par la fortune ou la faveur du prince. Le monde se figure maladroitement le contraire, et croit d'ordinaire que la noblesse ne peut exister sans la présence d'un titre ; c'est une grave erreur. (*La Noblesse en France*, par E. DE BARTHÉLEMY, p. 78. Paris, 1858.)

But the legal definition of nobility, as put forth by Sir Edward Coke, Lord Chief-Justice (d. 1634), is this :—"Nobiles sunt qui arma gentilitia antecessorum suorum proferre possunt." The foreign "noble" is in fact the equivalent of our "gentleman by birth," who bears *legally* the ensigns of that rank in the shape of an armorial escutcheon with its proper accompaniments. In the continental sense of the word our British gentry are as truly entitled to the appellation and rank of "noble" as are those by whom it is borne abroad. But the ignorant restriction of the term to those who sit in the Upper House of Parliament, and the consequent disclaimers of nobility in foreign courts and other places, even by those who were most fully entitled to its privileges, has led to the erroneous continental idea that our British *noblesse* is a thing of small importance, since we ourselves speak of a man who may have been made a Baron in the reign of Queen Victoria, as having been "ennobled," whereas the fact may very probably be that he is the head of a family of untitled nobility, who can trace their descent and have held their lands from the time of the Plantagenets, or even of the Conqueror and his sons.

Under the feudal system in Germany and Gaul nobility was attached to the possession of the soil. Besides the large districts held from the Crown by the nobles who were the *comites*, or companions of the Sovereign (hence the title of Count), other lands of less extent were held immediately from the Crown, and were the rewards of military service in the past, as their possession was the condition of military service in the future. The holders of all these noble fiefs had their tenants who held lands from them, and not from the Crown immediately, by payment of rent, etc. ; and there were also besides these the burghers of towns, and in the country large masses of population who were serfs, *adscripti glebæ*. Originally only a man who could prove his nobility, or descent from noble and free ancestors, could hold a noble or knightly fief; in later times the purchase of such a fief by a man free, but not noble, was held to confer nobility.. But the original nobility of Germany and Gaul was distinctly military in its character, and the military insignia of arms and crest were the outward and visible signs of noblemen. These only were admitted to take part in the chivalric exercises, the tournaments and jousts, which were the delight of the populace, and the opportunities for the exhibition of the personal prowess of the nobles in times of peace. Before a knight could take part in them his shield of arms and crest were exposed for days to official and to a not less stringent public criticism ; any one who should offer himself as a combatant without being able to prove his descent from four "noble" ancestors, that is from four grandparents entitled to bear coat-armour, was made to ride the barriers of the lists amid the jeers and hisses of the populace—sometimes was in danger of fine and imprisonment as the fit reward of his presumption. The arms of these four grandparents were exposed in a quartered shield, and hence came the technical heraldic term of "quarters."

In later times, when the Sovereign had no longer knightly fiefs to bestow, those who distinguished themselves in war or in the councils of the state were rewarded by being raised to noble rank independently of their possessions.

In the fifteenth century the descent required was carried back a generation further, and eight quarters were usually demanded. In the *preuves* of ARNOLD DE GELTWERT, who petitioned for reception as a Canon of LIÈGE in 1494, ULRIC DE WOLFERSDORF, one of the *témoins*, or official witnesses to the truth of his genealogical assertions, declared that he had seen the father of the candidate take part on several occasions in the Tourneys of Germany, where only gentlemen of eight lines were admitted. "In publico nobilium more torneasse, et hastiludiasse sæpius, et quod in Germaniâ non admittuntur ad hastiludium, nisi nobiles ad minimum ex octo lineis." (MENESTRIER, *Preuves de Noblesse.* Paris, 1683 p. 13.) By the old Saxon laws no one, whatever his rank or condition, could contract marriage with a person of lower station than his own except under the penalty that his progeny should descend to the condition of his bride. Thus a count who espoused a woman of baronial rank only left progeny of that rank, and a nobleman who married an ignoble wife forfeited thereby the privileges of his nobility, so far as his posterity were concerned. Even now the rules which restrict the alliances of princes and princesses of reigning German Houses to those who are *ebenbürtig* are the cause of those peculiar arrangements known as morganatic marriages, in which neither wife nor offspring have a right to the husband's or father's rank, title, or domains.

In spite of the Gospel declaration that in the Catholic Church of Christ the distinction of "bond and free" should not exist, many of the more important of the religious foundations only admitted to their fraternity the free born. This at first implied that not only the candidate himself but his ancestors had always been "*free.*" But when, as has been shown above, the word had undergone a change in its significance, the chapters extended their requirements to meet that change. Henceforth no one was admitted who could not prove a descent from four grandparents of free descent. The convenient proof of this was the exhibition of their armorial bearings since the right to use them was confined to the free and nobly born.

Later, when the Emperors conferred the privileges of nobility by diploma on those whom they considered deserving, the Chapters in many instances extended their requirements, at one time raising the number of quarters to eight, at another to sixteen ; or again stipulating that all the quarters should be those of families who bore the title of Prince or Count, or Baron, etc., etc. Of these, examples will be given as we proceed.

We have seen that the ancient people of Germany belonged to one or other of two classes, the free and the servile—*freie und leibeigene*. From the first class another emerged in course of time the *adelige*, who were entitled to a voice in the national council, and both these classes, whether they were *militares* or not, were designated *ingenui*. The union of the free and of the servile in marriage was strictly forbidden. If a free man married a servile girl he and their offspring became of her condition. The *Lex Salica* decreed : " Si quis ingenuus ancillam alienam in conjugium acceperit, ipse cum illa in servitium implicetur " (tit. 14, cap. 6). Even when a fief was held immediately from the Crown, but not by the *servitium militare*, if there were any condition of the tenure which had a ministerial or servile character, the holder sank into an inferior grade called *mittel-freie;* and his family sank with him, because each of them might be the inheritor of the obligation, and the over-lord, if he mortgaged the fief, included these his *ministeriales*, and their prospective services, in the obligation. The writer of an interesting paper on this subject in the *Gentleman's Magazine* of Dec. 1860, to which I desire to acknowledge my obligations, gives as an instance the case of the family of MALTITZ, fairly entitled to be counted "gentle," and ranked among the *nobiles minores;* one of its members, ELIZABETH VON MALTITZ, had actually been married to the Markgrave HEINRICH VON MEISSEN; in 1272. But it was afterwards discovered that the family held lands for which they owed some ministerial service to the Emperor, and accordingly in 1278 a formal letter of emancipation was obtained from the Emperor RUDOLF VON HAPSBURG, declaring the existing and future issue of the marriage "as noble and free as if they had been born of a *free* mother."

In process of time many slaves obtained their liberty, with or without the good will of the owners of the soil to which they had been *adscripti*. Some settled in the cities which were springing up, and obtained the rights of burgesses. These were called *liberti*, or *gefreite*, and afterwards they called themselves *freie* and *frei-geborne*, and claimed to rank with the ancient free families of the Empire, who, however, would not admit their claim, and excluded them from the tournaments, and usually from the Chapters. Accordingly we find in the old books of German jurisprudence such epithets as *immerfreie*, *völlig freie*, *semper liberi*,

liberi puri, and the like, used to distinguish families which had no taint of servile commixture. These *semper liberi* and the *militares* eventually claimed the title of *adelige*, which had been earlier appropriated by the families whose head had a voice in the national councils; and these latter, the original *adelige*, similarly called themselves *erlaucht*, or illustrious. This came to be the distinguishing epithet of those Counts and Barons who had a hereditary seat in the Diet; the *adelige* being the *nobiles minores* who had no parliamentary privileges; while the appellation *freie*, which had formerly been the distinguishing epithet of the most ancient races, was conceded to the burgesses of the Free Cities (a title assumed in the fourteenth century), and others who had become enfranchised. As to the "patrician families" of the free cities, such as AUGSBURG, NÜRNBERG, etc. (who are sometimes spoken of by ill-informed writers in England as if they were rather above than below the general run of German *armigeri* or *nobiles*), the fact is that while they claimed the right of ranking themselves with the other *free* families of the Empire, the latter altogether repudiated them, excluded them from the Tourneys and Chapters, and so late as 1754 refused recognition to their claims of social equality. Some indeed were of noble descent, as at AUGSBURG, where the families of LANGENMANTEL, REHLINGER, WELSER, HERWARDT (or HÖRWARTH), RAVENSPURGER, and ILSUNG were of ancient nobility, and their quarters had been in olden times admitted in the Chapters. But, later, the statutes made to exclude the *bourgeoisie*, and the creation by diploma of a large number of new patrician families (no less than fifty-four were created by the Senate of AUGSBURG, with the approval of CHARLES V., and fourteen were added later), caused the exclusion of the whole of them.

Regular "proofs of nobility" are not found before the thirteenth century, because up to that time all the nobles were a military class, accustomed, as has been shown, to marry only among themselves, so that it was only necessary for persons to prove that their parents belonged to the military nobility for them to be received into the Chapters and Colleges. And this "military nobility" was understood to date from time immemorial. There was in those days no means by which a man of servile descent could rise into the ranks of the *free*, the equivalent of the knightly and the noble.

The Chapters where the requirements were of the strictest kind were MENTZ, MÜNSTER, TRIER, WORMS, SPEYER, OSNABRÜCK, PADERBORN, HILDESHEIM, and BAMBERG. In these the investigation as to nobility of descent was so strict that an armorial quartering once admitted by any of them was received without further question by other Chapters.

At MENTZ there were forty-two Canons of whom the Dean and twenty-three senior Canons formed the Chapter proper, out of whose number the Prince-Archbishop and Elector was chosen. The other eighteen were "domicellaries." For admission to this Chapter sixteen quarters at least were required ; that is, the applicant had to prove his descent from four grandparents, all of whose grandparents on both sides were free and noble, members of families of name and arms, and who had been admitted to the tourneys. Later, a further limitation was made, and none were eligible who were not possessors of a noble fief in the circle of the Upper Rhine ; and at last thirty-two quarters, sixteen paternal, and as many maternal, were required.

At MÜNSTER the Chapter consisted of forty Canons. Pope BONIFACE IX., in a Bull dated in the 10th year of his pontificate (*i.e.*, in 1399) confirmed the statute which provided that only gentlemen of ancient knight families should be received: " Personas nobiles aut saltem militaribus parentibus procreatas ex utroque parente." Pope JULIUS II. confirmed the same statute in 1504. Up to 1576, therefore only four quarters were required, and the oath administered was in these terms : " Les quatre familles icy nommées sont les quatre plus proches Familles de pere et de mere, et d'icelles (un tel) est venu en droite ligne de legitime Mariage, et elles sont toutes de bonne Chevalerie, qu'ainsi Dieu m'aide, et ses Saints." A further limitation was made later with the object of excluding the patrician families of the city itself; and an educational qualification was required to the extent that the candidates must have studied at least a year and nine months in the University of Paris.

At TRIER (TRÈVES) there were forty Canons, of whom sixteen formed the Chapter, the others being Domicellaries. Here also ancient nobility originally sufficed but in process of time the sixteen quarters were increased to thirty-two.

At SPEYER (SPIRES) the Chapter consisted of fifteen full Canons and twelve Domicellaries. They had to prove sixteen quarters, eight paternal, and eight maternal. Similarly at PADERBORN, sixteen quarters were necessary, and the candidates must have studied in one of the universities of France or Italy.

At HILDESHEIM, where there were forty Canons ; and at BAMBERG, where there were twenty, with fifteen Domicellaries, sixteen quarters were required for admission to the Chapter. At BAMBERG the

Emperor held an honorary canonry. It was required that a newly elected Canon should not fail of attendance at Mass on a single day during the first two years of his tenure of his stall under penalty of the loss of two years seniority. Here also the Bishop elected from the Canons was usually a baron or gentleman (noble), rarely a prince or count.·

At EICHSTADT and at FULDA, sixteen quarters were needful. This was the case also in some of the great Chapters of Canonesses hereafter to be mentioned.

Some Chapters were less strict and only required the proof of eight quarters ; that is, the applicant had to prove that all his eight great-grandparents were of undoubted free and noble descent. This was the case at KEMPTEN (where the Chapter consisted of twenty Capitulars, besides expectants), and it was also the usual qualification for the Chapters of Canonesses, such as those of S. MARIA IN CAPITOLIO at Cologne, RHEINDORF, SUSTEREN, WILICH, MUNSTERBILSEN ; and the great abbeys in the Low Countries, such as NIVELLE, MONS, MAUBEUGE, etc.

At AUGSBURG, BASEL, BRIXEN, CHÜR, CONSTANCE, ELWAN-GEN, LIÈGE, PASSAU, REGENSBURG, and TRENT, the Chapters were not so exclusive, but while exacting the gentilitial qualification from a portion of their members they also admitted a certain number of persons who had graduated as Doctors in one or other faculty.

At AUGSBURG where the Chapter consisted of twenty Capitulars, ; and as many Domicellaries, not only Doctors but licentiates were received, so also at BRIXEN there were eighteen Canons, of whom half were nobles, and half were Doctors or at least licentiates. But these liberal Chapters were the exception. There was a continual tendency rather to strengthen than to diminish the exclusiveness of the Chapters, either through increasing the number of quarters by requiring another generation to be added ; or else by stipulating that the nobility proved should be of higher quality, or should be taken from the *noblesse* of a certain district.

For instance, it appears that the original qualification for admission to the Chapter at COLOGNE, as in many other places, was that the aspirant should be descended from four grandparents who were free and noble. After the year 1450, the requirements were carried a generation farther back, and eight quarters were demanded ; this extension was confirmed by Papal authority, and not only was the number of descents thus increased, but a new condition was inserted ; viz., that every one of them should be not merely of knightly rank, but of *ancient* knightly rank which demanded the proof of the nobility of *their* grandparents, and was of course equivalent to the requirement of at least thirty-two quarters.

But in process of time even this was not thought adequate. The statute of 1617 demands "sixteen *titled* quarters," that is, that all the quarters shown should be those of families who were princes, counts, or barons holding immediately from the Emperor. It does not appear that this statute ever received Papal sanction, and it could therefore only bind the Chapter by mutual agreement; as to the Pope he held himself free to disregard these later requirements whenever the patronage of a stall fell to him through the decease of a Cardinal, Canon, or in other ways. It is, however, necessary to say that the Chapter consisted of twenty - five full Canons, and of as many Domicellaries, and that eight of the full canonries were set apart for those who could not prove the nobility required from the others, but who were Doctors of Theology, or of Law; the latter of whom ranked as knights in Germany. Except these the Chapter soon came to consist only of those who belonged to princely or countly families.

The Chapter of WÜRZBURG, consisting of twenty-four full Canons, and of twenty-nine Domicellaries, at first demanded the proof of sixteen quarters, but afterwards raised it to thirty-two. In order to exclude all but natives of the district it further required that all the quarters approved should be those of families whose ancestors had been admitted to take part in the tourneys of FRANCONIA; and this stipulation virtually restricted eligibility to fill the WÜRZBURG canonries to the members of a very few families. In this Chapter there was the following curious custom. The person to be admitted was stripped to the waist, and obliged to pass before the Canons who were armed with rods and gave him blows at their pleasure. It was understood that this custom was instituted to keep out of the Chapter princes and counts, who would not submit to the indignity of a blow. As in the list of the later Bishops of WÜRZBURG we find such names as those of the Counts VON GLEICHEN, and VON SCHÖNBORN, it is pretty clear that, if this were the object of the usage, it was only very partially successful.

At SALZBURG the chapter consisted of twenty-four Canons, who at first proved eight quarters, but afterwards it seems that thirty-two were required, and to be all of countly families, or barons at least.

As has been stated, when the nobility of a far back progenitor had been accepted and recorded in one of the great Chapters, it was received without further question, not only in that Chapter but in the others. But with the newer quarters which required proof, the descent of the aspirant had to be asserted and confirmed on oath, not by

themselves only but by independent witnesses who were themselves
of ancient descent. Thus LOTHAIR REVENTLAW, Doctor of Medicine, wishing to serve as one of the witnesses for an aspirant to a
canonry in S. LAMBERTS at LIÈGE, declared that he was duly
qualified so to act, being himself of noble and knightly descent on
both the paternal and maternal sides : " Se qualificatum esse, juxta
tenorem et consuetudinem ecclesiæ Leodiensis, ad deponendum, et
se ex nobili militari genere procreatum ·esse ex utroque." In the
second statute relating to the reception of Canons at LIÈGE,
confirmed by Pope MARTIN V. in the year 1423 it is thus provided :
" Nobilis recipiendus si sit præsens, juret per se ; si absens per pro-
curatorem legitime constitutum, quod ipse recipiendus de utroque
parente, de nobili vel saltem militari genere procreatus existat."
In the original statutes it had been provided that the aspirant should
declare "Juro quod sum de libero genere et legitimo matrimonio
procreatus," and this requirement was confirmed by CLEMENT III.,
and by a Bull of INNOCENT IV., but the second statute required
the oath to run thus : " Juro quod ego sum de utroque parente,
de nobili vel saltem militari genere." MENESTRIER understands
by "nobili genere" in this place *titled noblesse*. (*Preuves de
Noblesse*, p. 15.) But the requirement is more clearly expressed in
the third statute of 1568, by which *nouveaux annoblis* are directly
excluded : " Titulo stemmatis et nobilitatis recipiendus debet esse
honestæ vitæ et moribus probatis. Item, habere-vel habuisse
patrem et matrem, avum, aviam, paternum, paternam, maternum,
maternam, legitimo matrimonio natos. Præterea nobiles antiqui
· et militaris ordinis, et qui vulgo semper apud nobiles et alios pro
talibus habiti et reputati forent vel fuissent. Item, si avus, paternus
vel maternus, alioqui non sufficienti familiâ seu genere natus,
Pontificiâ, Imperatoriâ, Regiâ, aut aliâ quacumque authoritate
nobilitatis, vel etiam Equitis titulo, jure et prærogativâ donatus
esset ; is ad Canonicatum et Prœbendam hujusmodi sub nobilitatis
titulo nullatenus recipiatur." The proof of eight quarters was
appointed at LIÈGE in 1614, but even in 1513 the witnesses of
GERARD VAN GROESBECK, who aspired to a canonry declared that
he was "nobili militari prosapia ortus, gerens insignia militaria
octo quarteriorum utriusque parentis." In 1503 JEAN VAN GROES-
BECK had already proved four descents : GROESBECK, RODINCK-
HAVEN (? RODENHAUSEN), FLODORP, and HAMAL-ELDEREN, " de
optima antiqua militia, præpotentioribus militaribus quarteriis."
(The Counts VAN GROESBECK still bear : *Argent, a fess entée
gules*.) ·
The best proof of the possession of ancient nobility was made

when the aspirant could trace an indisputable descent from an ancestor who had taken part in a tourney to which none were admitted who could not prove their eight quarters. Thus in the proofs of ARNOLD DE GELTWERT, received as Canon of LIÈGE in 1494, ULRIC DE WOLFERSDORF, one of his witnesses, declared on oath that he had often seen the father of the aspirant taking part in a tourney. "In publico more torneasse, et hastiludiasse sæpius, et quod in Germaniâ non admittuntur ad hastiludium nisi nobiles ad minimum ex octo lineis."

These attestations were sometimes made by Cities, represented by their magistrates. Thus PIERRE DE HOLAY of TUNGERN, being an aspirant for a canonry at LIÈGE, the City of TUNGERN gave a formal certificate that WALTER DE HOLAY, grandfather of the aspirant had the rank of knighthood. PIERRE FRIES, Esquire, made affirmation that the mother of the aspirant was of the knightly house of BETWE.

At SUSTEREN (where eight quarters were required), on the admission of a *Chanoinesse*, the following was the oath taken by the witnesses of the aspirant. "Je N.N., jure devant Dieu et sur les saintes Evangiles ; avec les doigts élevez, que la presente Demoiselle est née en legitime mariage, et qu'elle ne descend d'aucune bâtardise ny bourgeoisie, ny d'aucun état qui ne jouisse pleinement de la Noblesse, et qu'elle n'a point d'armes empruntées ; car elle est sortie d'une bonne et ancienne Chevalerie." At S. QUIRINUS DE NEWS (where eight quarters were demanded), the oath was in almost identical terms :—the sentence about the armorial bearings being somewhat amplified—"que ses armoiries ne sont ny empruneés d'ailleurs, ny inventeés à plaisir, mais qu'elles sont dans leurs couleurs véritables."

The Chapters of Canonesses which required sixteen quarters were ELTEN, ESSEN, GANDERSHEIM, GERNERODE, HERVORDEN, LANGENHORST, NOTELEN, QUEDLEMBURG, RELINCKHAUSEN, UTERSEN, and S. URSULA at COLOGNE.

Nearly all the others were content with eight only. At first sight it may seem that an infinity of trouble and research must have been required before any person, male or female, could have obtained admission to such close corporations by proving the nobility of his ancestors for four or five generations back. As a matter of fact this was by no means the case. Not only was much more attention paid than is the case among us, to accurate records of descent in a country where genealogical studies were not merely matters of sentimental interest, for their neglect of them would imperil privileges and advantages which were very real and matter

2 I

of fact ; but these canonries formed so desirable a provision for the younger or unmarried children of the nobility, that in the course of a few centuries nearly every noble family had, over and over again, some of its members in these noble foundations. Where this was the case a quartering once proved, especially if in one of the greater Chapters, was admitted with little or no questioning ; the aspirant had, so far as that particular quarter was concerned, only to prove a regular and legitimate descent from the family to which it belonged. Generally most, if not all, of his quarters could thus be traced with but little difficulty ; and an official attestation from other chapteral authorities to the effect that each quarter had been duly proved there under such and such circumstances, was all that would be required. The greater Chapters did not so easily accept the certificates of less strict ones. The form of such an attestation, without further examination, may be of interest. It was given in 1649, at the secularised house of MOUSTIER SUR SAMBRE, in proof of the five quarters of FENAL, SENSEILLES, BARLEMONT, BRECHT, and WALTHUISER, and ran thus :—" Nous, MARIE DE VAHA DE VACQUEMONT, Dame et Abbesse Seculiere du Noble et Illustre College de Moustier sur Sambre, au Comté de Namur, et les Dames Chanoinesses dudit, capituliairement assemblées certifions et attestons par cette à tous ceux qu'il appartiendra, que les quartiers de Fenal, Senseilles, Barlemont, et Brecht, ont esté prouvez et receus pour Nobles dans ce College en la reception de Mademoiselle Marie de Fenal, présentement Dame de Haren, et Chanoinesse dudit Moustier." " Certifions outre, les quartiers de Walthuiser avoir esté prouvez Nobles aux receptions de deux Demoiselles de Hil presentement encore Chanoinesses de ce College ; en témoinage de quoy, nous avous fait cacheter de nostre grand Cachet ordinaire, le 16 Juillet, 1649. (*Preuves de Noblesse*, pp. 30, 31.) When, however, a quarter had not received an attestation of this kind from any Chapter it was usual in the Chapters of the Low Countries to require proof of the nobility of the great grandfather and of the great great-grandfather of the applicant this was done at LIÈGE, and in the "Factum" of the Chanoinesses of MONS against the Marquis de Varignies it is declared that this is one of their statutes, as it was also in the case of the MOUSTIER SUR SAMBRE referred to above. We read also that on one occasion at MUNSTERBILSEN the reception of a lady, a member of the now well-known Austrian noble family of ALTHANN, was deferred because it had not been proved that one of her quarters (STREIN DE SCHWARTZENAU, now Barons and Counts), had been previously admitted in any Chapter or College.

Some Chapters did not receive the members of families who were of mediate nobility, that is who held their noble fiefs not immediately from the Emperor himself, but from some inferior prince or count.

On the whole I have found the Chapters of Chanoinesses much greater sticklers for purity or superiority of descent than the male ones. In some of them the rank of Chanoinesse conveyed, and still conveys, the secular rank of Countess. The Reformation even where it was accepted did not at first cause the suppression of these very useful provisions for the unmarried or widowed daughters of noble families : they were long continued, and here and there one still exists in a modified form. . But with the change of religion there was a laxer rule of life—in some cases there was none at all, for in some of the Protestant Chapters even marriage was permitted, but the genealogical requirements remained untouched, as in many cases did the comfortable pecuniary position. Thus the Chanoinesses of the (Catholic) Chapter of DENAIN, near ARRAS, proved their sixteen quarters of nobility, but took no vows at all. Those at POUSSEI, near TOUL, were in the same position.

Illegitimate descent from however distinguished a source, was a complete disqualification for any quartering in the *preuves* of Germany and of the Low Countries, until at least as many generations had elapsed as would enable the aspirant to declare a sufficient number of noble progenitors in the direct line without including the illegitimate ancestor. In the year 1555 the Conseil de Brabant ordained that a certain Chapter should not refuse admission to the daughter of HENRY D'YVE, chevalier, on the ground that the mother of her maternal grandfather had been an illegitimate daughter of a noble of high descent, Messire JEAN, Seigneur DE BERGHES (who was himself an illegitimate descendant of the Dukes of BRABANT). The Conseil gave judgment against the Chapter on the ground that, though the Emperor MAXIMILIAN had in 1495 confirmed the privileges of most of the Chapters of Canonesses in the Low Countries, he had expressly stated the limitation, which was that the aspirant should prove her own legitimacy and nobility on four sides paternal and maternal (*noble femme de quatre côtez de pere et de mere procrées en loyal mariage*). The proof demanded by the Chapter was excessive, as the alleged and admitted descent from an illegitimate ancestor was beyond the limits of the Imperial conditions.

There was, in some Chapters, a custom by which, though only a certain number of quarters were required to be strictly *proved*, another generation, or even two, had to be *shown*—thus doubling or quadrupling the requirements. This is one reason why there is sometimes an apparent discrepancy in the statements made by different authors as to the number of quarterings required for admission to a certain Chapter. An example may be found in the case of COLOGNE, the statute of 1450, confirmed by the Pope, only demanded as ,a qualification the proof of eight quarters, or four degrees of generation. But, as all these were required to be of " ancienne Chevalerie," the aspirant needed to be able to show thirty-two quarters (*i.e.*, six generations, or more). It was not, however, requisite that the *female* quarterings in excess of the stipulated eight should be of ancient knighthood.

It is not, perhaps, needful that I should further enlarge upon these genealogical proofs, but I ought to say that some of the minor Chapters were very sensibly satisfied with lesser requirements ; and, while desiring that those who were to be their daily associates should be of gentle birth and education, were content if the aspirant could prove that both parents were descended in the direct male line for three or four generations from gentlefolk of name and arms, without strictly requiring that there should be no trace of a female *mésalliance*.

In Italy the Chapters were freely open to men of all ranks. The old struggle between the GUELPHS and the GHIBELLINES contributed to this. The nobles were mostly on the side of the Emperor, from whom they or their ancestors had probably received their fiefs and their titles ; and it was the policy of the Popes therefore to take the side of popular interests. The Cathedral Chapter of MILAN was, so far as I am aware, the only Italian Chapter in which nobility of birth was ever a requisite for admission, and even there by the seventeenth century this condition had almost ceased, the archbishopric alone being reserved for a man of noble birth, and I believe that even this reservation no longer exists. In some Neapolitan convents only ladies of noble rank were eligible for admission. Probably in ancient times the requirements were stricter. The Abbé UGHELLI speaking of the election and confirmation of an Abbess of SALERNO in the year 1163, and describing the necessary qualifications says, it must not be omitted to inquire if the person to be confirmed as Abbess be of noble and legitimate birth :—" Ut generis etiam et ortus quæstio non prætereatur. Nobilioribus orta est natalibus, et legitimis nuptiis procreata." The Italian Language of the ORDER OF S. JOHN ; and the ORDER OF S. STEPHEN, in Tuscany, of course required proofs of nobility from their members.

In France the number of Chapters in which *preuves de noblesse* were required before admission was considerable. A list of the most important is appended here, and it is interesting to note how varied were their requirements.

THE CHAPTER OF S. JULIEN DE BRIOUDE. Here the King of France was the *Premier Chanoine Honoraire.* The twenty-two Canons had, by Royal grant, the title of Count, and ensigned their arms with the coronet. The proof required of them was sixteen quarters.

The arms of the Chapter were :—*Azure, the capital letter* B, *surmounted by a Royal crown, or.*

THE CHAPTER OF THE CATHEDRAL OF S. JEAN at Lyons, as early as the fourteenth century, admitted to their number none but gentlemen of eight quarters. In 1372 ELZIAS ALBERT, of the Seigneurs de BOULBON, was an aspirant, and his *témoins* made the necessary affirmation that his father, grandfather, and great-grandfather, and their wives, had all been *de genere militari.* The statutes of this celebrated Chapter had already been confirmed by Popes MARTIN V., LEO X., and GREGORY IX., were still further confirmed by a special Bull of CLEMENT VII., promulgated in the year 1532. (The text of this Bull is given at length in the Preface to MENÊTRIER'S scarce little volume on *Les Preuves de Noblesse,* published at Paris and Lyons in 1632.) The Bull is too long for reproduction here, but it bears that it has been issued on the special petition of FRANCIS, King of France, as *Premier Chanoine Honoraire.* It records that the customs of the church have been the same from time immemorial, indeed from the foundation of the church :—"ipsique Canonici ex tunc Comites in signum ipsius nobilitatis nuncupati fuerint, et de præsenti nuncupentur." It stipulates that in future none shall be received into that noble company, or hold any Canonry, Præbend, or other office therein, "nisi de nobili genere ex utroque parente procreatus, et cujus nobilitatis absque ignobilitatis commixtione ad quartum gradum ascendendo per Testes nobiles, et alios omni exceptione majores, in Capitulo dicti Ecclesiæ probata," etc.

The Canons were thirty-two in number. Their armorial privileges in the use of coronet, supporters, and badge, have been already referred to at pp. 45 and 467.

THE CHAPTER OF S. PIERRE AT MÂCON consisted of thirteen Canons who had the title and insignia of Count. They made proof of thirty-two quarters. This Chapter was secularised in the year 1557. It was originally a Benedictine foundation of the year 696. It then became a house of Augustinian, and finally of secular canons.

THE CHAPTER OF S. PIERRE DE ST. CLAUDE was composed of eighteen Canons who proved sixteen quarters. It was secularised in the year 1742.

THE CHAPTER OF S. PIERRE DE BAUME. Here the Abbot and ten Canons were required to make very strict proof of sixteen quarters. The date of its secularisation was 1759.

THE CHAPTER OF S. PIERRE DE VIENNE. This was originally a monastery of the ORDER OF S. BENEDICT, and the year 515 is assigned as that of its foundation. It was secularised by Pope PAUL V. in the year 1612, but in 1781 an union was effected between it and the ancient abbey of SAINT CHEF. The thirty-two Canons had to make proof of nine generations of direct noble descent on the paternal and on the maternal side. It will be noticed that this was a different kind of proof from the ordinary one of so many quarterings. It took no account of the nobility, or the reverse, of the wives. The *only* woman whose nobility required proof was the mother of the aspirant.

THE CHAPTER OF S. LOUIS DE GIGNY (at Saint Claude). Here the fourteen Canons had to prove eight paternal quarters, but only four maternal ones. The Chapter was secularised in 1757.

THE CHAPTER OF S. VICTOR AT MARSEILLES. This was originally a very ancient and illustrious Benedictine abbey. It was founded in, or about, the year 413 by JEAN CASSIEN, priest of MARSEILLES. This pious person founded two monasteries, one for men, of which the church was called the Basilica of SS. PETER and PAUL; the other for women, under the invocation of the BLESSED VIRGIN and S. JOHN THE BAPTIST. In the former the body of S. VICTOR, who afterwards gave his name to the monastery, was said to repose. The abbey was enriched by the gifts of PEPIN, CHARLEMAGNE, LOUIS THE PIOUS, and LOTHAIR, and became the mother-house of many other monasteries, some by its own foundation, some by affiliation. The abbey was secularised by a Bull of Pope CLEMENT XII. in the year 1739, which was confirmed in 1751 by Royal Letters-Patent which founded a "noble Chapter." LOUIS XV., in the year 1774, erected the prebends into dignities bearing the titles and privileges of Counts, and declared that the Chapter should consist of an *Abbé-Commendataire;* three Dignitaries—the Provost, Precentor, and Treasurer; sixteen Canons-Counts, and six aspirants. The members of the Chapter had to prove that their fathers were of Provençal birth, and of six degrees of nobility in direct paternal descent. (*See* the *Nobiliaire du Departement des Bouches du Rhone,* p. 193. Paris, 1863.) (*See* also p. 492, *infra.*)

THE CHAPTER OF ST. DIÉ in the Vosges, originated in an abbey founded in 669 by S. DEODATUS, Bishop of NEVERS. It followed originally the rule of S. COLUMBANUS, for which the Benedictine rule was substituted in later times. The abbey was secularised as early as the year 954, and became a celebrated Chapter of Canons, which became a Cathedral-Chapter on the foundation of the bishopric by Pope PIUS VII. in 1777. Out of the number of its twenty-six Canons, twenty-two had to prove nobility in the direct male line for eight generations ; the other four stalls were reserved for graduates without the genealogical qualification.

THE CHAPTER OF NOTRE DAME D'AMBOISE consisted of twelve Canons who were required to prove noble descent for a century.

THE CHAPTER OF S. MARTIN D'AINAI (Lyon), was composed of a Provost and nineteen Canons who were required to prove a century of noble descent, modified to the proof of the nobility of the grandfather of the aspirant, which was practically much the same thing.

THE FEMALE CHAPTERS in France had equally various requirements as will be seen by the following examples.

THE CHAPTER OF ALIX (Diocese of Lyons), founded in the twelfth century was composed of forty-one *Chanoinesses*, who all had the title and insignia of Countesses. Before admission they were required to prove noble descent for eight generations in direct male descent on the paternal side, and for three generations on the maternal side. (*See* also p. 493.)

THE CHAPTER OF NEUVILLE LES DAMES, EN BRESSE (also in the Diocese of LYONS), had fifty-eight *Chanoinesses-Comtesses*, who were required to prove nine generations of direct nobility on the paternal side, and also that their mothers were of noble descent. This Chapter was secularised by the Pope in 1751, and effected in the year 1755, and thenceforward consisted of a Doyenne, Chantre, Secrétaire, twenty full Chanoinesses, and some expectants (*vide post*, 493.)

THE CHAPTER OF POULANGY, in the Diocese of LANGRES, consisted of twenty-two *Chanoinesses-Comtesses*, who, as at Neuville, proved nine generations of paternal nobility, but only four on the maternal side.

THE CHAPTER OF S. MARTIN DE SÁLLES (in Beaujolais) had forty-three *Chanoinesses-Comtesses* who were required to prove eight generations of direct male nobility on the paternal side, and the nobility of their mothers.

But in some French Chapters the more stringent requirements of (so many) quarters, were made. Sixteen had to be proved at BOUXIERES AUX DAMES, in the Diocese of NANCY (originally a

Benedictine nunnery founded in 930, by GOSLIN, Bishop of TOUL, but secularised in the eighteenth century), and the same was the case at LONS LE SAULNIER, as well as at DENAIN and POUSSEI (*v.* pp. 483 and 494). Eight quarters were held to be sufficient at the Benedictine abbeys of NOTRE DAME DE RONCERAY (known as *La Charité des Nonnains*) at ANGERS, founded in 1028 ; at ESTRUN, near ARRAS in the Pas de Calais, founded, or (as some say) restored, about the year 1085 ; and of AVESNES DE BAPAUME, also near ARRAS. The proofs of eight generations of direct noble descent were required from the thirty *Chanoinesses*, unfettered by vows, who lived in community and replaced the Benedictine nuns, at MAUBEUGE, in the Diocese of CAMBRAY. (But MENÊTRIER tells us that eight quarters were required in 1545 ; and gives as an example those produced in that year for the Demoiselle FLORENCE DE DAVE, daughter of Messire WARNIER DE DAVE, Chevalier, Seigneur de MERLEMONT, and of his wife Dame MAXIMILIENNE DE ROMANCOURT. This nobility was affirmed " sur leur foy et honneur," by the *témoins* of the young lady.) Eight quarters were also required at NOTRE DAME de Coyse en Largentière, where the *Chanoinesses* reached the large number of eighty.

At the Chapter of LIEGNIEUX (LYON) (*v.* p. 493), the forty-five *Chanoinesses* were required to prove the nobility of their mothers, and five direct noble descents on the paternal side. At MONTFLEURY, near Grenoble, which was founded in the year 1342, the proof of four direct noble descents was held sufficient, and this also sufficed in the Benedictine Abbey of BLESLE in the Diocese of ST. FLOUR, founded before 910 by ERMENGARDE, Countess of AUVERGNE. In the Benedictine Abbey of NOTRE DAME DE BOURBOURG in the north of France (founded about the year 1099 by CLÉMENCE DE BOURGOGNE, wife of ROBERT, Count of FLANDERS), the nobility of the aspirant had to be proved as far back as the fourteenth century. In 1742 Queen MARIE ANTOINETTE, accepted the title of *première Chanoinesse*, and the Chapter, nineteen in number, the designation of " la Chapitre de la Reine " (*v.* p. 494).

I append here some brief notes of a similar character with regard to the noble Chapters in Alsace and Lorraine, which have been French but which are now re-included in the Germanic Empire.

THE CHAPTER OF S. JEAN AT BESANÇON (BISANTZ) consisted of four Dignitaries, four "*personnals*" and thirty-eight Canons. Here sixteen quarters were strictly required, except in the case of a few canonries which were reserved for graduates who were the sons of nobles or of graduates, and who underwent an examination before election, provisions which made it easy to exclude those who were in any way unacceptable.

THE CHAPTER OF NOTRE DAME AT STRASBURG. Members of the High Chapter (*vide ante*, p. 325) had to make proof of eight generations of noble descent both on the paternal, and on the maternal side. The statutes of 1687 required of the French Canons that their ancestors on both the paternal and the maternal side, should have borne for four generations the title of either Prince or Duke.

THE CHAPTER OF S. ETIENNE AT TOUL consisted of thirty-six Canons, from whom three descents of nobility on the paternal side were strictly exacted.

THE CHAPTER OF S. ETIENNE AT METZ had (besides eleven dignitaries) thirty-eight Canons out of whom seventeen had to prove a direct noble descent for three generations on the paternal side.

THE UNITED CHAPTERS OF LUDERS AND MURBACH (*vide ante*, p. 340) consisted of twenty-one Canons who all proved sixteen quarters.

THE CHAPTER OF BAUME LES DAMES or LES NONNAINS, arose from an ancient nunnery of the Diocese of Besançon, founded in the fifth century by two brothers, S. ROMAIN and S. LUPICIN. In it Saint ODILLE, the patron saint of Alsace, was brought up. It was at first an independent house but came under Benedictine rule, about the year 789. Since its secularisation it consisted of sixteen *Chanoinesses-Comtesses* who were required to make proof of sixteen quarters. They were permitted to introduce as aspirants to the like dignity one or two nieces from whom of course the same *preuves* were required.

THE CHAPTER OF CHÂTEAU CHALON in the Jura, about six miles north of LONS LE SAULNIER, in the Diocese of BESANÇON, but afterwards in that of ST. CLAUDE, was founded in the year 670, and was under the Benedictine rule. Later it was secularised, and became a noble Chapter of twenty-eight Canonesses, who all proved sixteen quarters. The like *preuves* were required from the Chapter of MIGETTE (Besançon), where eighteen ladies were prebendaries.

THE CHAPTER OF MONTIGNY, also in the Diocese of BESANÇON, was originally a monastery of "Urbanistes," women of the Order of Ste. Claire, and was founded in 1286. After its secularisation it required the *preuves* of eight quarters from its twenty-six *Chanoinesses*.

In the LOW COUNTRIES were several monasteries of note where *preuves* were required, some of them have already been mentioned incidentally, but we must include one or two others of importance.

ANDENNE, in the Diocese and County of Namur, half-way between Namur and Huy, was an ancient nunnery of the Benedictine Order, founded about. the year 690 by S. BEGGA, daughter of PEPIN DE LAUDEN and sister of S. GERTRUDE of NIVELLE. The Abbey was destroyed by the Northmen in the end of the ninth and early in the tenth century, but was rebuilt. The Counts of NAMUR held the office of *Avouez, Advocati,* of the Abbey, but misused their power and alienated its lands to their own advantage. The Emperor HENRY obliged ALBERT, Count of NAMUR, to a restoration, but allowed him to retain the Advocacy of the Abbey as a fief of the Empire. Henceforth the position of the Counts was rather that of *Abbés-Commendataires,* than of *Avouez.* The Chapter consisted of a *Dame-Prévôte,* a *Doyenne,* thirty Canonesses, and ten Canons, nominated by the Counts of NAMUR; from all the *preuves* of eight quarters were required, the families to have been recognised as noble from time immemorial.

The ABBEY OF SAINTE VAUDRU DE MONS, was a Benedictine nunnery founded in the year 640 by the Saint whose name it bears, who was sister of S. ALDEGONDA and daughter of WALBERT, a prince of THURINGIA. SIGEBERT, King of AUSTRASIA, soon increased its possessions, built a new church dedicated to the Blessed Virgin, and instituted thirty prebends for as many noble ladies; while in the former church, under the invocation of SS. PETER and PAUL, he placed a number of monks to perform the divine offices. In the tenth century Archbishop BRUNO of COLOGNE, with the Papal authority, transformed the nuns of STE. VAUDRU into Canonesses, and the monks of S. PIERRE into secular Canons.

In 821, the Advocacy of the Abbey was conferred on the Counts of HAINAULT, who were its vassals for certain fiefs. When the Netherlands were held by the Kings of Spain they held the office referred to as successors of the Counts of HAINAULT, and exercised the right of nomination to the canonries in "le Chapitre Royale des Chanoinesses de Sainte Vaudru." The ladies thus nominated were required to make proof of eight quarters. JOSEPH PELICER, in his genealogy of the Spanish SARMIENTOS, gives the pedigree of LEONORA DE GAND drawn up in order for her reception as a Canoness of ST. VALTRUDE, and says that it was necessary that the quarters of nobility proved should be those of families of four hundred years standing or more, in fact the commencement of the nobility should be in times immemorial.

MAUBEUGE. This convent in the Diocese of CAMBRAY was founded in 661, by Saint ALDEGONDA. It was originally Benedictine, but was afterwards secularised, it then became a Noble Chapter of Chanoinesses who were required to make proofs of eight quarters of immemorial nobility, and who enjoyed their prebends untrammelled by any vows.

NIVELLE. This famous Benedictine nunnery was founded in the year 645 by ITTA, wife of PEPIN, *maire du palais* of SIGEBERT, King of AUSTRASIA. Their daughter S. GERTRUDE was the first Abbess. The Abbey held immediately from the Empire although it was completely surrounded by the lands of the Duchy of BRABANT. About the year 1200 the Emperor ceded to the Duke of BRABANT certain lands which included the Abbeys of S. SERVAIS and NIVELLE, but the Abbess appealed to the Diet and was successful. But the Dukes of BRABANT often acted as Commissioners for the Emperor in the instalment of the Abbess, and gradually the sovereignty became vested in them. The Abbey was called *l'Abbaye Ducale de S. Gertrude*, and the election of the Abbess received the confirmation of the Duke of BRABANT. Nevertheless the Abbess claimed and received the empty title of Princess of the Empire, empty inasmuch as she had apparently neither seat nor vote in the Diet. The proof required was of eight quarters of immemorial nobility.

In this Chapter the Canonesses were all formally knighted on admission to their canonry. The aspirant, properly habited, was led by the *Prévôte* into the midst of the choir, attended by the four senior Canonesses, and there caused to kneel before the officiating knight; who was always a person of high dignity. He then gave her the accolade with his drawn sword, touching her three times upon the left shoulder with the words " Je vous fais Chevalière de Sainte Gertrude, par St. George au nom de Dieu et de Vierge Marie." He then held the cross-hilt of his sword to the lady, who kissed it, then rose and saluted the knight, and retired with the other members of the Chapter.

These noble Chapters, both of men and women, had usually a special cross or decoration worn round the neck, or on the breast, like the badge of an order of knighthood, suspended by its proper ribbon. Usually the badge was a cross of gold enamelled, resembling in general shape the eight-pointed cross of the ORDER OF S. JOHN OF JERUSALEM, but with variations of ornamentation and of colour.

Thus the Canons-Counts of the CHAPTER OF S. JOHN AT LYONS had by Royal Letters-Patent granted in March 4, 1745, registered in Parliament April 7, the privilege of wearing a golden cross of eight points, enamelled white, and having a golden fleur-de-lis in each of its four principal angles. Each arm of the cross terminated in a little golden coronet (that of a Count) ornamented with pearls, or silver balls ; and on a circular plate in the centre of the badge on a field of red enamel there was depicted the figure of S. JOHN THE BAPTIST within a motto-band bearing the legend "*Prima sedes Galliarum.*" The reverse bore the effigy of the proto-martyr S. STEPHEN, vested in a dalmatic and holding a palm-branch, within the circular band bearing the legend "*Ecclesia Comitum Lugduni.*" The ribbon by which the badge was suspended on the breast was of flame-coloured silk with a light blue border. Their shields of arms were also ornamented with this surrounding ribbon and pendant badge (*v.* Plate III., fig. 3).

In 1750 the King, by his Letters-Patent, conferred on the Canons of S. CLAUDE *en Franche Comté* a decoration to be worn instead of the *quasi*-episcopal cross which they had previously used. The new decoration was a Greek cross ✝ (*i.e.*, having equal arms) of gold, coticed with golden fleurs-de-lis, and engraved with the effigy of their patron, ST. CLAUDE. The whole badge was enclosed in a thin golden circle. Its ribbon was of black silk. The Abbey was erected into a Bishopric, and the monastery into a secular Chapter in 1742, and the old decoration which had been a cross similar to that used by Bishops but engraved with the effigy of S. CLAUDE was replaced by the Greek cross described above. The *preuves* required for admission into this Chapter were those of sixteen quarters.

By Letters-Patent granted in March 1760, the King granted to the Provost, Dignitaries, and sixteen Canons, Counts of the noble Chapter of S. VICTOR at Marseilles, the right to wear an eight-pointed cross of gold enamelled white, each point terminating in a little golden ball ; in each of the four principal angles of the cross was a golden fleur-de-lis. On the circular medallion in the centre of the cross was enamelled the figure of the Patron Saint, S. VICTOR, mounted on horseback and piercing with his lance the dragon overthrown. The motto band round the medallion bore the legend, "*Divi Victoris Massiliensis.*" Its reverse was enamelled with a representation of the old Church of S. VICTOR, surrounded by the device "*Monumentis et Nobilitate insignis.*" The whole badge was, after 1774, crowned with the coronet of a Count. The ribbon by which it was suspended from the neck was of flame-coloured watered silk. The Canons placed round the escucheons of their arms a motto band as on the obverse of the badge, and the cross was suspended thereto, as well as placed behind the escucheon (*v. ante*, p. 45).

Badges resembling the Crosses of Orders of Knighthood are still worn by the Canons of the Cathedral of S. DENIS, NOTRE DAME at PARIS, and some other French Cathedrals; at LUCERNE, and elsewhere.

In imitation of this custom FREDERICK THE GREAT in 1755 gave to the Chapter of BRANDENBURG consisting of a Dom-Probst, six Dom-Herren, and as many Canons, the right to wear an eight-pointed cross of gold, enamelled violet, having in the principal angles the Prussian eagle. In the centre of the cross was a round golden medallion bearing the Royal Cypher.

The Chapter of NEUVILLE LES DAMES en Bresse (*v. ante*, p. 487) had in 1755 the grant of a badge resembling that of the Canons of S. JEAN at Lyons described above but bearing on the obverse the effigy of the Blessed VIRGIN MARY, and on the reverse that of S. CATHARINE; the ribbon was of light blue silk with flame-coloured borders (*i.e.*, the reverse of that of the canons).

By Royal Letters-Patent, granted January 1755, the King granted to the Chanoinesses-Comtesses of ALIX (*vide ante*, p. 487), the right to wear a golden cross of eight points, enamelled white, and having four golden fleurs-de-lis in the principal angles.

The obverse bore on a circular medallion of gold in the centre of the cross the effigy of S. DENIS, decapitated, within a band bearing the legend "*Auspice Galliarum Patrono.*" The reverse had the figures of the Blessed Virgin and Holy Child, surrounded in like manner by the words "*Nobilis insignia voti.*" The whole badge was surmounted by a count's coronet and its ribbon (worn *en écharpe* over the right shoulder) was of flame-coloured silk. The ribbon and badge were placed around the escucheon of the arms.

In 1757 the "CHAPITRE NOBLE DE S. MARIE DE LIEGNEU" (*v.* p. 488) similarly obtained the Royal permission to wear a cross resembling that just described except that the central medallion bore on the obverse the effigy of the Blessed Virgin, and on the other that of S. BENEDICT, with the legend "LOUIS XV. *en a honoré le Chapitre en l'an* 1757." The ribbon was of white silk edged with blue, and was worn and used armorially in the preceding case.

At DENAIN, near VALENCIENNES, the eighteen *Chanoinesses* had all the title of Comtesse d'Ostrevant. They wore a white habit (with in choir a surplice of fine linen), and a mantle bordered with plain white ermine—that of the abbess was spotted. This was an ancient independent abbey founded in 764 for both sexes by ADEL-

BERT, Count of OSTREVANT, and REGNIA, his wife. After a time it embraced the Benedictine rule, but in 1029 it resumed its former constitution, as a college of noble Canonesses. The abbess, who was selected by the King from a list of three candidates elected by the Chapter, alone took the vows of a regular nun.

The Canonesses of BOURBOURG (*vide ante*, p. 488) had a decoration consisting of the usual gold cross of eight points enamelled white, and with golden fleurs-de-lis in the angles, bearing in the central medallion on the obverse the effigy of the Blessed Virgin ; on the reverse the portrait of the Queen. I have no note of the colour of the ribbon.

In Bavaria and in Austria noble Chapters still exist, usually without vows, as a provision for unmarried ladies of noble families.

At Prague the Abbess of the noble Chapter is always an Archduchess of the Imperial family, and resigns her dignity on her marriage.

The Bavarian ORDER OF S. ANNE was founded in 1784 by the Electress MARIA ANNA SOPHIA for ten single ladies and a Doyenne, who were to prove sixteen quarters and live in community. Later the number of ten was raised to eighteen. But in 1802 the obligation to the common life ceased. The number of members is now twenty-five in the first class, and forty-two in the second, who have respectively pensions of £80 and £40. The titular Abbess is always a princess of the Royal family, and on days of ceremony wears an ermine hood, in addition to the black dress with velvet mantle, common to all the ladies of the Order. The badge is a gold cross *patée-arrondie* of white enamel bordered with blue, in each angle a golden ring. The circular centre of white bordered with blue bears on the obverse the figure of the Blessed Virgin and on the reverse that of S. BENNO of Bavaria. On the arms of the cross are the words, *Sub tuum præsidium;* on the reverse. *Patronus noster.*

The Order of S. ANN at WÜRZBURG for Franconian ladies is similar, and its members, who originally lived in community, proved sixteen quarters, as the higher class of *pensionnaïres*, or *Chanoinesses*, still do. The badge nearly resembles that already described, but the border is of red, not blue ; and the figure in the centre is that of S. ANNE, and the words, "*In ihren edlen Tochtern.*" The ribbon is of red silk, with a double line of silver near either edge.

At WADSTENA in Sweden was a noble Chapter, founded for women by Queen LOUISA ULRICA (of Prussia), the mother of GUSTAVUS III.

In Denmark the noble Chapter of VALLÖE was founded by Queen MADALENA as late as 1738. The ladies rank as, but after,

Countesses, and before the wives of Counts' eldest sons. They have annual allowances varying from £60 to £120.

Other noble Chapters in Denmark were GISSELFELD, of which the eldest daughter of the House of DANNESKIOLD was born Abbess; and VANNETOFTE, founded in 1785 by Prince CARL (brother of FREDERICK IV.) and his sister Princess HEDWIG.

At ITZEHOE in Holstein the Abbess was a Princess of the Royal House.

APPENDIX C.

GRANT OF MITRE TO ABBOT.

POPE ALEXANDER III. in 1165 conferred this privilege on JOHN, Abbot of KELSO, and his successors. The grant is as follows :—
Alexander episcopus, servus servorum Dei, dilecto filio Johanni, Abbati de Calkou, salutem et apostolicam benedictionem : Devotionis tuæ sinceritatem, et quem circa nos et ecclesiam Dei geris affectum, diligenti studio attendentes, et quod ecclesia tuæ gubernationi commissa Romanæ ecclesiæ filia specialis existit, nihilominus, considerantes honorem et gratiam tibi, et eidem ecclesiæ tuæ in quibus cum Deo possumus libentius exhibemus, et prompto animo quantum honestas permiserit honoramus. Inde siquidem est, quod ad postulationem tuam, usum mitræ tibi, et successoribus tuis duximus indulgendum, auctoritate apostolica statuentes ut ad honorem Dei et ecclesiæ tuæ decorem, in solemniis missarum ·ea congruis temporibus utendi in ecclesia tua, et in processionibus in claustro tuo, et in concilio Romani Pontificis facultatem habeatis.

APPENDIX D.

ADDITIONAL NOTES ON THE ARMS OF THE . ENGLISH SEES.

AT p. 171 I have stated that the arms of the English Sees "were originally assumptions only . . . although after the institution of the College of Arms the arms in use were authoritatively confirmed; and in the case of Sees of later erection a regular armorial grant was made." The, passage quoted contains three distinct assertions, of which the first is indubitably correct; in this respect the custom in this country differed not from the custom on the Continent, and the arms borne were assumptions only at the will and pleasure of the occupant of the See. The third assertion that a regular armorial grant was made to Bishoprics of later erection must, I believe, be limited to the case of the Sees erected in the present century. The Post-Reformation Sees of BRISTOL, 1542; GLOUCESTER, 1541; CHESTER, 1542; OXFORD, 1542; and PETERBOROUGH, 1541; had not, so far as I can discover, any formal grant of arms at their foundation; and neither in their case nor in the arms of the elder Sees do I find that there were ever formal confirmations by the authority of the College of Arms. If there were this is a point on which I shall cordially welcome correction. In the case of the older Sees a long continuance in their use may have given a prescriptive authority to the arms usually employed (the earliest instance of the use of official arms on an Episcopal seal seems to be afforded by that of WILLIAM, Bishop of ELY, 1290-1298, as recorded at p. 180 *ante*), but this prescriptive right must clearly have been subject to the will and pleasure of the occupant of the See for the time being. In many cases, perhaps in most, he went on bearing what his predecessors had used; but the many variations of arms which meet us in the case of the arms of several of our most important bishoprics, *e.g.*, EXETER, WINCHESTER, YORK, WELLS, etc., show that the bishops retained and exercised the right of mutation, and it is only the most profound ignorance of the facts which can lead a person to say, *e.g.*, that the coat borne by Bishop BEKINTON of WELLS, and certain of his successors, is the one only true and authoritative coat, and is stereotyped for all time coming, while the one assumed and borne by later Bishops, as at present, is " entirely wanting in authority." We may prefer the older coat, we may hold that the present coat is a development not entirely according to knowledge, but it has at least as much *authority* as its predecessors. With regard to YORK, WINCHESTER, EXETER, LICHFIELD, and others, I have noticed some of the chief mutations; I have only here to append a few other examples in the case of other Sees.

As concerns GLOUCESTER, I have noted, at p. 181, the omission of the Pauline sword in later times; but I have omitted the fact that the original arms of the See are said to have been those of the CLARES, the old Earls of GLOUCESTER (*Or, three chevrons gules*), and that this coat was borne as recently as by Bishop FOWLER, 1691-1741, with the added difference of a mitre argent on the centre chevron, in fess point.

SALISBURY.—The seal of Bishop ROBERT HALLAM, 1407-1417, bears in the upper part of the *vesica* the effigy of the Blessed

Virgin and her Babe, which is now the charge in the arms of the See ; but it also contains in base two shields, the one for the Bishopric charged with either two keys, or a sword and key, in saltire ; the other of his personal arms (*Sable*), *a cross engrailed ermine, in the first quarter a crescent* (*argent*). (*Catalogue of Seals in British Museum*, i., No. 2206.)

BANGOR.—In the *Procession Roll* of 1512 the bend appears to be *argent*, charged with *larmes*.

HEREFORD.—The coat, *Gules, a bezant between three open crowns or,* said in COLE'S MS. to have been borne before the adoption of the arms of CANTELUPE, and probably the coat attributed in mediæval times to S. ETHELBERT, seems to be utterly without authority (DUNCUMB'S *Herefordshire* makes the arms of the DEANERY ; *Or, five chevronels azure*). (BEDFORD, *Blazon of Episcopacy*, p. 51.)

DURHAM.—It is worthy of notice that the arms of Bishop BEK (1283-1311), as Patriarch of JERUSALEM, are in the west window of the north aisle of Howden Church, Yorkshire, and form perhaps the earliest instance of an Episcopal coat in which the official are impaled with the personal arms. The dexter half contains what is probably intended for a cross-patriarchal, the head is a cross-*patée*, touching the upper border of the shield. The lower limb of the cross is supplied by the staff, from which lower down two arms of a cross-*patée* emerge. The cross is of rose colour, "on a tawny pink ground," perhaps for *Or.* The sinister half of the shield is occupied by the dimidiated coat of the bishop, who bore : *Gules, a cross-recercelé ermine.* (*See* the interesting paper on *The Old Heraldry of the Percies*, by W. H. DYER LONGSTAFFE, in *Archæologia Æliana*, 1860, p. 167 ; and the papers on *The Old Official Heraldry of Durham*, by the same able writer, in *The Herald and Genealogist*, vol. viii. p. 54.)

WELLS.—The earliest arms borne for the See of WELLS were probably a saltire only, the badge of its Patron S. ANDREW. *Azure, a saltire or*, may well have been the original coat, but we are singularly unfortunate in not finding on the seals of the mediæval bishops which remain to us in the British Museum collection any instance of the use of an official coat. That to which reference is made above and on p. 176, as being used by Bishop BEKINGTON (1443-1465), is said, by a writer in *N. and Q.*, 7th S., ix., 144, to be carved in stone in the chantry chapel of Bishop BUBWITH (d. 1424), and may therefore have been used by that prelate ; but of this there is, I believe, no other evidence. But we also read that this coat appears on the tomb of Dean GUNTHORPE, 1478 ; of Thomas CORNISH,

2 K

Provóst of ORIEL, who, as titular Bishop óf TENOS, *in partibus*, presided over the affairs of the See from 1486 to 1513, while its occupants were employed as ambassadors abroad, or as great Officers of State at home. The writer referred to states that the coat also appears on the monument of Bishop CREYGHTON, and on a lectern presented by him, as well as on the monument of Bishop HOOPER in 1727. But, if I remember rightly, the coat at present used is that which is inserted in the east window of WINCHESTER Cathedral, in connection with the arms of the other Sees successively filled by Bishop FOX, 1492-1494. GUILLIM assigns it to Bishop MONTAGU, 1608-1616 (but *see* p. 176); it was used by Bishop LAKE, 1616-1626, and it was probably used by Bishop WYNNE in 1729, in which year the saltire appears alone on the seal of the Archdeacon of TAUNTON. (*Catalogue of Seals, British Museum*, No. 1449.) It has been employed by all the bishops without exception, from Bishop MOSS, 1774, to the present venerable occupant of the See. Bishop BAGOT (1845-1854), with great propriety quartered the coat of BATH with that of WELLS. It is therefore simple nonsense to speak of the present coat as being "without authority," because a different one was borne at some other times. Numerous examples of such variations are recorded above. Even if it be admitted that the present coat originated in a misconception, and if it could be clearly traced to an instance in which the original plain saltire was, according to a general custom, represented in carvings as coped, or ridged, there would still be all the "authority" needed for its continuance in use at the pleasure of the Bishop ; and I am rather inclined to advise its retention, either impaled or quartered with the coat of BATH, than to approve of a reversion to the coat used by BEKINTON, which is not only somewhat overloaded, but on which the BATH charges are in such distinct subordination to the WELLS saltire.

It should be remarked that Bishop ROGER, 1244, was the first who, in obedience to the Papal command, assumed the designation of Bishop of BATH and WELLS.

CANTERBURY.—I may perhaps anticipate a criticism by saying that I have been asked on what ground I have given the tincture of the *pallium* in the arms of the Archbishops of ENGLAND and IRELAND, as *argent*, instead of leaving the *pallium* of its natural colour white. The answer is, because *argent* is its invariable tincture in all the blazons which have come under my notice. Had the *pallium* been "proper" it would of course have been tinctured white, but the pall in the arch-episcopal arms is not a "*pallium* proper ;*"* and, moreover, the vestment would not in that case have a golden border and fringe, nor would the crosses at the present day be *patées fitchées.*

The arms lately assumed by Cardinal Archbishop VAUGHAN are *Gules, an Archbishop's cross in pale or, over all a pall proper.* The Archbishop's eminent predecessors, Cardinals WISEMAN and MANNING, were content to use only their personal arms, and had no idea of assuming a coat, which (since no tinctures are marked on the archi-episcopal seal) *appears* to the ordinary observer to be a direct annexation of the arms of the archi-episcopal See of CANTERBURY! It is curious that even the appearance of such a thing should have had the sanction of an officer of the College of Arms. Up to the present time Roman Catholic prelates in England have very rarely adopted official arms. The present Bishop of SALFORD has lately assumed *Azure, a seated figure of the BLESSED VIRGIN (crowned, sceptred and having in her hand a scapular) supporting the HOLY CHILD proper.*

APPENDIX E.

SEALS, &c., OF AMERICAN BISHOPS.

A considerable number, perhaps all, of the American Bishops employ official seals, but, though in the majority of cases these are engraved with appropriate ecclesiastical devices, the assumptions are often wanting in heraldic fitness. There are, however, in some cases attempts at more regular armorial design ; and, as these are worthy of all encouragement, I very gladly comply with a special request to include in this volume some examples, in the hope that they may contribute to the formation of a better taste in future assumptions. The following are selected from a number of American Episcopal Seals, which were described in *Notes and Queries,* 6th Series, vii., pp. 484 and 502, by " H. W." (HENRY WAGNER, Esquire) in June 1883.

ALABAMA (1830). Argent, a key and pastoral staff in saltire, surmounted by a Latin cross in pale.

ARKANSAS (1871). Or, on a cross-patée-throughout, but couped in base, a human heart.

BUFFALO. Azure, a rainbow in fess proper, between three crosses patées ; in base a crosier and key in saltire.

CAROLINA (North) 1816. Two keys in saltire, wards in chief, and a pastoral staff in pale, over all an open book, thereon the letters A, and Ω.

COLORADO. Or, a cross, thereon a roundel between four cross-crosslets fitchées and charged with the monogram XP between the letters A, Ω.

CONNECTICUT (1783). Sable, a key and a crosier in saltire or.

EASTON (1868). . . . . A pastoral staff, and a long cross in saltire, between a mitre in chief, and an escroll in base, thereon the words *Esto Fidelis*.

FLORIDA (1838). The figure of S. John the Evangelist, between six palm trees (three on either side), in chief seven stars, in base an eagle displayed holding a cactus branch.

KANSAS (1854). A cross botonnée.

LONG-ISLAND (1868). A pastoral staff and key in saltire, surmounted by a sword in pale, in chief a mitre.

LOUISIANA (1838). A Latin cross coupé.

MAINE (1820). The Saviour holding a star and an orb, and walking between the seven candlesticks ; three in chief, two in either base.

MASSACHUSSETS (1781). A cross patonce, in chief a mitre.

MINNESOTA (1857). A Latin cross, in base a calumet and a broken tomahawk in saltire.

MISSOURI (1839). A crosier and olive branch in saltire, in chief a mitre.

NEBRASKA AND DAKOTA (1868). A Latin cross in pale, surmounted by a pastoral staff and key in saltire.

NEW YORK (CENTRAL) (1868). A sword and key in saltire, hilt and handle in chief, surmounted by a crosier in pale.

RHODE ISLAND (1790). Gules, a Latin cross argent.

TEXAS (1849). Two keys in saltire, wards in base, in chief a mitre.

VERMONT (1790). Two pastoral staves in saltire between a mitre in chief, and a chalice in base.

VIRGINIA (WEST) (1877). A key (wards uppermost) and a crosier in saltire, in chief a mitre.

It is obvious that nearly all of the above might be made into perfectly regular coats by the application of a very little heraldic knowledge. At present the tinctures are usually wanting. But all these are better by far than those assumptions in which the arms (and crest) of an English family have been appropriated ; in one case the entire arms of a British peer, with crest and supporters, were thus annexed. The writer of this book would very gladly give his assistance, when desired, in the formation of regular coats, which, while not departing from ancient precedent, might yet retain some national or provincial character.

APPENDIX F.

LIST OF THE SEES IN FRANCE.

BEFORE the revolution there were in France sixteen archbishoprics, of which (with their suffragans) a list is subjoined. Those included in brackets were suppressed by the Concordat of 1801.

1. AIX, Archbishopric, with five suffragans, viz. :
   (APT) FRÉJUS, GAP, (RIEZ, and SISTERON).
2. ALBI, Archbishopric, with five suffragans :
   CAHORS, (CASTRES), MENDE, RODEZ, (VABRES).
3. ARLES, Archbishopric, with four suffragans :
   MARSEILLE, (ORANGE), (ST. PAUL-TROIS-CHÂTEAUX) (TOULON).
4. AUCH, Archbishopric, with six suffragans :
   (LUÇON), PÉRIGUEUX, POITIERS, LA ROCHELLE, (SAINTES, and SARLAT).
5. BOURGES, Archbishopric, with five suffragans :
   CLERMONT, LIMOGES, LE PUY, ST. FLOUR, and TULLE.
6. CAMBRAI, Archbishopric, with four suffragans :
   ARRAS, (ST. OMER), NAMUR, and TOURNAI.
7. EMBRUN, Archbishopric, with six suffragans :
   DIGNE (GLANDÈVES, GRASSE, NICE, SENEZ, and VENCE).
8. LYON, Archbishopric, with six suffragans :
   AUTUN, (CHÂLONS-SUR-SAÔNE), DIJON, LANGRES, (MÂCON), ST. CLAUDE.
9. NARBONNE, Archbishopric, with eleven suffragans :
   (AGDE, ALAIS, ALETH, BÉZIERS), CARCASSONNE, (LODÈVE), MONTPELLIER, NÎMES, PERPIGNAN (S. PONS, and UZÈS).
10. PARIS, Archbishopric, with four suffragans :
    BLOIS, CHARTRES, MEAUX and ORLÉANS.
11. REIMS, Archbishopric, with eight suffragans :
    AMIENS, BEAUVAIS, (BOULOGNE), CHÂLONS-SUR-MARNE (LAON, NOYON, SENLIS) and SOISSONS.
12. ROUEN, Archbishopric, with six suffragans :
    (AVRANCHES), BAYEUX, COUTANCES, ÉVREUX, (LISIEUX) and SÉEZ.
13. SENS, Archbishopric, with three suffragans :
    AUXERRE, NEVERS, and TROYES.
14. TOULOUSE, Archbishopric, with seven suffragans :
    (LAVAUR, LOMBES, MIREPOIX), MONTAUBAN, PAMIERS, (RIEUX, and ST. PAPOUL).

15. TOURS, Archbishopric, with eleven suffragans :
ANGERS, (DOL), LE MANS, NANTES, QUIMPER, RENNES, ST. BRIEUC (ST. MALO, ST. PAUL DE LÉON), (TRÉGUIER), and VANNES.
16. VIENNE, Archbishopric, with six suffragans :
DIE (GENÈVE or ANNECY), GRENOBLE, (MAURIENNE), VALENCE, and VIVIERS.

METZ, TOUL, and VERDUN ; "*les trois Évêchés*" which had been united to France in 1552, still belonged ecclesiastically to the Archi-episcopal See of TRIER (TRÈVES) ; as did STRASBURG to that of MENTZ (MAYENCE).

The boundaries of the Sees were changed and they were re-grouped by the Concordat in 1801, as follows :—
1. PARIS, with five suffragans :
BLOIS, CHARTRES, MEAUX, ORLÉANS, and VERSAILLES.
2. CAMBRAY, with its suffragan :
ARRAS.
3. LYON and VIENNA, with five suffragans :
AUTUN, DIJON, GRENOBLE, LANGRES, ST. CLAUDE.
4. ROUEN, with four suffragans :
BAYEUX, COUTANCES, ÉVREUX, SÉEZ.
5. SENS and AUXERRE, with three suffragans :
MOULINS, NEVERS, TROYEZ.
6. REIMS, with four suffragans : '
AMIENS, BEAUVAIS, CHÂLONS-SUR-MARNE, and SOISSONS.
7. TOURS, with seven suffragans :
ANGERS, LE MANS, NANTES (QUIMPER, RENNES, ST. BRIEUC, and VANNES).
8. BOURGES, with five suffragans :
CLERMONT, LIMOGES, LE PUY, ST. FLOUR, TULLE.
9. ALBI, with four suffragans :
CAHORS, MENDE, PERPIGNAN, RODEZ.
10. BOURDEAUX, with six suffragans :
AGEN, ANGOULÊME, LUÇON, LA ROCHELLE, PÉRIGUEUX, POITIERS.
11. AUCH, with six suffragans :
AIRE, BAYONNE, TARBES.
12. TOULOUSE, and NARBONNE, with three suffragans :
CARCASSONNE, MONTAUBAN, PAMIERS.
13. AIX, ARLES, and EMBRUN, with six suffragans :
(ALGER, *v.i.*, No. 16), AJACCIO, DIGNE, FRÉJUS, (and TOULON), GAP, MARSEILLE, NICE (since its Cession).

14. BESANÇON, with six suffragans :
     BELLEY, (METZ), NANCY and TOUL, ST. DIÉ, (STRASBURG),
     VERDUN.   (METZ and STRASBURG were lost in the
     Franco-German War.)
15. AVIGNON, with four suffragans :
     MONTPELLIER, NÎMES, VALENCE, VIVIERS.

In more recent times :—
16. ALGIERS, with two suffragans (*vide supra*, No. 13) :
     CONSTANTINE, and ORAN.
17. CHAMBÉRY, with three suffragans :
     ANNECY, ST. JEAN DE MAURIENNE, TARENTAISE (as a
     result of the Cession of Savoy by Italy).
18. RENNES (Archbishopric restored, *vide ante*, No. 7), suffragans :
     QUIMPER, ST. BRIEUC, and VANNES.

INDEX.

BOUILLON, Duchy of, 297.
,,   *arms*, 296, 298, 470.
,,   Duke of, 296.
,,   EMMANUEL THÉODOSE DE LA TOUR D'AU-VERGNE, Cardinal de, *arms*, 470.
,,   Notre Dame de, Cistercian, *arms*, 405.
BOULBON, ELZIAS ALBERT, Seigneur de, 485.
BOULOGNE, *arms*, 470.
,,   See of, 501.
,,   STEPHEN, Earl of, 369.
BOURBON, CHARLES, Cardinal de, *arms*, 466.
,,   ,,   Duc de, 464.
,,   HENRI DE, Bishop of METZ, *arms*, 25.
,,   LANCEY, 422.
,,   ,,   *arms* of URSU-LINES of, 424.
,,   REYNAUD, Bâtard de Archbishop of NARBONNE, *arms*, 25.
BOURBOURG, Canonesses of, 494.
BOURDEAUX, Metropolitan of, 84.
,,   Archbishopric, with suffragan Sees, 502.
Bourdon, 15, 32.
,,   or knobbed staff, 51.
,,   use of, by priors and prioresses abroad, 52.
BOURG-EN-BRESSE, 422.
,,   ,,   *arms* of URSU-LINES at, 424.
,,   ,,   Chapter of Notre Dame, *arms*, 404.
,,   ,,   Franciscan Monastery at, *arms*, 418.
BOURGES, Archbishop of, and Primate, 85, 127.
,,   Archbishopric, with suffragan Sees, 501, 502.
,,   GUILLAUME, Archbishop of, *mitre*, Pl. VIII., fig. 6, p. 66.
,,   Metropolitan of, 84.
,,   Title of Patriarch given to Bishop of, 125.
BOURGEUIL EN ANJOU, LEONOR D'ESTAMPES, Abbé of, *arms*, 466.
BOURGOGNE, CLÉMENCE DE, 488.
,,   DAVID, Bâtard de, Bishop of TEROUENNE, *arms*, 24.
,,   JEAN, Bâtard de, Provost of St. OMER, *seal* and *arms*, 465.
,,   RENAUD III., Comte de, 405.
BOUSSEN, FRANÇOIS, Bishop of BRUGES, *arms*, 81.
BOUTELL, *Christian Monuments*, 8.
,,   *Heraldry, Historical and Popular*, 442, 461.
,,   quoted, 14.
BOUTILLIER DE RANCE, ARMAND JEAN LE, 414.
Bouvines, Battle of, 36, 37, 95.
BOUXIERES AUX DAMES, Chapter of, 487.
BOWETT, HENRY, Archbishop of York, *seal* and *arms*, 191, 458.

BOXLEY (Kent), Cistercian Abbey, *arms* 358.
BOYD, ANDREW, Bishop of ARGYLL *arms*, 24.
,,   THOMAS, Lord, 24.
BRABANT, *arms*, 276, 465.
,,   Dukes of, 483, 491.
,,   ,,   Honorary Canons at UTRECHT, 51.
BRABECK, THEODORE VON, Bishop of CORVEY, 280.
BRAGA, Archbishop of, in Portugal, claims Primacy of whole Peninsula, 127.
,,   GEORGE DA COSTA, Archbishop of, *arms*, 23.
,,   *mitre*, used by Canons at, 48.
,,   RODERIC DA CUNHA, Archbishop of, quoted, 126.
BRANDENBURG, ALBERT, Archbishop of MAGDEBURG, Markgrave of, 300.
,,   Bishopric, *arms*, 27.
,,   Chapter of, 493.
,,   CHRISTIAN WILLIAM, Archbishop of MAGDEBURG, Prince of, 300.
,,   Duchy of, 300.
,,   Elector JOACHIM II. of, 271.
,,   ,,   of, 289, 300, 332.
,,   ,,   of, Grand-Chamberlain, Bishop of BAMBERG, 266.
,,   Electorate of, 277, 288.
,,   Electors of, Cupbearers of TRIER, 260.
,,   FREDERICK, Archbishop of MAGDEBURG, Prince of, 300.
,,   JOACHIM, Duke of MUNSTERBERG, Bishop of, 271.
,,   JOACHIM FREDERICK, Archbishop of MAGDEBURG, Prince of, 300.
,,   JOACHIM FREDERICK, Bishop of LEBUS, Markgrave of, 293.
,,   Princes of the House of, 288, 303.
,,   Prussian Province of, 293.
,,   See of, suffragan to MAGDEBURG, 271, 300.
,,   See of, suffragan to MAINZ, 271.
,,   SIGISMUND, Archbishop of MAGDEBURG, Prince of, 300.
,,   WILHELM, Markgrave of, 317.
BRANDIS, *arms*, 314.
BRANSCOMBE, Bishop of EXETER, *tomb* of, 73.
BRASCHI, *arms*, 166.

2 N

SEVER, WILLIAM, Bishop of DUR-
HAM, seal, 192.
SÉVÉRIE, Duchy of, 351.
SEVILLE, ISIDORE of, 108.
,, Mitre used at, by Canons, 49.
SEYNA, See, 287.
SEYSSEL, CLAUDE DE, Bishop of
MARSEILLES, arms, 465.
SFONDRATI, arms, 163.
SFORZA, ASCANIO, Cardinal, tomb of,
154.
,, Cardinal, arms, 145.
SHAFTESBURY (Dorset), Benedictine
Abbey of SS. MARY and EDWARD,
arms, 385.
SHARDELOWE, Sir THOMAS, arms,
388.
SHERBORNE, Bishop, at CHICESTER,
arms, 99.
,, (Dorset) Benedictine Abbey
of S. MARY, arms,
385.
,, Monastery of, 413.
,, S. ALDHEM, Bishop of,
377.
,, See of, 174, 177.
SHREWSBURY (Shropshire) Benedictine
Abbey of SS. PETER and PAUL,
arms, 386.
SHIPLEY quoted, 14.
SHIRWOOD, JOHN, Bishop of DUR-
HAM, tomb and arms, 97, 98.
SIBTON, Abbots of, seal, 7.
SICILY; ROGER, Count of, Mitre
granted to, 65.
SIDNACESTER, Bishopric, 184.
SIDNEY, arms, 442.
,, FRANCIS, 442.
,, -SUSSEX COLLEGE (Cam-
bridge), arms, 442.
SIEBMACHER, Wappenbuch, quoted,
259, 273, 275, 289, 290, 293, 295, 302,
307, 315, 316, 320, 321, 326, 328, 334,
337, 389, 350, 410, 469.
SIELUN, Principality of, 351.
SIENA, 137.
SIERRA LEONE, See of, arms, 249 ; Pl.
XXXV., fig. 3, p. 250.
SIGBERT, King of the EAST ANGLES,
436.
SIGEBERT, King of AUSTRASIA,
343, 490, 491.
SILESIA, arms, 90, 272, 307.
SIMONCELLI, Cardinal, arms, 146.
SIMON'S, Armorial Général de l'Empire
Français, 133.
SIMOR, Cardinal, Archbishop of GRAN,
Prince-Primate of HUNGARY, 20.
SINGAPORE, LABUAN, and SARA-
WAK, See of, arms,
249.
,, See of, arms, Pl. XXXV.,
fig. 5, p. 250.
SION COLLEGE (London), arms, 445.
,, or SITTEN, 321.
,, suffragan to LYON, 322.
,, ,, MILAN, 322.
,, ,, TARENTAISE, 325.
SISTERON, See of, 501.
SITTEN, Bishop of, has title of Prince-
Bishop of the HOLY EM-
PIRE, 322.
,, or SION, Prince-Bishopric,
arms, 321.

SITTEN, THEODORE, Bishop of, 22.
SIXTUS IV., Pope, 329.
,, IV., Pope (DELLA ROVERE),
arms, 161.
,, IV., Pope (FRANCESCO DEL-
LA ROVERE), 145.
,, IV., Pope, tomb of, 154.
,, V., Pope, 134, 136, 416 421.
,, V., Pope (PERETTI), arms,
163.
SKEAT, Dictionary, 14.
SKENE, DR, Celtic Scotland, 216, 221,
226, 228.
,, Monastery, 415.
SKIRLAW, Bishop of DURHAM, seal
and crest, 102.
SLANE, See of, 202.
SLAPTON (Devon), College of S. MARY,
arms, 386.
SMITH, Bishop, arms, 431.
,, WILLIAM, Bishop of LICH-
FIELD, seal, 183.
,, WILLIAM, Bishop of LINCOLN,
431.
,, ,, ,, seal, 184.
SMITH'S Dictionary of Christian Anti-
quities, 58, 63.
SMYTH, Bishop of LIMERICK, etc.,
arms, 215.
SODOR AND MAN, Bishop of, has seat
but no vote in
House of Lords,
197.
,, ,, Bishops MARK and
JOHN of, seals,
196.
,, See of, 190.
,, ,, arms, 171,
196, 217.
,, Bishop ANDREW KNOX of, seal,
221.
,, ,, WALLACE of, seal 221.
,, See of arms, Pl. XXV., fig. 2,
p. 190.
SOISSONS, Bishop of, 84.
,, ,, had right of Coro-
nation in absence of Arch-
bishop, 84.
,, See of, 501, 502.
SOLTRE, see SALTREY.
SOMBERNON, GUI DE, 408.
SOMERSET, Diocese of, 177.
SONIUS, ANSELM VON, Abbot of
WERDEN, arms, 77.
,, arms, 77.
SONNENBERG, arms, 278.
SONNENTHURN, CHRISTOPH AN-
TON, Archbishop of VIENNA, Count
VON, arms, 329.
SONTAG, see LECH.
SOTERN, Chamberlainship of TRIER
hereditary in family of, 260.
SOUBISE, ARMAND DE ROHAN,
Prince-Bishop of STRASBURG,
Cardinal de, arms, 139.
SOUCILANGES, Priory of, 415.
SOUTHWELL, See of, 173.
,, ,, arms, 189 ; Pl.
XXV., fig. 3, p. 190.
SOUTHWICK (Hampshire) Priory of
Augustinian Canons, arms, 386.
SOUVIGNY, Priory of, 415.
SOUVRÉ, Abbess DE, arms, 76 ; Pl. VII.,
fig. 3, p. 60.

2 P

Lightning Source UK Ltd.
Milton Keynes UK
UKHW02f2229130818
327178UK00011B/562/P